D1603668

PHILOSTRATUS

HEROICUS
GYMNASTICUS
DISCOURSES

LCL 521

PHILOSTRATUS

HEROICUS
GYMNASTICUS
DISCOURSES 1 AND 2

EDITED AND TRANSLATED BY

JEFFREY RUSTEN
JASON KÖNIG

HARVARD UNIVERSITY PRESS
CAMBRIDGE, MASSACHUSETTS
LONDON, ENGLAND
2014

Library of Congress Control Number 2013948585
CIP data available from the Library of Congress

ISBN 978-0-674-99674-8

Composed in ZephGreek and ZephText by
Technologies 'N Typography, Merrimac, Massachusetts.
Printed on acid-free paper and bound by
The Maple-Vail Book Manufacturing Group

CONTENTS

HEROICUS

PREFACE

With the support of an NEH translation grant for the summer of 1985, I completed an annotated translation based on the excellent Teubner text by de Lannoy (1977) of the then little-known dialogue *Heroicus*, in a naive search for evidence about the continuity of Greek popular religion, the epic cycle and lost tragedies, and the state of the Troad under the Roman Empire—none of which, I eventually discovered, was really to be found there. What I found instead was a construction of great literary, cultural, and ideological sophistication, the full elucidation of whose background demanded a formidable range of expertise, which I could not acquire quickly; since in any case publishers were not interested in the project, I put my translation aside (though it circulated unofficially) and took up other work.

Two decades later the situation had changed: Greek literature from Trajan to Septimius Severus, and Philostratus in particular, had experienced a dramatic surge in scholarly interest from the UK to Europe and the US, and most of the gaps I had felt in the 1980s were splendidly filled in the 2000s with studies of archaeology and the Greek landscape under the Roman empire (Susan Alcock), Roman Ilion (Brian Rose), translations of Physiognomic texts from Arabic (Simon Swain), the historical context of imperial literature and hero cults under the empire (Christopher P. Jones), the visual and religious sensibility of imperial Greek literature (Jaś Elsner), and the integration of this age into the mainstream of Greek literary studies (Simon Goldhill, Tim Whitmarsh, Froma Zeitlin, and others), with the promise of a new generation of scholarly interest. Attention to *Heroicus* had grown also, resulting in a brave foray into the first published English translation (MacLean and Aitken 2002, with emphasis on its relation to Christianity), an international conference (Aitken and MacLean 2004), and an admirably thorough and careful German translation and scholarly commentary (Grossardt 2006a, with emphasis on its language and allusions to classical literature) to which my debt in the revision has been especially great.

In 2010, the chance to teach Greek imperial literature in a delightful collaboration with Verity Platt (a second-generation of the scholarly movement noted above) encouraged me to think my revised translation and introduction had not been superseded; and I am grateful to Jason König (another of the second-generation) for his willingness to add his *Gymnasticus* to a proposal to complete the Loeb Philostratus and to Jeffrey Henderson for his quick acceptance and support. Cornell's Society for the Humanities funded a collaborative visit of Jason to Ithaca in April 2013, when the final manuscript took shape. Samuel Kurland prepared the index. In the final stage, Christopher P. Jones and Peter Grossardt put me still further in their debt by sharing important forthcoming articles and by reading extensive sections of the proofs and alerting me to many errors not only of typing but also of substance.

J. S. R.

INTRODUCTION

1. *HEROICUS* AMONG THE WORKS
OF PHILOSTRATUS

The *Heroicus* presents a conversation at the site of Protesilaus' hero shrine near Elaious, on the Gallipoli peninsula, between a devout farmer and a skeptical Phoenician sailor about the powers and worship of the Homeric heroes.

Its author does not introduce himself, but the manuscripts and other sources ascribe the work to "Philostratus." There are three authors by that name, all associated with Lemnos, listed in the Suda, and of the many titles ascribed to them nine are preserved in manuscripts. The Suda's biographical entries are hopelessly confused;[1] but

---

Ancient authors and works are abbreviated as in *OCD*.

[1] They are listed in the wrong order, the wrong number of books is given for *Imagines* and *Lives of the Sophists* (of which the latter is assigned to two of the three), and there is a glaring contradiction with the preface of the second set of *Imagines*, where the author claims to be imitating a work of his *grandfather*, not his *uncle*. On problems with homonymous authors in this work, see Welcker (1865, 1.71–72) and A. Adler (*RE* 4.A.1.707). Text and translation of the entries for Philostratus (*Suda* nos. 421–23 Adler) in Anderson (1986, 291–96); discussion in Bowersock (1969, 2–4), Solmsen (*RE* 20.1.124ff.), de Lannoy (1997), and Bowie (2009).

from internal evidence, it seems close to certain that *Heroicus* was written by the Philostratus who began his career under Septimius Severus and who also wrote *The Life of Apollonius of Tyana*, *Lives of the Sophists*, *Gymnasticus*, and the first work known as *Imagines*. With the last two works, *Heroicus* shares a keen interest in anecdotes of Olympic victors (chs. 14–15)[2] and physical and artistic ekphrasis (see §11 below, and *Gymnasticus* Introduction §5), but also by the explicit testimony of Menander Rhetor, who speaks of the simple, plain style of "the Philostratus who wrote the *Heroicus* and the *Imagines*."[3]

The portrait of the sophist-hero Palamedes, and the biographical style of chapters 25.17–42, seems to prefigure the *Lives of the Sophists*. There we first find articulated the concept of a "Second Sophistic" age;[4] when the Greeks recovered their prosperity and self-esteem during the relative peace of the later-first through early-third centuries of our era, a new sort of intellectual leader emerged among them, who preserved the past and reinterpreted it for the new age. By profession such men might be rhetoricians, philosophers, or other savants;[5] but their celebrity entitled them to be called *sophists*, a term coined centu-

---

2 Jüthner (1902).

3 Russell and Wilson (1981, 117, 297).

4 Essential is Bowersock (1969); see now Goldhill (2001) and Whitmarsh (2005). On the existence of this and other diverse regional identity groups see most recently Whitmarsh (2010).

5 For example, the physician Galen might be reckoned among them (Bowersock 1969, 59–75).

ries before for a varied group of intellectual celebrities of fifth-century Greece.[6]

Some of these figures—such as Dio of Prusa, the friend of Titus and Trajan; the hermaphroditic Favorinus of Arelate, hated by Hadrian; or the rhetorician/memoirist Aelius Aristides—are known through surviving writings. But Philostratus' biographies include the millionaire Herodes Atticus; Hadrian's friend Polemon of Laodicea, who dabbled in physiognomy; Antipater of Hierapolis, who taught the children of Septimius Severus; Dionysius of Miletus; Scopelian of Smyrna; Lollianus of Ephesus; and many others.

Utterly different in many respects, these men were nonetheless alike in mastering the heritage of Greek literature, art, history, and religion, combined under the term *paideia*,[7] and in achieving an unparalleled public recognition in the eastern cultural capitals of Smyrna, Ephesus, and Pergamon, as well as in Athens and Rome. They also all came from privileged families, were deeply (though sometimes reluctantly) involved in politics and public service, and when they needed a patron, sought one no lower than the emperor himself.

The relationship between *Heroicus* and *The Life of Apollonius of Tyana* is especially close, since several episodes in it seem to have inspired the topic of conversation in *Heroicus*.

[6] See Kerferd (1981). For a survey of the word's range of meaning in the second and third centuries, see Bowersock (1969, 10–15).

[7] Essential is Bowie (1974); subsequently Borg (2004), Eshlemann (2012), Schmitz (1997).

The chronicler of the sophists was clearly a sophist himself, for there he hints at his own close relationship with the imperial family. Julia Domna, the Syrian wife of Septimius Severus, was a devoted student of philosophy and a patron of sophists, especially after she lost influence at court to the praetorian prefect Fulvius Plautianus in the late 190s (Dio 75.15.3–7);[8] Philostratus himself says "I belonged to her circle—for she encouraged and supported all rhetorical compositions."[9]

Julia's patronage drew him to the life of Apollonius, and perhaps thereby into the study of Greek hero cult also. In 215, Julia's son, the emperor Caracalla, paused on his expedition through the east at Tyana in Cappadocia to establish a hero shrine (*herôon*) to the first-century philosopher and mystic Apollonius.[10] It was probably about this time that Julia commissioned a biography of this ascetic miracle worker, putting into Philostratus' hands the unpublished memoirs of a disciple named Damis and instructing him to rework them into a full biography.

How much of the biography comes from "Damis," from Philostratus' other research on Apollonius' career, or

[8] On Julia Domna as patroness and the evidence for her circle, see Bowersock (1969, 101–9). See in general, Swain, Harrison, and Elsner (2007).

[9] *VA* 1.3. Other members are often claimed, but the only one definitely attested is the sophist Philiscus (*VS*, p. 622). As Whitmarsh (2007a, 32–34) points out, "circle" in Philostratus elsewhere does not indicate a formal association.

[10] Dio 77.18.4.

from free invention, is uncertain,[11] but at least one episode suits an interest of Caracalla's suspiciously well: earlier on the same expedition in 215, Caracalla had paid an extensive visit to Ilion; there he gave special honor to the tomb of Achilles and even began to imitate that hero to the extent of giving a Patroclean funeral to Festus, a member of his entourage who had just died.[12]

The emperor's interest in Apollonius doubtless derived from his mother, but his mimicry of Achilles had an entirely different source: an obsessive emulation of Alexander the Great, who had himself honored Achilles at the outset of his Asian campaigns.[13] In *VA* 4.11–16, Philostratus manages to combine the two briefly, when he makes the holy man visit Ilion and interview the spirit of Achilles himself. He is allowed to pose five questions on the Trojan War, and every one of the unusual answers he receives corresponds precisely with a statement in the *Heroicus*:[14]

- No Muses or Nereids were at the burial of Achilles (51.7)

[11] For a range of views, see Bowie (1978), Anderson (1986, 155–74), Jones (2005–6, 4–7), and Platt (2009, 140n33).

[12] Hdn. 4.8.4; cf. Dio 77.16.7. Whitmarsh (2009, 36) notes that the historical accounts do not flatter the emperor and argues convincingly that there is no reason to suppose *Heroicus* supports a Caracallan imperial program of hero cult.

[13] Ameling (1988).

[14] In addition, Achilles' anger at the Thessalians for neglecting his cult (*VA* 4.16, 4.23) is mentioned again at *Her.* 53.8–23 (cf. Huhn and Bethe 1917, 620–21). On the relation of this "interview" to Lucian's *True Histories* and biographical traditions of Homer, see Grossardt (2009b).

- Polyxena killed herself for love of Achilles (51.3–6)
- Helen was not at Troy (and the Greeks knew it!) (25.10–11)
- Palamedes was omitted by Homer to whitewash Odysseus (24.2)
- Achilles was especially grieved over Palamedes (who was buried opposite Methymna) (33.36 and 33.49)

On the basis of these and several other correspondences between the two works, F. Solmsen suggested that the *Heroicus* is in part an expansion of this episode of the *Life of Apollonius* by the same author, and this is surely correct.[15] And the *Lives of the Sophists*, which explicitly refers back to the Apollonius life (II, ch. 5; Kayser 1870, 570), can be added to this author's writings also. One might therefore expect their relative chronology to be *Apollonius-Heroicus-Sophists*,[16] which is not inconsistent with other evidence: the *Life of Apollonius* is likely to have been completed *after* the suicide of Julia Domna in 217, since it is not dedicated to her. The *Heroicus* might have been written before the athlete Helix had won at the Capitoline games in 219 (see 15.9n), or perhaps after an imperial edict on purple dye under Alexander Severus (222–235, see 53.23n), whereas the *Lives of the Sophists* is dedicated to a certain Gordian, which suggests an appearance in the 220s at the earliest.[17]

---

15 Solmsen (1940). For the way that the two works interweave their stories, see §§7 and 12 below.

16 So Solmsen (1940, 572).

17 Jones (2002) suggests this might even be the emperor Gordian whose reign was 238–244. Jüthner (1902) thought the *Gymnasticus* was later than the *Heroicus*.

These works reveal a man of diverse interests: intellectual history and famous athletes, myths of the Trojan War and mysticism, physiognomy and religious cult. All these topics are reflected in the *Heroicus*, but they are subordinated to a single theme, to which we now turn.

2. THE EARLIEST HERO CULTS TO THE FIFTH CENTURY

Despite its many different themes, *Heroicus* is mainly a discussion of the evidence for belief in the reality of the cults of Greek heroes, especially those from the Trojan War. Greek hero cults are a vast topic; we will touch here mainly on those aspects taken up by Philostratus himself, of which, however, there are many. In fact, much of what we know of hero cult is based not on documents of belief but on literary and philosophical adaptations; this is, indeed, one of the things that made it so appealing to Philostratus.

There are several modern theories for the origins of hero cult: cults of dead ancestors going back to the Mycenaean age,[18] post-Mycenaean co-opting of earlier burials by social or political groups,[19] an eighth-century reflection

---

[18] Nagy (1979, 114–15), Price (1973), Currie (2005, 48–57), and many older scholars (doxography in Bremmer [2006, 15]). Price notes that the offerings to Erechtheus (*Il.* 2.250–51) resemble hero sacrifices and that the tomb of the Trojan founder Ilos (*Il.* 10.415–16) is like a *herôon*—but neither of these is called a *hêrôs* in Homer.

[19] Snodgrass (1982), Antonaccio (1995), Boehringer (2001).

of the popularity of epic poetry,[20] or a late sixth-century political-religious-literary invention.[21] Each relies on different sorts of arguments, and each must concede its supporting evidence is only partial.

The Greek word *hêrôs* (pl. *hêrôes*) is found already in Mycenaean Greek,[22] and especially in Homer. Etymologically, a connection with Hera is likely,[23] and the word occurs in Mycenaean Greek in an apparently religious sense. But in Homer it is used of warriors, without any religious significance whatsoever.[24] Hesiod uses the word in the same way, for the warriors of the *Iliad*, together with preceding generations who fought at Thebes (and sailed on the Argo as well), are also called *hêrôes* by Hesiod,[25] and one can speak of the "heroic verses" of Homer.[26]

Hero cults in a religious sense can be documented archaeologically. In the Argolid (especially at Mycenae), Attica, Messenia, Phocis, Boeotia, and elsewhere, beginning in the eighth century BC,[27] graves of the Mycenaean pe-

---

[20] Coldstream (1976), who follows Farnell (1921).

[21] Bremmer (2006).

[22] Gérard-Rousseau (1968, 32).

[23] Pötscher (1961; 1965); M. L. West (1978, 370–73).

[24] Especially in the general formulae "Achaean (Danaan) *hêrôes*," and "of men who are *hêrôes*" (*andrôn hêrôôn*). Aristarchus already assumed it could designate any human; cf. schol. *Il.* 2.110a with Erbse's testimonia, Rohde (1925, 142n 26).

[25] *Op.* 156–73, on which see below.

[26] So called by Plato (*Resp.* 400b, *Leg.* 958e) and Aristotle (*Poet.* 1459b32, *Rh.* 1408b32).

[27] The sensational tenth-century BC burial at Lefkandi (Popham and Lemos 1996) of a male, including the bodies of a woman and two horses (compare Patroclus' burial in *Il.* 23), is

riod centuries before were uncovered and instead of being
cleared away were venerated with votive offerings and
animal sacrifice.[28] It seems that these are not a contin-
uation of a Mycenaean cult of the dead after so long an
interval; rather it was the *strangeness* of the newly dis-
covered burials, their revelation of a society so different
from geometric Greece, that evoked a religious response.[29]
These had once been men and were now dead, but they
seemed closer to the gods than their discoverers, and so
their remains were deemed holy.

The first appearance of these holy remains in literature
suggests that they were not originally identified as *hêrôes*,
or connected with epic poetry. In the *Works and Days*,
Hesiod describes four ages of men, of descending qual-
ity—gold, silver, bronze, and iron—and interpolates be-
tween the last two still another age of *hêrôes*, those who
fought at Thebes and Troy and were removed by Zeus to
everlasting happiness on the islands of the blessed. But of
the men of the golden age he says (121–26):

αὐτὰρ ἐπεὶ δὴ τοῦτο γένος κατὰ γαῖα κάλυψε,
τοὶ μὲν δαίμονες εἰσι Διὸς μεγάλου διὰ βουλάς
ἐσθλοί, ἐπιχθόνιοι, φύλακες θνητῶν ἀνθρώπων . . .
πλουτοδόται· καὶ τοῦτο γέρας βασιλήιον ἔσχον.

---

often considered to be the earliest *herôon*; but there is no evi-
dence of votive offerings or sacrifice.

[28] For a survey of the sites, see Boehringer (2001), Antonaccio
(1995), Coldstream (1976).

[29] Coldstream (1976, 14) argues that it was in precisely the
areas where burial customs had changed that these cults devel-
oped.

But now that the earth has covered this race
They are spirits (*daimones*), by the counsel of Zeus
   the great,
Of good on earth, and guardians of mortals . . . [30]
Givers of wealth: this is their honor, worthy of kings.

To the next generation of silver (which is more violent, and accordingly shorter lived), Hesiod allots a complementary fate (140–42):

αὐτὰρ ἐπεὶ καὶ τοῦτο γένος κατὰ γαῖα κάλυψε,
τοὶ μὲν ὑποχθόνιοι μάκαρες θνητοὶ καλέονται,
δεύτεροι, ἀλλ᾽ ἔμπης τιμὴ καὶ τοῖσιν ὀπηδεῖ.

But now that the earth has also covered this race,
They are called the blessed mortals beneath the
   earth,
second in rank, but nevertheless, honor also attends
   them.

Whereas the first group is called "spirits upon the earth," to distinguish them from gods, the second is "beneath the earth," to distinguish them from the first.[31] But they represent two sides of the same belief: that the un-

---

[30] The next two lines ("who guard lawsuits and unjust deeds/ wrapped up in mist, wandering all over the earth") are identical to *Op*. 254–55 and are judged by most editors to be interpolated.

[31] So M. L. West (1978) on these lines (following Rohde 1925, 85n37); he also notes their relevance to hero cult, as does Mantero (1973, 64–69).

known dead of the distant past retain the power, on earth or under it, to guard[32] or punish men of a later day.

By the sixth century, however, the word *hêrôs* itself is first used to describe the formerly living recipient of a religious cult. Heraclitus uses it to criticize men who pray:[33]

καὶ τοῖς ἀγάλμασι δὲ τουτέοισιν εὔχονται,
ὁκοῖον εἴ τις δόμοισι λεσχηνεύοιτο, οὔ τι γινώ-
σκων θεοὺς οὐδ᾽ ἥρωας οἵτινές εἰσι

and they pray to these images as if they were chatting with houses, not recognizing what gods or even heroes are like."

The same author speaks (as Hesiod did of the golden age) of *"guardians*, wakeful over the living and the dead."[34] Pindar gives a definition of its religious sense in his account of life after death for select mortals (fr. 133):[35]

οἷσι δὲ Φερσεφόνα ποινὰν παλαιοῦ πένθεος
δέξεται, ἐς τὸν ὕπερθεν ἅλιον κείνων ἐνάτῳ ἔτεϊ
ἀνδιδοῖ ψυχὰς πάλιν, ἐκ τᾶν βασιλῆες ἀγαυοί
καὶ σθένει κραιπνοὶ σοφίᾳ τε μέγιστοι

[32] "Guardian" (*phylax,* as in *Op.* 123) is a title of heroes also in Heraclitus (VS B 63) and frequently elsewhere (*Phylakos* at Delphi).

[33] VS 22 B 5, translated by Kahn (1979).

[34] φύλακας γίνεσθαι ἐγερτὶ ζώντων καὶ νεκρῶν (VS 22 F 63).

[35] Cf. Empedocles VS 31 B 146 and Currie (2005, 129–30, and 47–48 on Pindar's many reference to the cults of heroes).

ἄνδρες αὔξοντ'· ἐς δὲ τὸν λοιπὸν χρόνον ἥροες ἁ-
γνοὶ πρὸς ἀνθρώπων καλ‹έον›ται

For those from whom Persephone accepts requital
for her ancient grief, she surrenders up their souls
again to the upper sun in the ninth year. From
these are nurtured haughty kings and men swift in
strength and greatest in wisdom; and they are called
by men "holy heroes" for the rest of time.

He could also categorize the possible subjects of a victory
ode by asking (*Ol.* 2.1–2):

Ἀναξιφόρμιγγες ὕμνοι,
τίνα θεόν, τίν' ἥρωα, τίνα δ' ἄνδρα κελαδήσομεν;

Hymns that rule the lyre,
what god, what hero, and what man shall we
celebrate?

"Gods and heroes" is now a standard expression to in-
clude greater and lesser divinities,[36] and from this age
onward the *hêrôs* has his full religious significance and
becomes a pervasive and highly productive force in Greek
religion and society.[37] The characteristic features of a
"classical" cult of the hero are:

[36] *Theoi kai hêrôes*: e.g., Hdt. 2.45.3, 8.109.3; Thuc. 2.74.3,
4.87.2; Xen. *Symp.* 8.28, *Eq.* 11.8; Antiph. 1.27; Bremmer (2006,
18); for Plato, see Reverdin (1945, 136n3), Audollent (1904,
72.10, 76.10), and *SIG* 360, 527, 581.

[37] A summary of Pythagoras' thought (Diog. Laert. 8.32)
notes that he believed "that all the air is full of souls, and these
are considered to be spirits and heroes, and by them are sent
dreams and omens of disease and health, not only to mortals but

- a notable career, celebrated in myth;
- a memorable death;
- a tomb which houses the hero's remains,
- where offerings to him are received
- and from which he[38] acts to punish or reward those in his sphere of influence.

Yet few heroes seem to have all of these features.

3. PATTERNS OF MYTH AND CULT

Identifications of Heroes

Philostratus (*Her.* 7–8) describes how the discovery of superhuman remains in his own age was followed by an eager search for their identity, and the same seems to have happened in classical Greece: according to their sites, or the cultural or political preoccupations of their finders, they were often identified as the bodies of the heroes of epic—although not exclusively of the *Iliad* and *Odyssey*. Outside Mycenae there is a shrine identified by sixth-century graffiti as the grave of Agamemnon (although in fact there is no body there);[39] at Ithaca a cave with Bronze

---

also to cattle and other animals. And purifications, rites of aversion, prophecy, oracles and the like relate to these." See further, Detienne (1963) and Burkert (1972, 73).

[38] Female heroes (*Hêrôinai*) are few, though they definitely exist as a type (Larson 1995; *pace* Bremmer 2006).

[39] Cook (1953), Coldstream (1976, 15). The sacrifices offered to it on the 13th of Gameleion (until its capture by the Argives in

Age remains was alternately viewed as belonging to the nymphs or to Odysseus;[40] the bones of Pelops were kept in a chest at Olympia, and the hero's sanctuary received notorious blood sacrifices;[41] the Seven Against Thebes were buried at Eleusis;[42] Amphion at Thebes.[43] Even children's graves had power, like those of Medea's children at Corinth,[44] Archemoros/Opheltes at Nemea,[45] and Melicertes/Palaimon at the Isthmus.[46]

But many (if not most) such cults were for heroes without names: "I belong to the hero" is the graffito on a fifth-century shard in grave circle A at Mycenae.[47] A fourth-century cult-regulation specifies offering to "the hero at the saltworks," "the hero at Antisara," "the hero at Pyrgilion."[48] Others seem to have been named after their special functions: "the hero doctor," "the hero at the stern," and "the hero general" are all attested.[49]

---

468 BC) were well enough known to be mentioned in Soph. *El.* 278–81; *FGrHist* 306 (Deinias) F 2.

[40] Benton (1934).

[41] Paus. 6.22.1; Pind. *Ol.* 1.90–93; Burkert (1983, 93–103).

[42] See *Her.* 27 and note.

[43] Paus. 9.17.4, 7.

[44] Eur. *Med.* 1378–83.

[45] Paus. 2.15.2–3; Hyg. *Fab.* 74; and the fragments of Eur. *Hyps.*

[46] Paus. 2.1.3, 2.2.1; *IG* 4.203.8–9; Bravo (2006). For other children's cults, see Pfister (1909, 1.313–16) and Pache (2004).

[47] Jeffery (1990, 174n6, with pl. 31).

[48] Ferguson (1938, 22–23).

[49] See Farnell (1921, 71–94, "Functional Heroes and Sondergötter"). Hero doctor: Dow (1985).

Authorization for Hero Cult

When they were known, the stories of the heroes' lives were obviously an important element in their cult.[50] Yet in contrast to the Christian cult of the saints (with which it is first compared by Augustine[51]), these figures did not "earn" their holiness by their deeds in life; in fact more than a few, such as Oedipus, the Seven Against Thebes, or, in historical times, Cleomedes of Astypalaea (Paus. 6.9.6), committed terrible crimes.[52] It was more often the hero's *death* that made him holy, at the hands of a god, like Neoptolemus (killed by Apollo) or Hippolytus (by Aphrodite),[53] or in some other violent and unseemly way, like Hesiod at Orchomenos,[54] Medea's children, or Eurystheus at Athens (Eur. *Heracl.* 1026–44).

The most impressive heroic end—even though it left no body for veneration—was disappearance (*aphanismos*).[55] After being disqualified at the Olympics, Cleomedes of Astypalaea (Paus. 6.9.6) killed dozens of schoolchildren in a fit of rage and shut himself into a box in the

[50] The complex task of classifying the myths of heroes and relating them to cults is addressed by Brelich (1958).

[51] *De civ. D.* 10.21. For a Christian dialogue defending the powers of the saints, see Dal Santo (2012).

[52] Rohde (1925, 1.178ff.).

[53] In each case the dead hero's cult is joined to the god's shrine. Many joint god-hero cults are reflected in divine epithets, in which case the hero might be either friend or enemy: Aphrodite Aineias, Apollo Ptoos, Apollo Hyacinthus, Poseidon Erechtheus, Artemis Iphigeneia, Athena Skiras (derived from Skiron), Artemis Kalliste (fr. Kallisto).

[54] Scodel (1981).

[55] Pease (1942).

temple of Athena; when the townsmen pried it open, he was gone. According to some versions, Heracles had disappeared from his pyre during a thunderstorm,[56] as had Alcmene's corpse from her coffin (Paus. 9.16.7; Pfister 1909, 120n429, 124–25). Finally, the classical version of the establishment of a hero cult, Sophocles' *Oedipus at Colonus*, culminates in Oedipus' disappearance at a holy site that will remain known only to Theseus and subsequent rulers of Athens.[57]

The ultimate authority for the heroic status of a tomb or recently dead citizen was the Delphic oracle.[58] Men as diverse as Lycurgus,[59] Adrastos in Sicyon (Hdt. 5.67), Eurystheus (Eur., *Heracl.* 1026–44), the poet Hesiod at Orchomenos (Paus. 9.38.3), and Cleomedes were revealed in this way to be heroes. Once the pattern was established, it was possible to add the recently dead to the heroes also.

In accordance with Homer's frequent assertion (e.g., *Il.* 1.272, 5.304, 12.383, 12.449, 20.287) that men in the past were stronger than their descendants, heroic bodies were assumed to be of fantastic size:[60] the bones of Orestes, recovered from Tegea and returned to Sparta

---

[56] Apollod. *Bibl.* 2.7.7 (160); Diod. Sic. 4.38.4; Eur. *Heracl.* 910ff. For disappearance during a storm, note also Romulus, Livy 1.16.1. According to Servius, *Aen* 3.402, only Philoctetes knew the site of his disappearance.

[57] Compare the secret tomb of Dirce (Paus. 2.2.2).

[58] Bouché-Leclercq (1879, 3.143ff.).

[59] Hdt. 1.65.3; Plut. *Lyc.* 31 (here called loosely "god"; but "hero" at *FGrHist* 90 F 57); cf. Paus. 3.16.6, and Fraser (1972, ad loc).

[60] For the catalog of such discoveries by the vinedresser and possible sources, see Rusten (2004).

(Hdt. 1.68) were in a coffin seven cubits long, and those of Theseus transferred from Scyros to Athens (see below) were equally large. Thus Philostratus' vinedresser devotes much time to convincing the skeptical Phoenician with stories of such finds.[61] In addition, the presence of snakes near a tomb was considered a sign of heroic status.[62]

Shrines and Cults

That *hêrôa* were distinct from shrines of gods is usually reflected in their architecture and placement and in the vocabulary of their cult.[63] For example, sacrifice to a hero was termed *enagizein* rather than *thuein*, libations called *choai* rather than *spondai*; they were made not on an altar (*bômos*), but on a ground-level hearth (*eschara*) or in a pit (*bothros*).[64] Many of the oldest *hêrôa* had been round burial mounds (grave circles, or *tholoi*);[65] perhaps in imi-

---

[61] *Her.* 7–8, on which see notes. Suetonius (*Aug.* 72) reports that the emperor kept a collection of such relics, and Virgil (*G.* 1.497) predicts that such finds will someday occur again. See in general Pfister (1909, 2.425–28, 507–8) and Frazer (1972, on Paus. 8.29.1).

[62] E.g., Theophr. *Char.* 16.4; Ogilvie on Livy 1.56.4; Porph *Plot.* 2; Hdt. 8.41; Plut. *Cleom.* 39; *Suppl. Hellen.* 129 (Archelaus); Verg. *Aen* 5.84–95. See especially Küster (1913), Harrison (1955, 325–31), Fraser (1972, 1.778ff, 2.1086–89), Rohde (1925, 1.120–21n 2).

[63] It is important to remember, however, that these distinctions (basically between Olympian and chthonic cults) are not unbreakable: see Burkert (1985, 199–203) and §12 below.

[64] Hdt. 2.44; see especially Ekroth (2002).

[65] Pelon (1976).

tation of these, when shrines were built they tended to be round, like that of Palaemon at Corinth and the hero Phylakos at Delphi; altars were also round.[66]

Since the hero was powerful only in the vicinity of his tomb, tomb placement was important for the sort of cult it enjoyed; at the gate of a city or even within its walls, the hero could defend against invaders.[67] Public places, especially the agora, were equally popular, and the Athenian agora was thick with *herôa*.[68] Some of the most famous *hêrôa* shared precincts with gods, with whom they were said to have a special (often antagonistic) association.[69]

4. PATTERNS OF BELIEF

City Cults

To match its diverse origins, hero cult partakes of various patterns of religious belief: heroes can be viewed as intermediaries between god and man, honored ancestors, civic icons and benefactors, or as the anonymous vengeful or grateful dead.

The value of divine powers (however small) whose names, careers, and functions might be invented or manipulated must have been obvious to politicians from the

[66] Pfister (1909, 445–49, "Gräber auf dem Markt"). Plut. *Sol.* 9, says that, in contrast to temples of gods, *hêrôa* usually face west.

[67] The Aeacidae moved from Aegina to Salamis during the Persian wars (see on 53.15); Bérard (1970). Similarly, in *Oedipus Colonus*, Creon, aware of the prophecy of Oedipus' powers, wishes him to be buried at the Theban frontier.

[68] Broneer (1942) and H. Thompson (1978).

[69] Pfister (1909, 450–58).

start,[70] especially at Athens. We are told that Draco and Solon used local heroes in programs of religious or administrative reform[71] and Cleisthenes went even further by choosing (with the help of Delphi) ten heroes to serve as eponyms of his new tribal organization of the city.[72] The citizen's loyalty to his family or geographical area of Attica was to be replaced by that to his tribe, represented by the hero. Subsequent leaders who evoked the pride of the city as a whole, like founder-heroes of colonies[73] or victorious athletes,[74] could receive such cults also.

National heroes were also called on for defense.[75] They were invoked to accompany armies into battle and were often said to appear in moments of crisis.[76] The presence

[70] Snodgrass (1982).

[71] Draco: Porph *Abst.* 4.22, p. 380.

[72] Kron (1976).

[73] E.g., Battos in Cyrene, Pind. *Pyth.* 5.95; Brasidas in Amphipolis, Thuc. 5.11; Hdt. 6.38; Rohde (1925, 1.175ff); Pfister (1909, 295–302, 445ff.); Farnell (1921, 413–41).

[74] Brelich (1958, 99n81) is right to protest against the notion that this is a late and degenerate development—he remarks on the irony that two experts on Pindar (Wilamowitz and Farnell) have so little regard for the importance of the athlete. Existing heroes in turn became patrons of athletics: see Fontenrose (1968).

[75] Ajax and Telamon, see *Her.* 53; Phylakos and Autonoos at Delphi (Hdt. 8.37), Brennus' death at Delphi—Paus. 10.23; Justin Trogus, Book 24; cf. Achilles' rout of the Amazons, *Her.* 57. Perhaps the most bizarre is Cimon in Cition, Plut. *Cim.* 19.5.

[76] Pfister (1909, 510–11). For epiphanies of heroes in warfare, see in general Pritchett (1979, 3.14–46). Even Xerxes himself had libations offered to the heroes of Troy on his way to Greece (Hdt.

of a hero's bones strengthened his native city: thus Orestes' bones were stolen from Tegea and returned to Sparta, and in 469–468 BC the bones of Theseus were returned to Athens from Scyros and placed in a special shrine.[77] Disputes often arose between two cities for the right to possess a *hêrôon*.[78]

Cities called on heroes to heal disease or ease famine.[79] There were special heroes relating to safety at sea;[80] eventually some hero shrines (especially of Trophonius in Boeotia and Amphilochus in Cilicia) developed reputations for prophecy that rivaled Delphi.[81]

Heroes and the Individual[82]

But as a lesser power, more closely tied to a particular place or neighborhood, the hero was even better suited to

---

7.43), which Alexander did in reverse (to Greek heroes) years later on his way to attack the east.

[77] Podlecki (1971).

[78] Pfister (1909, 193–211).

[79] Kutsch (1913).

[80] Eitrem (1935, 53–67); Ferguson (1938, 25–27); *FGrHist* 328 (Philochorus) F 111.

[81] Bouché-Leclercq (1879, 3.315–62).

[82] I pass over here (as not relevant to Heroicus) the abundant inscriptional evidence for the importance of heroes to associations and groups of all kinds (see the many entries in Ascough, Harland, and Kloppenborg 2012). Also omitted are the entertaining stories of the attempts of Empedocles and Heraclides of Pontus to fabricate evidence to make them heroes after their deaths (Diog. Laert. 8.67ff., 5.91).

a personal, individual faith, as in the *Heroicus*. For his protégés, the activities of a "local hero"[83] might be rather mundane—guard their buried treasure, keep them safe from disease or financial catastrophe—but his presence was all the more vividly felt. Comic poets, for example, seem often to have taken advantage of the meddlesomeness of the heroes to influence their plots: Menander wrote a play (now lost) called *The Hero*, and no less than five other plays were called *Heroes*, probably after their choruses. The parabasis of one of these is now extant, with a detailed description of the heroes' powers:[84]

> Therefore, gentlemen, stay on your guard and worship the heroes, since we are the dispensers of good fortune and bad—we keep an eye on the unjust, the thieves and pickpockets, and give them diseases: enlarged spleens, coughs, dropsy, running noses, psoriasis, gout, insanity, genital infections, chills and fever. That's what we give to thieves.

They probably went on to tell the rewards they gave to the good; yet heroes were distinctly more prone to harm than help, as a fable of Babrius tells:

> There was a hero who had a shrine at the house of a pious man; and he, sacrificing there and garlanding the altar, and soaking it with wine, used always to pray, "hail, most beloved of heroes, and bring your neighbor abundant good fortune." But the hero appeared to him in the middle of the night and

83 Rusten (1983).
84 Aristophanes fr. 322 Kassel-Austin.

25

said "there's not one hero who can give you good luck—you must ask the gods for that. We are the givers of all the bad things which are man's lot. So if you want troubles, go ahead and pray; I'll give you even more than you ask for. From now on, then, whenever you sacrifice you'll know how things are." (Perry 1965, Fable 63)

A character in a Menandrian play seems to agree (fr. 322 *PCG*): "The heroes are keener at doing harm than at helping out." The hero of Temesa (Paus. 6.6.4–11; Callim. *Aet.*, Book 4, frr. 98–99) was known only for violence, and Philostratus' vinedresser asserts that both Hector (*Her.* 19) and Achilles (*Her.* 56) have killed mortals who displeased them.

Heroes in Hellenistic and Roman Greece

Over subsequent centuries the concept of the hero was bound to undergo some change, and it has been asserted that it became debased.[85] In numerous known cases the dead could be called heroes and received tomb cult—the most famous case is Hadrian's favorite Antinous[86]—but the word itself and many of its associations remained intact.[87] In hellenistic Cnidus, a hero was commemorated in an epigram with an athletic facility, which recalls Protesilaus' racecourse (ch. 3.6):[88]

[85] Quotations in Jones (2010, ch. 5).
[86] Vout and Moore (2006); Vout (2007); Jones (2010, 75–83).
[87] See especially Jones (2010, ch. 6).
[88] Merkelbach and Stauber (1998, 1:6).

βαιὸν ὁδοιπορίης ἔ[τ]ι λείπεται, ἀλλὰ πρὸς αἶπος
    τὴν ὀλίγην ἀνύσεις ἀτραπιτὸν διέπων
χειρὸς ἀφ᾽ ἡμετέρης λαιῆς, ξένε, κἀμὲ προσείπας
    χαίρειν, εἰ στείχεις πρὸς φιλίου τέμενος
ἥρωος Ἀντιγόνου· Μοῦσαι δέ σοι εἴ τι νέμουσιν
    ἐσθλόν, ἀπάρχεσθαι δαίμοσιν ἐγ μελέτης.
καὶ γὰρ ἀοιδοῖσιν θυμέλη καὶ σηκὸς ὑπ᾽ ἄγχει
    τῶι Ἐπιγόνου κούρωι ξυνὸς ὁμευνετίδος
καὶ δρόμος ἠϊθέοισιν ἱδρύεται ἠδὲ παλαίστρη
    λουτρά τε καὶ ταρσῶι Πὰν ὁ μελιζόμενος.
ἀλλ᾽ ἀσινὴς ἔρχευ καὶ ἀπ᾽ Ἀρκαδίης τεμενουρὸν
    Ἑρμῆν οὐ μέμψει τρηχέος ἐχ Φενέου.

A little way still remains, but at the height
you will soon arrive, following the path
on your left hand, stranger; and once you have bid
    me
hello, you enter the precinct of the friendly
hero Antigonus. If the Muses have granted you some
talent, make an offering from your training to the
    divinities;
For there is an altar for singers, and down in the
    valley a shrine
for the son of Epigonus, shared by his wife.
There is also a running track for youths, and a
    palaestra,
baths, and Pan playing on his pipes.
But go without harm, and with the precinct guard
    from Arcadia,
Hermes from rough Pheneus, you will find no fault.

Furthermore, in the religious thought of the first to the
third centuries AD, the Hesiodic and Platonic notion of

daimones, intermediate between god and man, was a popular concept. Speakers in two of Plutarch's dialogues (*On the Decline of Oracles* and *On the Face in the Moon*), advance the notion of *daimones* as the earthly servants of the more distant gods, or moon-dwelling spirits of the dead. Maximus of Tyre (*Or.* 9.7, Trapp 1997) extends the concept to the heroes of myth as well:

> Not all *daimones* perform all functions, however; now too, as in life, each is given a different job. It is here that we see the role of that susceptibility to the emotions that marks them off from God. They do not want to rid themselves entirely of the natures that were theirs when they lived on earth. Asclepius continues to heal the sick, Heracles to perform mighty deeds, Dionysus to lead the revels, Amphilochus to give oracles, the Dioscuri to sail the seas, Minos to dispense justice, and Achilles to wield his weapons. Achilles dwells on an island in the Black Sea opposite the mouth of the Ister, where he has a temple and altars. . . . According to the people of Troy, Hector remains on the site of his former home, and can be seen sweeping over the plain, flashing with light. I myself have never seen either Hector or Achilles, but I have seen the Dioscuri, in the form of bright stars, righting a ship in a storm. I have seen Asclepius, and that not in a dream. I have seen Heracles, in waking reality.

The vinedresser in the *Heroicus* has such a personal relationship with one hero, his rustic patron and his informant for the "true story" of the Trojan War, and especially with two other heroes—one the prototype of the sophists and the other the quintessential warrior, but also a poet, whose rage and cult live on beyond his death.

5. CORRECTING HOMER

In contrast to the first two heroes, who do not appear in Homer at all and whose deeds are new to the Phoenician stranger, Achilles dominates the *Iliad*, and his tomb was a site of pilgrimage since Alexander and, most recently, Caracalla. Yet the vinedresser's account of him is quite different from Homer's, interweaving details from the *Iliad* with sensational novelties, using two different methods of "Homer correction," to which we must now turn.[89]

In the Hellenistic period, writers of mythological romances had fictionalized "sources" for their original compositions: Euhemerus claimed that his revelation that the "gods" were actually just human kings who invented ruler cult was based on an inscription that he had discovered; Dionysius Scytobrachion claimed to have discovered poems of Linus and Thymoitas that authenticated his stories of the mortal Dionysus who ruled in Libya.[90] Out of this tradition come two works of the first to second centuries AD, which, like the *Heroicus*, claim to correct Homer's account of the Trojan War based on new sources. In the time of Nero, the "discovery" of a memoir of the Trojan War by a certain Dictys of Crete, the secretary to Idomeneus, was supposedly translated first into Greek,

---

[89] See in general Lamberton and Keaney (1992), Zeitlin (2001), and Kim (2010).

[90] Rusten (1982, 102–6). Cf. the sources claimed in Quintilian 1.8.21 or the obscure histories in Plut. *Quaest. conv.* 5.2.7

then Latin, containing a very different account than that of Homer's. The Latin translation is extant in medieval manuscripts, and there was skepticism about a Greek original until its discovery on papyrus.[91] The Greek version is parodied by Lucian (*Ver. hist.* 2.25–26), and *Heroicus* knows it also, since it explicitly corrects the version of Dictys in numerous places (Huhn and Bethe 1917, 618–19):

- ch. 26.10: Thrasymedes was not at Troy with Nestor (cf. Dictys 1.13)
- ch. 30: Idomeneus was never at Troy at all (thereby invalidating the entire premise of Dictys!)
- ch. 48.17: Achilles attacks Hector even though weakened (cf. Dictys 3.15)
- ch. 51: Polyxena died of love for Achilles (cf. Dictys 5.13)

A somewhat later work, known only in Latin translation, purports to be the memoir of Dares the Phrygian, mentioned by Homer (*Il.* 5.9) as a priest of Hephaestus at Troy. It tells the fall of Troy from the other side (Merkle 1996).[92] These works not only revised Homer, they often replaced him: in the Middle Ages, knowledge of the Trojan War was based entirely on Dictys (preferred in Byzantine literature) and Dares (preferred in the Latin west).[93]

The conceit of *Heroicus* is more complex. The fact that

91 Gainsford (2012).

92 Cf. the letter of Sarpedon discovered in Lycia by Mucianus, Plin. *HN* 13.88.

93 Homer is also debunked in Lucian, *The Dream* or *The Cock* 17 (by a cock who claims to have been at Troy in a past life).

the vinedresser relies for much of his information on the hero Protesilaus, and is withdrawn from the rest of the world, results in the paradox that within the dialogue the mythical events have the most immediate authority: an anecdote about Hadrian is oral tradition from one's grandfather (8.1), but for the events at Troy we have "firsthand" evidence. Further, Protesilaus is also a sensitive critic of Homer's poetry (ch. 25). He praises Homer's style and superiority to other hexameter poets and his philosophical treatment of the battles of gods, but he criticizes his tendency to make men more noble than gods, his suppression of the truth of Helen being in Egypt, and his invention of tall tales to magnify Odysseus. Protesilaus also frequently explains the meaning of individual Homeric verses (e.g., chs. 2, 12).

But the vinedresser also frequently corrects Homer on his own account, using the "rationalistic" method of assessing the "plausibility" (*eikos*) of the transmitted story versus an alternative.[94] This approach to myth had been practiced since the earliest Greek historians, Hecataeus and Herodotus, and it had been brilliantly applied by the late first-century sophist Dio of Prusa in his *Trojan Oration* to deduce that Hector had in fact killed Achilles, and Troy had not been taken by the Greeks.[95] The vinedresser knows this allegation as well and explicitly corrects it: Achilles *did* kill Hector (ch. 37, Huhn and Bethe 1917, 617, 619n1).

The vinedresser is also a critic of Homer's poetry, but less an aesthetic than a partisan one: he is angered that

[94] *Her.* 25.10, 33.33, 35.11, 45.8.
[95] See especially Hunter (2009) and Kim (2010, 85–139).

Homer suppressed the Telephus story, Palamedes, and others to magnify Achilles and Odysseus (ch. 24).

6. THE SETTING[96]

Like the Phoenician—who is originally interested only in finding a good wind to help him sail away—we learn only gradually the unusual qualities of the setting. The moment of greatest surprise is in 5.2, when he cannot contain himself over the spot where he has sat down: the fragrances, the colors, the artful plantings, are for him the perfect spot to talk. In the ancient literary tradition, fragrant flowers and trees, heavy shade, and clear streams were the invariable elements of the perfect natural setting for meeting a divinity (cf. Numa and Egeria, Livy 1.21.3, and especially Pl. *Phdr.*, 230 BC, near a sanctuary of Pan) as well as for holding a long conversation[97] throughout ancient literature. The hero even keeps his racecourse there.[98]

But beyond the inevitable *Phaedrus* reference,[99] there is further significance to the landscape. The countryside is a place to return to the simple pleasures of working the land (cf. Dio's *Euboicus*) and to find throwbacks to an earlier age, like Herodes' Agathion (see §11 below). It recalls a neglected philosophical and cultural past to

---

[96] See especially Jones (2001) and Whitmarsh (2009).

[97] Martin (2002) on similarities to the Greek novel.

[98] For the Hellenistic hero Antigonus' gift of a race course and athletic facilities in Cnidus, see §4 above.

[99] For *Phaedrus* in particular as a favorite of imperial literature, see Trapp (1990), and for *Heroicus* in particular, Hodkinson (2011).

which the reader feels drawn to make a personal pilgrimage.

The mound of Protesilaus,[100] his shrine,[101] and his statue[102] are also at the site. As the vinedresser admits, they are decayed with age and neglected (9.5), as many a Greek sacred site is described by Pausanias—beautiful as the Phoenician finds them, a sanctuary is not supposed to be covered with vines;[103] and the vinedresser's understated allusion to the shrine's history (9.5) will not conceal its fame in the penultimate episode of Herodotus' Persian wars (see §8 below).

In fact, this sanctuary stands on the crossing between Europe and Asia (Rutherford 2009, 230), the path of invasion (in both directions)[104] and travel. The vinedresser claims it has been frequently visited, even as an oracle and healing shrine.

Across the Hellespont from the vinedresser's territory but closely linked to it ("the sea is like a river for us," ch. 23.1), is the Troad, especially the contemporary town of

---

[100] Mound: Demangel (1926); Jones (2001); Grossardt (2006a, I, ch. 2, pp. 32–33) (see Strabo 13.1.31).

[101] Shrine: The shrine is mentioned as a landmark by Thuc. 8.102 (cited with other travelers' account in Pottier [1915, 141–46]).

[102] Used also to describe his appearance, §11 below.

[103] Some of the famous sites are covered by vines (Pisa, Paus. 6.22.1; Alcock 1993), like Elaious; many deserted shrines (Frazer 1966, on Pausanias, xiv n6).

[104] Evocative also for Gallipoli; the Elaious necropolis was excavated by French troops during that campaign; Pottier (1915).

Ilion, portrayed as inhabited by shepherds and cowherds amid the still-surviving monuments of the Trojan War:[105] statues of Hector[106] (honored with athletic contests) and other Trojan heroes, but also Greeks[107]—near the sea the tomb of Ajax,[108] and especially the mound of Achilles and Patroclus[109]—which have attracted regular visits from celebrities, some historical (Alexander,[110] Hadrian, Caracalla) some more fictionalized (Caesar, in Lucan; Julian, in a letter [Henning 1874]).[111]

Farther afield the speaker is familiar with the sites of the discovery of large heroic (or gigantic) bones in Sigeiun (8.6) or the islands of the northeast Aegean, south in Cos

[105] The Tübingen-Cincinnati excavations at Ilion show that Roman Ilion was far more developed and prosperous, and the worship of Athena more prominent (athletic contests actually hers) than of the heroes; see the annual reports by Rose. *Heroicus* has the same way of filtering out the contemporary population as Pausanias; see §7 below.

[106] Literary and numismatic testimonia for a statue of Hector in Erskine (2001, 103n44).

[107] Ilians sacrifice to Achilles, Patroclus, even Ajax, but not to Heracles (Strabo 13.1.32).

[108] Monument and temple of Ajax at Rhoeteaum: Strabo 13.1.30, his statue was restored by Augustus after taken by Antony.

[109] The mound of Achilles: *Her.* 51.12; Hdt. 5.94; Cook (1973, 177–79); Rose (2000, 65–66); Burgess (2009, 117–26 [114–17 on the literary evidence]); Graninger (2011, 149n141); Alcock (2004, 160–63), on imperial constructions connected with Achilles' tumulus.

[110] Arr. *Anab.* 1.12.

[111] Erskine (2001); Hertel (2003, 199–208 [graves of heroes], 274–301 [Roman Ilion]); Zwingmann (2012, 31–106).

or others (Follet 2004), or the oracle of Orpheus' head on
Lesbos (28.8–9) and of special significance in Lemnos,
home of the author and a place the vinedresser has visited
to confirm a heroic burial discovered by Menecrates of
Steiria, a historically attested prominent Lemnian (Follet
1974; 2004). The vinedresser also knows Lemnian lore:
the annual fire purification (53.3–7, [Burkert 1970]), the
powers of "terra Lemnia" (28.5), and the story of Philoc-
tetes (28 [Masciadri 2008]). Because the port of Elaious is
nearby, the vinedresser also claims knowledge of sailors'
stories of Leuke in the Black Sea (cf. §13 below).

7. VOICES OF THE DIALOGUE

The Vinedresser's Voices and Narrative Modes

If the primary setting of *Heroicus* owes something to
Phaedrus, it also resembles it in being an unframed dia-
logue with no external narrator, so that it is itself intrinsi-
cally resistant to the search for authorial voice, even
though it is dominated by one speaker.

This is a familiar problem with the Socratic dialogues,
but a new one for Philostratus, and the key character of
the vinedresser is an original and productive creation. In
him, Philostratus embodies a complex of traits that in a
past life has become a *pepaideumenos* but is now in rus-
tic retreat—rusticity, a simple life and occupation, piety
and morality, with high education and impeccable Attic
speech, narrative and descriptive skill.

Added to this is the vinedresser's unique access to Pro-
tesilaus as informant—he is profoundly devoted to his

patron hero (the similarity of this fictional religious relationship to that between Aristides and Asclepius, and the profound differences in the way it is expressed, are instructive for the limits of Philostratus' dialogue), and he can "combine aesthetic and literary sophistication with a profound engagement with lived religion" (Platt 2011, 241).

As an authority on the past, the vinedresser surpasses not only Dictys and Dares with their discovered documents but even the interviews of Apollonius with Achilles, Lucian with Homer in *True Histories* or that of Homer himself with Odysseus (*Her.* 43.12–16), so that he "facilitates a more direct engagement between the reader and the *daimon* that purports to bypass the very sources of information on which the dialogue is based" (Platt 2011, 241). He is the perfect intermediary between the contemporary world of Roman Greece and the literary, religious, and moral world of the Greek heroes.[112]

Since one might say he is "talking for two," the vinedresser makes use of ancient Greek's whole range of distancing-markers for indirect speech: accusative and infinitive, ὡς with the optative or indicative, but sometimes dispenses with these markers entirely.

But the vinedresser also interjects his own material, posing numerous questions to the Phoenician and giving answers to him in turn about his past life and his relation-

112 Although his relationship to Protesilaus owes something to the rustic "Heracles" of Herodes VS 2.552–54 (§11 below), his setting is indebted to Dio's *Euboicus* as well as Plato's *Phaedrus*.

ship to the hero. He has assembled the catalog of giant bones himself (even in one case verified with autopsy). As noted above (§5), the rationalistic arguments for and against the Homeric stories' truth are often his own, and on Leuke he supplements Protesilaus with travelers' tales he has collected himself.

Further, although the vinedresser is well informed on some things that we do not know (56.5, the famous vase whose story he declines to tell), the setting is made subordinate to his theme of the heroes of the age of Homer; as in Pausanias, the contemporary world is filtered out, and we are left only with what is relevant to his stories, as noted in §6 above.

And the vinedresser is not always a reliable narrator, at least of detail. He makes obvious slips (which are unlikely to be the author's or the result of textual corruption): Nemea for Tegea (8.3), Ariadne for Evadne (11.8), Theseus as founder of the Anthesteria (35.9), "in Troy" instead of "at Aulis" for Telephus' healing of Achilles (23.24), comparing the body of Protesilaus to a herm (10.4). Even in the case of Homer's texts we have obvious slips: at 18.2 ("the story in the *Madness*," as if referring to a section of the *Iliad* or a tragedy that is not known to exist), 51.7 ("in the Second Weighing of Souls" for "Second Nekyia"). Less obvious but still notable is 51.1, where he claims that *Il.* 22.359, which in our texts refers to Achilles' future death at the Scaean gates, is consistent with an ambush at the temple of Thymbraean Apollo, or his claim at 24.1–2 that Homer omitted the story of the battle with Telephus, when it would have been impossible for him to include it in the scope of the *Iliad*. Are we to assume that all these

37

are the vinedresser's inept adaptations of Protesilaus' correct reports?[113]

Once we realize that the vinedresser is not simply to be taken as the voice of the author, we can see that he manipulates his interlocutor by provoking him with an insulting characterization, by planting mentions of stories to elicit further requests, and above all by insisting on his declaration of faith before giving him any more stories.

All this means that the voice of the vinedresser can be that of a Homeric scholar/reinterpreter, teller of tall tales, ekphrast of statues and faces, repository of athletic anecdotes, exegete of cults, finally a witness to personal religion. This appropriation of other narrative modes within the dialogue enables two sophisticated elaborations.

First, the vinedresser's storytelling gives different kinds of narrative:[114]

[113] One result is that it is futile to attempt to trace Philostratus' "sources" in any case, since every conceivable "source" of Philostratus' is also filtered through the vineyard keeper's mouth (and sometimes through Protesilaus' as well) to remove it still farther from reality, so that the very intractability of the source search is a sign of his aesthetic success. Clearly, to speak of "sources" at all in *Heroicus* is much less valid than it would be for even another work from this fertile period of reworking classical texts.

[114] These sometimes enable the vinedresser to mimic some of the rest of Philostratus' works with biography (*VS, VA*), athletic anecdote (*Gym.*), and ekphrasis (*Gym.* and *Imag.*).

- "biographies" of the heroes
- battle narratives of two kinds (Iliad style, and divine rout of impious foreign invaders)
- Elaborate rituals
- Tales of Faraway uncanny places

Second, the same story can be told from different perspectives in different works:

- The Trojan War corrections come from Achilles to Apollonius in the *Life of Apollonius*, but from Protesilaus to the vinedresser in *Heroicus* (see §1 above).
- The story of Thessalian sacrifices is divided between *Heroicus* (53.8–17) and the *Life of Apollonius* (4.16 and 4.23.1), each from a different perspective: the beginning of the story (the oracle's command, the first sacrifices and subsequent decline) is told by Protesilaus through the vinedresser, then for the middle it shifts to the voice of Achilles through Apollonius (now in the first century AD and with Apollonius in the role of the oracle), before returning to Protesilaus and the vinedresser (53.18–23) for an update.
- Anecdotes about advice to an athlete (14 and 15) are given by Protesilaus as oracle in *Heroicus,* but attributed to trainers in *Gymnasticus.*

On one occasion (56.5), the vinedresser points to an "overlap" himself and declines to retell a story, with which the Phoenician seems to agree. But the story of the golden *kalpis* is a mystery to us; was it really already told, or is this just a tease?

The Phoenician and His "Conversion"

In contrast to the vinedresser, the Phoenician tells us nothing explicitly about his background or his beliefs.[115] But the vinedresser himself makes some initial, not flattering observations—on his haste and ignoring of his surroundings (1.2; Alcock 2004, 159), on his luxurious clothing and the reputation of Phoenicians not only for seafaring but also (relying on Homer)[116] for greed; in responding to them the Phoenician reveals that he is a merchant, anxious about his Aegean voyage and its profit, and he has had an unsettling dream about heroes that spurred him to this spot. He has heard Greek myths as a child, and seems to know Homer well. But on the heroes, he declares himself a definite skeptic, especially regarding their larger-than-human size.

This traveler is curious—one thinks of Apuleius' Lucius—about what he sees and hears, and the vinedresser exploits this well. Before the vinedresser will proceed to any more stories, he insists first on belief in the heroes' size, and overwhelms the Phoenician with examples from the distant past in distant places to this very region and just last year. This is the first step to the Phoenician's enthusiastic acceptance of the vinedresser's (and Protesilaus') stories, and at the end of the dialogue he is begging for more.

Modern scholars, intrigued by this change of heart,

---

115 In this way he is very different from the argumentative Phoenician encountered by Paus. 7.23.7, who asserts the superiority of his own religion.

116 Winter (1995).

have been inclined to see this Phoenician as a stand-in for some other political individual or ethnic or religious group that would be obvious to the emperor.[117] But Phoenicians are not so rare in imperial literature as to be necessarily allegorical, and along with other stereotypes not in play here (pirates, debauchery, strange rituals) in the novel in particular they are highly Hellenized and thus closer to Greeks than barbarians.[118]

Even apart from the Phoenician's identity, there is the question of how to interpret his change of heart. Nock (1972, 327) found it profoundly and traditionally religious and compared it with Christianity:

> The *Heroicus* of Philostratus illustrates well the concept of πίστις in the early third century A.D. A Phoenician visits a vine-tender who believes himself to have a special relation to the hero Protesilaus, who visits him and looks after him. The Phoenician is inclined to disbelieve things mystical, having met no eye-witnesses of their reality (17.9 φημὶ γὰρ ἀπίστως διακεῖσθαι πρὸς τὰ μυθώδη) but is sympathetic, having said earlier (3.1) "I'm sure the heroes would be much indebted to you, if I left here believing in them." The vine-tender's narratives convince him, and he says (18.1) "From now on, vinedresser, I shall be on your side, and

[117] Champlin (1981); Aitken and MacLean (2004) combine a number of associations with threats to Rome (Syrians, Carthaginians, Eastern religions) tied to eastern campaigns of Alexander Severus promoting Hellenized religion as a means to resist the Persian threat.

[118] Briquel-Chatonnet (1992); Millar (1983).

allow no one to doubt such stories." (Μετὰ σοῦ
λοιπόν, ἀμπελουργέ, τάττω ἐμαυτὸν καὶ οὐδεὶς ἔτι
τοῖς τοιούτοις ἀπιστήσει.) . . . It is like the effect
of an apostolic sermon.

Others have felt the same, pointing to the movement from
ἄπιστος to πείθομαι (σοι), and the parallel phrase used
to acknowledge Apollonius of Tyana who appeared after
his death (VA 8.31).[119]

The entire phenomenon of literary conversion, natu-
rally better known in Christian texts of this period than in
pagan ones, was studied by Nock (1933). The very first
Christian conversion-dialogue, from the first decades of
the third century, is the Latin work *Octavius* by Minucius
Felix, which doubles *Heroicus* in some formal aspects: it
begins with a chance meeting on the beach in Ostia, at a
beautiful and relaxing spot; a skeptic who is a critic of
Christian beliefs is converted after hearing the other side;
at the end, he postpones further discussion of the myster-
ies to tomorrow, because the sun is setting (*Oct.* 40).[120]

To some extent these similarities are misleading: the
two speakers are already known to each other (and there
exists considerable hostility between them), the skepti-
cism of the converted is of a philosophical kind, and the
substance of the dialogue, allowing each to make his case
in full in alternation, resembles a Ciceronian dialogue
more closely than the Platonic style of *Heroicus*.

---

[119] ἱδρῶτί τε πολλῷ ἐρρεῖτο καὶ ἐβόα "πείθομαί σοι." ἐρο-
μένων δ᾽ αὐτὸ τῶν παρόντων, ὅ τι πέπονθεν, "οὐχ ὁρᾶτε" ἔφη
"ὑμεῖς Ἀπολλώνιον τὸν σοφόν . . .

[120] Some of these elements occur also in Justin's *Dialogue
with Trypho*.

In any case, most scholars of early Christianity and secular literature would agree that it was Christians who adapted the pagan dialogues, not the other way around.[121] The "protreptic" dialogue was a form used by Aristotle and in Cicero's *Hortensius*, both now lost, but their forms are used (or parodied) by Lucian in four dialogues: *Nigrinus* (a conversion to philosophy so effective that even the man to whom the story is told is converted); *Hermotimus* (a student of philosophy is converted to "a normal life" [κοινὸς βίος] and abandons philosophy, a sort of "apotreptic" as Schäublin [1985] notes); and two conversions to absurd vocations, the life of the parasite (*de Parasito*) and a love of theatrical dance (*de Saltatione*). As Schäublin (1985) notes, these four dialogues have in common an initial declaration of criticism or disbelief, a willingness to listen to the case for it, and a concluding statement of belief. All these are of course to be found in *Heroicus*. But there is an additional link with a work of Lucian when we consider precisely what it is that the Phoenician embraces: it is not the religion of the heroes themselves, but the highly entertaining *stories* about them that the vine-dresser tells that captivate him. The inability to disbelieve captivating stories is the subject of Lucian's *Lover of Lies*, for which the title ἄπιστος is also preserved. There Tychiades (who is the one "converted" in *Parasite*) complains to his interlocutor of a host's insistence on telling him one tall tale after another, until he finally had to leave him in disgust. The tales Tychiades repeats, however, are so cap-

---

[121] Schäublin (1985). Grossardt (2006a, 41–61) finds at the beginning and the end of *Heroicus* and *VA* glimpses of an underlying Epicureanism at odds with their purported contents; see also ch. 4.6 n. 15.

tivating that his hearer confesses he himself is in danger of believing them. Now, the tale whose very beginning finally sends Tychiades packing promises to be about an oracle from the hero Amphilochus in Cilicia, mentioned early on by the vinedresser as a hero that the Phoenician probably knows already (17.1). In Lucian's *Assembly of the Gods* 12, Momus includes in his complaint to Zeus the fraudulent divinity of six heroes, all named in *Heroicus*:

> Trophonius, Zeus, and (what sticks in my gorge beyond everything) Amphilochus, who, though the son of an outcast and matricide, gives prophecies, the miscreant, in Cilicia, telling lies most of the time and playing charlatan for the sake of his two obols. That is why you, Apollo, are no longer in favor; at present, oracles are delivered by every stone and every altar that is drenched with oil and has garlands and can provide itself with a charlatan—of whom there are plenty. Already the statue of Polydamas the athlete heals those who have fevers in Olympia, Alcmaeon, son of Amphiaraus; he slew his mother Eriphyle, fled from Argos in frenzy, and never returned. And the statue of Theagenes does likewise in Thasos; they sacrifice to Hector in Troy and to Protesilaus on the opposite shore, in the Chersonnese. (Harmon 1936)

Two of the heroes are oracular, two are healers, and two are worshipped at Troy, including the vinedresser's favorite. Jones (1986, 35–37) suggested very plausibly that such an attack may have contributed to the motives for the *Heroicus* itself, which is in stark opposition to the failed

44

"conversion" of *Philopseudes*. The vinedresser is a much
more sophisticated storyteller, and with gradual revela-
tions, he reels the Phoenician in with apparent indiffer-
ence to his disbelief, until he is manipulated by the vine-
dresser into begging for more stories—and renouncing his
skepticism. To put the comparison another way, at the end
of *Octavius*, Caecilius professes his faith but breaks it off
at sunset to hear the rest tomorrow. At the end of *He-
roicus*, the Phoenician wants to continue to get stories of
the underworld but is put off by the vinedresser because
of sunset; he can come again tomorrow if the winds are
still against him, but he now prays to Poseidon that this
will happen so he can hear more stories. *Heroicus* in dif-
ferent ways has bested Lucian and Christian conversion
dialogues alike, since the vinedresser has used neither
argument nor conviction, but rather the power of his nar-
rative, to guide the restoration of the power of the heroes.

8. PROTESILAUS (Chs. 8.18–16)

The chief religious presence in the life of the vinedresser,
and the source for his information on heroes, is Protesi-
laus[122] of Thessaly. As we learn from Homer's catalog of
the Greek contingents before Troy, Protesilaus' career had
been brief (*Il.* 695–702):[123]

[122] His name is an epic form of Prôtolaos, "first of the people"
(Fick and Bechtel (1894, 408).

[123] According to Hesiod's *Catalog of Women* (fr. 199.6), he
had been one of the suitors of Helen; on Philostratus' invention
of his glorious role in the battle against Telephus in Mysia, see
§10 below.

Some lived in Phylake, and flowering Pyrasos
the holy place of Demeter, and Iton the mother of
    flocks,
and Antron on the seacoast and grassy Pteleos;
these warlike Protesilaus commanded
while he yet lived; but by then the black earth already
    covered him.
His wife, her cheeks torn with grief, had been left
    behind in Phylake,
and his house was half-built; but a Dardanian man[124]
    killed him,
as he leaped from his ship, by far the first of the
    Achaeans.

But the disappointment of his life as a warrior was com-
pensated with posthumous honors and powers. Tradition
assigned his burial to the land across the Hellespont—
on the Gallipoli peninsula, where in the First World War
many youthful invaders would be cut down, as he had
been—near the town on its western tip, Elaious (literally,
"The town of the Olive," modern Eski Kale). A neolithic
mound there is still known as the tomb of Protesilaus, and
there can be little doubt that this is the site where the

---

[124] Later writers tried to supply the name of this unspecified
Trojan. Most often it was Hector—in the epic cycle and Sopho-
cles' *Shepherds* (Kullmann [1960, 184–85])—but other possibili-
ties (Achates, Euphorbos, Aeneas) are reviewed in schol. (D) *Il.*
2.701. One ingenious interpreter (*FGrHist* 56 F 1) suggested that
Dardanos meant a Greek friend of Protesilaus' named Dardanos,
who "killed him" in the sense that he failed to tell him of the
prophecy of Thetis that the first to leave his ship would die.

people of Elaious erected his *herôon* and statue[125] and where Philostratus' dialogue is set in a vineyard near his sacred grove.[126]

In the final story of his *Histories*, Herodotus tells of a Persian's attempt in 480 BC[127] to desecrate Protesilaus' shrine and of the hero's revenge (9.116–21):

> The tyrant of this district was a subordinate of Xerxes named Artayktes, a clever and wanton Persian; as the king was marching toward Athens, he had tricked him and stolen the treasures of Protesilaus son of Iphiklos from Elaious. For Elaious in the Chersonnese was the site of Protesilaus' tomb and shrine, where there was much money, gold and silver goblets, bronze and clothing and other dedica-

[125] Tutelary deity of Elaious: Paus. 1.34.2. For the shrine see §6 above (Setting). The statue is described at *Her.* 9.5; for coinage depicting it see §11 below (ekphrasis). For shrines in Thessaly (16.4) one at Phylake is known from Pind. *Isthm.* 1.58–9, and Agon for Protesilaus in Thessaly: Schol. Pind. 1.1.11. For mockery of his supposed oracle in Lucian, *Parliament of the Gods* 12, see §7 above (on the Phoenician's "conversion").

[126] Grove, ch. 9.1. The trees surrounding Protesilaus' mound are described with less detail by Plin. *HN* 16.238; Antiphilus of Byzantium *A.P.* 7.141 (= Gow and Page 1968, Ep. 23); Philip of Thessalonica *A.P.* 7.385 (= Ep. 33); Quintus of Smyrna 7.408–11. As Gow and Page (1968) note, the scene is modeled on the tomb of Eetion, *Il.* 6.419ff. For heroic sacred groves, see Birge (1982, 39–42, 143 [Strabo]); particularly notable was the grove of Anagyros, Aristoph. frr. 41–66 Kassel-Austin.

[127] A coin from Scione soon after 480 BC (the time of Artayktes' desecration), Kraay (1976, 134).

tions, which, with the king's permission, Artayktes stole.

He deceived Xerxes with these words: "Master, here there is the house of a Greek who attacked your country, but received his just punishment and was killed. Give me this man's house, so that all may learn not to attack your land." Obviously such a request was bound to persuade Xerxes to give him the man's house, since he had no inkling of its real meaning: in saying that Protesilaus attacked the king's land, he implied that the Persians consider all of Asia to belong to them and to whoever is their king.

Once the award had been made, Artayktes removed the treasures from Elaious to Sestos and planted the land in the sacred precinct and farmed it, and whenever he made personal visits to Elaious, he had sex with women in the shrine.

[When the Athenians besieged Artayktes at Sestos, he was captured trying to escape and returned under guard.]

It is said by those who live in the Chersonnese that one of Artayktes' guards, when he was roasting some salted fish, saw a portent: the salt fish lying in the fire wriggled and squirmed as if they had been freshly caught. The bystanders were amazed, but when Artayktes saw it he told the man roasting the fish "don't be afraid of this omen; it isn't meant for you. Protesilaus from Elaious is showing me that despite being dead and dried up,[128] he has power

---

[128] *Tarichos* means not only "dried fish" but "mummy."

from the gods to punish an evildoer. I wish, therefore, to offer the following compensation: to pay to the god,[129] in return for the treasure I took from the shrine, 100 talents; and for myself and my son I shall pay the Athenians two hundred talents, if I am spared."

But his offer did not persuade the Athenian general Xanthippus. The people of Elaious demanded that Artayktes be executed to avenge Protesilaus, and the general agreed with them. They took Artayktes to the shore to which Xerxes had attached his bridge—others say it was the hill above the city of Madytus—there nailed him up onto a plank, and then stoned his son to death before his eyes.

This was the place of Alexander's visit in 334 (Arr. *Anab.* 1.11.5):

When he arrived at Elaious he sacrificed at the tomb of Protesilaus, because Protesilaus seemed to be the first of the Greeks on the expedition against Troy with Agamemnon to disembark; the intent of the sacrifice was for him to have a more successful landing than Protesilaus.

Later in the fifth century, Euripides in his tragedy *Protesilaus*[130] took up the story again, focusing on the grieving wife, Laodameia (Polydora in the *Cypria,* Paus. 4.2.5). The play is lost, and although it is likely that later mythographic

---

[129] The use of "god" for a hero is not uncommon; see Rusten (1983, 289n3).

[130] Collard and Cropp (2008, 8.106–17).

sources preserve its plot, they also give too many variants for the Euripidean version to be reconstructed with certainty. In one version, Protesilaus is allowed to visit his widow for one day from the underworld, and he persuades her to join him in death. In another, Laodameia turns to magic and attempts to bring a statue of the dead man to life,[131] but her father discovers and burns the statue, whereupon she takes her own life. Whether Euripides told one of these (or a combination of them, or one of the other minor variants) is impossible to say; Philostratus himself only alludes to the story, without giving any details (ch. 2.9–11).

Elaborated romantically by Ovid (*Her.* 13) and satirically by Lucian (*Dial. mort.* 23), Protesilaus' final visit to his wife is a common theme of sarcophagus reliefs.[132]

For Philostratus, what distinguishes Protesilaus from the other heroes (apart from his usefulness as a source of information) is his early death, which excluded him from receiving his due from Homer; his military greatness without the temperament of Achilles, and *sophia* (4.10) without the aloofness of Palamedes; his moral compass; and

[131] Burkert (1983, 245) stresses the affinity between this statue magic and the women's worship (represented on Lenaia vases) of the Dionysus mask and statue; he also compares the story of Philinnion of Amphipolis (*FGrHist* 257 F 36.1): she returned from the dead to visit a young lodger at her old house, until her parents broke in on them, whereupon she died once again, her young lover joining her in grief a few days later.

[132] Platt (2011, 388); Zanker, Ewald, and Slater (2011, 93–95).

his beneficent attitude to mortals. Protesilaus exercises all the powers characteristic of a local hero (see §4 above): favor (or punishment when merited) to his neighbors, athletic skill, and prophecy.

9. LIVES OF THE HEROES

The Catalog of Heroes

The center of *Heroicus* (chs. 25–51) constitutes a work not dissimilar to that undertaken in the *Lives of the Sophists*:[133] a series of biographical sketches, systematically covering a particular occupational type (as of emperors, artists, or poets) of the Greek and Trojan heroes of the Trojan War (interrupted by a biography of Homer himself [43–44]), then finally a biography of Achilles. Bowie (2004, 76–77) gives a "checklist" of items to be included in a sophistic biography, and *Heroicus* too has its standard elements, though of unequal length and emphasis:

- comparative estimates of their talents (including athletics as well as warfare)
- physical descriptions (on which see §11 below)
- anecdotes, especially those with moral value
- critique of Homer's treatment of them, and if necessary "corrections" of it

But Philostratus' favorite heroes receive special treatment, as has Protesilaus already.

---

[133] For Philostratus' methods in *Lives of the Sophists*, see Whitmarsh (2004) and Hägg (2012, 341–51).

Palamedes (Ch. 33)

In this catalog, Philostratus gives special attention to an intellectual hero (*sophistes*, 33.25, *sophos/sophia*, 33.1, 8, 10, 15, etc.). Palamedes had first appeared in the cyclic epic *Cypria* (M. L. West 2013, 102, 123–25), where he angers Odysseus by exposing his feigned madness, and while fishing he is drowned by Odysseus and Diomedes. But by the fifth century, when the development of civilization was seen as a series of technological advances, Palamedes acquired the role of the archetypical inventor, who is as wise, high-minded, and magnanimous as Odysseus is crafty, malicious. and jealous. He was the inventor of writing, games, astronomy, military formations, and strategy, and he was a savior from plague (public health) and famine.[134]

Aeschylus, Sophocles, and Euripides all wrote plays about Palamedes, of which plot summaries seem to be preserved in the mythographers.[135] They all tell of Odysseus' plot to have Palamedes falsely condemned and executed by the Greek army. In the most elaborate version, Odysseus captured a Phrygian slave carrying Trojan gold, then fabricated a dream in which Athena warned they must move their camp for one night; when Agamemnon ordered this, he buried the gold on the spot where Palamedes' tent had been. Next Odysseus ordered the captured slave to write a letter in Phrygian from Priam to Palamedes and made him carry it back to Troy, seeing to it that he was killed on the way and the letter captured.

[134] See in general Falcetto (2003), Hodkinson (2011), Romero Mariscal (2008a), Usener (1994a).
[135] Gantz (1996, 605).

Palamedes was tried for treason; when the gold was discovered under his tent, he was convicted and stoned to death, not only becoming the most famous victim of a kangaroo court but also the first man to be framed using his own invention—writing.

Palamedes thus became the archetype of the innocent philosopher-sophist, martyred by ignorant jurors at the hands of jealous rivals; he is cited as an example in the Socratic apologies of both Plato and Xenophon, and the quintessential sophist Gorgias wrote a fictional defense speech, using arguments from probability to demonstrate the emptiness of Odysseus' charges.[136] Near the close (chs. 30–31), Gorgias defended his own contributions (Dillon and Gergel 2003):

> I might indeed claim, and in doing so I would not
> be lying, nor could I be refuted, that I am not only
> blameless but actually a major benefactor of you
> and of the Greek nation and of mankind in general, not only of the present generation but of all
> those to come. For who else but I made human life
> viable instead of destitute, and civilized instead of
> uncivilized, by developing military tactics, a major
> contrivance for progress; written laws, the guarantees of justice; writing, the instrument of memory; weights and measures, the convenient means
> of commercial exchange; number, the guardian of
> goods; powerful beacons and very swift messenger

[136] A speech of prosecution by Odysseus is preserved with an ascription to Alcidamas; see O'Sullivan (2008).

services—and, last but not least, draughts, a harm-
less way of passing the time?

Unlike the extended story of Telephus with Protesilaus,
the "suppressed" plot to kill Palamedes and his trial itself,
as known from Euripides' play and the defense speech of
Gorgias, are not told in full by the vinedresser. We are thus
left with a concentrated focus on the man's character itself,
a combination of technological brilliance and political na-
ïveté.[137]

Apollonius of Tyana comes across a boy in India who is
the reincarnation of Palamedes (*VA* 3.22.2); later, when
he interviews Achilles at Troy (above, §1), he learns the
hidden location of Palamedes' burial, finds his tomb and
statue opposite Methymna, and establishes a shrine to him
there (*VA* 4.33.9).[138]

Achilles (Chs. 45–51)[139]

Unlike Protesilaus and Palamedes, Achilles is a major fig-
ure in the *Iliad*. The vinedresser's story of Achilles is

[137] In Dictys 2.15 by contrast, the Palamedes plot is simple
and quick—he is tricked into a well by Odysseus and Diomedes
and stoned, in a reminiscence of the Doloneia in *Il.* 10. In Dares
(chs. 25–30) Palamedes instigates a revolt and actually replaces
Agamemnon as commander (to the anger of Achilles) but is then
himself killed in battle by Paris, and Agamemnon re-takes com-
mand.

[138] The shrine is mentioned by Plin. *HN* 5.22, Strabo 13.1.51;
cf. Cook (1973, 239); Grossardt (2006a, 604–5).

[139] For his cults at Troy see §12 below, and for his life on
Leuke see §13 below.

marked by frequent corrections of that poem:[140] his anger against the Greeks was the result of Palamedes' death (48.6–8), he never lost his armor to Hector or received replacement armor from the gods (47.2), he was killed not in battle but in an ambush while expecting to marry Polyxena (47.4, see below). But we hear less about Achilles' career in war (and nothing about his being honored by Alexander and Caracalla) than about his childhood education in music and poetry (45.5–7) and his youthful mission to Scyros and marriage there (46.2–4). The major themes for Achilles are:

- his parents' plans for him (Thetis takes him to Aulis to fulfill his fate, and Peleus sends him to Scyros on a commission)
- his highly developed sense of honor in money matters
- his love for Deidameia and Polyxena (Patroclus is not so much in evidence)[141]
- his volatile temperament, which is the reason for the decision to educate him in music, and is explained by his loyalty to his friends Palamedes and Patroclus, but it surfaces later against the Thessalians, the Trojan girl, and also the Amazons

[140] For comparisons with Dictys, see Huhn and Bethe (1917). For all the extra-Homeric Achilles traditions, see Burgess (2009) and King (1987).

[141] For these traditions, see especially Fantuzzi (2012).

10. STORIES EXPURGATED
BY HOMER

Telephus (Ch. 23)

Onto Protesilaus' revelations Philostratus grafts an extensive narrative of the battle of the Greeks with Telephus of Mysia. The mythographers give four stages of his story:[142]

- illegitimate birth to Auge by Heracles and escape from exposure and execution of his mother by her hostile father
- both Telephus and mother escape to Mysia and Teuthras, where Telephus becomes his adopted son
- battle against the invading Greeks, where he repels them but receives an unhealable wound
- his trip back to Greece in disguise to follow the advice of an oracle that the healer will be the one who wounded him

The first of these was told in Euripides' tragedy *Auge*, the fourth in his *Telephus* (Collard and Cropp 2008, 7:259–77, 8:185–223). The second is known from Hesiod's *Catalogue of Women* (fr. 165 M-W), and may have occurred in various plays by Aeschylus and Sophocles.[143] The third forms the heart of the vinedresser's epic narrative of how Protesilaus came to possess Telephus' shield.

---

[142] Gantz (1996, 428–31, 526–80).

[143] Hyg. 99 and 100 preserve the description of a suspenseful plot in which mother and son recognize each other just as he is about to marry her, and she about to murder him.

But it seems likely that Philostratus is influenced by the recent discussion of Pausanias,[144] and especially by the great Hellenistic frieze at Pergamon, still preserved in Berlin today.[145] The Pergamene king Attalus II viewed Teuthras of Mysia and through him Telephus as an important ancestor,[146] and this frieze tells the entire story of his life, several pictures on which seem to match Protesilaus' descriptions, notably the death of two sons of the Danube and the woman fighter Hiera.

The episodes of the narrative are mostly built on resemblances or contrasts with other aspects of the *Heroicus* or the Trojan War:[147]

- the rationalistic dismissal of the notion that the Greeks thought they were at Troy (cf. the refutation of their motives at Troy in 25.12; for the method, see on Dio's *Troicus* and §5 above)
- the fiercely fought landing and leap onto shore by both Achilles and Protesilaus that succeeds here brilliantly, but misfires later at Troy (12.1)
- Protesilaus' stripping of Telephus' shield before his wounding parallels Apollo's of Patroclus (*Il.* 16.802), except that Telephus survives

---

[144] See Cohen (2001, 98–100), who notes that Telephus has a *herôon*.

[145] Bauchhenss-Thüriedl (1971); Dreyfus and Schraudolph (1996).

[146] Robert (1984).

[147] The battle with Telephus figured in Dictys (2.1–7, where Tlepolemus is an agent of peace after battle); in Dares ch. 16, Telephus is from the start a Greek ally.

- Haemus, son of Ares, is prominently killed here, as is another of his sons, Ascalaphus, in the *Iliad* (13.518–25, 15.104–42)
- the woman warrior Hiera, who is killed and whose body is so beautiful, is clearly based on Penthesileia, except that she is now Telephus' wife, and perhaps the eponym of Hierapolis

New elements are:

- The Arcadians' ineptitude during the landing (23.15) may be a hit at Pausanias 1.4.6 and Aelius Aristides 23.15, as Grossardt (2006a) notes.
- Ajax's rogue attack (23.22) on the sons of the Danube and use of his shield to make noise to frighten their horses[148] contrasts with (as Grossardt [2006a] notes) the rebuke he has just been described making to Menestheus for lack of obedience.
- The addition of troops from the "northern" Mysians, by an interpretation of *Il.* 13.4–7 (see *Her.* ch. 23.10 note), which allows the entrance of two sons of the river Danube.[149]

Although the participation of Hiera and the sons of the Danube is not attested by name before *Heroicus*, two panels of the Pergamon frieze depict two men fighting from a chariot (Dreyfus and Schraudolph 1996, catalog 66)

[148] For which Grossardt (2006a) aptly compares Xen. *An.* 1.8.18, and Philostr. *VA* 2.11.1, *VS* 1.21.5; though we should note that in Homer, Ajax's shield is not metal.

[149] For the theme of offspring of rivers fighting at Troy, see Fenno (2005, 482n19).

and a mounted woman attacked by a warrior (*LIMC* Hiera pl. 1).

Achilles and Polyxena (Ch. 51.1)

Philostratus refers to the unusual version of Achilles' death found in Dictys 4.9–10 and subsequently in mythographic scholia (see Frazer 1966, on Apollod. *Bibl. Epit.* 5.3) and in medieval romances of Troy (King 1987, 196–205): Achilles had been promised Polyxena as his bride by Priam and was lured unarmed to the temple of Apollo Thymbraeus to conclude the bargain, where he was ambushed and killed by Paris and Deiphobus. (*Il.* 22.359–60 refers the death of Achilles to the Scaean gates, and despite Philostratus' claim cannot possibly refer to this story.)

11. VERBALIZING THE VISUAL

The age of the Second Sophistic was greatly interested in the pseudoscience of physiognomy; indeed, the sophist Polemon even compiled a handbook of it (Swain 2007). Although the "science" was completely arbitrary and there was no standardized system, physical descriptions, especially the face, have their regular place in biographies by Plutarch and Suetonius. We would in any case expect the author of the *Imagines* to be ambitious in expressing visual sensations in words. But it is in the *Lives of the Sophists* that we find the closest analogue, where Philostratus gives Herodes' visual description of his rustic friend Agathion (2.552 tr. W. C. Wright):

He says that his hair grew evenly on his head, his eyebrows were bushy and they met as though they were but one, and his eyes gave out a brilliant gleam which betrayed his impulsive temperament; he was hooked-nosed, and had a solidly built neck, which was due rather to work than to diet. His chest, too, was well formed and beautifully slim, and his legs were lightly bowed outwards, which made it easy for him to stand firmly planted.

In *Heroicus* the Phoenician is constantly asking to "see" the heroes, i.e., to have a description of their appearance (see 10.1, 10.5 [Protesilaus], 26.13 [Nestor], 33.38 [Palamedes]). The vinedresser includes in his short "Lives" fifteen physiognomic sketches, mostly of just a few words but especially developed in the cases of his three favorites, and the fullest of these is Achilles (48.2–5). These most commonly describe the hair, nose, brow, eye color and emotions expressed, the neck, and the skin. Rarely are their bodies described, in contrast to *Gymnasticus*.

An occasion for further elaboration is comparison of hero to his statue. Like sophists,[150] proper heroes have statues (ἄγαλμα, ἀνδριάς used only of the athlete Helix [15.1]), and the descriptions of Protesilaus and Hector interweave consideration of the statue with the hero himself (Platt 2011, 241; Francis 2003). Euphorbus is himself compared to a statue of Apollo (42.3).

But the vinedresser indicates the limitations of ekphrasis in a piquant example (47.5). Protesilaus reports that the *Iliad*'s preeminent ekphrasis, the figures on the Shield

---

150 Chart in Bowie (2004, 76–77).

of Achilles, was an evasion. The real shield that Thetis fashioned for him (there was no replacement by the Hephaestus since it was never lent to Patroclus) had no figures on it; rather, it had colors only, which were so far beyond human powers that Homer was forced to substitute one with pictures instead.

12. RITUALS

Descriptions of Greek religious rituals had been part of ethnography since Herodotus on Egypt, and historiography since Thucydides on the public funeral; they are frequently deployed in Plutarch (the Plataean ritual in the *Life of Aristides*) and by such different authors as the mocking Lucian[151] and the devout Pausanias.[152] Apollonius of Tyana is said to have written a treatise on "how to sacrifice to any divinity appropriately and acceptably" (*VA* 3.41.2, cf. 4.19).

There are four descriptions of ritual in *Heroicus*; most relate to the chthonic offerings to the heroes or the dead, and all are dense with details of performance, symbolism, and specialized vocabulary.

Funerary Rites of Ajax of Locris (Ch. 31.8–.9)

The vinedresser skips the funerals of Patroclus and Achilles, and in the other notable deaths, Ajax and Palamedes, traditional rituals are not allowed: but in this one case there is an unusual procedure, which the vinedresser him-

151 Graf (2011).
152 Pirenne-Delforge (2001).

self informs us was an improvisation, apparently not tra-
ditional or commanded by any god. The unique "Viking
burial" for Locrian Ajax might be compared with Egyptian
(pyramid of Cheops) and Anglo-Saxon and Celtic (Scyld,
Beowulf 27–52, and Sutton Hoo) ship burials. It is re-
counted (doubtless from this passage of *Heroicus*) also by
Tzetzes on Lycophron Alexandra 368 (Scheer 1881, 141).
Within the Greek world one might compare the *ploiaphe-
sia* in the cult of Isis (Apul. *Met.* 11.17; Huhn and Bethe
1917, 622–24). Grossardt (2006a, 566) also compares a
funerary ritual described by Nicolaus of Damascus
(*FGrHist* 90 F 118). For the "black ship of death" as a
theme in lamentations, see Alexiou (1974, 192).

Ritual of New Fire at Lemnos (Ch. 53.5–7)

The second ritual is told by the vinedresser himself. Bur-
kert (1970) finds it has the ring of authenticity, as part of
the lore of nearby Lemnos, still maintained in the current
day (a "Philostratus" was a priest of Hephaestus); it relates
to purification but still juxtaposed to a sacrifice to the
dead.

Thessalian Ritual for Achilles in Troy[153] (Ch. 53.8–23)

There was a cult of Thetis in Thessaly (Burkert 1985,
417n30), but there is no other evidence for one of Achilles.

[153] See especially Rutherford (2009) and Aitken (2001). The
same story is told from a different perspective/authority/date in
VA 4.16 (the same mound but no blood sacrifice, anger at Thes-

This ritual begins with the command from an oracle for
a double offering to Achilles (53.8), which leads to a sa-
cred voyage with black sails (as at Lemnos) to a hostile
country[154] to make elaborate offerings. Their description
(53.11–12) evokes terminologically the opposition in sac-
rifice between offerings to heroes and the dead (*enagizein*,
which burns the entire victim) and those to the gods (*thy-
ein*, which sends smoke to the gods, but the meat is con-
sumed by the celebrants—see the note on 53.13). This
distinction[155] seems to have been extended from cults of
Heracles (Hdt. 1.167.2, 2.44; Thuc. 3.58.4, 5.11.1; Paus.
4.32.3) and applied here to Achilles (though later the
Olympian part is abandoned by the Thessalians). Another
elaboration of detail is the trenches (*bothroi*) with blood
for the hero.[156] Even the cult hymn is reproduced.

This passage is in many ways a model (although not
linguistically) for the long description of a Thessalian sac-
rifice to Neoptolemus at Delphi, including a hymn to The-
tis, by Heliod. *Aeth.* 3.35ff. (a work that also alludes to the
Life of Apollonius). Here there is the same opposition,

---

salians but now AD 1 and Apollonius plays the role of the oracle,
but no sacrificial description because the rite is forgotten; the
punishment-sequel is picked up again in *Heroicus*).

[154] Rutherford (2009) thinks of the ritual of the Locrian maid-
ens, but its rationale seems more like the inverse of that atone-
ment ritual. It is more like relatives from ANZAC armies to the
cemeteries of Gallipoli.

[155] Ekroth (2002, 74–128). The distinctiveness of *enagizein*
and *thuein* seems however to be absent elsewhere in the dialogue.

[156] Compare the dead in general in *Od.* 11 and *Her.* 43.14, and
in Paus. 9.39.6, 9.37.7; see Ekroth (2002, 67).

but now *thusia* for Apollo, *enagismata* for Neoptolemus (Rutherford 2009, 246).

Sacrifices on Leuke

One important feature of the stories of this fantastic island (see next section) is the fact that arrivals need provide no sacrificial victim: there is one standing ready for them at the altar.

Some judge these rituals to be fictions, others to be actual traditions. Even if we doubt them, we must admit that the author has a very a good ear for authentic-sounding descriptions. Paradoxically, the Delian-Lemnian ritual and the Thessalian-Trojan one are situated by the vine-dresser in the locality, and he seems to have direct knowledge of the first; yet their existence has been questioned (Rutherford 2009; cf. however Graninger 2011). The final cult site, known only by distant report and seeming utterly fantastic, turns out to possess a sound archaeological basis in reality.

13. AMAZING STORIES

That the spirit of Achilles was translated not to the Isles of the Blessed (as in Hesiod's *Works and Days,* §1 above) but to the Black Sea island of Leuke is told already in the *Aithiopis* (M. L. West 2013, 155–56) alluded to in Pindar (*Nem.* 4.49), Alcaeus (fr. 354 Lobel-Page), and Euripides (*Andr.* 1259–62, *IT* 435–38), and forms the background of a parody in Aristophanes' *Birds*.[157] The vinedresser's tale

---

[157] Rusten (2012); the proof is that the place where men can

alludes to details of these accounts, but it responds most immediately to two second-century AD authors on Leuke, both of whom use the story in confirmation of the existence of the divinity of heroes. After his assertions on the heroes as *daimones* (see above, §4), Maximus of Tyre (9.7) writes:

> Achilles dwells on an island in the Black Sea opposite the mouth of the Ister, where he has a temple and altars. No one would go there of his own free will, except to offer sacrifices; and it is only after offering sacrifices that he will set foot in the temple. Sailors passing the island have often seen a young man with tawny hair, clad in golden armour, exercising there. Others have not seen him, but have heard him singing. Yet others have both seen and heard him. One man even fell asleep inadvertently on the island. Achilles himself appeared to him, raised him to his feet, took him to his tent, and entertained him; Patroclus was there to serve the wine, Achilles played the lyre, and Thetis and a host of other *daimones* were present too.

Arrian's *Periplus of the Black Sea* (23.3–5), addressed to Hadrian, concluded his description of the island with this meditation (I add the Greek to show language which recalls the Phoenician's reaction):

---

associate with heroes by day but not at night corresponds to *Her.* 54.11–12.

τάδε μὲν ὑπὲρ τῆς νήσου τῆς τοῦ Ἀχιλλέως ἀκοὴν
ἀνέγραψα τῶν ἢ αὐτῶν προσχόντων ἢ ἄλλων
πεπυσμένων· καί μοι δοκεῖ οὐκ ἄπιστα εἶναι.
Ἀχιλλέα γὰρ ἐγὼ πείθομαι εἴπερ τινὰ καὶ ἄλλον
ἥρωα εἶναι, τῇ τε εὐγενείᾳ τεκμαιρόμενος καὶ τῷ
κάλλει καὶ τῇ ῥώμῃ τῆς ψυχῆς καὶ τῷ νέον
μεταλλάξαι ἐξ ἀνθρώπων καὶ τῇ Ὁμήρου ἐπ’
αὐτῷ ποιήσει καὶ τῷ ἐρωτικὸν γενέσθαι καὶ
φιλέταιρον, ὡς καὶ ἐπαποθανεῖν ἑλέσθαι τοῖς
παιδικοῖς.

I wrote these things about the island of Achilles
based on reports from those who landed there
themselves or heard stories from others; and they
seem to me not to be untrustworthy. For I believe
that Achilles is a hero, if anyone else is, basing my
judgment on his nobility, his beauty, the strength of
his spirit, his youthful departure from mankind,
Homer's poetry about him and his passionate and
loyal nature, which led him to choose to die after
his beloved boy.[158]

The appeal of Leuke as a home for Achilles since ar-
chaic times has doubtless been its remote isolation; and
yet a series of Russian excavators in the nineteenth and
twentieth centuries have identified the island as modern
Zmeinyj, which contains the remains of the Hellenistic
temple and hundreds of dedications (ostraca, coins, in-

[158] A reminder of Antinous here seems likely.

scriptions), especially to Achilles (sometimes under the name Pontarches).[159]

The vinedresser's story adapts Lucian's Isles of the Blessed in the true history in making Achilles and Helen sing the verses of Homer in an endless symposium, but it also continues themes raised earlier in *Heroicus*: Achilles' talent for poetry finally blossoms, and the final paradox is that the song of his that is transcribed is in praise of his praiser, Homer. There are also Protesilaus-like beneficent epiphanies to sailors with warnings of adverse winds or invitations to join them (except at night).

But the climax of the story is an instance of Achilles' savagery, and this too takes up an earlier theme (see §9 above). Achilles' request for a Trojan slave girl from a merchant is recognized too late to be a continuation of the search for the last virgin of the house of Priam that demanded the sacrifice of Polyxena (Fantuzzi [2012, 15], who compares also Agamemnon's threats in *Il.* 9.139–40). Her violent death recalls the hero of Temesa, recounted by Strabo 6.1.5; Paus. 6.6, 7–10; and Ael. *V. H.* 8.18, see Callimachus fr. 78 Pfeiffer. See above, §4.

The miraculous repulse of the Amazons from Leuke is not told elsewhere and is doubtless an amalgam of motifs of foolhardy impiety and supernatural punishment. It illustrates the heroic function of guarding against invasion (Introduction §4) and might recall the encounter of the Persians with the heroes Phylakos and Autonoos at Delphi (Hdt. 8.36–39). It is curious, however, that it is dated by the vinedresser to the Hellenistic period, which provides a clue to another approximate model, the attack of the

[159] Rusyaeva (2003); Ochotnikov (2006).

Gauls on Delphi in 279 BC narrated by Paus. 10.23 and Justin Trogus, Book 24.[160] In the first, the Gauls take over the sanctuary, Apollo sends supernatural obstacles (dead heroes, rocks fall on them, and irrational panic causes them to kill each other), and the local Phocians join the fight (Athens and Aetolians pursue them after this point, and Brennus, the Gallic leader, drinks himself to death). In Justin the god himself joins with Athena and destroys them with the help of the Delphians alone, and their leader Brennus kills himself.

The conversation that began with the description of the *locus amoenus* of the benign Protesilaus has ended in remote Leuke with the savage revenge of Achilles; it is little wonder the Phoenician listener cannot wait to hear more.

14. THE MANUSCRIPTS AND MODERN EDITIONS AND TRANSLATIONS

The dialogue was very popular in antiquity and thereafter, so that many manuscripts contain the text, often along with other works of Philostratus. The first printed edition was by Aldus Manutius in 1503. Of subsequent editions, the most important are those of Boissonade (1806, Heroicus alone with scholia and a commentary) and Kayser (all the works of Philostratus, first in 1844 and then the two-volume Teubner edition of 1870–71). Kayser reported thirty-eight manuscripts; the new Teubner edition of de Lannoy (1977) established that two of these were

---

[160] See also Callim. *Hymn* 4 171–84; Nachtergael (1977); Pritchett (1971–1985, 3.30–32). For an epigraphically attested pirate raid on Leuke, see S. West (2003, 166); Ochotnikov (2006, 78–79).

actually two parts of the same manuscript, and added eleven more witnesses, for a total of forty-eight (plus six fragments). Of these, seventeen are important sources, and all of them descend from a miniscule manuscript not earlier than the ninth century. Thereafter, there are two recensions, which de Lannoy names the Laurentian (divided into two families, F [Laurentian Plut. 58, 32 xii–xii century] and v [six other manuscripts]) and the Parisian (a [four manuscripts] and σ [six manuscripts]).

Because de Lannoy's edition is relatively recent and offers very full reports of manuscript readings and conjectures, textual notes here are minimal, and I follow his text with very few exceptions as noted (mostly in agreement with Grossardt [2006a]).

BIBLIOGRAPHY

There is an extensive bibliography, organized by topic, to all aspects of *Heroicus* in Grossardt 2006a, 1:245–98.

Abramson, Herbert. 1979. "A Hero Shrine for Phrontis at Sounion?" *California Studies in Classical Antiquity*: 1–19.

Aitken, Ellen Bradshaw. 2001. "The Cult of Achilles in Philostratos' *Heroikos.*" In *Between Magic and Religion: Interdisciplinary Studies in Ancient Mediterranean Religion and Society*, ed. Sulochana Ruth Asirvatham, Corinne Ondine Pache, and John Watrous, 127–38. Greek Studies. Lanham, MD.

Aitken, Ellen Bradshaw, and Jennifer K. Berenson Maclean. 2004. *Philostratos' Heroikos: Religion and Cultural Identity in the Third Century C.E.* Atlanta.

Alcock, Susan. 1993. *Graecia Capta: Landscapes of Roman Greece.* Cambridge.

———. 1994. "The Heroic Past in a Hellenistic Present." *Échos du monde classique* 13: 221–34.

———. 1997. *The Early Roman Empire in the East.* Oxford.

———. 2004. "Material Witness: An Archaeological Context for Philostratus' Heroikos." In Aitken and Maclean 2004, 159–68. Atlanta.

Alexiou, Margaret. 1974. *The Ritual Lament in Greek Tradition*. Cambridge.

Ameling, W. 1988. "Alexander und Achilleus." In *Zu Alexander dem grossen: Festschrift G. Wirth*, ed. W. Will, 657–92. Amsterdam.

Anderson, Graham. 1986. *Philostratus: Biography and Belles Lettres in the Third Century A.D.* London.

Antonaccio, Carla Maria. 1995. *An Archaeology of Ancestors: Tomb Cult and Hero Cult in Early Greece*. Lanham, MD.

Armstrong, A. Macc. 1958. "The Methods of the Greek Physiognomists." *Greece & Rome* 5: 52–56.

Ascough, Richard S., Philip A. Harland, and John S. Kloppenborg. 2012. *Associations in the Greco-Roman World: A Sourcebook*. Waco, TX.

Aslan, Carolyn Chabot. 2011. "A Place for Burning: Ancestor or Hero Cult at Troy." *Hesperia* 80 (3): 381–429.

Audollent, Auguste Marie Henri. 1904. *Defixionum tabellae. Quotquot innotuerunt tam in Graecis orientis quam in totius occidentis partibus praeter Atticas in corpore inscriptionum Atticarum editas*. Paris.

Austin, R. G. 1940. "Greek Board-Games." *Antiquity* 14: 257–71.

———. 1972. "Hector's Hair-Style." *The Classical Quarterly* 22 (2): 199.

Barringer, Judith M. 1995. *Divine Escorts: Nereids in Archaic and Classical Greek Art*. Ann Arbor.

Bauchhenss-Thüriedl, Christa. 1971. *Der Mythos von Telephos in der antiken Bildkunst*. Würzburg. Beitraege zur Archaeologie 3.

Baurain, C. 1986. "Portée chronologique et géographique du terme 'phénicien.'" *Studia Phoenicia* 4: 7–28.

Bean, George Ewart. 1966. *Aegean Turkey*. London.

Benner, A. R., and F. H. Fobes. 1949. *The letters of Alciphron, Aelian and Philostratus*. Cambridge.

Benton, S. 1934. "Excavations at Ithaca, III: The Cave at Polis I." *Annual of the British School at Athens* 35: 45–73.

Bérard, Claude. 1970. *L'Hérôon à la porte de l'ouest*. Berne.

Beschorner, Andreas. 2000. *Helden und Heroen, Homer und Caracalla: Übersetzung, Kommentar und Interpretationen zum Heroikos des Flavios Philostratos*. Bari.

Betz, Hans Dieter. 2004. "Hero Worship and Christian Beliefs: Observations from the History of Religion on Philostratus' *Heroikos*." In Aitken and Maclean 2004, 25–48.

Billault, Alain. 1993. "Le Γυμναστικός [Gymnastikos] de Philostrate: a-t-il une signification littéraire?" *Revue des Études Grecques* 106: 142–62.

———. 2000. *L'univers de Philostrate*. Brussels. Collection Latomus vol. 252.

Birge, Darice. 1982. "Sacred Groves in the Ancient Greek World." PhD diss., University of California at Berkeley.

Boehringer, David. 2001. *Heroenkulte in Griechenland von der geometrischen bis zur klassischen Zeit: Attika, Argolis, Messenien*. Berlin.

Boissonade, Jean Francois. 1806. *Philostrati Heroica*. Paris

Borg, Barbara. 2004. *Paideia: The World of the Second Sophistic*. Millennium Studies in the Culture and History of the First Millennium C.E., vol. 2. Berlin.

Bouché-Leclercq, Auguste. 1879. *Histoire de la divination dans l'antiquité*. Paris.

PHILOSTRATUS

Bowersock, G. W. 1969. *Greek Sophists in the Roman Empire.* Oxford.

Bowie, Ewen. L. 1974. "Greeks and Their Past in the Second Sophistic." In *Studies in Ancient Society*, ed. M. I. Finley, 166–209. London.

———. 1978. "Apollonius of Tyana. Tradition and Reality." *Aufstieg und Niedergang der römischen Welt* 2 (16.2): 1652–99.

———. 1994. "Philostratus as Writer of Fiction." In *Greek Fiction: The Greek Novel in Context*, ed. John R. Morgan and Richard Stoneman, 181–99. London.

———. 2004. "The Geography of the Second Sophistic: Cultural Variations." In Borg 2004, 65–84.

———. 2009. "Philostratus: The Life of a Sophist." In Bowie and Elsner 2009, 19–32.

Bowie, Ewen, and Jaś Elsner. 2009. *Philostratus.* Cambridge.

Boys-Stones, George R., and Johannes Haubold. 2010. *Plato and Hesiod.* Oxford.

Bravo, Jorge Jose III. 2006. "The Hero Shrine of Opheltes/Archemoros at Nemea: A Case Study of Ancient Greek Hero Cult." PhD diss., University of California at Berkeley.

Brelich, Angelo. 1958. *Gli eroi greci: un problema storico-religioso.* Rome.

Bremmer, J. N. 2006. "The Rise of the Hero Cult and the New Simonides." *Zeitschrift für Papyrologie und Epigraphik.* 158: 15–26.

Brenk, Frederick E. 1973. "A Most Strange Doctrine. Daimon in Plutarch." *Classical Journal* 69 (1): 1–11.

Briquel-Chatonnet, F. 1992. "L'Image des Phéniciens dans les Romans Grecs." In *Le Monde du Roman Grec*, ed. Marie-Françoise Baslez, 189–97. Études de Littérature ancienne. Paris.

Broneer, Oscar. 1942. "Hero-shrines in the Corinthian Agora." *Hesperia* 11: 128–61.

Brückner, A., and Wilhelm Dörpfeld. 1902. "Gechichte von Troja und Ilion." In *Troja und Ilion*, 549–93. Athens.

Buffière, Félix. 1956. *Les mythes d'Homère et la pensée grecque*. Paris.

Burgess, Jonathan S. 2009. *The Death and Afterlife of Achilles*. Baltimore.

Burkert, Walter. 1970. "Jason, Hypsipyle and New Fire at Lemnos." *Classical Quarterly* 20: 1–16.

———. 1972. *Lore and Science in Ancient Pythagoreanism*. Cambridge, MA.

———. 1983. *Homo Necans: The Anthropology of Ancient Greek Sacrificial Ritual and Myth*. Berkeley.

———. 1985. *Greek Religion*. Cambridge, MA.

Canciani, Fulvio. "Protesilaos." In *LIMC*, 554–60. VII.1.

Champlin, Edward. 1981. "Serenus Sammonicus." *Harvard Studies in Classical Philology* 85: 189–212.

Cohen, Ada. 2001. "Art, Myth and Travel in the Hellenistic World." In *Pausanias: Travel and Memory in Ancient Greece*, ed. Susan Alcock, John F. Cherry, and Jaś Elsner, 93–126. Oxford.

Coldstream, J. N. 1976. "Hero-Cults in the Age of Homer." *Journal of Hellenic Studies* 1976: 8–17.

Collard, Christopher, and Martin Cropp. 2008. *Euripides: Fragments*. Vol. 7. Loeb Classical Library 504. Cambridge, MA.

Cook, J. M. 1953. "Mycenae, 1939–1953. Part III: The Agamemnoneion." *Annual of the British School at Athens* 48: 30–68.

————. 1973. *The Troad: An Archaeological and Topographical Study.* Oxford.

————. 1988. "Cities In and Around the Troad." *Annual of the British School at Athens* 83: 7–19.

Currie, Bruno. 2005. *Pindar and the Cult of Heroes.* Oxford.

Dal Santo, Matthew. 2012. *Debating the Saints' Cults in the Age of Gregory the Great.* Oxford.

Danek, Georg. 2000. "Lukian und die Homer-Erklärung: (*Verae historiae* 1, 37 und *Odyssee* 10, 203–9)." *Acta antiqua Academiae Scientiarum Hungaricae* 40: 87–91.

de Lannoy, L. 1977. *Flavi Philostrati Heroicus.* Leipzig.

————. 1997. "Le problème des Philostrate (État de la question)." *Aufstieg und Niedergang der römischen Welt* 2.34.3: 2362–449.

Demangel, R. 1926. *Le tumulus dit de Protésilas.* Paris.

Deonna, W. 1925. "Orphée et l'oracle de la tête coupée." *Revue des Etudes Grecques* 38: 44–69.

Detienne, Marcel. 1963. *La notion de Daïmon dans le pythagorisme ancien* Bibliothèque de la faculté de philosophie et lettres de l' université de Liège, vol. 165. Paris.

Dierauer, Urs. 1977. *Tier und Mensch im Denken der Antike: Studien zur Tierpsychologie, Anthropologie und Ethik.* Studien zur antiken Philosophie. Amsterdam.

Dillon, John M., and Tania Gergel. 2003. *The Greek Sophists.* Penguin Classics. London.

Dover, K. J. 1968. *Aristophanes' Clouds.* Oxford.

Dow, S. 1985. "The Cult of the Hero Doctor." *Bulletin of the American Society of Papyrologists* 22: 33–47.

Dreyfus, Renée, and Ellen Schraudolph. 1996. *Pergamon:*

The Telephos Frieze from the Great Altar. San Francisco.

Eitrem, Sam O. 1929. "Zu Philostrats Heroikos." *Symbolae Osloenses* 8: 1–56.

———. 1935. "Heroen der Seefahrer," *Symbolae Osloenses* 14: 53–67.

Ekroth, Gunnel. 2002. *The Sacrificial Rituals of Greek Hero-Cults in the Archaic to the Early Hellenistic Periods.* Kernos, Supplément 12. Liége.

Elsner, Jaś. 2001. "Describing Self in the Language of Other: Pseudo (?) Lucian at the Temple of Hierapolis." In Goldhill 2001, 123–53.

———. 2009. "Beyond Compare: Pagan Saint and Christian God in Late Antiquity." *Critical Inquiry* 35 (3): 655–83.

Elsner, Jaś, and E. L. Bowie. 2009. *Philostratus.* Cambridge.

Elsner, Jaś, and Ian Rutherford. 2005. *Pilgrimage in Graeco-Roman & Early Christian Antiquity: Seeing the Gods.* Oxford.

Erskine, Andrew. 2001. *Troy between Greece and Rome: Local Tradition and Imperial Power.* Oxford.

Eshleman, Kendra. 2012. *The Social World of Intellectuals in the Roman Empire: Sophists, Philosophers, and Christians.* Greek Culture in the Roman World. Cambridge.

Evans, Elizabeth C. 1969. "Physiognomics in the Ancient World." *Transactions of the American Philosophical Society,* New Series,59pt. (5): 5–105.

Falcetto, Raffaella. 2003. "Il mito di Palamede nell' 'Heroikos' di Filostrato." In *Forme di comunicazione nel mondo antico e metamorfosi del mito: dal teatro al romanzo*, ed. Marcella Guglielmo and Edoardo Bona, 275–97. Allesandria, Italy.

Fantuzzi, Marco. 2012. *Achilles in Love*. Oxford.

Faraone, Christopher A. 2004. "Orpheus' Final Performance: Necromancy and a Singing Head on Lesbos." *Studi italiani di filologia classica* 4: 5–27.

Farnell, Lewis Richard. 1921. *Greek Hero Cults and Ideas of Immortality: The Gifford Lectures Delivered in the University of St. Andrews in the Year 1920*. Oxford.

Fenno, Jonathan Brian. 2005. "'A Great Wave Against the Stream': Water Imagery in Iliadic Battle Scenes." *American Journal of Philology* 126: 475–504.

Ferguson, W. S. 1938. "The Salaminioi of Heptaphylai and Sounion." *Hesperia* 7: 1–74.

FGrHist = Jacoby, F. 1923–. *Die Fragmente der griechischen Historiker*. Berlin-Leiden.

Fick, A., and F. Bechtel. 1894. *Die griechischen Personennamen*. Berlin.

Finkelberg, Margalit. 2011. *The Homer Encyclopedia*. Chichester, West Sussex.

Foerster, Richardus. 1893. *Scriptores physiognomici*. Teubner.

Follet, Simone. 1969. "Édition critique, avec introduction, notes et traduction, de l'Héroïque de Philostrate." *Annuaire de l'École pratique des Hautes Études, IVe sect., Sciences historiques et philologiques*: 747–48.

———. 1974. "Inscription inédite de Myrina." *Annuario della Scuola Archaeologica Italiana di Atene* 36–37: 309–12.

———. 1976. *Athènes au IIe et au IIIe siècle: Études chronologiques et prosopographiques*. Paris.

———. 1991. "Divers aspects de l'hellénisme chez Philostrate." In *Hellenismos: Quelques jalons pour une histoire de l'identité grecque*, ed. S. Saïd, 205–15. Leiden.

———. 1994. "Remarques sur deux valeurs de κατά dans l'Héroïque de Philostrate." In *Cas et prépositions en grec ancien: contraintes syntaxiques et interprétations sémantiques: actes du colloque international de Saint Etienne, 3–5 juin 1993*, edited by B. C. J. P. Jacquinod, 113–19. Saint-Etienne.

———. 2004. "Philostratus' *Heroikos* and the Regions of the Northern Aegean." In Aitken and Maclean 2004, 221–36.

Fontenrose, Joseph. 1968. "The Hero as Athlete." *Classical Antiquity* 1: 73–104.

Francis, James A. 2003. "Living Icons: Tracing a Motif in Verbal and Visual Representation from the Second to Fourth Centuries C.E." *American Journal of Philology* 124: 575–600.

Fraser, P. M. 1972. *Ptolemaic Alexandria*. Oxford.

Frazer, R. M. 1966. *The Trojan War: The Chronicles of Dictys of Crete and Dares the Phrygian*. Bloomington, IN.

Fredrich, C. 1908. "Imbros." *Ath. Mitt.* 33: 81–112.

Frisch, Peter. 1975. *Die Inschriften von Ilion*. Bonn.

Gainsford, Peter. 2012. "Dictys of Crete." *The Cambridge Classical Journal (New Series)* 58: 58–87.

Gantz, Timothy. 1996. *Early Greek Myth: A Guide to Literary and Artistic Sources*. Baltimore.

Gardiner, E. Norman. 1930. *Athletics of the Ancient World*. Oxford.

Gärtner, Thomas. 1999. *Klassische Vorbilder mittelalterlicher Trojaepen*. Stuttgart.

Gérard-Rousseau, M. 1968. *Les mentions religieuses dans les tablettes mycéniennes.* Incunabula Graeca 29. Roma.

Giannini, Alexander. 1966. *Paradoxographorum graecorum reliquiae.* Milan.

Gleason, Maud. 1995. *Making Men: Sophists and Self-Presentation in Ancient Rome.* Princeton.

Goebel, Maximilianus. 1915. *Ethnica: de graecarum civitatum proprietatibus proverbio notatis.* Breslau.

Goldhill, Simon. 2001. *Being Greek under Rome: Cultural Identity, the Second Sophistic, and the Development of Empire.* Cambridge.

———. 2008. *The End of Dialogue in Antiquity.* Cambridge.

Gomme, A. W., and F. H. Sandbach. 1973. *Menander: A Commentary.* Oxford.

Gorman, Robert J., and Vanessa B. Gorman. 2007. "The Tryphê of the Sybarites: A Historiographical Problem in Athenaeus." *The Journal of Hellenic Studies* 127: 38–60.

Gow, A. S. F., and D. L. Page. 1965. *The Greek Anthology: Hellenistic Epigrams.* Cambridge.

———. 1968. *The Greek Anthology: the Garland of Philip, and Some Contemporary Epigrams.* Cambridge.

Graf, Fritz. 2011. "A Satirist's Sacrifices: Lucian's *On Sacrifices* and the Contestation of Religious Traditions." In *Ancient Mediterranean Sacrifice*, edited by Jennifer Wright Knust and Várhelyi Zsuzsanna, 203–15. New York.

Graninger, Denver. 2011. *Cult and Koinon in Hellenistic Thessaly.* Leiden.

Grentrup, Henricus. 1914. *De Heroici Philostratei fabularum fontibus.* Münster.

Griffith, Mark. 1983. *Aeschylus: Prometheus Bound.* Cambridge.

Grossardt, Peter. 2002. "Der Ringer Maron und der Pankratiast 'Halter' in epigraphischen und literarischen Quellen: (*SEG* 41, 1407 A und B bzw. Philostr. *Gym.* 36 und *Her.* 14–15)." *Epigraphica Anatolica* 34: 170–72.

———. 2004. "Ein Echo in allen Tonarten: der 'Heroikos' von Flavius Philostrat als Bilanz der antiken Troia-Dichtung." *Studia Troica* 14: 231–38.

———. 2006a. *Einführung, Übersetzung und Kommentar zum 'Heroikos' von Flavius Philostrat.* Schweizerische Beiträge zur Altertumswissenschaft 33. 2 vols. Basel.

———. 2006b. "Die Kataloge der troischen Kriegsparteien: von Dares und Malalas zu Isaak Porphyrogennetos und Johannes Tzetzes—und zurück zu Diktys und Philostrat ?" In *Approches de la Troisième Sophistique: hommages à Jacques Schamp,* ed. Eugenio Amato, Alexandre Roduit, and Martin Steinrück, 449–59. Brussels.

———. 2009a. "Chronographische Fachsprache und biographische Tradition in Philostrat, *Her.* 43–Korrekturen und Nachträge." *MH* 66: 84–87.

———. 2009b. "How to Become a Poet: Homer and Apollonius Visit the Tomb of Achilles." In *Theios Sophistes: Essays on Flavius Philostratus' 'Vita Apollonii,'* ed. Kristoffel Demoen and Danny Praet, 75—94. Leiden.

———. 2013. "Sprachliche und mythologische Probleme in Philostrat *Her.* 51." *Rheinisches Museum* 156: 353–78.

———. forthcoming. "Phil. *VA* 8, 31 und die Frage nach der epikureischen Prägung des Corpus Philostrateum." *Würzburger Jahrbücher für die Altertumswissenschaft* 38.

Hägg, Tomas. 2012. *The Art of Biography in Antiquity.* Cambridge.

Hansen, William. 1996. *Phlegon of Tralles' Book of Marvels.* Exeter.

Harmon, A. M. 1936. *Lucian.* Vol. 5. Loeb Classical Library 302. Cambridge, MA.

Harrison, Jane Ellen. 1955. *Prolegomena to the Study of Greek Religion.* New York.

Hasluck, F. W. 1909. "Terra Lemnia." *The Annual of the British School at Athens* 16: 220–31.

Hedreen, Guy. 1991. "The Cult of Achilles in the Euxine." *Hesperia* 60: 313–30.

Henning, C. 1874. "Ein ungedruckter Brief Julians." *Hermes* 9: 257–66.

Heyden, Katharina. 2009. "Christliche Transformation des antiken Dialogs bei Justin und Minucius Felix." *Zeitschrift für Antikes Christentum = Journal of Ancient Christianity* 13 (2): 204–32.

Hind, John. 1996. "Achilles and Helen on the White Island in the Euxine Sea: Side B of the Portland Vase." In *New Studies on the Black Sea Littoral*, ed. Gocha Tsetskhladze, 59–62. Colloquia Pontica I. Oxford.

Hirzel, R. 1895. *Der Dialog.* 2 vols. Leipzig.

Hodkinson, Owen. 2011. *Authority and Tradition in Philostratus' Heroikos.* Vol. 8 of *Satura.* Lecce.

Hommel, Hildebrecht. 1980. *Der Gott Achilleus.* Heidelberg.

Huhn, F., and E. Bethe. 1917. "Philostrats Heroikos und Diktys." *Hermes* 52: 613–24.

Hunter, Richard. 2009. "The *Trojan Oration* of Dio Chrysostom and Ancient Homeric Criticism." In *Narratology and Interpretation: The Content of Narrative Form in Ancient Literature*, eds. Jonas Grethlein and Antonios Rengakos, 43–61. Berlin.

Hupe, Joachim, and Claudia von Behren. 2006. *Der Achilleus-Kult im nördlichen Schwarzmeerraum vom Beginn der griechischen Kolonisation bis in die römische Kaiserzeit: Beiträge zur Akkulturationsforschung*. Rahden.

Imhoof-Blumer, Friedrich. 1910. "Beiträge zur Erklärung griechischer Münzen." *Nomisma: Untersuchungen auf dem Gebiete der antiken Münzkunde* 5: 25–42.

Jeffery, L H. 1990. *The Local Scripts of Archaic Greece: A Study of the Origin of the Greek Alphabet and Its Development from the Eighth to the Fifth Centuries B.C.* Rev. ed. with a supplement by A. W. Johnston. Oxford.

Jones, C. P. 1986. *Culture and Society in Lucian*. Cambridge, MA.

———. 2000. "The Emperor and the Giant." *Classical Philology* 95 (4): 476–81.

———. 2001. "Philostratus' *Heroikos* and Its Setting in Reality." *Journal of Hellenic Studies* 121: 141–49.

———. 2002. "Philostratus and the Gordiani." *Mediterrano antico* 5: 759–67.

———. 2005–6. *Philostratus, the Life of Apollonius of Tyana*. Loeb Classical Library 16, 17, and 458. Cambridge, MA.

———. 2010. *New Heroes in Antiquity: From Achilles to Antinoos*. Cambridge, MA.

———. 2011. "The Historian Philostratus of Athens." *The Classical Quarterly (New Series)* 61 (1): 320–22.

Jones, C. P., and G. W. Bowersock. 1974. "The Reliability of Philostratus." In *Approaches to the Second Sophistic*. University Park, PA.

Jouan, F. 1966. *Euripide et les légendes des chants cypriens.* Paris

Jüthner, Julius. 1902. "Der Verfasser des Gymnastikos." In *Festschrift Theodor Gomperz dargebracht zum siebzigsten Geburtstage am 29. März 1902, von Schülern, Freunden, Collegen,* ed. Moritz von Schwind, 225–32. Vienna.

———. 1909. *Philostratos über Gymnastik.* Leipzig.

Kahn, Charles. 1979. *The Art and Thought of Heraclitus: A New Arrangement and Translation of the Fragments with Literary and Philosophical Commentary.* Cambridge.

Kalinka, Ernst, and Otto Schönberger. 1968. *Philostratos: Die Bilder.* München.

Kannicht, Richard. 2004. *Tragicorum graecorum fragmenta; Vol. 5: Euripides.* 2 parts. Göttingen.

Kayser, C. L. 1870. *Flavi Philostrati Opera.* 2 vols. Leipzig.

Keaney, John J., and Robert Lamberton. 1996. *Plutarch, De Homero: Essay on the Life and Poetry of Homer.* American Classical Studies. Atlanta.

Kerferd, G. B. 1981. *The Sophistic Movement.* Cambridge.

Kim, Lawrence. 2010. *Homer between History and Fiction in Imperial Greek Literature.* Cambridge.

Kindstrand, Jan Fredrik. 1973. *Homer in der zweiten Sophistik: Studien zu der Homerlektüre und dem Homerbild bei Dion von Prusa, Maximos von Tyros und Ailios Aristeides.* Uppsala.

King, Katherine Callen. 1987. *Achilles: Paradigms of the Hero from Homer to the Middle Ages.* Berkeley.

König, Jason. 2005. *Athletics and Literature in the Roman Empire.* Cambridge.

————. 2009. *Greek Literature in the Roman Empire*. London.

Kraay, Colin M. 1976. *Archaic and Classical Greek Coins*. Berkeley.

Krauss, Johannes. 1980. *Inschiften von Sestos und der thrakischen Chersones*. Bonn.

Kreider, Alan. 1999. *The Change of Conversion and the Origin of Christendom*. Christian Mission and Modern Culture. Harrisburg, PA.

Kron, Uta. 1976. *Die zehn attischen Phylenheroen: Geschichte, Mythos, Kult und Darstellungen*. Mitteilungen des deutschen Archäologischen Instituts, Athenische Abteilung: Beiheft 5. Berlin.

Kuhlmann, Peter Alois. 2002. *Religion und Erinnerung: die Religionspolitik Kaiser Hadrians und ihre Rezeption in der antiken Literatur*. Göttingen.

Kullmann, Wolfgang. 1960. *Die Quellen der Ilias (troischer Sagenkreis)*. Hermes Einzelschriften 14. Wiesbaden.

Kurke, Leslie. 1999. "Ancient Greek Board Games and How to Play Them." *Classical Philology* 94: 247–67.

Küster, Erich. 1913. *Die Schlange in der griechischen Kunst und Religion*. Giessen.

Kutsch, Ferdinand. 1913. *Attische Heilgötter und Heilheroen*. Giessen.

Lamberton, Robert, and John J. Keaney. 1992. *Homer's Ancient Readers: The Hermeneutics of Greek Epic's Earliest Exegetes*. Princeton.

Lambrinoudakis, V. K. 1988. "Veneration of Ancestors in Geometric Naxos." In *Early Greek Cult Practice: Proceedings of the Fifth International Symposium at the Swedish Institute at Athens*, Act.Ath. 38, ed. Robin

Hägg, Nanno Marinatos, and Gullög C. Nordquiest, 235-46.

Larson, Jennifer. 1995. *Greek Heroine Cults.* Madison, WI.

Liapis, Vayos. 2011. "The Thracian Cult of Rhesus and the Heros Equitans." *Kernos* 24: 95–104.

Lilja, Saara. 1976. *Dogs in Ancient Greek Poetry.* Commentationes Humanarum Litterarum 56. Helsinki.

LIMC = Kahil, Lilly. 1981–2000. *Lexicon iconographicum mythologiae classicae.* Zurich.

Lindner, Ruth. 1994. *Mythos und Identität: Studien zur Selbstdarstellung kleinasiaticher Städte in der römischen Kaiserzeit.* Schriften der wissenschaftlichen Gesellschaft an der Johann Wolfgang Goethe-Universität Frankfurt. Stuttgart.

MacDowell, Douglas M. 1971. *Aristophanes, Wasps.* Oxford.

Maclean, Jennifer K. Berenson, and Ellen Bradshaw Aitken. 2002. *Flavius Philostratus: On Heroes.* Writings from the Greco-Roman World, vol. 3. Atlanta.

Mantero, Teresa. 1966. *Ricerche sull'Heroikos di Filostrato.* Genova.

————. 1973. *Aspetti del culto degli eroi presso i greci.* Genoa.

Marangou-Lerat, Antigone. 1995. *Le vin et les amphores de Crète: de l'époque classique à l'époque impériale.* Athens.

Mari, Manuela. 1997. "Tributo a Ilio e prostituzione sacra: storia e riflessi sociali di due riti femminili locresi." *Rivista di Cultura Classica e Medioevale* 39: 131–77.

Martin, Richard. 2002. "A Good Place to Talk: Discourse and Topos in Achilles Tatius and Philostratus." In *Space in the Ancient Novel*, ed. Michael Paschalis and Stavros Frangoulidis, 143–60. Groningen.

Masciadri, Virgilio. 2008. *Eine Insel im Meer der Geschichten: Untersuchungen zu Mythen aus Lemnos.* Potsdamer altertumswissenschaftliche Beiträge. Stuttgart.

Mayor, Adrienne. 2000. *The First Fossil Hunters: Paleontology in Greek and Roman Times.* Princeton.

Méndez Lloret, and María Isabel. 1993. "El démon: la inteligencia en el mundo." *Faventia* 15 (2): 23–38.

Merkelbach, Reinhold, and Josef Stauber. 1998. *Steinepigramme aus dem griechischen Osten I: Die Westküste Kleinasiens von Knidos bis Ilion.* Stuttgart.

Merkle, Stefan. 1989. *Die Ephemeris belli Troiani des Diktys von Kreta.* Studien zur klassischen Philologie 44. Frankfurt.

———. 1994. "Telling the True Story of the Trojan War: The Eyewitness Acount of Dictys of Crete." In *The Search for the Ancient Novel*, ed. James Tatum. Baltimore.

———. 1996. "The Truth and Nothing But the Truth: Dictys and Dares." In *The Novel in the Ancient World*, ed. Gareth Schmeling, 563–80. Leiden.

Mestre, Francesca. 2005. "Héroes en Luciano." In *Actas del XI congreso español de estudios clásicos*, 435–42. Madrid.

Miles, Graeme. 2004. "Music and Immortality: The Afterlife of Achilles in Philostratus' 'Heroicus.'" *Ancient Narrative* 4: 66–78.

Millar, Fergus. 1983. "The Phoenician Cities: A Case-Study of Hellenisation." *Proceedings of the Cambridge Philology Society* 29: 55–71.

Minon, Sophie. 2012. *Dion de Pruse. Ilion n'a pas été prise: Discours troyen 11.* La roue à livres 61. Paris.

Moretti, Luigi. 1957. "Olympionikai, i vincitori negli antichi agoni olimpici." *Memoria della Classe di Scienze morali e storiche dell' Accademia dei Lincei* 8.8.

Morgan, Catherine. 1990. *Athletes and Oracles: The Transformation of Olympia and Delphi in the Eighth Century BC.* Cambridge.

Morris, Ian. 1988. "Tomb Cult and the "Greek Renaissance": The Past in the Present in the 8th Century BC." *Antiquity* 62: 750–61.

Münscher, Karl. 1907. "Die Philostrate." In *Philologus,* Suppl. 10.4, 469–567. Leipzig.

Nachtergael, Georges. 1977. *Les Galates en Grèce et les Sôtéria de Delphes: recherches d'histoire et d'épigraphie hellénistiques.* Mémoires de la Classe des lettres - Académie royale de Belgique 63. Brussels.

Nagy, Gregory. 1979. *The Best of the Achaeans: Concepts of the Hero in Archaic Greek Poetry.* Baltimore.

Nock, A. D. 1933. *Conversion: The Old and the New in Religion from Alexander the Great to Augustine of Hippo.* Oxford.

———. 1972. *Essays on Religion and the Ancient World.* Edited by Zeph Stewart. Oxford.

Oberhummer, E. 1898. "Imbros." In *Beiträge zur alten Geschichte und Geographie: Festschrift für Heinrich Kiepert,* 277–304. Berlin.

Ochotnikov, Sergei B. 2006. "Achilleus auf der Insel Leuke." In Hupe and von Behren 2006,49–87.

Ogden, Daniel. 2007. *In Search of the Sorcerer's Apprentice: The Traditional Tales of Lucian's Lover of Lies.* Swansea.

Ortiz, Victor Jay. 1993. "Athenian Tragedy and Hero-Cult: A Study of the Greek Poetic and Religious Imagination." PhD diss., University of California, Los Angeles.

O'Sullivan, Neil. 2008. "The Authenticity of [Alcidamas] 'Odysseus': Two New Linguistic Considerations." *Classical Quarterly* 58: 638–47.

Pache, Corinne Ondine. 2004. *Baby and Child Heroes in Ancient Greece.* Urbana.

Parker, R. 2005. "ὡς ἥρωι ἐναγίζειν." in *Greek Sacrificial Ritual, Olympian and Chthonian: Proceedings of the Sixth International Seminar on Ancient Greek Cult, Organized by the Department of Classical Archaeology and Ancient History, Göteborg University, 25–27 April 1997,* edited by Robin Hägg and Brita Alroth, 37–45. Stockholm.

Pease, A. S. 1942. "Some Aspects of Invisibility." *Harvard Studies in Classical Philology* 53: 12–18.

Pelliccia, Hayden. 2002. "The Interpretation of Iliad 6.145–9 and the Sympotic Contribution to Rhetoric." *Colby Quarterly* 38: 197–230.

Pelon, Olivier. 1976. *Tholoi, tumuli, et cercles funéraires: recherches sur les monuments funéraires de plan circulaire dans l'Égée de l'âge du bronze, IIIe et IIe millénaires av. J.-C.* Athens.

Perry, B. E. 1965. *Babrius and Phaedrus.* Loeb Classical Library 436. Cambridge, MA.

Petrakos, Vasileios Ch. 1968. Ὁ Ὠροπός καί τό ἱερόν τού Ἀμφιαράρου. Athens.

Petzl, Georg. 1969. *Antike Diskussionen über die beiden Nekyiai.* Beiträge zur klassischen Philologie 29. Meisenheim.

Pfister, Friedrich. 1909. *Der Reliquienkult im Altertum.* Giessen.

Pirenne-Delforge, V. 2001. "Les rites sacrificiels dans la Périégèse de Pausanias." In *Editer, traduire, commenter Pausanias en l'an 2000*: Actes du colloque de Neuchâtel et de Fribourg, 18–22 septembre 1998, autour des deux éditions en cours de la Périégèse, collection des universités de France, fondazione Lorenzo Valla, ed. Denis Knoepfler and Maurice Piérart, 109–34. Neuchâtel.

Pirenne-Delforge, Vinciane, Suárez de la Torre Emilio, and Université de Valladolid. 2000. *Héros et héroïnes dans les mythes et les cultes grecs: actes du colloque organisé à l'Université de Valladolid du 26 au 29 mai 1999.* Liège

Platt, Verity. 2009. "Virtual Visions: *Phantasia* and the Perception of the Divine in the *Life of Apollonius of Tyana.*" In Bowie and Elsner 2009, 131–54.

———. 2011. *Facing the Gods. Epiphany and Representation in Graeco-Roman Art, Literature and Religion.* Greek Culture and the Roman World. Cambridge.

Podlecki, A. J. 1971. "Cimon, Scyros and Theseus' Bones." *Journal of Hellenic Studies* 91: 141–43.

Poliakoff, Michael. 1986. *Studies in the Terminology of the Greek Combat Sports.* Frankfurt.

———. 1987. *Combat Sports in the Ancient World: Competition, Violence, and Culture.* Sport and History Series. New Haven.

Popham, Mervyn R., and Irene S. Lemos. 1996. *Lefkandi. 3, the Toumba Cemetery: The Excavations of 1981, 1984, 1986 and 1992–4. 2, Plates/Compiled by Mervyn R. Popham and Irene S. Lemos.* London.

Pötscher, W. 1961. "Hera und Heros." *Rheinisches Museum* 104: 302–55.

———. 1965. "Der Name der Göttin Hera." *Rheinisches Museum* 108: 317–20.

Pottier, Edmond. 1915. "Fouilles archéologiques sur l'emplacement de la nécropole d'Éléonte de Thrace (Juillet-Decembre 1915)." *Bulletin de correspondance hellénique* 39: 135–240.

Preller, Ludwig, Carl Robert, and Otto Kern. 1894–1926. *Griechische Mythologie*. Berlin.

Price, T. H. 1973. "Hero-Cult and Homer." *Historia* 22: 129–44.

Pritchett, W. K. 1971–1985. *The Greek State at War*. Berkeley.

Puiggali, J. 1983. "La démonologie de Philostrate." *Revue des sciences philosophiques et théologiques* 67: 117–30.

Radet, G. 1925. "Notes sur l'histoire d'Alexandre II: les théores Thessaliens au tombeau d' Achille." *Revue des études anciennes* 27: 81–96.

RE = Pauly, A., and G. Wissowa. 1894. *Paulys Real-Encyclopädie der classischen Altertumswissenschaft*. Stuttgart.

Reinhold, Meyer. 1970. *History of Purple as a Status Symbol in Antiquity*. Collection Latomus 116. Brussels.

Reitzenstein, R. 1906. *Hellenistische Wundererzählungen*. Leipzig.

Rempe, Johannes. 1927. *De Rheso Thracum heroe*. Munich.

Reverdin, Olivier. 1945. *La religion dans la cité platonicienne*. Paris.

Richardson, Nicholas J. 1984. "Innovazione poetica e mutamenti religiosi nell' antica grecia." *Studi classici e orientali* 33: 13–27.

Robert, Louis. 1984. "Héraclès à Pergame et une épigramme de l'Anthologie XVI,91." *Revue de philologie, de littérature et d'histoire anciennes* 58: 7–18.

Rohde, Erwin. 1901. *Kleine Schriften*. Tübingen.

———. 1925. *Psyche; the Cult of Souls and Belief in Immortality Among the Greeks*. Translated by W. B. Willis. London.

Romero Mariscal, Lucía Presentación. 2008a. "'Paideia' héroïque: Palamède et l'éducation des héros dans l'"Héroïque' de Philostrate." *Humanitas: revista do Instituto de Estudos clássicos* 60: 139–56.

———. 2008b. "El 'Heroico' de Filóstrato." In *En Grecia y Roma. 2, Lecturas pendientes*, ed. Andrés Pociña Pérez and Jesús María García González, 345–64. Granada.

———. 2011. "Ajax and Achilles Playing a Board Game: Revisited from the Literary Tradition." *The Classical Quarterly* 61 (2): 394–401.

Rommel, Hans. 1923. *Die naturwissenschaftlich-paradoxographischen Exkurse bei Philostratos, Heliodor und Achilles Tatios*. Stuttgart.

Rose, Brian. 1999. "The 1998 Post-Bronze Age Excavations at Troia." *Studia Troica* 9: 53–62.

———. 2000. "The 1999 Post-Bronze Age Excavations at Troia." *Studia Troica* 10: 53–62.

———. 2002. "Ilion in the Early Empire." In *Patris und imperium: kulturelle und politische Identität in den Städten der römischen Provinzen Kleinasiens in der frühen Kaiserzeit: Kolloquium Köln, November 1998*, ed. Christof Berns, 33–47. Leuven.

Russell, D. A., and N. G. Wilson. 1981. *Menander Rhetor.* Oxford.

Rusten, Jeffrey S. 1982. *Dionysius Scytobrachion.* Opladen.

———. 1983. "Γείτων ἥρως: Pindar's Prayer to Heracles (N. 7.86–101) and Greek Popular Religion." *Harvard Studies in Classical Philology* 87: 289–97.

———. 2004. "Living in the Past: Allusive Narratives and Elusive Authorities in the World of the *Heroikos.*" In Aitken and Maclean 2004, 143–58.

———. 2013. "The Mirror of Aristophanes: The Winged Ethnographers of *Birds* (1470–93, 1553–64, 1694–1705)." In *Greek Comedy and the Discourse of Genres*, ed. E. Bakola, L. Prauscello, and M. Telò, 298–318. Cambridge.

Rusyaeva, Anna S. 2003. "The Temple of Achilles on the Island of Leuke in the Black Sea." *Ancient Civilizations from Scythia to Siberia* 9: 1–16.

Rutherford, Ian. 2009. "Black Sails to Achilles: The Thessalian Pilgrimage in Philostratus' *Heroicus.*" In Bowie and Elsner 2009, 230–50.

Sánchez Jiménez, Francisco. 1992. "Protesilao en Escione: en torno a la utilización política de leyendas y cultos." *Baetica (Málaga Universidad de Málaga Facultad de Filosofía y Letras)* 14: 216–23.

Schäublin, Christoph. 1985. "Conversionen in antiken Dialogen." In *Catalepton: Festschrift für Bernhard Wyss zum 80 Geburtstag*, ed. Christoph Schäublin, 117–31. Basel.

Scheer, Eduard. 1881. *Lycophronis Alexandra.* Berlin.

Schmid, Wilhelm. 1887. *Der Atticismus in seinen Haupt-*

vertretern: von Dionysius von Halikarnass bis auf den zweiten Philostratus. Stuttgart.

Schmidt, Thomas S., and Pascale Fleury. 2011. *Perceptions of the Second Sophistic and Its Times*. Toronto.

Schmitz, Thomas. 1997. *Bildung und Macht: zur sozialen und politischen Funktion der zweiten Sophistik in der griechischen Welt der Kaiserzeit*. Munich.

————. 2011. "The Second Sophistic." In *The Oxford Handbook of Social Relations in the Roman World*, ed. Michael Peachin, 304–16. Oxford.

Séchan, Louis. 1953. "La légende de Protésilas." *Bulletin Assoc. Guillaum Budé* 4: 3–27.

Scodel, Ruth. 1980. *The Trojan Trilogy of Euripides. Hypomnemata*. Vol. 60. Göttingen.

————. 1981. "Hesiod Redivivus." *Greek, Roman and Byzantine Studies* 21: 301–20.

Shackleton Bailey, D. R. 1977. *Cicero, Epistulae ad familiares*. Cambridge.

Skiadas, Aristoxenos D. 1965. *Homer im griechischen Epigramm*. Athens.

Snodgrass, A. M. 1982. "Les origines du culte des héros dans la grèce antique." In *La mort, les morts dans les sociétés anciennes*, edited by G. Gnoli and J.-P. Vernant, 107–20. Cambridge.

Solmsen, Friedrich. 1941. "Philostratus (nos. 9–12)." In *RE* 20: 104–77.

————. 1940. "Some Works of Philostratus the Elder." *Transactions of the American Philological Association* 71: 556–72.

————. 1968. "Hesiodic Motifs in Plato." In *Kleine Schriften*, 82–105. Hildesheim.

Stelow, Anna Rachel Pease. 2005. "Not Quite the Best of

the Achaians: Menelaos in Archaic Greek Poetry and Art." PhD diss., University of Minnesota.

Swain, Simon. 1996. *Hellenism and Empire: Language, Classicism and Power in the Greek World AD 50–250.* Oxford.

————, ed. 2007. *Seeing the Face, Seeing the Soul: Polemon's Physiognomy from Classical Antiquity to Medieval Islam.* Oxford.

Swain, Simon, Stephen Harrison, and Jaś Elsner. 2007. *Severan Culture.* Cambridge.

Syme, Ronald. 1988. "Journeys of Hadrian." *Zeitschrift für Papyrologic und Epigraphik* 73: 159–70.

Szarmach, M. 1974. "Le mythe de Palamède avant la tragédie grecque." *Eos* 62: 35–47.

Thompson, D'Arcy Wentworth. 1936. *Glossary of Greek Birds.* Oxford.

Thompson, Eugene Taylor. 1985. "The Relics of the Heroes in Ancient Greece." PhD diss., University of Washington.

Thompson, Homer. 1978. "Some Hero Shrines in Early Athens." In *Athens Comes of Age: from Solon to Salamis*, ed. William Childs, 96–105. Princeton.

Trapp, M. B. 1990. "Plato's Phaedrus in Second-Century Greek Literature." In *Antonine Literature*, ed. D. A. Russell, 141–73. Oxford.

————. 1997. *Maximus of Tyre, The Philosophical Orations.* Oxford.

Uden, James. 2010. "The 'Contest of Homer and Hesiod' and the Ambitions of Hadrian." *The Journal of Hellenic Studies* 130: 121–35.

Usener, Knut. 1994a. "Diktys und Dares über den Troi-

schen Kriege: Homer in der Rezeptionskrise?" *Eranos*
92: 102–20.

―――. 1994b. "Palamedes: Bedeutung und Wandel
eines Heldenbildes in der antiken Literatur." *Würz-
burger Jahrbücher fur die Altertumswissenschaft* 20:
49–78.

Ustinova, Yulia. 2002. "'Either a Daimon, or a Hero, or
Perhaps a God': Mythical Residents of Subterranean
Chambers." *Kernos* 15: 267–88.

Van Leeuwen, Johannis. 1893. *Aristophanis Vespae*. Lei-
den.

Van Nijf, Onno. 2001. "Local Heroes: Athletics, Festivals
and Elite Self-Fashioning in the Roman East." In Gold-
hill 2001, 306–34.

Vermeule, Emily. 1979. *Aspects of Death in Early Greek
Art and Poetry.* Berkeley.

Villari, Elisabetta. 2003. "La physiognomonie comme
technè." In *"Ars et ratio": sciences, art et métiers dans
la philosophie hellénistique et romaine: actes du collo-
que international organisé à Créteil, Fontenay et Paris
du 16 au 18 octobre 1997,* ed. Carlos Lévy, Bernard
Besnier, and Alain Gigandet, 89–101. Brussels.

Vogt, Sabine. 2002. *Aristoteles Opuscula, Physiognomica.*
Werke in deutscher Übersetzung, vol. 18, pt 6. Berlin.

Vout, Caroline. 2007. "Romancing the Stone, Hadrian and
Antinous." In *Power and Eroticism in Imperial Rome.*
Cambridge.

Vout, Caroline, and Penelope Curtis. 2006. *Antinous: The
face of the Antique.* Leeds.

VS = Diels, Hermann, and Walther Kranz. 1951. *Die
Fragmente der Vorsokratiker, griechisch und deutsch.*
Berlin.

Walker, Susan, and Averil Cameron. 1989. *The Greek Renaissance in the Roman Empire: Papers from the Tenth British Museum Classical Colloquium.* London.

Waszink, J. H. 1974. *Biene und Honig als Symbol des Dichters und der Dichtung in der griechisch-römischen Antike.* Opladen.

Welcker, F. G. 1865. *Der epische Cyclus.* Part 1. Bonn.

West, M. L. 1978. *Hesiod: Works & Days,* edited with an introduction and commentary. Oxford.

———. 2003a. *Greek Epic Fragments from the Seventh to the Fifth Centuries BC.* The Loeb Classical Library 497. Cambridge, MA.

———. 2003b. *Homeric Hymns, Homeric Apocrypha, Lives of Homer.* The Loeb Classical Library 496. Cambridge, MA.

———. 2013. *The Epic Cycle: a Commentary on the Lost Troy Epics.* Oxford.

West, Stephanie. 2003. "'The Most Marvellous of All Seas': The Greek Encounter with the Euxine." *Greece & Rome* 50: 151–67.

Whitmarsh, Tim. 1999. "Greek and Roman in Dialogue: The Pseudo-Lucianic Nero." *Journal of Hellenic Studies* 119: 142–60.

———. 2004. "Philostratus." In *Narrators, Narratees, and Narratives in Ancient Greek Literature. Studies in Ancient Greek Narrative,* vol. 1, ed. Irene J. F. de Jong, René Nünlist, and Angus M. Bowie, 423–39. Leiden.

———. 2005. *The Second Sophistic.* Oxford.

———. 2006. "Quickening the Classics: The Politics of Prose in Roman Greece." In *Classical Pasts,* ed. James I. Porter, 353–74. Princeton.

————. 2007a. "Prose Literature and the Severan Dynasty." In Swain, Harrison, and Elsner (2007), 29–51.

————. 2007b. "Time in Philostratus." In *Time in Ancient Greek Literature. Studies in Ancient Greek Narrative*, vol. 2, ed. Irene J. F. de Jong and R. Nünlist, 413–000. Leiden.

————. 2009. "Performing Heroics: Language, Landscape and Identity in Philostratus' *Heroicus*." In Bowie and Elsner 2009, 205–29.

————. 2010. *Local Knowledge and Microidentities in the Imperial Greek World*. Cambridge.

Williamson, George. 2005. "Mucianus and a Touch of the Miraculous: Pilgrimage and Tourism in Roman Asia Minor." In Elsner and Rutherford 2005, 220–52.

Winter, I. J. 1995. "Homer's Phoenicians: History, Ethnography or Literary Trope?" In *The Ages of Homer: A Tribute to Emily Townsend Vermeule*, ed. Jane Carter and Sarah Morris, 247–71. Austin.

Woodford, Susan. 1994. "Palamedes Seeks Revenge." *The Journal of Hellenic Studies* 114: 164–69.

Woolf, Greg. 1994. "Becoming Roman, Staying Greek: Culture, Identity and the Civilizing Process in the Roman East." *Proceedings of the Cambridge Philology Association* 40: 116–43.

Zanker, Paul, Björn Ewald, and Julia Christian Slater. 2013. *Living with Myths: The Imagery of Roman Sarcophagi*. Oxford.

Zeitlin, Froma. 2001. "Visions and Revisions of Homer." In Goldhill 2001, 195–268.

Zwingmann, Nicola. 2012. *Antiker Tourismus in Kleinasien und auf den vorgelagerten Inseln: Selbstvergewisserung in der Fremde*. Antiquitas. Vol. 59. Bonn.

OUTLINE OF THE *HEROICUS*

Chapters 1–5: Introductory conversation. The scene is Protesilaus' grove. A Phoenician merchant, scanning the skies for an omen relating to his next voyage, meets a vinedresser somewhere near Elaious in the Thracian Chersonnese. In the course of their talk the vinedresser claims to meet regularly with the hero Protesilaus and receive his aid. The Phoenician is skeptical about all miracles attributed to heroes but would like to hear more; they choose to continue their conversation in the very grove where Protesilaus and the vinedresser meet.

5–8.17: The Phoenician's dream; skepticism on heroes. The Phoenician reveals that a dream has foretold their conversation; but he admits that he finds stories of oversize heroes too much to believe. The vinedresser convinces him with a long list of wonders, some from the past, others from his own day.

8.18–16: Protesilaus. The vinedresser introduces Protesilaus' shrine and its history, and describes the hero's appearance and the way he visits and helps him. The hero also gives prophecies to athletes (being a fine athlete himself), heals diseases, and punishes adulterers.

17–22: Other heroes at Troy. The vinedresser tells how Ajax, Hector, and Palamedes have all appeared at Troy to punish or reward mortals as they deserve.

100

52–57: Tales of the hero Achilles. The vinedresser describes the long history of Achilles worship at Troy by the Thessalians and the punishments for its neglect. He also describes the strange island of Leuke in the Black Sea, where he and Helen are immortal, the terrible punishments Achilles inflicted there on a slave girl of Trojan blood and on some Amazons who tried to plunder his shrine.

58: Conclusion. The Phoenician asks for tales of the underworld, but the vinedresser must break off at day's end. He suggests the Phoenician return tomorrow, which the stranger promises to do.

ΦΙΛΟΣΤΡΑΤΟΥ ΗΡΩΙΚΟΣ

(ΤΑ ΠΡΟΣΩΠΑ ΑΜΠΕΛΟΤΡΓΟΣ ΚΑΙ ΦΟΙΝΙΞ)

1. ΆΜΠ. Ἴων ὁ ξένος ἢ πόθεν;

ΦΟΙΝ. Φοῖνιξ, ἀμπελουργέ, τῶν περὶ Σιδῶνά τε καὶ Τύρον.

ΆΜΠ. Τὸ δὲ Ἰωνικὸν τῆς στολῆς;

ΦΟΙΝ. Ἐπιχώριον ἤδη καὶ ἡμῖν τοῖς ἐκ Φοινίκης.

ΆΜΠ. Πόθεν οὖν μετεσκευάσθε;

ΦΟΙΝ. Σύβαρις Ἰωνικὴ τὴν Φοινίκην κατέσχεν ὁμοῦ πᾶσαν, καὶ γραφὴν ἐκεῖ ἄν τις, οἶμαι, φύγοι μὴ τρυφῶν.

2 ΆΜΠ. Βαδίζεις δὲ ποῖ μετέωρός τε καὶ ὑπὲρ πάντα τὰ ἐν ποσί;

ΦΟΙΝ. Ξυμβόλου καὶ φήμης, ἀμπελουργέ, δέομαι περὶ εὐπλοίας· φασὶ· γὰρ ἡμᾶς ἀφήσειν ἐς τὸν Αἰγαῖον αὐτόν, δεινὴ δέ, οἶμαι, ἡ θάλαττα καὶ οὐ ῥᾳδία πλεῦσαι. βαδίζω δὲ τὴν ἐναντίαν ὁδὸν τῷ ἀνέμῳ· τὰ γὰρ ὑπὲρ εὐπλοίας πρὸς τουτονὶ τὸν σκοπὸν θεωροῦσι Φοίνικες.

3 ΆΜΠ. Σοφοί γε, ὦ ξένε, τὰ ναυτικὰ ὄντες· ὑμεῖς γάρ που καὶ τὴν ἑτέραν ἄρκτον ἐνεσημήνασθε τῷ

PHILOSTRATUS, *ON HEROES*

(The characters: A vinedresser and a Phoenician)

1. *Vinedresser.* Are you an Ionian, stranger, or from where?

Phoenician. A Phoenician, vinedresser, from around Tyre and Sidon.

Vinedresser. But your Ionian clothing. . . ?

Phoenician. That is native to us Phoenicians also.

Vinedresser. How did you come to adopt it?

Phoenician. The Sybaritic habits of Ionia[1] have influenced every bit of Phoenicia—and in Sybaris it was a crime, I imagine, *not* to be luxurious.

Vinedresser. But where are you going with your head in the clouds, ignoring everything in your path? 2

Phoenician. I am seeking a prophetic sign for a fair voyage, for I hear that we are setting sail on the Aegean itself—a formidable sea, I am sure, and not easy to sail. I am walking facing the wind, for that is the standard by which Phoenicians reckon the conditions for sailing.

Vinedresser. You are skilled in seafaring, stranger, I will 3 allow; for of course you Phoenicians located the other bear

---

[1] For the proverbial luxury of Sybaris, see Gorman and Gorman (2007). For the Hellenism of Phoenicians, see Introduction §7.

PHILOSTRATUS

οὐρανῷ καὶ πρὸς αὐτὴν πλεῖτε. ὥσπερ δὲ τὰς ναυτι-
λίας ἐπαινεῖσθε, οὕτω τὰς ἐμπορίας διαβέβλησθε ὡς
φιλοχρήματοί τε καὶ τρῶκται.

4   ΦΟΙΝ. Σὺ δὲ οὐ φιλοχρήματος, ἀμπελουργέ, ζῶν
ἐν ταύταις ταῖς ἀμπέλοις καὶ ζητῶν ἴσως ὅστις μὲν
ὀπωριεῖ καταβαλών σοι δραχμὴν τῶν βοτρύων, ὅτῳ
δὲ ἀποδώσῃ τὸ γλεῦκος ἢ ὅτῳ τὸν ἀνθοσμίαν; ὅν,
οἶμαι, καὶ κατορωρυγμένον φῂς ἔχειν ὥσπερ ὁ Μά-
ρων.

5   ΑΜΠ. Ξένε Φοῖνιξ, εἰ μέν εἰσί που τῆς γῆς Κύ-
κλωπες, οὓς λέγεται ἡ γῆ ἀργοὺς βόσκειν φυτεύοντας
οὐδὲν οὐδὲ σπείροντας, ἀφύλακτα μὲν τὰ φυόμενα εἴη
ἄν, καίτοι Δήμητρός γε καὶ Διονύσου ὄντα, πωλοῖτο
δ᾽ ἂν οὐδὲν ἐκ τῆς γῆς, ἀλλ᾽ ἄτιμά τε καὶ κοινὰ φύοιτ᾽
ἄν, ὥσπερ ἐν συῶν ἀγορᾷ· σπείρειν δὲ ὅπου χρὴ καὶ
ἀροῦν καὶ φυτεύειν καὶ ἄλλο ἐπ᾽ ἄλλῳ πονεῖν προσ-
κείμενον τῇ γῇ καὶ ὑποκείμενον ταῖς ὥραις, ἐνταῦθα
6   πωλεῖν τε χρὴ καὶ ὠνεῖσθαι. δεῖ γὰρ καὶ γεωργίᾳ

---

2 The "other bear" (in contrast to the "great" one) is Ursa
Minor, also called "the Wagon"; Philostratus' words echo Calli-
machus (*Iambi* fr. 99.55 Pfeiffer), who says that Thales intro-
duced it to Greece from Phoenicia.

3 Hom. *Od.* 14.289; Pl. *Resp.* 4.436a.

4 Maron was the priest of Apollo (later of Dionysus, Eur. *Cyc.*
143; Hesiod fr. 238 M–W), who gave Odysseus the potent wine
he carried into Polyphemus' cave; Homer does not say he buried
it, but only that he kept its existence secret from most of his
household (*Od.* 9.205–07). Maron was considered the mythical
founder of the Thracian town Maroneia, so the Phoenician may
be alluding to a local legend.

104

in the sky, and sail by it.[2] But with your good reputation as sailors goes an equally bad one as greedy and grasping merchants.[3]

Phoenician. Do you mean, then, that *you* have no inter- 4
est in money, vinedresser, even though you live amid this vineyard, and doubtless look for a man to pick your grapes and pay a drachma for them, or customers for your must and fragrant new wine? I suppose you claim to keep it buried underground, like Maron![4]

Vinedresser. Phoenician stranger, if anywhere on earth 5
there live Cyclopes, whom they say the earth feeds with no labor of planting or sowing on their part,[5] then plants would be unguarded—even though they belong to Demeter and Dionysus—and no produce of the earth would be sold; instead, they would grow free for all to share in, just as in a "pigs' marketplace."[6] But where it is necessary to sow and plow and plant and toil constantly, attached to the land and in thrall to the seasons, there one must buy and sell. Even farming takes money, and without it you can- 6

[5] The vinedresser answers one allusion to *Od.* 9 with another, to 9.107–11: the Cyclopes "relying on the immortal gods neither plant with their hands nor reap, but all things grow for them without sowing or harvesting." The "Cyclopean life" became proverbial.

[6] See Rusten (2004): Philostratus has in mind a passage from Pl. *Resp.* (2.372A–D), a work to which he alludes frequently. After Socrates describes an ideal rustic city of simple and unsophisticated pleasures, Adeimantus objects and demands more civilized foods: "If you were constructing a city of pigs (ὑῶν πόλις) wouldn't you give them this fodder also?" Philostratus' rebuke to the Phoenician's naïveté substitutes "market" for "city," because commercialism is the bone of contention between them.

χρημάτων, καὶ ἄνευ τούτων οὔτε ἀρότην θρέψεις οὔτε
ἀμπελουργὸν οὔτε βουκόλον οὔτε αἰπόλον, οὐδὲ κρα-
τὴρ ἔσται σοι πιεῖν ἢ σπεῖσαι. καὶ γὰρ τὸ ἥδιστον
τῶν ἐν γεωργίᾳ, τὸ τρυγᾶν ἀμπέλους, μισθοῦ χρὴ
πράττειν· εἰ δὲ μή, ἄοινοί τε καὶ ἀργοὶ ἑστήξουσιν,
7 ὥσπερ γεγραμμέναι. ταυτὶ μέν, ὦ ξένε, ὑπὲρ παντὸς
εἴρηκα τοῦ τῶν γεωργῶν κύκλου, τοὐμὸν δὲ πολλῷ
ἐπιεικέστερον· οὐ γὰρ ξυμβάλλω ἐμπόροις, οὐδὲ τὴν
δραχμὴν ὅ τι ἐστὶ γινώσκω, ἀλλὰ βοῦν σίτου καὶ
οἴνου τράγον καὶ τοιαῦτα τοιούτων ἢ ὠνοῦμαι ἢ αὐτὸς
ἀποδίδομαι σμικρὰ εἰπών τε καὶ ἀκούσας.

2. ΦΟΙΝ. Χρυσῆν ἀγορὰν λέγεις, ἀμπελουργέ, καὶ
ἡρώων μᾶλλον ἢ ἀνθρώπων. ἀλλὰ ὁ κύων οὗτος τί
ἐθέλει; περίεισι γάρ με προσκυνιζώμενος τοῖς ποσὶ
καὶ παρέχων τὸ οὖς ἁπαλόν τε καὶ πρᾶον.
2 ΑΜΠ. Τοὐμὸν ἦθος ἑρμηνεύει σοι, ξένε, καὶ ὅτι
πρὸς τοὺς δεῦρο ἀφικνουμένους οὕτω μετρίως καὶ
χρηστῶς ἔχομεν, ὡς μηδὲ τῷ κυνὶ ξυγχωρεῖν ὑλα-
κτεῖν αὐτούς, ἀλλὰ προσδέχεσθαί τε καὶ ὑποπίπτειν
ἥκοντας.
3 ΦΟΙΝ. Ἔξεστιν οὖν ἀμπέλῳ προσβαλεῖν;
ΑΜΠ. Φθόνος οὐδείς· εἰσὶ γὰρ ἡμῖν ἱκανοί γε
βότρυς.
4 ΦΟΙΝ. Τί δὲ συκάσαι;
ΑΜΠ. Καὶ τούτου ἄδεια· περίεστι γὰρ καὶ σύκων.
καὶ κάρυα δοίην καὶ μῆλα δοίην καὶ μυρία ἀγαθὰ
ἕτερα· φυτεύω δὲ αὐτὰ οἷον παροψήματα τῶν ἀμπέ-
λων.

106

not keep a plowman, a Vinedresser, a cowherd or a goat-herd, nor will you have a bowl of wine to drink or pour a libation. Even the pleasantest part of farming, harvesting the grapes, has to be done for a wage; otherwise the vines will stand wineless and idle, as in a picture. That much, 7 stranger, I've said on behalf of all farmers, but I myself am much more praiseworthy; for I keep no company with merchants, and I don't even know what a drachma is, since I either buy or sell a cow for grain, or a goat for wine or such other things, with little conversation.

2. *Phoenician.* The market you describe, vinedresser, is of a golden age and more suited to heroes than men.[7] But what is this dog after? He is circling and whimpering fondly at my feet, and listening to me calmly and quietly.

Vinedresser. He is showing you what we're like here, 2 stranger; I treat new arrivals so gently and humanely that I don't even allow my dog to bark at them,[8] but fall at their feet in welcome when they come.

Phoenician. May I have a go at the vines, then? 3

Vinedresser. Of course; I have plenty of grapes.

Phoenician. What about picking some figs? 4

Vinedresser. Feel free; I have more than enough of them too. I can also offer you walnuts and apples and much else that is good, which I grow as a sort of garnish for the wines.

---

[7] Actually the "golden age" and that of the heroes are separate in Hes. *Op.* 106–201, but the Phoenician refers in general to the blessed past. "Golden" applied to persons may also mean "naive."

[8] Farmers and shepherds kept dogs primarily for security (Hes. *Op.* 605–6; Verg. *G.* 3.404–8), and a traveler might expect to be troubled by them (e.g., *Od.* 14.29–38).

5   ΦΟΙΝ. Τί ἂν οὖν καταβάλοιμι;

ΑΜΠ. Τί δ᾽ ἄλλο γε ἢ φαγεῖν τε ἡδέως καὶ ἐπισιτίσασθαι καὶ ἀπελθεῖν χαίρων;

6   ΦΟΙΝ. Ἀλλ᾽ ἦ φιλοσοφεῖς, ἀμπελουργέ;

ΑΜΠ. Καὶ σύν γε τῷ καλῷ Πρωτεσίλεῳ.

7   ΦΟΙΝ. Σοὶ δὲ τί καὶ τῷ Πρωτεσίλεῳ κοινόν, εἰ τὸν ἐκ Θετταλίας λέγεις;

ΑΜΠ. Ἐκεῖνον λέγω, τὸν τῆς Λαοδαμείας· τουτὶ γὰρ χαίρει ἀκούων.

8   ΦΟΙΝ. Τί δὲ δὴ δεῦρο πράττει;

ΑΜΠ. Ζῇ καὶ γεωργοῦμεν.

9   ΦΟΙΝ. Ἀναβεβιωκὼς ἢ τί;

ΑΜΠ. Οὐδὲ αὐτὸς λέγει, ὦ ξένε, τὰ ἑαυτοῦ πάθη, πλήν γε δὴ ὅτι ἀποθάνοι μὲν δι᾽ Ἑλένην ἐν Τροίᾳ, ἀναβιῴη δὲ ἐν Φθίᾳ Λαοδαμείας ἐρῶν.

10   ΦΟΙΝ. Καὶ μὴν ἀποθανεῖν γε μετὰ τὸ ἀναβιῶναι λέγεται καὶ ἀναπεῖσαι τὴν γυναῖκα ἐπισπέσθαι οἷ.

11   ΑΜΠ. Λέγει καὶ αὐτὸς ταῦτα, ἀλλ᾽ ὅπως καὶ μετὰ τοῦτο ἀνῆλθε, πάλαι μοι βουλομένῳ μαθεῖν οὐ λέγει, Μοιρῶν τι ἀπόρρητον, ὥς φησι, κρύπτων. καὶ οἱ συστρατιῶται δὲ αὐτοῦ οἱ ἐν τῇδε τῇ Τροίᾳ, ἔτι ἐν τῷ πεδίῳ φαίνονται μάχιμοι τὸ σχῆμα καὶ σείοντες τοὺς λόφους.

3. ΦΟΙΝ. Ἀπιστῶ, νὴ τὴν Ἀθηνᾶν, ἀμπελουργέ, καίτοι οὕτω βουλόμενος ταῦτα ἔχειν. εἰ δὲ μὴ πρὸς τοῖς φυτοῖς εἶ μηδὲ ὀχετηγεῖς, ἤδη δίελθέ μοι ταῦτά τε καὶ ὅσα τοῦ Πρωτεσίλεω γινώσκεις· καὶ γὰρ ἂν χαρίζοιο τοῖς ἥρωσιν, εἰ πιστεύων ἀπέλθοιμι.

Phoenician. What might I pay you for them? 5

Vinedresser. You need only eat your fill, take a good supply for later and enjoy the rest of your journey.

Phoenician. Are you then a philosopher, vinedresser? 6

Vinedresser. I am, with the help of the good Protesilaus.

Phoenician. What have you to do with *him*? You mean 7 the one from Thessaly?

Vinedresser. Yes, the husband of Laodameia—as he likes to be called.

Phoenician. But what is he doing here? 8

Vinedresser. He lives here, and helps me farm.

Phoenician. Has he come back to life, or what? 9

Vinedresser. As to his sufferings, not even he himself speaks of them, stranger, except that he died at Troy because of Helen and came back to life in Phthia because of his love for Laodameia.

Phoenician. But they also say he died after his resur- 10 rection, and persuaded his wife to follow him.[9]

Vinedresser. He says that himself as well; but how he 11 came back again after that he hasn't told me, although I've long desired to know it—he claims to be keeping a secret of the Fates. His fellow soldiers at Troy here also still appear on the plain, looking very warlike and shaking their crests.

3. *Phoenician.* By Athena, vinedresser, *that* I cannot believe—although I wish it were so. But if you aren't working at your crops or watering them, please tell me about it, and all you know of Protesilaus. I'm sure the heroes would be much indebted to you, if I left here believing in them.

[9] In Euripides' play *Protesilaus*; see Introduction §8.

2   ΑΜΠ. Οὐκέτ᾽, ὦ ξένε, κατὰ μεσημβρίαν τὰ φυτὰ
πίνει· μετόπωρον γὰρ ἤδη καὶ ἄρδει αὐτὰ ἡ ὥρα.
σχολὴ οὖν μοι διελθεῖν πάντα. μηδὲ γὰρ λανθάνοι
τοὺς χαρίεντας τῶν ἀνθρώπων θεῖα οὕτω καὶ μεγάλα
ὄντα. βέλτιον δὲ καὶ ἐν καλῷ τοῦ χωρίου ἱζῆσαι.

     ΦΟΙΝ. Ἡγοῦ ὡς ἑψομένου καὶ ὑπὲρ τὰ μέσα τῆς
Θρᾴκης.

3   ΑΜΠ. Παρέλθωμεν εἰς τὸν ἀμπελῶνα, ὦ Φοῖνιξ·
καὶ γὰρ ἂν καὶ εὐφροσύνης τι ἐν αὐτῷ εὕροις.

     ΦΟΙΝ. Παρέλθωμεν· ἡδὺ γάρ που ἀναπνεῖ τῶν
φυτῶν.

4   ΑΜΠ. Τί λέγεις; ἡδύ; θεῖον· τῶν μὲν γὰρ ἀγρίων
δένδρων αἱ ἄνθαι εὔοσμοι, τῶν δὲ ἡμέρων οἱ καρποί.
εἰ δὲ ἐντύχοις ποτὲ φυτῷ ἡμέρῳ παρὰ τὴν ἄνθην εὐώ-
δει, δρέπου τῶν φύλλων μᾶλλον· ἐκείνων γὰρ τὸ ὀδω-
δέναι.

5   ΦΟΙΝ. Ὡς ποικίλη σοι ἡ ὥρα τοῦ χωρίου, καὶ ὡς
ἐκδεδώκασιν ἱλαροὶ οἱ βότρυς, τὰ δένδρα τε ὡς διά-
κειται πάντα καὶ ὡς ἀμβροσία ἡ ὀσμὴ τοῦ χωρίου.
τοὺς δρόμους δέ, οὓς ἀνῆκας, χαρίεντας μὲν ἡγοῦμαι,
τρυφᾶν δέ μοι δοκεῖς, ἀμπελουργέ, τοσαύτη γῇ ἀργῷ
χρώμενος.

6   ΑΜΠ. Ἱεροί, ξένε, οἱ δρόμοι· γυμνάζεται γὰρ ἐν
αὐτοῖς ὁ ἥρως.

---

10 Cf. the letters of Aristaenetus 1.3 (a lover in a garden):
"I picked a leaf to crush it in my fingers, but when I held it near
my nose I could breathe a much sweeter fragrance (than the
flowers)."

110

Vinedresser. The crops no longer need water at noon, 2
stranger, now that it is autumn and the season itself sees
to their irrigation; so I have time to tell you everything. I
wouldn't in any case want such sacred and important mat-
ters to be unknown to men of culture. But it would be
better to find a pleasant spot and sit down.

Phoenician. Lead on; I shall follow you even beyond
the interior of Thrace.

Vinedresser. Let us go into the vineyard, Phoenician; it 3
might be an enjoyable place for you.

Phoenician. By all means; for the vines have a sweet
fragrance.

Vinedresser. It is better than sweet, it is divine! For on 4
wild trees it is the flowers that smell sweet, on cultivated
ones it is the fruit. If you ever find a cultivated plant that
is fragrant while in blossom, then you must pick not the
flowers but the leaves—for the sweet smell belongs to
them.[10]

Phoenician. What variety your beautiful garden has! 5
There is a fine crop of grapes, the trees are beautifully
arranged, and the garden's fragrance is ambrosial! And the
racecourse you've set out is very delightful, although I
think you must be quite well-off if you can leave so much
land uncultivated.

Vinedresser. The racecourse is sacred,[11] stranger; the 6
hero takes his exercise there.

---

[11] The vinedresser pleads piety rather than extravagance. It
was not unusual for an individual to set aside a grove or some
other spot if he had reason to believe it was holy ground (see on
9.1). For the running track and other athletic facilities at Cnidus
for the hero Antigonus, see Introduction §4.

4. ΦΟΙΝ. Ἐρεῖς ταῦτα ἐπειδὰν ἱζήσωμεν οὗ ἄγεις. νυνὶ δέ μοι ἐκεῖνο εἰπέ· οἰκεῖα γεωργεῖς ταῦτα ἢ δεσπότης μὲν αὐτῶν ἕτερος, σὺ δὲ τρέφοντα τοῦτον τρέφεις, ὥσπερ τὸν τοῦ Εὐριπίδου Οἰνέα;

2   ΑΜΠ. Ἓν τοῦτ' ἐκ πολλῶν γήδιον λείπεταί μοι τρέφον οὐκ ἀνελευθέρως, τοὺς δὲ ἄλλους ἀγροὺς ἀφείλοντό με οἱ δυνατοὶ κομιδῇ ὀρφανόν. καὶ τουτὶ δὲ τὸ χωρίδιον ὑπὸ Ξείνιδος ἤδη τοῦ Χερρονησίτου κατεχόμενον ἐξείλετο ὁ Πρωτεσίλεως προσβαλών τι αὐτῷ ἑαυτοῦ φάσμα, ὑφ' οὗ τὰς ὄψεις ἀνακοπεὶς ἀπῆλθε τυφλός.

3   ΦΟΙΝ. Ἀγαθόν γε τοῦ ἀγροῦ φύλακα ἐκτήσω, καὶ οὐδὲ λύκου τινὸς ἔφοδον, οἶμαι, δέδιας ἐγρηγορότος οὑτωσὶ τοῦ φίλου.

4   ΑΜΠ. Ἀληθῆ λέγεις· οὐδὲ γὰρ θηρίῳ ξυγχωρεῖ ἐσφοιτᾶν οὐδενί· οὐδὲ ὄφις ἐνταῦθα, οὐδὲ φαλάγγιον, οὐδὲ συκοφάντης ἡμῖν περὶ τοῦ ἀγροῦ ἐπιτίθεται. τὸ δὲ θηρίον τοῦτο δεινῶς ἀναιδές· ἀπόλλυσι γοῦν ἐν ἀγορᾷ.

5   ΦΟΙΝ. Τὴν δὲ φωνήν, ἀμπελουργέ, πῶς ἐπαιδεύθης; οὐ γάρ μοι τῶν ἀπαιδεύτων φαίνῃ.

---

12 = fr. 561, Kannicht (2004); Collard, and Cropp (2008, 8.35). Oineus, king of Calydon, had been deposed and expelled by a rival family in his old age; Euripides seems to have represented him as reduced to abject poverty (scholia to Ar. *Ach.* 418) until restored to power by his grandson Diomedes (cf. [*Apollodorus*], *Bibl.* 1.8.6 [77–79]; Hyg. *Fab.* 175). The speaker and exact context of the Phoenician's quotation are unknown.

4. *Phoenician. That* you must tell me about when we sit down at our destination; but for the moment tell me this: do you farm this land for yourself, or is someone else the owner, while you "feed the man who feeds you," as in Euripides' *Oineus*?[12]

Vinedresser. This plot is all I have left of a great num-   2
ber, although it feeds me fairly well; the rest was stolen from me by powerful men, when I was an utterly helpless orphan. Even this field had already been taken over, by Xeinis of the Chersonnese, but Protesilaus got it back by appearing to him in a vision, as a result of which his eyes were stricken and he lost his sight.[13]

Phoenician. You've acquired a fine guardian for your   3
land; I don't suppose you even fear the attack of any wolf, with such a watchful friend.

Vinedresser. That is true, for he does not allow any   4
beast even to enter; nor is there a snake or poisonous spider to be found here, nor does the sycophant attack me for my farm—this last animal is terribly ruthless, since he does his killing right in the center of town.[14]

Phoenician. Where did you learn to speak, vinedresser?   5
You seem to be quite well educated.

[13] Xeinis' blinding by the hero is perhaps modeled on the story of Epizelos, who lost his sight when he saw a hero at the battle of Marathon (Hdt. 6.117); comparable also is the blindness inflicted on Homer and Stesichorus by an angry Helen (Pl. *Phdr.* 243A).   [14] For the vinedresser's characterization of the corruption of the city and the innocence of the countryside, see Introduction §7. Grossardt (2006a) notes the characterization of the sycophant (a venal informer) as a dangerous animal is from Dem. 25.52.

113

6 ΑΜΠ. Ἐν ἄστει, ξένε, τὸ πρῶτον ἐτρίβομεν τοῦ
βίου, διδασκάλοις χρώμενοι καὶ φιλοσοφοῦντες. πο-
νήρως οὖν τὰ ἐμὰ εἶχεν· ἐπὶ δούλοις γὰρ ἦν τὰ γεωρ-
γούμενα, οἱ δ᾽ ἀπέφερον ἡμῖν οὐδέν, ὅθεν δανείζεσθαί

7 τε ἐπὶ τῷ ἀγρῷ ἔδει καὶ πεινῆν. καὶ δῆτα ἀφικόμενος
ἐνταῦθα ξύμβουλον ἐποιούμην τὸν Πρωτεσίλεων, ὁ δ᾽
ὀργήν μοι δικαίαν ἔχων, ἐπειδὴ καταλιπὼν αὐτὸν ἐν

8 ἄστει ἔζων, ἐσιώπα. λιπαροῦντος δέ μου καὶ ἀπολεῖ-

9 σθαι φάσκοντος εἰ ἀμεληθείην, "μεταμφίασαι" ἔφη.
τοῦτ᾽ ἐπ᾽ ἐκείνης μὲν τῆς ἡμέρας ἀργῶς ἤκουσα· μετὰ
ταῦτα μέντοι βασανίζων αὐτό, ξυνῆκα ὅτι μεταβαλεῖν

10 κελεύει με τὸ τοῦ βίου σχῆμα. ὅθεν διφθέραν τε ἐναρ-
μοσάμενος καὶ σμινύην φέρων καὶ οὐδὲ τὴν ἐς ἄστυ
ὁδὸν ἔτι γινώσκων, βρύει μοι τὰ ἐν τῷ ἀγρῷ πάντα,
κἂν νοσήσῃ προβάτιον ἢ σμῆνος ἢ δένδρον, ἰατρῷ
χρῶμαι τῷ Πρωτεσίλεῳ· συνών <τε> αὐτῷ καὶ τῇ γῇ
προσκείμενος, σοφώτερος {τε} ἐμαυτοῦ γίνομαι· περί-
εστι γὰρ καὶ σοφίας αὐτῷ.

11 ΦΟΙΝ. Μακάριε τῆς ξυνουσίας καὶ τοῦ ἀγροῦ, εἰ
μὴ μόνον ἐλάας καὶ βότρυς ἐν αὐτῷ τρυγᾷς, ἀλλὰ καὶ
σοφίαν δρέπῃ θείαν τε καὶ ἀκήρατον. καὶ ἴσως ἀδικῶ
τὴν ἐν σοὶ σοφίαν, καλῶν γε ἀμπελουργόν.

12 ΑΜΠ. Οὕτω κάλει· καὶ γὰρ ἂν χαρίζοιο τῷ Πρω-
τεσίλεῳ γεωργόν τε ἐμὲ καὶ κηπουρὸν καὶ τὰ τοιαῦτα
ὀνομάζων.

---

15 Grossardt (forthcoming) finds a glimpse of Epicureanism
here and in "gardener" (4.12, below), and on the latter notes Si-
monides test. 47K Campbell: "Simonides said that Hesiod was a
gardener and Homer a garland-weaver, the one having planted

Vinedresser. I spent the first part of my life in town, 6
attending lectures and studying philosophy.[15] That is why
my affairs were in such a disastrous state. The farming was
in the hands of slaves, and they produced no profit for me,
so that I had to take out loans on the land and live as a
pauper. Then I finally came here and sought advice from 7
Protesilaus. At first he was justly angry with me because I
had left him to live in town, so he said nothing. But when 8
I pleaded, saying I was lost if he ignored me, he told me,
"Change your clothes." What he said made no impression 9
on me that day; but later, thinking it over, I realized he was
telling me to change the way I lived. Now that I've put on 10
a leather cloak[16] and carry a hoe, and don't even remem-
ber the way back to town, everything on my land is burst-
ing with life. If my animals take sick or my bees or crops,
Protesilaus acts as their doctor;[17] and while I keep com-
pany with him and work the land I become wiser than ever,
because his wisdom is abundant.

Phoenician. In your farm and your companion you are 11
blessed; not only do you pick grapes and olives, you also
reap a harvest of wisdom, divine and pure—perhaps my
calling you a Vinedresser offends your wisdom.

Vinedresser. But that is what you *should* call me; Pro- 12
tesilaus would be pleased if you also called me "farmer,"
"gardener," or the like.

the mythologies of the heroes, the other having woven the garland
of *Iliad* and *Odyssey*."

[16] The cloak, called a *diphthera*, marks the farmer; see
Gomme and Sandbach (1973) on Men. *Epit.* 229. (The Greek
sentence is a "nominative absolute," on which see Schmid [1887,
4.113ff.].)

[17] For the hero as healer, see Introduction §4.

PHILOSTRATUS

5. ΦΟΙΝ. Ἐνταῦθα οὖν, ἀμπελουργέ, ξύνεστε ἀλ-
λήλοις;

ΑΜΠ. Ἐνταῦθα, ξένε. πῶς δὲ ἐτεκμήρω;

2   ΦΟΙΝ. Ὅτι μοι δοκεῖ τὸ μέρος τοῦ ἀγροῦ τοῦτο
ἥδιστόν τε εἶναι καὶ θεῖον. καὶ εἰ μὲν ἀναβιῴη ἄν τις
ἐνταῦθα, οὐκ οἶδα· βιῴη δ' ἂν ἥδιστά που καὶ ἀλυπό-
3   τατα ἐξελθὼν τοῦ ὁμίλου. δένδρα τε γὰρ ὑπερμήκη
ταῦτα χρόνου αὐτὰ ἄραντος, ὕδωρ τε ἐκ πηγῶν τουτὶ
ποικίλον, καὶ ἀρύεσθε, οἶμαι, αὐτὸ ὥσπερ ἄλλου καὶ
ἄλλου ἀνθοσμίου πίνοντες. σὺ δὲ καὶ σκηνὰς φυτεύ-
εις ξυμπλέκων τὰ δένδρα καὶ συναρμόττων, ὡς οὐδ'
ἂν στέφανόν τις ἐκ λειμῶνος ἀκηράτου ξυμβάλοι.

4   ΑΜΠ. Καὶ οὔπω, ξένε, τῶν ἀηδόνων ἤκουσας, οἷον
τῷ χωρίῳ ἐναττικίζουσιν, ἐπειδὰν δείλη τε ἤκῃ καὶ
ἡμέρα ἄρχηται.

5   ΦΟΙΝ. Δοκῶ μοι ἀκηκοέναι ξυντίθεσθαί τε μηδὲ
θρηνεῖν αὐτάς, ἀλλὰ ᾄδειν μόνον. πλὴν εἰπὲ τὰ τῶν
ἡρώων· ἥδιον γὰρ ἂν τούτων ἀκούοιμι. ξυγχωρεῖς δέ
που καὶ ἱζῆσαι;

ΑΜΠ. Ξυγχωρεῖ ὁ ἥρως χρηστὸς ὢν ξενίζων του-
τοισὶ τοῖς θάκοις.

6   ΦΟΙΝ. Ἰδοὺ ἀναπαύομαι· τὸ γὰρ ξένιον ἡδὺ τῷ γε
ἀκροασομένῳ λόγου σπουδαιοτέρου.

---

18 Quoted from Eur. *Hipp.* 73. For the literary pedigree of the
grove setting, see Introduction §6.

19 The first nightingale was Procne, daughter of Pandion, king
of Athens; she was transformed into the bird after she killed

116

5. *Phoenician.* Is this where you talk to each other?

Vinedresser. Yes, how did you guess?

Phoenician. Because I think this part of your land is the 2 most pleasant, even divine. Whether it is a place where someone might come *back* to life I don't know, but at least one could *live* here, far from the crowd, in utter enjoyment and freedom from care. Look at these trees, which have 3 grown tall with the years! And the springs, with all sorts of water—I imagine you draw it like drinking various sweet wines in alternation. And you are planting arbors by interweaving and combining the trees; one could not compare it even to a garland "from an undefiled meadow."[18]

Vinedresser. You haven't yet heard how the nightin- 4 gales make the place like Attica,[19] in the afternoon or at daybreak.

Phoenician. I think I *have* heard them, and agree that 5 they are not even lamenting, but only singing.[20] But tell me about the heroes, for I would rather hear that. Do I have your permission to sit?

Vinedresser. You have the hero's permission; for he is our kind host in these seats.

Phoenician. There, I am resting. The hospitality is wel- 6 come, while I listen to this important story.

---

her child in rage at her husband's (Tereus) rape of her sister Philomela. The nightingale's famous song is supposed to be her lament for her son Itys. It is called the "Attic song" by Himer. *Or.* 6.3; cf. Plaut. *Rud.* 604, and Mart. 1.53.9.

[20] Grossardt (2006a) notes he is "agreeing" with Socrates in *Phdr.* 84e–85b that the swans' and nightingales' songs are not really laments for death.

6. ΑΜΠ. Ἐρώτα, ξένε, ὅ τι βούλει, καὶ οὐ μάτην
ἀφῖχθαι φήσεις. Ὀδυσσεῖ μὲν γάρ, ὁπότε πόρρω τῆς
νεὼς ἤλυεν, ἐντυχὼν ὁ Ἑρμῆς ἤ τις τῶν παρὰ Ἑρμοῦ
σοφῶν, ἐς κοινωνίαν λόγου τε καὶ σπουδῆς ἀφίκετο
(τουτὶ γὰρ ἡγεῖσθαι προσήκει τὸ μῶλυ), σὲ δὲ ὁ Πρω-
τεσίλεως ἱστορίας τε δι' ἐμοῦ ἐμπλήσει καὶ ἡδίω ἀπο-
φανεῖ καὶ σοφώτερον. τὸ γὰρ πολλὰ γινώσκειν πολ-
λοῦ ἄξιον.

2   ΦΟΙΝ. Ἀλλ' οὐκ ἀλύω, βέλτιστε, κατὰ δὲ θεόν, νὴ
τὴν Ἀθηνᾶν, ἥκω. ξυνίημι γὰρ λοιπὸν τοῦ ἐνυπνίου.

ΑΜΠ. Καὶ πῶς ἔχει σοι τὸ ἐνύπνιον; θεῖον γάρ τι
ὑποδηλώσεις.

3   ΦΟΙΝ. Πλέω μὲν ἐξ Αἰγύπτου καὶ Φοινίκης πέμ-
πτην καὶ τριακοστὴν ἤδη που ταύτην ἡμέραν. κατα-
σχούσης δὲ τῆς νεὼς εἰς Ἐλεοῦντα τοῦτον ἔδοξα τὰ
Ὁμήρου ἔπη ἀναγινώσκειν, ἐν οἷς τὸν κατάλογον τῶν
Ἀχαιῶν φράζει, καὶ ξυνεκάλουν τοὺς Ἀχαιοὺς ἐμβῆ-
4   ναι τὴν ναῦν ὡς ἀποχρῶσαν ὁμοῦ πᾶσιν. ἐπεὶ δὲ ἐξ-
έθορον τοῦ ἐνυπνίου (καὶ γάρ με καὶ φρίκης τι ὑπ-
εληλύθει), ξυνεβαλόμην μὲν αὐτὸ ἐς βραδυτῆτα τοῦ
πλοῦ καὶ μῆκος· αἱ γὰρ τῶν ἀποθανόντων ὄψεις ἀργοὶ
5   τοῖς ἐσπουδακόσι. βουληθεὶς δὲ ξυμβόλῳ περὶ τοῦ
ἐνυπνίου χρήσασθαι (οὐδὲ γὰρ τὸ πνεῦμά πω ξυν-
6   εχώρει πλεῖν), ἐξαλλάττω δεῦρο ἀπὸ τῆς νεώς. βαδί-

---

21 Hom. Od. 10.234–306. Grossardt (2006a) notes that Stoics
and Homeric allegorists interpreted "moly" as reason; on its sym-
bolism here see Platt (2011, 243–45).

6. *Vinedresser.* Ask whatever you like, stranger, and you won't say you came in vain. For just as Odysseus, when he was wandering far from his ship, was met by Hermes or one of his wise pupils, who shared with him speech and support (for we must imagine the "moly" as this),[21] so Protesilaus, through my agency, will fill you with knowledge, and make you happier and wise—for great knowledge is a thing of great value.

Phoenician. But I'm not wandering—rather I've come 2 with a god's favor by Athena. For henceforth I understand my dream.

Vinedresser. What was in your dream? For what you tell me will be sent from the gods.

Phoenician. This is the thirty-fifth day of my voyage 3 from Egypt and Phoenicia. As we put in here at Elaious, I dreamed I was reading the verses of Homer where he recites the catalog of the Achaeans, and I started to invite the Achaeans to come on board the ship as if it were big enough for them all at once. When I started awake from 4 the dream—a sort of shudder had come over me—I interpreted it as referring to the long and slow voyage. For to 5 those who are in pursuit of something, dreams of the dead imply failure.[22] But I wished to receive a sign about the dream and so, since the wind did not yet allow me to sail, I left the ship and came here.[23] You of course have seen 6

---

[22] Grossardt (2006a) compares Artemidorus 2.62 and a fragment of Astrampsychus, "when you see the dead, you will have the death of your projects" (νεκροὺς ὁρῶν νέκρωσιν ἕξεις πραγμάτων).

[23] Encounters with animals or humans along the road were widely held to portend the future. See Griffith's (1983) commentary on Aesch. *PV*, 486–87; Xen. *Mem.* 1.1.12–19.

PHILOSTRATUS

ζῶν δέ, ὡς εἶδες, πρώτῳ ἐντετύχηκα σοὶ καὶ περὶ τοῦ
Πρωτεσίλεω διαλεγόμεθα. διαλεξόμεθα δὲ καὶ περὶ
τοῦ καταλόγου τῶν ἡρώων· φῂς γὰρ οὕτω ποιήσειν.
καὶ τὸ καταλέγειν σφας ἐς τὴν ναῦν εἴη ἂν τὸ συλ-
λεξαμένους τὸν περὶ αὐτῶν λόγον εἶτα ἐμβῆναι.

7   ΑΜΠ. Κατὰ θεὸν ἥκεις ἀληθῶς, ξένε, καὶ ὑγιῶς
ἐξηγῇ τὴν ὄψιν. περαίνωμεν οὖν τὸν λόγον, μὴ καὶ
θρύπτεσθαί με φῂς διάγοντά σε ἀπ᾽ αὐτοῦ.

        7. ΦΟΙΝ. Ἃ ποθῶ μαθεῖν, ξυνίης δή γε· αὐτὴν γὰρ
τὴν ξυνουσίαν, ἥτις ἐστί σοι πρὸς τὸν Πρωτεσίλεων,
καὶ ὁποῖος ἥκει καὶ εἴ τι παραπλήσιον τοῖς ποιηταῖς
ἢ διηγνοημένον αὐτοῖς περὶ τῶν Τρωικῶν οἶδεν, ἀκοῦ-
2 σαι δέομαι. Τρωικὰ δὲ λέγω τὰ τοιαῦτα· τήν τε ἐν
Αὐλίδι ξυλλογὴν τοῦ στρατοῦ καὶ καθ᾽ ἕνα τοὺς ἥρως
εἰ καλοί τε, ὡς ᾄδονται, καὶ ἀνδρεῖοι καὶ σοφοὶ ἦσαν.
τὸν γὰρ πόλεμον, ὃς περὶ τῇ Τροίᾳ ἐγένετο, πῶς ἂν
διηγοῖτο μήτε διαπολεμήσας αὐτόν, ἀποθανών τε
πρῶτος τοῦ Ἑλληνικοῦ παντὸς ἐν αὐτῇ, φασί, τῇ
ἀποβάσει;

3   ΑΜΠ. Εὔηθες τουτί σοι, ξένε. ψυχαῖς γὰρ θείαις
οὕτω καὶ μακαρίαις ἀρχὴ βίου τὸ καθαρεῦσαι τοῦ
σώματος· θεούς τε γάρ, ὧν ὀπαδοί εἰσι, γινώσκουσι
τότε οὐκ ἀγάλματα θεραπεύουσαι καὶ ὑπονοίας, ἀλλὰ
ξυνουσίας φανερὰς πρὸς αὐτοὺς ποιούμεναι, τά τε

24 For heroes as *daimones* in Maximus of Tyre (usually they
are a separate category of divinity), see Introduction §4. Protesi-
laus is called a *daimon* at 43.3, below. Despite his separation from

120

that, as I walked, you were the first one I met, and we have
been talking about Protesilaus. We shall also talk about the
catalog of heroes, as you have promised; and cataloging
them onto the ship and collecting their story before em-
barking amount to the same thing.

   Vinedresser. You have indeed come with a god's favor,   7
stranger, and your interpretation of the dream is sound.
We must therefore proceed with our talk, so that you don't
imagine I'm making difficulties and diverting you from it.

   7. *Phoenician.* You know what I wish to learn; I desire
to hear of the meetings you have with Protesilaus, in what
form he comes, and whether what he knows about the
stories of Troy is the same as what the poets say, or un-
known to them. By "stories of Troy" of course I mean only   2
the army's mustering at Aulis, and whether the individual
heroes were as handsome, brave and wise as the poems
say. For how could he tell me about the war that took place
at Troy when he didn't fight in it, but was, as they say, the
first Greek to be killed at the very moment he landed?

   Vinedresser. That is a silly question, stranger; for souls   3
that are so divine and blessed, purification from the body
is only the beginning of life.[24] On the one hand, their
knowledge of gods they obtain not by worshipping statues
and approximations,[25] but by speaking with them openly;

the body, Protesilaus is experienced physically by the vinedresser
(11.2, 11.9; Platt [2011, 247]; Whitmarsh [2009, 219–225]) and
travels on board ship (53.18).
   [25] Contrast Dio, *Olympian Oration* 21.45, who says these ar-
tistic conceptions (*hyponoiai*) of the gods are the best humans can
attain (Platt 2011, 228–30, 243).

τῶν ἀνθρώπων ὁρῶσιν ἐλεύθεραι νόσων τε καὶ σώμα-
τος, ὅτε δὴ καὶ μαντικῆς σοφίας ἐμφοροῦνται καὶ τὸ
4 χρησμῶδες αὐταῖς προσβακχεύει. τὰ γοῦν Ὁμήρου
ποιήματα τίνα φήσεις οὕτως ἀνεγνωκέναι τῶν σφό-
δρα βασανιζόντων Ὅμηρον, ὡς ἀνέγνωκέ τε ὁ Πρω-
5 τεσίλεως καὶ διορᾷ αὐτά; καίτοι, ξένε, πρὸ Πριάμου
καὶ Τροίας οὐδὲ ῥαψῳδία τις ἦν, οὐδὲ ᾔδετο τὰ μήπω
πραχθέντα· ποιητικὴ μὲν γὰρ ἦν περί τε τὰ μαντεῖα
περί τε τὸν Ἀλκμήνης Ἡρακλέα, καθισταμένη τε ἄρτι
καὶ οὔπω ἡβάσκουσα, Ὅμηρος δὲ οὔπω ᾖδεν, ἀλλ' οἱ
μὲν Τροίας ἁλούσης, οἱ δὲ ὀλίγαις ἢ ὀκτὼ γενεαῖς
6 ὕστερον ἐπιθέσθαι αὐτὸν τῇ ποιήσει λέγουσιν. ἀλλ'
ὅμως οἶδεν ὁ Πρωτεσίλεως τὰ Ὁμήρου πάντα, καὶ
πολλὰ μὲν ᾄδει Τρωικὰ μεθ' ἑαυτὸν γενόμενα, πολλὰ
δὲ Ἑλληνικά τε καὶ Μηδικά, τήν τε γοῦν στρατείαν
τὴν Ξέρξου τρίτην ὀνομάζει φθορὰν ἀνθρώπων μετὰ
τὴν ἐπὶ Δευκαλίωνός τε καὶ Φαέθοντος ξυμβᾶσαν,
ἐπειδὴ πλεῖστα ἔθνη ἐν αὐτῇ ἐφθάρη.
7   ΦΟΙΝ. Κέρας Ἀμαλθείας ἐμπλήσεις, ἀμπελουργέ,
τοσαῦτα εἰδότος τοῦ ἑταίρου. ὑγιῶς γάρ που ἀπαγγε-
λεῖς αὐτὰ καὶ ὡς ἤκουσας.
8   ΑΜΠ. Νὴ Δί', ἢ ἀδικοίην φιλόσοφόν τε καὶ φιλα-
λήθη ἥρωα μὴ τιμῶν ἀλήθειαν, ἣν ἐκεῖνος μητέρα
ἀρετῆς ὀνομάζειν εἴωθε.
9   ΦΟΙΝ. Δοκῶ μοι καὶ κατ' ἀρχὰς τῶν λόγων ὡμο-
λογηκέναι πρὸς σὲ τὸ ἐμαυτοῦ πάθος· φημὶ γὰρ ἀπί-
στως διακεῖσθαι πρὸς τὰ μυθώδη. τὸ δὲ αἴτιον· οὐδενί
πω ἑωρακότι αὐτὰ ξυγγέγονα, ἀλλ' ὁ μὲν ἑτέρου ἀκη-

122

on the other hand, they observe mortal affairs, free from the illnesses of the body, now that they are filled with prophetic wisdom and oracular inspiration comes upon them.[26] Which of the most acute Homeric critics can you 4 say has read the poems in the way that Protesilaus has read and examines them? Of course before Priam and Troy, 5 stranger, there was not even any singing of tales, nor were there poems about what had not yet taken place; for poetry, which had just come into being and was still in its infancy, was concerned with oracles or with Heracles, son of Alcmene, while Homer was not yet singing—some say he first attempted a poem either after Troy's capture, others either several or eight generations later. Nevertheless 6 Protesilaus is acquainted with all of Homer's stories, and he sings of much that took place at Troy after him, as well as Greek and Persian history; at any rate he calls Xerxes' expedition the third great destruction of mankind (after those in the time of Deucalion and Phaethon) because so many peoples perished in it.

Phoenician. You will fill the horn of Amaltheia, vine- 7 dresser, since your companion has such wide knowledge: you will of course report it faithfully, exactly as you heard it.

Vinedresser. So I shall, by Zeus, or else I would wrong 8 a hero who is wise as well as truthful by disregarding the truth, which he is accustomed to call the mother of virtue.

Phoenician. I believe I admitted to you my feeling, as 9 we started our talk: I declare I am inclined to distrust mythical stories. The reason is this: I've never yet met anyone who was an eyewitness to them, but rather one

[26] For Protesilaus and prophecy, see ch. 15, below, and for hero oracles, Introduction §4.

κοέναι φησίν, ὁ δὲ οἴεσθαι, τὸν δὲ ποιητὴς ἐπαίρει. καὶ τὰ λεγόμενα δὲ περὶ τοῦ μεγέθους τῶν ἡρώων, ὡς δεκαπήχεις ἦσαν, χαρίεντα μὲν κατὰ μυθολογίαν ἡγοῦμαι, ψευδῆ δὲ καὶ ἀπίθανα τῷ γε θεωροῦντι αὐτὰ πρὸς τὴν φύσιν, ἧς μέτρα οἱ νῦν ἄνθρωποι.

10 ΑΜΠ. Ταυτὶ δὲ ἡγεῖσθαι ἀπίθανα πότε ἤρξω;

ΦΟΙΝ. Πάλαι, ἀμπελουργέ, κἂν μειρακίῳ ἔτι. παῖς μὲν γὰρ ὢν ἔτι ἐπίστευον τοῖς τοιούτοις, καὶ κατεμυθολόγει με ἡ τίτθη χαριέντως αὐτὰ ἐπᾴδουσα καί τι καὶ κλάουσα ἐπ᾽ ἐνίοις αὐτῶν· μειράκιον δὲ γενόμενος οὐκ ἀβασανίστως ᾠήθην χρῆναι προσδέχεσθαι ταῦτα.

11 ΑΜΠ. Τὸ δὲ τοῦ Πρωτεσίλεω, καὶ ὅτι ἐνταῦθα φαίνοιτο, ἀκηκοώς ποτε ἔτυχες;

ΦΟΙΝ. Πῶς, ἀμπελουργέ, ὅς γε καὶ σοῦ τήμερον ἀκούων ἀπιστῶ;

12 ΑΜΠ. Οὐκοῦν ἀρχὴ τοῦ λόγου σοι γινέσθω τὰ πάλαι σοι ἀπιστούμενα· φῂς δέ που ἀπιστεῖν, εἰ δεκαπήχεις ἐγένοντο ἄνθρωποι. ἐπειδὰν δὲ τούτου ἱκανῶς ἔχῃς, ἀπαίτει λοιπὸν τὸν περὶ τοῦ Πρωτεσίλεω λόγον καὶ ὁπόσα βούλει τῶν Τρωικῶν· οὐδὲν γὰρ αὐτῶν ἀπιστήσεις.

ΦΟΙΝ. Καλῶς λέγεις καὶ οὕτω ποιῶμεν.

8. ΑΜΠ. Ἄκουε δή· πάππος ἦν μοι, ξένε, πολλὰ

27 Homer had asserted that his heroes were stronger than men of his own day, and so heroic bones were usually reported to be of great size; see Introduction §3.

28 He means not the story of his death (which the Phoenician obviously knows) but of his size (10.4, below) and epiphanies,

124

says he heard it from someone else; another says he imagines it so, and still another is excited by some poet. As for what is said about the height of the heroes, that they were ten cubits tall, I find it charming as myth, but when one compares it to the standard of reality of which the men of today are the measure it seems an incredible falsehood.[27]

Vinedresser. When did you begin to consider these 10 things incredible?

Phoenician. Long ago, vinedresser, while still in my youth. Of course as a child I still believed in such stories, and my nurse used to tell me myths charmingly, soothingly, even weeping over some of them; but when I became a youth, I decided I must not accept these things uncritically.

Vinedresser. Have you ever actually heard about Pro- 11 tesilaus, and that he makes appearances here?[28]

Phoenician. How could I have, since I am listening to you today with such disbelief?

Vinedresser. Then we shall have to begin with what 12 you've doubted for so long; you admit you don't believe that men have ever been ten cubits tall. Only when you are satisfied on that point, should you go on to ask for the story of Protesilaus, and as much as you like about Troy. I guarantee you'll doubt none of it.

Phoenician. I agree; let us so proceed.

8. *Vinedresser.* Then listen:[29] I had a grandfather,

which are of course known only to the vinedresser (Eitrem's corrections to the text are thus unnecessary).

[29] For the correspondences of this catalog of giant bones with Pausanias and other sources, see Rusten (2004).

τῶν ἀπιστουμένων ὑπὸ σοῦ γινώσκων, ὃς ἔλεγε δια-
φθαρῆναι μέν ποτε τὸ τοῦ Αἴαντος σῆμα ὑπὸ τῆς
θαλάσσης, πρὸς ᾗ κεῖται, ὀστᾶ δὲ ἐν αὐτῷ φανῆναι
κατὰ ἑνδεκάπηχυν ἄνθρωπον· καὶ ἔφασκεν Ἀδριανὸν
βασιλέα περιστεῖλαι αὐτὰ ἐς Τροίαν ἐλθόντα καὶ τὸν
νυνὶ τάφον περιαρμόσαι τῷ Αἴαντι ἔστιν ἃ καὶ προσ-
πτυξάμενον τῶν ὀστῶν καὶ φιλήσαντα.

2   ΦΟΙΝ. Οὐ μάτην ἀπιστεῖν ἔοικα τοῖς τοιούτοις,
ἀμπελουργέ· καὶ σὺ γὰρ πάππου μέν τι ἀκηκοέναι
φῂς καὶ ἴσως μητρὸς ἢ τίτθης, σεαυτοῦ δὲ ἀπαγγέλ-
λεις οὐδέν, εἰ μὴ ἄρα περὶ τοῦ Πρωτεσίλεω εἴποις.

3   ἈΜΠ. Καὶ μήν, εἰ μυθολογικὸς ἦν, τόν τε τοῦ
Ὀρέστου νεκρὸν διῄειν, ὃν ἑπτάπηχυν ἐν Νεμέᾳ Λα-
κεδαιμόνιοι εὗρον, καὶ τὸν ἐν τῷ χαλκῷ ἵππῳ τῷ Λυ-
δίῳ, ὃς κατωρώρυκτο μὲν ἐν Λυδίᾳ πρὸ Γύγου ἔτι,
σεισμῷ δὲ τῆς γῆς διασχούσης θαῦμα τοῖς περὶ Λυ-
δίαν ὤφθη ποιμέσιν, οἷς ἅμα ὁ Γύγης ἐθήτευσεν. ἐς
γὰρ κοῖλον τὸν ἵππον θυρίδας ἐν ἑκατέρᾳ πλευρᾷ
4 ἔχοντα νεκρὸς ἀπέκειτο μείζων ἢ ἀνθρώπου δόξαι. εἰ
δὲ ταῦτα οἷα ἀπιστεῖσθαι διὰ τὸν χρόνον, ἀλλὰ τοῖς
5 γε ἐφ᾽ ἡμῶν οὐκ οἶδ᾽ ὅ τι ἀντερεῖς. Ἀρνάδην γάρ, ὃν

30 For the damage to the tomb of Ajax (and the great size of
the body it contained), see Paus. 1.35.3; Plin. *HN* 5.125; Antipater
(Gow and Page 1965, no. 7); and Strabo 13.1.30. On its current
site see Cook (1973, 88). For Hadrian's restoration activity at
Troy, see Frisch (1975, no. 94). For Ajax' burial, see ch. 35.15.

stranger, who knew as fact many of the stories you don't believe, and he used to tell that the tomb of Ajax was once destroyed by the sea near which it was located, and that in it a skeleton was revealed about eleven cubits tall. And he said that the emperor Hadrian went to Troy, laid it out for burial, and built for it the tomb which now exists—he even embraced and kissed some of the bones.[30]

Phoenician. It seems I was right to disbelieve such sto- 2 ries, vinedresser; for you too say that you've heard something from your grandfather—or perhaps your mother or nurse—but you say nothing on your own authority, unless you talk about Protesilaus.

Vinedresser. If I were fond of telling stories I would 3 indeed have told you about Orestes' body, which the Spartans discovered in Nemea—it was seven cubits tall[31]—or about the body in the Lydian bronze horse, which had been buried in Lydia still before Gyges' time, and miraculously appeared after an earthquake to some shepherds in Lydia, together with whom Gyges was a servant. In the hollow of the horse, which contained windows on both sides, lay a body, which was greater than a man could imagine.[32] But if these stories are the sort to be disbe- 4 lieved because they happened so long ago, still I don't know how you can contradict events of our own day. Not long ago a rupture on the banks of the river Orontes brought to light Aryades—thirty cubits tall—who had been buried in Assyria; some say he was an Ethiopian, 5

---

[31] Hdt. 1.68. "Nemea" for "Tegea" here seems the vinedresser's mistake rather than a manuscript corruption; see Introduction §7.

[32] Pl. *Resp.* 359c–60b.

οἱ μὲν Αἰθίοπα, οἱ δὲ Ἰνδὸν ἔφασαν, τριακοντάπηχυν
ἐν τῇ Ἀσσυρίων γῇ κείμενον οὐ πάλαι ἀνέφηνεν ἡ τοῦ
6 Ὀρόντου ποταμοῦ ὄχθη σχισθεῖσα. τουτὶ δὲ τὸ Σί-
γειον πρὸ πεντήκοντα οὔπω ἐτῶν ἐν προβολῇ τοῦ
ἀκρωτηρίου σῶμα ἀνέδειξε γίγαντος, ὃν αὐτὸς Ἀπόλ-
λων ἀπεκτονέναι φησὶν ὑπὲρ Τροίας αὐτῷ¹ μαχόμε-
νον· καὶ εἶδον, ξένε, πλεύσας εἰς τὸ Σίγειον αὐτό τε
τὸ πάθος τῆς γῆς καὶ τὸν γίγαντα ὅσος ἦν. ἔπλεον
δὲ καὶ Ἑλλησποντίων πολλοὶ καὶ Ἰώνων καὶ νησι-
ῶται πάντες καὶ τὸ Αἰολικὸν ἅπαν· ἐπὶ γὰρ μῆνας δύο
μέγας ἐν μεγάλῳ ἀκρωτηρίῳ προὔκειτο παρέχων ἄλ-
λον ἄλλῳ λόγον οὔπω δηλοῦντος αὐτὸν τοῦ χρησμοῦ.
7   ΦΟΙΝ. Εἴποις ἂν οὖν ἔτι, ἀμπελουργέ, περί τε
μεγέθους αὐτοῦ περί τε ὀστῶν ἁρμονίας περί τε τῶν
λεγομένων ὄφεων ξυμπεφυκέναι τοῖς γίγασιν, οὓς
ὑπογράφουσιν οἱ ζωγράφοι τῷ Ἐγκελάδῳ καὶ τοῖς
ἀμφ᾽ αὐτόν;
8   ΑΜΠ. Εἰ μὲν τερατώδεις ἐγένοντο ἐκεῖνοι, ξένε, καὶ
ξυμβεβλημένοι θηρίοις, οὐκ οἶδα. ὁ δὲ ἐν τῷ Σιγείῳ
δύο μὲν καὶ εἴκοσι πήχεις ἐπεῖχεν, ἔκειτο δὲ ἐν πετρώ-
δει σήραγγι, τὴν κεφαλὴν μὲν πρὸς τὴν ἤπειρον

---

¹ αὐτῶι Grossardt (2006a), taking μαχόμενον of the giant, but
see Schmid (1887, 4.83) for the construction.

---

33 Paus. 8.29.3 tells of the same discovery, but says that the
oracle of Apollo at Clarus identified the body as Orontes of India.
34 The Giants (Grk. *gigantes*) were a semidivine race sprung
from earth that challenged Zeus for supremacy of heaven and was

others an Indian.[33] And less than fifty years ago, Sigeium   6
over there disclosed on an outcropping of the cape the
body of a giant,[34] whom Apollo himself said he had killed
while fighting him to defend Troy. I myself sailed to
Sigeium, stranger, and witnessed exactly what had hap-
pened to the land as well as the giant's size. Many others
sailed there also, from the Hellespont, Ionia, and all of the
islands and Aeolia, since for two months this huge body
lay on the huge cape; provoking different explanations
from everyone before the oracle cleared things up.[35]

Phoenician. Could you than say something more about   7
its size, and the arrangement of the bones, and about the
snakes that are said to form part of the bodies of giants,
which the painters always attach to the bodies of Encela-
dus and such?[36]

Vinedresser. Whether they were monstrous or joined   8
with snakes, I don't know. But the one on Sigeium mea-
sured twenty-two cubits. He lay in a rocky cave, his head

defeated by the Olympian gods in a battle—the "gigantomachy"
—famous in art. In what follows, Philostratus makes little distinc-
tion between giants and heroes, evidently believing like Pausanias
(8.29.3) that both were mortals of an earlier age. For discover-
ies of giant-bones (most likely mastodon skeletons), see Mayor
(2000), and for the catalogs of them, Rusten (2004).

[35] Philostratus gives no exact name, perhaps because the ora-
cle of Apollo had not mentioned one. The giant Porphyrion (Pind.
Pyth. 8.12–18) was killed by Apollo, but he had no connection
with Troy.

[36] Artistic representations often make the lower part of giants'
bodies into snakes; for the snake as a familiar of the hero, see
Introduction §3.

ἔχων, τοὺς δὲ πόδας συναπολήγων τῷ ἀκρωτηρίῳ·
δρακόντων δὲ οὐδὲν σημεῖον περὶ αὐτὸν ἑωρῶμεν,
οὐδὲ ἔστιν ὅ τι τῶν ὀστῶν παρήλλαττεν ἀνθρώπου.

9 καὶ μὴν καὶ Ὕμναιος ὁ Πεπαρήθιος, ἐπιτηδείως μοι
ἔχων, ἔπεμψέ τινα τῶν ἑαυτοῦ υἱέων πρὸ ἐτῶν ἐνταῦθά
που τεττάρων, ἐρησόμενον δι' ἐμοῦ τὸν Πρωτεσίλεων
περὶ ὁμοίου θαύματος· ἐν <Ἴ>κῳ γὰρ τῇ νήσῳ (κέκτη-
ται δὲ αὐτὴν μόνος) ἔτυχε μὲν ὀρύττων ἀμπέλους, ἡ
γῆ δὲ ὑπήχησε τοῖς ὀρύττουσιν οἷον κενή. διανοίξαν-
τες οὖν, δωδεκάπηχυς μὲν ὁ νεκρὸς ἔκειτο, τὸ δέ γε
10 κρανίον ᾤκει δράκων. ὁ μὲν δὴ νεανίας ἀφίκετο ἐπ-
ερησόμενος ἡμᾶς ὅ τι χρὴ πράττειν ἐπ' αὐτῷ, ὁ δὲ
Πρωτεσίλεως "τὸν ξένον" ἔφη "συγκαλύπτωμεν," κε-
λεύων δήπου ἐπιθάπτειν τὸν νεκρὸν καὶ μὴ γυμνοῦν
11 ἑκόντας· εἶπε δὲ καὶ ὡς γίγας εἴη τῶν βεβλημένων. ὁ
δὲ ἐν Λήμνῳ φανείς, ὃν Μενεκράτης ὁ Στειριεὺς εὗρε,
μέγιστός τε ἦν καὶ εἶδον αὐτὸν πέρυσιν ἐξ Ἴμβρου
πλεύσας· δι' ὀλίγου γὰρ ἦν ἐς τὴν Λῆμνον. τὰ μὲν οὖν
ὀστᾶ οὐκέτι ἐν κόσμῳ ἑωρᾶτο· καὶ γὰρ οἱ σπόνδυλοι
ἀπ' ἀλλήλων ἔκειντο σεισμοῖς, οἶμαι, διενεχθέντες,
καὶ τὰ πλευρὰ ἐξήρμοστο τῶν σπονδύλων. ἐνθυμου-
μένῳ δὲ αὐτὰ ὁμοῦ τε καὶ κατὰ ἕν, φρικῶδες ἐδόκει τὸ
μέγεθος καὶ οὐ ῥάδιον ἀνατυποῦσθαι· τὸ γοῦν κρανίον
ἐμφορησάντων ἡμῶν ἐς αὐτὸ οἶνον οὐδὲ ὑπὸ δυοῖν
12 ἀμφορέοιν ἐνεπλήσθη τῶν ἐκ Κρήτης. ἔστι δέ τι κατὰ

---

37 Paus. 8.29.3 also rejects the idea that giants had serpentine
bodies.

38 Evidently identical to one of the speakers in the dialogue,

in the inland side, and his feet extended to the end of the cape. There was no sign of a snake on him, and nothing on his skeleton deviated from the human.[37] And yet, about 9 four years ago, Hymnaios of Peparethos, a friend of mine, sent one of his sons to have me ask Protesilaus about a similar wonder. For on the island of Ikos (he was its sole owner) he happened to be digging up some vines, when the earth rang under the shovel, as if hollow. When they cleaned it away, there lay exposed a body twelve cubits tall, and in its skull was living a snake. Now the boy came to 10 ask us what should be done with it, and Protesilaus' answer was "let us veil our guest," meaning of course they should rebury the corpse and be careful to take nothing from it. He also said it was one of the giants who was laid low. But the largest of all was the one on Lemnos, which 11 Menecrates of Steiria[38] discovered, and I myself sailed over last year from Imbros (it was a short trip to Lemnos) to see it. It wasn't any longer possible to see the bones in their proper position, because the backbone lay in pieces —separated by earthquakes, I imagine—and the ribs had been wrenched from the vertebrae. But as I examined them, both all together and one by one, I received an impression of terrifying size, one I found impossible to describe. The skull alone, when we poured wine into it, was not filled even by two Cretan amphoras.[39] There is 12

Nero (ascribed to an older Philostratus), and appearing as a magistrate in an inscription from Lemnos (Follet 1974).

[39] It is uncertain why they poured wine into the skull in the first place: the Scythians (Hdt. 4.65) used their enemies' skulls as drinking vessels; but here they might simply have been washing out the skull for reburial. For the Cretan amphora, mentioned only here in the literary sources, see Marangou-Lerat (1995).

νότον ἄνεμον ἀκρωτήριον τῆς Ἴμβρου, Ναύλοχος, ᾧ
πηγὴ ὑφώρμισται τὰ μὲν ἄρσενα τῶν ζῴων εὐνού-
χους ἐργαζομένη, τὰ δὲ θήλεα οὕτω μεθύσκουσα, ὡς
καθεύδειν αὐτά. τρύφος οὖν ἐνταῦθα τῆς γῆς ἀπορρα-
γὲν συνεπέσπαστο σῶμα μεγίστου γίγαντος· κἂν
ἀπιστῇς, πλεύσωμεν· πρόκειται γὰρ γυμνὸς ἔτι καὶ ὁ
ἐς Ναύλοχον πλοῦς βραχύς.

13   ΦΟΙΝ. Ἐβουλόμην μὲν ἂν καὶ ὑπὲρ τὸν Ὠκεανὸν
ἐλθεῖν, ἀμπελουργέ, θαῦμα εἴ που τοιοῦτον εὕροιμι· ἡ
δὲ ἐμπορία οὐ ξυγχωρεῖ τοσοῦτον ἀποφοιτᾶν ἑαυτῆς,
ἀλλὰ δεῖ προσδεδέσθαι τῇ νηί, καθάπερ τὸν Ὀδυσ-
σέα· εἰ δὲ μή, καὶ τὰ ἐκ πρῴρας, φασί, καὶ τὰ ἐκ
πρύμνης ἀπολεῖται.

14   ΑΜΠ. Ἀλλὰ μήπω, ξένε, πιστὰ ἡγοῦ ἃ εἶπον, πρὶν
ἔς τε τὴν νῆσον τὴν Κῶ πλεύσῃς, ἐν ᾗ τὰ τῶν γη-
γενῶν ὀστᾶ ἀνάκειται, Μερόπων, φασί, τῶν πρώτων,
ἐν Φρυγίᾳ δὲ τά τε Ὕλλου τοῦ Ἡρακλέους ἴδῃς, καὶ
νὴ Δί' ἐν Θετταλίᾳ τὰ τῶν Ἀλωαδῶν, ὡς ἐννεόργυιοι
15   ἀτεχνῶς ἐγένοντο καὶ ὁποῖοι ᾄδονται. Νεαπολῖται δὲ
Ἰταλίαν οἰκοῦντες θαῦμα πεποίηνται τὰ τοῦ Ἀλκυο-
νέως ὀστᾶ. λέγουσι γὰρ δὴ πολλοὺς τῶν γιγάντων
ἐκεῖ βεβλῆσθαι καὶ τὸ Βέσβιον ὄρος ἐπ' αὐτοὺς τύ-
16   φεσθαι. καὶ μὴν καὶ ἐν Παλλήνῃ, ἣν Φλέγραν οἱ ποι-
ηταὶ ὀνομάζουσι, πολλὰ μὲν σώματα ἡ γῆ τοιαῦτα
ἔχει γιγάντων στρατοπεδευσάντων ἐκεῖ, πολλὰ δὲ
ὄμβροι τε καὶ σεισμοὶ ἀνακαλύπτουσι. θαρσεῖ δὲ

also a cape on Imbros to the southwest called Naulochos, and in it is nestled a spring that makes eunuchs[40] of all male animals that drink of it, and so intoxicates the females that they fall asleep. Here a broken off piece of earth had carried with it the body of a huge giant. If you don't believe me, we can sail there; for the body is still stripped and lying there, and it is a short trip to Naulochos.

Phoenician. I would have been willing to travel even 13 beyond the ocean to find such a marvel, vinedresser, but a merchant's trade allows not a moment's neglect. I must stay lashed to my ship, like Odysseus, otherwise all is lost "from stem to stern."[41]

Vinedresser. But you must not believe what I say, 14 stranger, until you sail to the island of Cos, where they say the house of the first earthborn Meropes lie; and until you see those of Heracles' son Hyllus in Phrygia, or by Zeus even those of the Aloadae in Thessaly—They were actually nine fathoms tall, just as the poet says (*Od.* 11.312). And in Italy the Neapolitans have made a wonder of the 15 bones of Alkyoneus; for they say that many of the giants were laid low there, and that Mt. Vesuvius smolders over them.[42] Furthermore in Pallene, which the poets call 16 Phlegra, the earth still contains the bodies of many such giants, since that was their camp; thunderstorms and earthquakes have brought many others to the surface. Not

---

[40] I.e., sterilizes them. The same is said of the tomb of Aepytos, scholia to Theoc. 1.125.   [41] *Od.* 12.159; on the nautical proverb, see Shackleton Bailey (1977) on Cicero, *Fam.* 16.24.

[42] Grossardt (2006a) notes that the Campanian Phlegraean fields are well-established by the early years of Augustus (Diodorus 5.71.4; Strabo 5.4.4, 5.4.6, 6.3.5).

PHILOSTRATUS

οὐδὲ ποιμὴν περὶ μεσημβρίαν ἐκεῖνο τὸ χωρίον ὑπο-
17 παταγούντων εἰδώλων, ἃ ἐν αὐτῷ μαίνεται. τὸ δὲ ἀπι-
στεῖν τοῖς τοιούτοις ἴσως που καὶ ἐπὶ τοῦ Ἡρακλέους
ἦν, ὅθεν τὸν Γηρυόνην ἐν τῇ Ἐρυθείᾳ ἀποκτείνας καὶ
μεγίστῳ αὐτῷ ἐντετυχηκέναι λεγόμενος, ἀνέθηκε τὰ
ὀστᾶ ἐς Ὀλυμπίαν, ὡς μὴ ἀπιστοῖτο τοῦ ἄθλου.

18   ΦΟΙΝ. Εὐδαιμονίζω σε τῆς ἱστορίας, ἀμπελουργέ.
ἐγὼ δὲ μεγάλα μὲν ἠγνόουν, ἀνοήτως δὲ ἠπίστουν.
ἀλλὰ τὰ τοῦ Πρωτεσίλεω πῶς ἔχει; καιρὸς γάρ που
ἐπ᾽ ἐκεῖνα ἥκειν μηκέτ᾽ ἀπιστούμενα.

9. ΑΜΠ. Περὶ τῶν τοιούτων ἄκουε, ξένε. κεῖται μὲν
οὐκ ἐν Τροίᾳ ὁ Πρωτεσίλεως ἀλλ᾽ ἐν Χερρονήσῳ
ταύτῃ, κολωνὸς δὲ αὐτὸν ἐπέχει μέγας οὑτοσὶ δήπου
ὁ ἐν ἀριστερᾷ, πτελέας δὲ ταύτας αἱ νύμφαι περὶ τῷ
κολωνῷ ἔφυσαν καὶ τοιόνδε ἐπὶ τοῖς δένδρεσι τούτοις
2 ἔγραψάν που αὗται νόμον· τοὺς πρὸς τὸ Ἴλιον τε-
τραμμένους τῶν ὄζων ἀνθεῖν μὲν πρωί, φυλλορροεῖν
δὲ αὐτίκα καὶ προαπόλλυσθαι τῆς ὥρας (τοῦτο δὴ τὸ
τοῦ Πρωτεσίλεω πάθος), τῷ δὲ ἑτέρῳ μέρει ζῆν τὸ
3 δένδρον καὶ εὖ πράττειν. καὶ ὁπόσα δὲ τῶν δένδρων
μὴ περὶ τὸ σῆμα ἕστηκεν, ὥσπερ καὶ ταυτὶ τὰ ἐν
κήπῳ, πᾶσιν ἔρρωται τοῖς ὄζοις καὶ θαρσεῖ τὸ ἴδιον.

4   ΦΟΙΝ. Ὁρῶ, ἀμπελουργέ, καὶ θαυμάζειν ἔχων οὐ
τεθαύμακα· σοφὸν γὰρ τὸ θεῖον.

---

43 For the dangers of noonday to the superstitious, see Ogden
(2007, 168n2); on the shepherd's boldness then see Gow and Page
(1965) on Theocritus 1.15ff.

134

even the shepherd takes courage at noonday[43] when the
angry spirits of that land clatter about underneath it. But   17
disbelief in such things must have been common even in
Heracles' day, since after he killed Geryones—the larg-
est being he reportedly ever encountered—in Erythia, he
dedicated the bones at Olympia so that his feat would not
be dismissed as incredible.

Phoenician. You are truly fortunate, vinedresser, in   18
your knowledge. As for me, my ignorance was great, and
my disbelief was foolish. But what about Protesilaus? For
it is time to proceed to that part, about which I no longer
have any doubts.

9. *Vinedresser.* That is what you should listen to,
stranger. To start with, Protesilaus is buried not in Troy,
but here in the Chersonnese; of course this large mound
on our left[44] holds his body, and these elms around it were
planted by the nymphs; they also established for these
trees the following rule: the branches which face Ilion   2
blossom too early, then immediately lose their leaves and
die before their time.[45] for this is what happened to Pro-
tesilaus, while all the rest of the tree remains alive and
flourishes. And all the trees which don't stand around the   3
tomb, such as these ones here in the garden, are healthy
in all their branches and uniquely confident.

Phoenician. I have noticed that, and although I was   4
tempted to express astonishment, I refrained; for what is
done by divine will must be wise.

---

[44] For the possible location of this mound, see Introduc-
tion §6.   [45] For the "miracle" of these trees and Protesilaus'
sacred grove, see Introduction §8, and compare the grove of
Achilles on Leuke, chs. 54.9, 57, below.

5 ΆΜΠ. Τὸ δέ γε ἱερόν, ἐν ᾧ κατὰ τοὺς πατέρας ὁ
Μῆδος ὕβριζεν, ἐφ᾽ ᾧ καὶ τὸ τάριχος ἀναβιῶναί
φασι, τοῦτο ἡγοῦ, ὦ ξένε· καταλείπεται δὲ αὐτοῦ ὁρᾷς
ὡς ὀλίγα. τότε δέ, οἶμαι, χαρίεν τε ἦν καὶ οὐ μικρόν,
6 ὡς ἔστι τοῖς θεμελίοις ξυμβαλέσθαι. τὸ δὲ ἄγαλμα
τοῦτο βέβηκε μὲν ἐπὶ νεώς, τὸ γὰρ τῆς βάσεως
σχῆμα πρῷρα, ἵδρυται δὲ ναύαρχος. περιτρίψας δὲ
αὐτὸ ὁ χρόνος καὶ νὴ Δί᾽ οἱ ἀλείφοντές τε καὶ
ἐπισφραγιζόμενοι τὰς εὐχὰς ἐξηλλάχασι τοῦ εἴδους.
7 ἐμοὶ δὲ οὐδὲν τοῦτο· αὐτῷ γὰρ ξύνειμι καὶ αὐτὸν
βλέπω καὶ οὐδὲν ἄν μοι γένοιτο ἄγαλμα ἐκείνου
ἥδιον.

10. ΦΟΙΝ. Ἦ καὶ διαγράψεις μοι αὐτὸν καὶ κοινω-
νήσεις τοῦ εἴδους;

2 ΆΜΠ. Χαίρων γε, νὴ τὴν Ἀθηνᾶν, ὦ ξένε. γέγονε
μὲν γὰρ ἀμφὶ τὰ εἴκοσί που μάλιστα ἔτη. τηλίκος δὲ
ἐλάσας ἐς Τροίαν, ἁβρῷ ἰούλῳ βρύει καὶ ἀπόζει
αὐτοῦ ἥδιον ἢ τὸ μετόπωρον τῶν μύρτων. φαιδρὰν δὲ
ὀφρῦν περὶ τὸ ὄμμα βέβληται· τὸ γὰρ ἐπίχαρι αὐτῷ
φίλον. βλέπει δὲ ἐν μὲν ταῖς σπουδαῖς σύντονον καὶ
σφοδρόν, εἰ δὲ ἀνειμένου τύχοιμεν, φεῦ τῶν ὀφθαλ-
3 μῶν ὡς ἐπαφρόδιτοί τε καὶ φιλικοὶ φαίνονται. καὶ
μὴν καὶ κόμης ξανθῆς ἔχει τὸ μέτριον· ἔστι γὰρ ὡς
ἐπικρέμασθαι τῷ μετώπῳ μᾶλλον ἢ κατ᾽ αὐτοῦ πί-
πτειν. καὶ τετράγωνος ἡ ἰδέα τῆς ῥινός, οἷον ἀγάλμα-
τος. φθέγγεται δὲ γεγωνότερον ἢ αἱ σάλπιγγες καὶ
4 ἀπὸ μικροῦ γε τοῦ στόματος. γυμνῷ δὲ ἐντυχεῖν ἥδι-

Vinedresser. As for the sanctuary, that in our ancestors' day was the scene of the Mede's arrogance, at which they say the salted fish returned to life,[46] this is it, stranger. But you see how little is left of it. To judge from its foundations, though, it used to be a fine and large area in those days. The statue is standing on a ship, for its base is in the shape of a prow, and he is set up as the ship's captain.[47] But the workings of time and also, by Zeus, those who have anointed it and hang their vows on it, have totally altered its appearance. But that doesn't concern me; for I can see and talk with Protesilaus himself, and no statue could be more beautiful than he is.

10. *Phoenician.* Can you then describe him, and share with me what you've seen?

Vinedresser. By Athena, with pleasure, stranger. I suppose he is about twenty years old. As suits the age at which he campaigned against Troy, a light down grows on his chin, and he smells sweeter than myrtle in the fall. He puts on his face a bright expression, because he loves a cheerful disposition; when things are serious he looks alert and intense, but if I find him relaxed, and oh, his eyes are so charming and friendly! His hair is blond, and of moderate length; it seems to overhang his forehead rather than cover it. The shape of his nose is angular, just like a statue's. His voice carries farther than trumpets, although his mouth is small. He looks most handsome nude, for he is well-pro-

---

[46] For this story, see Introduction §8.

[47] See the coin depicting Protesilaus on the prow of a ship from the time of Commodus (Introduction §11; Imhoof-Blumer [1910]).

στον· εὐπαγὴς γὰρ καὶ κοῦφος, ὥσπερ οἱ δρομικοὶ
τῶν ἑρμῶν. τὸ δὲ μῆκος δεκάπηχυς τάχα, δοκεῖ δ᾽ ἄν
μοι καὶ ὑπὲρ τοῦτο ἀναδραμεῖν εἰ μὴ ἐν μειρακίῳ ἀπ-
έθανεν.

5   ΦΟΙΝ. Εἶδον τὸν νεανίαν, ἀμπελουργέ, καὶ ἄγαμαί
σε τοῦ ἑταίρου. ὥπλισται δὲ ἢ τί;

ΑΜΠ. Χλαμύδα ἐνῆπται, ξένε, τὸν Θετταλικὸν τρό-
πον, ὥσπερ τὸ ἄγαλμα τοῦτο. ἁλουργὴς δὲ ἡ χλαμύς,
θείου ἄνθους. ἄρρητον γὰρ τὸ τῆς πορφύρας ἄνθος.

11. ΦΟΙΝ. Ὁ δὲ δὴ ἔρως, ὃν τῆς Λαοδαμείας ἤρα,
πῶς ἔχει αὐτῷ νῦν;

ΑΜΠ. Ἐρᾷ, ξένε, καὶ ἐρᾶται, καὶ διάκεινται πρὸς
ἀλλήλους ὥσπερ οἱ θερμοὶ τῶν νυμφίων.

2   ΦΟΙΝ. Περιβάλλεις δὲ ἥκοντα ἢ διαφεύγει σε
καπνοῦ δίκην, ὥσπερ τοὺς ποιητάς;

ΑΜΠ. Χαίρει περιβάλλοντι καὶ ξυγχωρεῖ φιλεῖν
τε αὐτὸν καὶ τῆς δέρης ἐμφορεῖσθαί γε.

3   ΦΟΙΝ. Θαμίζει δὲ ἢ διὰ πολλοῦ ἥκει;

ΑΜΠ. Τετράκις τοῦ μηνὸς ἢ πεντάκις οἶμαι αὐτοῦ
μετέχειν, ὁπότ᾽ ἢ φυτεῦσαί ποτε τουτωνὶ τῶν φυτῶν
βούλοιτο ἢ τρυγῆσαι ἢ ἄνθη κεῖραι. φιλοστέφανος
γάρ τις καὶ ἡδίω ἀποφαίνων τὰ ἄνθη ὁπότε περὶ αὐτὰ
εἴη.

4   ΦΟΙΝ. Ἱλαρόν γε τὸν ἥρω λέγεις καὶ ἀτεχνῶς
νυμφίον.

portioned and graceful, like the herms[48] one sees at race-courses. He is perhaps ten cubits tall—I think he would have grown even beyond that if he hadn't died in his youth.

Phoenician. I can picture the youth, vinedresser, and I   5
am in awe of your friend. Does he wear armor?

Vinedresser. Just as this statue, he wears a soldier's mantle as they do in Thessaly; it is purple, the color of the gods—for the shade of purple is sacred.[49]

11. *Phoenician.* How fares now the love he used to feel for Laodameia?

Vinedresser. He loves her as much as she does him. They treat each other like passionate newlyweds.

Phoenician. Do you embrace him when he comes, or   2
does he elude your grasp like smoke, as he does the po-ets?[50]

Vinedresser. He is glad to be embraced by me, and allows me to kiss him and linger on his neck.

Phoenician. Does he come often, or only occasionally?   3

Vinedresser. I suppose I meet him four or five times a month, whenever he wishes to plant or harvest something, or to cut flowers; for he likes garlands, and makes the flowers more beautiful when he is among them.

Phoenician. This hero is cheerful, as you describe him,   4
and quite the newlywed.

---

[48] Evidently another slip by the vinedresser (Introduction §7), since a Herm is a statue type with only a head and erect phallus, i.e., no body at all (Platt 2011, 246–47).

[49] The purple soldier's mantle had first been adopted by Alexander the Great (Reinhold 1970, 29).

[50] Like the ghost of Patroclus, *Il.* 23.99–101, which however eludes Achilles, not the poet.

ΆΜΠ. Καὶ σώφρονά γε, ὦ ξένε. φιλόγελως γὰρ ὢν
ὑφ᾽ ἡλικίας, ὕβρει οὐδὲν πράττει. καὶ σμινύης δὲ
ἅπτεται πολλάκις εἴ που ὀρύττων πέτρᾳ ἐντύχοιμι,
καὶ ξυλλαμβάνει μοι τῶν δυσέργων, κἂν ἀγνοήσω τι
5 τῶν κατὰ γεωργίαν, διορθοῦταί με. τά τε δένδρα ἐγὼ
μὲν παρακηκοὼς τοῦ Ὁμήρου μακρὰ ἐφύτευον μεῖον
τοῦ ἄνω τὸ ἐς τὴν γῆν ἐμβιβάζων, καὶ ὁπότε ἐπελά-
βετό μου ὁ Πρωτεσίλεως, ἐχρώμην τοῖς τοῦ Ὁμήρου
πρὸς αὐτόν, ὁ δὲ ὑπολαβὼν "αὐτὸς μέντοι Ὅμηρος
τὸν ἐναντίον" ἔφη "κελεύει τρόπον ἢ σὺ πράττεις·
μακρὰ γὰρ ὑπὸ σοφίας τὰ βαθέα οἶδεν, ὥς που τὰ
φρέατα μακρὰ ὀνομάζει, βαθέα ὄντα"· καὶ τὰ δένδρα
δὲ εἶπεν ἐμβιώσεσθαι τῇ γῇ μᾶλλον, εἰ τῷ μὲν πλεί-
6 ονι ἑστήκοι, τῷ δὲ ὀλίγῳ κινοῖτο. ἐπιστὰς δέ μοί ποτε
ἄνθη ποτίζοντι "τὸ μύρον" εἶπεν, "ὦ τᾶν, οὐ δεῖται
ὕδατος," διδάσκων δήπου μὴ ἔκπλυτα ποιεῖν τὰ ἄνθη.

7 ΦΟΙΝ. Τὸν δὲ ἄλλον χρόνον, ὦ ἀμπελουργέ, ποῦ
διαιτᾶται;

ΆΜΠ. Ποτὲ μὲν ἐν Ἅιδου, φησί, ποτὲ δὲ ἐν Φθίᾳ,
ποτὲ δὲ αὖ ἐν Τροίᾳ, οὗ οἱ ἑταῖροι, καὶ πρὸς θήρα
συῶν τε καὶ ἐλάφων γινόμενος, ἀφικνεῖται κατὰ με-
σημβρίαν καὶ καθεύδει ἐκταθείς.

8 ΦΟΙΝ. Ποῦ δὲ τῇ Λαοδαμείᾳ ξύνεστιν;

ΆΜΠ. Ἐν Ἅιδου, ξένε. καὶ λέγει αὐτὴν εὐδοκιμώ-
τατα γυναικῶν πράττειν, ἀριθμουμένην ἐν αἷς Ἄλκη-
στίς τε ἡ Ἀδμήτου καὶ Ἀριάδνη ἡ Καπανέως καὶ αἱ
ταύταις ἴσαι σώφρονές τε καὶ χρησταί.

Vinedresser. He is moderate as well, stranger, for although he loves a joke, like any young man, he never does anything unkind. If I happen to strike a rock while digging, he often grabs a hoe himself, and pitches in when the work is hard, and corrects me if I am misguided on anything to do with farming. Misreading Homer, I was trying to "plant 5 trees tall" (*Od.* 18.359) by placing much less of them into the soil than above it, and when Protesilaus stopped me, I quoted Homer's verses to him; he, however, answered, "But Homer himself commands the opposite of what you're doing. For by 'tall' he cleverly means 'deep,' just as of course he speaks of 'tall' i.e., deep, 'wells'" (*Il.* 21.197). He said that the trees would take root in the earth better if they were anchored with more of their length, and could be moved only with a small part. Once also he stood beside 6 me as I was irrigating the flowering plants and said, "My good man, don't water down the perfume";[51] he meant of course that I should not drown the blossoms.

Phoenician. Where does he spend the rest of his time? 7

Vinedresser. Partly in the underworld, he says, partly in Phthia, and partly also in Troy, where his comrades are; when he is hunting wild boar and deer, he comes here at midday and stretches out for a nap.

Phoenician. Where does he meet Laodameia? 8

Vinedresser. In the underworld, stranger. He also says that she is most honored of women, being numbered in the group which includes Admetus' wife Alcestis and Capaneus' wife Ariadne[52] and others equally moderate and noble.

---

[51] So Grossardt (2006a).   [52] An error for "Evadne" (for the vinedresser's slips, see Introduction §7); all these wives decided to die rather than survive their husbands.

9   ΦΟΙΝ. Ξυσσιτοῦνται δὲ ἀλλήλοις ἢ οὐ θέμις;

ΑΜΠ. Οὔπω, ξένε, σιτουμένῳ ἐνέτυχον οὐδὲ πί-
νοντα ἔγνων. καίτοι σπένδω γε αὐτῷ κατὰ ἑσπέραν
ἀπὸ τουτωνὶ τῶν Θασίων ἀμπέλων, ἃς φυτεύει αὐτός,
καὶ τρωκτὰ ὡραῖα τίθεμαι κατὰ μεσημβρίαν, ἐπειδὰν
θέρος τε ἥκῃ καὶ μετόπωρον ἱστῆται· σελήνης τε ἰού-
σης ἐς κύκλον ἐν τῇ τοῦ ἦρος ὥρᾳ, γάλα ἐγχέας ἐς
τὸν ψυκτῆρα τοῦτον "ἰδού σοι" λέγω "τὸ τῆς ὥρας
νᾶμα, σὺ δὲ πῖνε"· κἀγὼ μὲν εἰπὼν ταῦτα ἀπαλλάτ-
τομαι, τὰ δὲ βέβρωταί τε καὶ πέποται θᾶττον ἢ κατα-
μῦσαι.

12. ΦΟΙΝ. Περὶ δὲ τῆς ἡλικίας ἣν γεγονὼς ἀπ-
έθανε, τί φησιν;

ΑΜΠ. Ἐλεεῖ, ξένε, τὸ ἑαυτοῦ πάθος καὶ τὸν δαί-
μονα, ἐφ᾽ ᾧ τότε ἦν, ἄδικόν τε ἡγεῖται καὶ βάσκανον
μὴ συγχωρήσαντα οἱ τὸν γοῦν πόδα ἐς τὴν Τροίαν
ἐρεῖσαι· μὴ γὰρ ἂν μήτε Διομήδους τι ἐλαττωθῆναι
μαχόμενος, μήτ᾽ ἂν Πατρόκλου, μήτ᾽ ἂν τοῦ δευτέρου
2   Αἴαντος. τῶν γὰρ Αἰακιδῶν λελεῖφθαι τὰ πολέμια δι᾽
ἡλικίαν φησίν· αὐτὸς μὲν γὰρ εἶναι μειράκιον, ἐκεί-
νων δὲ τὸν μὲν Ἀχιλλέα εἶναι νεανίαν, τὸν δὲ Αἴαντα
3   ἄνδρα. καὶ τὰ ἔπη τὰ ἐς αὐτὸν Ὁμήρῳ εἰρημένα ἐπαι-
νεῖ, καίτοι μὴ πάντα ἐπαινῶν τὰ Ὁμήρου, ὡς ἀμφί-
δρυφον μὲν αὐτῷ τὴν γυναῖκα εἶπεν, ἡμιτελῆ δὲ τὴν
οἰκίαν, περιμάχητον δὲ τὴν ναῦν ἐφ᾽ ἧς ἔπλευσε, πο-
4   λεμικόν τε αὐτὸν καλεῖ. ἑαυτὸν δὲ ὀλοφύρεται μηδὲν
ἐν Τροίᾳ ἐργασάμενον, ἀλλὰ πεσόντα ἐν γῇ ἧς οὐδὲ

Phoenician. Do they take meals together, or is that   9
unlawful?

Vinedresser. I have never encountered him eating, nor
have I known him to drink. I do, however, pour him a liba-
tion in the evening with wine from these Thasian vines,
which he himself planted. When summer comes or fall
begins I serve him fruits of the season at noon; in the
spring when the moon is full I pour milk into this cooler
and say, "Here is the liquid of the season for you to drink."
When I've said this I depart, and what I've left is eaten and
drunk quick as a wink.

12. *Phoenician.* What does he say about the age at
which he died?

Vinedresser. He mourns about his sufferings and be-
lieves that the fortune which had him in its power in those
days was unjust and malicious in not allowing him to plant
at least his foot on Trojan soil. He says he would have been
in no way inferior to Diomedes in fighting, nor to Patro-
clus, nor to the lesser Ajax—he admits he fell short of the   2
Aeacidae in warfare because of his age—he himself was a
youth, but among these Achilles was a young man, and
Ajax fully adult. Although he doesn't approve everything   3
in Homer, he praises the verses written by Homer about
himself, since he wrote that his wife had cheeks torn in
mourning, that his house was half-built, that the ship on
which he sailed was a scene of fierce fighting, and called
him warlike. He laments that he accomplished nothing at   4
Troy, but fell on land on which he had not even stood. He

PHILOSTRATUS

ἐπέβη. καὶ τὴν οὐλὴν δὲ ἐντετύπωται τῷ μηρῷ· τὸ
γὰρ τραῦμα συναπορρύψασθαί φησι τῷ σώματι.

13. ΦΟΙΝ. Γυμνάζεται δέ, ὦ ἀμπελουργέ, τίνα τρό-
πον; ἐπειδὴ ἔφασκες αὐτὸν καὶ τοῦτο ἐξασκεῖν.

ΑΜΠ. Γυμνάζεται, ξένε, τὰ πολεμικὰ πλὴν τοξι-
κῆς, τὰ δὲ γυμναστικὰ πλὴν πάλης· τὸ μὲν γὰρ το-
ξεύειν δειλῶν ἡγεῖται, τὸ δὲ παλαίειν ἀργῶν.

2   ΦΟΙΝ. Παγκρατιάζει δὲ πῶς ἢ πυκτεύει;

ΑΜΠ. Σκιᾶς, ὦ ξένε, τούτων γυμνάζεται, καὶ δι-
σκεύει μεῖζον ἢ ἐφικέσθαι ἄνθρωπον. ἀνακρούει μὲν
γὰρ ὑπὲρ τὰς νεφέλας τὸν δίσκον, ῥίπτει δὲ ὑπὲρ τοὺς
ἑκατὸν πήχεις καὶ ταῦθ', ὡς ὁρᾷς, διπλάσιον τοῦ
Ὀλυμπικοῦ ὄντα. δραμόντος δὲ αὐτοῦ οὐκ ἂν εὕροις
ἴχνος, οὐδ' ἂν ἐνσημήναιτό τι τῇ γῇ ὁ πούς.

3   ΦΟΙΝ. Καὶ μὴν καὶ ἴχνη μεγάλα ἐντετύπωται τοῖς
δρόμοις, ἐς τὸ δεκάπηχυ μέγεθος τοῦ ἥρω.

ΑΜΠ. Βαδίζοντος, ξένε, τὰ ἴχνη ἐκεῖνα καὶ γυμνα-
ζομένου τι ἕτερον· δραμόντος δὲ ἄσημος ἡ γῆ· μετέ-
ωρος γάρ τις καὶ οἷον ἐπικυματίζων αἴρεται. φησὶ δὲ
καὶ παραδραμεῖν ἐν Αὐλίδι τὸν Ἀχιλλέα ἐν ἄθλοις,
γυμναζομένης ἐπὶ Τροίαν τῆς Ἑλλάδος, καὶ ὑπὲρ τὸ
4   πήδημα τὸ ἐκείνου ἀρθῆναι. τὰ δὲ πολέμια ξυγχωρεῖ,
ὡς ἔφην, τῷ Ἀχιλλεῖ πλὴν τῆς ἐν Μυσοῖς μάχης· ἐκεῖ

---

53 Protesilaus may have defeated Achilles in the long jump at
Aulis, but Philostratus is doubtless alluding to the famous "jump
of Achilles" at Troy: he was the last to leave the ship there (he
obeyed the same oracle that Protesilaus ignored), but when he

144

has the scar imprinted on his thigh; for he says he washed the wound away along with the rest of his body.

13. *Phoenician.* How does he engage in exercise, vine-dresser? For you said that he does that as well.

Vinedresser. He practices all the arts of war except for the bow, and all athletics except for wrestling; he considers archery a coward's art, and wrestling for the lazy.

Phoenician. Where does he find an opponent for box- 2 ing or the pankration?

Vinedresser. In those events he exercises by shadow-boxing. His discus-throwing far surpasses anything a man could attain, for he throws it up and beyond the clouds, and farther than one hundred cubits, even though the discus is twice the size of the one used at Olympia. When he runs, one can't even find his tracks, and his foot makes no impression on the earth.

Phoenician. But there are footprints sunk into the race- 3 course large enough to fit a ten-cubit-tall hero.

Vinedresser. Those are from when he is walking or ex-ercising in some other way. When he runs, the earth re-mains unmarked, for he is almost suspended, and lifted up as if he were skipping across the waves. He says that he even ran against Achilles in the games held at Aulis, when the Greeks were exercising in preparation to fight Troy, and that his jump was farther than that of Achilles.[53] In 4 the skills of warfare he yields to Achilles, as I said, except

finally disembarked he leaped out with such force that a spring was produced at the spot where he landed, henceforth called "Achilles' jump." See Scholia to Lycophron 246; scholia to Eur. *Andr.* 1139; *addenda* to *FGrHist* 48 (p. 19), with Jacoby's com-mentary.

γὰρ πλείους ἀπεκτονέναι τῶν Μυσῶν ἢ ἐκεῖνος, ἀρι-
στεῖα δὲ ἀπενηνέχθαι· κεκρατηκέναι δὲ αὐτοῦ καὶ τὸν
ἀγῶνα τὸν περὶ τῆς ἀσπίδος.

14. ΦΟΙΝ. Καὶ τί ἂν εἴη, ἀμπελουργέ, τὸ τῆς ἀσπί-
δος; οὔτε γὰρ ποιητῇ εἴρηταί πω, οὔτε ἐς λόγον τινὰ
τῶν Τρωικῶν ἥκει.

ΑΜΠ. Περὶ πολλῶν, ξένε, τοῦτ' ἐρεῖς· πολλὰ γὰρ
2 περί τε ἀνδρῶν περί τε πολεμικῶν ἔργων ὁ ἥρως λέγει
μήπω τοῖς πολλοῖς δῆλα ὄντα. τὸ δὲ αἴτιον· φησὶν
αὐτούς, κατὰ ἔκπληξιν τῶν Ὁμήρου ποιημάτων, ἐς
μόνους Ἀχιλλέα τε καὶ Ὀδυσσέα βλέψαντας ἀμελῆ-
σαι καλῶν καὶ ἀγαθῶν ἀνδρῶν, καὶ τῶν μὲν οὐδὲ ἐπι-
μνησθῆναι τὸ παράπαν, τοῖς δὲ ἀναθεῖναι τριήρη
τεττάρων ἐπῶν. τὸν μὲν δὴ Ἀχιλλέα φησὶν ἐπαξίως
3 ὑμνῆσθαι, τὸν δὲ Ὀδυσσέα μειζόνως. καὶ ὁπόσα δὲ
Σθενέλου τε καὶ Παλαμήδους καὶ τῶν τοιῶνδε ἀνδρῶν
παραλέλειπται, δίειμί σοι μικρὸν ὕστερον· μὴ γὰρ
ἀγνοήσας γε ἀπέλθοις τι τούτων. καὶ τὸν λόγον δὲ
τὸν Μύσιον, ἐς ὃν ἥκει ἡ ἀσπίς, αὐτίκα ἀποτελοῦμεν.
4 νῦν δέ, ἐπειδὴ παγκρατίου καὶ πυγμῆς καὶ δίσκου
μνημονεύοντες ἐς τὴν ἀσπίδα ἀπηνέχθημεν, ἄκουε
τοῦ ἥρω θαύματα πρὸς ἀθλητὰς οἳ ἐχρήσαντο αὐτῷ
συμβούλῳ. τὸν Κίλικα, οἶμαι, παγκρατιαστὴν ἀκού-
εις, ὃν Ἁλτῆρα ἐκάλουν οἱ πατέρες, ὡς μικρὸς ἦν καὶ
τῶν ἀντιπάλων παρὰ πολύ.

15. ΦΟΙΝ. Οἶδα τεκμαιρόμενος δήπου τοῖς ἀνδρι-
ᾶσι· χαλκοῦς γὰρ πολλαχοῦ ἕστηκε.

for the battle in Mysia; for there he says he killed more Mysians than Achilles, and won the prize for valor, and also defeated him in the contest for the shield.

14. *Phoenician.* What is this about the shield, vine-dresser? It has never yet been told of by any poet, nor does it figure in any account of the Trojan War.

Vinedresser. You are going to say that about many things, stranger, for the hero tells many stories about men and 2 their feats in war which are as yet unknown to most poets. Here is the reason: he claims that they, awed by the Homeric poems, pay attention only to Achilles and Odysseus, and neglect fine, good men, some not recounting at all, to others assigning a trireme of four verses. He says that Achilles has received his due measure of praise, and Odysseus more than his due. As for what has been left out about 3 Sthenelus, Palamedes and their like, I shall tell you a little later; you should not leave here without knowing about them. The story about Mysia, on which the shield figures, we shall finish presently. But now, since we digressed to 4 the shield while on the subject of the pankration, boxing and the discus, let me tell you about the miracles he has here performed for the athletes who have sought his advice. I imagine you have heard of the Cilician pankratiast, whom our fathers used to call the "jumping man," because he was short and so much more so than his opponents.[54]

15. *Phoenician.* I had of course realized that to judge from his statues; his likeness in bronze can be found in many places.

---

[54] Grossardt (2002 and 2006a, 426) compares *Gym.* ch. 36 on short athletes and plausibly identifies this unnamed athlete with the Cilician wrestler Maron, whose career and honors are described in a Cilician inscription (*SEG* 52 1464 bis).

ΆΜΠ. Τούτῳ, ξένε, περιῆν μὲν καὶ ἐπιστήμης,
περιῆν δὲ καὶ θυμοῦ, καὶ μάλα ἐρρώννυ αὐτὸν ἡ εὐαρ-
2 μοστία τοῦ σώματος. ἀφικόμενος οὖν ἐς τὸ ἱερὸν
τοῦτο ὁ παῖς (ἔπλει δὲ εὐθὺ Δελφῶν ἀγωνιούμενος τὴν
κρίσιν) ἠρώτα τὸν Πρωτεσίλεων, ὅ τι πράττων περι-
3 έσοιτο τῶν ἀντιπάλων· ὁ δὲ "πατούμενος" ἔφη. ἀθυ-
μία οὖν αὐτίκα τὸν ἀθλητὴν ἔσχεν ὡς καταβεβλημέ-
νον ὑπὸ τοῦ χρησμοῦ· τὸ δ' ἀποπτερνίζειν ἐν ἀγωνίᾳ
πρῶτος εὑρὼν ξυνῆκεν ὕστερον ὅτι κελεύει αὐτὸν μὴ
μεθίεσθαι τοῦ ποδός· τὸν γὰρ προσπαλαίοντα τῇ
πτέρνῃ πατεῖσθαί τε ξυνεχῶς χρὴ καὶ ὑποκεῖσθαι τῷ
ἀντιπάλῳ. καὶ τοῦτο πράττων ὁ ἀθλητὴς οὗτος ὀνό-
4 ματος λαμπροῦ ἔτυχε καὶ ἡττήθη οὐδενός. ἀκούεις δέ
που καὶ Πλούταρχον ἐκεῖνον τὸν δεξιόν;

ΦΟΙΝ. Ἀκούω. τὸν γὰρ πύκτην, ὡς τὸ εἰκός, λέγεις.

5 ΆΜΠ. Οὗτος ἀνιὼν τὴν δευτέραν Ὀλυμπιάδα ἐπὶ
τοὺς ἄνδρας ἱκετεύει τὸν ἥρω χρῆσαι οἷ περὶ τῆς νί-
κης· ὁ δὲ αὐτὸν κελεύει Ἀχελῴῳ ἐναγωνίῳ εὔχεσθαι.

6 ΦΟΙΝ. Τί οὖν τὸ αἴνιγμα;

ΆΜΠ. Ἠγωνίζετο μὲν ἐν Ὀλυμπίᾳ πρὸς Ἑρμείαν
τὸν Αἰγύπτιον τὴν περὶ τοῦ στεφάνου νίκην. ἀπειρη-
κότες δὲ ὁ μὲν ὑπὸ τραυμάτων, ὁ δὲ ὑπὸ δίψης (καὶ
γὰρ ἀκμάζουσα μεσημβρία περὶ τὴν πυγμὴν εἱστή-
κει), νεφέλη ἐς τὸ στάδιον καταρρήγνυται καὶ διψῶν
ὁ Πλούταρχος ἔσπασε τοῦ ὕδατος ὃ ἀνειλήφει τὰ

---

55 I.e., by putting his feet behind the opponent's heel to trip

Vinedresser. He had plenty of skill, stranger, and spirit, and his well-shaped body made him quite strong. Well, he came to this sanctuary as a boy; he was sailing straight to Delphi, to compete in a contest—and asked Protesilaus what he should do to defeat his opponents. The answer was "be trampled."[55] Well, the athlete was discouraged at first, thinking the oracle had rejected him; but later, when in a contest he was the first to discover the use of heel tripping, he understood that Protesilaus was telling him not to disengage from the other's feet, since someone who wrestles against the heel must constantly be stepped on and stay under his opponent. By doing so, this athlete made a glorious name for himself and was undefeated. I suppose you have heard of the talented Plutarch?

Phoenician. I have indeed. You must be talking about the boxer.

Vinedresser. When he was going to Olympia for the second time, to compete among the men, he asked the hero to prophesy how he could win. Protesilaus told him to pray to Achelous, "god of the contest."

Phoenician. What riddle was that?

Vinedresser. He was competing against Hermeias of Egypt in the final match at Olympia, and when both men were exhausted, one from his wounds, the other from thirst—the boxing was taking place in the full midday heat[56]—a cloud burst over the stadium, and Plutarch, the one who was thirsty, drank some of the water which the

him; see Poliakoff (1987, 57, 172n8) and Gardiner (1930, 215); and cf. Pind. *Isthm.* 4.48; Theoc. 24.113–14.

[56] For the legendary heat at Olympia, see Poliakoff (1987, 165n6).

περὶ τοῖς πήχεσι κῴδια· καὶ τὸν χρησμὸν ἐνθυμηθείς,
ὡς μετὰ ταῦτα ἔφασκεν, εἰς θάρσος ὥρμησε καὶ ἔτυχε
7   τῆς νίκης. Εὐδαίμονα δὲ τὸν Αἰγύπτιον θαυμάζεις τῆς
καρτερίας ἴσως, εἰ πυκτεύοντί που παρέτυχες. τούτῳ
ἐρομένῳ πῶς ἂν μὴ ἡττηθείη, "θανάτου" ἔφη "κατα-
φρονῶν."

ΦΟΙΝ. Καὶ πείθεταί γε, ὦ ἀμπελουργέ, τῷ χρη-
σμῷ· παρασκευάζων γὰρ οὕτως ἑαυτόν, ἀδαμάντινος
τοῖς πολλοῖς καὶ θεῖος δοκεῖ.

8   ΑΜΠ. Ἕλιξ δὲ ὁ ἀθλητὴς αὐτὸς μὲν οὔπω προσ-
πέπλευκε τῷ ἱερῷ τούτῳ, πέμψας δέ τινα τῶν ἑαυτοῦ
ἑταίρων ἤρετο ποσάκις νικήσει τὰ Ὀλύμπια· ὁ δὲ
"δὶς" ἔφη "νικήσεις, ἐὰν μὴ ἐθέλῃς τρίς."

9   ΦΟΙΝ. Δαιμόνιον, ἀμπελουργέ· λέξεις γάρ που τὸ
ἐν Ὀλυμπίᾳ πραχθέν· προϋπαρχούσης γὰρ αὐτῷ νί-
κης μιᾶς, ὅτ᾽ ἀνὴρ ἐκ παίδων ἐνίκα πάλην, ἀπεδύσατο
τὴν ἐπ᾽ ἐκείνῃ Ὀλυμπιάδα πάλην τε καὶ παγκράτιον,
ἐφ᾽ ᾧ δυσχεράναντες οἱ Ἠλεῖοι διενοοῦντο μὲν ἀμ-
φοῖν εἴργειν αὐτὸν ἐγκλήματα Ὀλυμπικὰ ξυντιθέντες
10   αὐτῷ· μόγις δ᾽ οὖν ἀνέδησαν τὸ παγκράτιον. καὶ τοῦ-
τον ἄρα τὸν φθόνον ὁ Πρωτεσίλεως φυλάξασθαι
προὔλεγεν, εἰδὼς αὐτὸν ἀντίπαλον τοῖς ἐξῃρημένοις
ὄντα.

---

57 Death was a real possibility for boxers wearing the spiked
caestus (Poliakoff 1987, 87–88).

58 So Grossardt (2006a).

sheepskins on his arms had absorbed. When he remembered the oracle, as he said later, he regained his confidence, and won. Perhaps you also are an admirer of the   7
endurance of Eudaimon of Egypt, if you've ever seen him box. When *he* asked Protesilaus how he could remain undefeated, the answer was "by scorning death."[57]

Phoenician. He obeys the oracle too, vinedresser. His attitude is so impressive that the crowds find him hard as adamant and like a god.

Vinedresser. As for the athlete Helix, he has never   8
sailed to this the sanctuary himself, but he sent one of his companions to ask how often he would win at the Olympic games. Protesilaus' answer was "you will win twice, if you don't want to win three times."

Phoenician. That is astounding, vinedresser; obviously   9
you will go on to say what happened at Olympia: he already had one victory wrestling in the men's, though belonging to the boys,[58] and in the Olympiad after that he entered both the wrestling and the pankration, which so angered the Eleans that they intended to bar him from both, charging him with infringement of the Olympic rules; they barely crowned him for the pankration.[59] It was this envy   10
that Protesilaus predicted he should guard against, since he knew it opposes men of achievement.[60]

[59] According to Dio Cass. 80 [79] 10.2–3, they simply canceled the wrestling.

[60] For the athlete Aurelius Helix, see Introduction to *Gymnasticus.* Helix' two Olympic victories were probably in 213 and 217; it seems likely that the present passage was written before his most famous victory, in the Pancration at the Capitoline games in 219.

ΆΜΠ. Ἄριστα, ξένε, τοῦ χρησμοῦ ἐτεκμήρω.

16. ΦΟΙΝ. Τῶν δὲ δὴ νόσων τίνας ἰᾶται; πολλοὺς γὰρ αὐτῷ φῂς εὔχεσθαι.

ΆΜΠ. Πάσας ἰᾶται ὁπόσαι εἰσί, μάλιστα δὲ τὰς φθόας τε καὶ τοὺς ὑδέρους καὶ τὰς τῶν ὀφθαλμῶν
2 νόσους καὶ τοὺς τεταρταίῳ πυρέσσοντας. ἔστι καὶ ἐρῶντι τυχεῖν αὐτοῦ ξυμβούλου· ξυναλγεῖ γὰρ σφόδρα τοῖς τὰ ἐρωτικὰ ἀτυχοῦσι καὶ ὑποτίθεται αὐτοῖς ἐπῳδὰς καὶ τέχνας, αἷς τὰ παιδικὰ θέλξουσι. μοιχοῖς δὲ οὔτε προσδιαλέγεται οὐδὲν οὔτε ὑποτίθεταί τι ἐρωτικόν· φησὶ γὰρ ἀπηχθῆσθαι αὐτοῖς, ἐπειδὴ τὸ ἐρᾶν
3 διαβάλλουσιν. ἀφικομένου γοῦν ἐνταῦθα μοιχοῦ ποτε αὐτῇ γυναικὶ ἣν ἐπείρα, καὶ ξυνομνύναι βουλομένων ἐπὶ τὸν ἄνδρα παρόντα μέν, ξυνιέντα δὲ οὔπω—ὁ μὲν γὰρ ἔτυχε καθεύδων μεσημβρίας ἐνταῦθα, οἱ δ' ὤμνυσαν ἤδη προσεστηκότες τῷ βωμῷ. . . .

ΦΟΙΝ. Τί οὖν ὁ Πρωτεσίλεως;

4 ΆΜΠ. Ἐξορμᾷ τοῦτον τὸν κύνα καίτοι χρηστόν, ὡς ὁρᾷς, ὄντα προσπεσεῖν τε αὐτοῖς κατόπιν καὶ δακεῖν ἔτι ὀμνύντας· καὶ τὸν ὅρκον οὑτωσὶ ξυγχέας ἐφίσταται τῷ ἀνδρὶ καὶ κελεύει αὐτὸν ἐκείνων μὲν ἀμελεῖν, τὸ γὰρ δῆγμά σφων ἀνίατον εἶναι, σῴζειν δὲ νῦν γοῦν αὐτόν τε καὶ τὸν αὐτοῦ οἶκον· τοὺς μὲν γὰρ θεοὺς πάντα γινώσκειν, τοὺς δὲ ἥρωας θεῶν μὲν
5 ἐλάττω, πλείω δὲ ἀνθρώπων—πολὺς ἐπιρρεῖ τῶν τοιούτων ὄχλος εἰ πάντων ἀπομνημονεύοιμι, ὄντων γε καὶ τῶν ἐν Φθίᾳ τε καὶ Φυλάκῃ φανερῶν πᾶσιν ὅσοι Θετταλίαν οἰκοῦσι· καὶ γὰρ τὸ ἐκείνῃ ἱερὸν ἐνεργὸν

Vinedresser. That is an excellent interpretation of the oracle, stranger.

16. *Phoenician.* What diseases does he heal? You said that many people pray to him.

Vinedresser. He heals every sort that exists, especially tuberculosis, dropsy, eye diseases, and malaria. A lover 2 may seek his counsel also; he is very sympathetic to those unlucky in love, and suggests to them incantations and rituals to win their beloved boys. But he doesn't talk to adulterers, nor offer them any advice on love; he says he hates them, because they give love a bad name. At any 3 rate, when once there came here an adulterer with the very woman he was seducing, and they wanted to conspire against her husband, who was here also, but knew nothing, well, he happened to be taking a midday nap here, while they had already taken their places before the altar and were taking their oath. . . .

Phoenician. What did Protesilaus do?

Vinedresser. He stirred up this dog—who as you know 4 is very well-behaved—to attack them from behind and bit them, while they swore their oaths; after ruining their pledges in this way Protesilaus appeared to the husband in a dream and told him not to concern himself with them. The bite they had received would be incurable, but at least to save himself and his house; for the gods (he said) know everything, while heroes have less knowledge than gods, but more than men—but the mass of such stories swamps 5 us if I should recount them all, since there are also incidents from Phthia and Phylake, well known to the inhabitants of Thessaly. The sanctuary there keeps Protesilaus

153

τῷ Πρωτεσίλεῳ, καὶ πολλὰ τοῖς Θετταλοῖς ἐπισημαί-
νει φιλάνθρωπά τε καὶ εὐμενῆ, καὶ ὀργίλα αὖ εἰ ἀμε-
λοῖτο.

6   ΦΟΙΝ. Πείθομαι, νὴ τὸν Πρωτεσίλεων, ἀμπε-
λουργέ· καλὸν γάρ, ὡς ὁρῶ, καὶ ὀμνύναι τοιοῦτον
ἥρω.

17. ΑΜΠ. ῍Η ἀδικήσεις γε ἀπιστῶν, ξένε, τόν τε
Ἀμφιάρεων, ὃν λέγεται ἡ γῆ ἐν σοφῷ ἀδύτῳ ἔχειν,
Ἀμφίλοχόν τε τὸν τούτου παῖδα πλείω ἴσως ἢ ἐγὼ
2   γινώσκεις, οὐ πολὺ ἀπέχων τῆς Κιλίκων ἠπείρου. καὶ
Μάρωνα δὲ τὸν Εὐάνθους ἀδικοίης ἂν ἐπιφοιτῶντα
ταῖς ἐν Ἰσμάρῳ ἀμπέλοις καὶ ἡδυοίνους αὐτὰς ἐργα-
ζόμενον φυτεύοντά τε καὶ κυκλοῦντα, ὅτε δὴ ὁρᾶται
τοῖς γεωργοῖς ὁ Μάρων καλός τε καὶ ἁβρὸς καὶ ἀνα-
3   πνέων πότιμόν τε καὶ οἰνῶδες. γινώσκειν δὲ χρὴ καὶ
τὰ τοῦ Θρᾳκὸς Ῥήσου· Ῥῆσος γάρ, ὃν ἐν Τροίᾳ Δι-
ομήδης ἀπέκτεινε, λέγεται οἰκεῖν τὴν Ῥοδόπην καὶ
πολλὰ αὐτοῦ θαύματα ᾄδουσιν· ἱπποτροφεῖν τε γὰρ
4   φασιν αὐτὸν καὶ ὁπλιτεύειν καὶ θήρας ἅπτεσθαι. ση-
μεῖον δὲ εἶναι τοῦ θηρᾶν τὸν ἥρω τὸ τοὺς σῦς τοὺς
ἀγρίους καὶ τὰς δορκάδας καὶ ὁπόσα ἐν τῷ ὄρει θη-
ρία φοιτᾶν πρὸς τὸν βωμὸν τοῦ Ῥήσου κατὰ δύο ἢ
τρία, θύεσθαί τε οὐδενὶ δεσμῷ ξυνεχόμενα καὶ παρ-

---

61 For this sanctuary, see Introduction §8.
62 While fleeing from the battle of Thebes, Amphiaraus was
swallowed by the earth at Oropus on the border between Boeotia
and Attica (Sophocles fr. 958 Radt); for his shrine and oracle

busy, and he makes many kind and beneficial pronounce-
ments for the Thessalians and many angry ones also, if he
is slighted.[61]

Phoenician. I believe you, vinedresser—by Protesilaus,   6
I do; for I see this hero is a good one to swear by.

17. *Vinedresser.* Indeed if you continue to disbelieve
you will offend not only Amphiaraus, whom the earth is
said to keep in a wise sanctuary, but also his son Amphilo-
chus—you know him perhaps better than I, since you live
not far from Cilicia.[62] You would also offend Maron, Euan-   2
thes' son, who visits the vineyards at Ismaros and makes
the wine so pleasant, when he plants and encircles[63] them;
that is when visions of Maron, handsome, fair, and fra-
grant with fresh wine, appear to the farmers. You must   3
also know about Rhesus the Thracian, for it's said that he,
whom Diomedes killed at Troy, has his abode at Rhodope;
and they praise many of his miracles. They say he keeps
horses and wears heavy armor and joins in the hunt. It is   4
said that the hero's hunting is confirmed by the fact that
wild boar, roe deer and all animals living in the mountains
visit Rhesus' altar in groups of two or three and without
any restraint upon them, offer themselves to the knife and

---

there, see Petrakos (1968). On the even more famous oracle of
his son Amphilochus at Mallos in Cilicia, see Latte, *RE* 18 (1939,
862ff.); Bouché-Leclercq (1879, 3:341–45). That oracle was a fa-
vorite target of Lucian's skepticism (Jones 1986, 37). The discus-
sion of humans who are honored with city-sanctuaries at Paus.
1.34.2 also adduces Amphiaraus at Oropus, Amphilochus in Cili-
cia, and Protesilaus at Elaious (as well as Trophonius at Leba-
deia).

[63] Perhaps with trenches (Grossardt 2006a).

PHILOSTRATUS

5 ἔχειν τῇ μαχαίρᾳ ἑαυτά. λέγεται δὲ ὁ ἥρως οὗτος καὶ
λοιμοῦ ἐρύκειν τοὺς ὅρους· πολυανθρωποτάτη δὲ ἡ
6 Ῥοδόπη καὶ πολλαὶ περὶ τὸ ἱερὸν αἱ κῶμαι. ὅθεν μοι
δοκεῖ καὶ βοήσεσθαι ὑπὲρ τῶν ἑαυτοῦ συστρατιωτῶν
ὁ Διομήδης, εἰ τὸν μὲν Θρᾷκα τοῦτον, ὃν ἀπέκτεινεν
αὐτὸς μηδὲν εὐδόκιμον ἐν Τροίᾳ ἐργασάμενον, μηδὲ
δείξαντά τι ἐκεῖ λόγου ἄξιον πλὴν ἵππων λευκῶν, εἶ-
ναί τε ἡγοίμεθα καὶ θύοιμεν αὐτῷ διὰ Ῥοδόπης τε καὶ
Θρᾴκης πορευόμενοι, τοὺς δὲ θεῖά τε καὶ λαμπρὰ εἰρ-
γασμένους ἔργα ἀτιμάζοιμεν, μυθώδη τὴν περὶ αὐτοὺς
δόξαν ἡγούμενοι καὶ κεκομπασμένην.

18. ΦΟΙΝ. Μετὰ σοῦ λοιπόν, ἀμπελουργέ, τάττω
ἐμαυτὸν καὶ οὐδεὶς ἔτι τοῖς τοιούτοις ἀπιστήσει· οἱ δὲ
ἐν τῷ πεδίῳ τῷ ἐν Ἰλίῳ, οὓς ἔφασκες τὸν μάχιμον
τρόπον δι᾽ αὐτοῦ στείχειν, πότε ὤφθησαν;

2 ΑΜΠ. Ὁρῶνται, ἔφην, ὁρῶνται ἔτι βουκόλοις τε
τοῖς ἐν τῷ πεδίῳ καὶ νομεῦσι μεγάλοι καὶ θεῖοι, καὶ
θεῶνται ἔστιν ὅτε ἐπὶ κακῷ τῆς γῆς· εἰ μὲν γὰρ κεκο-
νιμένοι φαίνοιντο, αὐχμοὺς ἐπισημαίνουσι τῇ χώρᾳ,
εἰ δὲ ἱδρῶτος πλέοι, κατακλυσμούς τε καὶ ὄμβρους, εἰ
δὲ αἷμα περὶ αὐτοῖς ἢ τοῖς ὅπλοις φαίνοιτο, νόσους
τῷ Ἰλίῳ ἀναπέμπουσιν· εἰ δὲ μηδὲν τούτων περὶ τοῖς
εἰδώλοις ὁρῷτο, ἀγαθὰς ἤδη ἄγουσι τὰς ὥρας καὶ
σφάττουσιν αὐτοῖς τότε οἱ νομεῖς, ὁ μὲν ἄρνα, ὁ δὲ
3 ταῦρον, ὁ δὲ πῶλον, ὁ δ᾽ ἄλλο τι ὧν νέμει. φθορὰς δέ,
ὁπόσαι περὶ τὰς ἀγέλας γίνονται, πάσας ἐξ Αἴαντος

64 This hero cult of Rhesus (introduced somewhat artificially

156

are sacrificed. This hero is said to keep his borders safe 5
from plague and Rhodope is in fact very populous, with
many villages near the sanctuary.[64] That is why I think 6
Diomedes is likely to come to the aid of his comrades in
arms if this Thracian, whom he killed although at Troy
though totally undistinguished in valor or even (apart from
his white horses) in appearance, we believe to exist and
sacrifice to him when we travel through Rhodope and
Thrace, and yet dishonor those who performed such god-
like and glorious deeds, and consider their reputations
fabulous and inflated.

18. *Phoenician.* From now on, vinedresser, I shall be
on your side, and allow no one to doubt such stories. But
about the heroes you said walk upon the plain of Troy
looking warlike, when were they seen?

Vinedresser. I said that they *are* seen; they are still seen 2
today, tall and godlike, by the cowherds and shepherds in
the plain, and sometimes their appearances portend harm
for the land. If they appear covered with dust, they pres-
age drought for the territory; if they are drenched with
sweat, floods and thunderstorms; if there is blood on them
or their weapons, they are sending diseases upon Ilion.
But if none of these things accompanies their visions, they
are bringing good weather, and then the shepherds sacri-
fice to them a ram, a bull, a colt, or something else from
their flocks. When losses occur among their flocks they 3

as a confirmation of the power of Diomedes his killer) was estab-
lished at Amphipolis in 437 according to Polyaenus 6.53 (Pfister
1909, 1.197–98), but the additional details may be an attempt to
equate him with the "Thracian rider hero" well known from many
inscriptions; see Liapis (2011).

ἥκειν φασίν, οἶμαι διὰ τὸν ἐν τῇ μανίᾳ λόγον, ὅτε δὴ
ὁ Αἴας λέγεται ταῖς ἀγέλαις ἐμπεσὼν διαφορῆσαί
σφας οἷον κτείνων τοὺς Ἀχαιοὺς ἐπὶ τῇ κρίσει· καὶ
οὐδὲ νέμει περὶ τὸ σῆμα οὐδεὶς φόβῳ τῆς πόας· νο-
4 σώδης γὰρ δὴ ἀναφύεται καὶ πονηρὰ βόσκειν. ἔστι
δέ τις λόγος ὡς Τρῶές ποτε ποιμένες ἐς τὸν Αἴαντα
ὕβριζον νενοσηκότων αὐτοῖς τῶν προβάτων, καὶ περι-
στάντες τὸ σῆμα πολέμιον μὲν Ἕκτορος τὸν ἥρωα
ἐκάλουν, πολέμιον δὲ Τροίας τε καὶ ποιμνίων· καὶ ὁ
μὲν μανῆναι αὐτόν, ὁ δὲ μαίνεσθαι, ὁ δ᾽ ἀσελγέστα-
τος τῶν ποιμένων "Αἴας δ᾽ οὐκέτ᾽ ἔμιμνε," μέχρι τού-
του τὸ ἔπος αὐτῷ ἐπερραψῴδει ὡς δειλῷ· ὁ δὲ "ἀλλὰ
ἔμιμνον" εἶπε βοήσας ἐκ τοῦ τάφου φρικῶδές τι καὶ
ὄρθιον· λέγεται δὲ καὶ δουπῆσαι τοῖς ὅπλοις, οἷον ἐν
5 ταῖς μάχαις εἰώθει. τὸ μὲν δὴ τῶν κακοδαιμόνων ἐκεί-
νων πάθος οὐ χρὴ θαυμάζειν, εἰ Τρῶές τε καὶ νομεῖς
ὄντες ἐξεπλάγησαν ὁρμὴν Αἴαντος, καὶ οἱ μὲν ἔπεσον
αὐτῶν, οἱ δ᾽ ἔτρεσαν, οἱ δ᾽ ᾤχοντο φεύγοντες οὐ ἐποί-
μαινον· τὸν δὲ Αἴαντα θαυμάσαι ἄξιον· ἀπέκτεινε γὰρ
οὐδένα αὐτῶν, ἀλλὰ τὴν παροινίαν, ᾗ ἐχρῶντο, ἐκαρ-
6 τέρησε μόνον ἐνδειξάμενος αὐτοῖς τὸ ἀκούειν. ὁ δὲ
Ἕκτωρ οὐκ ἐγίνωσκεν, οἶμαι ξένε, τὴν ἀρετὴν ταύτην·
ὑβρίσαντος γὰρ ἐς αὐτὸν πέρυσι μειρακίου τινὸς (ἦν
δ᾽ ὥς φασι κομιδῇ νέον καὶ ἀπαίδευτον), ὥρμησεν ἐπὶ
τὸ μειράκιον καὶ ἀπέκτεινεν αὐτὸ ἐν ὁδῷ, ποταμῷ τὸ
ἔργον προσθείς.

65 Philostratus refers loosely to sections of Homer's work this

attribute them all to Ajax, probably because of this story in the *Madness*[65] [of Ajax], where he is said to have attacked the flocks and cut them to pieces, thinking he was killing the Achaeans in revenge for their verdict. And no one even grazes his flock around the monument, because they fear the unhealthy and indigestible grass that grows there. There is a story that the Trojan shepherds once 4 insulted Ajax when their animals were sick, by standing around his tomb and calling him an enemy of Hector and of Troy, and of their flocks. One of them said he had been insane, another added that he still was, and the most shameless of the shepherds recited to him, "Ajax remained no more" (*Il.* 14.727)—using only enough of the verse to imply he was a coward. Ajax, however, answered from his tomb with a loud and terrifying shout, "But I *did* remain," and is said to have shaken his armor, just as he used to do in battle. What those poor men felt next isn't surprising— 5 being Trojans and shepherds, they were terrified at Ajax' onset, and some of them fell down, others fled in terror, and others went running back to were they had left their flocks. But Ajax' action is surprising, since he killed not one of them, but put up with their drunken behavior, except to show them he was listening. But Hector knew no 6 such restraint, I think, stranger; for last year, when a youth behaved disrespectfully to him—they say he was very young and uneducated—Hector attacked the lad on a road and killed him, though he delegated the task to a river.

---

way (25.3, 51.7); however, the madness of Ajax is not told in Homer, but rather in the epic cycle (M. L. West 2013, 159–62, 166–67), then in Sophocles' *Ajax*. No work entitled "The Madness [of Ajax]" is known. (Astydamas' *Ajax mainomenos* is closest.)

PHILOSTRATUS

19. ΦΟΙΝ. Ἀγνοοῦντι λέγεις, ἀμπελουργέ, καὶ σφό-
δρα ἐκπληττομένῳ τὸν λόγον· ᾤμην γὰρ μηδαμοῦ
φαίνεσθαι τὸν ἥρω τοῦτον; καὶ ὁπότε μοι τὰ τῶν Ἑλ-
λήνων ἀπήγγελλες, ὑπερήλγουν τοῦ Ἕκτορος, εἰ
μήτε ἀρότης τι ὑπὲρ αὐτοῦ λέγει μήτε αἰπόλος, ἀλλ᾽
2 ἀφανής ἐστι τοῖς ἀνθρώποις καὶ ἀτεχνῶς κεῖται. περὶ
μὲν γὰρ τοῦ Πάριδος οὐδ᾽ ἀκούειν ἀξιῶ οὐδέν, δι᾽ ὃν
τοιοίδε καὶ τοσοίδε ἔπεσον· περὶ δὲ τοῦ Ἕκτορος, ὃς
ἔρεισμα μὲν τῆς Τροίας καὶ τοῦ ξυμμαχικοῦ παντὸς
ἦν, ἵππους δὲ ξυνεῖχε τέτταρας, ὃ μηδεὶς τῶν ἡρώων
ἕτερος, τὰς δὲ τῶν Ἀχαιῶν κατεπίμπρη ναῦς, ἐμάχετο
δὲ πρὸς αὐτοὺς ὁμοῦ πάντας ἐφορμῶντάς τε καὶ ξυν-
ταττομένους ἐπ᾽ αὐτόν, οὐκ ἂν ἐροίμην γέ τι, οὐδ᾽ ἂν
ἀκούσαιμι χαίρων, εἰ μὴ διαπηδῴης αὐτὰ μηδ᾽ ἀμε-
λῶς λέγοις;

3   ΑΜΠ. Ἄκουε διὰ πλειόνων, ἐπειδὴ τοῦτο ἡγῇ τὸ
μὴ ἀμελῶς φράζειν· τὸ ἐν Ἰλίῳ ἄγαλμα τοῦ Ἕκτορος
ἡμιθέῳ ἀνθρώπῳ ἔοικε καὶ πολλὰ ἤθη ἐπιφαίνει τῷ
θεωροῦντι αὐτὸ ξὺν ὀρθῷ λόγῳ· καὶ γὰρ φρονηματῶ-
δες δοκεῖ καὶ γοργὸν καὶ φαιδρὸν καὶ ξὺν ἁβρότητι
σφριγῶν καὶ ἡ ὥρα μετ᾽ οὐδεμιᾶς κόμης. ἔστι δ᾽ οὕτω
τι ἔμπνουν, ὡς τὸν θεατὴν ἐπισπάσασθαι θιγεῖν.
4 τοῦτο ἵδρυται μὲν ἐν περιβλέπτῳ τοῦ Ἰλίου, πολλὰ δὲ
ἐργάζεται χρηστὰ κοινῇ τε καὶ ἐς ἕνα, ὅθεν εὔχονται
αὐτῷ καὶ ἀγῶνα θύουσιν· ὅτε δὴ θερμὸν οὕτω καὶ
ἐναγώνιον γίνεται, ὡς καὶ ἱδρῶτα ἀπ᾽ αὐτοῦ λείβε-
5 σθαι. μειράκιον οὖν Ἀσσύριον ἧκον ἐς τὸ Ἴλιον ἐλοι-
δορεῖτο τῷ Ἕκτορι, προφέρον αὐτῷ τάς τε ἕλξεις, αἱ

19. *Phoenician.* What you say is entirely new to me, vinedresser, and I am very surprised to hear it. I thought he was one hero who never was seen, and when you were telling about the Greeks, I felt badly for Hector, if neither farmer nor goatherd has anything to say about him, but instead he has disappeared and is totally neglected. About Paris, who caused the deaths of so many noble and strong men, I don't wish to hear a word; but about Hector, who was the bulwark of Troy and her allies, and drove four horses—a thing which no other hero did—and set the Achaeans' ships on fire, and fought the whole enemy army when they made a concerted attack against him, shouldn't I ask any questions, and hear the answers gladly, so long as you don't skip over them or speak offhandedly?

Vinedresser. I shall tell you in exhaustive detail—since that is what you mean by "not speaking offhand." The statue of Hector in Ilion looks like a demigod, and reveals much of his character if one looks at it properly: for it seems self-confident, fierce, and alert, bursting with splendor, and its elegance doesn't need long hair.[66] It is so lifelike that it attracts the observer to touch it. The statue is set up on a spot in Ilion visible to all, and has performed many good deeds both for the city and individuals, which is why they address prayers to him and celebrate games in his honor. During these he becomes so excited and involved in the contest that the sweat drips off him. Well, an Assyrian youth arrived in Ilion and started to insult Hector, bringing up the draggings which had been inflicted on

[66] For Hector's short-cropped front hair, see ch. 37.2n. For his statue see Introduction §§6 and 11.

ἐξ Ἀχιλλέως ποτὲ ἐς αὐτὸν ἐγένοντο, καὶ τὸν τοῦ Αἴ-
αντος λίθον, ᾧ βληθεὶς ἀπέθανε πρὸς βραχύ, καὶ ὡς
Πάτροκλον τὰ πρῶτα ἔφυγε, καὶ ὡς οὐδὲ ἀπέκτεινεν
ἀλλὰ ἕτεροι. μετεποίει δὲ τὸ ἄγαλμα τοῦ Ἕκτορος·
Ἀχιλλέως γὰρ ἔφασκεν εἶναι αὐτὸ μετὰ τὴν κόμην,
6 ἣν ἐκείρατο ἐπὶ τῷ Πατρόκλῳ. τούτων ἐμφορηθὲν ἐξ-
ήλασεν ἐκ τοῦ Ἰλίου, καὶ πρὶν ἢ δέκα πορευθῆναι
σταδίους, ποταμὸς οὕτω βραχύς, ὡς μηδὲ ὄνομα αὐ-
τοῦ ἐν Τροίᾳ εἶναι, μέγας ἐκ μικροῦ αἴρεται, καὶ ὡς
ἀπήγγελλον οἱ διαφυγόντες τῶν ὀπαδῶν, ὁπλίτης
ἡγεῖτο τοῦ ποταμοῦ μέγας, παρακελευόμενος αὐτῷ
βαρβάρῳ τῇ φωνῇ καὶ σφοδρᾷ ἐπιστρέφειν τὸ ὕδωρ
εἰς τὴν ὁδόν, δι' ἧς τὸ μειράκιον ἤλαυνεν ἐπὶ τεττά-
7 ρων ἵππων οὐ μεγάλων· οὓς ὑπολαβὼν ὁ ποταμὸς
ὁμοῦ τῷ μειρακίῳ βοῶντί τε καὶ ξυνιέντι λοιπὸν τοῦ
Ἕκτορος, ἀπήγαγεν ἐς τὰ ἑαυτοῦ ἤθη καὶ οὕτως ἀπ-
ώλεσεν ὡς μηδὲ ἀνελέσθαι ξυγχωρῆσαι τὸ σῶμα·
ᾤχετο γὰρ οὐκ οἶδ' ὅποι ἀφανισθέν.

8   ΦΟΙΝ. Οὔτε τὸν Αἴαντα χρὴ θαυμάζειν, ἀμπε-
λουργέ, καρτερήσαντα τὰ ἐκ τῶν ποιμένων, οὔτε τὸν
Ἕκτορα ἡγεῖσθαι βάρβαρον μὴ ἀνασχόμενον τὰ ἐκ
9 τοῦ μειρακίου· τοῖς μὲν γὰρ καὶ ξυγγνώμη ἴσως, οἳ
Τρῶες ὄντες, ἔτι καὶ πονήρως ἐχόντων σφίσι τῶν
προβάτων, ἐπεπήδων τῷ τάφῳ· μειρακίῳ δὲ Ἀσσυρίῳ
πομπεύοντι ἐς τὸν τοῦ Ἰλίου ἥρω τίς συγγνώμη; οὐ
γὰρ δὴ Ἀσσυρίοις ποτὲ καὶ Τρωσὶ πόλεμος ἐγένετο,
οὐδὲ τὰς ἀγέλας σφῶν ὁ Ἕκτωρ ἐπόρθησεν, ὥσπερ
τὰς τῶν Τρώων ὁ Αἴας.

him by Achilles, the rock thrown by Ajax which hit and nearly killed him, and that at first he ran from Patroclus, and did not even kill him himself, but let others do it. He even tried to change the statue's identity, saying it was one of Achilles after he had cut his hair in mourning for Patroclus. When he had enough of that he drove out of Ilion, 6 but before he had traveled ten stades a river, so small that it had no name at Troy, grew suddenly large; those of his servants who escaped said later that a tall man in armor led the river on, commanding it loudly in a barbarian language, to divert its water into the road along which the youth was driving with his four small horses. The river 7 caught them together with the youth, who gave a shout in recognition at last of who Hector really was, and swept them away into its depths, doing away with him so completely as not to permit the body's recovery. He was gone, disappeared, I don't know where.

Phoenician. I think we should neither be surprised at 8 Ajax' forbearance toward the shepherds nor think Hector a barbarian for not enduring the youth's behavior. The 9 shepherds could be forgiven if they, being Trojans whose flocks were failing, attacked the tomb; but who could forgive an Assyrian youth abusing the hero of Ilion? There was never a war between Trojans and Assyrians, and Hector hadn't ravaged their flocks, as Ajax had those of the Trojans.

PHILOSTRATUS

20. ἈΜΠ. Πεπονθέναι τι πρὸς τὸν Ἕκτορα, ὦ ξένε,
δοκεῖς, καὶ οὐκ ἀξιῶ διαφέρεσθαι, ἀλλ᾽ ἐπανίωμεν ἐπὶ
τὰ τοῦ Αἴαντος· ἐκεῖθεν γὰρ οἶμαι τὴν ἐκβολὴν τοῦ
λόγου πεποιῆσθαι.

ΦΟΙΝ. Ἐκεῖθεν, ἀμπελουργέ, καὶ ὡς δοκεῖ, ἐπανί-
ωμεν.

2 ἈΜΠ. Πρόσεχε οὖν, ξένε· νηός ποτε καθορμισα-
μένης ἐς τὸ Αἰάντειον δύο τῶν ξένων πρὸ τοῦ σήμα-
τος ἤλυόν τε καὶ πεττοῖς ἔπαιζον, ἐπιστὰς δὲ ὁ Αἴας
"πρὸς θεῶν" ἔφη, "μετάθεσθε τὴν παιδιὰν ταύτην·
ἀναμιμνήσκει γάρ με τῶν Παλαμήδους ἔργων σοφοῦ
τε καὶ μάλ᾽ ἐπιτηδείου μοι ἀνδρός. ἀπολώλεκε δὲ κἀμὲ
κἀκεῖνον ἐχθρὸς εἰς ἄδικον εὑρὼν ἐφ᾽ ἡμῖν κρίσιν."

3 ΦΟΙΝ. Δεδάκρυκα, νὴ τὸν Ἥλιον, ἀμπελουργέ· τὰ
γὰρ ἀμφοῖν πάθη παραπλήσιά τε καὶ ἐοικότα εἰς εὔ-
νοιαν. ἀγαθῶν μὲν γὰρ κοινωνία τίκτει ποτὲ καὶ φθό-
νον, ὅσοι δ᾽ ἂν κοινωνήσωσι συμφορῶν, ἀγαπῶσιν
4 ἀλλήλους τὸν ἔλεον τοῦ ἐλέου ἀντιδιδόντες. Παλαμή-
δους δὲ εἴδωλον ἔχοις ἄν τινα εἰπεῖν ἑωρακότα ἐν
Τροίᾳ;

21. ἈΜΠ. Τὰ μὲν ὁρώμενα εἴδωλα οὔπω δῆλα ὅτου
ἕκαστον· πολλὰ γὰρ καὶ ἄλλοτε ἄλλα, διαλλάττει δὲ
2 ἀλλήλων καὶ ἰδέᾳ καὶ ἡλικίᾳ καὶ ὅπλοις. ἀκούω δὲ
ὅμως καὶ περὶ τοῦ Παλαμήδους τοιαῦτα· ἦν γεωργὸς
ἐν Ἰλίῳ ταὐτόν ποτ᾽ ἐμοὶ πράττων· οὗτος ἐπεπόνθει τι
πρὸς τὸ τοῦ Παλαμήδους πάθος καὶ ἐθρήνει αὐτὸν
ἥκων ἐπὶ τὴν ἠιόνα πρὸς ᾗ λέγεται ὑπὸ τῶν Ἀχαιῶν

20. *Vinedresser.* You seem somehow sympathetic to Hector, stranger, and I have no desire to quarrel with you, but let us return to Ajax—for we were speaking of him before we digressed.

Phoenician. We were indeed, vinedresser; let us return, if you wish.

Vinedresser. Listen carefully, then. Once when a ship 2 had put in at the Aianteion, two foreigners were bored and playing backgammon in front of the monument, when Ajax appeared to them and said, "By the gods, leave off this game. It reminds me of the career of Palamedes, a wise man and a good friend of mine, for an enemy had both him and me killed, by contriving an unjust verdict against us."[67]

Phoenician. You have made me weep, by Helios, for 3 both their fates are indeed alike, and appropriate for mutual goodwill; shared good fortune sometimes produces envy, but those who share sorrows love each other and feel mutual sympathy. Could you say whether anyone has seen 4 Palamedes' spirit at Troy?

21. *Vinedresser.* Although spirits have been seen, it's not yet clear to which hero each of them belongs, since different ones appear at different times, with variations in appearance, age, and armor. But I have heard about Pala- 2 medes the following story: there was in Ilion a farmer, such as I, who had been moved by Palamedes' fate, and used to go to the beach on which the Achaeans are said to

---

[67] I.e., Odysseus. For Palamedes' invention of backgammon, see 33.2, below, and Paus. 10.31.1, 2.20.3 (dedication of *pessoi* in a temple).

βεβλῆσθαι, καὶ ὁπόσα νομίζουσιν ἐπὶ σημάτων ἄν-
θρωποι, ἐπέφερε τῇ κόνει, τάς τε ἡδίους τῶν ἀμπέλων
ἐξαιρῶν αὑτῷ κρατῆρα ἐτρύγα, καὶ ξυμπίνειν τῷ Πα-
3 λαμήδει ἔφασκεν ὅτε ἀναπαύοιτο τῶν ἔργων. ἦν δὲ
αὐτῷ καὶ κύων τέχνῃ αἰκάλλων καὶ ὑποκαθήμενος
τοὺς ἀνθρώπους· τοῦτον Ὀδυσσέα ἐκάλει καὶ ἐπαίετο
ὑπὲρ τοῦ Παλαμήδους ὁ Ὀδυσσεὺς οὗτος προσ-
4 ακούων κακὰ μυρία. δοκεῖ δὴ τῷ Παλαμήδει ἐπιφοι-
τῆσαί ποτε τῷ ἐραστῇ τούτῳ καὶ ἀγαθόν τι αὐτῷ
5 δοῦναι. καὶ δῆτα ὁ μὲν πρὸς ἀμπέλῳ τινὶ ἦν γόνυ
αὐτῆς ἰώμενος, ὁ δὲ ἐπιστὰς αὐτῷ "σὺ γινώσκεις με"
ἔφη "γεωργέ;"—"καὶ πῶς" εἶπεν, "ὃν οὔπω εἶδον;"—"τί
6 οὖν" ἔφη, "ἀγαπᾷς ὃν μὴ γινώσκεις;" ξυνῆκεν ὁ γε-
ωργὸς ὅτι Παλαμήδης εἴη· καὶ τὸ εἶδος ἐς ἥρω ἔφερε
μέγαν τε καὶ καλὸν καὶ ἀνδρεῖον, οὔπω τριάκοντα ἔτη
γεγονότα· καὶ περιβαλὼν αὐτὸν μειδιῶν "φιλῶ σε, ὦ
Παλάμηδες" εἶπεν, "ὅτι μοι δοκεῖς φρονιμώτατος ἀν-
θρώπων γεγονέναι καὶ δικαιότατος ἀθλητὴς τῶν κατὰ
σοφίαν πραγμάτων, πεπονθέναι τε ὑπὸ τῶν Ἀχαιῶν
ἐλεεινὰ διὰ τὰς Ὀδυσσέως ἐπὶ σοὶ τέχνας, οὗ τάφος
εἴ τις ἦν ἐνταῦθα, ἐξωρώρυκτ' ἂν ὑπ' ἐμοῦ πάλαι· μι-
αρὸς γὰρ καὶ κακίων τοῦ κυνός, ὃν ἐπ' αὐτῷ τρέ-
7 φω."—"φειδώμεθα λοιπὸν τοῦ Ὀδυσσέως" ὁ ἥρως
ἔφη, "τούτων γὰρ ἐπραξάμην αὐτὸν ἐγὼ δίκας ἐν
8 Ἅιδου· σὺ δέ, ἐπειδὴ φιλεῖς που τὰς ἀμπέλους, εἰπέ
μοι τί μάλιστα περὶ αὐταῖς δέδοικας."—"τί δ' ἄλλο
γε" εἶπεν "ἢ τὰς χαλάζας ὑφ' ὧν ἐκτυφλοῦνταί τε καὶ
ῥήγνυνται;"—"ἱμάντα τοίνυν" εἶπεν ὁ Παλαμήδης

have thrown his body,[68] and used to mourn him and offer the customary tomb offerings to his dust; he even chose the sweetest grapes and mixed him a bowl of wine, saying that he was having a drinking party with Palamedes when he rested from work. He also had a dog who was clever at 3 fawning, and also at sneaking up on people; him he called Odysseus, and this Odysseus used to be beaten and reviled constantly for what had been done to Palamedes. One day, Palamedes decided to visit his admirer and do 4 him some good turn; while he straightened out a kink 5 on some vine, Palamedes appeared to him, and said, "Do you recognize me, farmer?" "How could I," he answered, "when I've never seen you?" "Why then," the other said, "do you love someone you don't recognize?" The farmer 6 realized it was Palamedes—his appearance suggested a hero of great size, beauty and courage, not yet thirty years old—and embraced him with a smile, "I admire you, Palamedes, because I think you were the most sensible of men, and the most just competitor in the contest of wisdom, and because you suffered a pitiable death at the Achaeans' hands because of Odysseus' plots against you—if his tomb were here, I would have dug it up long ago, for he was foul and more evil than this dog, whom I keep under his name." The hero answered, "Let us torment Odysseus no further, 7 since I have exacted from him the penalty for that in the world below; but as for you, tell me, since you obviously 8 take care of your vines, what do you most fear concerning them?" "Why, the hailstorms of course, which tear off the buds or break them." "Then," said Palamedes, "let us tie

---

[68] The actual burial spot was discovered by Apollonius of Tyana and honored with a shrine. Cf. 33.48 and Introduction §9.

"περιάπτωμεν μιᾷ τῶν ἀμπέλων καὶ οὐ βεβλήσονται
αἱ λοιπαί."

9   ΦΟΙΝ. Σοφός γε ὁ ἥρως, ἀμπελουργέ, καὶ ἀεί τι
εὑρίσκων ἀγαθὸν τοῖς ἀνθρώποις. Ἀχιλλέως δὲ πέρι
τί ἂν εἴποις; τοῦτον γὰρ θειότατον τοῦ Ἑλληνικοῦ
παντὸς ἡγούμεθα.

22. ΑΜΠ. Τὰ μὲν ἐν τῷ Πόντῳ, ξένε, εἰ μήπω ἐς
αὐτὸν πέπλευκας, καὶ ὅσα ἐν τῇ ἐκεῖ νήσῳ λέγεται
πράττειν, ἐγώ σοι ἀπαγγελῶ ὕστερον ἐν τῷ περὶ αὐ-
τοῦ λόγῳ μακροτέρῳ ὄντι, τὰ δὲ ἐν Ἰλίῳ παραπλήσια
τοῖς ἄλλοις ἥρωσι· καὶ γὰρ προσδιαλέγεταί τισι καὶ
2   ἐπιφοιτᾷ καὶ θηρία διώκει. ξυμβάλλονται δὲ αὐτὸν
Ἀχιλλέα εἶναι τῇ τε ὥρᾳ τοῦ εἴδους καὶ τῷ μεγέθει
καὶ τῇ ἀστραπῇ τῶν ὅπλων· κατόπιν δὲ αὐτοῦ ζάλη
ἀνέμων εἰλεῖται πομπὸς τοῦ εἰδώλου.

3   ἐπιλείψει με ἡ φωνή, ξένε, τῶν τοιούτων μνημονεύ-
οντα· καὶ γάρ τι καὶ περὶ Ἀντιλόχου ᾄδουσιν, ὡς
κόρη Ἰλιὰς φοιτῶσα ἐπὶ τὸν Σκάμανδρον εἰδώλῳ τοῦ
Ἀντιλόχου ἐνέτυχε καὶ προσέκειτο τῷ σήματι ἐρῶσα
τοῦ εἰδώλου, καὶ ὡς βουκόλοι μειράκια περὶ τὸν τοῦ
Ἀχιλλέως βωμὸν ἀστραγαλίζοντες ἀπέκτεινεν ἂν ὁ
ἕτερος τῇ καλαύροπι τὸν ἕτερον πλήξας, εἰ μὴ ὁ Πά-
τροκλος αὐτοὺς διεπτόησεν, "ἀρκεῖ μοι" εἰπὼν "ὑπὲρ
4   ἀστραγάλων αἷμα ἕν." γινώσκειν δὲ ὑπάρχει ταῦτα
καὶ παρὰ τῶν βουκόλων καὶ πάντων τῶν οἰκούντων
τὸ Ἴλιον· ἐπιμίγνυμεν γὰρ ἅτε τὰς ὄχθας οἰκοῦντες
τῶν τοῦ Ἑλλησπόντου ἐκβολῶν καὶ ποταμόν, ὡς
ὁρᾷς, πεποιημένοι τὴν θάλατταν.

a strap around one of the vines, so the rest will not be struck."

Phoenician. The hero is wise, vinedresser, and as usual   9
he invented something to benefit mankind. But what could you say about Achilles? For we consider him the most godlike of the Greek army.

22. *Vinedresser.* As for his presence in the Black Sea, if you've never sailed to it, and his reports of activities on the island there, I shall speak of that later when I tell you of Achilles, which is a longer story; but in Ilion he is like the other heroes, since he visits and holds conversations with a few people and hunts wild animals. They assume   2
it is Achilles because of his physical grace, his size and the brilliance of his armor, and behind him there swirls a windstorm accompanying his spirit.

If I go on telling such stories my voice will fail me,   3
stranger; but there is also a legend about Antilochus, that a girl from Ilion on her way to the river Scamander met his spirit, fell in love with it and devoted herself to his tomb. It is also said some young shepherds were playing dice near Achilles' altar, and one struck the other with his staff and would have killed him if Patroclus had not frightened them: "One murder over a dice game is enough."[69]
You may hear these stories from the cowherds and all the   4
inhabitants of Ilion, since we keep in close touch, living as we do on the banks of the mouth of the Hellespont. For us, as you see, the sea is like a river.

[69] Patroclus had been forced into exile after killing a companion over a dice game (*Il.* 23.89–90).

23. Ἄγε δή, ξένε, τὴν ἀσπίδα ἤδη ἀναλάβωμεν, ἣν ὁ Πρωτεσίλεως Ὁμήρῳ τε ἠγνοῆσθαί φησι καὶ ποιηταῖς πᾶσι.

2   ΦΟΙΝ. Ποθοῦντι ἀποδίδως, ἀμπελουργέ, τὸν περὶ αὐτῆς λόγον· σπάνιον δὲ οἶμαι ἀκούσεσθαι.

ΑΜΠ. Σπανιώτατον· προσέχων δὲ ἀκροῶ.

ΦΟΙΝ. Προσέχων λέγεις; οὐδὲ τὰ θηρία ἐς τὸν Ὀρφέα οὕτως ἐκεχήνει ᾄδοντα, ὡς ἐγώ σου ἀκούων τά τε ὦτα ἵστημι καὶ τὸν νοῦν ἐγρήγορα καὶ ξυλλέγομαι ἐς τὴν μνήμην πάντα. ἡγοῦμαι δὲ καὶ τῶν ἐπὶ Τροίαν ἐστρατευκότων εἷς εἶναι· τοσοῦτον κατέσχημαι τοῖς ἡμιθέοις ὑπὲρ ὧν διαλεγόμεθα.

3   ΑΜΠ. Οὐκοῦν, ἐπειδὴ φρονεῖς οὕτω, αἴρωμεν ἐξ Αὐλίδος, ὦ ξένε. τὸ γὰρ ἐκεῖ ξυνειλέχθαι σφᾶς ἀληθές. τὰ δ' ἐμβατήρια τοῦ λόγου τῷ Πρωτεσίλεῳ εὔ-
4   χθω. ὡς μὲν δὴ τὴν Μυσίαν οἱ Ἀχαιοὶ πρὸ Τροίας ἐπόρθησαν ἐπὶ Τηλέφῳ τότε οὖσαν, καὶ ὡς ὁ Τήλεφος ὑπὲρ τῶν ἑαυτοῦ μαχόμενος ἐτρώθη ὑπὸ Ἀχιλλέως, ἔστι σοι καὶ ποιητῶν ἀκούειν· οὐ γὰρ ἐκλέλειπται αὐτοῖς ταῦτα.

5   τὸ δὲ πιστεύειν ὡς ἀγνοήσαντες οἱ Ἀχαιοὶ τὴν χώραν τὰ τοῦ Πριάμου ἄγειν τε καὶ φέρειν ᾤοντο, διαβάλλει τὸν Ὁμήρου λόγον ὃν περὶ Κάλχαντος ᾄδει τοῦ μάντεως· εἰ γὰρ ἐπὶ μαντικῇ ἔπλεον καὶ τὴν τέχνην ἡγεμόνα ἐποιοῦντο, πῶς ἂν ἄκοντες ἐκεῖ καθ-
6   ωρμίσθησαν; πῶς δ' ἂν καθορμισθέντες ἠγνόησαν ὅτι μὴ ἐς Τροίαν ἥκουσι, καὶ ταῦτα πολλοῖς μὲν βουκόλοις ἐντετυχηκότες, πολλοῖς δὲ ποιμέσι; νέμεταί τε

23. But now, stranger, let us take up the story of the shield, which Protesilaus says is unknown to Homer and to all the other poets.

Phoenician. I am very eager for you to tell me about it,   2
vinedresser—I expect I am going to hear an unusual story.

Vinedresser. Very unusual, so listen attentively.

Phoenician. Attentively? Not even the beasts gaped at Orpheus' singing such as I do—my ears strained, my mind alert and ready to commit everything to memory. I feel as if I were one of the army which has sailed for Troy, so possessed am I by the demigods we are discussing.

Vinedresser. Since you feel that way, stranger, let us set   3
sail from Aulis—for the story that they mustered there first is true—and let the embarkation offerings for our story be made to Protesilaus. Now then, as to the story that   4
before Troy the Achaeans ravaged Mysia which was then under Telephus' rule, and that Telephus was wounded by Achilles while fighting to defend his people, you can learn that even from the poets, who haven't left out this part.[70]

But to believe that the Achaeans, in ignorance of the   5
country, thought they were plundering Priam's land, does an injustice to Homer's account of Calchas the prophet. For if they sailed after consulting a seer and allowed his skill to guide them, then how could they have landed in Mysia unless they wanted to? And once they had landed,   6
how could they not have known they weren't at Troy, although they encountered many cowherds and shepherds?

[70] On the narrative of the battle with Telephus, see Introduction §10.

171

γὰρ ἡ χώρα μέχρι θαλάσσης καὶ τοὔνομα ἐρωτᾶν τῆς
7 ξένης ξύνηθες, οἶμαι, τοῖς καταπλέουσιν. εἰ δὲ καὶ
μηδενὶ τούτων ἐνέτυχον, μηδὲ ἤροντο τῶν τοιούτων
οὐδέν, ἀλλ᾽ Ὀδυσσεύς γε καὶ Μενέλεως ἐς Τροίαν ἤδη
ἀφιγμένω τε καὶ πεπρεσβευκότε καὶ τὰ κρήδεμνα τοῦ
Ἰλίου εἰδότε, οὐκ ἄν μοι δοκοῦσι περιιδεῖν ταῦτα, οὐδ᾽
ἂν ξυγχωρῆσαι τῷ στρατῷ διαμαρτάνοντι τῆς πολε-
8 μίας. ἑκόντες μὲν δὴ οἱ Ἀχαιοὶ τοὺς Μυσοὺς ἐληί-
ζοντο, λόγου ἐς αὐτοὺς ἥκοντος ὡς ἄριστα ἠπειρωτῶν
πράττοιεν, καί πῃ καὶ δεδιότες μὴ πρόσοικοι τῷ Ἰλίῳ
9 ὄντες ἐς κοινωνίαν τῶν κινδύνων μετακληθῶσι. Τη-
λέφῳ δὲ Ἡρακλείδῃ τε ὄντι καὶ ἄλλως γενναίῳ καὶ
ὡπλισμένης γῆς ἄρχοντι, οὐκ ἀνεκτὰ ταῦτα ἐφαίνετο,
ὅθεν πολλὴν μὲν ἀσπίδα παρέταττε, πολλὴν δὲ ἵππον.
10 ἦγε δὲ τοὺς μὲν ἐκ τῆς ὑπ᾽ αὐτῷ Μυσίας (ἦρχε δέ,
οἶμαι πάσης, ὁπόση ἐπὶ θαλάττῃ), οἱ δὲ ἐκ τῶν ἄνω
Μυσῶν ξυνεμάχουν, οὓς Ἀβίους τε οἱ ποιηταὶ κα-
λοῦσι καὶ ἵππων ποιμένας καὶ τὸ γάλα αὐτῶν πίνον-
11 τας· τῆς τε γὰρ τῶν Ἀχαιῶν διανοίας καθ᾽ ἣν ἐποιοῦ-
ντο τοὺς περίπλους οὐκ οὔσης ἀδήλου, Τληπολέμου
τε πέμψαντος ἐπὶ Ῥοδίας ὁλκάδος ἄγγελον ὡς ἀδελ-
φὸν καὶ κελεύσαντος ἀπὸ γλώττης αὐτῷ σημαίνειν
ὁπόσα τῶν Ἀχαιῶν ἐν Αὐλίδι διῄσθετο (γράμματα

71 Although he could have simply asserted the "authority" of
Protesilaus, the vinedresser prefers to employ rationalistic argu-
ments; see Introduction §5.   72 According to Od. 11.517–22
(cf. Little Iliad, M. L. West 2013, 190–91), Telephus' son Eury-
pylos did in fact join the Trojans at a later stage in the war.

For the country is inhabited right to the coast, and of
course those who arrive somewhere by sea customarily ask
the name of the foreign country. But even if they met   7
no one, and asked no such questions, still Odysseus and
Menelaus, who had both already gone to Troy as ambas-
sadors, and knew the battlements of Ilion, wouldn't have
stood by and allowed the army to miss the enemy com-
pletely.[71] No, the Achaeans were raiding Mysia deliber-   8
ately, since word had reached them that these were the
wealthiest people on the mainland, probably also because
they were afraid that, as Troy's neighbors, the Mysians
would be summoned to join in the war.[72] Now Telephus,   9
who was a son of Heracles, a man of spirit and ruler of a
powerful country, wouldn't stand for this; so he collected
a large force of infantry and cavalry against them. His   10
army was drawn from his part of Mysia. I believe he ruled
all the coastal areas—and there came from upper Mysia
as allies those whom the poets call the Abioi, the shep-
herds of horses and drinkers of their milk.[73] Not only was 11
the intent behind the Achaeans' expedition obvious, but
also Telephus' brother Tlepolemos had sent him a mes-
senger on a Rhodian merchant ship with orders to report
verbally—writing hadn't yet been invented—all he had

[73] Cf. *Il.* 13.4–7, where the "close-fighting Mysians" are listed
along with "horse-rearing Thracians, the noble Horse-milkers
and the milk-eating Abioi, the most just of men." These are nor-
mally taken as far northern barbarian tribes, but Posidonius
(Strabo 7.3.2 = fr. 277a Edelstein-Kidd) interpreted them as
northern kinsman to the southern Mysians, and the vinedresser
adds them to the army of Telephus.

γὰρ οὔπω εὔρητο), πᾶσα ἡ μεσόγεια ἐς ξυμμαχίαν
καταβεβήκει καὶ τῷ πεδίῳ ἐπεκύμαινε τὰ Μύσιά τε
12 καὶ Σκυθικὰ ἔθνη. λέγει δὲ ὁ Πρωτεσίλεως ὅτι καὶ
μέγιστος αὐτοῖς ἀγώνων γένοιτο τῶν τε ἐν αὐτῇ τῇ
Τροίᾳ καὶ ὁπόσοι πρὸς βαρβάρους ὕστερον διεπολε-
13 μήθησαν Ἕλλησι. καὶ γὰρ κατὰ πλῆθος εὐδόκιμοι
καὶ κατ᾽ ἄνδρα ἦσαν ἡ ξυμμαχία τοῦ Τηλέφου, καὶ
ὥσπερ ὑπὸ τῶν Ἀχαιῶν Αἰακίδαι τε ᾔδοντο καὶ Διο-
μήδεις καὶ Πάτροκλοι, οὕτω Τηλέφου τε ὄνομα ἦν καὶ
Αἴμου τοῦ Ἄρεος· ὀνομαστότατοι δὲ ἦσαν Ἕλωρός
τε καὶ Ἀκταῖος ποταμοῦ παῖδες τοῦ κατὰ Σκυθίαν
14 Ἴστρου. τὴν μὲν δὴ ἀπόβασιν οὐ ξυνεχώρουν οἱ Μυ-
σοὶ ποιεῖσθαι τοξεύοντες ἀπὸ τῆς γῆς καὶ ἀκοντίζον-
τες, οἱ δὲ Ἀχαιοὶ καὶ μὴ ξυγχωρούντων ἐβιάζοντο,
καί τινας καὶ ὤκελλον τῶν νεῶν οἱ Ἀρκάδες ἅτε
πρῶτον πλέοντες καὶ θαλάσσης οὔπω γεγυμνασμέ-
15 νοι. φησὶ γάρ, ὥς που γινώσκεις, Ὅμηρος ὅτι μήτε
ναυτικοὶ ἦσαν πρὸ Ἰλίου Ἀρκάδες μήτε ἔργων θαλατ-
τίων ἥπτοντο, ἀλλ᾽ ἐπὶ νεῶν ἑξήκοντα ὁ Ἀγαμέμνων
ἐσηγάγετο αὐτοὺς ἐς τὴν θάλασσαν, αὐτὸς ἐπιδοὺς
ναῦς οὔπω πεπλευκόσιν. ὅθεν ἐπιστήμην μὲν ὁπόση
πολεμικὴ καὶ ῥώμην ἐς τὰ πεζὰ παρείχοντο, πλέοντες
16 δὲ οὔτε ὁπλῖται ἀγαθοὶ ἦσαν οὔτε ἐρέται. τὰς μὲν δὴ
ναῦς ἀπειρίᾳ τε καὶ τόλμῃ ὤκελλον καὶ πολλοὶ μὲν

74 Tlepolemos was, like Telephus, a son of Heracles, who had
colonized Rhodes when forced to flee Greece after murdering a
kinsman (Il. 2.653–70; Pind. Ol. 7); thus he might be imagined to

174

heard the Achaeans say at Aulis.[74] As a result, all the peoples of the interior came west to join the army, and waves of Mysian and Scythian tribes covered the plain. Protesilaus says it was the largest battle of all, including not only those fought at Troy but also those fought later by Greeks against barbarians. The army of Telephus and his allies was glorious both in magnitude and in individuals, and the glory of the Aeacidae and men like Diomedes and Patroclus on the Achaean side was matched by the names of Telephus and Haimus, son of Ares. The most famous were Heloros and Actaeus, the sons of the river Danube in Scythia.[75] The Mysians resisted their attempt to land. They covered them with arrows and spears from the shore. The Achaeans, on the other hand, had to force their landing because of the fierce resistance, but also the Arcadians among them, who were at sea for the first time and inexperienced in sailing, ran aground some of their ships. You know of course that Homer says the Arcadians had not sailed or learned anything of seafaring before Ilion, but that Agamemnon had brought them to sea in sixty ships, which he himself provided, to men who had never yet sailed.[76] As infantry therefore they contributed military skill and strength, but on board ship they were neither good soldiers nor oarsmen. At any rate, through inexperience and rashness they had run aground their ships, and

have been one of the Greek allies who assembled at Aulis but who was not averse to giving secret information to his neighbor and half brother, Telephus.

[75] They can be identified also in the frieze of the Pergamon altar (Introduction §10).

[76] Following *Il.* 2.603–14.

PHILOSTRATUS

αὐτῶν ἐτρώθησαν ὑπὸ τῶν ἐπὶ τῇ ῥαχίᾳ τεταγμένων,
ὀλίγοι δὲ ἀπέθανον· Ἀχιλλεὺς δὲ καὶ Πρωτεσίλεως
δείσαντες ὑπὲρ τῶν Ἀρκάδων ὥσπερ ἀπὸ συνθήματος
ἄμφω ἅμα ἐς τὴν γῆν ἐπεπήδησαν καὶ ἀπεώσαντο
τοὺς Μυσοὺς εὐοπλοτάτω ὀφθέντε καὶ καλλίστω τοῦ
Ἑλληνικοῦ, τοῖς δ᾽ ἄγαν βαρβάροις καὶ δαίμονες
17 ἐδοξάτην. ἐπεὶ δὲ ὁ Τήλεφος ἐπανήγαγε τὴν στρατιὰν
ἐς τὸ πεδίον καὶ προσέπλευσαν οἱ Ἀχαιοὶ καθ᾽ ἡσυ-
χίαν, ἐξεπήδων αὐτίκα τῶν νεῶν πλὴν κυβερνήτου καὶ
περίνεω πάντες οὓς ἡ ναῦς ἦγεν, ἐτάττοντο δὲ ὡς ἐς
18 μάχην κόσμον καὶ σιωπὴν ἐν θυμῷ ἔχοντες. ὀρθῶς
γὰρ τοῦτο τὸν Ὅμηρον περὶ αὐτῶν εἰρηκέναι φησὶν
ἐπαινοῦντα τὸ τῆς Ἑλληνικῆς μάχης ἦθος, ἧς ξύμ-
19 βουλον γενέσθαι Αἴαντα τὸν Τελαμῶνος λέγει. Μενε-
σθέως γὰρ τοῦ Ἀθηναίου τακτικωτάτου τῶν βασι-
λέων ἐς Τροίαν ἐλθόντος καὶ διδάσκοντος ἐν Αὐλίδι
τὴν στρατιὰν πᾶσαν ὡς χρὴ συνηρμόσθαι, κραυγῇ
τε χρωμένοις μὴ ἐπιπλήττοντος, οὐ ξυνεχώρει ὁ Αἴας
ἀλλ᾽ ἐπετίμα, γυναικεῖόν τε ἀποφαίνων καὶ ἄτακτον.
ἔλεγε γὰρ ὅτι καὶ τὸν θυμὸν ἡ κραυγὴ κακῶς ἑρμη-
νεύει.
20   ταχθῆναι δὲ πρὸς μὲν τοὺς Μυσοὺς ἑαυτόν τε καὶ
τὸν Ἀχιλλέα φησὶν ὁμοῦ τῷ Πατρόκλῳ, πρὸς δὲ τὸν
τοῦ Ἄρεος Αἷμον Διομήδην τε καὶ Παλαμήδην καὶ
Σθένελον· πρὸς δὲ τοὺς ἀπὸ τοῦ Ἴστρου ἥκοντας οἱ
Ἀτρεῖδαί τε καὶ ὁ Λοκρὸς καὶ οἱ λοιποὶ ἐτάχθησαν.
21 Αἴας δὲ ὁ μέγας τοὺς μὲν τὰ πλήθη ἀποκτείνοντας
θεριστὰς ἡγεῖτο μέγα οὐδὲν ἀμῶντας, τοὺς δὲ τῶν

176

many of them were wounded by the Mysian troops stationed on the rocky shore; but few were killed, because Achilles and Protesilaus became alarmed at their situation and both at the same moment, as if it had been prearranged, leaped ashore and routed the Mysians. They were the fairest and most impressively armed of the Greeks, and to these simple barbarians they seemed like gods. When Telephus had retired with his army to the plain, and 17 the Achaeans had landed without further resistance, the whole force on each ship, except for a helmsman and noncombatant, immediately came ashore and arranged themselves for battle, remaining emotionally disciplined and quiet. Protesilaus says Homer relates about them this cus- 18 tom of Greek battle correctly and praises it, which he says was the idea of Ajax son of Telamon; when Menestheus of 19 Athens, as the best tactician among the kings, had joined the expedition to Troy and taught the whole army at Aulis how to take up their positions, but didn't rebuke them when they raised a shout, Ajax objected and criticized this as being womanly and undisciplined. Shouting, he said, was a coward's way of showing spirit.

Protesilaus says that he himself, Achilles and Patroclus 20 were drawn up against the Mysians, while Diomedes, Palamedes and Sthenelus faced Haimus, son of Ares; the Atreidae, Ajax the Locrian and the rest were opposite the troops from the Danube. The greater Ajax, however, used 21 to consider soldiers who slew large numbers as reapers who harvested the small crops, and called those who over-

ἀρίστων κρατοῦντας δρυτόμους ἐκάλει καὶ ταύτης

22 αὐτὸν τῆς μάχης ἠξίου μᾶλλον. ταῦτά τοι καὶ ἐπὶ
τοὺς τοῦ ποταμοῦ παῖδας ᾖξεν οὔτε τοῦ μέρους ἑαυτοῦ
ὄντας καὶ τὸν τοῦ Ἕκτορος τρόπον ἀπὸ τεττάρων μα-
χομένους ἵππων, βαίνων τε σοβαρὸν μετὰ τῆς αἰχμῆς
πρὸς τὴν ἀσπίδα ἐδούπησε ταραχῆς ἕνεκα τῶν ἵπ-
πων· οἱ δὲ ἵπποι ἔκφρονές τε αὐτίκα ἐγένοντο καὶ ὀρ-
θοὶ ἀνεσκίρτησαν, ὅθεν ἀπιστήσαντες οἱ Σκύθαι τῷ
ἅρματι ἀπεπήδησάν τε αὐτοῦ ἀτακτοῦντος καὶ ξυν-
έπεσον τῷ Αἴαντι, λόγου τε ἀξίως μαχόμενοι ἄμφω

23 ἀπέθανον. μνημονεύει ὁ Πρωτεσίλεως καὶ τῶν τοῦ
Παλαμήδους ἔργων ὡς μεγάλων, οἷς αὐτός τε καὶ
Διομήδης καὶ Σθένελος τὸν Αἶμον καὶ τοὺς ἀμφ'
αὐτὸν ἀποκτείναντες, οὐδὲ ἀριστείων ὁ Παλαμήδης
ἠξίου τυγχάνειν ἀλλ' ἐκεῖνα μὲν τῷ Διομήδει ξυνεχώ-
ρει ἔχειν, ἐπειδὴ πάνθ' ὑπὲρ τῆς τῶν πολεμικῶν τιμῆς
τε καὶ δόξης ἐγίνωσκεν αὐτὸν πράττοντα· σοφίας δὲ
εἴ τινα στέφανον προθείη τὸ Ἑλληνικόν, οὐκ ἂν ἐκ-
στῆναι τούτου ἑτέρῳ, σοφίας τε ἀπ' ἀρχῆς ἐρῶν καὶ
μελετῶν τοῦτο.

24 Τηλέφῳ δὲ ὁ Πρωτεσίλεως αὐτὸς μὲν συμπλακῆναί
φησι καὶ τὴν ἀσπίδα ζῶντος περισπάσαι, τὸν δὲ
Ἀχιλλέα γυμνῷ προσπεσόντα τρῶσαι αὐτὸν εὐθὺ τοῦ
μηροῦ καὶ ἰατρὸν μὲν ὕστερον ἐν Τροίᾳ γενέσθαι τοῦ
τραύματος, τότε δὲ λειποθυμῆσαί τε ὑπ' αὐτοῦ ὁ Τή-
λεφος καὶ ἀποθανεῖν ἄν, εἰ μὴ οἱ Μυσοὶ ξυνδραμόν-
τες ἀνείλοντο αὐτὸν ἐκ τῆς μάχης· ὅτε δὴ λέγονται
πολλοὶ τῶν Μυσῶν ἐπ' αὐτῷ πεσεῖν, ὑφ' ὧν ἡματω-

came their champions the woodcutters. He thought this
share of the fighting more worth his attention; therefore   22
he rushed upon the sons of the river, even though they
were not on his side of the field and were fighting, like
Hector did, from a four-horse chariot. As he came on, he
beat his spear violently against his shield to frighten the
horses, who were immediately terrified and reared straight
up. At that point the two Scythians lost confidence in their
chariot, leaping from it as it went out of control, and at-
tacked Ajax—they struggled bravely, but he killed them
both. Protesilaus also told of the noble deeds of Palame-   23
des, in which he joined Diomedes and Sthenelus in slay-
ing Haimus and his men, though Palamedes declined the
prize for valor, conceding it to Diomedes because he knew
his sole concern to be military glory and recognition. If the
Greek army should ever offer a prize for wisdom, he said,
he would yield it to no one, since this was what he had
always loved and followed.

Protesilaus said that he himself came to grips with   24
Telephus and stripped him of his shield while he was still
alive. When he had been disarmed, Achilles attacked and
wounded him in the thigh—the wound he was later to
heal at Troy,[77] but at that time Telephus lost consciousness
from it, and would have been killed if the Mysians had not
joined to rescue him from the battle. It was then that many
of the Mysians are said to have fallen in the fight over him,

[77] Told in Euripides' *Telephus* (see Introduction §10). "Troy"
here for "Aulis" looks like another slip by the vinedresser (see
Introduction §7) rather than a variant version.

25 μένον ῥυῆναι τὸν Κάικον. λέγει δὲ ὡς καὶ δικάσαιτο
μὲν πρὸς αὐτὸν ὁ Ἀχιλλεὺς περὶ τῆς ἀσπίδος, ἐπειδὴ
ἐτετρώκει τὸν Τήλεφον, οἱ δὲ Ἀχαιοὶ ψηφίσαιντο
αὐτῷ μᾶλλον προσήκειν τὴν ἀσπίδα, ὡς οὐκ ἂν τοῦ
26 Τηλέφου τρωθέντος εἰ μὴ ἐκείνης ἐγυμνώθη. φησὶ δὲ
ὅτι καὶ Μυσαὶ γυναῖκες ἀφ' ἵππων ξυνεμάχοντο τοῖς
ἀνδράσιν, ὥσπερ Ἀμαζόνες, καὶ ἦρχε τῆς ἵππου ταύ-
27 της Ἱέρα γυνὴ Τηλέφου. ταύτην μὲν δὴ λέγεται Νι-
ρεὺς ἀποκτεῖναι (τὸ γὰρ μειρακιῶδες τοῦ στρατοῦ καὶ
οὔπω εὐδόκιμον πρὸς αὐτὰς ἔταξαν), πεσούσης δὲ
ἀνέκραγον αἱ Μυσαὶ καὶ ξυνταράξασαι τὴν ἑαυτῶν
28 ἵππον ἐς τὰ τοῦ Καΐκου ἕλη ἀπηνέχθησαν. τὴν δὲ
Ἱέραν ταύτην ὁ Πρωτεσίλεως μεγίστην τε ὧν εἶδε
γυναικῶν γενέσθαι λέγει, καλλίστην τε ἁπασῶν ὁπό-
σαι ὄνομα ἐπὶ κάλλει ἤραντο. Ἑλένην μὲν γὰρ τὴν
Μενέλεω γυναῖκα ἰδεῖν οὔ φησιν ἐν Τροίᾳ, νυνὶ δὲ
ὁρᾶν μὲν αὐτὴν τὴν Ἑλένην καὶ οὐ μέμφεσθαι τὸ
ὑπὲρ αὐτῆς ἀποθανεῖν· εἰ δὲ ἐνθυμηθείη τὴν Ἱέραν,
τοσοῦτον αὐτήν φησι πλεονεκτεῖν τῆς Ἑλένης, ὅσον
29 κἀκείνη τῶν Τρωάδων. καὶ οὐδὲ αὕτη, ξένε, Ὁμήρου
ἐπαινέτου ἔτυχεν, ἀλλὰ Ἑλένῃ χαριζόμενος οὐκ ἐσή-
γάγετο ἐς τὰ ἑαυτοῦ ποιήματα θείαν γυναῖκα, ἐφ' ᾗ
καὶ παθεῖν τι Ἀχαιοὶ καὶ πεσούσῃ λέγονται, καὶ
παρακελεύσασθαι πρεσβύτεροι νέοις μὴ σκυλεύειν
30 Ἱέραν μηδὲ προσάπτεσθαι κειμένης. ἐν ταύτῃ, ξένε,
τῇ μάχῃ πολλοὶ τῶν Ἀχαιῶν ἐτρώθησαν, καὶ λουτρὰ

---

78 According to *Il.* 2.671, Nireus was "the most beautiful man

with whose blood the Kaikos river flowed red. He says that   25
Achilles disputed with him over the shield on the grounds
that it was he who had wounded Telephus, but the Achae-
ans voted that the shield belonged more properly to him,
since Telephus would not have been wounded if he hadn't
been stripped of it. He says that the women of Mysia also   26
helped their husbands to fight on horseback, like Ama-
zons, and the commander of this cavalry was Telephus'
wife Hiera. She is said to have been killed by Nireus—   27
the youngest and least well-known part of the army had
been assigned to oppose the women[78]—and when she had
fallen the Mysian women shouted in alarm, frightening
their horses, and were carried away to the marshy ground
around the Kaikos. This Hiera, claims Protesilaus, was the   28
tallest woman he had ever seen, and the fairest of all who
were famous for beauty. As for Menelaus' wife Helen, he
didn't see her at Troy, but he sees her now and finds no
fault with dying for her; but when he remembers Hiera,
she seems to him to surpass Helen by as far as Helen did
the women of Troy. Yet not even such a woman, stranger,   29
received Homer's praises, but in deference to Helen he
did not introduce into his poems the godlike woman over
whom the Achaeans are said to have been moved even
when she had died, and the older soldiers commanded the
younger ones not to strip the arms from Hiera, or even to
touch her corpse.[79] Many of the Achaeans were wounded   30

before Troy" after Achilles, but he was weak and his army was
small; he is not mentioned again in Homer.

[79] Hiera is identifiable also in the Pergamon frieze and clearly
modeled after the beautiful Amazon Penthesileia, who fought and
died at Troy (Introduction §10).

τοῖς τετρωμένοις μαντευτὰ ἐγένετο, πηγαὶ θερμαὶ ἐν
Ἰωνίᾳ, ἃς ἔτι καὶ νῦν Ἀγαμεμνονείους καλοῦσιν οἱ
Σμύρναν οἰκοῦντες. ἀπέχουσι δέ, οἶμαι, τετταράκοντα
στάδια τοῦ ἄστεος καὶ ἀνῆπτό ποτε αὐτοῖς αἰχμά-
λωτα κράνη Μύσια.

24. ΦΟΙΝ. Τί οὖν, ἀμπελουργέ, φῶμεν ἑκόντα τὸν
Ὅμηρον ἢ ἄκοντα παραλιπεῖν ταῦτα οὕτως ἡδέα καὶ
ποιητικὰ ὄντα;

2 ΑΜΠ. Ἑκόντα ἴσως, ξένε· βουληθεὶς γὰρ τὴν Ἑλέ-
νην ὡς ἀρίστην γυναικῶν ὑμνῆσαι ἐπὶ τῷ κάλλει καὶ
τὰς Τρωικὰς μάχας ὡς μεγίστας τῶν ἀλλαχοῦ διαπο-
λεμηθεισῶν ἐπαινέσαι, Παλαμήδην τε τὸν θεῖον ἐξαι-
ρῶν ἅπαντος λόγου δι᾿ Ὀδυσσέα, Ἀχιλλεῖ τε μόνῳ τὰ
μαχιμώτατα τῶν ἔργων οὕτως ἀνατιθεὶς ὡς ἐκλανθά-
νεσθαι τῶν ἄλλων Ἀχαιῶν ὅτε Ἀχιλλεὺς μάχοιτο,
οὔτε Μύσια ἐποίησεν ἔπη, οὔτε ἐς μνήμην κατέστη
τοῦ ἔργου τούτου ἐν ᾧ καὶ γυνὴ καλλίων Ἑλένης
εὕρητο ἂν καὶ ἄνδρες οὐ παρὰ πολὺ Ἀχιλλέως τὴν
ἀνδρείαν καὶ ἀγὼν εὐδοκιμώτατος· Παλαμήδους δὲ
μνημονεύσας οὐκ ἂν εὗρεν ὅτῳ ποτὲ κρύψει τὸ τοῦ
Ὀδυσσέως ὄνειδος ἐπ᾿ αὐτῷ.

25. ΦΟΙΝ. Πῶς οὖν ὁ Πρωτεσίλεως περὶ τοῦ Ὁμή-
ρου φρονεῖ; βασανίζειν γάρ που αὐτὸν ἔφασκες τὰ
τούτου ποιήματα.

2 ΑΜΠ. Τὸν Ὅμηρόν φησι, ξένε, καθάπερ ἐν ἁρμο-

in this battle, and a healing bath for the wounded was revealed to them by an oracle: the hot springs in Ionia, which the Smyrnaeans even to this day call the springs of Agamemnon.[80] They are forty stades away from the city, and they used to be decorated with captured Mysian helmets.

24. *Phoenician* Well, vinedresser, shall we say that it was against his will or on purpose that Homer left out such a fine story, and quite suited to a poem?

Vinedresser. It was probably intentional. He wished to glorify Helen as the best for her beauty, and to exalt the battles at Troy war as the greatest ever fought; he also expunged the godlike Palamedes from the entire story for Odysseus' sake, and attributed the greatest feat of arms to Achilles alone, so that when he was fighting we should forget about everyone else. So he neither composed a poem about the Mysian war, nor made any mention of this event, in which would have been found a more beautiful than Helen, men not far from[81] Achilles in bravery, and a most glorious struggle. Also, if he once mentioned Palamedes he could not have found any way to conceal Odysseus' disgraceful act against him.[82]

25. *Phoenician.* What does Protesilaus think of Homer? You said that he goes over his poems carefully.

Vinedresser. He says that, to borrow a phrase from mu-

---

[80] Bean (1966, 52, 272). Most warm springs were called "baths of Heracles" (Ath. 11.512f; Dover [1968] on Ar. *Nub.* 1051); Paus. 7.5.11 says that Agamemnon is honored at baths near Clazomenae.

[81] Grossardt (2006a) disputes this meaning, but see Schmid (1887, 4:461–62).   [82] The same observation in *VA* 4.16 (see Introduction §1; cf. Strabo 8.6.2) and in 43.15 it is made the result of an agreement with the ghost of Odysseus.

νία μουσικῇ πάντας ψῆλαι τοὺς ποιητικοὺς τῶν τρό-
πων, καὶ τοὺς ποιητὰς ἐφ᾽ οἷς ἐγένετο ὑπερβεβλῆσθαι
πάντας ἐν ὅτῳ ἕκαστος ἦν αὐτῶν κράτιστος· μεγα-
λορρημοσύνην τε γὰρ ὑπὲρ τὸν Ὀρφέα ἀσκῆσαι,
ἡδονῇ τε ὑπερβαλέσθαι τὸν Ἡσίοδον καὶ ἄλλῳ ἄλ-
3 λον· καὶ λόγον μὲν ὑποθέσθαι Τρωικόν, ἐς ὃν ἡ τύχη
τὰς πάντων Ἑλλήνων τε καὶ βαρβάρων ἀρετὰς ξυνή-
νεγκεν, ἐσαγαγέσθαι δὲ ἐς αὐτὸν πολέμους τοὺς μὲν
πρὸς ἄνδρας, τοὺς δὲ πρὸς ἵππους καὶ τείχη, τοὺς δὲ
πρὸς ποταμούς, τοὺς δὲ πρὸς θεοὺς καὶ θεάς, καὶ
ὁπόσα κατ᾽ εἰρήνην εἰσὶ καὶ χοροὺς καὶ ᾠδὰς καὶ
ἔρωτας καὶ δαῖτας, ἔργα τε ὧν γεωργία ἅπτεται, καὶ
ὥρας, αἳ σημαίνουσιν ὁπόσα χρὴ ἐς τὴν γῆν πράτ-
τειν, καὶ ναυτιλίας καὶ ὁπλοποιίαν τὴν ἐν Ἡφαίστῳ,
4 εἴδη τε ἀνδρῶν καὶ ἤθη ποικίλα. πάντα ταῦτα τὸν
Ὅμηρον δαιμονίως ἐξειργάσθαι φησὶ καὶ τοὺς μὴ
5 ἐρῶντας αὐτοῦ μαίνεσθαι. καλεῖ δὲ αὐτὸν καὶ οἰκι-
στὴν Τροίας, ἐπειδὴ εὐδοκίμησεν ἐκ τῶν Ὁμήρου ἐπ᾽
6 αὐτῇ θρήνων. θαυμάζει δὲ αὐτοῦ καὶ ὅσα ἐπιτιμᾷ τοῖς
ὁμοτέχνοις, ὅτι μὴ τραχέως διορθοῦταί σφας ἀλλ᾽
7 οἷον λανθάνων· Ἡσίοδον μὲν ἐν ἄλλοις τε οὐκ ὀλίγοις
καὶ νὴ Δί᾽ ἐν τοῖς ἐκτυπώμασι τῶν ἀσπίδων· ἑρμη-
νεύων γὰρ οὗτός ποτε τὴν τοῦ Κύκνου ἀσπίδα, τὸ τῆς
Γοργοῦς εἶδος ὑπτίως τε καὶ οὐ ποιητικῶς ᾖσεν, ὅθεν
ἐπιστρέφων αὐτὸν ὁ Ὅμηρος

τῇ δ᾽ ἐπὶ μὲν Γοργὼ βλοσυρῶπις ἐστεφάνωτο
δεινὸν δερκομένη, περὶ δὲ Δεῖμός τε Φόβος τε

sic, Homer played all the modes of poetry, and surpassed all the poets preceding him in their strongest qualities. He practices much more forceful expressions than Orpheus, in charm he surpasses Hesiod, and so on. He chose for his 3 subject the story of Troy, in which fate brought together the virtues of Greeks and barbarians. To it he added warfare against men, against horses and walls, against rivers, gods and goddesses, as well as all the pursuits of peace: dancing, song, love, banqueting, the life of the farmer and the seasons which show him his agricultural tasks, seafaring, the making of armor in his section on Hephaestus, the types of men and their varied characters. All these he 4 worked out with divine skill, and those who do not love him are out of their minds. He calls Homer the founding 5 hero of Troy, since it was through his lament for it that its fame began. He admires in Homer also the way he points 6 out faults in his fellow poets, since he does not correct them harshly, but almost imperceptibly. He corrects Hes- 7 iod, for example, in many other passages, but especially in the reliefs on the shields. That poet, describing Cycnus' shield (*Shield of Heracles* 223–24) had composed the Gorgon's appearance flat and unpoetically, and Homer converted it to tell of the Gorgon this way (*Il.* 10.36–37):

> Upon the shield was set a grim-faced Gorgon,
> with terrible glance, around her fright and fear.

8 οὑτωσὶ τὴν Γοργὼ ᾄδει. Ὀρφέα δὲ ἐν πολλοῖς τῶν
κατὰ θεολογίαν ὑπερῆρε, Μουσαῖον δὲ ἐν ᾠδαῖς χρη-
σμῶν, καὶ μὴν καὶ Παμφὼ σοφῶς μὲν ἐνθυμηθέντος
ὅτι Ζεὺς εἴη τὸ ζῳογονοῦν καὶ δι᾽ οὗ ἀνίσταται τὰ ἐκ
τῆς γῆς πάντα, εὐηθέστερον δὲ χρησαμένου τῷ λόγῳ
καὶ καταβεβλημένα ἔπη ἐς τὸν Δία ᾄσαντος. ἔστι
γὰρ τὰ τοῦ Παμφὼ ἔπη·

Ζεῦ κύδιστε, μέγιστε θεῶν, εἰλυμένε κόπρῳ
μηλείῃ τε καὶ ἱππείῃ καὶ ἡμιονείῃ

τὸν Ὅμηρον ὁ Πρωτεσίλεώς φησιν ἐπάξιον τοῦ Διὸς
ᾆσαι ὕμνον.

Ζεῦ κύδιστε, μέγιστε, κελαινεφές, αἰθέρι ναίων,

ὡς οἰκοῦντος μὲν αὐτοῦ τὸ καθαρώτατον, ἐργαζομένου
9 δὲ ἔμβια τὰ ὑπὸ τῷ αἰθέρι. καὶ τὰς μάχας δέ, ὁπόσαι
Ποσειδῶνι μὲν πρὸς Ἀπόλλω, Λητοῖ δὲ πρὸς Ἑρμῆν
ἐγένοντο, καὶ ὡς ἐμάχοντο ἡ Ἀθηνᾶ τῷ Ἄρει καὶ ὁ
Ἥφαιστος τῷ ὕδατι, ταῦτα τὸν Ὀρφέως τρόπον πε-
φιλοσοφῆσθαι τῷ Ὁμήρῳ φησὶ καὶ οὐ μεμπτὰ εἶναι
πρὸς ἔκπληξιν καὶ θεῖα, ὥσπερ τὸ

ἀμφὶ δὲ σάλπιγξε μέγας οὐρανός,

καὶ <ὡς> ἀνεπήδησεν Ἀϊδωνεὺς τοῦ θρόνου τινασσο-
μένης τῆς γῆς ἐκ Ποσειδῶνος.

10 μέμφεται δὲ τοῦ Ὁμήρου ἐκεῖνα· πρῶτον μὲν ὅτι
θεοὺς ἐγκαταμίξας ἀνθρώποις, περὶ μὲν τῶν ἀνθρώ-
πων μεγάλα εἴρηκε, περὶ δὲ τῶν θεῶν μικρὰ καὶ

186

Orpheus he surpassed in many ways in his descriptions of   8
the gods, Musaeus in his poetic oracles, and even Pam-
phos, who sagely realized that it was Zeus who engenders
life and through whom all things on earth came into being,
but expressed himself rather clumsily and addressed Zeus
in vulgar verses. Pamphos' verses run:

> Zeus most glorious, greatest of gods, in dung
>   enfolded
> of sheep and horse and ass. . . .

Whereas Homer, Protesilaus says, sang a hymn worthy of
Zeus (*Il.* 2.412):

> Zeus most glorious, greatest, dark-clouded, dwelling
>   in heaven. . . .

because he lives in the purest air, and gives life to all under
heaven. As for the battles between Poseidon and Apollo,   9
Leto and Hermes, Athena's fight against Ares, and that
of Hephaestus against the river, he says these have been
treated by Homer philosophically in the manner of Or-
pheus, and faultless in their breathtakingness and divinity,
for example the passage beginning

> great heaven trumpeted around (*Il.* 21.388)

and when Aidoneus leaped from his throne as the earth
was shaken by Poseidon (*Il.* 20.61–65).
    He finds fault with Homer, however, in the following:
first, because he confuses the gods with men, and says   10
great things about men, but about the gods petty and in-

187

φαῦλα· εἶτα ὅτι σαφῶς γινώσκων ὡς ἐν Αἰγύπτῳ ἡ
Ἑλένη ἐγένετο ἀπενεχθεῖσα ὑπὸ ἀνέμων ὁμοῦ τῷ Πά-
ριδι, ὁ δὲ ἄγει αὐτὴν ἐπὶ τὸ τοῦ Ἰλίου τεῖχος ὀψομέ-
νην τὰ ἐν τῷ πεδίῳ κακά, ἣν εἰκός, εἰ καὶ δι᾽ ἑτέραν
γυναῖκα ταῦτα ἐγίνετο, ξυγκαλύπτεσθαί τε καὶ μὴ
11 ὁρᾶν αὐτὰ διαβεβλημένου τοῦ γένους. ἐπαινουμένου
δὲ οὐδὲ ἐν αὐτῇ τῇ Τροίᾳ Πάριδος ἐπὶ τῇ ἁρπαγῇ τῆς
Ἑλένης, οὔτ᾽ ἂν Ἕκτορα τὸν σωφρονέστατον καρ-
τερῆσαί φησι τὸ μὴ οὐκ ἀποδοῦναι αὐτὴν τῷ Μενέ-
λεῳ ἐν Ἰλίῳ οὖσαν, οὔτ᾽ ἂν Πρίαμον ξυγχωρῆσαι τῷ
Πάριδι τρυφᾶν, πολλῶν ἤδη ἀπολωλότων αὐτῷ παί-
δων, οὔτ᾽ ἂν τὴν Ἑλένην διαφυγεῖν τὸ μὴ οὐκ ἀπο-
θανεῖν ὑπὸ τῶν Τρωάδων ὁπόσων ἤδη ἄνδρες ἀπωλώ-
λεισαν καὶ ἀδελφοὶ καὶ παῖδες· ἴσως δ᾽ ἂν καὶ
ἀποδρᾶναι αὐτὴν παρὰ τὸν Μενέλεων διὰ τὸ ἐν τῇ
12 Τροίᾳ μῖσος. ἐξηρήσθω δὴ ὁ ἀγὼν ὅν φησιν Ὅμηρος
ἀγωνίσασθαι τῷ Μενέλεῳ τὸν Πάριν ἐπὶ σπονδαῖς
τοῦ πολέμου· κατ᾽ Αἴγυπτόν τε γὰρ τὴν Ἑλένην εἶναι
καὶ τοὺς Ἀχαιοὺς πάλαι τοῦτο γινώσκοντας, ἐκείνῃ
μὲν ἐρρῶσθαι φράζειν, μάχεσθαι δὲ ὑπὲρ τοῦ ἐν
Τροίᾳ πλούτου.

13 οὐδὲ ἐκεῖνα ὁ Πρωτεσίλεως ἐπαινεῖ τοῦ Ὁμήρου,
ὅτι λόγον ὑποθέμενος Τρωικόν, ἀποπηδᾷ τοῦ λόγου
μετὰ τὸν Ἕκτορα, καθάπερ σπεύδων ἐπὶ τὸν ἕτερον

83 Cf. "Longinus," *Subl.* 9.7 (conflating the same two Homeric passages cited separately here): "In relating the wounds of the gods, their civil wars, vendettas, weeping, kidnapping and all sorts

significant things;[83] secondly, although he knew perfectly well that Helen was in Egypt—she and Paris had been carried there by a storm—he makes her go up on the wall of Troy to watch the sufferings on the field, although it is plausible that if any other woman had caused such things she would have veiled herself and refused to watch, when it was a disgrace to her sex. Since Paris' kidnapping of Helen was viewed with disapproval even in Troy itself, Protesilaus says that such a prudent man as Hector would never have condoned not giving her back to Menelaus if she had really been there, nor would Priam have permitted Paris such license when many of his sons had already died, nor would Helen have escaped death at the hands of the Trojan women whose husbands, brothers, and children had perished. Perhaps she would even have deserted to Menelaus because of her unpopularity at Troy. Indeed, the single combat which Homer says Menelaus had against Paris during a truce in the fighting must be canceled, since Helen was in Egypt, as the Achaeans had long known. They couldn't have cared less about her—they were fighting for Troy's wealth.[84]

Protesilaus also disapproves of Homer in this, that although his subject was Troy, he drops this story after Hector's death because he is in a hurry to get to the other

of sufferings, Homer seems to me to have done his best to make the men in the Trojan War into gods, and the gods into men."

[84] The allegation that Helen was not really in Troy at all is as old as Stesichorus (fr. 192), Hdt. 2.112–20, and Eur. *Hel.*, although in those accounts the Greeks attacked in the belief that she *was* there. The shade of Achilles in *VA* 4.16 tells the same story as Protesilaus here (see Introduction §1).

PHILOSTRATUS

τῶν λόγων, ᾧ τὸν Ὀδυσσέα ἐπιγράφει, καὶ ᾄδει μὲν
ἐν ᾠδαῖς Δημοδόκου τε καὶ Φημίου τήν τε τοῦ Ἰλίου
πόρθησιν καὶ τὸν Ἐπειοῦ τε καὶ Ἀθηνᾶς ἵππον, δίεισι
δὲ αὐτὰ ἀποτεμὼν τοῦ λόγου καὶ ἀνατιθεὶς Ὀδυσσεῖ
μᾶλλον, δι᾽ ὃν Κυκλώπων τε αὐτῷ ἐπενοήθη γένος
οὐδαμοῦ τῆς γῆς φύντες, Λαιστρυγόνες τε ἀνετυπώ-
θησαν, οὓς οὐδεὶς οἶδεν ὅπου γενόμενοι, Κίρκη τε δαί-
μων ἐξεποιήθη ⟨ἡ⟩ σοφὴ ἐπὶ φαρμάκοις καὶ θεαὶ ἕτε-
ραι ἐρᾶν αὐτοῦ καίτοι προήκοντος ἤδη ἐς ὠμὸν γῆρας,
ὅτε καὶ τὰς ὑακινθίνας κόμας, αἳ ἐπὶ τὴν Ναυσικάαν
αὐτῷ ἤνθησαν, φαίνεται ἔχων.

14   ὅθεν ὁ Πρωτεσίλεως παίγνιον τὸν Ὀδυσσέα καλεῖ
τοῦ Ὁμήρου· οὐδὲ γὰρ τῆς λεγομένης αὐτοῦ σοφίας
ἦρα ἡ κόρη· τί γὰρ σοφὸν ἢ εἶπε πρὸς τὴν Ναυσι-
κάαν ἢ ἔπραξε; καλεῖ δὲ αὐτὸν Ὁμήρου παίγνιον καὶ
ἐν τῇ ἄλῃ· καθεύδων τε γὰρ πολλαχοῦ ἀπόλλυται καὶ
ἐκφέρεται τῆς νεὼς τῶν Φαιάκων ὥσπερ ἀποθανὼν ἐν
15   τῇ εὐπλοίᾳ. τὴν δὲ τοῦ Ποσειδῶνος μῆνιν, δι᾽ ἣν οὔτε
ναῦς ὑπελείφθη τῷ Ὀδυσσεῖ οὐδεμία καὶ οἱ ἄνδρες οἱ
πληροῦντες αὐτὰς ἀπώλοντο, οὐχ ὑπὲρ τοῦ Πολυφή-
μου γενέσθαι φησίν· οὔτε γὰρ ἀφικέσθαι τὸν Ὀδυσ-
σέα ἐς ἤθη τοιαῦτα, οὔτ᾽ ἄν, εἰ Ποσειδῶνι Κύκλωψ
παῖς ἐγένετο, μηνῖσαι τὸν Ποσειδῶ ποτε ὑπὲρ τοῦ
τοιούτου παιδός, ὃς λέοντος ὠμοῦ δίκην τοὺς ἀνθρώ-
πους ἤσθιεν, ἀλλ᾽ ὑπὲρ Παλαμήδους υἱωνοῦ ὄντος
ἄπλουν μὲν τὴν θάλασσαν τῷ Ὀδυσσεῖ ἐποίει, δια-
φυγόντα δὲ αὐτὸν τὰ ἐκεῖ πάθη ἀπώλεσεν ⟨ἐν⟩ αὐτῇ
Ἰθάκῃ ὕστερον, θαλαττίαν, οἶμαι, αἰχμὴν ἐπ᾽ αὐτὸν

190

one—which he named after Odysseus—and he sings only
in the poems given to Demodocus and Phemius Troy's fall
and the horse built by Epeius and Athena, while his nar-
ration of these events is separated from the story and con-
nected rather with Odysseus, the man for whose sake the
race of Cyclopes (which don't exist anywhere) was in-
vented, and Laestrygonians were imagined (although no
one knows where they are), and the divine Circe who
knew all about magic potions, as well as other goddesses
were made to fall in love with him, although he was al-
ready reaching a premature old age, even when he was
made to appear with the hyacinth hair which blossomed
on him while he was with Nausicaa.

That is why Protesilaus calls Odysseus "Homer's play-
thing," since the girl didn't fall in love with his so-called
wisdom either; for what wise thing did he do or say in
Nausicaa's presence? He also calls him Homer's plaything
in his wanderings; for he was constantly being undone
when he fell asleep, and he was carried asleep off the
Phaeacians' ship as if he had died during a calm crossing.
As for the anger of Poseidon which made all his ships lost
and their crews perish, he says it was not on account of
Polyphemus; for Odysseus never reached such haunts,
and even if the Cyclops had been his child, Poseidon
would never have felt indignant on behalf of a son who ate
men like a savage lion. No it was for the sake of his grand-
son Palamedes that Poseidon made the sea impassable to
Odysseus, and after he had escaped his sufferings at sea
Poseidon had him killed in Ithaca itself, since it must have

14

15

16 δούς. λέγει δὲ καὶ τὴν Ἀχιλλέως μῆνιν οὐχ ὑπὲρ τῆς
τοῦ Χρύσου θυγατρὸς ἐμπεσεῖν τοῖς Ἕλλησιν, ἀλλὰ
17 κἀκεῖνον ὑπὲρ τοῦ Παλαμήδους μηνῖσαι. καὶ ἀποκεί-
σθω μοι ὁ λόγος οὗτος ἐς τὰ τοῦ Ἀχιλλέως ἔργα·
δίειμι γὰρ καὶ κατὰ ἕνα τοὺς ἥρως, ἀπαγγέλλων ὅσα
τοῦ Πρωτεσίλεω περὶ αὐτῶν ἤκουσα.
18   ΦΟΙΝ. Ἥκεις ἐπὶ τὸν ἥδιστον ἐμοὶ τῶν λόγων.
ἵππων γὰρ ἤδη δή με καὶ ἀνδρῶν "ἀμφὶ κτύπος οὔατα
βάλλει" καὶ μαντεύομαί τι ἀγαθὸν ἀκούσεσθαι μέγα.
    ΑΜΠ. Ἄκουε, ξένε· παρέλθοι δέ με, ὦ Πρωτεσίλεω,
μηδέν, μηδὲ ἐκλαθοίμην τινὸς ὧν ἤκουσα.
    26. Πρεσβύτατον μὲν τοίνυν τοῦ Ἑλληνικοῦ φησιν
ἐλθεῖν ἐς Τροίαν τὸν Νηλέως Νέστορα, πολέμων τε
πολλῶν γεγυμνασμένον, οἳ ἐφ᾽ ἡλικίας αὐτῷ ἐπολε-
μήθησαν, ἀγώνων τε γυμνικῶν, ἐν οἷς πυγμῆς καὶ
πάλης ἆθλα ἐτίθετο, τακτικήν τε ὁπόση ὁπλιτῶν τε
καὶ ἵππων ἄριστα δὴ ἀνθρώπων γινώσκοντα, δημα-
γωγίᾳ τε ἐκ μειρακίου ξυμβεβηκότα, μὰ Δί᾽ οὐ τῇ
κολακευούσῃ τοὺς δήμους ἀλλὰ τῇ σωφρονιζούσῃ·
πράττειν δὲ αὐτὸ ξὺν ὥρᾳ τε καὶ ἡδονῇ τῶν λόγων,
ὅθεν καὶ τὰς ἐπιπλήξεις, ἃς ἐποιεῖτο, μὴ ἀγροίκους
μηδὲ ἀηδεῖς φαίνεσθαι.
2   καὶ ὁπόσα Ὁμήρῳ περὶ αὐτοῦ εἴρηται, ξὺν ἀληθείᾳ

---

85 *Od.* 11.134 prophecies a death to Odysseus from the sea;
the cyclic *Telegony* (M. L. West 2003a, 166–71) had his unknown
son, Telegonus, kill him with a spear made from a stingray. For

been he who provided the seaborne spear.[85] He says that the anger of Achilles fell upon the Greeks not for Chryses' daughter, but that he too was enraged about Palamedes. But let that story be reserved for the account of Achilles' deeds; for I shall tell about the heroes one by one, and report whatever Protesilaus has told me about them. 16 17

Phoenician. You are coming to what is for me the best part of your story. For "there assaults my ears the din" (*Il.* 10.535) of horses and men even now, and I foresee that I am going to hear something impressive. 18

Vinedresser. Then listen, stranger. I pray to Protesilaus that I not omit or forget any of what I have heard.[86]

26. He says that the oldest in the Greek army that came to Troy was Nestor son of Neleus, who had been trained not only in many wars fought by him in his youth, but also in athletic competitions in which prizes had been awarded for boxing and wrestling; furthermore he was most knowledgeable of men in infantry and cavalry tactics, and had engaged in public oratory since his youth—not, by Zeus, the kind that caters to the rabble, but chastens it—and did it with such elegance pleasantness that the rebukes he made[87] never seemed crude or insulting.

He says that what is said about him by Homer is cor- 2

---

an attempt to sort out these details, see M. L. West (2013, 307–15), but no source other than *Heroicus* attributes the death to Poseidon.

[86] For the following biographies of heroes, see Introduction §9. In each case, for the hero's presentation in Homer, see the article under each name in Finkelberg (2011), and for the mythographic tradition, see the index in Gantz (1996).

[87] To fellow soldiers in the *Iliad*.

3 φησὶν εἰρῆσθαι. καὶ μὴν καὶ ὁπόσα ἕτεροι περὶ τῶν
τοῦ Γηρυόνου βοῶν εἶπον, ὡς ἀφείλοντο αὐτὰς τὸν
Ἡρακλέα Νηλεύς τε καὶ οἱ Νηλεῖδαι πλὴν Νέστορος,
ἐπαινεῖ ὁ Πρωτεσίλεως ὡς ἀληθῆ καὶ μὴ παρευρη-
μένα· τὸν γάρ τοι Ἡρακλέα δικαιοσύνης μισθὸν τῷ
Νέστορι δοῦναι τὴν Μεσσήνην, ἐπεὶ μηδὲν ὧν οἱ ἀδελ-
4 φοὶ περὶ τὰς βοῦς ἥμαρτε. λέγεται δὲ καὶ ἁλῶναι
αὐτοῦ ὁ Ἡρακλῆς σωφρονεστάτου τε ὄντος καὶ καλ-
λίστου, ἀγαπῆσαί τε αὐτὸν μᾶλλον ἢ τὸν Ὕλλαν τε
καὶ τὸν Ἄβδηρον· οἱ μὲν γὰρ παιδάρια ἦσαν καὶ κο-
μιδῇ νέοι, Νέστορι δὲ ἐφήβῳ ἤδη ἐντυχεῖν αὐτὸν καὶ
ἀρετὴν ἀσκοῦντι ὁπόση ψυχῆς τε καὶ σώματος, ὅθεν
5 ἀγαπῆσαί τε καὶ ἀγαπηθῆναι. τό τοι διομνύναι τὸν
Ἡρακλέα οὔπω ξύνηθες τοῖς ἀνθρώποις ὄν, πρῶτόν
γε νομίσαι φησὶ τὸν Νέστορα καὶ παραδοῦναι τοῖς
ἐν Τροίᾳ.

6 γενέσθαι δὲ αὐτῷ καὶ παῖδα Ἀντίλοχον, ὃν μεσοῦν-
7 τος ἤδη τοῦ πολέμου ἐλθεῖν. νέον μὲν γὰρ εἶναι τὸν
Ἀντίλοχον καὶ οὐκ ἐν ὥρᾳ τῶν πολεμικῶν ὁπότε ξυν-
ελέγοντο ἐς Αὐλίδα, βουλομένῳ δὲ αὐτῷ στρατεύειν
οὐ ξυγχωρῆσαι τὸν πατέρα, τὸν δ᾽, ἐπειδὴ πέμπτον
ἔτος ἤδη προβεβήκει τῷ πολέμῳ, νεώς τε ἐπιβάντα
ἀφικέσθαι καὶ παρελθόντα ἐς τὴν τοῦ Ἀχιλλέως σκη-
νήν, ἐπειδὴ τοῦτον ἐπιτηδειότατον εἶναι τῷ πατρὶ
ἤκουεν, ἱκετεῦσαι τὸν Ἀχιλλέα παραιτήσασθαι αὐτὸν
8 τοῦ πατρός, εἴ πως ἀπειθήσαντι μὴ ἄχθοιτο. ὁ δὲ
ἡσθεὶς τῇ τοῦ Ἀντιλόχου ὥρᾳ καὶ τῆς προθυμίας
ἀγασθεὶς αὐτόν, "οὔπω τὸν πατέρα" εἶπεν, "ὦ μειρά-

rect. And also what others wrote, that it was Neleus and 3
his children, without Nestor's help, who stole Geryon's
cattle from Heracles, he approves as the unvarnished
truth, because Heracles in fact gave Messene to Nestor as
a reward for his fairness, since he did not join his brothers
in the cattle crime.[88] Heracles is rumored to have been 4
captivated by his goodness and beauty, and loved him
more than he did Hyllas and Abderos,[89] they being quite
young and little more than children, whereas Nestor was
a youth who sought moral and physical excellence; it was
from this that their mutual affection developed. Inciden- 5
tally, Protesilaus adds that oaths by Heracles, which were
not yet widespread, were first practiced and popularized
among the troops at Troy by Nestor.

Nestor's son was Antilochus, who arrived only when the 6
war was halfway over. He was still not of age for military 7
service when the troops were mustered at Aulis, and
even though he wanted to campaign his father would not allow
it. But when the war had already entered its fifth year, the
boy took ship and on arrival went to the tent of Achilles,
whom he heard was his father's closest friend, and begged
him to intercede himself for him so that his father not
grow angry at his disobedience. Achilles was delighted and 8
impressed by this youthful zeal, and told him, "You don't

---

[88] Heracles' killing of the sons of Neleus (except for Nestor)
is told, without his motive, in *Il.* 11.689–92. The idea that Nestor
alone had refused to steal is found in Isoc. 6.19 (Gantz 1996,
426–27).

[89] Hylas was stolen by nymphs while accompanying Heracles
with the Argonauts. Abderos was torn apart by some man-eating
horses that Heracles had captured (Gantz 1996, 348, 396).

κιον, τὸν σεαυτοῦ γινώσκεις, εἰ μὴ ὑπ' αὐτοῦ ἐπαινε-
θήσεσθαι μᾶλλον οἴει ἔργον φιλότιμόν τε καὶ νεανι-
9 κὸν εἰργασμένος." καὶ ὀρθῶς εἶπεν ὁ Ἀχιλλεὺς ταῦτα·
ὑπερησθεὶς γὰρ τῷ παιδὶ ὁ Νέστωρ καὶ ἐπ' αὐτῷ
φρονήσας ἄγει αὐτὸν παρὰ τὸν Ἀγαμέμνονα, ὁ δὲ
αὐτίκα ξυγκαλεῖ τοὺς Ἀχαιοὺς καὶ λέγεται ἄριστα
10 ἑαυτοῦ διαλεχθῆναι τότε ὁ Νέστωρ. ξυνελθεῖν μὲν
γὰρ αὐτοὺς χαίροντας ἐπὶ τῷ παιδὰ ὄψεσθαι Νέστο-
ρος (οὐδὲ γὰρ εἶναι αὐτῷ ἐν Τροίᾳ υἱόν, οὔτε Θρα-
συμήδην τινὰ οὔτε ἕτερον), ἑστάναι δὲ τὸν Ἀντίλοχον
ἐρυθριῶντά τε καὶ ἐς τὴν γῆν βλέποντα καὶ θαυ-
μαστὰς κτήσασθαι τοῦ κάλλους οὐκ ἐλάττους ἢ
11 Ἀχιλλεὺς ἐκέκτητο. τὸ μὲν γὰρ ἐκείνου εἶδος ἐκπλη-
κτικόν τε φαίνεσθαι καὶ θεῖον, τὸ δὲ τοῦ Ἀντιλόχου
12 τερπνόν τε καὶ ἥμερον δοκεῖν πᾶσι. καὶ τοὺς Ἀχαιοὺς
ὁ Πρωτεσίλεως οὐδὲ ἄλλως ἐκλελησμένους τότε δὴ
μάλιστα εἰς ἔννοιαν ἑαυτοῦ ἀφικέσθαι λέγει, ξυμβαί-
νοντος ἑαυτῷ τοῦ Ἀντιλόχου τὴν ἡλικίαν τε καὶ τὸ
μέγεθος· πολλοῖς δὲ αὐτῶν καὶ δάκρυα ἐπελθεῖν φη-
σιν οἴκτῳ τῆς ἀμφοῖν ἡλικίας, εὐφημίαις τε χρήσα-
σθαι τοὺς Ἀχαιοὺς ἐς τὸν Νέστορα ἐφ' οἷς εἶπε· δι-
έκειντο γὰρ ὡς παῖδες πρὸς πατέρα.
13 ἔστι σοι καὶ ἄγαλμα παραγαγεῖν τοῦ Νέστορος. ὁ
γὰρ Πρωτεσίλεως αὐτὸν ὧδε ἑρμηνεύει, ὡς φαιδρὸς
μὲν ἀεὶ φαίνοιτο καὶ ἐν ὁρμῇ μειδιάματος, γενειῶν δὲ
σεμνῶς τε καὶ ξυμμέτρως, τὰ δὲ ἀμφὶ παλαίστραν
αὐτῷ πεπονημένα τὰ ὦτα κατηγοροίη καὶ ὁ αὐχὴν
ὑπονεάζων ἔτι· καὶ γὰρ δὴ καὶ ὀρθὸν εἶναι τὸν Νέ-

know your father yet, young man, if you don't think that
you will rather be *praised* by him, for acting with such
ambition and boldness." And he was right; Nestor was   9
overjoyed with his son, and proudly led him to meet
Agamemnon, who in turn assembled all the Greeks, and
in addressing them Nestor surpassed himself. For the   10
Greeks assembled full of joy at the prospect of seeing
Nestor's son (for he had not had a son with him at Troy—
not a Thrasymedes or any other one[90]); and there stood
Antilochus, blushing, staring at the ground and gaining as
many admirers of his beauty as of Achilles'; Achilles' ap-   11
pearance was striking and godlike, but Antilochus was
universally judged pleasantly gentle. Protesilaus says that   12
at that moment the Greeks, although they had always been
mindful of him, thought back to Protesilaus himself more
strongly than ever, because Antilochus' age and stature
were so similar. He says tears of grief for the two youths
came to the eyes of many, and the Greeks praised Nestor
for his speech as warmly as if he had been their father.

I can also present to you Nestor's statue, for Protesi-   13
laus expresses him as follows: He always looks cheerful
and about to smile, with a dignified and symmetrical
beard, ears that betray his experience in wrestling, and a

---

[90] In disagreement with Homer, who makes Thrasymedes
fight alongside his brother in the *Iliad*.

στορα καὶ μὴ ἡττώμενον ὑπὸ τοῦ γήρως, εἶναι δὲ καὶ
μελανόφθαλμον καὶ μὴ ἀποκρεμώμενον τὴν ῥῖνα.
ταυτὶ δὲ ἐν γήρᾳ μόνοι ἴσχουσιν οὓς μὴ ἐπιλίποι τὸ
14 ἐρρῶσθαι. τὸν δὲ Ἀντίλοχον τὰ μὲν ἄλλα ὅμοιόν
φησι γενέσθαι τῷ Νέστορι, δρομικώτερον δὲ καὶ
περιεπτισμένον τὸ εἶδος καὶ μὴ φρονοῦντα ἐπὶ τῇ
κόμῃ.
15   κἀκεῖνά μοι τοῦ Ἀντιλόχου ἑρμηνεύει· φιλιππότα-
τόν τε γενέσθαι αὐτὸν καὶ κυνηγετικώτατον καὶ ταῖς
τῶν πολέμων ἀνοχαῖς ἐπὶ τὰ θηρία χρώμενον· ἀνα-
φοιτᾶν γοῦν ἐς τὴν Ἴδην τὸν Ἀντίλοχον ξὺν Ἀχιλλεῖ
καὶ Μυρμιδόσι, καὶ ἐφ᾽ ἑαυτοῦ μετὰ Πυλίων τε καὶ
Ἀρκάδων, οἳ θηρίων ἀγορὰν παρεῖχον τῷ στρατῷ διὰ
πλῆθος τῶν ἁλισκομένων· τὰ δὲ πολέμια γενναῖόν τε
εἶναι καὶ πτηνὸν τὼ πόδε καὶ ταχὺν τὴν ἐν τοῖς ὅπλοις
κίνησιν, εὐξύνετόν τε τοῖς παραγγελλομένοις χρῆσα-
σθαι καὶ τὸ ἐπίχαρι μηδὲ ἐν ταῖς μάχαις ἀπολεί-
16 ποντα. ἀποθανεῖν δὲ οὐχ, ὡς οἱ πολλοὶ ᾄδουσιν, ὑπὸ
Μέμνονος ἐξ Αἰθιοπίας ἥκοντος· Αἰθίοπα μὲν γὰρ
γενέσθαι Μέμνονα, δυναστεύσαντα ἐπὶ τῶν Τρωικῶν
ἐν Αἰθιοπίᾳ, ἐφ᾽ οὗ καὶ τὸ ψάμμινον ὄρος ἀναχωσθῆ-
ναι λέγεται ὑπὸ τοῦ Νείλου, καὶ θύουσιν αὐτῷ κατὰ
Μερόην καὶ Μέμφιν Αἰγύπτιοι καὶ Αἰθίοπες, ἐπειδὰν
ἀκτῖνα πρώτην ὁ ἥλιος ἐκβάλῃ, παρ᾽ ἧς τὸ ἄγαλμα
φωνὴν ἐκρήγνυσιν ᾗ τοὺς θεραπεύοντας ἀσπάζεται·
17 Τρῶα δὲ ἕτερον γενέσθαι Μέμνονα, νεώτατον τοῦ

youthful neck. Nestor stands erect, not burdened by age; his eyes are dark and his nose is not crooked—the sort of things that only continued vigor allows one to maintain in old age. Antilochus resembled his father, except that he 14 was a faster runner and more trim in build, and not as proud of his hair.

And he also expresses this about Antilochus: he was a 15 superb horseman and hunter, and spent every respite from the war hunting; he went regularly to Mt. Ida with Achilles and Patroclus, and also by himself joined the men of Pylos and Arcadia, who sold game to the troops because they caught so much of it. In fighting he was noble, with great speed and agility in moving fully armed, alert in executing orders, and even in battle he never lost his cheerful disposition. He says that he was killed not by 16 Memnon who came from Ethiopia, as many poets have sung;[91] there *was* an Ethiopian Memnon, but he was a king in that country at the time of the Trojan war, in whose time the sand mountain is said to have been constructed by the Nile.[92] It is to this Memnon that the Egyptians and Ethiopians sacrifice around Memphis and Meroe whenever the sun casts its first light, which causes his statue to speak and greet his worshippers.[93] But there was also another 17

[91] Among them Homer (*Od.* 4.187–88), and the cyclic poem *Aithiopis* (M. L. West 2013, 145–46).   [92] Hdt. 2.8.2, 2.99.2.
[93] The hypothesis of multiple Memnons (a common technique in "revisionist" mythography [Pfister 1909, 221–23] and the description of the so-called *Memnoneion* in Thebes [on which see Tac. *Ann.* 2.61.1; Strabo 17.1.46, *CIL* 3.1.30–66; it was restored by Septimius Severus, after which it ceased to "sing"]) are presented in greater detail in *VA* 6.4 and *Imag.* 1.7.3; see Platt (2009, 136–49).

PHILOSTRATUS

Τρωικοῦ, ὃν ζῶντος μὲν Ἕκτορος οὐδὲν βελτίω δόξαι
τῶν ἀμφὶ Δηίφοβόν τε καὶ Εὔφορβον, ἀποθανόντος
δὲ προθυμότατόν τε καὶ ἀνδρειότατον νομισθῆναι, καὶ
τὴν Τροίαν ἐς αὐτὸν βλέψαι κακῶς ἤδη πράττουσαν.

18 οὗτος, ξένε, τὸν καλόν τε καὶ χρηστὸν Ἀντίλοχον
ἀποκτεῖναι λέγεται προασπίζοντα τοῦ πατρὸς Νέστο-
ρος, ὅτε δὴ τὸν Ἀχιλλέα πυράν τε νῆσαι τῷ Ἀντιλόχῳ
καὶ πολλὰ ἐς αὐτὴν σφάξαι, τά τε ὅπλα καὶ τὴν κε-

19 φαλὴν τοῦ Μέμνονος ἐπικαῦσαι αὐτῷ· τὸ γὰρ τοῦ
ἀγῶνος, ὃν ἐπὶ Πατρόκλῳ {τε καὶ Ἀντιλόχῳ} ὁ Ἀχιλ-
λεὺς ἔθηκεν, ἐπὶ πλέον τοῖς ἀρίστοις νενομίσθαι φη-
σίν· ὅθεν τεθῆναι μὲν ἐφ᾽ ἑαυτῷ ἐνταῦθα, τεθῆναι δὲ
ἐπ᾽ Ἀχιλλεῖ τε καὶ ἐπὶ Πατρόκλῳ καὶ Ἀντιλόχῳ ἐν

20 Ἰλίῳ. λέγεται δὲ καὶ ἐπὶ τῷ Ἕκτορι τεθῆναι ἀγῶνα
δρόμου καὶ τόξου καὶ αἰχμῆς, πάλην δὲ καὶ πυγμὴν
μηδένα ἀποδύσασθαι Τρώων· τὸ μὲν γὰρ οὔπω ἐγί-
νωσκον, τὸ δὲ οἶμαι ἐφοβοῦντο.

27. Διομήδης καὶ Σθένελος ἡλικίας μὲν ταὐτὸν εἶ-
χον, ἤστην δὲ ὁ μὲν Καπανέως, ὁ δὲ Τυδέως, οἳ λέ-
γονται τειχομαχοῦντες ἀποθανεῖν ὁ μὲν ὑπὸ Θηβαίων,

2 ὁ δ᾽ οἶμαι κεραυνωθείς. κειμένων δὲ ἀτάφων τῶν νε-
κρῶν, τὸν μὲν ὑπὲρ τῶν σωμάτων ἀγῶνα Ἀθηναῖοι

---

94 The detail that Antilochus died rescuing his father (whose
chariot had been broken by Memnon) is known also from Pind.
Pyth. 6.28–42 (cf. Quintus of Smyrna 2.243).

95 Achilles killed the Ethiopian Memnon in the *Aithiopis*
(M. L. West 2013, 143–49); he had promised Patroclus the head
and armor of Hector (*Il.* 18.334) but did not carry this out.

200

Memnon, a Trojan and the youngest of their army; he was
thought no better than Deiphobus and Euphorbus and the
rest while Hector was alive , but after their champion's
death he was accounted their fiercest and bravest fighter,
and it was to him that Troy turned in its hour of need.
It was this man, stranger, who killed the noble and stead-   18
fast Antilochus while he was protecting Nestor with his
shield,[94] and it was on this occasion that Achilles built
Antilochus a funeral pyre and offered on it many sacrificial
victims, and even burned for his ghost the armor and the
head of Memnon.[95] He says that the competition, which   19
Achilles held for Patroclus, was generally customary for
the best warriors; that is why Protesilaus himself received
one here in Elaious, and Achilles, Patroclus and Antilo-
chus at Troy. It is said that even Hector's death was fol-   20
lowed by contests in running, archery and the javelin,
although no Trojan ever stripped for wrestling or boxing—
the first they hadn't yet learned, the second (as I suspect)
they feared.

27. Diomedes and Sthenelus[96] were the same age; their
fathers had both been killed while attacking cities. Tydeus
was killed by the Thebans, Capaneus I believe was struck
by a bolt of lightning.[97] Their bodies lay unburied, and   2
the struggle for them was undertaken by the Athenians,

[96] Diomedes is one of the foremost fighters in the *Iliad*; in his
greatest exploit (*Il.* 5), Athena helps him not only kill Pandarus
and wound Aeneas but even wound Aphrodite and Ares himself.
Sthenelus is his lesser companion.

[97] Philostratus avoids the grisly story (Gantz 1996, 518) that
Tydeus, despite being mortally wounded by Melanippus, decap-
itated him and sucked out his brains.

201

ἤραντο καὶ ἔθαψαν αὐτοὺς νικῶντες· τὸν δὲ περὶ τῶν
ψυχῶν οἱ παῖδες ὑπὲρ τῶν πατέρων ἐνίκησαν ὅτε
ἥβησαν, καὶ τὸ κράτος τῆς μάχης εἰς Διομήδην τε
καὶ Σθένελον ἦλθεν ὡς ἀρίστω τε καὶ ὁμοίω ἄνδρε.

3 Ὅμηρος δὲ οὐκ ἀξιοῖ σφας τῶν ἴσων· τὸν μὲν γὰρ
λέοντί τε εἰκάζει καὶ ποταμῷ γεφύρας ἀπάγοντι καὶ
ἀνθρώπων ἔργα (καὶ γὰρ οὕτως ἐμάχετο), ὁ δ' οἷον
θεατὴς τοῦ Διομήδους ἔστηκε, φυγῆς τε ξύμβουλος

4 αὐτῷ γινόμενος καὶ ἄρχων φόβου. καίτοι φησὶν ὁ
Πρωτεσίλεως μὴ ἐλάττω τοῦ Διομήδους ἔργα τὸν
Σθένελον μηδὲ ἐκεῖ δρᾶσαι· φιλίαν μὲν γὰρ σφισιν
εἶναι οὐ μείω ἢ Ἀχιλλεῖ τε καὶ Πατρόκλῳ ἐγένετο,
φιλοτιμεῖσθαι δὲ οὕτω πρὸς ἀλλήλους ὡς ξὺν ἀθυμίᾳ
ἐπανήκειν ἐκ τῆς μάχης τὸν ἀπολειφθέντα τοῦ ἑτέρου.

5 καὶ τὸ ἔργον δὲ τὸ ἐς Αἰνείαν τε καὶ Πάνδαρον πε-
πρᾶχθαι αὐτοῖς φησιν ὁμοῦ· τὸν μὲν γὰρ τῷ Αἰνείᾳ
προσπεσεῖν μεγίστῳ τοῦ Τρωικοῦ ὄντι, τὸν Σθένελον
δὲ τῷ Πανδάρῳ προσαγωνίσασθαι καὶ κρατῆσαι αὐ-

6 τοῦ. ἀλλὰ τὸν Ὅμηρον Διομήδει μόνῳ ἐξῃρηκέναι
ταῦτα ὥσπερ ἐκλαθόμενον ὧν πρὸς τὸν Ἀγαμέμνονα
ὑπὲρ τοῦ Σθενέλου εἶπε· τὸ γὰρ

ἡμεῖς τοι πατέρων μέγ' ἀμείνονες εὐχόμεθ' εἶναι,
ἡμεῖς καὶ Θήβης ἕδος εἵλομεν

---

98 As described in Euripides' *Suppliants* (in Aeschylus' lost play *Eleusinians*, the Athenians won back the bodies by diplomacy alone, without military action). The so-called "graves of the seven" were to be seen at Eleusis (Paus. 1.39.2; Plut. *Thes.* 29).

who buried them after their victory;[98] the struggle to avenge their fathers' spirits was won by the sons, when they grew up;[99] in that battle Diomedes and Sthenelus, equally matched in bravery, were superior.

Homer doesn't rank them equally; Diomedes he compares to a lion (*Il.* 5.136, 161; 10.485), or a river which washes away bridges and the works of men (*Il.* 5.87–92)—for that is how he fought—but Sthenelus stands like a mere spectator of Diomedes, urging him to run away and starting to be afraid (*Il.* 5.249–50). And yet Protesilaus asserts that even at Troy Sthenelus did deeds no less than Diomedes'; their friendship was as strong as that of Achilles and Patroclus, but they were so competitive against each other that if one was surpassed by the other he returned from the fighting in poor spirits. And he adds that the exploits against Aeneas and Pandarus were performed by them both, when Diomedes attacked Aeneas, the greatest in the Trojan army, while Sthenelus fought against Pandarus as well, and defeated him. But Homer reserved this exploit for Diomedes alone, as if he had forgotten the words he had made Sthenelus say to Agamemnon. For his words (*Il.* 4.405–6):

We are the ones who claim to be better by far than
    our fathers;
We are the ones who captured the seat of Thebes. . . .

[99] For the expedition of the *Epigonoi* (successors) to avenge their fathers' deaths at Thebes, see Gantz (1996, 522–25) and M. L. West (2003a, 9–10, 54–57).

ἀνδρός πού ἐστι παραπλήσια τούτοις καὶ ἐν Ἰλίῳ
πράττοντος.

7   ἔστω σοι κἀκεῖνα περὶ Σθενέλου εἰδέναι, ὡς τεῖχος
μὲν οὐδὲν τοῖς Ἀχαιοῖς ἐξεποιήθη ἐν Τροίᾳ, οὐδὲ
ἔστιν ᾧ ἐφράξαντο ἢ τὰς ναῦς ἢ τὴν λείαν, ἀλλὰ
τειχομαχίας ᾠδαὶ ταῦτα Ὁμήρῳ ἐπενοήθησαν, δι᾽ ἃς
8   καὶ τὸ τεῖχος αὐτῷ ξυνετέθη. ὁρμὴ μέντοι τειχοποιίας
ὁμολογεῖται τὸν Ἀγαμέμνονα εἰσελθεῖν μηνίοντος
Ἀχιλλέως, ᾗ πρῶτον ἀντειρηκέναι τὸν Σθένελον εἰ-
πόντα "ἐγὼ μέντοι ἐπιτηδειότερος τείχη καθαιρεῖν ἢ
ἐγείρειν"· ἀντειρηκέναι δὲ καὶ τὸν Διομήδη τῷ τείχει
φήσαντα μεγάλων ἀξιοῦσθαι τὸν Ἀχιλλέα "εἰ ξυγ-
κλείσαιμεν ἑαυτοὺς λοιπὸν ἐπειδὴ ἐκεῖνος μηνίει."
Αἴας δὲ λέγεται ταυρηδὸν ὑποβλέψας τὸν βασιλέα
9   "δείλαιε" εἰπεῖν, "τί οὖν αἱ ἀσπίδες;" καὶ τὸν ἵππον δὲ
τὸν κοῖλον παρῃτεῖτο Σθένελος, οὐ τειχομαχίαν τοῦτο
φάσκων εἶναι ἀλλὰ κλοπὴν τῆς μάχης.

10   τὰ μὲν δὴ μάχιμα ὁμοίω ἤστην καὶ ἴσου τοῖς
Τρωσὶ φόβου ἄξιοι, ἐλείπετο δὲ τοῦ Διομήδους ὁ Σθέ-
νελος ξύνεσίν τε καὶ λόγου ἰσχὺν καὶ καρτερήσεις,
ὁπόσαι ψυχῆς τέ εἰσι καὶ σώματος· ὀργῆς τε γὰρ
ἥττων ἦν καὶ ὑπέρφρων τοῦ ὁμίλου καὶ τραχὺς ἐπι-
πλήττεσθαι καὶ τὰ ἐς τὴν δίαιταν ἁβρότερον ἢ ἐπὶ

100 A reference to two distinct sections of the *Iliad*: "The wall
building" (*teichopoiia*, cf. scholia to *Il.* 21.446a²) is the passage in
Il. 7.433–464 in which the Greeks build a stockade to defend their
camp; the "battle at the wall" or "siege" (*teichomachia*, cf. Pl. *Ion*
539B) is the Trojan attack on that wall in *Il.* 12. An ancient Homer
commentator gives the same view expressed here (scholia to [T]

are surely those of a man whose deeds are the same at Troy also.

There is one more thing you should know in connection with Sthenelus: no wall was built by the Greeks at Troy, nor did they protect their ships and booty with anything; this was rather invented by Homer as the poetic episodes of the battle at the wall, and it was for their sake that he added a fortification.[100] Protesilaus agrees that the plan of building a wall occurred to Agamemnon while Achilles had withdrawn in anger, but Sthenelus was the first to speak against it, saying, "I am better at tearing walls down than erecting them." Diomedes spoke against the wall also, saying they valued Achilles too highly "if we are locking ourselves up forever just because he is angry." Ajax is said to have given the king an angry look and said, "What do you think our shields are for, you coward?" Sthenelus disagreed with the wooden horse as well, saying that this was not siegecraft but battle by theft.

In fighting they were both alike and equally terrifying to the Trojans, but Sthenelus was inferior to Diomedes in intellect, forcefulness in speaking and mental and physical endurance; for he was emotional, scornful at conversation and harsh at being rebuked,[101] and his lifestyle was some-

7

8

9

10

Il. 12.3–35): "Obviously Homer wishes to convert the battle on the plain into a *teichomachia*, and for this reason he added the *teichopoiia*, so that he could introduce contests as part of a siege; this would have been impossible in relation to the Trojan wall, since it had been built by a god." (For the construction of Troy's walls by Poseidon and Apollo, see *Il.* 7.452–53, 21.446–9, and ch. 35.12, below.)

[101] As when Agamemnon rebukes them both (*Il.* 4.401–18) and Sthenelus (unlike Diomedes) responds angrily.

11 στρατοπέδου ἐχρῆν κατεσκεύαστο. Διομήδει δὲ τά-
ναντία τούτων ἐπράττετο· μετρίως τε γὰρ πρὸς τὰς
ἐπιπλήξεις εἶχε καὶ ἐκόλαζε τὸ ἐξοιδοῦν τῆς ὀργῆς,
ὑβρίζειν τε οὐ ξυνεχώρει τοῖς πλήθεσιν οὐδὲ ἀθυμεῖν,
αὐτός τε αὐχμῶν φαίνεσθαι στρατιωτικὸν ἡγεῖτο καὶ
τὸ ὡς ἔτυχε καθεύδειν ἐπῄνει, σιτία τε ἦν αὐτῷ τὰ
ἐπιτυχόντα, καὶ οὐδὲ οἴνῳ ἔχαιρεν εἰ μὴ καθίκοιντο
12 αὐτοῦ οἱ πόνοι. τὸν δὲ Ἀχιλλέα ἐπῄνει μέν, οὐ μὴν
ἐξεπέπληκτό γε οὐδὲ ἐθεράπευεν, ὥσπερ οἱ πολλοί·
καὶ ἀνέκραγέ ποτε ὁ Πρωτεσίλεως ἐπ᾽ ἐκείνοις τοῖς
ἔπεσιν, οἷς ὁ Διομήδης πεποίηται λέγων·

μὴ ὄφελες λίσσεσθαι ἀμύμονα Πηλεΐωνα
μυρία δῶρα διδούς· ὁ δ᾽ ἀγήνωρ ἐστὶ καὶ ἄλλως.

ταῦτα γὰρ τὸν Ὅμηρον ὡς συστρατιώτην ἔφη εἰρη-
κέναι, καὶ οὐχ ὡς ὑποτιθέμενον ἀλλ᾽ αὐτὸν ξυγγεγο-
νότα τοῖς Ἀχαιοῖς ἐν Τροίᾳ· τὸν γὰρ Διομήδη καθ-
άπτεσθαι τοῦ Ἀχιλλέως παρὰ τὴν μῆνιν τρυφῶντος
ἐς τοὺς Ἕλληνας.

13 τὰ δὲ εἴδη ἀμφοῖν, τὸν μὲν Σθένελον εὐμήκη ὁ
Πρωτεσίλεως οἶδε καὶ ἀνεστηκότα, γλαυκόν τε καὶ
γρυπὸν καὶ οἷον κομῶντα, ὑπέρυθρόν τε καὶ ἕτοιμον
τὸ αἷμα· τὸν Διομήδη δὲ βεβηκότα τε ἀναγράφει καὶ
χαροπὸν καὶ οὔπω μέλανα καὶ ὀρθὸν τὴν ῥῖνα, καὶ
οὔλη δὲ ἡ κόμη καὶ σὺν αὐχμῷ.

28. Φιλοκτήτης δ᾽ ὁ Ποίαντος ἐστράτευσε μὲν ὀψὲ

---

102 Alluded to briefly in the catalog of ships (*Il.* 2.718–28). His
wound and abandonment were told in the *Cypria* (M. L. West

what more luxurious than suited an army. Diomedes did   11
just the opposite of all this, being temperate when re-
buked, restrained in his anger, good at keeping the men
from extremes of exhilaration or discouragement. Being
himself of the opinion that appearing unwashed suited a
soldier, he advised them to sleep as they could, his food
was indifferent to him, and he enjoyed wine only if his
troubles were weighing on him. He used to admire Achil-   12
les, but was not an awestruck flatterer of him as most were;
and Protesilaus once expressed outrage over those verses
which Diomedes is made to speak (*Il.* 9.698–99):

> You ought not to beg and entreat Achilles the
>   blameless
> Giving him endless gifts; he is prideful even without
>   this.

For he says that Homer spoke here as a fellow soldier, not
as if he were a poet but *himself* one of the Greeks in Troy.
For Diomedes criticized Achilles only while he was acting
spoiled toward the Greeks because of his anger.

As for their appearance, Protesilaus knows that Sthen-   13
elus stood tall and erect, with blue eyes, a hooked nose and
rather long hair, and a complexion that was ruddy and
quick to color. Diomedes he describes as steady, with clear
eyes, a complexion just short of dark, and a straight nose;
his hair was curly and dirty.

28. Philoctetes son of Poias[102] joined the Trojan expedi-

2013, 112–13), and his return and killing of Paris in the *Little
Iliad* (M. L. West 2013, 181–85). His return from Lemnos was
the subject of plays by Aeschylus and Euripides as well as by
Sophocles (Dio Chrys. 52.1). For connections with Lemnos in
particular, see Masciadri (2008, 38–111).

τῶν Τρωικῶν, ἄριστα δὲ ἀνθρώπων ἐτόξευσεν, Ἡρα-
κλέους, φασί, τοῦ Ἀλκμήνης μαθὼν αὐτό. καὶ κληρο-
νομῆσαι λέγεται τῶν τόξων ὁπότε Ἡρακλῆς, ἀπιὼν
τῆς ἀνθρωπείας φύσεως, αὐτόν τε παρεστήσατο καὶ
2   τὸ ἐν τῇ Οἴτῃ πῦρ. τοῦτον ἐν Λήμνῳ καταλειφθῆναί
φασιν ἄτιμον τοῖς Ἀχαιοῖς, ὕδρου ἐνσκήψαντος αὐτῷ
ἐς τὸν πόδα, ὑφ' οὗ νοσεῖν αὐτὸν ἐπὶ ἀκτῆς ὑψηλῆς
ἐν πέτρᾳ κείμενον, καὶ μαντευτὸν τοῖς Ἀχαιοῖς ἐλθεῖν
ὕστερον ἐπὶ τὸν Πάριν, ὃν ἀποκτείνας τὴν μὲν Τροίαν
ἑλεῖν τοῖς Ἡρακλέους τόξοις αὖθις, ἰαθῆναι δὲ ὑπὸ
τῶν Ἀσκληπιαδῶν αὐτός.

3   ταῦτά φησιν ὁ Πρωτεσίλεως οὐ παρὰ πολὺ τῆς
ἀληθείας εἰρῆσθαι· τά τε γὰρ {τόξα} τοῦ Ἡρακλέους
εἶναι ὁποῖα ὕμνηται, καὶ τὸν Φιλοκτήτην ξυλλαβεῖν
αὐτῷ τοῦ ἐν τῇ Οἴτῃ ἄθλου, τὰ τόξα τε ἀπελθεῖν
ἔχοντα καὶ μόνον ἀνθρώπων γινώσκειν ὡς χρὴ ἕλκειν
αὐτά, τυχεῖν τε ἀριστείων λαμπρῶν ἐπὶ τῇ ἁλώσει τοῦ
4   Ἰλίου. τὰ δὲ τῆς νόσου καὶ τῶν ἰασαμένων αὐτὸν ἑτέ-
ρως λέγει· καταλειφθῆναι μὲν γὰρ ἐν Λήμνῳ τὸν Φι-
λοκτήτην, οὐ μὴν ἔρημον τῶν θεραπευσόντων οὐδὲ
ἀπερριμμένον τοῦ Ἑλληνικοῦ· πολλούς τε γὰρ τῶν
Μελίβοιαν οἰκούντων ξυγκαταμεῖναι (στρατηγὸς δὲ
τούτων ἦν), τοῖς τε Ἀχαιοῖς δάκρυα ἐπελθεῖν ὅτι ἀπ-
έλιπε σφᾶς ἀνὴρ πολεμικὸς καὶ πολλῶν ἀντάξιος·
5   ἰαθῆναι δὲ αὐτὸν αὐτίκα ὑπὸ τῆς βώλου τῆς Λημνίας,

---

103 An allusion to Heracles' apotheosis: his wife Deianeira had
unwittingly given him a robe that devoured his flesh; in agony, he

tion late, but was the best archer alive; he is said to have
learned his skill from Heracles, and inherited his bow
when, as he was leaving his mortal life, he made his wit-
nesses both Philoctetes and the fire on Mount Oita.[103]
Philoctetes is supposed to have been scorned and aban-   2
doned by the Greeks on Lemnos, after a water snake had
attacked his foot and made him sick; he lay in a cave high
on the coast, and returned in response to an oracle to seek
Paris, by killing whom he captured Troy with Heracles'
weapons a second time.[104] Then he was healed by the sons
of Asclepius.

Protesilaus says that this is not far from[105] the truth.   3
For Heracles' deeds are described correctly, and Philoc-
tetes really did help him in his struggle at Mt. Oita and
leave with the bow, which he alone of men could draw, and
won glory at the fall of Troy. But he tells the story of his   4
illness and those who healed him differently, saying that
Philoctetes was left behind at Lemnos, but not without
people to care for him or an outcast from the army; for
many of the inhabitants of Meliboea (whose contingent he
commanded) stayed with him, and the Greeks shed many
tears to think that such a warlike and worthy man was
staying behind. He was healed immediately by the Lem-   5

commanded Philoctetes to light a funeral pyre for him to be
burned alive and gave him his bow (Gantz 1996, 459). The story
is not in Sophocles' *Philoctetes* or *Trachiniae*.

[104] Heracles had sacked Troy in an earlier generation to force
its king, Laomedon, to pay him for rescuing his daughter Hesione
(*Il.* 5.640–642; Gantz 1993, 442–44).

[105] For the translation, see 24.2n.

εἰς ἣν λέγεται πεσεῖν ὁ Ἥφαιστος· ἡ δὲ ἐλαύνει μὲν
τὰς μανικὰς νόσους, ἐκραγὲν δὲ αἷμα ἴσχει, ὕδρου δὲ
ἰᾶται μόνου δῆγμα ἑρπετῶν.

6   ὃν δὲ ἐτρίβοντο οἱ Ἀχαιοὶ χρόνον ἐν τῷ Ἰλίῳ,
τοῦτον ὁ Φιλοκτήτης Εὐνέῳ τῷ Ἰάσονος συνεξῄρει
τὰς μικρὰς τῶν νήσων, Κᾶρας ἐξελαύνων ὑφ᾽ ὧν κατ-
είχοντο, καὶ μισθὸς τῆς συμμαχίας αὐτῷ μοῖρα τῆς
Λήμνου ἐγένετο, ἣν Ἄκεσαν ὁ Φιλοκτήτης ἐκάλεσεν
7   ἐπειδὴ ἐν Λήμνῳ ἰάθη. ἐκεῖθεν αὐτὸν Διομήδης καὶ
Νεοπτόλεμος ἑκόντα ἐς Τροίαν ἤγαγον, ἱκετεύσαντες
ὑπὲρ τοῦ Ἑλληνικοῦ καὶ ἀναγνόντες αὐτῷ τὸν ὑπὲρ
τῶν τόξων χρησμόν, ἐκ Λέσβου ὥς φησιν ἥκοντα.
8   χρῆσθαι μὲν γὰρ καὶ τοῖς οἴκοι μαντείοις τοὺς Ἀχαι-
ούς, τῷ τε Δωδωναίῳ καὶ τῷ Πυθικῷ καὶ ὁπόσα μαν-
τεῖα εὐδόκιμα Βοιωτιά τε ἦν καὶ Φωκικά· Λέσβου δὲ
ὀλίγον ἀπεχούσης τοῦ Ἰλίου, στέλλειν ἐς τὸ ἐκεῖ μαν-
9   τεῖον τοὺς Ἕλληνας. ἔχρα δέ, οἶμαι, ἐξ Ὀρφέως· ἡ
κεφαλὴ γὰρ μετὰ τὸ τῶν γυναικῶν ἔργον ἐς Λέσβον
κατασχοῦσα, ῥῆγμα τῆς Λέσβου ᾤκησε καὶ ἐν κοίλῃ
10   τῇ γῇ ἐχρησμῴδει. ὅθεν ἐχρῶντό τε αὐτῇ τὰ μαντικὰ
Λέσβιοί τε καὶ τὸ ἄλλο πᾶν Αἰολικὸν καὶ Ἴωνες Αἰο-
λεῦσι πρόσοικοι, χρησμοὶ δὲ τοῦ μαντείου τούτου καὶ
11   ἐς Βαβυλῶνα ἀνεπέμποντο. πολλὰ γὰρ καὶ ἐς τὸν

106 Cf. the *Lithica* ascribed to Orpheus, 346–56, and for this
prized remedy see Hasluck (1909). This and the following stories
might be local traditions, since Philostratus was a native of Lem-
nos (Masciardi 2008, 306–7).

210

nian earth, into which Hephaestus is said to have fallen.[106]
It drives away madness, clots blood, and heals the bite of
one particular reptile, the water snake.

While the Greeks were in Troy Philoctetes joined Eue- 6
nus the son of Jason in subduing the smaller islands by
driving out the Carians by whom they were being op-
pressed, and as a reward for his help he was given a part
of Lemnos which he named Akesa, because he had been
healed in Lemnos.[107] From there Diomedes and Neoptol- 7
emus brought him back to Troy voluntarily, appealing to
him on behalf of the army and reading him the oracle
about the bow, which Protesilaus says came from Lesbos.
He says the Greeks usually employed the oracles near 8
their home, like Dodona, Delphi and other well-known
oracles of Boeotia and Phocis; but since Lesbos was near
Troy they sent to the oracle there. I suppose that the
prophecy in this case came from Orpheus.[108] For after the 9
women had done their work, his head drifted to Lesbos,
lodged in a chasm on Lesbos and sang its prophecies in an
earthen chamber. Therefore it was used for prophecies 10
not only by the Lesbians, but also by all the Aeolians and
their neighbors the Ionians; oracles from this shrine were
even sent to Babylon, and the head sang many prophecies 11

[107] *Akos* is the Greek word for "cure."
[108] Legend said that Orpheus was torn apart by the women of
Thrace and his parts cast into the sea; his head floated to Antissa
in Lesbos, where it used to sing prophecies, until silenced by
order of Apollo; see *VA* 4.14, and (especially for the theme in art)
Faraone (2004).

ἄνω βασιλέα ἡ κεφαλὴ ᾖδε, Κύρῳ τε τῷ ἀρχαίῳ χρη-
σμὸν ἐντεῦθεν ἐκδοθῆναι λέγεται· "τὰ ἐμά, ὦ Κῦρε,
σά"· καὶ ὁ μὲν οὕτως ἐγίνωσκεν, ὡς Ὀδρύσας τε καὶ
τὴν Εὐρώπην καθέξων, ἐπειδὴ Ὀρφεύς ποτε, μετὰ τοῦ
σοφοῦ καὶ δυνατὸς γενόμενος, ἀνά τε Ὀδρύσας ἴσχυ-
σεν ἀνά τε Ἕλληνας ὁπόσοι τελεταῖς ἐθείαζον, ὁ δ᾽
12 οἶμαι τὰ ἑαυτοῦ πείσεσθαι ἐδήλου τὸν Κῦρον. ἐλάσας
γὰρ Κῦρος ὑπὲρ ποταμὸν Ἴστρον ἐπὶ Μασσαγέτας
καὶ Ἰσσηδόνας (τὰ δὲ ἔθνη ταῦτα Σκύθαι), ἀπέθανέ
τε ὑπὸ γυναικὸς ἣ τούτων ἦρχε τῶν βαρβάρων, καὶ
ἀπέτεμεν ἡ γυνὴ τὴν Κύρου κεφαλήν, καθάπερ αἱ
13 Θρᾷτται τὴν Ὀρφέως. τοσαῦτα, ξένε, περὶ τοῦ μαν-
τείου τούτου Πρωτεσίλεώ τε καὶ Λεσβίων ἤκουσα.

14 ἐλθεῖν δὲ ἐς Τροίαν τὸν Φιλοκτήτην οὔτε νοσοῦντα
οὔτε νενοσηκότι ὅμοιον, ἀλλὰ πολιὸν μὲν ὑφ᾽ ἡλικίας
(ἑξήκοντα γάρ που ἔτη γεγονέναι), σφριγῶντα δὲ
παρὰ πολλοὺς τῶν νέων, βλέπειν δεινότατα ἀνθρώ-
πων καὶ φθέγγεσθαι βραχυλογώτατα καὶ ὀλίγοις τῶν
βουλευμάτων ξυντίθεσθαι.

29. Ἀγαμέμνονα δὲ καὶ Μενέλεων οὔτε τὸ εἶδος
2 ὁμοίω γενέσθαι φησὶν οὔτε τὴν ῥώμην. τὸν μὲν γὰρ
ἐν αὐτουργίᾳ τῶν πολεμικῶν εἶναι, μαχόμενόν τε
οὐδενὸς τῶν ἀρίστων ἧττον καὶ ὁπόσα ἐς βασιλέα
ἥκει πράττοντα· γινώσκειν τε αὐτὸν ἃ χρὴ τὸν ἄρ-
χοντα, καὶ ὅ τι ἕτερος γνοίη πείθεσθαι, πρέπειν τε τῇ
τῶν Ἑλλήνων ἀρχῇ καὶ δι᾽ αὐτὸ τὸ εἶδος· σεμνὸν γὰρ

relating to the king of Persia. And a prophecy from there
is said to have been given to Cyrus the great: "What was
mine, O Cyrus, will be yours." He understood by this that
he was going to conquer the Odrysians and Europe, since
Orpheus had been powerful as well as poetic, with author-
ity among Odrysians and all the Greeks who were inspired
by his rituals; but Orpheus seems rather to have meant
that Cyrus would suffer his own fate. For when the king   12
crossed the Danube to attack the Massagetai and Isse-
dones (these tribes are Scythians), he was killed by the
woman who ruled these barbarians and the woman cut off
Cyrus' head, just as the Thracian women had done with
Orpheus.[109] That, stranger, is what I have learned about   13
this oracle from Protesilaus and the Lesbians.

Well, he says that when Philoctetes went to Troy he was   14
not sick at all—a little gray from his age (he was about sixty
years old), but stronger than many of the youths; with a
fierce look in his eye, he spoke little, and agreed with very
few of their plans.

29. He says that Agamemnon and Menelaus were dif-
ferent both in appearance and in physical strength. Aga-   2
memnon participated in hand to hand combat, not only
fighting as well as any of the champions but also doing
what pertained to a king also. He himself knew what a king
should do, and if someone else did, Agamemnon followed
his advice. He was suited to rule the Greeks for his ap-

[109] The story of Cyrus' defeat by Tomyris, the queen of the
Massagetae, is told (without reference to Orpheus' oracle) by
Hdt. 1.201–15.

PHILOSTRATUS

καὶ μεγαλοπρεπῆ φαίνεσθαι καὶ οἷον ταῖς Χάρισι θύ-
οντα.

3   τὸν δὲ Μενέλεων μάχεσθαι μὲν μετὰ πολλοὺς τῶν
Ἑλλήνων, ἀποχρῆσθαι δὲ τῷ ἀδελφῷ πάντα, καὶ τυγ-
χάνοντα προθύμου τε καὶ εὔνου τοῦ Ἀγαμέμνονος
ὅμως βασκαίνειν αὐτῷ καὶ ὧν ὑπὲρ αὐτοῦ ἔπραττεν,
ὑπὸ τοῦ ἄρχειν μὲν αὐτὸς ἐθέλειν, μὴ ἀξιοῦσθαι δέ.

4   τὸν γοῦν Ὀρέστην, Ἀθήνησι μὲν καὶ παρὰ τοῖς Ἕλ-
λησιν εὐδοκιμοῦντα, ἐπειδὴ τῷ πατρὶ ἐτιμώρησεν, ἐν
δὲ τῷ Ἄργει κινδυνεύοντα, βληθέντα ἂν περιεῖδεν ὑπὸ
τῶν Ἀργείων, εἰ μὴ Ὀρέστης ἐμπεσὼν τούτοις μετὰ
ξυμμάχων Φωκέων, τοὺς μὲν ἐτρέψατο, τὴν δὲ ἀρχὴν
τοῦ πατρὸς καὶ ἄκοντος τοῦ Μενέλεω κατεκτήσατο.

5   κομᾶν τὸν Μενέλεων μειρακιωδῶς φησιν, ἐπεὶ δὲ ἡ
Σπάρτη ἐκόμα, ξυγγινώσκειν αὐτῷ τοὺς Ἀχαιοὺς ἐπι-
χωριάζοντι. (οὐδὲ γὰρ τοὺς ἀπ᾽ Εὐβοίας ἥκοντας ἐτώ-
6   θαζον, καίτοι γελοίως κομῶντας.) διαλεχθῆναι δὲ
αὐτὸν ῥᾷστα ἀνθρώπων φησὶ καὶ βραχυλογώτατα,
ξυγκεραννύοντα ἡδονὴν τῷ λόγῳ.

30. Κρῆτα Ἰδομενέα ὁ Πρωτεσίλεως οὐκ εἶδεν ἐν

---

110 Adapting the advice that Plato is said to have given his
student, the austere and conscientious Xenocrates: "Sacrifice to
the Muses" (Diog. Laert. 4.11; Plut. Mor. 141f, 769c). Plut. Lyc.
21.7 reports that Spartan kings sacrificed to the Muses before
battle. Agamemnon's portrait here follows Il. 3.166–80.

111 The negative characterization of Menelaus is derived from
tragedy; see Sophocles' Ajax and (for his attitude to his nephew)
Euripides' Orestes. See in general Stelow (2005, 271).

214

pearance alone: he says he looked august and noble, as if
he sacrificed to the Graces.[110]

He says that Menelaus fought worse than many of the 3
Greeks, and exploited his brother in everything; even
though he was treated with kindness and concern he was
jealous of him, even for the things Agamemnon did for
him; this was because he wanted to rule himself, but was
considered unworthy. At any rate he says that when Ores- 4
tes, glorious in Athens and throughout Greece, because
he had avenged his father, was in danger in Argos, Mene-
laus would have allowed him to be stoned by the Argives;
but Orestes attacked and routed them with allies from
Phocis, and regained his father's throne even against
Menelaus' will.[111]

He says that Menelaus wore a rather juvenile long hair- 5
style, but since long hair was the fashion at Sparta the
Greeks tolerated this practice of his local custom. (They
even refrained from ridiculing those who came from Eu-
boea, though their long hair was quite absurd.)[112] He says 6
he was the most facile speaker of them all and the most
concise, and mixed charm into his words.[113]

30. Protesilaus did not see Idomeneus of Crete[114] at

[112] *Il.* 2.542; according to Strabo 10.3.6 and Archemorus of
Euboea (*FGrHist* 424 F 9) they wore it very long in back and
shaved in front (Grossardt 2006a). The vinedresser adds this de-
tail on his own, not from Protesilaus.

[113] *Il.* 3.212–15 (Antenor's report of a speech Menelaus made
at Troy).

[114] Philostratus denies that Idomeneus was ever at Troy, thus
implicitly rejecting the whole of the Dictys story, for which
Idomeneus' secretary was the source; see Introduction §5.

Ἰλίῳ, ἀλλ' ἐν Αὐλίδι ὄντων πρεσβείαν ἀφικέσθαι
παρ' Ἰδομενέως φησίν, ὑπισχνουμένου τὸ Κρητῶν
συμμαχικόν, εἰ συμμετέχοι τῆς ἀρχῆς τῷ Ἀγα-
2 μέμνονι. τὸν μὲν δὴ Ἀγαμέμνονα σωφρόνως ἀκοῦσαι
ταῦτα καὶ παραγαγεῖν τὸν ἥκοντα, τὸν δὲ λαμπρᾷ τῇ
φωνῇ καὶ φρονιμώδει "ὦ Ἀχαιοὶ" φάναι, "ἀνὴρ τὴν
Μίνω τοῦ Κρητὸς ἀρχὴν ἔχων δίδωσιν ὑμῖν ξυμμά-
χους ἑκατὸν πόλεις ὡς καὶ τὴν Τροίαν ἑλεῖν παίζον-
τας, ἀξιοῖ δὲ συντετάχθαι τῷ Ἀγαμέμνονι καὶ ἄρχειν
3 ὑμῶν ὥσπερ οὗτος." πρὸς ταῦτα εἰπόντος τοῦ Ἀγα-
μέμνονος· "ἐγὼ δὲ καὶ πάσης τῆς ἀρχῆς παραχωρεῖν
ἕτοιμος εἰ βελτίων ἐμοῦ φαίνοιτο," παρελθεῖν φησι
τὸν Τελαμῶνος Αἴαντα καὶ διαλεχθῆναι ὧδε· "ἡμεῖς,
Ἀγάμεμνον, ἐδώκαμέν σοι τὴν ἡγεμονίαν ὑπὲρ εὐ-
ταξίας τοῦ στρατοῦ καὶ τοῦ μὴ πολλοὺς ἄρχειν,
στρατεύομεν δὲ οὐχ ὑπὲρ τοῦ δουλεύειν ἢ σοὶ ἢ ἑτέρῳ,
ἀλλ' ὑπὲρ τοῦ καταδουλώσασθαι Τροίαν, ἣν λάβοι-
μεν, ὦ θεοί, λαμπρὰ καὶ καλὰ ἐργασάμενοι. τοιοῦτοι
γάρ ἐσμεν τὰς ἀρετάς, οἷοι Τροίαν μὲν ἐσπουδακότες
λαβεῖν, Κρήτην δὲ παίζοντες."

31. Αἴαντα δὲ τὸν Λοκρὸν τὰ μὲν πολέμιά φησι
κατὰ Διομήδη τε καὶ Σθένελον γεγονέναι, ξυνετὸν δὲ
ἧττον δόξαι, προσέχειν δὲ οὐδὲν τῷ Ἀγαμέμνονι· πα-
τρός τε γὰρ εἶναι Λοκρῶν δυνατωτάτου, στρατιάν τε
οὐκ ἀφανῆ ἄγειν, οὐδὲ δουλεύσειν ποτὲ ἑκὼν οὔτ' ἂν
Ἀτρείδαις οὔτε ἄλλῳ οὐδενί, "ἔστ' ἂν ἥδε ἀστράπτῃ."
τὴν αἰχμὴν δεικνὺς ταῦτα ἔλεγε, γοργὸν βλέπων καὶ

Troy; when the Greeks were at Aulis an embassy came from Idomeneus, who promised an allied force of Cretans if he could share the command with Agamemnon; Agamemnon listened to him politely and introduced the arrival, who spoke loudly and boldly: "Greeks, the man who holds the empire of Minos of Crete offers you a hundred cities as allies such that it is child's play to capture even Troy; but he demands that he be ranked equal to Agamemnon, and rule you as he does." Agamemnon responded, "For my part, I am ready to withdraw entirely from command if you think this man better." But then Ajax son of Telamon stepped forth and spoke as follows: "Agamemnon, we gave you the command to keep the army in good order and to avoid having too many rulers. We are not going to war to become the slaves of you or any man, but to enslave Troy—may the gods grant we do it, and do fine and noble deeds. We are brave enough to capture Troy if we work hard—Crete we can capture like child's play."

31. He says that Ajax of Locris[115] was as good a warrior as Diomedes and Sthenelus, but seemed less intelligent, and paid no attention to Agamemnon; he was the son of the most powerful man in Locris and he himself led a considerable army, and would never be the slave of the Atreidae or anyone if he could help it, "until this (pointing

[115] Sometimes called Ajax "the lesser" to distinguish him from the homonymous son of Telamon. Philostratus retains his traditional arrogance but gives him distinctive features (familiar snake, fighting for Europe against barbarians, ship burial) and alters the story of his death to make him, like Palamedes, an innocent victim of slander.

ἀναχαιτίζων τὴν κόμην ὑπὸ τοῦ τῆς γνώμης ἑτοίμου.
2 καὶ τοὺς μὲν ἄλλους ἔφασκεν, ὅσοι προσεῖχον τῷ
Ἀγαμέμνονι, ὑπὲρ τῆς Ἑλένης ἥκειν, ἑαυτὸν δ' ὑπὲρ
τῆς Εὐρώπης· δεῖν γὰρ δὴ Ἕλληνας ὄντας κρατεῖν
3 βαρβάρων. εἶναι δὲ αὐτῷ καὶ χειρόηθη δράκοντα πεν-
τάπηχυν τὸ μέγεθος, ὃν ξυμπίνειν τε καὶ συνεῖναι τῷ
Αἴαντι καὶ ὁδῶν ἡγεῖσθαι καὶ ξυνομαρτεῖν οἷον κύνα.
4   τὴν δὲ Κασσάνδραν ἀποσπάσαι μὲν ἀπὸ τοῦ τῆς
Ἀθηνᾶς ἕδους προσκειμένην τῇ θεῷ καὶ ἱκετεύουσαν,
οὐ μὴν βιάσασθαί γε, οὐδὲ ὑβρίσαι ἐς αὐτὴν ὁπόσα
οἱ μῦθοι ἐς αὐτὸν ψεύδονται, ἀλλ' ἀπαγαγεῖν μὲν ἐς
τὴν ἑαυτοῦ σκηνήν, τὸν δὲ Ἀγαμέμνονα ἰδόντα τὴν
Κασσάνδραν (πρὸς γὰρ τῇ ὥρᾳ καὶ κατέστεπτο παρὰ
τῆς τέχνης) ἁλῶναί τε αὐτίκα τῆς κόρης καὶ ἀφελέ-
σθαι αὐτὴν τὸν Αἴαντα,
    ἔριδός τε αὐτοῖς ἐν τῷ δασμῷ γενομένης ὁ μὲν
ἠξίου ἑαυτοῦ εἶναι ἃ εἷλεν, ὁ δὲ οὔτε ἀπεδίδου καὶ
5 ἀσεβῆσαι αὐτὸν ἐς τὴν Ἀθηνᾶν ἔφασκε. καθεῖντο δὲ
τῷ Ἀγαμέμνονι λογοποιοὶ ἐς τὸ Ἑλληνικὸν διὰ τὸ ἀεὶ
πρὸς τὸν Αἴαντα ἔχθος, τὴν θεὸν πολλὰ καὶ ἄτοπα
ἐπισημαίνειν ὑπὲρ τῆς κόρης, καὶ ἀπολεῖσθαι τὴν
6 στρατιὰν εἰ μὴ ἀπολέσειεν αὐτόν. ὁ δ' ἐνθυμηθεὶς
ὅπως Αἴαντα μὲν ἀπώλεσεν ἄδικος κρίσις, Παλαμήδη
δὲ οὐδὲν ἡ σοφία ὤνησε τὸ μὴ οὐκ ἀποθανεῖν δια-
βληθέντα, ἀποδρᾶναι νύκτωρ ἐν πορθμείῳ οὐ μεγάλῳ

116 For snakes and hero cult, see Introduction §3.
117 In the cyclic *Sack of Troy* (Proclus in M. L. West 2003a,

to his spear) flashes like lightning." He used to tell them this with a fierce look, shaking his long hair with a bold attitude. He used to say that the others who had obeyed 2 Agamemnon had come for Helen, but he had come for Europe, since as Greeks it was their duty to conquer barbarians. As a drinking and living companion he had a tame 3 snake that was five cubits long, which led the way when he traveled and otherwise followed him like a dog.[116]

Ajax dragged Cassandra out of the temple of Athena 4 when she was kneeling and supplicating the goddess, but did not rape her, or treat her in any way violently as the stories falsely have it; he took her away to his own tent, but Agamemnon had seen her and had to have her—for her natural beauty had been crowned by art—and took her away from Ajax.

They quarreled over the division of spoils, one claiming as his right what he had captured, the other refusing to return her, and charging Ajax with impiety to Athena. Agamemnon sent his agents through the army to exploit 5 their hostility to Ajax, saying that Athena was giving many strange portents for the girl, and that the army would be destroyed if they did not destroy Ajax first.[117] The 6 Locrian remembered that an unjust verdict had killed the other Ajax, and that Palamedes' wisdom had not prevented him from being slandered and killed,[118] fled by night in a small troop transport, although it was winter

146, and M. L. West 2013, 235–37), Ajax, while dragging Cassandra away, also dislodges Athena's statue, for which he was condemned to be stoned but escaped by taking refuge at Athena's altar. Athena herself contrives his later death at sea. For later versions see Gantz (1996, 651–55).   [118] Compare Dictys 5.15.

χειμῶνός τε καὶ ὡς ἔτυχεν, ὅτε δὴ πλέων εὐθὺ Τήνου
τε καὶ Ἄνδρου πρὸς Γυραῖς ἀπέθανεν.

7   ἀγγελίας δὲ τοῦ πάθους ἐς τοὺς Ἀχαιοὺς ἐλθούσης
ὀλίγους μὲν αὐτῶν σίτου ἅψασθαι, πάντας δὲ ὡς ἐπ'
ἀνδρὶ ἀγαθῷ χεῖρας ἄρασθαι, προσεσχηκότας τε τῇ
θαλάσσῃ ἀνακαλεῖν αὐτὸν καὶ ὀλοφύρεσθαι καὶ τὸν
Ἀγαμέμνονα ἐν ὀργῇ ἔχειν μονονοὺ χερσὶ πράξαντα
τὴν ἀπώλειαν τοῦ Αἴαντος.

8   ἐναγισμάτων τε αὐτὸν τυχεῖν ἃ μήπω ἐπηνέχθη
πρότερον μήτε μὴν ὕστερον ἀνθρώπῳ τινί, μηδὲ ὁπό-
9 σους ναυμαχίαι ἀφανεῖς ἔσχον· ἐς γὰρ Λοκρίδα ναῦν,
ἣ τὸν Αἴαντα ἦγε, ξύλα νήσαντες ὥσπερ ἐς πυράν,
ἔσφαξαν μέλανα πάντα, καὶ στείλαντες αὐτὴν ἱστίοις
μέλασι καὶ τοῖς ἄλλοις ὁπόσα ἐς τὸ πλεῖν εὕρηται,
ξυνεῖχον πείσμασιν ἔστε πνεῦσαι τὸν ἀπὸ τῆς γῆς
ἄνεμον, ὃν περὶ ὄρθρον μάλιστα ἡ Ἴδη ἀποστέλλει·
ἐπεὶ δὲ ἡμέρα διεφαίνετο καὶ κατῄει τὸ πνεῦμα, πῦρ
ἐς κοίλην τὴν ναῦν ἐνῆκαν. ἔπλει τε δὴ μετεωρίζουσα
ἐς τὸ πέλαγος, καὶ οὔπω ἡλίου ἀνίσχοντος αὐτή τε
κατεφλέχθη καὶ ὁπόσα τῷ Αἴαντι ἔφερεν.

32. Χείρωνα δὲ τὸν ἐν Πηλίῳ γενέσθαι μέν φησιν
ἀνθρώπῳ ὅμοιον, σοφὸν δὲ καὶ λόγους καὶ ἔργα (θή-

---

119 In *Od.* 4.499–510 Ajax dies on these same rocks, but in a
storm that sinks the returning Greek fleet. The Gyraean rocks
were variously placed at Cape Caphareus on the southern tip of
Euboea, on the island of Mykonos (where one version had it that
his body had been saved for burial), or on Tenos, as evidently

and he had made no preparations; it was then, as he was
sailing for Tenos and Andros, that he was killed on the
rocks of Gyrai.[119]

When the news of his fate reached the Greeks few of
them touched their food, and every one of them raised his
hand for the death of this brave man,[120] and gazing at the
sea called out his name and grieved; they were enraged at
Agamemnon, who had virtually murdered him.

Ajax received a funeral ceremony that was given to no
one before or after, not even among those who are lost in
sea battles: they stacked a sort of pyre of wood on the
Locrian ship on which he had sailed to Troy, slaughtered
in sacrifice only black victims, and fitted it out with sails
and all the other sailing gear which was black. They held
it with lines until there blew the offshore wind which
Mount Ida emits about dawn; but when day broke and the
wind descended, they set a fire in the hull. It sailed high
above the water toward open sea, and before the sun had
risen the boat itself, and the offerings it carried for Ajax,
were consumed by the flames.[121]

32. Protesilaus says that Chiron of Mt. Pelion[122] looked
like a man, and was wise in both words and deeds (for he

here; see Preller, Robert, and Kern (1894–1926, vol. 2, pt. 2,
1450–52), and Gantz (1996, 695–97).

[120] For this gesture of grief, see *Il.* 18.317, 23.18, 23.136,
24.712, 24.724; Collard on Eur. *Supp.* 772–73.

[121] For this unusual ritual see Introduction §12.

[122] The centaur Chiron did not of course go to Troy, but the
discussion of him here forms a transition to Palamedes. It is based
on Xenophon's *On Hunting*, preface (cf. 1.11), with which Philostratus however disagrees by making Palamedes largely self-taught
(not a student of Chiron).

ρας τε γὰρ ποικίλης ἥπτετο καὶ τὰ πολεμικὰ ἐπαίδευε
καὶ ἰατροὺς ἀπέφαινε καὶ μουσικοὺς ἥρμοττε καὶ δι-
καίους ἐποίει), βιῶναί τε ἐπὶ μήκιστον, φοιτῆσαι δὲ
αὐτῷ Ἀσκληπιὸν Τελαμῶνά τε καὶ Πηλέα καὶ Θησέα,
θαμίζειν δὲ καὶ Ἡρακλέα τῷ Χείρωνι, ὅτε μὴ ἀπά-
2 γοιεν αὐτὸν οἱ ἆθλοι. μετασχεῖν δὲ τῆς τοῦ Χείρωνος
ὁμιλίας καὶ αὐτός φησι Παλαμήδει ἅμα καὶ Ἀχιλλεῖ
καὶ Αἴαντι.

33. Καὶ τὰ τοῦ Παλαμήδους ὧδε ἀπαγγέλλει· αὐτο-
μαθῆ ἀφικέσθαι αὐτὸν καὶ σοφίας ἤδη γεγυμνασμέ-
νον καὶ πλείω γινώσκοντα ἢ ὁ Χείρων· πρὸ γὰρ δὴ
Παλαμήδους ὧραι μὲν οὔπω ἦσαν οὖσαι, μηνῶν δὲ
οὔπω κύκλος, ἐνιαυτὸς δὲ οὔπω ὄνομα ἦν τῷ χρόνῳ,
οὐδὲ νόμισμα ἦν, οὐδὲ σταθμὰ καὶ μέτρα, οὐδὲ ἀριθ-
μεῖν, σοφίας τε οὔπω ἔρως, ἐπεὶ μήπω ἦν γράμματα.
2 βουλομένου δὲ τοῦ Χείρωνος ἰατρικὴν διδάσκειν αὐ-
τόν, "ἐγὼ" ἔφη, "ὦ Χείρων, ἰατρικὴν μὲν ἡδέως οὐκ
οὖσαν ἂν εὗρον, εὑρημένην δὲ οὐκ ἀξιῶ μανθάνειν,
καὶ ἄλλως τὸ ὑπέρσοφόν σου τῆς τέχνης ἀπήχθηται
μὲν Διί, ἀπήχθηται δὲ Μοίραις, καὶ διῄειν ἂν τὰ
3 Ἀσκληπιοῦ, εἰ μὴ ἐνταῦθα ἐβέβλητο." ὄντων δὲ τῶν
Ἀχαιῶν ἐν Αὐλίδι πεττοὺς εὗρεν, οὐ ῥάθυμον παιδιὰν
ἀλλ' ἀγχίνουν τε καὶ εἴσω σπουδῆς.

---

123 See, in general, Introduction §9.   124 The story is
told by Pind. *Pyth.* 3: Asclepius had learned to heal from Chiron
on Mt. Pelion, but he was eventually induced by a large sum of
money to bring back a man from the dead. For this offense against
the gods, he was struck with a thunderbolt by Zeus.

used to practice all sorts of hunting and teach the art of war, train doctors, mold musicians and make men just). He lived to a great age, and among his students were Asclepius, Telamon, Peleus and Theseus, and Heracles when labors did not distract him; Protesilaus himself says he enjoyed his company, as did Palamedes and Achilles and Ajax.

33. As for Palamedes,[123] he reports as follows: he arrived at Chiron's already self-taught and practiced in wisdom, indeed with more of it than Chiron; for before Palamedes there were not yet any "seasons," nor the progression of the months, and "year" did not yet exist as a customary designation of time, nor was there currency or weights and measures or counting, nor was there any desire for learning since there was as yet no writing. When Chiron wanted to teach him medicine, he said, "I would gladly have discovered it if it had not yet existed, but since it does I do not think I want to learn it; in any case your excessively wise craft is hated by Zeus and the Fates—I would remind you of the story of Asclepius, if it were not exactly here that he had been struck down."[124] When the Greeks were at Aulis he invented backgammon,[125] not as an idle pastime but as a game requiring skill and concentration.

[125] Probably the closest modern equivalent to the Greek *pessoi*; see Austin (1940, 265–66) and Kurke (1999). Eur. *IT* 195–97 also places the invention of this game at Aulis, but most other sources consider it a device to kill time at Troy, and numerous vases depict Ajax and Achilles playing it (Romero Mariscal 2011; and see on 33.34 below). The rock he used for a playing board was still shown at Ilion in the time of Polemon the Periegete (fr. 32 Preller from Eustathius, quoted by Radt on Sophocles fr. 479).

4   τὸν δὲ λόγον, ὃς πολλοῖς τῶν ποιητῶν εἴρηται, ὡς
στρατεύοι μὲν ἐπὶ Τροίαν ἡ Ἑλλάς, Ὀδυσσεὺς δὲ ἐν
Ἰθάκῃ μανίαν πλάττοιτο καὶ πρὸς ἀρότρῳ εἴη βοῦν
ἵππῳ ξυμβαλών, Παλαμήδης τε αὐτὸν ἐλέγξειε τῷ
Τηλεμάχῳ, οὗ φησιν ὑγιᾶ εἶναι· προθυμότατα γὰρ δὴ
τὸν Ὀδυσσέα ἐς Αὐλίδα ἐλθεῖν καὶ ὄνομα ἤδη αὐτοῦ
5   παραδεδόσθαι τοῖς Ἕλλησιν ἐπὶ δεινότητι. διενεχθῆ-
ναι δὲ αὐτὸν τῷ Παλαμήδει ἐντεῦθεν· ἔκλειψις ἡλίου
ἐν Τροίᾳ ἐγένετο καὶ ὁ στρατὸς ἄθυμοι ἦσαν λαμβά-
6   νοντες τὴν διοσημίαν ἐς τὰ μέλλοντα. παρελθὼν οὖν
ὁ Παλαμήδης αὐτό τε τὸ πάθος τοῦ ἡλίου διεξῆλθε
καὶ ὅτι τῆς σελήνης ὑποτρεχούσης αὐτὸν ἐξαμαυ-
ροῦται καὶ ἀχλὺν ἕλκει· "κακὰ δὲ εἴ τινα σημαίνοι,
ταῦτα δήπου οἱ Τρῶες πείσονται· οἱ μὲν γὰρ ἀδίκων
ἦρξαν, ἡμεῖς δὲ ἀδικούμενοι ἥκομεν. προσήκει δὲ καὶ
ἀνίσχοντι τῷ Ἡλίῳ εὔχεσθαι, πῶλον αὐτῷ κατα-
7   θύσαντας λευκόν τε καὶ ἄνετον." ταῦτα τῶν Ἀχαιῶν
ἐπαινεσάντων (καὶ γὰρ ἥττητο τῶν τοῦ Παλαμήδους
λόγων), παρελθὼν ὁ Ὀδυσσεὺς "ἃ μὲν χρὴ θύειν"
ἔφη, "ἢ ὅ τι εὔχεσθαι ἢ ὅτῳ, Κάλχας ἐρεῖ· μαντικῆς
γὰρ τὰ τοιαῦτα· τὰ δὲ ἐν τῷ οὐρανῷ καὶ ἥτις τῶν
ἄστρων ἀταξία τε καὶ τάξις, Ζεὺς οἶδεν, ὑφ' οὗ ταῦτα
κεκόσμηταί τε καὶ εὕρηται. σὺ δέ, Παλάμηδες, ἥττονα
ληρήσεις προσέχων τῇ γῇ μᾶλλον ἢ τὰ ἐν τῷ οὐρανῷ
8   σοφιζόμενος." ὑπολαβὼν οὖν ὁ Παλαμήδης "εἰ σοφὸς
ἦσθα, ὦ Ὀδυσσεῦ" εἶπε, "ξυνῆκας ἂν ὅτι μηδεὶς ἂν
δύναιτο λέγειν σοφόν τι περὶ τῶν οὐρανίων μὴ πλείω
περὶ τῆς γῆς γινώσκων. σὲ δὲ ἀπολελεῖφθαι τούτων

224

The story told by most of the poets, that the rest of 4
Greece was sailing against Troy, but Odysseus feigned
madness in Ithaca and had yoked an ox to a horse for plow-
ing, and that Palamedes had exposed him by using Telema-
chus, all this Protesilaus says is misguided; for Odysseus
came to Aulis with the greatest enthusiasm, and his repu-
tation for cleverness was already established among the
Greeks. His hostility to Palamedes came rather from this: 5
a solar eclipse occurred at Troy and the army, taking it as
a portent for the future, was nervous; but Palamedes stood 6
up and explained to them exactly what had happened to
the sun, and that when the moon passed in front of it the
result was darkness and difficulty in seeing. "If it portends
any harm," he said, "I think that the Trojans will suffer it,
since it was they who first wronged us, and we have come
as the injured party. It is best to pray to the rising sun and
sacrifice to it a consecrated white colt." When the Greeks 7
had been persuaded by his reasoning and approved his
plan, Odysseus came forward and said, "It is Calchas who
will determine what we must sacrifice and what to pray
and to whom, since that is the task of prophecy. And it is
Zeus, by whom all this was put together and invented, who
knows what is in heaven, and what constitutes order or
disorder among the stars. As for you, Palamedes, you will
talk less nonsense if you spend more time looking at the
earth than being wise about the heavens." Palamedes an- 8
swered, "If you were wise, Odysseus, you would know that
no one can say anything wise about the heavens unless he
first knows much more about the earth. I have no doubt

οὐκ ἀπιστῶ· φασὶ γὰρ ὑμῖν τοῖς Ἰθακησίοις μήτε
9 ὥρας μήτε γῆν εἶναι." ἐκ τούτων ὁ μὲν Ὀδυσσεὺς ἀπ-
ῆλθεν ὀργῆς πλέως, Παλαμήδης δὲ ὡς πρὸς βασκαί-
νοντα ἤδη παρασκευάζων ἑαυτόν.

10 ἐν ἐκκλησίᾳ δέ ποτε τῶν Ἀχαιῶν ὄντων γέρανοι
μὲν ἔτυχον πετόμεναι τὸν εἰωθότα ἑαυταῖς τρόπον, ὁ
δὲ Ὀδυσσεὺς ἐς τὸν Παλαμήδη βλέψας "αἱ γέρανοι"
ἔφη "μαρτύρονται τοὺς Ἀχαιοὺς ὅτι αὐταὶ γράμματα
11 εὗρον, οὐχὶ σύ." καὶ ὁ Παλαμήδης "ἐγὼ γράμματα
οὐχ εὗρον" εἶπεν, "ἀλλ᾽ ὑπ᾽ αὐτῶν εὑρέθην· πάλαι γὰρ
ταῦτα ἐν Μουσῶν οἴκῳ κείμενα ἐδεῖτο ἀνδρὸς τοιού-
του, θεοὶ δὲ τὰ τοιαῦτα δι᾽ ἀνδρῶν σοφῶν ἀναφαί-
νουσι. γέρανοι μὲν οὖν οὐ μεταποιοῦνται γραμμάτων
ἀλλὰ τάξιν ἐπαινοῦσαι πέτονται· πορεύονται γὰρ ἐς
Λιβύην ξυνάψουσαι πόλεμον μικροῖς ἀνθρώποις. σὺ
δ᾽ οὐδὲν ἂν περὶ τάξεως εἴποις· ἀτακτεῖς γὰρ τὰς μά-
12 χας." αἰτίαν δὲ οἶμαι, ξένε, Ὀδυσσεὺς εἶχεν ὡς, εἴ που
Ἕκτορα ἢ Σαρπηδόνα ἢ Αἰνείαν ἴδοι, καταλείπων τὴν
τάξιν καὶ μεθιστάμενος πρὸς τὰ ῥᾳστώνην ἔχοντα
τοῦ πολέμου.

13 μειρακιώδης δὲ ἐπὶ τῆς ἐκκλησίας δόξας καὶ πρε-
σβύτερος νέου τοῦ Παλαμήδους ἡττηθείς, ἐπετείχιζεν
αὐτῷ τὸν Ἀγαμέμνονα ὡς πρὸς τὸν Ἀχιλλέα τοὺς
Ἀχαιοὺς μεθιστάντι.

---

126 Ithaca's lack of land for horses and field crops is admitted
by Telemachus (*Od.* 4.600–608) and Athena (*Od.* 13.242–47).

that you are somewhat backward in all this, for they say that in Ithaca you have neither seasons nor land."[126] Odysseus stalked off in a rage, while Palamedes became cautious against a man who now bore him a grudge. 9

Once while the Greeks were in assembly some cranes happened to be flying in their customary formation,[127] and Odysseus looked at Palamedes and said, "The cranes call the Greeks to witness that it was they who discovered writing, not you." Palamedes answered, "I did not discover writing—I was discovered *by* writing, since it had long been stored in the house of the muses waiting for the right man; the gods customarily make known such things through wise men. The cranes, however, do not claim to make letters; they show their admiration for military order and arrangement in their flight; in fact, they are flying to Libya to fight with some tiny men.[128] But then, arrangement is something you can't speak of, since you always ignore it in battle." I believe that Odysseus was commonly charged with deserting the formation, and moving to where the fighting was slow whenever he saw Hector, Sarpedon or Aeneas.[129] 11 12

Odysseus was senior to the young Palamedes, but had been overcome by him in the assembly and made to look childish; so he began to turn Agamemnon against Palamedes, by claiming that he was urging the Greeks to favor Achilles. 13

[127] That is, in the shape of a delta (or some other letter); see D. Thompson (1936, 72). [128] For the battle of the cranes and pygmies, see *Il.* 3.6; D. Thompson (1936, 72–73).
[129] Odysseus is rebuked by Agamemnon in *Il.* 4.339–48 for lagging behind the ranks, and he ignores Diomedes' call to return to face Hector in 8.97.

14   διενεχθῆναι πάλιν αὐτοὺς ἐκ τοιούτου φησί· λύκοι
καταβαίνοντες ἐκ τῆς Ἴδης ἐσίνοντο τὰ σκευοφόρα
παιδάρια καὶ τῶν ὑποζυγίων τὰ περὶ τὰς σκηνάς· ὁ
μὲν δὴ Ὀδυσσεὺς ἐκέλευσεν ἀραμένους τόξα καὶ
ἀκόντια φοιτᾶν ἐς τὴν Ἴδην ἐπὶ τοὺς λύκους, ὁ δὲ
Παλαμήδης "ὦ Ὀδυσσεῦ" ἔφη, "τοὺς λύκους ὁ Ἀπόλ-
λων προοίμιον λοιμοῦ ποιεῖται καὶ τοξεύει μὲν αὐτοὺς
καθάπερ τοὺς ὀρέας τε καὶ τοὺς κύνας ἐνταῦθα, πέμ-
πει δὲ πρότερον παρὰ τοὺς νοσήσοντας εὐνοίας εἵ-
νεκα τῶν ἀνθρώπων καὶ τοῦ φυλάξασθαι. εὐχώμεθα
οὖν Ἀπόλλωνι Λυκίῳ τε καὶ Φυξίῳ, τὰ μὲν θηρία
ταῦτα τοῖς ἑαυτοῦ τόξοις ἐξελεῖν, τὴν νόσον δὲ ἐς αἶ-
γας, φασί, τρέψαι. καὶ ἡμεῖς δέ, ὦ ἄνδρες Ἕλληνες,
ἐπιμελώμεθα ἡμῶν αὐτῶν· δεῖ δὲ τοῖς φυλαττομένοις
τὰ λοιμώδη διαίτης λεπτῆς καὶ κινήσεων συντόνων.
ἰατρικῆς μὲν γὰρ οὐχ ἡψάμην, σοφίᾳ δὲ καταληπτὰ

15   ἅπαντα." εἰπὼν ταῦτα τὴν μὲν τῶν κρεῶν ἀγορὰν
ἐπέσχε καὶ τὰ στρατιωτικὰ τῶν σιτίων ἐκέλευσε παρ-
αιτήσασθαι, τραγήμασι δὲ καὶ λαχάνοις ἀγρίοις δι-
ῆγε τὸν στρατὸν πειθομένους αὐτῷ καὶ πᾶν τὸ ἐκ

16   Παλαμήδους θεῖόν τε ἡγουμένους καὶ χρησμῶδες· καὶ
γὰρ δὴ ὁ λοιμὸς ὃν προὔλεγεν ἐνέσκηψε μὲν ἐς τὰς
Ἑλλησποντικὰς πόλεις, ἀρξάμενος, φασίν, ἐκ τοῦ

---

130 When Apollo sent a plague upon the Greeks in *Il.* 1.50, he
"first attacked the mules and the idle dogs." Scholia (A) *Il.* 1.50c
explains "the god kills first mules and dogs and dumb animals
because he loves mankind, so that by using them to frighten the
Greeks he can make them pious." The Homeric idea that a god

Protesilaus says that bad feelings arose from another 14
incident also: wolves from Mount Ida were attacking the
slaves who carried the baggage and the pack animals in
camp. Odysseus ordered the Greeks to take their bows
and spears and go to Mount Ida to attack the wolves, but
Palamedes said, "Odysseus, Apollo is starting the plague
with the wolves and striking them down first, just as he is
doing to the mules and dogs here;[130] and he is sending
them to those who are going to suffer the plague next
because he cares for men, and to help us take precautions.
Let us pray therefore to Apollo Lykios and Phyxios, not
only to destroy these wolves with his own arrows, but also
to direct the disease, as they say, to the goats.[131] But we,
men of Greece, must take care of ourselves, and if we want
to keep away disease we must have a light diet and vigor-
ous movement. For even though I haven't studied medi-
cine, anything can be learned by wisdom." Following these 15
words he stopped the sale of meat and commanded them
to reject their army rations of food, and fed them wild
fruits and vegetables; they obeyed, thinking every word he
said like an oracle from god. In fact, the plague he had 16
predicted actually devastated the cities of the Hellespont
—they say it began in Pontus—and Ilion as well, but it

would kill innocent animals and spare guilty humans had been
criticized in antiquity; see Buffière (1956, 196) and *FGrHist* 71
(Zoilus of Amphipolis, F 5). Palamedes means that, since the
wolves are driven from the mountain by the beginnings of a
plague, it is better to *avoid* Mt. Ida and concentrate on remaining
healthy themselves.

[131] "Send it to the wild goats" was proverbial for consigning
something to oblivion; see Pfeiffer on Callimachus fr. 75.13.

PHILOSTRATUS

Πόντου, προσέπεσε δὲ καὶ τῷ Ἰλίῳ, τῶν δὲ Ἑλλήνων
οὐδενὸς ἥψατο καίτοι στρατοπεδευόντων ἐν γῇ νο-
σούσῃ.

17 πρὸς γὰρ τῇ διαίτῃ καὶ τὰς κινήσεις αὐτῶν ὧδε
ἐσοφίσατο· καθελκύσας ἑκατὸν ναῦς ἐνεβίβαζε τὸν
στρατὸν κατὰ μέρος, ἐρέττοντάς τε καὶ ἁμιλλωμένους
ἀλλήλοις ἢ ἀκρωτήριον περιβαλεῖν ἢ σκοπέλου ἅψα-
σθαι ἢ προκατᾶραι τῶν πέλας ἐς λιμένα τινὰ ἢ ἀκτήν,
ἔπεισε δὲ καὶ τὸν Ἀγαμέμνονα προθεῖναί σφισι τοῦ
18 ταχυναυτεῖν ἆθλα. χαίροντες οὖν ἐγυμνάζοντο καὶ
ξυνιέντες τὸ ὑγιαίνειν· καὶ γὰρ ἐδίδασκεν αὐτοὺς ὅτι
τῆς γῆς παρεφθορυίας τε καὶ οὕτως ἐχούσης ἡδίων ἡ
θάλαττα καὶ ἀσφαλεστέρα ἀναπνεῖν.

19 ἐπὶ τούτοις ὁ μὲν σοφίας ἀριστεῖα ἐστεφανοῦτο
ὑπὸ τῶν Ἑλλήνων, ὁ δὲ Ὀδυσσεὺς ἀτίμως τε ἡγεῖτο
πράττειν καὶ πανουργίας ὅ τι εἶχεν ἐπὶ τὸν Παλα-
20 μήδη ἔστρεφεν. ἐπὶ τούτοις ὁ Πρωτεσίλεως τοιαῦτα
ἀπαγγέλλει· τὸν Ἀχιλλέα στρατεύοντα ἐπὶ τὰς νή-
σους καὶ τὰς ἀκταίας πόλεις, αἰτῆσαι τοὺς Ἀχαιοὺς
21 ξὺν Παλαμήδει στρατεῦσαι. ἐμάχοντο δὲ ὁ μὲν Πα-
λαμήδης γενναίως καὶ σωφρόνως, ὁ δὲ Ἀχιλλεὺς οὐ
καθεκτῶς· ὁ γὰρ θυμὸς ἐξαίρων αὐτὸν εἰς ἀταξίαν
ἦγεν, ὅθεν ἔχαιρε τῷ Παλαμήδει συνασπίζοντι καὶ
ἀπάγοντι μὲν αὐτὸν τῆς φορᾶς, ὑποτιθεμένῳ δὲ ὡς
χρὴ μάχεσθαι. καὶ γὰρ δὴ καὶ ἐῴκει λεοντοκόμῳ λέ-
οντα γενναῖον πραΰνοντί τε καὶ ἐγείροντι, καὶ οὐδὲ

230

touched none of the Greeks even though they were en-
camped in the territory of the disease.

After seeing to their diet, he devised exercise for them   17
as follows: he launched one hundred ships and put the
army on as crew in teams, to compete against each other
to round a cape, or reach a headland, or to put in at some
harbor or shore before the others, and he persuaded
Agamemnon to offer prizes for speed in sailing. They en-   18
joyed the exercise, as well as knowing they were staying
healthy. He also taught then that when the earth was in
such a corrupt condition the sea was better, and its air was
safer to breathe.

For these services Palamedes was awarded the prize   19
for wisdom by the Greeks—while Odysseus felt shamed,
and turned all his villainy against him. On this Protesilaus   20
reports in this way: when Achilles was leading an expedi-
tion against the islands and the coastal cities,[132] he re-
quested from the Greeks to campaign with Palamedes. In   21
battle Palamedes was noble and restrained, but Achilles
was unchecked—his emotions sometimes led him into
carelessness, so that he was glad to have Palamedes beside
him in battle, who would prevent him from being carried
away, and also instruct him in tactics. For he was like a
trainer alternately calming and rousing a noble lion, nor

[132] Achilles says in *Il.* 9.327–33, "I sacked twelve cities of men
with my ships, and eleven on foot, around fertile Troy; from all of
these I took much fine booty, all of it I brought and gave to
Agamemnon son of Atreus. He took it , though he stayed behind
by the swift ships, and distributed little, but kept much." These
expeditions must have been narrated in full in the *Cypria* (M. L.
West 2013, 120–21; cf. Dictys 2.16–17).

ἐκκλίνων ταῦτ᾽ ἔπραττεν, ἀλλὰ καὶ βάλλων καὶ φυ-
λαττόμενος βέλη καὶ ἀσπίδα ἀντερείδων καὶ διώκων
στῖφος.

22   ἐξέπλευσαν μὲν δὴ χαίροντες ἀλλήλοις, εἵποντο
δὲ αὐτοῖς Μυρμιδόνες τε καὶ οἱ ἐκ Φυλάκης Θετταλοί.
(ταχθῆναι γὰρ μετὰ ταῦτα τὴν ἑαυτοῦ δύναμιν ὁ
Πρωτεσίλεως ὑπ᾽ Ἀχιλλεῖ, καὶ Μυρμιδόνας οὕτως
23 ὀνομασθῆναι πάντας Θετταλούς.) αἱ μὲν οὖν πόλεις
ἡλίσκοντο καὶ εὐδόκιμα τοῦ Παλαμήδους ἔργα ἀπηγ-
γέλλετο· ἰσθμῶν διορυχαὶ καὶ ποταμοὶ ἐς τὰς πόλεις
ἐπιστρεφόμενοι καὶ σταυροὶ λιμένων καὶ ἐπιτει-
χίσματα νυκτομαχία τε ἡ περὶ Ἄβυδον, ὁπότε τρωθέν-
τες ὁ μὲν Ἀχιλλεὺς ἀνεχώρησεν, ὁ Παλαμήδης δὲ οὐκ
ἀπεῖπεν ἀλλὰ πρὶν μέσην ἑστάναι νύκτα, εἷλε τὸ χω-
ρίον.

24   ὁ δὲ Ὀδυσσεὺς ἐν Τροίᾳ ξυνετίθει λόγους πρὸς τὸν
Ἀγαμέμνονα, ψευδεῖς μέν, πιθανοὺς δὲ πρὸς τὸν εὐ-
ήθως ἀκούοντα, ὡς ἐρῴη μὲν ὁ Ἀχιλλεὺς τῆς τῶν Ἑλ-
λήνων ἀρχῆς, μαστροπῷ δὲ τῷ Παλαμήδει χρῷτο·
25 "καὶ ἀφίξονται μὲν" ἔφη "μικρὸν ὕστερον, σοὶ μὲν
βοῦς τε ἀπάγοντες καὶ ἵππους καὶ ἀνδράποδα, ἑαυ-
τοῖς δὲ χρήματα, οἷς ὑποποιήσονται δήπου τοὺς δυ-
νατοὺς τῶν Ἑλλήνων ἐπὶ σέ· Ἀχιλλέως μὲν οὖν ἀπ-
έχεσθαι χρὴ καὶ γινώσκοντας αὐτὸν φυλάττεσθαι,
τὸν σοφιστὴν δὲ ἀποκτεῖναι τοῦτον. εὕρηται δέ μοι
κατ᾽ αὐτοῦ τέχνη, δι᾽ ἧς μισηθήσεταί τε ὑπὸ τῶν Ἑλ-
26 λήνων καὶ ἀπολεῖται ὑπ᾽ αὐτῶν." καὶ διεξῆλθεν, ὡς
ἡτοίμασται αὐτῷ τὰ περὶ τὸν Φρύγα καὶ τὸ χρυσίον

did he hang back while he did so, but followed the thick of the fighting, throwing and fending off spears and thrusting his shield forward.

They sailed together joyfully, in command of the Myr- 22 midons and the Thessalians from Phylake (Protesilaus says his men were later under Achilles' command, the whole group now being called Myrmidons). The cities 23 were captured, and there were reports of great deeds by Palamedes: of channels dug through isthmuses, rivers diverted toward cities, piles driven in harbors, forts in enemy territory, and a night battle at Abydos in which Achilles and Palamedes were both wounded: the former had to retire, but Palamedes stayed on, and captured the place before midnight came.[133]

At Troy, meanwhile, Odysseus was telling Agamemnon 24 stories that were false, but persuasive to a foolish listener: that Achilles lusted after the Greek command, and was using Palamedes as his pimp to have it. "Soon they will 25 return bringing cattle and horses and slaves for you, but for themselves money, with which of course they intend to turn the most powerful on the army against you. As for Achilles, we must not touch him and be on guard, knowing who he is; but the sophist we must kill, and I have discovered a trick by which he will become hated by the Greeks and be killed at their hands." He then explained to him 26 how everything concerning the Phrygian and the gold cap-

---

[133] Grossardt (2006a) notes that Abydos is not usually included in other lists of the cities captured on this expedition, and it put up fierce resistance to Philip V (Polyb. 16.33).

27 τὸ ληφθὲν ὑπὸ τῷ Φρυγί. σοφῶς δὲ τούτων ἐπινενοῆ-
σθαι δοκούντων καὶ ξυνθεμένου τῇ ἐπιβουλῇ τοῦ
Ἀγαμέμνονος, "ἄγε δή, ὦ βασιλεῦ" ἔφη, "τὸν μὲν
Ἀχιλλέα φύλαττέ μοι περὶ τὰς πόλεις ἐν αἷς ἐστι νῦν,
τὸν Παλαμήδη δὲ ὡς τειχομαχήσοντα τῷ Ἰλίῳ καὶ
μηχανὰς εὑρήσοντα μεταπέμπου ἐνταῦθα· ἄνευ γὰρ
τοῦ Ἀχιλλέως ἥκων, οὐκ ἐμοὶ μόνῳ ἔσται ἁλωτὸς
ἀλλὰ καὶ ἄλλῳ ἧττον σοφῷ."

28 ἔδοξε ταῦτα καὶ ἔπλεον οἱ κήρυκες ἐς Λέσβον·
ἑαλώκει δ' οὔπω πᾶσα, ἀλλ' ὧδε τὰ περὶ αὐτὴν εἶχε·
πόλις Αἰολὶς Λυρνησσὸς ᾠκεῖτο τειχήρης τὴν φύσιν
καὶ οὐδὲ ἀτείχιστος, ᾗ φασι τὴν Ὀρφέως προσεν-
εχθῆναι λύραν καὶ δοῦναί τινα ἠχὴν ταῖς πέτραις, καὶ
μεμούσωται ἔτι καὶ νῦν τῆς Λυρνησσοῦ τὰ περὶ τὴν
29 θάλατταν ὑπ' ᾠδῆς τῶν πετρῶν. ἐνταῦθα προσκαθη-
μένων δεκάτην ἡμέραν (χαλεπὸν γὰρ ἦν ἁλῶναι τὸ
χωρίον), ἀπήγγειλαν μὲν οἱ κήρυκες τὰ τοῦ Ἀγα-
μέμνονος, ἐδόκει δὲ πείθεσθαι καὶ τὸν μὲν καταμένειν,
τὸν Παλαμήδη δὲ ἀπιέναι, καὶ ἀπῆλθον ἀλλήλων
δακρύοις ἅμα.

30 ἐπεὶ δὲ κατέπλευσεν ἐς τὸ στρατόπεδον καὶ τὰ τῆς
στρατιᾶς ἀπήγγειλεν ἀνατιθεὶς ἅπαντα Ἀχιλλεῖ, "ὦ
βασιλεῦ" ἔφη, "κελεύεις με τειχομαχεῖν τῇ Τροίᾳ; ἐγὼ
δὲ μηχανήματα μὲν γενναῖα ἡγοῦμαι τοὺς Αἰακίδας

---

134 Philostratus assumes that readers know of Odysseus' plot
more or less as it was told in tragedy, although there Agamemnon
was not usually an accomplice; see Introduction §9.

tured by the Phrygian had been arranged. This seemed   27
to have been cleverly devised, and Agamemnon agreed to
the plan.[134] "In that case, my king," said Odysseus, "keep
Achilles in the cities where he is now, but send for Pala
medes to come to help you invent siege machines to take
Troy. For if he comes without Achilles, not just I but even
a man less wise can take him."

This was agreed, and heralds sailed for Lesbos, but this   28
place had not yet been entirely conquered. Things in that
region stood like this: there was an Aeolian city called
Lyrnessus which was not only well-protected by nature
but had man-made walls also, where they say Orpheus'
lyre was carried, and resounded among the rocks; even
today the seacoast around Lyrnessus is full of music from
the song of the cliffs.[135] Here they had been encamped for   29
ten days (the place was difficult to capture), when the
heralds gave them Agamemnon's orders, and they decided
to obey. One stayed behind while Palamedes went away,
and they took a tearful leave of each other.

When Palamedes had sailed back to the camp and re-   30
ported on the expedition, giving all the credit to Achilles,
he said, "King, do you really want me to plan the siege of
Troy? In my opinion the Aeacidae,[136] the sons of Capaneus

[135] There are many references in the *Iliad* to Achilles' capture
of the mainland city of Lyrnessus, which was described in the
Cypria (M. L. West 2013, 120). It was there that Achilles cap-
tured Briseis (*Il.* 2.688, 19.59–60) and nearly killed Aeneas (*Il.*
20.90–91, 191–94). For remains of Orpheus in the area, cf. 28.9,
above.

[136] Achilles and the greater Ajax.

PHILOSTRATUS

καὶ τὸν Καπανέως τε καὶ Τυδέως καὶ τοὺς Λοκρούς,
Πάτροκλόν τε δήπου καὶ Αἴαντα· εἰ δὲ καὶ ἀψύχων
μηχανημάτων δεῖσθε, ἤδη ἡγεῖσθε τὴν Τροίαν τό γε
ἐπ᾽ ἐμοὶ κεῖσθαι."

31   ἀλλ᾽ ἔφθησαν αὐτὸν αἱ Ὀδυσσέως μηχαναὶ σοφῶς
ξυντεθεῖσαι, καὶ χρυσοῦ μὲν ἥττων ἔδοξε προδότης τε
εἶναι κατεψεύσθη, περιαχθεὶς δὲ τὼ χεῖρε κατελιθώθη,
βαλλόντων αὐτὸν Πελοποννησίων τε καὶ Ἰθακησίων·
ἡ δὲ ἄλλη Ἑλλὰς οὐδὲ ἑώρα ταῦτα ἀλλὰ καὶ δο-
32 κοῦντα ἀδικεῖν ἠγάπα. ὠμὸν καὶ τὸ ἐπ᾽ αὐτῷ κή-
ρυγμα· μὴ γὰρ θάπτειν τὸν Παλαμήδη μηδὲ ὁσιοῦν
τῇ γῇ, ἀποθνήσκειν δὲ τὸν ἀνελόμενόν τε καὶ θά-
33 ψαντα. κηρύττοντος δὲ ταῦτα τοῦ Ἀγαμέμνονος, Αἴας
ὁ μέγας ἐπιρρίψας ἑαυτὸν τῷ νεκρῷ πολλὰ μὲν δά-
κρυα περὶ αὐτῷ ἀφῆκεν, ἀναθέμενος δὲ αὐτὸν διεξ-
έπαισε τοῦ ὁμίλου γυμνῷ τῷ ξίφει καὶ ἑτοίμῳ· θάψας
οὖν ὡς εἰκὸς ἦν τὸν εἰργόμενον, οὐ προσῄει τῷ κοινῷ
τῶν Ἑλλήνων, οὐδὲ βουλῆς ἢ γνώμης ἥπτετο, οὐδὲ
ἐξῄει ἔτι ἐς τὰς μάχας.

34   Ἀχιλλέως τε ἀφικομένου μετὰ τὴν τῆς Χερρονήσου
35 ἅλωσιν, ἄμφω ἐπὶ τῷ Παλαμήδει ἐμήνισαν. ὁ μὲν
Αἴας οὐκ ἐπὶ πολύ· ὡς γὰρ ᾔσθετο τῶν ξυμμάχων
κακῶς πραττόντων, ἤλγησέ τε καὶ τὴν ὀργὴν μετέθη-
36 κεν. ὁ δὲ Ἀχιλλεὺς ἐπεμήκυνε τὴν μῆνιν· ᾠδήν τε γὰρ
τῆς λύρας τὸν Παλαμήδην ἐπεποίητο καὶ ᾖδεν αὐτὸν
ὅσα τοὺς προτέρους τῶν ἡρώων, ἐδεῖτό τε ὄναρ ἐφί-

236

and Tydeus, and the Locrians (obviously I mean Patroclus and Ajax) are splendid siege machines; but if you need inanimate machines as well, then rest assured that, as far as is in my power, Troy is already fallen."

But the machinery of Odysseus' plot had been inge-   31
niously constructed before he realized it, and Palamedes was framed for accepting bribes and falsely accused of treason. His hands were tied behind his back and he was stoned to death by the Peloponnesians and Ithacans; the rest of the Greeks did not witness the trial, but went along with his presumed guilt.[137] Even the announcement of his death sentence was harsh: that no one must bury Pala-   32
medes or sanctify him with earth, but whoever should raise him up and bury him would die. As Agamemnon   33
announced this, the greater Ajax threw himself on the body with a flood of tears, raised it and burst through the crowd, his sword drawn and ready. When he had buried him appropriately in spite of the edict, he stopped contact with the rest of the Greeks, did not join in their plans and councils, nor even go into battle any more.

When, after the capture of the Chersonnese, Achilles   34
returned, they both were in a rage over Palamedes.[138] For Ajax this did not last long, for when he saw that his allies   35
were in desperate straits he was pained, and altered his anger. But Achilles was angry for a long time: he composed   36
a song for the lyre on Palamedes, and sang of him as of the heroes of old; and he prayed that he visit him in a dream,

[137] Again Philostratus avoids the details, for which see Introduction §9.   [138] Romero Mariscal (2011) notes that it is precisely these two heroes who are so often depicted playing the board game that Palamedes invented.

στασθαι οἷ, σπένδων ἀπὸ κρατῆρος οὗ Ἑρμῆς ὑπὲρ
ὀνείρων πίνει.

37   ἔοικέ τε ὁ ἥρως οὗτος οὐκ Ἀχιλλεῖ μόνον, ἀλλὰ καὶ
πᾶσιν οἷς ῥώμης τε καὶ σοφίας ἔρως, παρέχειν ἑαυτὸν
ζήλου τε καὶ ᾠδῆς ἄξιον, ὅ τε Πρωτεσίλεως, ἐπειδὰν
ἐς μνήμην αὐτοῦ ἀφικώμεθα, ἀστακτὶ δακρύει, τήν τε
ἄλλην ἀνδρείαν τοῦ ἥρω ἐπαινῶν καὶ τὴν ἐν τῷ
θανάτῳ· οὐ γὰρ δὴ ἱκετεῦσαι τὸν Παλαμήδη, οὐδὲ
οἰκτρόν τι εἰπεῖν οὐδὲ ὀδύρασθαι, ἀλλ' εἰπὼν "ἐλεῶ
σε, ἀλήθεια· σὺ γὰρ ἐμοῦ προαπόλωλας," ὑπέσχε τὴν
κεφαλὴν τοῖς λίθοις, οἷον ξυνιεὶς ὅτι ἡ Δίκη πρὸς
αὐτοῦ ἔσται.

38   ΦΟΙΝ. Ἔστι καὶ τὸν Παλαμήδη ἰδεῖν, ἀμπελουργέ,
καθάπερ καὶ τὸν Νέστορα εἶδον καὶ τὸν Διομήδη καὶ
τὸν Σθένελον, ἢ οὐδὲν περὶ τῆς ἰδέας αὐτοῦ ὁ Πρωτε-
σίλεως ἑρμηνεύει;

39   ΑΜΠ. Ὑπάρχει, ξένε, καὶ ὅρα· μέγεθος μὲν τοίνυν
αὐτὸν κατὰ Αἴαντα τὸν μείζω γενέσθαι, κάλλος δὲ
Ἀχιλλεῖ τε ἁμιλλᾶσθαι καὶ Ἀντιλόχῳ καὶ ἑαυτῷ φη-
σιν ὁ Πρωτεσίλεως καὶ Εὐφόρβῳ τῷ Τρωΐ· γένεια μὲν
γὰρ αὐτῷ ἁπαλὰ ἐκφύεσθαι καὶ ξὺν ἐπαγγελίᾳ βο-
στρύχων, τὴν κόμην δὲ ἐν χρῷ εἶναι, τὰς δὲ ὀφρῦς
ἐλευθέρας τε καὶ ὀρθὰς καὶ ξυμβαλλούσας πρὸς τὴν
40   ῥῖνα τετράγωνόν τε οὖσαν καὶ εὖ βεβηκυῖαν. τὸν δὲ
τῶν ὀφθαλμῶν νοῦν ἐν μὲν ταῖς μάχαις ἄτρεπτόν τε
φαίνεσθαι καὶ γοργόν, ἐν δὲ τῇ ἡσυχίᾳ φιλέταιρόν τε
καὶ εὐπροσήγορον τὰς βολάς· λέγεται δὲ καὶ μεγί-
41   στοις ἀνθρώπων ὀφθαλμοῖς χρήσασθαι. καὶ μὴν καὶ

offering wine from the bowl where Hermes drinks to send dreams.[139]

This hero appeared not only to Achilles, but to all those 37 who loved strength and wisdom, to be worthy of song and admiration; and whenever I discuss him with Protesilaus he weeps profusely, praising especially his courage in the face of death. He did not beg for his life, or speak words of misery or lament, but said, "I pity you, truth; for you have died even before I do." He held his head out to receive the stones, as if he understood that justice was with him.

Phoenician. Is it possible to behold Palamedes as I did 38 with Nestor, Diomedes and Sthenelus? Or does Protesilaus give no interpretation of his appearance?

Vinedresser. Yes you may, so behold: Protesilaus says 39 he is as tall as the greater Ajax, in beauty he rivals Achilles or Antilochus, or himself, or Euphorbus of Troy. He is growing a light beard, just beginning to curl, with hair shaved to the skin; his eyebrows are free and straight, and meet at a four-cornered and solid nose. The look in his 40 eyes seems unshakeable and fierce in battle, but when relaxed is amiable and friendly in its glance. It is said that he had the largest eyes of any mortal. Stripped, they say 41

---

[139] For Hermes receiving the final libation before sleep, cf. *Od.* 7.136–38; *PCG* Strattis fr. 23. For his control of sleep and dreams, cf. *Hymn to Hermes* 14, scholia *Od.* 23.198V = *FGrHist* 244 (Apollodorus of Athens) F 129. The mysterious "bowl where Hermes drinks to send dreams" may have meant for Philostratus something like the jar pictured in a fifth-century *lekythos* now in Jena (Vermeule [1979, 26], from which Hermes sent forth winged creatures [souls or dreams? or, like Palamedes, both?] into the light).

PHILOSTRATUS

γυμνόν φησι τὸν Παλαμήδη μέσα φέρεσθαι βαρέος
ἀθλητοῦ καὶ κούφου, καὶ αὐχμὸν περὶ τῷ προσώπῳ
ἔχειν πολὺν ἡδίω τῶν Εὐφόρβου πλοκάμων τῶν χρυ-
σῶν. αὐχμοῦ δὲ ἐπεμεμέλητο ὑπὸ τοῦ καθεύδειν τε ὡς
ἔτυχεν, αὐλίζεσθαί τε πολλάκις ἐν τῇ ἀκρωνυχίᾳ τῆς
Ἴδης ἐν σχολῇ τῶν πολεμικῶν· τὴν γὰρ κατάληψιν
τῶν μετεώρων ἐντεῦθεν ἀπὸ τῶν ὑψηλοτάτων οἱ σοφοὶ
ποιοῦνται.

42   ἦγε δὲ εἰς Ἴλιον οὔτε ναῦν οὔτε ἄνδρα, ἀλλ᾽ ἐν
πορθμείῳ ξὺν Οἴακι τῷ ἀδελφῷ ἔπλευσε, πολλῶν,
43   φασί, βραχιόνων ἀντάξιον ἑαυτὸν ἡγούμενος. οὐδὲ
ἀκόλουθος ἦν αὐτῷ οὐδὲ θεράπων οὐδὲ Τέκμησσά τις
ἢ Ἶφις λούουσα ἢ στρωννῦσα τὸ λέχος, ἀλλ᾽ αὐτουρ-
44   γὸς βίος καὶ ἔξω τοῦ κατεσκευάσθαι. εἰπόντος γοῦν
ποτε πρὸς αὐτὸν Ἀχιλλέως "ὦ Παλάμηδες, ἀγροικό-
τερος φαίνῃ τοῖς πολλοῖς, ὅτι μὴ πέπασαι τὸν θερα-
πεύσοντα," "τί οὖν, ὦ Ἀχιλλεῦ, ταῦτα;" ἔφη τὼ χεῖρε
45   ἄμφω προτείνας. διδόντων δὲ αὐτῷ τῶν Ἀχαιῶν ἐκ
δασμοῦ χρήματα καὶ κελευόντων αὐτὸν πλουτεῖν, "οὐ
λαμβάνω" ἔφη, "κἀγὼ γὰρ ὑμᾶς κελεύω πένεσθαι καὶ
46   οὐ πείθεσθε." ἐρομένου δέ ποτε αὐτὸν Ὀδυσσέως ἐξ
ἀστρονομίας ἥκοντα "τί πλέον ἡμῶν ὁρᾷς ἐν τῷ οὐ-
ρανῷ;" "τοὺς κακοὺς" εἶπεν. ἀμείνων δ᾽ ἂν ἦν τοὺς
Ἀχαιοὺς ἐκδιδάξας ὅτῳ ποτὲ τῶν τρόπων φανεροὶ οἱ
κακοί· οὐ γὰρ ἂν προσήκαντο τὸν Ὀδυσσέα ἐπαν-
τλοῦντα αὐτῷ ψευδεῖς οὕτω καὶ πανούργους τέχνας.

he was somewhat between a lightweight and heavyweight athlete, and he had a great deal of dirt on his face that was more pleasant than Euphorbus' golden locks; he cultivated the dirt as the result of sleeping wherever he found himself, and of spending many nights, during lulls in the fighting, at the summit of Mt. Ida; for since that time seekers of knowledge make their observations of the sky from the highest places.

He brought to Troy neither a ship nor men, but sailed 42
in a troop transport with his brother Oiax, thinking himself "a match for many arms," as they say.[140] He had no fol- 43
lower, no attendant, no Tecmessa or Iphis to wash him or lay his bed;[141] his life was self-sufficient and free of any trappings. Once Achilles said to him, "Palamedes, people 44
think you a dolt, because you have no attendant." But he held out his two hands and said, "What, Achilles, are these for?" Once when the Greeks awarded him a share of booty 45
and desired to make him wealthy, he said, "I cannot accept this; for I keep urging you to be poor, and you do not obey me either." Once as he was returning from study 46
of the stars Odysseus asked him, "What more do you see in the sky than we do?" Palamedes replied, "Evil men." He would have been more valuable if he had taught the Greeks by what character traits evil men can be recognized, for they would not have believed Odysseus when he covered him with his arts of deceit and villainy.

[140] Cf. *Il.* 11.514. Scodel (1980, 62–63) compares the use of "arm" for "strength" in Eur. *Supp.* 478 and *Antiope* fr. 199, and she suggests that this phrase echoes his *Palamedes*.

[141] Iphis was the slave girl of Patroclus (*Il.* 9.667); Tecmessa the captive wife in Sophocles' *Ajax*.

47 τὸ δὲ λεγόμενον πῦρ ὑπὸ Ναυπλίου περὶ κοίλην
Εὔβοιαν ἐπὶ τοὺς Ἀχαιοὺς ἀρθῆναι, ἀληθές τέ φησιν
εἶναι καὶ ὑπὲρ Παλαμήδους ἐκ Μοιρῶν πεπρᾶχθαι
καὶ Ποσειδῶνος, ἴσως, ξένε, μηδὲ βουλομένης τῆς
Παλαμήδους ταῦτα ψυχῆς· σοφὸς γὰρ ὢν ξυνεγί-
48 νωσκέ που αὐτοῖς τῆς ἀπάτης. ἔθαψαν δὲ αὐτὸν Ἀχιλ-
λεύς τε καὶ Αἴας εἰς τὴν ὅμορον τῇ Τροίᾳ τῶν Αἰο-
λέων ἤπειρον, ὑφ' ὧν καὶ ἱερὸν αὐτῷ τι ἐξῳκοδόμητο
μάλα ἀρχαῖον καὶ ἄγαλμα Παλαμήδους ἵδρυται γεν-
ναῖόν τε καὶ εὔοπλον, καὶ θύουσιν αὐτῷ ξυνιόντες οἱ
49 τὰς ἀκταίας οἰκοῦντες πόλεις. μαστεύειν δὲ χρὴ τὸ
ἱερὸν κατὰ Μήθυμνάν τε καὶ Λεπέτυμνον· ὄρος δὲ
τοῦτο ὑψηλὸν ὑπερφαίνεται τῆς Λέσβου.

34. Τὰ δὲ Ὀδυσσέως οὑτωσὶ φράζει· γενέσθαι μὲν
αὐτὸν ῥητορικώτατον καὶ δεινόν, εἴρωνα δὲ καὶ ἐρα-
στὴν φθόνου καὶ τὸ κακόηθες ἐπαινοῦντα, κατηφῆ τε
ἀεὶ καὶ οἷον ἐπεσκεμμένον, τὰ πολέμιά τε δοκοῦντα
μᾶλλον γενναῖον ἢ ὄντα, οὐ μὴν ἐπιστήμονα ὁπλί-
σεως, ἢ τοῦ τάξαι ναυμαχίας τε καὶ τειχομαχίας, καὶ
2 αἰχμῆς καὶ τόξων ἕλξεως. τὰ δὲ ἔργα αὐτοῦ εἶναι
πολλὰ μέν, οὐ μὴν θαυμάσαι ἄξια πλὴν ἑνός, τοῦ ἐς
τὸν ἵππον τὸν κοῖλον, οὗ τέκτων μὲν Ἐπειὸς σὺν
Ἀθηνᾷ ἐγένετο, Ὀδυσσεὺς δὲ εὑρετής· καὶ ἐν αὐτῷ δὲ
λέγεται τῷ λόχῳ θαρσαλεώτερος ὀφθῆναι τοῦ πληρώ-
ματος.

3 εἰς Ἴλιον μὲν οὖν παρηβηκὼς ἦλθεν, ἐς δὲ Ἰθάκην
γεγηρακώς· μακροτέρᾳ γὰρ ἐχρήσατο τῇ ἄλῃ διὰ τὸν

Protesilaus says that the beacon that is said to have   47
been lit against the Greeks around hollow Euboea by Nau-
plius really existed, but was made for Palamedes' sake by
the fates and Poseidon, perhaps even against the will of
Palamedes' spirit; wise man that he was, I expect he for-
gave them for being tricked. Achilles and Ajax buried him   48
on the Aeolians' mainland bordering Troy, and there had
been a very old shrine built by these people, and is now a
noble statue of Palamedes in full armor; the cities along
the coast join together to give him sacrifice. His shrine   49
can be found opposite Methymna and Lepetymnos, a tall
mountain which overlooks Lesbos.[142]

34. Protesilaus describes Odysseus[143] as follows: he was
a clever master of persuasion, deceitful, he relished envy,
an admirer of wickedness, always avoiding one's gaze and
like one meditating. As a soldier he seemed more noble
than he was, having no skill in infantry fighting, naval tac-
tics or siegecraft, or discharging spear or arrows. He did
many things, but the only one which was especially im-   2
pressive was that of the wooden horse, which Epeius built
with Athena's help, but Odysseus invented; and during
that ambush he is said to have proved himself braver than
the rest of the crew.

He was already past his youth when he went to Troy,   3
and returned to Ithaca only in his old age; his wanderings

---

[142] *VA* 4.12.2–3 tells of the rediscovery of his statue (seen by
Philostratus himself) and the reestablishment of the shrine by
Apollonius of Tyana. For its location on the mainland *opposite*
Methymna on Lesbos, see Follet (1994) and Grossardt (2006a).
See Introduction §9.   [143] Philostratus takes to an extreme
the negative portrait of Odysseus found in tragedy and of course
accepts none of the fabulous adventures in *Od.* 9–12 as genuine.

πόλεμον ὃς πρὸς Κίκονας αὐτῷ διεπολεμήθη κατα-
4 τρέχοντι τὰ ἐπὶ θαλάττῃ τοῦ Ἰσμάρου. τὰ γὰρ Πολυ-
φήμου καὶ Ἀντιφάτου καὶ Σκύλλης καὶ τὰ ἐν Ἅιδου
καὶ ὁπόσα αἱ Σειρῆνες ᾖδον, οὐδὲ ἀκούειν ξυγχωρεῖ
ὁ Πρωτεσίλεως, ἀλλ' ἐπαλείφειν ἡμᾶς κηρὸν τοῖς ὠσὶ
καὶ παραιτεῖσθαι αὐτά, οὐχ ὡς οὐ πλέα ἡδονῆς καὶ
ψυχαγωγῆσαι ἱκανά, ἀλλ' ὡς ἀπίθανά τε καὶ παρευ-
5 ρημένα. καὶ τὴν νῆσον δὲ τὴν Ὠγυγίαν καὶ τὴν
Αἰαίαν καὶ ὡς ἤρων αὐτοῦ αἱ θεαί, παραπλεῖν κελεύει
καὶ μὴ προσορμίζεσθαι τοῖς μύθοις· ἔξωρόν τε γὰρ
τῶν ἐρωτικῶν εἶναι τὸν Ὀδυσσέα, καὶ ὑπόσιμον καὶ
οὐ μέγαν καὶ πεπλανημένον τοὺς ὀφθαλμοὺς διὰ τὰς
6 ἐννοίας τε καὶ ὑπονοίας. ἐνθυμουμένῳ γὰρ ἐῴκει,
τοῦτο δὲ ἄχαρι ἐς τὰ ἐρωτικά. οἷος μὲν δὴ οἷον καὶ
ὡς σοφώτερόν τε καὶ ἀνδρειότερον ἑαυτοῦ τὸν Παλα-
μήδη ὁ Ὀδυσσεὺς ἀπέκτεινεν, ἱκανῶς ἐκ τούτου διδά-
7 σκει ὁ Πρωτεσίλεως· ὅθεν καὶ τὸν θρῆνον τὸν παρ'
Εὐριπίδῃ ἐπαινεῖ, ὁπότε Εὐριπίδης ἐν Παλαμήδους
μέλεσιν·

ἐκάνετε" φησίν, "ἐκάνετε
τὸν πάνσοφον, ὦ Δαναοί,
τὰν οὐδὲν ἀλγύνουσαν
ἀηδόνα Μουσᾶν

καὶ τὰ ἐφεξῆς μᾶλλον, ἐν οἷς φησι καὶ ὅτι πεισθέντες
ἀνθρώπῳ δεινῷ καὶ ἀναιδεῖ ταῦτα δράσειαν.
35. Αἴαντα δὲ τὸν Τελαμῶνος ἐκάλουν οἱ Ἀχαιοὶ

were long because he had to fight against the Cicones
while he was raiding along the coast of Ismaros.[144] As for   4
Polyphemus, Antiphates, Scylla or what happened in Ha-
des and the Sirens' song, Protesilaus does not allow listen-
ing to it, but to put wax in our ears and reject it, not be-
cause it was not enjoyable and entertaining, but because
it was an incredible series of fictions. The islands of Ogygia   5
and Aiaia and the tale that goddesses loved him he advises
me to give a wide berth to, and not anchor at these myths.
Odysseus was too old for love affairs, and anyway he was
short with a snub nose, and shifty eyes because he was
always scheming or suspicious. He always seemed to be   6
calculating—an unattractive trait in a lover. Protesilaus
thinks this a sufficient account of how such a man killed
the wiser and braver Palamedes. And so he approves the   7
Euripidean dirge in the lyrics of *Palamedes*:[145]

> You all killed, you killed
> the wisest man, Greeks,
> nightingale of the Muses,
> who did you no harm

and he likes even better what follows, where Euripides
says they did this persuaded by a clever and shameless
man.

35. The Greeks called Ajax son of Telamon "the great"

---

[144] Cf. *Od.* 9. 39–61, where this episode only lasts a few days.
The Cicones are a Thracian tribe that had been allied with Troy.

[145] Fr. 588 Kannicht (2004); Collard and Cropp (2008, 8.59);
cf. Scodel (1980, 59).

μέγαν, οὐκ ἀπὸ τοῦ μεγέθους, οὐδ' ἐπειδὴ μείων ὁ
ἕτερος, ἀλλ' ἀφ' ὧν ἔπραττε, καὶ ἐποιοῦντο αὐτὸν ξύμ-
βολον τοῦ πολέμου ἀγαθὸν ἐκ πατρῴου ἔργου· τὸν
γὰρ Λαομέδοντα τὸν Ἡρακλῆ ἀπατήσαντα μετῆλθε

2 ξὺν Ἡρακλεῖ ὁ Τελαμὼν καὶ αὐτῷ Ἰλίῳ εἷλεν. ἔχαι-
ρον μὲν οὖν αὐτῷ καὶ ἀόπλῳ (πελώριος γάρ τις ἦν
καὶ ὑπὲρ τὴν στρατιὰν πᾶσαν καὶ φρόνημα αἴρων
εὐήνιόν τε καὶ σῶφρον) ὡπλισμένου τε ἐξεκρέμαντο,
μετέωρόν τε βαίνοντος ἐπὶ τοὺς Τρῶας καὶ τὴν
ἀσπίδα εὖ μεταχειριζομένου τοσαύτην οὖσαν, βλέπο-
ντός τε χαροποῖς τοῖς ὀφθαλμοῖς ὑπὸ τὴν κόρυν, οἷον
οἱ λέοντες ἐν ἀναβολῇ τοῦ ὁρμῆσαι.

3   τὰς μάχας δὲ πρὸς τοὺς ἀρίστους ἐποιεῖτο, Λυκίους
μὲν καὶ Μυσοὺς καὶ Παίονας ἀριθμοῦ φάσκων ἕνεκα
ἐς Τροίαν ἥκειν, τοὺς δὲ τούτων ἡγεμόνας ἀξιομάχους
τε ἡγούμενος καὶ οἵους ἀποκτείναντι μὲν ὄνομα δοῦ-
ναι, τρωθέντι δὲ οὐκ ἄδοξον τραῦμα. πολέμιόν τε
ἑλὼν ἀπείχετο τῶν ὅπλων· τὸ μὲν γὰρ ἀποκτείνειν
ἀνδρὸς εἶναι, τὸ δὲ σκυλεύειν λωποδύτου μᾶλλον.

4 ἀκόλαστον δὲ οὐδὲν οὐδὲ ὑβριστικὸν ἐφθέγξατο ἂν
οὐδεὶς ἐν ἐπηκόῳ τοῦ Αἴαντος, οὐδὲ ὁπόσοις ἦν δια-
φορὰ πρὸς ἀλλήλους, ἀλλὰ καὶ θάκων ὑπανίσταντο
αὐτῷ καὶ ὁδῶν ὑπεξίσταντο, οὐχ οἱ πολλοὶ μόνον,
ἀλλὰ καὶ οἱ τῆς εὐδοκίμου μοίρας.

5   πρὸς δὲ Ἀχιλλέα φιλία ἦν αὐτῷ καὶ βασκαίνειν
ἀλλήλοις οὔτε ἐβούλοντο οὔτε ἐπεφύκεσαν, τάς τε λύ-
πας ὁπόσαι περὶ τὸν Ἀχιλλέα, εἰ καὶ μὴ μικρῶν ἕνε-
κεν ἐγίνοντο, πάσας ἐπράυνε, τὰς μὲν ὡς ἂν ξυναλ-

not because of his height, nor because the other Ajax was shorter, but from his achievements, and they considered him a good omen for the war because of what his father had done: after Laomedon had deceived Heracles, Telamon went after him with Heracles and took him Ilion and all.[146] Therefore they were pleased with him even when he was not armed (for he was a giant who towered above all the rest of the army, but bore a temperament that was pliant and restrained); but when he was armed they depended on him, as he strode tall against the Trojans wielding his shield well despite its size, watching with gleaming eyes beneath his helm, like lions when they are about to pounce.

He used to fight only against the best men, saying that Lycians, Mysians and Paeonians had come to Troy only because of their numbers; it was their leaders who were worth fighting, since they offered fame to the man who killed them, and at least an honorable wound to the man they defeated. When he killed an opponent he did not touch his armor, in the belief that killing was a man's work, stripping a corpse that of a thief. No one would have spoken a boastful or arrogant word within Ajax's hearing, not even those who had been quarreling; they offered him their seats and got out of his way, not only the common soldiers but even those of high rank.

Between him and Achilles there was a friendship, and mutual jealousy they neither wished, nor was it in their nature; he lightened all Achilles' griefs even if for great reasons, sometimes with sympathy, sometimes with a sort

[146] Cf. ch. 28 n. 104, above.

γῶν τις, τὰς δ' οἷον ἐπιπλήττων, καθημένων τε ὁμοῦ
καὶ βαδιζόντων ἐπεστρέφετο ἡ Ἑλλάς, ἐς ἄνδρε
6   ὁρῶσα οἴω μετὰ Ἡρακλέα οὔπω ἐγενέσθην. τὸν μέν
γε Αἴαντα καὶ τρόφιμον τοῦ Ἡρακλέους εἶναι ἔφασαν
καὶ βρέφος ὄντα ἐνειληθῆναι τῇ λεοντῇ τοῦ ἥρωος,
ὅτε ἀνασχὼν αὐτὸν τῷ Διί, ἀνάλωτον ᾔτει γενέσθαι
κατὰ τὴν δορὰν τοῦ λέοντος, ἀετός τε εὐξαμένῳ ἀφ-
ίκετο φέρων ἐκ Διὸς τῷ μὲν παιδὶ ὄνομα, ταῖς δὲ εὐ-
χαῖς νεῦμα.
7   δῆλός τε ἦν καὶ ἁπλῶς βλέψαντι μὴ ἀθεεὶ φῦναι,
διά τε τὴν ὥραν διά τε τὴν ῥώμην τοῦ εἴδους, ὅθεν ὁ
8   Πρωτεσίλεως ἄγαλμα πολέμου καλεῖ αὐτόν. ἐμοῦ δὲ
εἰπόντος "καὶ μὴν κατεπαλαίσθη ἀεὶ ὑπὸ τοῦ Ὀδυσ-
σέως ὁ μέγας οὗτος καὶ θεῖος," "εἰ Κύκλωπες" ἔφη
"ἐγεγόνεισαν καὶ ἀληθὴς ἦν ὁ περὶ αὐτῶν μῦθος,
μᾶλλον ἂν τῷ Πολυφήμῳ διεπάλαισεν Ὀδυσσεὺς ἢ
τῷ Αἴαντι."
9   ἤκουσα τοῦ Πρωτεσίλεω, ξένε, κἀκεῖνα περὶ τοῦ
ἥρω τούτου, ὡς ἄρα ἐκόμα ποταμῷ Ἰλισσῷ τῷ Ἀθή-
νησι, καὶ ἠγάπων αὐτὸν οἱ ἐν Τροίᾳ Ἀθηναῖοι καὶ
ἡγεμόνα ἡγοῦντο καὶ ὅ τι εἴποι ἔπραττον, ἠττίκιζέ τε
ἅτε, οἶμαι, Σαλαμῖνα οἰκῶν, ἣν Ἀθηναῖοι δῆμον πε-
ποίηνται, παῖδά τε αὐτῷ γενόμενον, ὃν Εὐρυσάκην οἱ
Ἀχαιοὶ ἐκάλουν, τήν τε ἄλλην ἔτρεφε τροφὴν ἣν Ἀθη-
ναῖοι ἐπαινοῦσι καὶ ὅτε Ἀθήνησιν οἱ παῖδες ἐν μηνὶ
ἀνθεστηριῶνι στεφανοῦνται τῶν ἀνθέων, τρίτῳ ἀπὸ
γενεᾶς ἔτει, κρατῆράς τε τοὺς ἐκεῖθεν ἐστήσατο καὶ

of reproof. When they sat or walked together all the Greeks were in rapt attention, seeing two men whose like there had never yet been since Heracles. They said that 6 Ajax had actually been brought up by Heracles and once, as a baby, wrapped up in the hero's lion skin, when he raised him to Zeus and prayed that the child be invulnerable just like the skin of the lion, an eagle (*aietos*) flew down from Zeus as he prayed and brought the baby his name (*Aias*) and approved the prayer.

From his appearance of beauty and strength it was 7 clear even to a casual onlooker that a god had some part in his birth, and Protesilaus calls him a statue of warfare. When I answered, "But this great and godlike man was 8 always outwrestled by Odysseus!"[147] he said, "If there had been Cyclopes and the story about them were true, Odysseus could sooner have wrestled with Polyphemus than with Ajax."

I heard from Protesilaus , stranger, also the following 9 about this hero: that he wore his hair long for the river Ilissos at Athens,[148] and that the Athenians at Troy loved him, considered him their leader and did whatever he commanded; he spoke Attic, I suppose, because he lived in Salamis which the Athenians have made a deme,[149] and he brought up the child born to him (called Eurysakes by the Greeks) just as the Athenians approve in other respects, and, when, in the third year of their birth, in the month Anthesterion the Athenians have their children crowned with flowers, he set up the bowls of wine from

---

[147] *Il.* 23.700–39.   [148] It was customary for Greek boys and girls coming of age to dedicate their hair to their local river (Burkert 1985, 373, 374n29).

[149] Actually, Salamis was never really a deme of Athens.

ἔθυσεν ὅσα Ἀθηναίοις ἐν νόμῳ· μεμνῆσθαι δὲ καὶ
αὐτὸν ἔφασκε τουτωνὶ τῶν Διονυσίων κατὰ Θησέα.

10 ὁ δὲ τοῦ θανάτου λόγος, ὃν ὑφ' ἑαυτοῦ ἀποσφαγεὶς
ἀπέθανεν, ἀληθὴς μέν, ἐλεεινὸς δὲ καὶ Ὀδυσσεῖ τάχα,
τά τε ἐν Ἅιδου·

μὴ ὄφελον νικᾶν τοιῷδ' ἐπ' ἀέθλῳ·
τοίην γὰρ κεφαλὴν ἕνεκ' αὐτῶν γαῖα κατέσχεν

ἐκεῖ μὲν οὔ φησιν εἰρῆσθαι τῷ Ὀδυσσεῖ, μὴ γὰρ
καταβῆναι αὐτὸν ζῶντα, πάντως δὲ εἰρῆσθαί που. πι-
θανὸν γάρ που παθεῖν τι καὶ τὸν Ὀδυσσέα καὶ ἀπεύ-
ξασθαι τὴν ἑαυτοῦ νίκην ἐλέῳ τοιοῦδε ἀνδρὸς ἐπ'
αὐτῇ ἀποθανόντος.

11 ἐπαινῶν δὲ ὁ Πρωτεσίλεως τοῦ Ὁμήρου ταῦτα,
πολὺ μᾶλλον ἐπαινεῖ τὸ ἐπ' αὐτῷ ἔπος ἐν ᾧ φησι·
"παῖδες δὲ Τρώων δίκασαν·" καὶ γὰρ τῶν Ἀχαιῶν
ἀφεῖλε τὴν ἄδικον κρίσιν καὶ δικαστὰς ἐκάθισεν οὓς
εἰκὸς ἦν καταψηφίσασθαι τοῦ Αἴαντος· συγγενὲς γὰρ
12 φόβῳ μῖσος. μανέντα δὲ αὐτὸν οἱ μὲν Τρῶες ἔδεισαν
πλείω ἢ εἰώθεσαν, μὴ προσβαλὼν τῷ τείχει ῥήξῃ
αὐτό, καὶ ηὔχοντο Ποσειδῶνί τε καὶ Ἀπόλλωνι, ἐπειδὴ
ἐς τὸ τεῖχος ἐθήτευσαν, προβεβλῆσθαι τῶν περγά-
μων τοῦ ἄστεος καὶ σχεῖν τὸν Αἴαντα εἰ τῶν ἐπάλ-
ξεων ἅπτοιτο·

οἱ δὲ Ἕλληνες οὐκ ἐπαύοντο ἀγαπῶντες αὐτόν,

---

150 For the participation of children in the Anthesteria, see
Burkert (1983, 221).

Athens and sacrificed in their manner.[150] Protesilaus says
that Ajax observed this Dionysiac festival just as Theseus
had.[151]

The story that he died self-slaughtered Protesilaus says   10
is true, and he was lamented soon even by Odysseus; and
the words in the underworld (*Od.* 11.548–49):

> . . . I ought not to have won in so awful a contest;
> For such a warrior the grave now holds because of it

were not said by him *there*—since he never went there
alive—but were nonetheless probably said by him; it is
plausible that even Odysseus should have had some feel-
ing, and condemned his own victory out of pity for the
great man whose death it had caused.

While Protesilaus finds this sentiment of Homer's   11
praiseworthy, he finds even more so the adjacent verse
"the children of the Trojans judged them" (*Od.* 11.547),
since it exonerates the Greeks from the unjust vote and
makes the judges the ones who would more plausibly have
condemned Ajax; for fear often breeds hate. When Ajax   12
became insane the Trojans had an even greater fear than
usual, that he would attack their wall and tear it apart; they
prayed to Poseidon and Apollo, since they had performed
their servitude on the wall,[152] to guard the city's towers
and push him back if he should attack the battlements.

The Greeks' affection for him never ceased; but they

---

[151] Grossardt (2006a) notes this as another of the vinedresser's
errors (Introduction §7), since Theseus founded the Panathe-
naea.

[152] See ch. 27.7, 27.8n.

ἀλλὰ πένθος τε τὴν τοῦ Αἴαντος μανίαν ἐποιοῦντο καὶ
τὰ μαντεῖα ἱκέτευον χρῆσαι πῶς ἂν μεταβάλοιτο καὶ
13 εἰς νοῦν ἔλθοι. ἐπεὶ δὲ ἀποθανόντα εἶδον καὶ περὶ τῷ
ξίφει κείμενον, ὤμωξαν μὲν οὕτως ἀθρόον, ὡς ἀνή-
κοοι γενέσθαι μηδὲ τῷ Ἰλίῳ· προύθεντο δὲ Ἀθηναῖοι
τὸ σῶμα καὶ Μενεσθεὺς ἐπ᾽ αὐτῷ λόγον ἠγόρευσεν ᾧ
νομίζουσιν Ἀθήνησι τιμᾶν τοὺς ἐκ τῶν πολέμων τε-
14 λευτῶντας. ἔργον ἐνταῦθα εὐδόκιμον τοῦ Ὀδυσσέως ὁ
Πρωτεσίλεως οἶδε· προκειμένῳ γὰρ τῷ Αἴαντι τὰ
ὅπλα ἐπενεγκὼν τοῦ Ἀχιλλέως καὶ δακρύσας, "θά-
πτου τοι" ἔφη "ἐν οἷς ἠγάπησας καὶ τὴν νίκην τὴν ἐπ᾽
αὐτοῖς ἔχε, μηδὲν εἰς μῆνιν βαλόμενος." ἐπαινούντων
δὲ τῶν Ἀχαιῶν τὸν Ὀδυσσέα ἐπῄνει μὲν καὶ ὁ
Τεῦκρος, τὰ δὲ ὅπλα παρῃτεῖτο· μὴ γὰρ ὅσια εἶναι
15 ἐντάφια τὰ τοῦ θανάτου αἴτια. ἔθαψαν δὲ αὐτὸν κατα-
θέμενοι ἐς τὴν γῆν τὸ σῶμα, ἐξηγουμένου Κάλχαντος
ὡς οὐχ ὅσιοι πυρὶ θάπτεσθαι οἱ ἑαυτοὺς ἀποκτεί-
ναντες.

36. Τὸν δὲ Τεῦκρον νέον μὲν ἡγοῦ, μέγεθος δὲ καὶ
εἶδος καὶ ῥώμην ἔχειν.

2   ΦΟΙΝ. Τὰ δὲ τῶν Τρώων γινώσκει ὁ Πρωτεσίλεως,
ἀμπελουργέ, ἢ οὐκ ἀξιοῖ μνημονεύειν αὐτῶν, ὡς μὴ
ἄξιοι σπουδῆς φαίνοιντο;

3   ΑΜΠ. Οὐκ ἔστι, ξένε, τὸ τοῦ Πρωτεσίλεω τοιοῦτον·
ἄπεστι γὰρ αὐτοῦ φθόνος. ἀπαγγέλλει δὲ δὴ καὶ τὰ

153 Actually the later funeral orations (Thuc. 2.41) were not
given for an individual, but for all the dead as a group.

grieved for his madness and sent to oracles to tell them
how he could change and return to sanity. When they   13
saw him lying dead on his sword they joined in lament so
loud it could be heard even at Troy. It was the Athenians
who prepared him for burial, and Menestheus delivered
over him the oration in which the Athenians customarily
honor those who have fallen in war.[153] Protesilaus knows   14
of a noble gesture on that occasion by Odysseus: he placed
on the body of Ajax the arms of Achilles and said, amid his
tears, "Be buried amid the things you so wanted, and bear
no anger; you have won them." Odysseus was praised by
all the Greeks and even Teucer, who nonetheless declined
the weapons, because he thought it unholy that what had
caused his death should be buried with him. They buried   15
his body in the ground, since Calchas had explained that
it was unholy for suicides to be burned.[154]

36. You can conclude that Teucer was young and had
stature, beauty and strength.

Phoenician. Does Protesilaus know about the Trojans?   2
Or does he disdain to discuss them as unworthy of atten-
tion?

Vinedresser. That is not his way; jealousy is not in his   3
nature. He talks of the Trojans with serious interest, and

---

[154] In the *Little Iliad* (M. L. West 2013, 178–79), an enraged
Agamemnon forbade Ajax's body to be burned; in Philostratus the
whole Greek army pities him, but the pollution of suicide prohib-
its fire. There were indeed often ritual punitive measures against
suicide (Grossardt [2009b] compares Lucian *Ver. hist.* 2.7 on the
religious objections to suicides), but burial without cremation
also conveniently explains how Ajax' body could be found whole
in the time of Hadrian; see ch. 8.1.

τῶν Τρώων ἐσπουδακυίᾳ τῇ γνώμῃ· φησὶ γὰρ κἀκεί-
4 νους πολὺν πεποιῆσθαι λόγον ἀρετῆς. δίειμι δέ σοι
πρὸ τοῦ Ἀχιλλείου λόγου ταῦτα· εἰ γὰρ μετ᾽ ἐκεῖνον
λέγοιτο, οὐ θαυμαστὰ εἶναι δόξει.

37. Ἐπαινῶν τοίνυν τὸν Ἕκτορα ὁ Πρωτεσίλεως
ἐπαινεῖ καὶ τὸν Ὁμήρου ἐπ᾽ αὐτῷ λόγον· ἄριστα γὰρ
τὸν Ὅμηρον τάς τε ἡνιοχήσεις αὐτοῦ διελθεῖν καὶ τὰς
μάχας καὶ τὰς βουλὰς καὶ τὸ ἐπ᾽ αὐτῷ καὶ μὴ ἐπ᾽
ἄλλῳ εἶναι τὴν Τροίαν, καὶ ὁπόσα δὲ κομπάζει ἐν τῇ
τοῦ Ὁμήρου ποιήσει ὁ Ἕκτωρ ἀπειλῶν τοῖς Ἀχαιοῖς
τὸ ἐπὶ τὰς ναῦς πῦρ, πάνυ φησὶν ἐοικέναι τῇ φορᾷ
τοῦ ἥρω· πολλὰ γὰρ τοιαῦτα λέγειν αὐτὸν ἐν ταῖς
μάχαις, ἐκπληκτικώτατα δὲ ἀνθρώπων βλέψαι καὶ
φθέγξασθαι μέγα.

2 εἶναι δὲ τοῦ μὲν Τελαμωνίου μείω, κακίω δὲ οὐδὲν
τὰς μάχας, ἐν αἷς ἐνδείκνυσθαί τι αὐτὸν καὶ τῆς τοῦ
3 Ἀχιλλέως θερμότητος. διεβέβλητο δὲ πρὸς τὸν Πάριν
ὡς δειλὸν καὶ ἥττω τοῦ κοσμεῖσθαι· τό τοι κομᾶν,
καίτοι σπουδαζόμενον βασιλεῦσί τε καὶ βασιλέων
4 παισίν, ἀνάξιον ἑαυτοῦ δι᾽ ἐκεῖνον ἡγεῖτο. τὰ δὲ ὦτα
κατεαγὼς ἦν, οὐχ ὑπὸ πάλης (τουτὶ γάρ, ὡς ἔφην,
οὔτ᾽ αὐτὸς ἐγίνωσκεν οὔθ᾽ οἱ βάρβαροι), ἀλλὰ ταύ-
ροις ἀντήριζε καὶ τὸ συμπλέκεσθαι τοῖς θηρίοις τού-
τοις πολεμικὸν ἡγεῖτο· παλαίοντος μὲν γὰρ καὶ ταῦτα

---

155 For his cult at Troy, see Lucian, *Council of the Gods* 12;
Strabo 13.1.29. According to other accounts (Paus. 9.18.5;
FGrHist 383 [Aristodemus of Thebes] F 7), his tomb was in

says that they too set great store by bravery. I will tell these 4
things before the story of Achilles—if it is told afterward
it will not seem so impressive.

37. Protesilaus praises not only Hector[155] but also what
Homer says about him: he says Homer has described
splendidly his riding the chariot, fighting or taking coun-
sel, and the fact that Troy depended on him and no one
else. And the boasts that Hector delivers in Homer's
poem, threatening to burn the Greeks' ships, are just like
the hero's impetuosity; for he used to say many such things
during the fighting, with an extremely terrifying look and
a loud voice.

He was smaller than Ajax the son of Telamon, but no 2
worse in the fighting, where he demonstrated something
of Achilles' fervor. He reviled Paris for cowardice, and for 3
being too devoted to his looks; even though wearing one's
hair long was a common practice for the kings and their
sons, Hector considered it beneath him because Paris did
so.[156] His ears were battered, not from wrestling[157]— 4
which, as I've said (ch. 26.20), neither he nor any of
the barbarians knew about—rather he used to try his
strength against bulls, and for him grappling with these
beasts was related to warfare: this was a form of wrestling,

Thebes. Philostratus revises the Homeric portrait of Hector only
slightly; Dio's *Troicus* (Introduction §5) claimed that Hector had
killed Achilles, won the war, and lived to a ripe old age as the king
of Troy.   [156] He wore his hair long at the back but close-
cropped in front; cf. 19.3, above, and see Austin (1972, 199) and
PCG, Anaxilas fr. 37.

[157] For "cauliflower ears" among ancient wrestlers, see Polia-
koff (1987, 166n17).

ἦν, ὁ δὲ τοῦτο μὲν ἠγνόει πράττων, τὸ δὲ ὑφίστασθαι
μυκωμένους καὶ θαρσεῖν τὰς αἰχμὰς τῶν κεράτων καὶ
ἀπαυχενίσαι ταῦρον καὶ τρωθεὶς ὑπ' αὐτοῦ μὴ ἀπει-
πεῖν, ὑπὲρ μελέτης τῶν πολεμικῶν ἤσκει.

5   τὸ μὲν δὴ ἄγαλμα τὸ ἐν Ἰλίῳ νέον τὸν Ἕκτορα καὶ
μειρακιώδη φέρει, ὁ Πρωτεσίλεως δὲ γενέσθαι μὲν
αὐτὸν κἀκείνου ἡδίω φησὶ καὶ μείζω, ἀποθανεῖν δὲ
τριακοντούτην ἴσως, οὐ μὴν φεύγοντα ἢ παρεικότα
τὰς χεῖρας (ταυτὶ γὰρ συκοφαντεῖσθαι τὸν Ἕκτορα
ὑπὸ τοῦ Ὁμήρου), ἀλλὰ καρτερῶς ἀγωνισάμενον καὶ
μόνον τῶν Τρώων καταμείναντα ἔξω τοῦ τείχους πε-
σεῖν ὀψὲ τῆς μάχης· ἀποθανόντα δὲ ἑλχθῆναι μὲν
ἠρτημένον τοῦ ἄρματος, ἀποδοθῆναι δέ, ὡς Ὁμήρῳ
εἴρηται.

38. Αἰνείαν δὲ μάχεσθαι μὲν τούτου ἧττον, συνέσει
δὲ περιεῖναι τῶν Τρώων, ἀξιοῦσθαι δὲ τῶν αὐτῶν
Ἕκτορι, τὰ δὲ τῶν θεῶν εὖ εἰδέναι, ἃ δὴ ἐπέπρωτο
αὐτῷ Τροίας ἁλούσης, ἐκπλήττεσθαι δὲ ὑπ' οὐδενὸς
φόβου· τὸ γὰρ ἔννουν τε καὶ λελογισμένον ἐν αὐτοῖς
2 μάλιστα τοῖς φοβεροῖς ἔχειν. ἐκάλουν δὲ οἱ Ἀχαιοὶ
τὸν μὲν Ἕκτορα χεῖρα τῶν Τρώων, τὸν δὲ Αἰνείαν
νοῦν, καὶ πλείω παρέχειν αὐτοῖς πράγματα Αἰνείαν
σωφρονοῦντα ἢ μεμηνότα Ἕκτορα.

3   ἤστην δὲ ἰσήλικές τε καὶ ἰσομήκεις. τὸ δὲ εἶδος
τοῦ Αἰνείου φαιδρὸν μὲν ἧττον ἐφαίνετο, καθεστηκότι
δὲ ἐῴκει μᾶλλον· ἐκόμα τε ἀνεπαχθῶς· οὐ γὰρ ἤσκει
τὴν κόμην οὐδὲ ὑπέκειτο αὐτῇ, ἀλλὰ μόνην τὴν ἀρε-
τὴν ἐποιεῖτο κόσμημα, σφοδρὸν δὲ οὕτω τι ἔβλεπεν,

but he did not know that he was practicing it, he used rather to practice for battle by standing up to their bellowing, daring the tips of their horns, turning back a bull's neck or, if wounded by him, not giving up.

His statue at Ilion depicts Hector as a young stripling, 5 but Protesilaus says that he was handsomer and taller than that; he died at perhaps the age of thirty, not while running away or having dropped his arms (this is Homeric slander), but he died after a long battle, having fought with all his might, the only one of the Trojans to stay outside the walls. After his death he was hung from a chariot and dragged, but his body was returned, as Homer says.

38. Aeneas could not fight like Hector, but he was the foremost Trojan in intelligence, was valued as highly as Hector, knew well what the gods had in store for him when the city fell, and felt no fear whatsoever: since his intelligence and good sense were never more in evidence than when danger was at its worst. The Greeks used to call 2 Hector the Trojans' hand, but Aeneas their brain; and he did more harm with his wisdom than Hector with his fury.

They were the same age and size, but Aeneas looked 3 less cheerful and more calm, and wore his hair moderately long; he did not cultivate or was distracted by his hairstyle, but considered bravery his only adornment. His look was

ὥστε ἀποχρῶν εἶναί οἱ πρὸς τοὺς ἀτακτοῦντας καὶ
αὐτὸ τὸ βλέψαι.

39. Σαρπηδόνα δὲ Λυκία μὲν ἤνεγκε, Τροία δὲ ἦρεν·
ἦν μὲν γὰρ κατὰ τὸν Αἰνείαν τὰς μάχας, ἦγε δὲ Λυ-
κίους ξύμπαντας καὶ ἀρίστω ἄνδρε, Γλαῦκόν τε καὶ
2 Πάνδαρον. ἦν δὲ αὐτοῖν ὁ μὲν ὁπλιτεύειν εὐδόκιμος,
ὁ δὲ Πάνδαρος τὸν Ἀπόλλω τὸν Λύκιον ἐπιστάντα οἷ
μειρακίῳ ἔτι κοινωνῆσαι ἔφη τοῦ τοξεύειν, καὶ ηὔχετο
ἀεὶ τῷ Ἀπόλλωνι ὅτε τοῦ τόξου ἐπὶ μεγάλῳ ἅπτοιτο.

3   καὶ πανστρατιᾷ δὲ ὁ Πρωτεσίλεως ἀπαντῆσαί
φησι τῷ Σαρπηδόνι τοὺς Τρῶας· πρὸς γὰρ τῇ ἀν-
δρείᾳ καὶ τῷ εἴδει θείῳ τε καὶ γενναίῳ ὄντι ἀνήρτητο
τοὺς Τρῶας καὶ τῷ λόγῳ τῷ περὶ τοῦ γένους· ἀπὸ
Διὸς μὲν γὰρ Αἰακίδας τε ᾄδεσθαι καὶ Δαρδανίδας
καὶ τοὺς Ταντάλου, τὸ δ' αὐτοῦ Διὸς γεγονέναι μόνῳ
τῶν ὑπὲρ Τροίας τε καὶ ἐπὶ Τροίαν ἐλθόντων ἐκείνῳ
ὑπάρξαι, τουτὶ δὲ καὶ τὸν Ἡρακλέα μείζω ποιῆσαι
καὶ θαυμασιώτερον τοῖς ἀνθρώποις.

4   ἀποθανεῖν δὲ ὡς Ὁμήρῳ εἴρηται, καὶ εἶναι ἀμφὶ τὰ
τετταράκοντα ἔτη καὶ τάφου ἐν Λυκίᾳ τυχεῖν, ἐς ὃν
παρέπεμψαν οἱ Λύκιοι δεικνύντες τὸν νεκρὸν τοῖς
ἔθνεσι δι' ὧν ἤγετο. ἐσκεύαστο δὲ ἀρώμασι καὶ ἐῴκει
καθεύδοντι, ὅθεν οἱ ποιηταὶ πομπῷ φασιν αὐτὸν τῷ
Ὕπνῳ χρήσασθαι.

40. Ἄκουε καὶ τὰ Ἀλεξάνδρου τοῦ Πάριδος, εἰ μὴ
ἄχθῃ αὐτῷ σφόδρα.

---

[158] For his death, see Il. 16.419–83.

so intense that, if his men were out of formation, merely to stare at them was enough.

39. Sarpedon was produced by Lycia, but made great by Troy. He was as good a fighter as Aeneas, and led the whole Lycian contingent that included two fine men, Glaucus and Pandarus: the former was renowned at close combat, while Pandarus said that Apollo *Lycios* had helped him while still a boy to learn archery, and he used to pray to Apollo whenever he aimed his bow at an important target.

Protesilaus says the Trojans came out to meet Sarpedon with all their army, since besides his courage and his noble, even godlike appearance, he engaged the Trojans with the tale of his descent; for although the Aeacidae, the Dardanians and the children of Tantalus were hymned as descendants of Zeus, he alone of those coming to defend or attack Troy had the distinction of being the son of Zeus himself, and this fact had also made Heracles seem to men greater and more amazing.

Sarpedon died as Homer describes it,[158] and was at about the age of forty; he was buried in Lycia, and the Lycians accompanied him there, displaying the body to the tribes on their route. It had been anointed with aromatics and looked like it was asleep, which is why the poets say that he had Sleep to carry him away.[159]

40. You can also hear about Alexander called Paris,[160] if it doesn't trouble you.

---

[159] A rationalistic explanation (Introduction §5) of the Homeric story that Zeus had sent Sleep and Death themselves to carry his body to the underworld (*Il.* 16.666–83).

[160] For the phrase *Alexandros ho Paris* (to distinguish him from Alexander the great), cf. Plut. *Thes.* 34.3; Chariton 1.8.1; Cornutus, *Rh.* 87.1.

PHILOSTRATUS

ΦΟΙΝ. Ἄχθομαι μέν, οὐ χεῖρον δὲ ἀκοῦσαι.

2   ΑΜΠ. Φησὶ τοίνυν Ἀλέξανδρον Τρωσὶ μὲν ἀπ-
ηχθῆσθαι πᾶσι, κακὸν δ' οὐκ εἶναι τὰ πολέμια, τὸ δὲ
εἶδος ἥδιστον ἐπίχαρίν τε τὴν φωνὴν καὶ τὸ ἦθος ἅτε
τῇ Πελοποννήσῳ ἐπιμίξαντα, μάχεσθαι δὲ πάντας
τρόπους καὶ τὴν ἐπιστήμην ὁπόση τόξων μὴ λείπε-
3   σθαι τοῦ Πανδάρου. καὶ πλεῦσαι μὲν ἐς τὴν Ἑλλάδα
ἔφηβον, ὅτε δὴ ξένον τοῦ Μενέλεω γενέσθαι αὐτὸν
καὶ τὴν Ἑλένην ἑλεῖν τῷ εἴδει, ἀποθανεῖν δὲ οὔπω
τριακοντούτην.

4   γάννυσθαι δὲ τῷ ἑαυτοῦ κάλλει καὶ περιβλέπεσθαι
μὲν ὑφ' ἑτέρων, περιβλέπειν δὲ ἑαυτόν, ὅθεν χαρι-
5   έστατα ὁ ἥρως ἐς αὐτὸν παίζει· τοῦτον γὰρ τὸν ταῶ
(χαίρει δὲ ὁ Πρωτεσίλεως τῇ ἄνθῃ καὶ τῇ ὥρᾳ τοῦ
ὄρνιθος) ἰδών ποτε ὑπερανεστηκότα καὶ περιβεβλη-
μένον τὰ πτερὰ περιβλέποντά τε αὐτὰ καὶ καθαί-
ροντα, ἔστι δ' ἃ καὶ διατιθέντα, ἵν' ὥσπερ οἱ τῶν λί-
θων ὅρμοι κεκοσμημένα φαίνοιτο, "ἰδοὺ" ἔφη, "οὗ
πρῴην ἐμνημονεύομεν, Πάρις ὁ τοῦ Πριάμου." ἐμοῦ
δὲ ἐρομένου αὐτόν· "τί ἔοικεν ὁ ταὼς τῷ Πάριδι;" "τὸ
6   φίλαυτον" εἶπε. καὶ γὰρ δὴ κἀκεῖνος κόσμου ἕνεκεν
περιήθρει μὲν ἑαυτόν, περιεσκόπει δὲ τὰ ὅπλα. δορὰς
δὲ παρδάλεων ἐνῆπτο τοῖς ὤμοις, αὐχμὸν δὲ προσιζά-
νειν ταῖς κόμαις οὐδὲ ὁπότε μάχοιτο ἠνείχετο, ἔστιλβε
δὲ καὶ τοὺς ὄνυχας τῶν χειρῶν, καὶ ὑπόγρυπος ἦν καὶ
λευκὸς καὶ τὸ ὄμμα ἐγέγραπτο, ἡ δὲ ἑτέρα ὀφρῦς
ὑπερῆρε τοῦ ὄμματος.

Phoenician. It *does* trouble me, but it is right to hear it.

Vinedresser. Well, Protesilaus says that Paris was hated 2 by all the Trojans. He was not a bad fighter, and he was extremely good-looking, with a pleasant voice and manner. Since he had visited the Peloponnese, he could fight in every style, and in his skill with a bow he was the equal of Pandarus. His voyage to Greece, when he was Menelaus' 3 guest and captivated Helen with his beauty, was while he was still a youth, and he died before he reached thirty.

He preened himself on his good looks, and admired 4 himself no less than others did, which led Protesilaus to some clever mockery:[161] for when he saw this peacock 5 here (a bird he enjoys for its ravishing beauty) puffed up and opening out its feathers,[162] inspecting and cleaning them, and rearranging some to look like necklaces of precious stones, he said, "Do you see the man we were recently talking about, Paris son of Priam?" When I asked him how the peacock was like Paris, he answered, "In his vanity." For evidently Paris too used to take great care for 6 his looks, and fuss over the appearance of his armor. He wore leopard skins on his shoulders, and even in the battle would never allow dirt to settle on his hair; he polished his fingernails; he was pale with a slightly hooked nose, wore eye makeup, and one of his eyebrows was always raised.[163]

---

[161] For comparisons as party jokes, see MacDowell (1971) on Ar. *Vesp.* 1308–13, and Pelliccia (2002).

[162] For the vanity of the peacock, who displays his tail feathers when he hears them praised, see D. Thompson (1936, 280).

[163] For the raising of one or both eyebrows in arrogance, see Van Leeuwen (1893) on Ar. *Vesp.* 655.

PHILOSTRATUS

41. Ἕλενος δὲ καὶ Δηίφοβος καὶ Πολυδάμας ξυν-
έβαινον μὲν ἀλλήλοις τὰς μάχας καὶ ταὐτὸν ἐφέροντο
τῆς ῥώμης, εὐδόκιμοι δὲ τὰς ξυμβουλίας ἦσαν· ὁ δὲ
Ἕλενος καὶ μαντικῆς ἥπτετο ἴσα τῷ Κάλχαντι.

42. Περὶ δὲ Εὐφόρβου τοῦ Πάνθου καὶ ὡς γένοιτό
τις ἐν Τροίᾳ Εὔφορβος καὶ ἀποθάνοι ὑπὸ τοῦ Μενέ-
λεω, τὸν Πυθαγόρου, οἶμαι, τοῦ Σαμίου λόγον ἤκου-
σας· ἔλεγε γὰρ δὴ ὁ Πυθαγόρας Εὔφορβος γεγονέναι
μεταφῦναί τε Ἴων μὲν ἐκ Τρωός, σοφὸς δὲ ἐκ πολε-
μικοῦ, κεκολασμένος δὲ ἐκ τρυφῶντος· τήν τε κόμην,
ἣν σοφὸς γενόμενος ἐκόσμει τῷ αὐχμῷ, χρυσῆν ἐν
2 Τροίᾳ ἐποιεῖτο ὁπότ᾽ ἦν Εὔφορβος. ὁ δὲ Πρωτεσίλεως
τὸν Εὔφορβον ἥλικα ἑαυτοῦ ἡγεῖται καὶ ἐλεεῖ καὶ
ὁμολογεῖ τὸν Πάτροκλον ὑπ᾽ αὐτοῦ τρωθέντα παρα-
δοθῆναι τῷ Ἕκτορι. εἰ δὲ εἰς ἄνδρας ἦλθεν, οὐδὲν ἂν
3 φησιν αὐτὸν κακίω νομισθῆναι τοῦ Ἕκτορος. τὴν μέν
γε ὥραν αὐτοῦ καὶ τοὺς Ἀχαιούς φησι θέλγειν· ἐοικέ-
ναι γὰρ αὐτὸν ἀγάλματι, ὁπότε κάλλιστα ἑαυτοῦ ὁ
Ἀπόλλων ἀκερσεκόμης τε καὶ ἁβρὸς φαίνοιτο.

4 Τοσαῦτα, ξένε, περὶ Τρώων δίεισιν ὁ θεῖός τε καὶ
ἀγαθὸς ἥρως. λοιπὸν δ᾽ ἡμῖν ἴσως τὸν τοῦ Ἀχιλλέως
ἀποτελέσαι λόγον, εἰ μὴ ἀπείρηκας πρὸς τὸ μῆκος.

43. ΦΟΙΝ. Εἰ οἱ τοῦ λωτοῦ παρ᾽ Ὁμήρῳ φαγόντες,
ὦ ἀμπελουργέ, προθύμως οὕτω προσέκειντο τῇ πόα
ὡς ἐκλελῆσθαι τῶν οἴκοι, μὴ ἀπίστει κἀμὲ προσκεῖ-
σθαι τῷ λόγῳ καθάπερ τῷ λωτῷ, καὶ μήτ᾽ ἂν ἑκόντα
ἀπελθεῖν ἐνθένδε, ἀπαχθῆναι δὲ μόγις ἂν ἐπὶ τὴν
ναῦν καὶ δεθῆναι δὲ αὖ ἐν αὐτῇ κλάοντα καὶ ὀλοφυ-

262

41. Helenus, Deiphobus and Polydamas were equal to each other in fighting, contributed equal strength, and were famed for their counsel; in addition, Helenus was as skilled in prophecy as Calchas.

42. As for Euphorbus son of Panthous, that he was at Troy, and was killed by Menelaus, you have probably heard the story of Pythagoras of Samos; since Pythagoras claimed that in a past life he *was* Euphorbus, but was later reborn as an Ionian instead of a Trojan, a philosopher instead of a warrior, and an ascetic instead of a wastrel; he adds that the hair which he smeared with dirt as a philosopher he kept golden while he was Euphorbus.[164] Protesilaus thinks Euphorbus was his own age, and mourns him; he agrees with Homer (*Il.* 16.806–50) that Patroclus was first wounded by him and then passed on to Hector. He says that if he had reached manhood he would have been considered as good as Hector, and that his beauty charmed even the Greeks; he was like a statue of long-haired and delicate Apollo more beautiful than ever.

That, stranger, is what this holy and good hero says about the Trojans. It remains for me to complete perhaps the story of Achilles, if you are not weary at such length.

43. *Phoenician.* If those who ate of the lotus in Homer were so mad about the plant that they forgot their homes, you can rest assured that I am as taken with your story as with the lotus; far from ever leaving, I would have to be carried off to my ship and bound there, crying and

---

[164] Cf. *VA* 8.7. It was said that Pythagoras had seen the shield of Euphorbus dedicated in a temple at Argos and recognized it as belonging to him in a past life; for this notorious (and often ridiculed) claim, see Burkert (1972, 139–41).

2 ρόμενον ἐπὶ τῷ μὴ ἐμπίπλασθαι τοῦ λόγου. καὶ γάρ
με καὶ πρὸς τὰ τοῦ Ὁμήρου ποιήματα οὕτω διατέθει-
κας, ὡς θεῖά τε αὐτὰ ἡγούμενον καὶ πέρα ἀνθρώπου
δόξαι, νῦν ἐκπεπλῆχθαι μᾶλλον, οὐκ ἐπὶ τῇ ἐποποιίᾳ
μόνον, οὐδ᾽ εἴ τις ἡδονὴ διήκει σφων, ἀλλὰ πολλῷ
μᾶλλον ἐπί τε τοῖς ὀνόμασι τῶν ἡρώων ἐπί τε τοῖς
γένεσι καὶ νὴ Δί᾽ ὡς ἕκαστος αὐτῶν ἔλαχε τοῦ κτεῖναί
3 τινα ἢ ἀποθανεῖν ὑφ᾽ ἑτέρου. τὸν μὲν γὰρ Πρωτεσί-
λεων δαίμονα ἤδη ὄντα οὐδὲν οἶμαι θαυμαστὸν εἰδέ-
ναι ταῦτα, Ὁμήρῳ δὲ πόθεν μὲν Εὔφορβος, πόθεν δὲ
Ἑλενοί τε καὶ Δηίφοβοι καὶ νὴ Δί᾽ ἐκ τῆς ἀντικειμέ-
νης στρατιᾶς οἱ πολλοὶ ἄνδρες οὓς ἐν καταλόγῳ φρά-
4 ζει; τὸ γὰρ μὴ ὑποτεθεῖσθαι ταῦτα τὸν Ὅμηρον, ἀλλὰ
γεγονότων τε καὶ ἀληθινῶν ἔργων ἀπαγγελίαν ποιεῖ-
σθαι μαρτυρεῖ ὁ Πρωτεσίλεως, πλὴν ὀλίγων, ἃ δοκεῖ
μᾶλλον ἑκὼν μετασκευάσαι ἐπὶ τῷ ποικίλην τε καὶ
5 ἡδίω ἀποφῆναι τὴν ποίησιν· ὅθεν τὸ ὑπὸ ἐνίων λεγό-
μενον, ὡς Ἀπόλλων αὐτὰ ποιήσας τὸν Ὅμηρον ἐπέ-
γραψε τῇ ποιήσει, σφόδρα μοι δοκεῖ ἐρρῶσθαι· τὸ
γὰρ γινώσκειν ταῦτα θεῷ μᾶλλον ἢ ἀνθρώπῳ ἔοικε.

6 ΑΜΠ. Τὸ μὲν θεοὺς ἡγεμόνας εἶναι τοῖς ποιηταῖς,
ξένε, πάσης ᾠδῆς, αὐτοί που οἱ ποιηταὶ ὁμολογοῦσιν,
οἱ μὲν τὴν Καλλιόπην, οἱ δὲ πάσας, οἱ δὲ καὶ τὸν
Ἀπόλλω πρὸς ταῖς ἐννέα παρατυχεῖν αἰτούμενοι τῷ
λόγῳ· τὰ δὲ Ὁμήρου ταῦτα οὐκ ἀθεεὶ μὲν εἴρηται, οὐ
7 μὴν Ἀπόλλωνί γε αὐτῷ ἢ Μούσαις αὐταῖς ᾖσται. γέ-
γονε γάρ, ξένε, γέγονε ποιητὴς Ὅμηρος καὶ ᾖδεν, ὡς
μέν φασιν ἕτεροι μετὰ τέτταρα καὶ εἴκοσιν ἔτη τῶν

grieving because I hadn't had my fill of stories. You've 2
already persuaded me to believe that Homer's poetry is
divine, beyond human powers; but I now am struck not
only by the poetry and its pervasive charm, but much more
at the names and families of the heroes, and how it was
each one's lot to kill someone or be killed by someone else.
It doesn't seem to be so remarkable that Protesilaus, who 3
is after all divine, should know this; but where did Homer
get Euphorbus, or men like Helenus or Deiphobus, or the
many others from the opposing side that he mentions in
the catalog? For Protesilaus attests that Homer has not 4
invented this, but reported what actually happened—the
few exceptions seem intentional reworking, to give his
poetry greater variety and charm. So when some people 5
say that Apollo wrote it and merely put Homer's name on
it, it seems to me to have some force; it would take a god
to know all this, not a mere man.

Vinedresser. The poets themselves admit that the gods 6
initiate all their song, and some pray to Calliope to attend
their words, others pray to all the Muses, others to Apollo
besides the nine; obviously Homer's poems are divine, but
that does not mean that Apollo himself or the Muses ac-
tually wrote them. No, there really was a Homer who sang 7

PHILOSTRATUS

Τρωικῶν, οἱ δὲ μετὰ ἑπτὰ καὶ εἴκοσι πρὸς τοῖς ἑκατόν, ὅτε τὴν ἀποικίαν ἐς Ἰωνίαν ἔστειλαν·

οἱ δὲ ἐξήκοντα καὶ ἑκατὸν ἔτη γεγονέναι μετὰ τὴν Τροίαν ἐπὶ Ὅμηρόν τέ φασι καὶ Ἡσίοδον, ὅτε δὴ ᾆσαι ἄμφω ἐν Χαλκίδι, τὸν μὲν τὰ ἑπτὰ ἔπη τὰ περὶ τοῖν Αἰάντοιν καὶ ὡς αἱ φάλαγγες αὐτοῖς ἀραρυῖαί τε ἦσαν καὶ καρτεραί, τὸν δὲ τὰ πρὸς τὸν ἀδελφὸν τὸν ἑαυτοῦ Πέρσην, ἐν οἷς αὐτὸν ἔργων τε ἐκέλευεν ἅπτε- σθαι καὶ γεωργίᾳ προσκεῖσθαι, ὡς μὴ δέοιτο ἑτέρων
8 μηδὲ πεινῴη. καὶ ἀληθέστερα, ξένε, περὶ τῶν Ὁμήρου χρόνων ταῦτα· ξυντίθεται γὰρ αὐτοῖς ὁ Πρωτεσίλεως.
9 δύο γοῦν ποιητῶν ὕμνον ποτὲ εἰπόντων ἐς αὐτὸν ἐν- ταυθοῖ καὶ ἀπελθόντων, ἤρετό με ὁ ἥρως ἀφικόμενος ὅτῳ αὐτῶν ψηφιζοίμην· ἐμοῦ δὲ τὸν φαυλότερον ἐπαι- νέσαντος (καὶ γὰρ μᾶλλον ἔτυχεν ᾑρηκώς), γελάσας ὁ Πρωτεσίλεως "καὶ Πανίδης" εἶπεν, "ἀμπελουργέ, ταὐτόν σοι πέπονθε· Χαλκίδος γὰρ τῆς ἐπ' Εὐρίπῳ βασιλεὺς ὢν ἐκεῖνος Ἡσιόδῳ κατὰ Ὁμήρου ἐψηφί- σατο, καὶ ταῦτα τὸ γένειον ἔχων μεῖζον ἢ σύ."
10 γέγονε μὲν δή, ξένε, ποιητὴς Ὅμηρος καὶ τὰ ποι-
11 ήματα ἀνθρώπου ταῦτα. τὰ δὲ ὀνόματα ᾔδει καὶ τὰ ἔργα ξυνελέξατο μὲν ἐκ τῶν πόλεων ἃς ἕκαστοι ἦγον· ἦλθε μὲν γὰρ περὶ τὴν Ἑλλάδα μετὰ χρόνον τῶν Τρωικῶν οὔπω ἱκανὸν ἐξαμαυρῶσαι τὰ ἐν τῇ Τροίᾳ.

---

165 Attempts to write the "biography" of Homer began with Theagenes in the sixth century BC and Alcidamas in the fourth; for a collection of the extant ancient biographies, see M. L. West (2003b).

266

them[165]—some say 24 years after the Trojan war, others 127 years after, at the time of the Ionian migration.

Others say that 160 years elapsed after Troy until Homer and Hesiod, when both sang at Chalcis:[166] the one with his seven verses[167] about the two Ajaxes and how firm and strong their columns were, the other those to his brother Perses, commanding him to work and attend to his farming, to avoid indigence and hunger.[168] And this seems the truest date for Homer, since Protesilaus confirms it—once when two poets had sung hymns to praise him, Protesilaus came to me after they had left and asked me which one I voted for. I gave the preference to the one that was less impressive (he had happened to be more compelling). He laughed and said, "Panides made the same mistake as you, Vinedresser; for when he was king of Chalcis on the Euripus he voted for Hesiod against Homer, and he had a longer beard than you."[169]

So then, there really was a Homer, and these poems were written by a man. He knew the names, and he collected the events from the cities which each warrior led, since he traveled around Greece soon enough after

8

9

10

11

---

[166] A reference to the *Contest Between Homer and Hesiod*, text and translation in M. L. West (2003b, 318–53); see also Uden (2010).

[167] A slight error, since this section of the *Contest of Homer and Hesiod* (ch. 12; M. L. West 2003b, 338–39) quotes eight verses (*Il.* 13.126–33) and adds to them six more (*Il.* 13.339–44).

[168] *Contest*, ch. 12 (M. L. West 2003b, 336–37), quoting Hes. *Op.* 383–92.

[169] *Contest*, ch. 13 (M. L. West 2003b, 341), where he is called Panedes.

12 ἔμαθε δὲ αὐτὰ καὶ τρόπον ἕτερον δαιμόνιόν τε καὶ
σοφίας πρόσω· εἰς Ἰθάκην γάρ ποτε τὸν Ὅμηρον
πλεῦσαί φασιν ἀκούσαντα ὡς πέπνυται ἔτι ἡ ψυχὴ
τοῦ Ὀδυσσέως, καὶ ψυχαγωγίᾳ ἐπ' αὐτὸν χρήσασθαι.

13 ἐπεὶ δὲ ἀνελθεῖν τὸν Ὀδυσσέα, ὁ μὲν ἠρώτα αὐτὸν τὰ
ἐν Ἰλίῳ, ὁ δὲ εἰδέναι μὲν πάντα ἔλεγε καὶ μεμνῆσθαι
αὐτῶν, εἰπεῖν δ' ἂν οὐδὲν ὧν οἶδεν εἰ μὴ μισθὸς αὐτῷ
παρ' Ὁμήρου γένοιτο εὐφημίαι τε ἐν τῇ ποιήσει καὶ

14 ὕμνος ἐπὶ σοφίᾳ τε καὶ ἀνδρείᾳ. ὁμολογήσαντος δὲ
τοῦ Ὁμήρου ταῦτα καὶ ὅ τι δύναιτο χαριεῖσθαι αὐτῷ
ἐν τῇ ποιήσει φήσαντος, διῄει ὁ Ὀδυσσεὺς πάντα ξὺν
ἀληθείᾳ τε καὶ ὡς ἐγένετο· ἥκιστα γὰρ πρὸς αἵματί

15 τε καὶ βόθροις αἱ ψυχαὶ ψεύδονται. ἀπιόντος δὲ ἤδη
τοῦ Ὁμήρου, βοήσας ὁ Ὀδυσσεὺς "Παλαμήδης με"
ἔφη "δίκας ἀπαιτεῖ τοῦ ἑαυτοῦ φόνου καὶ οἶδα ἀδικῶν
καὶ πάντως μὲν πείσομαί τι· οἱ γὰρ θεμιστεύοντες
ἐνταῦθα δεινοί, Ὅμηρε, καὶ τὰ ἐκ Ποινῶν ἐγγύς. εἰ δὲ
τοῖς ἄνω ἀνθρώποις μὴ δόξω εἰργάσθαι τὸν Παλα-
μήδη ταῦτα, ἧττόν με ἀπολεῖ τὰ ἐνταῦθα· μὴ δὴ ἄγε
τὸν Παλαμήδη ἐς Ἴλιον, μηδὲ στρατιώτῃ χρῶ, μηδὲ
ὅτι σοφὸς ἦν εἴπῃς. ἐροῦσι μὲν γὰρ ἕτεροι ποιηταί,

16 πιθανὰ δὲ οὐ δόξει μὴ σοὶ εἰρημένα." αὕτη, ξένε, ἡ
Ὀδυσσέως τε καὶ Ὁμήρου ξυνουσία, καὶ οὕτως Ὅμη-
ρος τὰ ἀληθῆ μὲν ἔμαθε, μετεκόσμησε δὲ πολλὰ ἐς
τὸ συμφέρον τοῦ λόγου ὃν ὑπέθετο.

44. ΦΟΙΝ. Πατρίδα δὲ Ὁμήρου, ὦ ἀμπελουργέ, καὶ
τίνων ἐγένετο, ἤρου ποτὲ τὸν Πρωτεσίλεων;

ΑΜΠ. Καὶ πολλάκις, ξένε.

the Trojan war that its events had not been forgotten. He learned of the events in one other way also, which was 12 more magical and extremely wise. He sailed to Ithaca, it is said, since he had heard that Odysseus' soul still retained its faculties, and conjured it up from the dead. When it 13 appeared, he asked about the events at Troy: Odysseus replied that he knew and still remembered them, but would say nothing he knew unless rewarded by Homer with good treatment in his poetry, and praise for his wisdom and courage. When Homer agreed to do this and said 14 he would do everything to please him in his poetry, Odysseus recalled it all exactly as it had happened—souls are least prone to lying when they are at the pit filled with blood. As Homer was going away, Odysseus shouted, "Palamedes is demanding justice for his murder; I know I am guilty, and that I will assuredly suffer for it. The judges here are terrifying, and the work of the Punishments is at hand. But if the men in the upper world do not think that I did this to Palamedes, my doom will be less harsh. Therefore you must not say that Palamedes went to Troy, nor speak of his fighting or his wisdom. Other poets will tell of this—but they will not be believed if you have not said it." This, stranger, is what happened between Homer and 16 Odysseus; thus it came about that Homer knew the truth, but changed much of it to benefit the subject he had chosen.

44. *Phoenician.* Did you ever ask Protesilaus about Homer's birthplace, or who his parents were?

Vinedresser. Many times.

ΦΟΙΝ. Ὁ δὲ τί;

2 ΑΜΠ. Φησὶ μὲν εἰδέναι, Ὁμήρου δὲ παραλιπόντος
αὐτὰ ἵνα αἱ σπουδαῖαι τῶν πόλεων πολίτην αὐτὸν
σφῶν αὐτῶν ποιοῖντο, ἴσως δὲ καὶ θεσμοῦ Μοιρῶν
ἐπὶ Ὁμήρῳ ὄντος ἄπολιν αὐτὸν δοκεῖν, οὔτ᾽ ἂν ταῖς
Μοίραις οὔτ᾽ ἂν ταῖς Μούσαις φίλα γε ἔφη αὐτὸν
πράττειν εἰ τοῦτ᾽ ἐκφέροι, περιεστηκὸς λοιπὸν εἰς

3 ἔπαινον τῷ Ὁμήρῳ. προστίθενται μὲν γὰρ αὐτῷ πᾶ-
σαι μὲν πόλεις, πάντα δὲ ἔθνη, καὶ δικάσαιντο δ᾽ ἂν
περὶ αὐτοῦ πρὸς ἀλλήλας, ἐγγράφουσαι τῷ Ὁμήρῳ

4 ἑαυτὰς οἷον πολίτῃ. τοῦ δὲ μηδ᾽ ἂν τοῦτον σιωπῆσαι
τὸν λόγον πρὸς σέ, ὦ Φοῖνιξ, μηδ᾽ ἂν κρύψαι εἴπερ
ἐγίνωσκον αὐτόν, τεκμήρια ἔστω σοι ἃ εἴρηκα· ἀφθό-
νως γὰρ οἶμαι διεληλυθέναι σοι ὁπόσα οἶδα.

5 ΦΟΙΝ. Πιστεύω, ἀμπελουργέ, καὶ ἑπώμεθα τῷ
λόγῳ δι᾽ ὃν σιωπᾶται ταῦτα. τὸν δὲ Ἀχιλλέα ὥρα σοι
ἀναφαίνειν, εἰ μὴ καὶ ἡμᾶς ἐκπλήξει, ὥσπερ τοὺς
Τρῶας ὅτ᾽ ἔλαμψεν ἐπ᾽ αὐτοὺς ἀπὸ τῆς τάφρου.

45. ΑΜΠ. Μὴ δέδιθι τὸν Ἀχιλλέα, ὦ ξένε· παιδὶ
γὰρ ἐντεύξῃ αὐτῷ παρὰ τὴν πρώτην τοῦ λόγου.

ΦΟΙΝ. Μεγάλα δώσεις διεξελθὼν αὐτὸν ἐκ νηπίου·
μετὰ ταῦτα γὰρ ὁπλιζομένῳ που ἐντευξόμεθα καὶ μα-
χομένῳ.

2 ΑΜΠ. Οὕτως ἔσται καὶ πάντα φήσεις τὰ Ἀχιλλέως
εἰδέναι. ἤκουσα δὲ περὶ αὐτοῦ τοιάδε· Πηλεῖ φάσμα
ἐφοίτα θαλαττίας δαίμονος καὶ ἐρῶσα αὐτοῦ ἡ δαί-
μων ξυνῆν τῷ Πηλεῖ ἐν Πηλίῳ, αἰδοῖ τοῦ ὁμίλου οὔπω

Phoenician. What did he say?

Vinedresser. He said that he knew; but since Homer 2
himself had not said, to keep all ambitious cities claim-
ing him as their own, and since perhaps some law of the
fates ordained that Homer should seem to have no city, he
would not please the Muses if he revealed the secret which
had redounded to Homer's glory ever after. For all cities 3
and all peoples connect themselves to him, and they would
take each other to court to enter themselves under his
name as their citizen.[170] If I knew it, I would not have kept 4
silent or hidden the story of this from you either. What I've
told you already should convince you of that; for I'm sure
I've told you everything I know without reserve.

Phoenician. I believe you. Let us follow the story for 5
whose sake this is kept secret: it is time for you to tell me
of Achilles, unless he is going to terrify us as he did the
Trojans, when he gleamed at them from the trench (*Il.*
18.203–31).

45. *Vinedresser.* You need not fear Achilles; at the be-
ginning of my story he is only a child.

Phoenician. It will be excellent if you describe him
from his infancy; we can meet him in full fighting gear a
little later.

Vinedresser. All right; you will be able to say you know 2
everything about Achilles. What I have heard about him
is this: the phantom of a sea goddess had fallen in love with
Peleus, and the divinity used to visit and lie with Peleus
on Mount Pelion; but out of fear of publicity she told him

---

[170] For the rivalry of Greek cities for Homer's birthplace, see
Skiadas (1965) and M. L. West (2003b, 309–10).

3 τὰ ἑαυτῆς λέγουσα, οὐδὲ ὁπόθεν ἥκοι. γαλήνης δ᾽
ἐπεχούσης τὴν θάλατταν ἡ μὲν ἔτυχεν ἐπὶ δελφίνων
τε καὶ ἱπποκάμπων ἀθύρουσα, ὁ δὲ ἐκ περιωπῆς τοῦ
Πηλίου ὁρῶν ταῦτα ξυνῆκε τῆς θεοῦ καὶ ἔδεισεν
ἥκουσαν. ἡ δὲ ἐς θάρσος ἦγε τὸν Πηλέα Ἠοῦς τε
μνημονεύουσα ὡς Τιθωνοῦ ἤρα, καὶ Ἀφροδίτης ὡς
ἥττητο τοῦ Ἀγχίσου, καὶ Σελήνης ὡς Ἐνδυμίωνι ἐπ-
εφοίτα καθεύδοντι· "ἐγὼ δέ σοι καὶ παῖδα" εἶπεν, "ὦ
Πηλεῦ, δώσω κρείττω ἀνθρώπου."

4 ἐπεὶ δ᾽ Ἀχιλλεὺς ἐγένετο, ποιοῦνται αὐτοῦ τροφέα
τὸν Χείρωνα· ὁ δὲ ἔτρεφεν αὐτὸν κηρίοις τε καὶ μυε-
λοῖς νεβρῶν, ἐς ἡλικίαν τε ἥκοντα ἐν ᾗ οἱ παῖδες ἁμα-
ξίδων καὶ ἀστραγάλων δέονται, εἶργε μὲν οὐδὲ τῶν
τοιούτων, ἀκοντίοις δὲ εἴθιζε καὶ παλτοῖς καὶ δρόμοις.
ἦν δὲ αὐτῷ καὶ μελία μικρὰ τετμημένη ὑπὸ τοῦ Χεί-
ρωνος, καὶ ἐῴκει ψελλιζομένῳ ἐς τὰ πολεμικά.

5 ἐφήβου δὲ ἁπτόμενος ἀκτῖνα μὲν ἀπὸ τοῦ προσώ-
που ἔπεμπεν, ὑπερφυὴς δὲ τὸ σῶμα ἐφαίνετο, αὐξη-
θείς τε ῥᾷον ἢ τὰ πρὸς ταῖς πηγαῖς δένδρα, πολὺς μὲν
6 ἐν συμποσίοις ᾔδετο, πολὺς δὲ ἐν σπουδαῖς. ἐπεὶ δὲ
θυμοῦ ἥττων ἐφαίνετο, μουσικὴν αὐτὸν ὁ Χείρων ἐδι-
δάξατο· μουσικὴ γὰρ ἱκανὴ πραΰνειν τὸ ἕτοιμόν τε
καὶ ἀνεστηκὸς τῆς γνώμης· ὁ δὲ οὐδενὶ πόνῳ τάς τε
ἁρμονίας ἐξέμαθε καὶ πρὸς λύραν ᾖσεν. ᾖδε δὲ τοὺς
ἀρχαίους ἥλικας, τὸν Ὑάκινθον καὶ τὸν Νάρκισσον
καὶ εἴ τι Ἀδώνιδος. προσφάτων δὲ ὄντων τῶν περὶ
Ὕλα τε καὶ Ἀβδήρῳ θρήνων, ἐπειδὴ ἄμφω ἐφήβω
ὄντε ὁ μὲν ἐς πηγὴν ᾤχετο ἀφανισθείς, τὸν δὲ αἱ τοῦ

nothing about herself or where she came from. One day,   3
when the sea was calm and she chanced to be playing,
riding on dolphins and seahorses, he looked down from
the summit of mount Pelion and saw her, and recognized
her as a goddess; when she next came to him, he was afraid.
But she encouraged him by reminding him of the love of
Dawn for Tithonus, of how Aphrodite succumbed to An-
chises, and how Selene visited Endymion while he slept.
She added, "I shall give you a child greater than any mortal."

When Achilles was born they chose Chiron to bring him   4
up; as a baby he fed him honey and the marrow of fawns.[171]
At the age when other children want toy wagons and knuck-
lebones to play with, Chiron did not keep him away from
these, but trained him in spears, javelins and running. He
had a small spear of ash that Chiron had cut for him; one
might say he was in the baby-talk phase of training for war.

By the time he was a youth his face gleamed and his   5
size was prodigious (he had grown more rapidly than the
trees around springs), and his praises were sung much at
drinking parties, but also much on serious occasions. Since   6
he tended to be emotional, Chiron taught him music,
which was able to soften his agile and excitable mind. He
learned the harmonies with no difficulty, and sang and
played the lyre.[172] He used to sing of youths of long ago,
like Hyacinthus, Narcissus or anything about Adonis. The
dirges for Hyllas who had disappeared by falling into a
stream, and Abderus who had been eaten by Diomedes'

[171] As in *Imag.* 2.2, an *ekphrasis* of an episode in the education
of Achilles.

[172] Achilles' musical talent is fulfilled in his song to Echo on
Leuke (55.3; Miles 2004).

Διομήδους ἵπποι ἐδαίσαντο, οὐκ ἀδακρυτὶ ταῦτα
7 ᾖδεν. ἤκουσα δὲ κἀκεῖνα, θύειν μὲν αὐτὸν τῇ Καλ-
λιόπῃ μουσικὴν αἰτοῦντα καὶ τὸ ἐν ποιήσει κράτος,
τὴν θεὸν δὲ ἐπιστῆναι καθεύδοντι καὶ "ὦ παῖ" φάναι,
"μουσικῆς μὲν καὶ ποιητικῆς δίδωμί σοι τὸ ἀποχρῶν
ὡς ἡδίους μὲν τὰς δαῖτας ἐργάζοιο, κοιμίζοις δὲ τὰς
λύπας· ἐπειδὴ δὲ ἐμοί τε καὶ Ἀθηνᾷ δοκεῖ πολεμικὸν
εἶναί σε καὶ δεινὸν ἐν δεινοῖς {ἐν στρατοπέδοις}, Μοῖ-
ραί τε οὕτω κελεύουσι, σὺ μὲν ἐκεῖνα γυμνάζου κἀκεί-
νων ἔρα. ποιητὴς δὲ ἔσται χρόνοις ὕστερον ὃν ἐγὼ
ἀνήσω τὰ σὰ ὑμνεῖν ἔργα." ταυτὶ μὲν αὐτῷ περὶ Ὁμή-
ρου ἐχρήσθη.

8   μειράκιον δὲ γενόμενος οὐχ, ὥσπερ οἱ πολλοὶ φα-
σιν, ἀπόθετος ἐν Σκύρῳ ἐτρέφετο, τοῦτο δὴ τὸ ἐν ταῖς
παρθένοις· οὔτε γὰρ τὸν Πηλέα εἰκὸς ἄριστον τῶν
ἡρώων γενόμενον ὑπεκπέμψαι ποι τὸν υἱὸν πολέμους
τε καὶ κινδύνους ἀποδράντα, καὶ ταῦτα τοῦ Τελα-
μῶνος ἐξορμῶντος τὸν Αἴαντα, οὔτ' ἂν Ἀχιλλεὺς
ἠνέσχετο ἐς γυναικωνῖτιν ἐσβεβλῆσθαι, παρεὶς ἑτέ-
ροις τὸ θαυμάζεσθαί τε καὶ εὐδοκιμεῖν ἐν Τροίᾳ· τὸ
γὰρ φιλότιμον πλεῖστον δὴ καὶ ἐν αὐτῷ ἦν.

46. ΦΟΙΝ. Τί οὖν δὴ ὁ Πρωτεσίλεως, ἀμπελουργέ,
περὶ τούτων οἶδε;

2   ΑΜΠ. Πιθανώτερα, ξένε, καὶ ἀληθέστερα· φησὶ
γὰρ Θησέα ἐξ Ἀθηνῶν φεύγοντα ἐπὶ τῇ ἀρᾷ τῇ ἐς τὸν

---

173 Euripides' *Scyrioi* (probably not the *Cypria*; see M. L.
West 2003a, 104) had said that Achilles tried to avoid fighting by

horses, were still new, and he sang them with much weeping. I have also heard that he sacrificed to Calliope and prayed for the gift of music and greatness as a poet, and that the goddess appeared in a dream to him and said, "My boy, I am giving you enough of music and poetry that you can make banquets sweeter and calm your grief; but since it is my will and Athena's, and the decree of the fates, that you be a warrior, a terror amid the terrors of battle, it is this that you must practice and love; later there will be a poet, whom I shall command to praise your deeds." Thus the coming of Homer was prophesied to him.

When he became a young man he was not, as most claim, brought up in hiding—and among maidens at that —on Scyros; for it is not plausible that the best of heroes, Peleus, packed his son away to escape warfare and danger at a time when his brother Telamon was sending Ajax forth to war. Nor would Achilles have stood for being thrown into women's quarters, and letting others gain admiration and glory at Troy; the most prominent quality was ambition in him too.[173]

46. *Phoenician.* What then does Protesilaus have to say about this?

Vinedresser. He tells a more persuasive and truer story. Theseus, in exile from Athens because he had cursed his

---

disguising himself as a daughter of king Lycomedes on Scyros—it was there that he fathered Neoptolemus with one of the daughters. The *Little Iliad*, however, had made him the husband of Deidameia (M. L. West 2003a, 107). For the rationalistic reinterpretation here, see Introduction §5. It is also adopted by Libanius and Tertullian (Fantuzzi 2012, 63–64).

υἱὸν ἀποθανεῖν ὑπὸ Λυκομήδους ἐν Σκύρῳ, Θησεῖ δὲ
ξένον ὄντα τὸν Πηλέα καὶ κοινωνὸν τοῦ Καλυδωνίου
ἔργου στεῖλαι τὸν Ἀχιλλέα ἐς τὴν Σκῦρον τιμωρὸν τῷ
Θησεῖ, τὸν δὲ ἐκπλεύσαντα ὁμοῦ τῷ Φοίνικι μόνα ὑπὸ
γήρως τὰ ξυμβουλευτικὰ εἰδότι κατασεῖσαι τὴν Σκύ-
ρον ἐκ προσβολῆς μετέωρον οὖσαν καὶ ἀνῳκισμένην
ἐπ᾽ ὄχθου πετραίου, τὸν Λυκομήδη δὲ σχεῖν μέν, οὐ
μὴν ἀποκτεῖναι, ἀλλ᾽ ἐρέσθαι τί παθὼν ἄνδρα ἑαυτοῦ
3 βελτίω ἀπέκτεινεν· εἰπόντα δὲ ὅτι "ἐπ᾽ ἀδίκοις, ὦ
Ἀχιλλεῦ, ἥκοντα καὶ πειρῶντα τὴν ἀρχὴν τὴν ἐμήν,"
ἀφῆκεν ὡς ἐν δίκῃ ἀποκτείναντα καὶ ἀπολογήσεσθαι
4 ὑπὲρ αὐτοῦ ἔφη πρὸς τὸν Πηλέα. Δηιδάμειαν δὲ
θυγατέρα τοῦ Λυκομήδους ἔγημε καὶ γίνεται αὐτοῖς
Νεοπτόλεμος, ὀνομασθεὶς τοῦτο διὰ νεότητα τοῦ
Ἀχιλλέως καθ᾽ ἣν ἐς τὸ πολεμεῖν ὥρμησεν.
5   ἐνταῦθα τῷ Ἀχιλλεῖ διαιτωμένῳ παρεγίνετο ἡ Θέ-
τις καὶ ἐθεράπευε τὸν υἱὸν ὥσπερ αἱ θνηταὶ τῶν μη-
τέρων, ξυλλεγομένου δὲ ἐς τὴν Αὐλίδα τοῦ στρατοῦ
διεπόρθμευσεν αὐτὸν ἐς τὴν Φθίαν διὰ τὰ ἐπ᾽ αὐτῷ
κεκλωσμένα, τὸν Πηλέα ποιουμένη κύριον τοῦ παιδός·
6 λέγεται καὶ ὅπλα ἐκποιῆσαι αὐτῷ οἷα μήπω τις
ἤνεγκε, ξὺν οἷς ἐς τὴν Αὐλίδα ἀφικόμενος ἐλπίδος τε
ὑπέπλησε τὸν στρατόν, θεοῦ τε οὕτω τι ἐνομίσθη
παῖς, ὡς θύειν αὐτοὺς τῇ Θέτιδι ἐπὶ θαλάττῃ καὶ προ-
σκυνεῖν τὸν Ἀχιλλέα ἄττοντα ἐν τοῖς ὅπλοις.
7   ἠρόμην τὸν Πρωτεσίλεων καὶ περὶ τῆς μελίας, ὅ τι
ἦν τὸ περὶ αὐτῇ θαῦμα, καί φησι μῆκος μὲν εἶναι τῇ
μελίᾳ ὃ μὴ ἄλλη αἰχμῇ, εὐθὺ δὲ τὸ ξύλον καὶ οὕτω

son, was killed in Scyros by Lycomedes, and since Peleus
had been a friend of Theseus and joined him in the hunt
for the Calydonian boar, he sent Achilles to Scyros to
avenge Theseus' death. He sailed with Phoenix (who has
too old to participate in anything but the planning), and
even though Scyros was very high, and founded on a rocky
cliff, he captured it by assault. He seized Lycomedes but
did not kill him, asking instead what had driven him to kill
a man so much his better; "He came to injure me," said 3
Lycomedes, "and to steal my kingdom," and so Achilles
released him as justified in the killing, and said he would
take his side before Peleus. He married Lycomedes' 4
daughter Deidameia and they had a son Neoptolemus (=
"young war"), so named because of Achilles' youthful en-
thusiasm for warfare.

It was while Achilles was living there that Thetis joined 5
him and cared for him just like mortal mothers. When the
army gathered at Aulis she carried him over to Phthia and
gave him to Peleus' charge, because of what was fated for
him; she is also said to have made him arms the like of 6
which no one had ever carried. When he arrived with
these at Aulis he filled the army with hope, and was so
obviously the child of a goddess that they sacrificed to
Thetis along the shore, and prostrated themselves before
Achilles when he ran in his armor.

I also asked Protesilaus what had been so miraculous 7
about his ash spear (*Il.* 16.140–44; 19.387–91); he said that
it was longer than any other spear; its shaft was straight,

τι ἐρρωμένον ὡς μὴ ἂν κλασθῆναι, τὸ δὲ στόμα τῆς
αἰχμῆς ἀδάμαντός τε εἶναι καὶ παντὸς διεκπαίειν, τὸν
δὲ στύρακα ἐκ τοῦ ἐπὶ θάτερα ὀρειχάλκου ἐμβεβλῆ-
σθαι, ἵνα πᾶσα δὴ ἀστράπτουσα ἐμπίπτοι.

47. ΦΟΙΝ. Τὰ δὲ ὅπλα, ὦ ἀμπελουργέ, πῶς φησιν
αὐτῷ κεκοσμῆσθαι;

2   ΑΜΠ. Οὐ τὸν Ὁμήρου τρόπον, ὦ ξένε· θεῖα μὲν
κἀκεῖνα ἐξευρῆσθαι τῷ Ὁμήρῳ, πόλεις τε ἀναγρά-
φοντι καὶ ἄστρα καὶ πολέμους καὶ γεωργίας καὶ γά-
3   μους καὶ ᾠδάς, ἀλλ᾽ ἐκεῖνα περὶ αὐτῶν φησιν· Ἀχιλ-
λεῖ ὅπλα μὴ γεγονέναι ἄλλα ἢ ἃ ἐς Τροίαν ἤνεγκε,
μηδὲ ἀπολωλέναι ποτὲ Ἀχιλλεῖ ὅπλα, μηδὲ τὸν Πά-
τροκλον ἐνδῦναι αὐτὰ παρὰ τὴν μῆνιν· ἀποθανεῖν μὲν
γὰρ ἐν τοῖς ἑαυτοῦ ὅπλοις εὐδοκιμοῦντα τῇ μάχῃ
καὶ ἁπτόμενον ἤδη τοῦ τείχους, τὰ δὲ τοῦ Ἀχιλλέως
4   ἄσυλα μεῖναι καὶ ἀνάλωτα. οὐδὲ γὰρ ἐν τοῖς ὅπλοις
τελευτῆσαι αὐτόν, ἀλλὰ ἐς γάμον ἥκειν δοκοῦντα,
γυμνὸν ἀποθανεῖν ἐστεφανωμένον ὥσπερ οἱ νυμφίοι.
5   τὰ δὲ ὅπλα κατεσκευάσθαι μὲν ἄσημα καὶ σώ-
φρονα, συγκεκρᾶσθαι δὲ αὐτοῖς ποίκιλμα ὕλης, μεθ-
ιστάμενον ἐς αὐγὰς ἄλλοτε ἄλλας, ὅσας ἡ ἶρις· ὅθεν
δοκεῖν αὐτὰ πέρα τέχνης καὶ Ἡφαίστου ᾄδεσθαι.

48. ΦΟΙΝ. Ἦ καὶ δείξεις αὐτόν, ἀμπελουργέ, καὶ
ἀναγράψεις ἀπὸ τοῦ εἴδους;

2   ΑΜΠ. Τί δὲ οὐ μέλλω φιληκόου γέ σου τυγχάνων;
τὴν μὲν δὴ κόμην ἀμφιλαφῆ αὐτῷ φησιν εἶναι καὶ

and so strong it could never be broken; its point was of adamant and penetrated anything; the shaft on its opposite end had been coated with brass, so that the whole thing glistened as it approached the target.

47. *Phoenician.* How does he say his armor was decorated?

Vinedresser. Not as Homer describes it.[174] Those divine arms were an invention of Homer, who puts on them cities and stars, wars, farming, marriages, and singing, but Protesilaus says this about them: Achilles had no other arms than those he brought with him to Troy, and they were never lost, nor did Patroclus ever wear them while Achilles was angry. Patroclus died wearing his own arms after a glorious fight in which he had already reached the Trojan wall, and Achilles' arms were not stolen or captured. Achilles himself did not die in his armor either, rather he thought that he was going to a wedding, and so died unarmed, wearing a garland like bridegrooms.

His armor was made simply and without pictures, although different materials were combined on it which changed colors like a rainbow; it was for this reason that it seemed to surpass human skill, and was poetically called the work of Hephaestus.

48. *Phoenician.* Will you present him to me, and describe how he looked?

Vinedresser. Since you are so eager to hear, of course I will. His hair was bushy, more beautiful than gold, and

---

[174] Philostratus seems to follow Eur. *IA* 1068ff. In the *Iliad*, Patroclus dies wearing the arms of Achilles, which are captured by the Trojans. Thetis asks Hephaestus to make her son new arms, whose elaborate decoration is described in *Il.* 18.468–613.

χρυσοῦ ἡδίω καὶ εὐσχήμονα, ὅπῃ καὶ ὅπως κινοίη
αὐτὴν ἢ ἄνεμος ἢ αὐτός, τὴν δὲ ῥῖνα οὔπω γρυπὴν
ἀλλ᾽ οἷον μέλλουσαν, τὴν δὲ ὀφρῦν μηνοειδῆ, τὸν θυ-
μὸν δὲ τὸν ἐν τοῖς ὄμμασι χαροποῖς οὖσιν ἡσυχάζον-
τος μὲν ἀναβάλλεσθαί τινα ὁρμήν, ὁρμήσαντος δὲ
συνεκπηδᾶν τῇ γνώμῃ, τοῖς τε ἐρῶσιν ἡδίω αὐτὸν
3 φαίνεσθαι. πεπονθέναι γάρ τι τοὺς Ἀχαιοὺς πρὸς
αὐτὸν οἷόν τι πρὸς τοὺς ἀλκίμους τῶν λεόντων· ἀσπα-
ζόμενοι γὰρ αὐτοὺς ἐν ἡσυχίᾳ, μᾶλλον αὐτοῖς χαίρο-
μεν ἐπὰν θυμοῦ ὑποπλησθέντες ἐπὶ σῦν ὁρμήσωσιν
4 ἢ ταῦρον ἤ τι τῶν μαχίμων θηρίων. τὸ δὲ λῆμα τοῦ
Ἀχιλλέως δηλοῦσθαί φησι καὶ παρὰ τοῦ αὐχένος· εἶ-
ναι γὰρ δὴ ὀρθὸν καὶ ἀνεστηκότα.
5   δικαιότατον δὲ αὐτὸν ἡρώων γενέσθαι φύσει τε καὶ
ξυνουσίᾳ τοῦ Χείρωνος. τό τοι διαβεβλῆσθαι πρὸς
χρήματα ἐκεῖθεν τῷ Ἀχιλλεῖ φοιτῆσαι· διεβέβλητο
γὰρ οὕτω πρὸς αὐτά, ὡς ἐκ τριῶν καὶ εἴκοσι πόλεων,
ἃς αὐτὸς εἷλε, λαβεῖν μὲν πλεῖστα αἰχμάλωτα, μηδε-
νὸς δὲ αὐτῶν ἡττηθῆναι πλὴν κόρης, ἣν οὐδὲ αὐτὸς
ἑαυτῷ δέδωκεν, ἀλλὰ τοὺς Ἀχαιοὺς ᾔτησεν· ἀδικίαν
δὲ τοῖς Ἀχαιοῖς ἐπικαλοῦντος τοῦ Νέστορος εἰ μὴ τὰ
πλείω Ἀχιλλεὺς λήψοιτο, "ἐμὸν ἔστω" ἔφη "τὸ πλέον
τῶν ἔργων, χρήμασι δὲ πλεονεκτείτω ὁ βουλόμενος."
6 ἐπ᾽ ἐκείνης τῆς ἐκκλησίας, ὦ ξένε, καὶ ἡ πρὸς τὸν
Ἀγαμέμνονα τῷ Ἀχιλλεῖ μῆνις ὑπὲρ τοῦ Παλαμήδους
7 ἤρξατο. μνημονεύων γὰρ τῶν πόλεων ἃς ἄμφω
ἐξεῖλον, "τοιαύτη μὲν" εἶπεν "ἡ τοῦ Παλαμήδους προ-
δοσία, κἀμὲ δὲ κρινέτω ὁ βουλόμενος· ἀπὸ γὰρ τῶν

always in place no matter how or where it was shaken by the wind or his own movements. His nose was not yet curved, but tending toward it. His brows were crescent shaped; the fierceness in his gray eyes hinted at his vigor even when he was quiet, and when in action it matched his temperament, and this was what his lovers found more attractive: for the Greeks thought of him as of strong lions, 3 whom we cherish when they are at rest, but enjoy more when they are full of spirit and attacking a boar or bull or some other fighting animal. Protesilaus says Achilles' tem- 4 perament was also clear from his straight and erect neck.

He was the most fair-minded of the heroes, both natu- 5 rally and through his training from Chiron, from whom an aversion to wealth had been passed on to Achilles: he was so uninterested in it that out of the great plunder he took from the twenty-one cities he captured he succumbed to none except a girl, and even her he did not simply take, but asked the Greeks for permission to have her. When Nestor said the Greeks would be criminals if they did not let him take more Achilles said, "I want the greater share of the work; anyone who wishes can have more of the pos- sessions." It was at this meeting that Achilles began his 6 anger at Agamemnon about Palamedes. After telling of 7 the cities which they had captured together, he said, "This was the so-called 'treachery' of Palamedes, and anyone who wishes must judge me too; for I have come from do-

8   αὐτῶν ἥκω.” δεξαμένου δὲ εἰς αὐτὸν ταῦτα τοῦ
Ἀγαμέμνονος καὶ λοιδορουμένου τῷ Ἀχιλλεῖ, τοῦ τε
Ὀδυσσέως εἰπόντος ὡς εἴη προδοσία καὶ τὸ ὑπὲρ
προδότου λέγειν, ἐκεῖνον μὲν ἀπήλασε τῆς ἐκκλησίας
οὐδὲ τοῖς Ἀχαιοῖς φίλα εἰπόντα, καθικόμενος δὲ τοῦ
Ἀγαμέμνονος λοιδορίαις πλείοσιν ἔξω βελῶν διῃτή-
σατο μήτ’ ἔργον τι πράττων ἐς τὸ κοινὸν φέρον μήτε
φοιτῶν ἐς τὰ βουλεύματα,

    ὅτε δὴ ἀφίκοντο αὐτῷ λιταὶ παρὰ τοῦ Ἀγαμέμνονος
9   ἐν παντὶ ἤδη τῶν Ἀχαιῶν ὄντων. ἐπρέσβευον δὲ
αὐτὰς Αἴας τε καὶ Νέστωρ, ὁ μὲν διὰ τὸ ξυγγενές τε
καὶ τὸ διηλλάχθαι ἤδη σφίσι μηνίσας ἐφ’ οἷσπερ ὁ
Ἀχιλλεὺς ἐμήνισεν, ὁ δὲ σοφίας τε ἕνεκα καὶ ἡλικίας,
10 ἣν ἐτίμων οἱ Ἀχαιοὶ πάντες. ἐπεὶ δὲ τὸν γοῦν Πάτρο-
κλον ξυμμαχῆσαι σφίσι παρ’ αὐτοῦ εὕραντο, ὁ μὲν
δράσας τε καὶ παθὼν ὁπόσα Ὅμηρός φησιν, ἀπέθανε
μαχόμενος τῇ Τροίᾳ ὑπὲρ τοῦ τείχους, ὁ δ’ ἔπραξε
μὲν οὐδὲν ἀγεννὲς ἐπ’ αὐτῷ οὐδὲ εἶπεν, ἀπολοφυράμε-
νος δὲ αὐτὸν ἐρρωμένως καὶ θάψας ὡς αὐτός τε ἐβούλε-
το κἀκείνῳ χαριεῖσθαι ᾤετο, ἐχώρει ἐπὶ τὸν Ἕκτορα.

11   τὰς μὲν δὴ ὑπερβολὰς αἷς κέχρηται Ὅμηρος περί
τε τοὺς ἀπολλυμένους αὐτοῖς ἅρμασιν ὁπότε Ἀχιλ-
λεὺς ἐφάνη, περί τε τοὺς ἐν ποταμῷ σφαττομένους,
τήν τε τοῦ ποταμοῦ κίνησιν ὅτ’ ἐπανίστη τῷ Ἀχιλλεῖ
τὸ ἑαυτοῦ κῦμα, ἐπαινεῖ μὲν καὶ ὁ Πρωτεσίλεως ὡς
12 ποιητικά, διαγράφει δὲ ὡς κεχαρισμένα· μήτε γὰρ τῷ

ing the same things." Agamemnon took this as a personal   8
attack and reviled him, and Odysseus said even defending
a traitor was treason. As for Odysseus, who was saying
things that not even the Greeks wanted to hear, Achilles
chased him out of the meeting. Agamemnon he assaulted
with even more insults; and afterward he kept away from
the missiles, doing nothing to help the common cause, nor
attending their councils.

This was when the entreaties came to him from Aga-
memnon, the Greeks being now in desperate straits: they   9
were brought by Ajax and Nestor, the first chosen for his
kinship and the fact that he had been angry for the same
reason as Achilles, but had now been reconciled with
them; the other for his wisdom and age, which all the
Greeks respected. They obtained from Achilles at least the   10
concession that Patroclus should help them; as a result, he
was killed fighting to broach Troy's walls, after the achieve-
ments and sufferings that Homer describes; Achilles how-
ever did or said nothing ignoble over his friend,[175] but
lamented him with great feeling, and buried him as he
himself thought best, and as he thought Patroclus would
have wanted. Then he went after Hector.

As for Homer's extravagance in describing men who   11
perished, chariots and all, when Achilles appeared, or who
were slaughtered in the river, or the movement of the river
itself when it raised its waters against Achilles, Protesilaus
praises this as poetic, but he rejects it as mere show;[176]

[175] Grossardt (2006a) points to Achilles' human sacrifice of
twelve Trojan youths (*Il.* 23.175–76).   [176] For the battle of
Achilles against the river Scamander itself, see *Il.* 21.212–97.

Ἀχιλλεῖ τηλικούτῳ ὄντι ἄπορον ἂν γενέσθαι τὸν Σκά-
μανδρον καὶ ταῦτα ἥττω ἢ οἱ μεγάλοι τῶν ποταμῶν
ὄντα, μήτ᾽ ἂν τὸν Ἀχιλλέα ἐς μάχην τῷ ποταμῷ ὁρ-
μῆσαι· εἰ γὰρ καὶ σφόδρα ἐπ᾽ αὐτὸν ἐμόρμυρεν, ἤλυ-
13 ξεν ἂν ἐκκλίνων καὶ μὴ ὁμόσε χωρῶν τῷ ὕδατι. πιθα-
νώτερα δὲ τούτων ἐκεῖνα, οἶμαι, δίεισι· ξυνελαθῆναι
μὲν ἐς τὸν ποταμὸν τοὺς Τρῶας καὶ πλείους ἀπολέ-
σθαι σφῶν ἢ ἐν ἅπαντι τῷ πολέμῳ ἀπώλοντο, οὐ μὴν
μόνῳ γε Ἀχιλλεῖ πεπρᾶχθαι ταῦτα, ἀλλὰ θαρσήσαν-
τας ἤδη παρ᾽ αὐτοῦ τοὺς Ἕλληνας ἐπικαταβαίνειν
14 καὶ τοὺς ἐν τῷ ποταμῷ σφάττειν. Ἀχιλλέα δὲ τούτων
μὲν ἀμελεῖν, ἀγωνίσασθαι δὲ ἀγῶνα τοιόνδε· ἦν ἀνὴρ
ἐκ Παιονίας ἥκων, οὗ καὶ Ὅμηρος ἐπεμνήσθη· Ἀστε-
ροπαῖον δὲ αὐτὸν καλεῖ καὶ Ἀξίου τοῦ ποταμοῦ υἱωνὸν
καὶ δεξιὸν ἄμφω τὼ χεῖρε, μέγιστον δ᾽ Ἀχαιῶν τε καὶ
Τρώων ὄντα τὸν Παίονα καὶ θηρίου δίκην ὁμόσε χω-
ροῦντα ταῖς αἰχμαῖς παρῆκεν Ὅμηρος τουτουὶ τοῦ
15 λόγου. ἦγε δὲ καὶ ἀκραιφνῆ δύναμιν Παίονας ἱππέας
ἄρτι ἐς Τροίαν ἥκων, οὓς ἐτρέψατο μὲν ὁ Ἀχιλλεὺς
ἐκπλήξας· δαίμονα γὰρ ἐμπεπτωκέναι σφίσιν ᾤοντο
16 οὔπω ἀνδρὶ τοιῷδε ἐντετυχηκότες. ὑποστάντος δὲ
Ἀστεροπαίου μόνου, πλείω περὶ ἑαυτοῦ ἔδεισεν ἢ
ὁπότε τῷ Ἕκτορι ἐμάχετο, καὶ οὐδὲ ἄτρωτος εἷλε τὸν
17 Παίονα· ὅθεν τῶν συμμάχων ἀπαγορευόντων αὐτῷ
μὴ μάχεσθαι τὴν ἡμέραν ἐκείνην τῷ Ἕκτορι, οὐκ
ἠνέσχετο τῶν λόγων τούτων ἀλλὰ εἰπὼν "ἰδέτω με
κρείττω καὶ τραυμάτων," ὥρμησεν ἐπὶ τὸν Ἕκτορα
προτεταγμένον τοῦ τείχους.

for the Scamander would not have been difficult for a man   12
of Achilles' size to cross, especially since it is not as big as
the great rivers; nor would Achilles have rushed to fight a
river—even if it had boiled up against him he could have
avoided it by leaning aside without charging to meet the
water. Protesilaus tells a story I find more plausible: the   13
Trojans had been driven into the river and more of them
had been killed than in all the rest of the war, nor only by
Achilles; the Greeks had been aroused by him, and were
attacking and slaughtering those in the river. Yet Achilles   14
did not care about this, but was involved in another con-
test. A man had come from Paeonia, who is mentioned by
Homer as Asteropaeus, the grandson of the river Axius,
and was ambidextrous.[177] Though he was the tallest man
on either side, and rushed like an animal against the
spears, Homer kept him out of this story. In fact, having   15
just arrived at Troy, he was leading a strong contingent of
cavalry from Paeonia, which Achilles routed and terrified;
they had never before met such a man, and thought a god
must have attacked them. When Asteropaeus alone re-   16
mained to fight him, Achilles had more to fear than when
he was fighting Hector, nor did he kill the Paeonian with-
out being wounded himself; for this reason his allies told   17
him not to fight with Hector that day, but he rejected their
words and said, "Let him see that even wounds do not
bother me," and rushed against Hector who was stationed
in front of the wall.

[177] *Il.* 21.139–204.

18   ἀποκτείνας δ᾽ αὐτὸν γενόμενον οἷον ἐν τῷ περὶ
       αὑτοῦ λόγῳ εἴρηκα, περιείλξε τῷ τείχει βάρβαρον
       μέν τινα καὶ ἀηδῆ τρόπον, ξυγγνωστὸν δέ, ἐπειδὴ τῷ
19   Πατρόκλῳ ἐτιμώρει. δαιμονίᾳ γὰρ δή τινι τὸν Ἀχιλ-
       λέα φύσει χρώμενον ἀεί τι μέγα ὑπὲρ τῶν φίλων
       πράττειν, ὅθεν μηνῖσαι μὲν ὑπὲρ Παλαμήδους ὁμοῦ
       πᾶσιν Ἕλλησι, τιμωρῆσαι δὲ Πατρόκλῳ τε καὶ Ἀντι-
20   λόχῳ. τά τοι πρὸς τὸν Τελαμῶνος Αἴαντα περὶ φίλων
       αὐτῷ εἰρῆσθαι λεγόμενα σφόδρα χρὴ γινώσκειν· ἐρο-
       μένου γὰρ αὐτὸν μετὰ ταῦτα τοῦ Αἴαντος ποῖα τῶν
       ἔργων ἐπικινδυνότατα αὐτῷ γένοιτο, "τὰ ὑπὲρ τῶν
21   φίλων" ὁ Ἀχιλλεὺς ἔφη. πάλιν δὲ ἐπερομένου ποῖα
       ἡδίω τε καὶ ἀπονώτερα, ταὐτὸν ἀπεκρίνατο· θαυμάσαν-
       τος δὲ τοῦ Αἴαντος πῶς ἂν ταὐτὸ ἔργον χαλεπόν τε
       γένοιτο καὶ ῥᾴδιον, "ὅτι" ἔφη "τὰ ὑπὲρ τῶν φίλων
       κινδυνεύματα μεγάλα ὄντα προθύμως πράττων, τῆς
22   ἐπ᾽ αὐτοῖς λύπης παύομαι."—"τραῦμα δέ, ὦ Ἀχιλλεῦ,
       ποῖον μάλιστά σε ἐλύπησεν;" ἦ δ᾽ ὅς. "ὃ ἐτρώθην ὑπὸ
       τοῦ Ἕκτορος."—"καὶ μὴν ὑπ᾽ αὐτοῦ γε οὐκ ἐτρώθης"
       ὁ Αἴας ἔφη. "νὴ Δία κεφαλὴν" ὁ Ἀχιλλεὺς εἶπε, "τάς
       τε χεῖρας· σὲ μὲν γὰρ κεφαλὴν ἐμαυτοῦ ἡγοῦμαι, Πά-
       τροκλος δέ μοι χεῖρες ἦν."

       49. Τὸν δὲ Πάτροκλον ὁ Πρωτεσίλεως, ὦ ξένε,
       πρεσβύτερον μὲν τοῦ Ἀχιλλέως οὐ πολὺ γενέσθαι
       φησί, θεῖον δὲ ἄνδρα καὶ σώφρονα, τῷ τε Ἀχιλλεῖ
       ἐπιτηδειότατον τῶν ἑταίρων· χαίρειν τε γὰρ ὁπότε καὶ
       ὁ Ἀχιλλεὺς ἔχαιρε, λυπεῖσθαί τε τὸν αὐτὸν τρόπον
       καὶ ξυμβουλεύειν ἀεί τι καὶ ἀκούειν ᾄδοντος, καὶ οἱ

After he killed him, as I have described (ch. 37.5), he   18
dragged him around the wall—which was awful and bar-
barous, but understandable since he was taking revenge
for Patroclus. It was the divine element in Achilles' nature   19
that made him so loyal to his friends, and that led him to
anger against all the Greeks for Palamedes, and to such
great revenge for Patroclus and Antilochus.[178] You ought   20
to know what he said about friends to Ajax son of Telamon,
who asked him after it was all over[179] which of his deeds
he thought most dangerous. "Those for my friends," he
said; and when asked which were most pleasant and easi-   21
est, he gave the same answer. When Ajax wondered how
the same task could be both difficult and easy, he an-
swered, "Because when I eagerly undertake dangers for
friends, no matter how great, I am relieved of my grief for
them." "And which of your wounds hurt you the most," he   22
asked next. "The wound I was given by Hector," he said.
"But he did not wound you," said Ajax. "Yes he did, by
Zeus," said Achilles, "in the head and the hands; for I
consider you my head, and Patroclus was my hands."

49. Protesilaus says that Patroclus, a fine and moderate
man, was a little older than Achilles, to whom he was the
perfect friend: he joined him in his joys and his sorrows,
gave him advice, and listened when he sang. Achilles'

[178] For the decapitation of Antilochus' killer, Memnon, see
ch. 26.18.

[179] Presumably this conversation takes place when both are
dead in the underworld, since the "wound" Hector inflicted on
Achilles must have been the gift of the sword (*Il.* 7.303–4) that
Ajax used to kill himself.

ἵπποι δὲ αὐτὸν ἔφερον χαίροντες ὥσπερ καὶ τὸν
2 Ἀχιλλέα. ἦν δὲ καὶ τὸ μέγεθος καὶ τὴν ἀνδρείαν
μεταξὺ τοῖν Αἰάντοιν· τοῦ μὲν Τελαμωνίου πάντα
3 ἐλείπετο, ἐκράτει δὲ ἄμφω τοῦ Λοκροῦ. καὶ μελίχλω-
ρος ἦν ὁ Πάτροκλος καὶ τὼ ὀφθαλμὼ μέλας καὶ
ἱκανῶς εὔοφρυς καὶ μέτρα ἐπαινῶν κόμης, ἡ κεφαλὴ
δὲ ἐβεβήκει ἐπ᾿ αὐχένος οἷον αἱ παλαῖστραι ἀσκοῦ-
σιν, ἡ δὲ ῥὶς ὀρθή τε ἦν καὶ τοὺς μυκτῆρας ἀνευρύ-
νετο, καθάπερ οἱ πρόθυμοι τῶν ἵππων.

50. ΦΟΙΝ. Εἰς καλόν με τῶν τοῦ Ἀχιλλέως ἵππων
ἀνέμνησας, ὦ ἀμπελουργέ· σφόδρα γὰρ δέομαι μα-
θεῖν τί βελτίους ὄντες ἑτέρων ἵππων θεῖοι ἐνομίσθη-
σαν.

2 ΑΜΠ. Ἠρόμην κἀγώ, ξένε, τὸν ἥρω αὐτὸ τοῦτο καὶ
φησι τὴν μὲν λεγομένην ἀθανασίαν περὶ αὐτοὺς εἶναι
μεμυθολογῆσθαι τῷ Ὁμήρῳ, τὴν Θετταλίαν δέ, εὔιπ-
πόν τε οὖσαν καὶ ἀγαθήν, τότε δύ᾿ ἵππους, λευκόν τε
καὶ ξανθόν, δαιμονίους τὴν ταχυτῆτα καὶ τὸ ἦθος
λαμπρούς, ἱπποτροφῆσαι κατὰ θεὸν δή τινα, ὁπότε ὁ
3 Ἀχιλλεὺς ἤνθει· καὶ πάντων ὅσα θείως ἐπὶ τῷ Ἀχιλ-
λεῖ ἐλέγετο πιστευομένων, ἤδη ἐδόκει καὶ τὸ τῶν ἵπ-
πων θεῖόν τε εἶναι καὶ ἐπέκεινα τοῦ θνητοῦ φαίνεσθαι.

51. Τελευτὴ δὲ τῷ Ἀχιλλεῖ ἐγένετο ἣν καὶ Ὅμηρος
ἐπιγινώσκει· φησὶ γὰρ αὐτὸν ἐκ Πάριδός τε καὶ
Ἀπόλλωνος ἀποθανεῖν, εἰδώς που τὰ ἐν τῷ Θυμβραίῳ
καὶ ὅπως πρὸς ἱεροῖς τε καὶ ὅρκοις, ὧν μάρτυρα τὸν
2 Ἀπόλλω ἐποιεῖτο, δολοφονηθεὶς ἔπεσεν. ἡ θυσία δὲ
τῆς Πολυξένης ἡ ἐπὶ τῷ σήματι καὶ ὅσα περὶ τοῦ

horses did not mind carrying him too. In his size and brav-   2
ery he stood between the two Ajaxes: he was entirely in-
ferior to the son of Telamon, but surpassed the Locrian in
both. He had an olive complexion and brown eyes with   3
fairly wide brows; he liked moderate length hair, and his
head was set as firmly on his neck as wrestling-schools like
to have it. His nose was straight and his nostrils flared like
spirited horses.

50. *Phoenician.* You have brought up Achilles' horses
at just the right time; I am very curious why they were
thought to be so much better than others, even divine.[180]

Vinedresser. I asked the hero that very question, and   2
he said that their immortality was a fable of Homer's; it
merely happened that Thessaly, a fine land famed for its
good horses, with the help of some god produced two
horses, a white one and a golden one of unbelievable
speed and notable temperament just at the time when
Achilles was mature. Since everything said to be divine   3
about Achilles was found credible, his horses also were
thought divine and supernatural.

51. Achilles died in the way that Homer acknowl-
edges:[181] for he says that he was killed by Paris and Apollo
(*Il.* 22.359), doubtless thinking of what happened in the
temple of Apollo Thymbraeus, and how it was at the sac-
rifice and oaths of which he was making Apollo witness
that he was treacherously killed. As to the sacrifice of Poly-   2
xena over his tomb, and the rest that you may have heard

---

[180] For the immortality of Achilles' horses, Balius and Xan-
thus, see *Il.* 16.148–51, 23.276–78; the latter speaks to him and
foretells his death at *Il.* 19.404–17.   [181] See Introduction
§10, and the discussion in Grossardt (2013).

3 ἔρωτος ἐκείνου ποιητῶν ἀκούεις, ὧδε ἔχει· Πολυξένης
ὁ Ἀχιλλεὺς ἦρα καὶ τὸν γάμον τοῦτον ἑαυτῷ ἔπραττεν
ἐπὶ τῷ τοὺς Ἀχαιοὺς ἀναστῆσαι τοῦ Ἰλίου, ἦρα δὲ
4 καὶ ἡ Πολυξένη τοῦ Ἀχιλλέως. εἶδον δ' ἀλλήλους ἐν
λύτροις Ἕκτορος· ὁ γὰρ Πρίαμος ἥκων παρὰ τὸν
Ἀχιλλέα χειραγωγὸν ἑαυτοῦ τὴν παῖδα ἐποιεῖτο νεω-
τάτην οὖσαν ὧν ἡ Ἑκάβη αὐτῷ ἔτεκεν, ἐθεράπευον δὲ
ἀεὶ τὸ βάδισμα τῶν πατέρων οἱ νεώτεροι τῶν παίδων.
5 καὶ οὕτω δή τι ὁ Ἀχιλλεὺς ἐσωφρόνει ὑπὸ δικαιοσύ-
νης καὶ τὰ ἐρωτικά, ὡς μήτε ἀφελέσθαι τὴν κόρην ἐφ'
ἑαυτῷ οὖσαν, γάμον τε αὐτῆς ὁμολογῆσαι τῷ Πριάμῳ,
πιστεῦσαί τε ἀναβαλλομένῳ τὸν γάμον.

6   ἐπεὶ δὲ ἀπέθανε γυμνὸς ἐν τοῖς περὶ τούτων ὅρκοις,
λέγεται ἡ Πολυξένη φευγουσῶν ἐκ τοῦ ἱεροῦ τῶν
Τρωάδων καὶ τῶν Τρώων ἐσκεδασμένων (οὐδὲ γὰρ τὸ
πτῶμα τοῦ Ἀχιλλέως ἀδεῶς ἤνεγκαν) αὐτομολίᾳ χρή-
σασθαι καὶ φυγεῖν ἐς τὸ Ἑλληνικόν, ἀναχθεῖσά τε τῷ
Ἀγαμέμνονι ζῆν μὲν ἐν κομιδῇ λαμπρᾷ τε καὶ σώ-
φρονι καθάπερ ἐν πατρὸς οἰκίᾳ, τριταίου δὲ ἤδη κει-
μένου τοῦ νεκροῦ δραμεῖν ἐπὶ τὸ σῆμα ἐν νυκτὶ ξίφει
τε αὐτὴν ἐπικλῖναι πολλὰ εἰποῦσαν ἐλεεινὰ καὶ γα-
μικά, ὅτε δὴ καὶ δεῖσθαι τοῦ Ἀχιλλέως ἐραστήν τε
μεῖναι καὶ ἀγαγέσθαι αὐτὴν μὴ ψευσαμένην τὸν γά-
μον.

7   ἃ δὲ τῷ Ὁμήρῳ ἐν δευτέρᾳ ψυχοστασίᾳ εἴρηται, εἰ

from the poets about his love for her, the truth is this: Achilles *did* love Polyxena and was negotiating his marriage to her on condition that he lead the Greeks away from Troy. Polyxena loved him too. They first saw each other when Hector's body was ransomed; for when he visited Achilles, Priam made the youngest of his children by Hecuba his guide—in general, the youngest children used to tag along with their fathers. Achilles' fairness was so restrained even in love that he did not simply take her then even though she was in his power, but made an agreement with Priam to marry her, and trusted him when he wished to delay the marriage.

Well, after Achilles was killed while unarmed during the marriage oaths, this is what is said to have happened to Polyxena: as the women of Troy were fleeing from the shrine and the men had been routed (even the corpse of Achilles terrified them) she became a deserter and fled to the Greek camp, was presented to Agamemnon and allowed to live, treated with respect and restraint, as if she were in her father's house. But then, on the third night after his body's being laid to rest, she ran to his tomb and, after a long, pitiful, wifely speech, begging Achilles to remain her lover, and to take her as his bride since she herself had not lied about the marriage, she braced herself against a sword.[182]

What Homer says in the second *Weighing of the*

---

[182] This version of her death contradicts Dictys; see Huhn-Bethe (1917, 619n1) and Grossardt (2013).

PHILOSTRATUS

δὴ Ὁμήρου ἐκεῖνα, ὡς ἀποθανόντα Ἀχιλλέα Μοῦσαι
μὲν ᾠδαῖς ἐθρήνησαν, Νηρηίδες δὲ πληγαῖς τῶν
στέρνων, οὐ παρὰ πολύ φησι κεκομπάσθαι· Μούσας
μὲν γὰρ οὔτε ἀφικέσθαι οὔτε ᾆσαι, οὐδὲ Νηρηίδων
τινὰ ὀφθῆναι τῷ στρατῷ καίτοι γινωσκομένας ὅτι
ἥκουσι, θαυμαστὰ δὲ ξυμβῆναι ἕτερα καὶ οὐ πόρρω
8 τῶν Ὁμήρῳ εἰρημένων. ἐκ γὰρ τοῦ κόλπου τοῦ Μέλα-
νος ἡ θάλασσα ἀνοιδήσασα τὰ μὲν πρῶτα ἐμυκᾶτο,
μετ᾽ οὐ πολὺ δὲ ἀρθεῖσα λόφῳ μεγάλῳ ἴση ἐχώρει ἐς
τὸ Ῥοίτειον, ἐκπεπληγμένων τῶν Ἀχαιῶν καὶ ἀπορούν-
9 των ὅ τι αὐτοί τε καὶ ἡ γῆ πείσονται. ἐπεὶ δὲ πλησίον
ἐγίνετο καὶ προσεκύμαινε τῷ στρατοπέδῳ, θρῆνον
ἤχησεν ὀξύν τε καὶ ἀθρόον, καθάπερ γυναικῶν ὅμι-
10 λος ὃν ἐς τὰ κήδη ἀναφθέγγονται. τούτου δὲ θείου τε
καὶ δαιμονίου φανέντος, καὶ πάντων ὁμολογούντων
ὅτι Νηρηίδας ἦγε τὸ κῦμα (οὐδὲ γὰρ ἐπέκλυσεν οὐ-
δέν, ἀλλὰ πρᾷόν τε καὶ λεῖον τῇ γῇ προσευνάσθη),
11 πολλῷ θειότερα τὰ ἐφεξῆς ἔδοξεν. ἐπειδὴ γὰρ νὺξ
ὑπέλαβεν, οἰμωγὴ τῆς Θέτιδος διεφοίτα τὸν στρατὸν
ἀνευφημούσης τε καὶ τὸν υἱὸν βοώσης. ἐβόα δὲ τορόν

183 What the vinedresser (or Philostratus, cf. VA 8.7.48) mis-
takenly calls a Psychostasia (the title of a play by Aeschylus [frr.
279–80 Radt] referring to a different incident), the "weighing
of souls" to determine a warrior's fate, is actually the "second
Nekyia (= visit to the dead)" in Od. 24.1–204.
184 The Hellenistic scholar Aristarchus and others claimed the
second Nekyia was not by Homer; for their reasons see Petzl
(1969, 44–66).

Dead[183]—if it *is* by Homer at all[184]—that the Muses sang songs of mourning for Achilles' death, and the Nereids beat their breasts, has not, he says, been much[185] exaggerated. For though the Muses neither came nor sang,[186] and not a one of the Nereids was seen by the army (although they are now known to visit),[187] yet other things happened which *were* surprising, and not too different from Homer's story. From the gulf of Melas[188] the sea bubbled up and 8 began to roar, then it rose, like a huge crest, and began to move toward Rhoetaeum. The Greeks were terrified, not knowing what was to become of themselves or the land on which they stood. When the wave was close by and hover- 9 ing over the camp, it gave off a piercing shriek all at once, like what a group of women cries out at a funeral. This 10 was a divine and supernatural event, and everyone agreed that the wave must have brought the Nereids, because it swept nothing away, but settled gently and gradually back to earth. But what happened next seemed even more the act of a god: when night had fallen, Thetis' lament of griev- 11 ing and cries for her son passed over all the army. It was a piercing cry that rang in the ear, like an echo in the moun-

---

185 See 24.2n.

186 The fact that the nine Muses are not mentioned otherwise in Homer was used in antiquity as a reason for declaring this passage spurious; see Petzl (1969, 59–60), where the evidence of the *Heroicus* should be added.

187 Cf. *VA* 4.16, Barringer (1995, 49–58). Grossardt (2013) suggests that a contemporary cult of the Nereids existed near Ilion.

188 Literally, the "black gulf"; it is the gulf of Saros, between Thrace and the Chersonnese. Rhoetaeum was a coastal town northeast of Ilion.

{μέγα} τε καὶ ἔναυλον καθάπερ ἡ ἐν τοῖς ὄρεσιν ἠχώ,
καὶ τότε μάλιστα οἱ Ἀχαιοὶ ξυνῆκαν ὅτι τέκοι τὸν
Ἀχιλλέα ἡ Θέτις, οὐδὲ ἄλλως ἀπιστοῦντες.

12   τὸν μὲν δὴ κολωνόν, ξένε, τοῦτον, ὃν ἐπὶ τοῦ μετώ-
που τῆς ἀκτῆς ὁρᾷς ἀνεστηκότα, ἤγειραν οἱ Ἀχαιοὶ
ξυνελθόντες ὅτε τῷ Πατρόκλῳ ξυνεμίχθη ἐς τὸν τά-
φον, κάλλιστον ἐντάφιον ἑαυτῷ τε κἀκείνῳ διδούς·
13   ὅθεν ᾄδουσιν αὐτὸν οἱ τὰ φιλικὰ ἐπαινοῦντες. ἐτάφη
δὲ ἐκδηλότατα ἀνθρώπων πᾶσιν οἷς ἐπήνεγκεν αὐτῷ
ἡ Ἑλλάς, οὐδὲ κομᾶν ἔτι μετὰ τὸν Ἀχιλλέα καλὸν
ἡγούμενοι, χρυσόν τε καὶ ὅ τι ἕκαστος εἶχεν ἢ ἀπ-
άγων ἐς Τροίαν ἢ ἐκ δασμοῦ λαβών, νήσαντες ἐς τὴν
πυρὰν ἀθρόα, παραχρῆμά τε καὶ ὅτε Νεοπτόλεμος ἐς
Τροίαν ἦλθε· λαμπρῶν γὰρ δὴ ἔτυχε πάλιν παρά τε
τοῦ παιδὸς παρά τε τῶν Ἀχαιῶν ἀντιχαρίζεσθαι αὐτῷ
πειρωμένων, οἵ γε καὶ τὸν ἀπὸ τῆς Τροίας ποιούμενοι
πλοῦν περιέπιπτον τῷ τάφῳ καὶ τὸν Ἀχιλλέα ᾤοντο
περιβάλλειν.

52. ΦΟΙΝ. Τὸν Νεοπτόλεμον δέ, ὦ ἀμπελουργέ,
ποῖόν τινα γενέσθαι φησί;

2   ΑΜΠ. Γενναῖον, ξένε, καὶ τοῦ μὲν πατρὸς ἥττω,
φαυλότερον δὲ οὐδὲν τοῦ Τελαμωνίου. ταὐτὸ δὲ καὶ
περὶ τοῦ εἴδους φησί· καλὸν μὲν γὰρ εἶναι καὶ προσ-
εοικότα τῷ πατρί, λείπεσθαι δ' αὐτοῦ τοσοῦτον ὅσον
3   τῶν ἀγαλμάτων οἱ καλοὶ λείπονται. καὶ μὴν καὶ
ὕμνων ἐκ Θετταλίας ὁ Ἀχιλλεὺς ἔτυχεν, οὓς ἀνὰ πᾶν
ἔτος ἐπὶ τὸ σῆμα φοιτῶντες ᾖδον ἐν νυκτί, τελετῆς τι

tains; then the Achaeans realized for certain, although they never really doubted it, that Thetis was Achilles' mother.

The mound which you see rising on the edge of the shore[189] is what the Greeks came together to raise when he was joined with Patroclus in the tomb, through which he gave the fairest of funeral gifts both to Patroclus and himself; this is why those who praise friendship celebrate him. His burial was the most notable among men for all the offerings with which the Greeks presented him: they decided it would never be right again to wear long hair after his death, and their gold, or whatever they had either brought with them to Troy or received from the booty there, they heaped up onto the pyre, both at that time and also after Neoptolemus had come to Troy. Then he received glorious honors once again both from his son and, in an effort to repay thanks to him, from the Greeks who also, as they prepared to sail away from Troy, fell on his tomb and imagined they were embracing Achilles.

52. *Phoenician.* What sort of man does he say Neoptolemus was?

Vinedresser. A fine one—not as great as his father, but every bit as good as the son of Telamon. And of his appearance he says the same; he is good-looking and resembles his father, but falls short of him just as beautiful men fall short of statues. Achilles also received hymns from Thessaly; they used to visit his tomb every year and sing them at night, combining religious rites with their offerings to

---

[189] For the location of this mound, see Introduction §6.

ἐγκαταμιγνύντες τοῖς ἐναγίσμασιν, ὡς Λήμνιοί τε νο-
μίζουσι καὶ Πελοποννησίων οἱ ἀπὸ Σισύφου.

53. ΦΟΙΝ. Ἄλλος αὖ λόγος ἥκει, ἀμπελουργέ, οὗ
μὰ τὸν Ἡρακλέα οὐκ ἂν μεθείμην, οὐδ᾽ εἰ πάνθ᾽ ὑπὲρ
τοῦ παραπτῆναι αὐτὸν πράττοις.

2   ΑΜΠ. Ἀλλὰ τὰς ἐκβολὰς τῶν λόγων ἀδολεσχίας
ἔνιοι, ξένε, ἡγοῦνται καὶ λῆρον πρὸς τοὺς μὴ σχολὴν
ἄγοντας. σὲ δὲ ὁρῶ δοῦλον μὲν τῆς νεὼς ἧς ἄρχεις,
δοῦλον δὲ τῶν ἀνέμων, ὧν εἰ καὶ μικρὰ αὔρα κατὰ
πρύμναν σταίη, δεῖ τὰ ἱστία ἀνασείειν καὶ συνεξαί-
ρεσθαι τῇ νηΐ, πάντα δεύτερα ἡγουμένους τοῦ πλεῖν.

3   ΦΟΙΝ. Ἐρρώσθω λοιπὸν ἡ ναῦς καὶ τὰ ἐν αὐτῇ·
τὰ γὰρ τῆς ψυχῆς ἀγώγιμα ἡδίω τέ μοι καὶ κερδαλε-
ώτερα, τὰς δὲ ἐκβολὰς τῶν λόγων μὴ λῆρον ἀλλ᾽ ἐπι-
κέρδειαν ἡγώμεθα τῆς ἐμπορίας ταύτης.

4   ΑΜΠ. Ὑγιαίνεις, ξένε, οὕτω γινώσκων, καὶ ἐπειδὴ
βούλει, ἄκουε· τὰ μὲν γὰρ Κορινθίοις ἐπὶ Μελικέρτῃ
(τούτους γὰρ δὴ τοὺς ἀπὸ Σισύφου εἶπον), καὶ ὁπόσα
οἱ αὐτοὶ δρῶσιν ἐπὶ τοῖς τῆς Μηδείας παισίν, οὓς
ὑπὲρ τῆς Γλαύκης ἀπέκτειναν, θρήνῳ εἴκασται τελε-
στικῷ τε καὶ ἐνθέῳ· τοὺς μὲν γὰρ μειλίσσονται, τὸν
δὲ ὑμνοῦσιν.

5   ἐπὶ δὲ τῷ ἔργῳ τῷ περὶ τοὺς ἄνδρας ὑπὸ τῶν ἐν
Λήμνῳ γυναικῶν ἐξ Ἀφροδίτης ποτὲ πραχθέντι καθ-
αίρεται μὲν ἡ Λῆμνος καθ᾽ ἕκαστον ἔτος καὶ σβέννυ-
ται τὸ ἐν αὐτῇ πῦρ ἐς ἡμέρας ἐννέα, θεωρὶς δὲ ναῦς
ἐκ Δήλου πυρφορεῖ, κἂν ἀφίκηται πρὸ τῶν ἐναγισμά-
των, οὐδαμοῦ τῆς Λήμνου καθορμίζεται, μετέωρος δὲ

the dead, as is the custom of the Lemnians and the descendants of Sisyphus in the Peloponnese.

53. *Phoenician.* Here comes another story! By Heracles, I will not miss this one no matter what you try to make it fly past me.

Vinedresser. But some consider these discursive stories 2 to be idle chatter and a nuisance to people who are busy. I know that you are in thrall to the ship you command, and to the winds—if even a small wind blows seaward you must unfurl the sails and cast off, thinking of nothing but your voyage.

Phoenician. My ship and everything in it can take care 3 of itself; my soul's cargo is a greater pleasure and profit, so let us consider the discursive stories not a nuisance, but the real profit from this voyage.

Vinedresser. That's the right attitude! Since you are 4 willing, listen: what the Corinthians do to commemorate Melicertes (for these are the ones I meant by Sisyphus' descendants), and what they also do for the children of Medea, whom they killed to avenge Glauke, are similar to a dirge that is mystical and ecstatic:[190] Medea's children they attempt to appease, Melicertes they praise.

Because of the deed performed once by the Lemnian 5 women at Aphrodite's bidding against the men, the island of Lemnos is purified every year and all fire is extinguished on it for nine days; a sacred ship bears fire from Delos, and if it arrives before the sacrifices to the dead it does not

---

[190] On the hero cults of these children, see Introduction §3.

PHILOSTRATUS

ἐπισαλεύει τοῖς ἀκρωτηρίοις ἔστε ὅσιον τὸ εἰσπλεῦ-
6 σαι γένηται. θεοὺς γὰρ χθονίους καὶ ἀπορρήτους κα-
λοῦντες τότε, καθαρόν, οἶμαι, τὸ πῦρ τὸ ἐν τῇ θα-
7 λάττῃ φυλάττουσιν. ἐπειδὰν δὲ ἡ θεωρὶς ἐσπλεύσῃ
καὶ νείμωνται τὸ πῦρ ἔς τε τὴν ἄλλην δίαιταν ἔς τε
τὰς ἐμπύρους τῶν τεχνῶν, καινοῦ τὸ ἐντεῦθεν βίου
ἄρχεσθαι.
8   τὰ δὲ Θετταλικὰ ἐναγίσματα φοιτῶντα τῷ Ἀχιλλεῖ
ἐκ Θετταλίας ἐχρήσθη Θετταλοῖς ἐκ Δωδώνης· ἐκέ-
λευσε γὰρ δὴ τὸ μαντεῖον Θετταλοὺς ἐς Τροίαν πλέ-
οντας θύειν ὅσα ἔτη τῷ Ἀχιλλεῖ καὶ σφάττειν τὰ μὲν
9 ὡς θεῷ, τὰ δὲ ὡς ἐν μοίρᾳ τῶν κειμένων. κατ' ἀρχὰς
μὲν δὴ τοιάδε ἐγίνετο· ναῦς ἐκ Θετταλίας μέλανα
ἱστία ἠρμένη ἐς Τροίαν ἔπλει, θεωροὺς μὲν δὶς ἑπτὰ
ἀπάγουσα, ταύρους δὲ λευκόν τε καὶ μέλανα, χειροή-
θεις ἄμφω, καὶ ὕλην ἐκ Πηλίου, ὡς μηδὲν τῆς πόλεως
δέοιντο· καὶ πῦρ ἐκ Θετταλίας ἦγον καὶ σπονδὰς καὶ
ὕδωρ τοῦ Σπερχειοῦ ἀρυσάμενοι· ὅθεν καὶ στεφάνους
ἀμαραντίνους ἐς τὰ κήδη πρῶτοι Θετταλοὶ ἐνόμισαν,
ἵνα, κἂν ἄνεμοι τὴν ναῦν ἀπολάβωσι, μὴ σαπροὺς
10 ἐπιφέρωσι μηδὲ ἐξώρους. νυκτὸς μὲν δὴ καθορμίζε-
σθαι ἔδει καὶ πρὶν ἅψασθαι τῆς γῆς ὕμνον ἀπὸ τῆς
νεὼς ᾄδειν ἐς τὴν Θέτιν ὧδε ξυγκείμενον·

Θέτι κυανέα, Θέτι Πηλεία,
τὸν μέγαν ἃ τέκες υἱὸν Ἀχιλλέα, τοῦ

298

enter the harbor, but stays at sea anchored off the capes, until it is holy to sail in. I believe that while they invoke 6 the unspeakable gods of the underworld they keep the fire pure out on the ocean. But when the sacred ship sails in, 7 and they distribute the fire for the rest of their daily uses and especially for those crafts which need fire, from that point on they begin a new life.[191]

The Thessalian offerings to the dead that travel to 8 Achilles from Thessaly were prophesied to the Thessalians from Dodona.[192] The oracle ordered the Thessalians to sail to Troy and burn and slaughter every year to Achilles some offerings as to a god, others as proper to burials. At 9 the beginning it took place as follows: a ship raised black sails and used to sail from Thessaly to Troy, carrying twice seven celebrants, one white and one black bull, both tame, and wood from Mount Pelion, so that they would require no help from Troy. They even carried fire and libations from Thessaly and water drawn from the Spercheius. For the same reason, the Thessalians also were the first to adopt the custom of amaranth garlands[193] for mourning, to avoid bringing rotten or faded flowers if the winds delayed them. They had to anchor at night and, before they 10 could disembark, sing the following hymn to Thetis:

Sea-blue Thetis, Pelean Thetis,
who bore your son great Achilles, of whom

[191] The annual purification of the island and sacrifices to the dead commemorate the myth of the murder of all males by their wives. [192] For these cults, see Introduction §12.

[193] Amaranth garlands, also in Plin. *HN* 21.8.47; Dioscorides, *Materia medica* 4.57; Paul, *Epistle to Peter* 1.5.4; Rutherford (2009, 243).

θνατὰ μὲν ὅσον φύσις ἤνεγκε,
Τροία λάχε· σᾶς δ' ὅσον ἀθανάτου
γενεᾶς πάις ἔσπασε, Πόντος ἔχει.
βαῖνε πρὸς αἰπὺν τόνδε κολωνὸν
μετ' Ἀχιλέως ἔμπυρα,
βαῖν' ἀδάκρυτος μετὰ Θεσσαλίας.
Θέτι κυανέα, Θέτι Πηλεία.

11   προσελθόντων δὲ τῷ σήματι μετὰ τὸν ὕμνον ἀσπὶς
μὲν ὥσπερ ἐν πολέμῳ ἐδουπεῖτο, δρόμοις δὲ ἐρρυθ-
μισμένοις συνηλάλαζον ἀνακαλοῦντες τὸν Ἀχιλλέα,
στεφανώσαντες δὲ τὴν κορυφὴν τοῦ κολωνοῦ καὶ βό-
θρους ἐπ' αὐτῇ ὀρύξαντες τὸν ταῦρον τὸν μέλανα ὡς
12   τεθνεῶτι ἔσφαττον. ἐκάλουν δὲ καὶ τὸν Πάτροκλον ἐπὶ
τὴν δαῖτα, ὡς καὶ τοῦτο ἐς χάριν τῷ Ἀχιλλεῖ πράττον-
13   τες. ἐντεμόντες δὲ καὶ ἐναγίσαντες κατέβαινον ἐπὶ
τὴν ναῦν ἤδη, καὶ θύσαντες ἐπὶ τοῦ αἰγιαλοῦ τὸν ἕτε-
ρον τῶν ταύρων Ἀχιλλεῖ πάλιν, κανοῦ τε ἐναρξάμενοι
καὶ σπλάγχνων ἐπ' ἐκείνῃ τῇ θυσίᾳ (ἔθυον γὰρ τὴν
θυσίαν ταύτην ὡς θεῷ), περὶ ὄρθρον ἀπέπλεον ἀπά-
γοντες τὸ ἱερεῖον, ὡς μὴ ἐν τῇ πολεμίᾳ εὐωχοῖντο.

14   ταῦτα, ξένε, τὰ οὕτω σεμνὰ καὶ ἀρχαῖα καταλυθῆ-
ναι μὲν καὶ ὑπὸ τῶν τυράννων φασὶν οἱ λέγονται

---

194 I.e., Achilles has the tomb of a mortal at Troy but also the
shrine of an immortal on the island of Leuke in the Black Sea (see
below).

195 For *empura*, see Ekroth (2002, 118, 120, 181).

what mortal nature provided
Troy obtained ; but what from your immortal
race the boy derived, Pontus has.[194]
Journey to this steep mound
to the offerings[195] of Achilles;
Journey without weeping, join Thessaly.
Sea-blue Thetis, Pelean Thetis.

After the hymn they approached the tomb; a shield was   11
rattled as if in war, and while running in rhythm they cried
out and invoked Achilles; they placed garlands on the peak
of the mound and dug pits in it, into which they cut the
throat of the black bull as an offering to the dead. They   12
invited Patroclus to the meal also, to gratify Achilles. After   13
cutting it into the fire and devoting it, they next returned
to their ship and on the shore they sacrificed the other bull
to Achilles also, using for that sacrifice the ritual basket
and organs—for they were sacrificing as if to a god. At
dawn they sailed away and took the meat of the victim with
them, to avoid celebrating the banquet in enemy terri-
tory.[196]

He says that these holy and original rituals were abol-   14
ished, stranger, by the tyrants who are said to have ruled

---

[196] Judging from the different terminology, Philostratus envi-
sions (1) a blood-offering into pits at the tomb as a "banquet" to
the dead, followed by the burning of all the animal's parts (Ekroth
2002, 74–128), and (2) the typical Greek sacrificial ritual at the
shore, including sprinkling grain (from a basket) on the victim,
cutting its throat, butchering it, and burning the inedible parts
for the gods, while cooking and eating the organs immediately,
but taking away the meat for later. See Introduction §§3 and 12.

μετὰ τοὺς Αἰακίδας ἄρξαι Θετταλῶν, ἀμεληθῆναι δὲ
καὶ ὑπὸ τῆς Θετταλίας· αἱ μὲν γὰρ ἔπεμπον τῶν πό-
λεων, αἱ δ᾽ οὐκ ἠξίουν, αἱ δ᾽ εἰς νέωτα πέμψειν ἔφα-
15 σαν, αἱ δὲ κατέβαλον τὸ πρᾶγμα. αὐχμῷ δὲ τῆς γῆς
πιεσθείσης καὶ κελευούσης τῆς μαντείας τιμᾶν τὸν
Ἀχιλλέα ὡς θέμις, ἃ μὲν ὡς θεῷ ἐνόμιζον ἀφεῖλον τῶν
δρωμένων, ἐξηγούμενοι ταύτῃ τὸ ὡς θέμις, ἐνήγιζον
δὲ ὡς τεθνεῶτι καὶ ἐνέτεμνον τὰ ἐπιτυχόντα, ἔστε ἡ
Ξέρξου ἔλασις ἐπὶ τὴν Ἑλλάδα ἐγένετο, ἐν ᾗ Θεττα-
λοὶ μηδίσαντες ἐξέλιπον πάλιν τὰ ἐς τὸν Ἀχιλλέα
νόμιμα, ἐπειδὴ ναῦς ἐς Σαλαμῖνα ἐξ Αἰγίνης ἔπλευ-
σεν ἄγουσα ἐπὶ ξυμμαχίᾳ τοῦ Ἑλληνικοῦ τὸν τῶν
Αἰακιδῶν οἶκον.

16   ἐπεὶ δὲ Ἀλέξανδρος ὁ Φιλίππου χρόνοις ὕστερον
τὴν μὲν ἄλλην Θετταλίαν ἐδουλώσατο, τὴν δὲ Φθίαν
τῷ Ἀχιλλεῖ ἀνῆκεν, ἐπί τε Δαρεῖον στρατεύων ξύμμα-
χον τὸν Ἀχιλλέα ἐν Τροίᾳ ἐποιήσατο, ἐπεστράφησαν
οἱ Θετταλοὶ τοῦ Ἀχιλλέως καὶ ἵππον τε, ὁπόσην
Ἀλέξανδρος ἐκ Θετταλίας ἦγε, περιήλασαν τῷ τάφῳ,
ξυνέπεσόν τε ἀλλήλοις ὥσπερ ἱππομαχοῦντες, καὶ
ἀπῆλθον εὐξάμενοί τε καὶ θύσαντες, ἐκάλουν δὲ αὐτὸν
ἐπὶ Δαρεῖον αὐτῷ Βαλίῳ τε καὶ Ξάνθῳ, βοῶντες
ταῦτα ἀπὸ τῶν ἵππων.

17   ἐπεὶ δὲ Δαρεῖος ἥλω καὶ πρὸς τοῖς Ἰνδικοῖς Ἀλέξ-
ανδρος ἦν, ξυνέστειλαν οἱ Θετταλοὶ τὰ ἐναγίσματα

---

197 Because the shrine of the family of Achilles had now been
moved to protect the Athenians. The transfer of these Aiginetan

the Thessalians after the Aeacidae, and were neglected by Thessaly; some cities sent offerings, others declined, others promised to send them the next year, and others abolished them. But when the land was oppressed by a drought 15 and the oracle commanded them to honor Achilles as was proper, they removed from the performance of the ritual what they practiced for a god (interpreting "as was proper" in this way), but continued to cut into the fire and devote as for the dead anything they had, until the expedition of Xerxes against Greece: during this the Thessalians surrendered to the Persians and abandoned once again their customs for Achilles, when a ship sailed from Aigina to Salamis, carrying the shrine of the Aeacidae to help the Greeks.[197]

Later, when Alexander the Great enslaved the rest of 16 Thessaly, but spared Phthia for Achilles' sake and made Achilles his ally at Troy when he attacked Darius, the Thessalians took an interest in Achilles, and rode around his tomb all the horses which Alexander was bringing from Thessaly; then they attacked each other in a mock cavalry battle. After a prayer and a sacrifice, they departed and shouted from their horses for Achilles, with Balius and Xanthus as well,[198] to join them against Darius.

Once Darius was dead and Alexander reached India, the Thessalians cut back on offerings and sent only a 17

hero helpers (cf. Hdt. 5.80; Diod. 8.32; Justin 20.2) to the Greek fleet at Salamis is told by Hdt. 8.64 and 83, and Plut. *Them.* 15. See Pritchett (1971–1985, 3:16).

[198] The names of Achilles' immortal horses (*Il.* 16.149, 19.400, ch. 50.1, above).

0

καὶ ἔπεμπον ἄρνα μέλανα. τῶν δὲ ἐναγιζόντων οὔτε
ἀφικνουμένων ἐς Τροίαν, εἴ τε ἀφίκοιντο μεθ᾽ ἡμέραν
ἕκαστα καὶ οὐκ ἐν κόσμῳ πραττόντων, ἐμήνισεν ὁ
Ἀχιλλεύς, καὶ ὁπόσα τῇ Θετταλίᾳ ἐνέσκηψεν εἰ διεξί-
οιμι, ἀδολεσχίας πλέως ὁ λόγος ἔσται.

18   πρὸ ἐτῶν δέ που τεττάρων ἐντυχὼν ἐνταῦθά μοι ὁ
Πρωτεσίλεως ἐκ Πόντου μὲν ἥκειν ἔφη· νεὼς γὰρ ἐπι-
τυχὼν πλεῦσαι παρὰ τὸν Ἀχιλλέα ξένῳ εἰκασθείς,
19   τουτὶ δὲ θαμὰ πράττειν. ἐμοῦ δὲ εἰπόντος ὡς φιλέται-
ρός τε καὶ χρηστὸς εἴη φιλῶν τὸν Ἀχιλλέα, "ἀλλὰ
νῦν" ἔφη "διενεχθεὶς αὐτῷ ἥκω. Θετταλοῖς γὰρ ὑπὲρ
τῶν ἐναγισμάτων μηνίοντα αἰσθόμενος, 'ἐμοὶ ἔφην,
'ὦ Ἀχιλλεῦ, πάρες τοῦτο'. ὁ δ᾽ οὐ πείθεται, φησὶ δ᾽
αὐτοῖς κακόν τι ἐκ θαλάττης δώσειν. καὶ δέδια μὴ
παρὰ τῆς Θέτιδος εὕρηταί τι αὐτοῖς ὁ δεινὸς ἐκεῖνος
20   καὶ ἀμείλικτος." κἀγὼ μέν, ξένε, ταῦτα ἀκούσας τοῦ
Πρωτεσίλεω, ἐρυσίβας τε ᾤμην καὶ ὁμίχλας προσβε-
βλήσεσθαι τοῖς Θετταλῶν ληΐοις ὑπὸ τοῦ Ἀχιλλέως
ἐπὶ φθορᾷ τοῦ καρποῦ· ταυτὶ γὰρ τὰ πάθη δοκεῖ πως
ἐκ θαλάττης ἐπὶ τὰς εὐκάρπους τῶν ἠπείρων ἱζάνειν.
21   ᾤμην δὲ καὶ ἐπικλυσθήσεσθαί τινας τῶν ἐν Θετταλίᾳ
πόλεων, οἷα Βοῦρά τε καὶ Ἑλίκη καὶ ἡ περὶ Λοκροὺς
Ἀταλάντη ἔπαθε· τὴν μὲν γὰρ καταδῦναί φασι, τὴν δ᾽
22   αὖ ῥαγῆναι. ἐδόκει δ᾽ ἄλλα τῷ Ἀχιλλεῖ καὶ τῇ Θέτιδι,
ὑφ᾽ ὧν ἀπολώλασι Θετταλοί· μεγάλων γὰρ δὴ ἐπιτι-

black lamb. Since they no longer came to Troy to make their offerings or, if they did so, performed them during the day and without any ceremony, Achilles was enraged— if I were to tell you all the miseries he inflicted on Thessaly, my story would be full of idle chatter.

About four years ago Protesilaus met me here and said 18 he had come from the Black Sea; disguised as a foreigner, he had found a ship and sailed to see Achilles, as he often did. When I had remarked how kind it was of him to be 19 so friendly to Achilles, he said, "At the moment you find me quite estranged from him. I noticed he was enraged at the Thessalians because of the offerings, and said, 'Achilles, please overlook this for my sake.' But he refuses, and says he will send them some harm from the sea. I am afraid the dreadful man may contrive something from Thetis against them." When I heard this from Protesilaus, I 20 thought that blight[199] or hailstorms would be inflicted by Achilles on the Thessalian crops to destroy their harvest, since these things usually seemed to afflict fertile lands from the sea. I also thought that some cities in Thessaly 21 would be destroyed by flood, just as Boura and Helice, and Atalante in Lokris had been; the first they say sank into the ground, the other was torn apart.[200] But Achilles and The- 22 tis decided to ruin the Thessalians in another way: great

[199] Grossardt (2006a, 733) notes that a grain very susceptible to such fungus was called "Achillean" (Theophr. *Hist. pl.* 8.10.2, *Caus. pl.* 3.22.2).

[200] An earthquake and tidal wave submerged the Achaean towns of Boura and Helice in 373–372 BC (see Gow and Page 1968, on 1737 = *A.P.* 9.423.7 [Bianor]). The island of Atalante suffered from an earthquake in 426 BC (Thuc. 3.89.3; cf. Strabo 1.3.20, and Diod. 12.59).

PHILOSTRATUS

μίων ὄντων ἐπὶ τῇ κόχλῳ παρ' ἧς οἱ ἄνθρωποι σοφί-
ζονται τὴν πορφύραν, αἰτίαν ἔσχον οἱ Θετταλοὶ
23 παρανομῆσαί τι ἐς τὴν βαφὴν ταύτην. εἰ μὲν ἀληθῆ,
οὐκ οἶδα· λίθοι <δ'> οὖν ἐπικρέμανταί σφισιν, ὑφ' ὧν
ἀποδίδονται μὲν τοὺς ἀγρούς, ἀποδίδονται δὲ τὰς
οἰκίας· τῶν δὲ ἀνδραπόδων τὰ μὲν ἀποδέδρακέ σφας,
τὰ δὲ πέπραται, καὶ οὐδὲ τοῖς γονεῦσιν οἱ πολλοὶ ἐν-
αγίζουσιν· ἀπέδοντο γὰρ καὶ τοὺς τάφους. ὥστε τὸ
κακόν, ὃ ἠπείλει τοῖς Θετταλοῖς ἐκ θαλάττης ὁ Ἀχιλ-
λεὺς δώσειν, ξένε, τοῦτο ἡγώμεθα.

54. ΦΟΙΝ. Οὐλομένην, ἀμπελουργέ, μῆνιν λέγεις
καὶ δυσίατον. ἀλλά μοι εἰπὲ τί περὶ τῆς ἐν τῷ Πόντῳ
νήσου θαυμάσιον ὁ Πρωτεσίλεως οἶδεν· ἐκεῖ γάρ που
αὐτῷ ξυγγίνεται.

2 ἈΜΠ. Ἐκεῖ, ξένε, καὶ λέγει περὶ αὐτῆς τοιαῦτα· ὡς
νῆσος μὲν εἴη μία τῶν ἐν τῷ Πόντῳ πρὸς τῇ ἀξένῳ
πλευρᾷ μᾶλλον, ἣν τίθενται ἀριστερὰν οἱ τὸ στόμα
τοῦ Πόντου ἐσπλέοντες, ἐπέχοι δὲ στάδια μῆκος μὲν
τριάκοντα, εὖρος δὲ οὐ πλείω τεττάρων, δένδρα τε ἐν
αὐτῇ πεφύκοι λεῦκαί τε καὶ πτελέαι, τὰ μὲν ἄλλα ὡς
3 ἔτυχε, τὰ δὲ περὶ τὸ ἱερὸν ἐν κόσμῳ ἤδη. τὸ δὲ ἱερὸν

201 Radet (1925, 91–93) noted that Alexander Severus inter-
ested himself especially in this government monopoly and that an
inscription of his time (CIL III inscr, ILS 1575) mentioned regu-
lation of purple production in Thessaly; hence, he dates the He-
roicus to his reign, 222 at the earliest, followed by Follet (1969)
and Jones (2010, 143). But Grossardt (2006a) notes this regula-
tion might have existed earlier. Nero is said to have profited from

fines had been imposed on the shell from which men fabricate purple dye, and the Thessalians were convicted of producing this dye illegally.[201] Whether this was true or not, I do not know; but fines hang over them that force them to sell their fields and their homes, some of their slaves have run away, others were sold, and many do not perform funeral offerings to their parents; for they had to sell even their tombs. We should conclude that this is the evil that Achilles had threatened against them from the sea.

54. *Phoenician.* I can see that the wrath of Achilles is destructive,[202] and difficult to heal. But tell me what Protesilaus knows of the wonders on the island in the Black Sea, since I presume that is where he visits Achilles. [203]

Vinedresser. Yes, he does, and he says this about it: that it is one of the islands close to the unfriendly shore[204] of the Black Sea, which those sailing up the mouth of the Black Sea[205] have on their left. It is thirty stades long but not more than four wide. Poplars and elms grow wild throughout but around his shrine are arranged in order.

23

2

---

a similar measure (Suet., *Ner.* 32); for later restrictions on purple (as an imperial prerogative), see Reinhold (1970, 63–67).

[202] Quoting the *Iliad's* first line.

[203] For the island (modern Zmeinyi) and the cult of Achilles there, see Introduction §13, and S. West (2003, 162–64).

[204] I.e., the north, where the Taurians practiced human sacrifice (Eur. *IT*) and the Amazons live (57.3, below). *Axenos* was another name for what the Persians called the *Aksaina* (dark) sea, S. West (2003, 157).

[205] From the vinedresser's Aegean perspective, sailing eastward through the sea of Marmara.

ἴδρυται μὲν πρὸς τῇ Μαιώτιδι (ἡ δὲ ἴση τῷ Πόντῳ ἐς
αὐτὸν βάλλει), τὰ δὲ ἐν αὐτῷ ἀγάλματα Ἀχιλλεύς τε
4 καὶ Ἑλένη ὑπὸ Μοιρῶν ξυναρμοσθέντες. κειμένου
γὰρ δὴ ἐν ὀφθαλμοῖς τοῦ ἐρᾶν καὶ ποιητῶν τὸν ἔρωτα
ἀπὸ τούτου ᾀδόντων, πρῶτοι Ἀχιλλεύς τε καὶ Ἑλένη,
μηδὲ ὀφθέντες ἀλλήλοις ἀλλ' ἡ μὲν κατ' Αἴγυπτον, ὁ
δὲ ἐν Ἰλίῳ ὄντες, ἐρᾶν ἀλλήλων ὥρμησαν γένεσιν
ἱμέρου σώματος ὦτα εὑρόντες.

5   πεπρωμένης δὲ αὐτοῖς ἐς τὸ ἀθάνατον τῆς διαίτης
οὐδεμιᾶς γῆς τῶν ὑπὸ ἡλίῳ, Ἐχινάδων τῶν κατ'
Οἰνιάδας καὶ Ἀκαρνανίαν ἤδη μεμιασμένων ὅτε δὴ
Ἀλκμαίων ἀποκτείνας τὴν μητέρα τὰς ἐκβολὰς τοῦ
Ἀχελῴου ᾤκησεν ἐν γῇ νεωτέρᾳ τοῦ ἔργου, ἱκετεύει
τὸν Ποσειδῶνα ἡ Θέτις ἀναδοῦναί τινα ἐκ τῆς θαλάτ-
6 της νῆσον ἐν ᾗ οἰκήσουσιν· ὁ δὲ ἐνθυμηθεὶς τὸ μῆκος
τοῦ Πόντου καὶ ὅτι νήσου οὐδεμιᾶς ἐν αὐτῷ κειμένης
ἀοίκητος πλεῖται, τὴν Λευκὴν νῆσον, ὁπόσην εἶπον,
ἀνέφηνεν Ἀχιλλεῖ μὲν καὶ Ἑλένῃ οἰκεῖν, ναύταις δὲ
7 ἵστασθαι καὶ τῷ πελάγει ἐγκαθορμίζεσθαι. ξυμπά-
σης δὴ ἄρχων ὁπόση ὑγρὰ οὐσία καὶ τοὺς ποταμοὺς
ἐννοήσας τὸν Θερμώδοντα καὶ τὸν Βορυσθένην καὶ
τὸν Ἴστρον, ὡς ἀμηχάνοις τε καὶ ἀεννάοις ῥεύμασιν
ἐς τὸν Πόντον ἐκφέρονται, προὔχωσε τὴν ἰλὺν τῶν
ποταμῶν ἣν ἀπὸ Σκυθῶν ἀρξάμενοι σύρουσιν ἐς τὸ
πέλαγος, νῆσόν τε ὁπόσην εἶπον ἀπετόρνευσε, συ-
στησάμενος αὐτὴν ἐν τῷ πυθμένι τοῦ Πόντου.

8   ἐνταῦθα εἶδόν τε πρῶτον καὶ περιέβαλον ἀλλήλους
Ἀχιλλεύς τε καὶ Ἑλένη, καὶ γάμον ἐδαίσαντο σφῶν

The shrine faces Lake Maeotis (which is as large as the 3
Black Sea and empties into it), and contains statues of
Achilles and Helen, who were joined by the Fates: love 4
comes from the eyes, and the poets sing of love from this
source; but Achilles and Helen had never been seen by
each other (she being in Egypt and he at Troy), and began
to love each other after discovering the source of physical
desire in their hearing.

Yet for their immortal life together no land beneath the 5
sun had been destined, and the Echinades islands oppo-
site Oeniadae and Acarnania had already been polluted
when Alcmaeon, after killing his mother, settled on the silt
deposits of the River Achelous, territory that had not yet
existed at the time of his crime;[206] Thetis asked Poseidon
to create a new island from the sea in which they could
settle; he remembered how long the Black Sea was, and 6
that sailing it offered no lodging because there was no is-
land in it; and so brought forth the island of Leuke, whose
size I have described, as a home for Achilles and Helen
and as a stopping point and anchorage in the sea for sail-
ors. Poseidon controls all liquid substance everywhere, so 7
he noticed that the rivers Thermodon, Borysthenes, and
Danube empty with irresistible and ever-flowing streams
into the Black Sea, and heaped up the silt which they
sweep from their Scythian headlands into the sea and fash-
ioned an island of the size I have described, and fastened
it to the floor of the Black Sea.

There Achilles and Helen first saw and embraced each 8
other. Their wedding was celebrated by Poseidon himself

---

[206] As told by Thuc. 2.102.

PHILOSTRATUS

Ποσειδῶν τε αὐτὸς καὶ Ἀμφιτρίτη, Νηρηίδες τε ξύμ-
πασαι καὶ ὁπόσοι ποταμοὶ καὶ δαίμονες ⟨ἐσ⟩έρχονται
τὴν Μαιῶτίν τε καὶ τὸν Πόντον.

9   οἰκεῖν μὲν δὴ λευκοὺς ὄρνιθας ἐν αὐτῇ φασιν, εἶναι
δὲ τούτους ὑγρούς τε καὶ τῆς θαλάττης ἀπόζοντας,
οὓς τὸν Ἀχιλλέα θεράποντας αὐτοῦ πεποιῆσθαι
κοσμοῦντας αὐτῷ τὸ ἄλσος τῷ τε ἀνέμῳ τῶν πτερῶν
καὶ ταῖς ἀπ᾽ αὐτῶν ῥανίσι· πράττειν δὲ τοῦτο χαμαὶ
πετομένους καὶ μικρὸν τῆς γῆς ὑπεραίροντας.

10   ἀνθρώποις δὲ πλέουσι μὲν τὸ τοῦ πελάγους χάσμα
ὁσία ἡ νῆσος ἐσβαίνειν, κεῖται γὰρ ὥσπερ εὔξεινος
νεὼν ἑστία· οἶκον δὲ μὴ ποιεῖσθαι αὐτὴν πᾶσί τε
ἀπείρηται τοῖς πλέουσι καὶ τοῖς περὶ τὸν Πόντον Ἕλ-

11   λησί τε καὶ βαρβάροις. δεῖ γὰρ προσορμισαμένους
τε καὶ θύσαντας ἡλίου δυομένου ἐσβαίνειν μὴ ἐννυ-
χεύοντας τῇ γῇ, κἂν μὲν τὸ πνεῦμα ἔπηται, πλεῖν, εἰ
δὲ μή, ἀναψαμένους τὸ πλοῖον ἐν κοίλῳ ἀναπαύεσθαι.

12   ξυμπίνειν γὰρ δὴ λέγονται τότε ὁ Ἀχιλλεύς τε καὶ ἡ
Ἑλένη καὶ ἐν ᾠδαῖς εἶναι, τὸν ἔρωτά τε τὸν ἀλλήλων
ᾄδειν καὶ Ὁμήρου τὰ ἔπη τὰ ἐπὶ τῇ Τροίᾳ καὶ τὸν
Ὅμηρον αὐτόν. τὸ γὰρ τῆς ποιητικῆς δῶρον, ὃ παρὰ
τῆς Καλλιόπης τῷ Ἀχιλλεῖ ἐφοίτησεν, ἐπαινεῖ ὁ
Ἀχιλλεὺς ἔτι καὶ σπουδάζει μᾶλλον, ἐπειδὴ πέπαυται

13   τῶν πολεμικῶν. τὸ γοῦν ᾆσμα τὸ ἐπὶ τῷ Ὁμήρῳ θείως
αὐτῷ, ξένε, καὶ ποιητικῶς ξύγκειται· καὶ γὰρ ἐκεῖνο
γινώσκει τε καὶ ᾄδει ὁ Πρωτεσίλεως.

     55. ΦΟΙΝ. Ἐμοὶ δ᾽ ἂν γένοιτο, ἀμπελουργέ, ἀκοῦ-
σαι τοῦ ᾄσματος, ἢ οὐ θέμις ἐκφέρειν αὐτό;

310

and Amphitrite, and all the Nereids and rivers and their divinities that flow into Lake Maeotis and the Black Sea.

It is said that the island is inhabited by white birds, 9 which are wet and smell of the salt air. Achilles has made them his servants, and they clean his grove with the breeze from their wings and the moisture from them, which they do by flying low and a little raised off the ground.[207]

The island may be visited by men who sail this vast sea, 10 and stands as a hospitable haven for their ships; but neither sailors nor dwellers in the region, Greek or barbarian, may ever make it their home. If they anchor and sacrifice 11 there, they must board their ships at sunset and not spend the night on land; if the wind is favorable they sail away, otherwise they tie up and sleep below deck. For it is then 12 that Achilles and Helen drink together, engage in song, and sing their love for each other, Homer's verses about Troy, and Homer himself. The poetic talent which came to Achilles from Calliope he still prizes and practices even more now that his fighting is over. His song for Homer is 13 quite finely and poetically composed; Protesilaus knows it, and has sung it to me.

55. *Phoenician.* Might I hear it, or may it not be divulged?

---

[207] For the flight of the shearwaters on Leuke, cf. Arr. *Periplus* 21, S. West (2003, 163); for the self-offering victims (56.4, below), cf. *Periplus* 22.

PHILOSTRATUS

2   ΆΜΠ. Καὶ μήν, ξένε, πολλοὶ τῶν προσελθόντων
τῇ νήσῳ καὶ ἄλλα τοῦ Ἀχιλλέως ᾄδοντος ἀκούειν
φασί, τουτὶ δὲ πέρυσιν, οἶμαι, τὸ ᾆσμα ἡρμόσατο
3 χαριέστατα τῆς γνώμης καὶ τῶν διανοιῶν ἔχον. ξύγ-
κειται δὲ ὧδε·

    Ἀχώ, περὶ μυρίον ὕδωρ
    μεγάλου ναίοισα πέρα Πόντου,
    ψάλλει σε λύρα διὰ χειρὸς ἐμᾶς·
    σὺ δὲ θεῖον Ὅμηρον ἄειδέ μοι,
    κλέος ἀνέρων,
    κλέος ἀμετέρων πόνων
    δι᾽ ὃν οὐ θάνον,
    δι᾽ ὃν ἔστι μοι
    Πάτροκλος, δι᾽ ὃν ἀθανάτοις ἴσος
    Αἴας ἐμός,
    δι᾽ ὃν ἁ δορίληπτος ἀειδομένα σοφοῖς
    κλέος ἤρατο κοὺ πέσε Τροία.

4   ΦΟΙΝ. Δαιμονίως γε ὁ Ἀχιλλεύς, ἀμπελουργέ, καὶ
ἐπαξίως ἑαυτοῦ τε καὶ τοῦ Ὁμήρου. καὶ ἄλλως σοφὸν
ἐν τοῖς λυρικοῖς ᾆσμασι τὸ μὴ ἀποτείνειν αὐτά, μηδὲ
σχοινοτενῆ ἐργάζεσθαι. καὶ ἐκ παλαιοῦ ἄρα εὐδόκι-
μόν τε καὶ σοφὸν ἦν ἡ ποίησις.
5   ΆΜΠ. Ἐκ παλαιοῦ, ξένε. καὶ γὰρ τὸν Ἡρακλέα
φασὶν ἀνασταυρώσαντα τὸ Ἀσβόλου τοῦ κενταύρου
σῶμα, ἐπιγράψαι αὐτῷ τόδε τὸ ἐπίγραμμα·

312

Vinedresser. Of course; many travelers to the island say 2
they hear Achilles singing other songs, but I believe this
one, composed last year, is the best in expression and con-
tent.[208] It goes like this: 3

> Echo, who live beyond great Pontus
> Over endless water,
> The lyre in my hands plays you;
> Sing for me divine Homer,
> The glory of men,
> The glory of my labors,
> Because of whom I did not die;
> Because of whom I still
> Have Patroclus; because of whom my Ajax
> Is like the immortals;
> Because of whom conquered Troy, sung by the wise,
> Won her glory, and never fell

Phoenician. That is marvelous, quite worthy of Achilles 4
and of Homer. It is always best not to make lyrics too long
or try to roll them out. Poetry must have been a glorious
and wise profession even long ago.

Vinedresser. Yes, it was, and they say even Heracles 5
composed these verses when he had hung up the body of
the Centaur Asbolus:[209]

[208] Achilles' musical skills were described in 45.6. For this
song, see Miles (2004).

[209] For the centaur Asbolus, see the pseudo-Hesiodic *Shield
of Heracles* 185.

Ἄσβολος οὔτε θεῶν τρομέων ὄπιν οὔτ᾽
    ἀνθρώπων,
ὀξυκόμοιο κρεμαστὸς ἀπ᾽ εὐλιπέος κατὰ πεύκης
ἄγκειμαι μέγα δεῖπνον ἀμετροβίοις κοράκεσσιν.

6   ΦΟΙΝ. Ἀθλητής γε καὶ τούτων ὁ Ἡρακλῆς ἐγένετο,
μεγαληγορίαν ἐπαινῶν, ἀμπελουργέ, παρ᾽ ἧς δεῖ δή-
που τὸν ποιητὴν φθέγγεσθαι. ἀλλ᾽ ἐπανίωμεν ἐπὶ τὴν
νῆσον· ῥεῦμα γὰρ δὴ ὑπολαβὸν ἡμᾶς, οἷα πολλὰ περὶ
τὸν Πόντον εἰλεῖται, παρέπλαγξε τοῦ λόγου.

56. ΑΜΠ. Ἐπανίωμεν, ὦ ξένε. τὰ μὲν γὰρ ᾄσματα
ἐν αὐτῇ τοιαῦτα, καὶ ἡ φωνὴ δὲ ἣν ᾄδουσι θεῖά τε
ἠχεῖ καὶ λαμπρά· διήκει γοῦν τοσαύτη ἐς τὸ πέλαγος,
ὡς φρίκην ἀνίστασθαι τοῖς ναύταις ὑπὸ ἐκπλήξεως.
2 φασὶ δ᾽ οἱ προσορμισάμενοι καὶ κτύπου ἀκούειν
ἵππων καὶ ἤχου ὅπλων καὶ βοῆς οἷον ἐν πολέμῳ
3 ἀναφθέγγονται. εἰ δ᾽ ὁρμισαμένων ἐς τὰ βόρεια ἢ τὰ
νότια τῆς νήσου μέλλοι τις ἄνεμος ἐναντίος τῷ ὅρμῳ
πνεῖν, κηρύττει ὁ Ἀχιλλεὺς κατὰ πρύμναν τοῦτο καὶ
4 κελεύει μεθορμισαμένους ἐκστῆναι τῷ ἀνέμῳ. πολλοὶ
δὲ καὶ τῶν ἐκπλεόντων τοῦ Πόντου προσπλέουσί τέ
μοι καὶ ἀπαγγέλλουσι ταῦτα, καὶ νὴ Δί᾽ ὡς, ἐπειδὰν
προΐδωσι τὴν νῆσον, ἅτε ἐν ἀπείρῳ πελάγει ἐμφερό-
μενοι, περιβάλλουσί τε ἀλλήλους καὶ ἐς δάκρυα ὑφ᾽
ἡδονῆς ἔρχονται, καταπλεύσαντες δὲ καὶ τὴν γῆν
ἀσπασάμενοι βαδίζουσιν ἐπὶ τὸ ἱερὸν προσευξόμενοί
τε τῷ Ἀχιλλεῖ καὶ θύσοντες. τὸ δὲ ἱερεῖον αὐτόματον
τῷ βωμῷ προσέστηκε κατὰ τὴν ναῦν τε καὶ τοὺς

Asbolus never feared wrath of god or mortal;
now, hung from a sharp-needled resinous pine,
My body is a great feast for the ravening crows.

Phoenician. Heracles was an athlete also in this, and 6
approved the eloquence with which the poet has to speak.
But let us return to the island; for the current has taken
us like it presses around much of the Black Sea, and driven
us off the course of our story.

56. *Vinedresser.* All right, stranger. These are the songs
there, and the voice in which they sing them resounds
divine and clear; it travels so far over the sea that it puts
a shudder of amazement in the sailors. Those who have 2
anchored there claim to hear the hoof beats of horses, the
clash of armor, and the cries like those at war. If sail- 3
ors anchor on the north or south side of the island and
a wind is going to strike their anchorage, Achilles ap-
pears at their stern to announce it and tell them to change
their mooring and escape the wind. Many of those who 4
have sailed out of the Black Sea put in here and report
these things to me; and further, by Zeus, that whenever,
traveling on this endless sea, they see the island in the
distance, they embrace each other and cry tears of joy.
After landing and kissing the earth they go to the shrine
to pray and sacrifice to Achilles, and the victim stands
ready beside the altar opposite the ship and its crew. The 5

315

5 ἐμπλέοντας. τὸ μὲν δὴ περὶ τὴν κάλπιν τὴν χρυσῆν
τὴν ἐν Χίῳ ποτὲ φανεῖσαν τῇ νήσῳ εἴρηται, ξένε,
σοφοῖς ἀνδράσι, καὶ τί ἄν τις ἀριζήλως εἰρημένων
αὖθις ἅπτοιτο;

6 ἐμπόρῳ δὲ λέγεται θαμίζοντί ποτε ἐς τὴν νῆσον
φαίνεσθαι μὲν ὁ Ἀχιλλεὺς αὐτός, διηγεῖσθαι δὲ τὰ ἐν
τῇ Τροίᾳ, ξενίσαι δ' αὐτὸν καὶ ποτῷ, κελεῦσαί τε ἐκ-
πλεύσαντα ἐς Ἴλιον ἀναγαγεῖν οἷ κόρην Τρωάδα, τὴν

7 δεῖνα εἰπὼν δουλεύουσαν τῷ δεῖνι ἐν Ἰλίῳ. θαυμάσαν-
τος δὲ τοῦ ξένου τὸν λόγον καὶ διὰ τὸ θαρσεῖν ἤδη
ἐρομένου αὐτὸν τί δέοιτο δούλης Ἰλιάδος, "ὅτι" ἔφη,
"ξένε, γέγονεν ὅθενπερ ὁ Ἕκτωρ καὶ οἱ πρὸ αὐτοῦ
ἄνω, λοιπὴ δ' ἐστὶ τοῦ Πριαμιδῶν τε καὶ Δαρδανιδῶν

8 αἵματος." ὁ μὲν δὴ ἔμπορος ἐρᾶν τὸν Ἀχιλλέα ᾤετο
καὶ πριάμενος τὴν κόρην ἐς τὴν νῆσον ἀνέπλευσεν, ὁ
δὲ Ἀχιλλεὺς ἐπαινέσας αὐτὸν ἥκοντα τὴν μὲν προσ-
έταξε φυλάττειν ἑαυτῷ ἐν τῇ νηὶ δι' οἶμαι τὸ μὴ ἐσβα-
τὸν εἶναι γυναιξὶ τὴν νῆσον, αὐτὸν δὲ ἑσπέρας ἥκειν
ἐς τὸ ἱερὸν καὶ εὐωχεῖσθαι μεθ' αὑτοῦ τε καὶ Ἑλένης·

9 ἀφικομένῳ δὲ πολλὰ μὲν χρήματα ἔδωκεν, ὧν ἥττους
ἔμποροι, ξένον δ' αὐτὸν ποιεῖσθαι ἔφη διδόναι τέ οἱ

10 τὴν ἐμπορίαν ἐνεργὸν καὶ τὴν ναῦν εὐπλοεῖν. ἐπεὶ δὲ
ἡμέρα ἐγένετο, "σὺ μὲν πλεῖ" ἔφη "ταῦτ' ἔχων, τὴν
κόρην δὲ ἐπὶ τοῦ αἰγιαλοῦ λίπε μοι." οὔπω στάδιον
ἀπεῖχον τῆς γῆς καὶ οἰμωγὴ προσέβαλεν αὐτοῖς τῆς
κόρης, διασπωμένου αὐτὴν τοῦ Ἀχιλλέως καὶ μελιστὶ
ξαίνοντος.

316

story of the golden pitcher which once appeared on the island of Chios has been told by wise men, stranger, and why would anyone repeat something perspicuously said?[210]

It is said that Achilles once visited a merchant who 6 frequented the island, and told him what had happened in Troy; he also entertained him with drink, and commanded him to sail to Ilion and bring back to him a specific Trojan girl who was the slave of a particular master. The stranger 7 was amazed, and made bold to ask why he needed a slave from Ilion. He answered, "Because, stranger, she is from the same line as Hector and his ancestors and is the last of the blood of the children of Priam and Dardanus." The 8 merchant thought that Achilles was in love, so he bought the girl and returned to the island; Achilles was pleased at his arrival and told him to keep the girl on his ship (I suspect because no women were allowed on the island), but to come himself at night to the shrine to feast with him and Helen. When he came, he gave him a great deal of 9 money, always pleasing to merchants, and said he made him his guest friend, and granted him a prosperous voyage and fair sailing. At daybreak Achilles said, "Now take 10 these things and sail, but leave the girl on the shore for me." They were not more than a stade away from shore, when the girl's scream reached them—Achilles was tearing her apart, and ripping limb from limb.[211]

---

[210] "Perspicuously said" quotes Odysseus in Homer, *Od.* 12.453. For the principle, cf. Hdt. 6.55, and Philostr. *VA* 2.33.2. But the story is in fact unknown. Grossardt (2006a) suggests it might have been another story of the spontaneous appearance of an offering.   [211] In *VA* 4.12, Achilles forces the sophist to dismiss a follower of Trojan descent.

PHILOSTRATUS

11   Ἀμαζόνας δέ, ἃς ἔνιοι τῶν ποιητῶν φασιν ἐλθεῖν
ἐς Τροίαν Ἀχιλλεῖ μαχουμένας, οὐκ ἀπέκτεινεν ὁ
Ἀχιλλεὺς ἐν Τροίᾳ· πιθανὸν γὰρ οὐκ οἶδ' ὅπως Πρι-
άμου πολεμήσαντος αὐταῖς ὑπὲρ Φρυγῶν κατὰ
Μυγδόνα, ξυμμάχους Ἀμαζόνας ὕστερον ἐλθεῖν Ἰλίῳ,
ἀλλ' οἶμαι κατὰ τὴν Ὀλυμπιάδα ἣν τὸ πρῶτον ἐνίκα
στάδιον Λεωνίδας ὁ Ῥόδιος, ἀπώλεσεν αὐτῶν ὁ Ἀχιλ-
λεὺς τὸ μαχιμώτατον ἐν αὐτῇ, φασί, τῇ νήσῳ.

57. ΦΟΙΝ. Μεγάλου, ἀμπελουργέ, ἤψω λόγου, καὶ
τὰ ὦτά μοι ἤγειρας καὶ ἄλλως ἑστηκότα πρὸς τοὺς
σοὺς λόγους· ἥκειν δέ σοι καὶ ταῦτα εἰκὸς παρὰ τοῦ
Πρωτεσίλεω.

2   ΑΜΠ. Παρὰ τούτου, ξένε, τοῦ χρηστοῦ διδασκά-
λου· πολλοῖς δὲ καὶ τῶν ἐς τὸν Πόντον ἐσπεπλευκό-
3 των δῆλα δὴ ταῦτα. κατὰ γὰρ τὴν ἄξενον τοῦ Πόντου
πλευράν, ᾗ τὰ ὄρη τὰ Ταυρικὰ τέταται, λέγονταί τινες
οἰκεῖν Ἀμαζόνες ἣν Θερμώδων τε καὶ Φᾶσις ἐξερχό-
μενοι τῶν ὁρῶν περιβάλλουσιν ἤπειρον, ἃς ὁ πατήρ
τε καὶ φυτουργὸς αὐτῶν Ἄρης ἐπαίδευσεν ἐν ὁμιλίᾳ
τῶν πολεμικῶν εἶναι καὶ ζῆν ἔνοπλόν τε καὶ ἔφιππον
βίον· βουκολεῖσθαι δὲ αὐταῖς ἵππον ἐν τοῖς ἕλεσιν
4 ἀποχρῶσαν τῷ στρατῷ. ἀνδράσι μὲν δὴ ἐνομιλεῖν οὐ
παρέχειν σφᾶς τὴν ἑαυτῶν χώραν, αὐτὰς δ', ἐπειδὰν
δέωνται τέκνων, κατιούσας ἐπὶ ποταμὸν Ἅλυν ἀγορά-
ζειν τε καὶ ξυγγίνεσθαι τοῖς ἀνδράσιν ἔνθα ἔτυχεν,

212 For Penthesileia, see in the *Aithiopis* (M. L. West 2003a,
130–41).

As to the Amazons, who some poets say went to Troy   11
to fight against Achilles,[212] it was not there that he killed
them; for I know it is implausible, that after Priam had
fought against them to help the Phrygians at the time of
Mygdon, the Amazons would later come to Troy as al-
lies.[213] I think it was in the year that Leonidas of Rhodes
won his first race at the Olympic Games that Achilles
killed their fiercest warriors, so they say, on this island.[214]

57. *Phoenician.* You have touched on quite a story, and
aroused my attention which was already keen for your
stories. Probably this too came to you from Protesilaus.

Vinedresser. Yes, he is an excellent source; but this is   2
quite familiar to many of those who have sailed into the
Black Sea. They say that along the unfriendly side[215]   3
where the Taurus Mountains extend, the Amazons live in
the land which the Thermodon and the Phasis Rivers de-
scend from the mountain to surround;[216] their founding
father, Ares, taught them to be well acquainted with war,
and live in armor and on horseback (in the nearby swamps
they herd enough horses for their army). They don't allow   4
men to become acquainted with their country; when they
need children, they travel down to the River Halys to trade
and to have random sex with men; then they return to their

---

[213] Once again, rationalistic critiques of myths (Introduc-
tion §5).

[214] In 164 BC. (For Leonidas of Rhodes, see on *Gym.* 33.) The
Hellenistic date is perhaps influenced by the model of another
famous northern attack on a sanctuary, that of Brennus and the
Gauls on Delphi in 279 BC (see Introduction §13).

[215] See 54.2n.

[216] Cf. Herodotus' description of the Amazons (4.110–17).

ἀπελθούσας τε ἐς ἤθη καὶ οἴκους, ἃ μὲν ἂν τέκωσιν
ἄρρενα, φέρειν ἐπὶ τὰ ὅρια τῆς χώρας ὅπως ἀνέλοιντο
αὐτὰ οἱ φύσαντες, τοὺς δὲ ἀναιρεῖσθαί τε ὧν ἕκαστος
5 ἔτυχε, καὶ ποιεῖσθαι δούλους· ἃ δ' ἂν ἀποτέκωσι θή-
λεα, φιλεῖν τε ἤδη λέγονται καὶ ὁμόφυλα ἡγεῖσθαι,
θεραπεύειν τε ᾗ φύσις μητέρων, πλὴν τοῦ ἐπισχεῖν
γάλα· τουτὶ δὲ πράττουσι διὰ τὰς μάχας, ὡς μήτε
6 αὐτὰ θηλύνοιντο μήτε τοὺς μαζοὺς ἀποκρεμῶντο. τὸ
μὲν δὴ ὄνομα ταῖς Ἀμαζόσιν ἐκ τοῦ μὴ μαζῷ τρέ-
φεσθαι κεῖσθαι ἡγώμεθα· τρέφουσι δὲ τὰ βρέφη γά-
λακτί τε φορβάδων ἵππων καὶ δρόσου κηρίοις, ἢ μέ-
λιτος δίκην ἐπὶ τοὺς δόνακας τῶν ποταμῶν ἱζάνει.

7   τὰ δὲ ποιηταῖς τε καὶ μυθολόγοις περὶ τῶν Ἀμα-
ζόνων τούτων εἰρημένα παραιτησώμεθα τοῦ λόγου·
πρόσφορα γὰρ οὐκ ἂν τῇ παρούσῃ σπουδῇ γένοιτο·
τὸ δὲ περὶ τὴν νῆσον ἔργον, ὁποῖόν τι αὐταῖς ἐπρά-
χθη καὶ ἐς ὅ τι ἐτελεύτησε, λεγέσθω μᾶλλον ἐπειδὴ
8 τῶν τοῦ Πρωτεσίλεω λόγων ἐστί. ναῦται γὰρ ἐπὶ νεῶν
ποτε πλειόνων καὶ ναυπηγοὶ τῶν ἐς Ἑλλήσποντον
ἀπαγόντων ἐκ τοῦ Πόντου ὤνια κατηνέχθησαν ἐς τὴν
ἀριστερὰν τοῦ πελάγους ὄχθην, περὶ ἣν αἱ γυναῖκες
9 οἰκεῖν λέγονται. ληφθέντες δὲ ὑπ' αὐτῶν χρόνον μέν
τινα ἐδέδεντο σιτούμενοι πρὸς φάτναις, ἵν' ἀποδῶνταί
σφας ὑπὲρ τὸν ποταμὸν ἄγουσαι τοῖς ἀνδροφάγοις
10 Σκύθαις. ἐπεὶ δὲ μειράκιον σὺν αὐτοῖς ληφθὲν μία
τῶν Ἀμαζόνων ἐπὶ τῇ ὥρᾳ ἠλέησε καί τις ἔρως ἐκ
τούτου ἐγένετο, παραιτεῖται τὴν δυναστεύουσαν ἀδελ-
11 φὴν οὖσαν μὴ ἀποδόσθαι τοὺς ξένους· λυθέντες δὲ

haunts and homes. Male children they carry to the border of their country for their fathers to take, and they accept anyone they find and make them their slaves. But any fe- 5
male children they are said to love and consider their own and raise them as is natural for a mother, except for with-holding their milk; this they do because of their warfare, to avoid making them effeminate or their breasts sag. We 6
should conclude that the Amazons have their name from their not being fed from the breast (*mazos*). They feed their children on mare's milk and honeydew,[217] which settles like honey on the reeds of the river.

Let us omit from our discussion what the poets and 7
mythographers have to say about the Amazons; it would not suit our current interests. But their attack on the is-land, what they did and what it led to we must discuss, all the more so since it is part of Protesilaus' stories. Once a 8
group of sailors and shipbuilders, on many ships, carrying merchant goods from the Black Sea to the Hellespont, were carried off course to the left bank of the sea, where the women are said to live. They were captured by them, 9
bound, and fattened up for some time, so that they could take them to the other side of the river and sell them to Scythian cannibals. But when one of the Amazons took 10
pity on a young man captured with them for his youth and it led to love, she asked the queen, who was her sister, not to sell the foreigners. After the sailors were released and 11

---

[217] For ancient beliefs about honey on plant leaves, see Waszink (1974, 8).

321

καὶ πρὸς αὐτὰς συγκραθέντες ἐφθέγγοντο ἤδη τὸν
ἐκείνων τρόπον, τόν τε χειμῶνα καὶ τὰ ἐν τῇ θαλάττῃ
διηγούμενοι παρῆλθον ἐς μνήμην τοῦ ἱεροῦ προσπε-
πλευκότες οὐ πάλαι τῇ νήσῳ, καὶ διῇεσαν τὸν ἐν
12 αὐτῷ πλοῦτον. αἱ δ᾽ εὕρημα ποιησάμεναι τοὺς ξένους,
ἐπειδὴ ναῦταί τε ἦσαν καὶ νεῶν τέκτονες, οὔσης καὶ
ἄλλως ναυπηγησίμου σφίσι τῆς χώρας, ποιοῦνται
ναῦς τὸν ἱππαγωγῶν τρόπον ὡς τὸν Ἀχιλλέα σχή-
σουσαι ταῖς ἵπποις· καταβᾶσαι γὰρ ἵππων Ἀμαζόνες
13 θῆλύ τέ εἰσι γένος καὶ ἀτεχνῶς γυναῖκες. εἰρεσίας
μὲν δὴ πρῶτον ἥψαντο καὶ πλεῖν ἐμελέτησαν, ὡς δ᾽
ἐπιστήμην τοῦ πλεῖν ξυνελέξαντο, ἄρασαι περὶ ἔαρ
ἀπὸ τῶν ἐκβολῶν τοῦ Θερμώδοντος ἀφῆκαν ἐς τὸ
ἱερὸν σταδίους μάλιστα δισχιλίους ἐπὶ νεῶν, οἶμαι,
πεντήκοντα, καὶ προσορμισάμεναι τῇ νήσῳ πρῶτον
μὲν ἐκέλευσαν τοὺς Ἑλλησποντίους ξένους ἐκκόπτειν
14 τὰ δένδρα, οἷς κεκόσμηται κύκλῳ τὸ ἱερόν· ἐπεὶ δὲ οἱ
πελέκεις ἐς αὐτοὺς ἀνακοπέντες τοῖς μὲν ἐς κεφαλὴν
ἐχώρησαν, τοῖς δὲ ἐς αὐχένα, πάντες δὲ πρὸς τοῖς
δένδρεσιν ἔπεσον, ἐπεχύθησαν αἱ Ἀμαζόνες τῷ ἱερῷ
15 βοῶσαί τε καὶ τὰς ἵππους ἐλαύνουσαι. ὁ δὲ θερμόν τε
καὶ δεινὸν ἐς αὐτὰς ἰδὼν καὶ πηδήσας οἷον ἐπὶ Σκα-
μάνδρῳ τε καὶ Ἰλίῳ πτοίαν μὲν χαλινοῦ κρείττω ταῖς
ἵπποις ἐνέβαλεν, ὑφ᾽ ἧς ἀνεσκίρτησαν ἀλλότριόν τε
καὶ περιττὸν ἄχθος ἡγούμεναι τὰς γυναῖκας, ἐς δὲ
θηρίων ἤθη μετέστησαν καὶ κειμέναις ἐμπεσοῦσαι
ταῖς Ἀμαζόσι τάς τε ὁπλὰς ἐνήρειδον καὶ τὰς χαίτας
ἔφριττον καὶ τὰ ὦτα ἐπ᾽ αὐτὰς ἵστασαν καθάπερ τῶν

lived among them and spoke their language, telling the Amazons of the storm and their adventures at sea, they came to recounting the sanctuary on the island that they had visited not long before, and described its wealth. The 12 women decided to take advantage of the foreigners, since they were sailors and builders of boats—their country happened to have the resources to build boats—and constructed ships for horse transport to attack Achilles on horseback. (Dismounted from their mares, Amazons are a womanly race, and as weak as other women.) In the spring, 13 when they had taken up rowing and practiced sailing and consolidated their skill in sailing, they cast off from the mouth of the Thermodon on I believe fifty ships and sailed to the shrine about two thousand stades distant. They landed on the island, and first commanded their captives from the Hellespont to chop down the trees arranged in a circle around the shrine; but when the axes 14 bounced back against them, striking some in the head, some in the neck, and all those at the trees fell, the Amazons thronged the shrine on horseback with a cry. But 15 Achilles glared back at them with terrible ferocity, and leaped as he had at the River Scamander and at Troy,[218] and cast on the mares a terror stronger than any bridle, which made them rear up against their riders, considering the women an alien and excessive burden; they reacted by reverting to their wild natures, attacking the fallen Amazons, trampling them with their hooves, shaking their manes, ears perked up against them like ravening lions.

---

[218] Not in the story he rationalizes away in 48.11, but evidently in Homer himself, *Il.* 21.233.

λεόντων οἱ ὠμοί, κειμένων τε γυμνὰς ὠλένας ἤσθιον
καὶ τὰ στέρνα ῥηγνῦσαι προσέκειντο τοῖς σπλάγ-
χνοις καὶ ἐλάφυσσον, ἐμφορηθεῖσαι δὲ ἀνθρωπείου
βρώσεως ἐκρόαινον περὶ τὴν νῆσον καὶ ἐμαίνοντο
μεσταὶ λύθρου, στᾶσαι δὲ ἐπὶ τῶν ἀκρωτηρίων καὶ τὰ
νῶτα τοῦ πελάγους ἰδοῦσαι πεδίῳ τε ᾤοντο ἐντετυχη-
κέναι καὶ κατὰ τῆς θαλάττης ἑαυτὰς ἧκαν.

16   ἀπώλοντο δὲ καὶ αἱ νῆες τῶν Ἀμαζόνων ἀνέμου
σφοδροῦ ἐς αὐτὰς πνεύσαντος· ἅτε γὰρ κεναὶ καὶ οὐ-
δενὶ κόσμῳ ὡρμισμέναι προσέπιπτον ἀλλήλαις καὶ
ξυνηράττοντο, ναῦς τε ὥσπερ ἐν ναυμαχίᾳ κατέδυε
ναῦν καὶ ἀνερρήγνυ, καὶ ὁπόσας ἐγκαρσίους τε καὶ
ἀντιπρῴρους ἐμβολὰς ποιοῦνται κυβερνῆται ναυ-
μάχοι, πᾶσαι ξυνέπεσον ἐν ναυσὶ κεναῖς καὶ οὐκ ἐκ
17   προνοίας πλεούσαις. πολλῶν δὲ ναυαγίων τῷ ἱερῷ
προσενεχθέντων καὶ ἀνθρώπων ἐν αὐτῷ κειμένων ἐμ-
πνεόντων ἔτι καὶ ἡμιβρώτων, μελῶν τε ἀνθρωπείων
ἐσπαρμένων καὶ σαρκῶν ἃς διέπτυσαν αἱ ἵπποι, κάθ-
αρσιν ὁ Ἀχιλλεὺς ποιεῖται τῆς νήσου ῥᾳδίαν· κορυ-
φὴν γὰρ τοῦ πόντου ἐπισπασάμενος ἀπένιψέ τε καὶ
ἀπέκλυσε ταῦτα.

58. ΦΟΙΝ. Ὅστις, ἀμπελουργέ, μὴ θεοφιλῆ σε
ἡγεῖται σφόδρα, αὐτὸς ἀπήχθηται τοῖς θεοῖς· τὸ γὰρ
τοιούτους τε καὶ θείους λόγους εἰδέναι οὕτω, παρ᾽
ἐκείνων οἶμαί σοι ἥκειν, οἳ καὶ τῷ Πρωτεσίλεῳ φίλον
τέ σε καὶ ἐπιτήδειον ἐποίησαν.

2   ἀλλ᾽ ἐπεὶ τῶν ἡρωικῶν ἡμᾶς λόγων ἐμπέπληκας,
τὸ μὲν ὅπως αὐτὸς ἀναβεβίωκεν οὐκέτ᾽ ἂν ἐροίμην,

They gnawed at the bare arms of the fallen, tore open their chests and mauled and devoured their intestines. Intoxicated with human flesh the mares thundered around the island in a frenzy of blood; once they stood on the summit and saw the crest of the waves, thinking they had reached the plain, they cast themselves down into the sea.

The Amazons' ships were also destroyed, when a strong 16 wind blew against them. Since they were empty and moored haphazardly, they crashed into each other and were broken; just as in a naval battle one ship tries to sink or smash another, now all the sideways or head-on collisions that captains produce in war, these happened to ships empty and sailing without guidance. Many wrecks 17 were carried ashore to the sanctuary with women still on board breathing and half-alive, or with scattered human limbs and pieces of flesh which the horses had spit out. Achilles cleaned the island easily by pulling in the tide and cleaning and washing it away.

58. *Phoenician.* Anyone who does not see how dear you are to the gods, vinedresser, must himself be their enemy; I think that such knowledge of divine stories like this comes to you from the same gods who have made you Protesilaus' friend and companion.

But since you have lavished on me stories of heroes, I 2 won't ask you any more how he came back to life, since

ἐπειδὴ ἀβεβήλῳ τε καὶ ἀπορρήτῳ φῂς αὐτὸν χρῆ-
3 σθαι τούτῳ τῷ λόγῳ· τοὺς δὲ Κωκυτούς τε καὶ Πυρι-
φλεγέθοντας καὶ τὴν Ἀχερουσιάδα καὶ τὰ τοιαῦτα
τῶν ποταμῶν τε καὶ τῶν λιμνῶν ὀνόματα καὶ νὴ Δία
τοὺς Αἰακοὺς καὶ τὰ τούτων δικαστήριά τε καὶ δικαι-
ωτήρια αὐτός τε ἴσως ἀπαγγελεῖς καὶ ξυγχωρεῖ διη-
γεῖσθαι.

4   ΑΜΠ. Ξυγχωρεῖ μέν, ἑσπέρα δὲ ἤδη καὶ βοῦς πρὸς
ἀναπαύλῃ· τὰ γοῦν ζευγάρια ὁρᾷς ὡς ἐκ βουλυτοῦ
ἥκει καὶ χρή με αὐτὰ ὑποδέξασθαι καὶ ὁ λόγος
5 πλείων τοῦ καιροῦ. νῦν μὲν δὴ ἐπὶ τὴν ναῦν χαίρων
ἴθι, πάντα ἔχων ὁπόσα ὁ κῆπος φέρει, κἂν μὲν τὸ
πνεῦμα ὑμέτερον, πλεῖ, ξένε, σπείσας ἀπὸ τῆς νεὼς
τῷ Πρωτεσίλεῳ· τουτὶ γὰρ τοὺς ἐνθένδε λύοντας νε-
νόμισται πράττειν· εἰ δ᾽ ἐναντίον εἴη τὸ πνεῦμα, χώρει
δεῦρο ἅμα ἡλίῳ ἀνίσχοντι καὶ τεύξῃ ὧν βούλει.

6   ΦΟΙΝ. Πείθομαί σοι, ἀμπελουργέ, καὶ οὕτως ἔσται·
πλεύσαιμι δὲ μήπω, Πόσειδον, πρὶν ἢ καὶ τοῦδε
ἀκροάσασθαι τοῦ λόγου.

you say that he considers this off-limits and a forbidden topic; but perhaps he allows you to tell and you yourself 3 will report things like Cocytus and Pyriphlegethon, and the Acherousian lake, and such names of rivers and lakes, or, by Zeus, of people like Aeacus and their courts and places of punishment.

Vinedresser. Yes, he allows it; but it is already evening 4 and the oxen are at the stopping point. You see at least that the teams have returned from the end of their plowing, I must meet them, and the story would last too long. For 5 now, return to your ship content, taking as much as the garden offers, and if the wind favors you, give a libation to Protesilaus and set sail—for that is the customary action for those departing from our harbor—but if the wind is unfavorable, come back at sunrise tomorrow and you will obtain what you want.

Phoenician. I obey you, vinedresser, and it will be so; 6 but may I not sail, by Poseidon, until I hear this story as well.

GYMNASTICUS

PREFACE

I have been puzzling over Philostratus' *Gymnasticus* for many years now, but it had never occurred to me to sit down and translate it for publication. I am very grateful to Jeff Rusten for suggesting that I might do so and for proposing this collaboration, as well as for organizing a visit to Cornell in April 2013, which gave me an opportunity to clarify the arguments laid out in the introduction, and provided a helpful deadline for finishing my final draft of the translation. I am grateful also to Jaś Elsner for comments on the translation, and to Jeffrey Henderson for his support and assistance.

J. P. K.

INTRODUCTION

The *Gymnasticus* is probably the least well known of Philostratus' surviving works. That is perhaps not surprising: structurally speaking it is a rather disjointed text. The Greek is often difficult, especially in the second half, which is full of specialized medical and athletic vocabulary. It has been discussed most frequently in publications whose primary aim is the reconstruction of ancient athletic practice and athletic history. There has been a tendency in those works to take Philostratus' evidence too much at face value[1] and to neglect the challenge of understanding the text on its own terms.[2] That is not to deny that it is an important source for the development of the Olympic program and for ancient training techniques, but it is also much more. It is an important landmark in Philostratus' lifelong project of defending and exploring Greek tradition: it has a great deal in common with his other

Ancient authors and works are abbreviated as in *OCD*.

[1] However, see Golden (1998, 48–50) and Potter (2011, 141–52) for more cautious recent accounts.

[2] See König (2005, 301–44; and 2009a) for one recent pair of attempts to fill that gap. This introduction recaps briefly on some of the conclusions of that earlier work but also aims to cover a range of other issues not dealt with there, particularly in sections 4 and 5.

PHILOSTRATUS

works in its treatment of that theme, although it is also in some respects quite unusual and distinctive. It is also a fascinating example of the richness and flexibility of the traditions of ancient technical and scientific writing as they were treated within Greek imperial prose.

1. DATE AND AUTHORSHIP

The work is hard to date precisely. It was written probably in the 220s or 230s AD. The only secure indication comes from *Gym.* 46, where we hear that "this [massage accompanied by clapping] was the type of exercise used by the Phoenician Helix, not only when he was a boy, but also when he had come into the men's age category, and he was an indescribably wonderful athlete, more so than any of those whom I know to be practicing that kind of recreation." Helix, we know, was Olympic victor in the *pankration* in AD 213 and 217; he also won a double victory at the Capitoline games of 219.[3] From the use of the past tense, and from the adulatory tone of his praise of Helix, it seems highly likely (although impossible to prove) that Philostratus was writing in the decade or so after those victories, when Helix's fame would have been at its height.[4]

Philostratus' authorship of the work is also hard to prove beyond doubt, especially since we know of a num-

[3] See Moretti (1957, no. 915), and Cass. Dio 79.10.2–3 for the Capitoline victories.
[4] See de Lannoy (1997, 2405–7) and Bowie (2009, 30), among others. Cf. p. 10, above, on the similar role of Helix in dating the *Heroicus.*

334

ber of different Philostrati from the same family.[5] The
Gymnasticus is assigned by the *Suda* to the so-called first
Philostratus. But the current consensus is that the author
of this work is the "second" Philostratus, probably identi-
cal with the sophist Flavius Philostratus, who was honored
by Athens with a statue at Olympia[6] and who is thought
to have been the author of the *Heroicus* and also of the
Imagines, the *Life of Apollonius,* the *Lives of the Sophists,*
and the *Nero* (traditionally ascribed to Lucian). That con-
sensus is based not least on the fact that it shares so many
similarities of athletic subject matter with those other
works, some of them discussed further below.[7]

2. ATHLETIC TRAINERS AND
ATHLETIC TRAINING IN
IMPERIAL CULTURE

Philostratus opens his work with the claim that "athletic
training (*gymnastikê*) . . . is a form of wisdom (*sophia*), and
one which is inferior to none of the other skills (*technai*)."
How plausible would that claim have seemed to his con-
temporaries?

Athletics broadly defined had a prominent position in
the cultural life of the Roman Empire. The second and
early third centuries AD were arguably the great heyday

[5] See pp. 5–6, above, for more details.

[6] *Syll.*[3] 878 = *IVO* 476.

[7] Among others, see Billault (1993, 158–61), Flinterman
(1995, 5–14), de Lannoy (1997, 2404–10), and König (2005, 304–
5, esp. n. 4).

of the Greek athletic tradition.[8] Greek athletic and musical festivals flourished right across the Mediterranean world. Victorious athletes in the more prestigious festivals could win great fame and fortune. They prided themselves on their membership of the Universal Athletic Guild, an institution that protected the interests of victors and competitors and was regularly involved in the foundation of new festivals. The guild had its headquarters in Rome and enjoyed the protection of successive emperors.[9] Benefactors won renown from their home cities by funding festivals (as "agonothetes") or by paying for the running of the gymnasia (as "gymnasiarchs"). All of this athletic activity was popular in part as a celebration of the classical heritage and of its continuing relevance for the present day.

The culture of the gymnasium also continued to flourish. Central to this was the institution of the *ephebeia* (the institution of higher education in which young members of the elite were trained in the gymnasium between the ages of seventeen and nineteen), which played an important role in civic life in cities throughout the Greek east. We have a rich body of epigraphical evidence for gymnasium activity for both the Hellenistic and the Roman periods.[10] The gymnasium was an official building, owned

---

[8] See among many others Robert (1984), van Nijf (2001), König (2005), and Newby (2005).

[9] See König (2005, 221–24), with further bibliography, on the formation of the guild from two separate Mediterranean-wide guilds in the mid-second century AD and on its relationship with various local athletic guilds.

[10] See Gauthier (2010) for the Hellenistic world and König (2005, 47–72), with further bibliography; also Miller (2004, no.

by the city, but the day-to-day administration of gymnasium education was generally left in the hands of the gymnasiarch. It generally involved a mixture of athletic and military training, but that was sometimes combined with rhetorical and literary education. We know from many surviving inscriptions that the gymnasium would typically have a permanent teaching staff attached to it, with specialists in these different disciplines. Gymnasia and private *palaistrai* (wrestling schools) were also used for private exercise for health, and in the imperial period facilities for exercise were increasingly combined with bath buildings.

Athletic trainers played an prominent role within that wider athletic culture. It is clear, however, that there was a considerable amount of variation in their social and intellectual status, and that they performed a range of different functions and laid claim to many different areas of expertise.[11] In the context of day-to-day festival competition and gymnasium education, the word most often used for the athletic trainer was *paidotribês*, alternatively sometimes *aleiptês* or *epistatês*.[12] In many cases these men seem to have been well respected. The tradition of praising trainers for their contributions to athletic victory dates

---

185 [pp. 137–42]) for translation of the gymnasium law of Beroia (*SEG* 27.261), a long inscription dating from the early second century BC, which gives us some of our best evidence for the day-to-day running of ancient gymnasia.

[11] See König (2005, esp. 305–15); also König (2009a, 262–64, and forthcoming).

[12] See König (2005, 305–6).

back at least to Pindar and Bacchylides.[13] Clearly a trainer
was viewed as an important part of the entourage of any
star athlete in the Hellenistic and Roman periods, and
trainers are frequently mentioned in passing in victory
inscriptions.[14] The following example, a statue base from
Smyrna recording the successes of a runner from the sec-
ond century AD, is typical: ". . . M. Aur . . . , best of the
Hellenes, first of runners, having won sixty-six sacred con-
tests under the instruction of the trainer Areius the Alex-
andrian, son of Hermeius (ὑπὸ ἀλείπτην Ἄρειον)" (the
opening of the inscription and the full name of the ath-
lete have not survived). This is clearly an athlete of the
very highest ability, with plenty to boast about: to have
won sixty-six victories in sacred contests (the more presti-
gious of the two categories of ancient agonistic festival,
where victory was rewarded with a wreath rather than just
a money prize) would have required many years of domi-

---

[13] See especially Pind. *Ol.* 8.54, *Nem.* 4.93, and *Nem.* 6.65 for
the trainer Melesias; Pind. *Nem.* 5.48 and Bacchyl. 13.190–98, for
the trainer Menander; and Nicholson (2005, 119–210), who ar-
gues, however, that there was a tendency in victory odes to down-
play the contribution of athletic trainers so as to avoid detracting
from the glory of the victorious athletes being celebrated, as well
as a tendency, in cases where trainers are mentioned, to downplay
the professional quality of their assistance, in order to avoid the
impression that their athletes have paid for the skills needed to
win victory. Cf. Burnett (2005, 51–53) for a more skeptical treat-
ment of the claim that Pindar and his patrons felt uncomfortable
with celebration of athletic trainers.

[14] See also Paus. 6.3.6 for a statue honoring a *paidotribês* at
Olympia, and *Inscriptions de Délos* 1924 for a similar example
from Delos.

nance over his rivals. And yet this athlete, or whoever is responsible for the inscription, devotes two whole lines of the inscription to the contribution of his trainer, who stands prominently at the end.[15] The key phrase ὑπὸ ἀλεί-πτην (under the instruction of the trainer x), or sometimes ὑπὸ παιδοτρίβην or ὑπ᾽ ἐπιστάτην, occurs over and over again in other inscriptions too.[16]

There is also evidence for trainers holding political office in their home cities[17] and using rhetorical skills, for example, in presenting requests for funding.[18] Some trainers clearly moved in intellectually elevated company. For example, Plutarch's *Quaestiones Convivales* includes one account of a symposium in Athens—"Pretty well all of our friends were present, and many other scholarly people in addition" (9.1.1, 736d)—where one of the guests is an athletic trainer (*paidotribês*) (9.15.1, 747a–b).[19] At the same time, however, trainers are presented as relatively subordinate figures in many of the surviving gymnasium

[15] See Robert (1937, 138–42).

[16] See König (2005, 308), drawing on Robert (1967, 31n3; 1974, 520–23; and 1937, 139n1).

[17] E.g., see van Nijf (1997, 42n54 and 59n144) on *Inschriften von Smyrna* 246.

[18] See *Inschriften von Ephesos* 1416 and 2005, from the fourth or third centuries BC; König (2005, 313–14); and Golden (2008, 25–26), as part of a wider discussion (23–39) of the increasing willingness to acknowledge the contribution of trainers to victory through the Hellenistic and Roman periods.

[19] However, see also Plut. *Precepts of Healthcare* 133b–d, with van Hoof (2010, 238–39), for a passage that criticizes the anti-intellectual conversation of *aleiptai* and *paidotribai* at dinner parties.

inscriptions, instructing young men in athletics without
any exceptional expertise and earning (relatively modest)
wages in the process.[20] We do have some evidence for
written instruction in the techniques of the combat events,
in a surviving papyrus fragment of a treatise on wrestling,
but it gives the impression of being very functional and is
lacking in any rhetorical embellishment, focusing mainly
on bare description of different wrestling moves.[21] The
paidotribês, in other words, was a figure who tended to
hover on the edge of the intellectual mainstream.

The picture is slightly different when we look at the
long tradition of medicalized gymnastic writing by people
who set themselves up as experts in preservative medicine,
often referred to as dietetics or regimen, using techniques
like massage and diet as well as exercise for the mainte-
nance of health.[22] It is in relation to these experts that we
tend to find the word *gymnastês* (which is rare in the in-
scriptional record) rather than *paidotribês*.[23] The medi-

[20] See König (2005, 309–12), with reference among others to
*Syll.*³ 577 and 578.

[21] *P Oxy.* 3.466; for translation, see Miller (2004, no. 36, p. 32)
and Poliakoff (1986, 161–63, and commentary at 165–71).

[22] The fullest survey is Wöhrle (1990); see also Jüthner (1909,
3–60) and Lehmann (2009).

[23] For example, Arist. *Pol.* 1338b offers explicit, though cau-
tious, approval of the *gymnastês* and the *paidotribês* as important
contributors to the education of the young, the former as overall
supervisors of the condition of the body, the latter as supervisors
of its actions. For rare exceptions, where *gymnastês* is used in
documentary texts, see *P London* 1178, line 63; *FD* 3.1.220; and
further discussion at König (2005, 306).

calized school of athletic training stretches back to Iccus of Tarentum[24] in the fifth century BC, and Herodicus of Selymbria, his near contemporary, whose work seems to have involved among other things innovations in the uses of diet for the preservation of health.[25] Another later *gymnastês* who seems to have been influential was Theon, who wrote among other things on massage (discussed further below), although our only detailed evidence for his work is from Galen, and his date is not certain.[26] There was also a great deal of work on regimen by authors who would have identified themselves not as *gymnastai* but as philosophers or doctors. The most important example is the Hippocratic work *On Regimen*.[27] From the early Hellenistic period we know of work along these lines by Diocles of Carystus, Mnesitheus of Athens, Praxagoras of Cos, Erasistratus of Ceos, and Dieuches, thanks to surviving fragments and later testimonies.[28]

Even this medicalized strand of gymnastic expertise, however, could be vulnerable to negative judgments, in cases where it was thought to prioritize training for competition over day-to-day good health. Plato's work is a case in point,[29] and especially his lengthiest discussion of the

[24] See Pl. *Prt.* 316d; Paus. 6.10; Jüthner (1909, 8–9).

[25] See Pl. *Prt.* 316d, *Phdr.* 227d, and *Resp.* 3, 406a; Jüthner (1909, 9–16).

[26] See Jüthner (1909, 16–22).

[27] See Jüthner (1909, 14–16) and Jouanna (1999, 166–68, 324–25, and 408–9).

[28] See Wöhrle (1990, 158–89) for survey.

[29] See Jüthner (1909, 37–43) for a survey of Plato's views on athletic training. Related to Plato's ambivalent attitude is a wider

subject, in *Republic* 3, 403c–12b. There he is clearly open to a positive role for athletic training so long as it is balanced with intellectual and musical education, but he is also very scathing about the effectiveness of Herodicus' views on regimen (at 406a) and more generally about some of the techniques used to train athletes for competition. For example, at 404a Socrates suggests that the condition of athletes is "a sleepy condition and dangerous for health: do you not see how these athletes sleep away their lives, and how they fall prey to great and violent diseases if they depart even a little from their prescribed regimen?" The Hippocratic writings similarly give an ambivalent assessment of the value of gymnastic training, partly, though perhaps not only, because of the varied authorship of the corpus. *Ancient Medicine* 4, for example, offers a fairly positive assessment: "Even today, those who give their attention to exercises and training are always making some additional discovery by the same method, investigating what foods and drinks a person will best overcome so as to become as strong as possible." Some ancient writers even thought that Hippocrates had been the pupil of Herodicus.[30] Elsewhere, by contrast, as in Plato, we find signs of anxiety about the dangerous, unhealthy character of the athletic condition. *Aphorisms* 1.3 is typical: "In athletes (*gymnastikoi*—literally, those involved in athletic training), good condition which is at its highest pitch is dan-

---

tradition of criticism of athletes by intellectuals in the classical period: e.g., Xen. *IE* 2.186–87; Eur. *Autolycus*, fr. 282 (*TGF*, 441–42); Isoc. *Paneg.* 1–2.

[30] E.g., see Soranus, *Life of Hippocrates* 2.

gerous." The Hippocratic work *On Regimen* falls halfway between these two extremes, embracing the power of exercise to improve the human constitution but also keeping training for competition rather at arm's length, stressing that the goal of exercise should always be the preservation of the correct constitutional balance within the human body.

Most vehement of all in his criticism of *gymnastai* is the great medical writer Galen, whose work dates from the second century AD.[31] Galen is notoriously combative in his interactions with other medical professionals, regularly denouncing rivals who fall short in education and in the skills of reasoning that he deems necessary to any kind of medical expertise or who attempt to practice without an adequate degree of personal experience. His strongest criticism of all is reserved for athletic trainers, who threaten to encroach on his medical expertise by claiming medical skills they do not possess and in the process do enormous damage to the bodies of their charges. For Galen, in other words, the trainers are an extreme example of the way in which medical incompetence can masquerade as expertise. The most vehement version of those criticisms comes in his *Protrepticus*.[32] That work is an exhortation to study the liberal arts and especially medicine, which is contrasted with a series of false arts. The worst of those, Galen suggests, in a denunciation that lasts for more than half the work as it survives, is athletics, which leads to a dangerous obsession with glory and also dam-

[31] See Jüthner (1909, 51–59); König (2005, 254–300).
[32] See König (2005, 291–300).

ages the health of the human body (he makes similar points in another brief work entitled *Good Condition*). In this work and others he aligns himself repeatedly with Hippocrates and Plato, although at times rather opportunistically, in a way that tends to overestimate the convergence of their views with his own.[33] Galen's *Thrasybulus: Is Health a Part of Medicine or Gymnastics* offers a more sustained justification of his negative judgment.[34] He argues at great length that the expertise of the *gymnastês*, as an expert in the exercises of the gymnasium, should be viewed as just one tiny part of the half of medicine that is concerned with maintaining good condition (the other half being curative or therapeutic medicine) and so should be subordinate to the medical expert. Here he is resisting an alternative view that takes the *gymnastês* as the expert with primary responsibility for preserving the health of the body and the doctor as responsible only for curing disease and injury. Even in this more measured work, however, a more antagonistic tone sometimes bursts into view, in a way that seems to be partly explained by the context of public debate between doctors and trainers, or at least between Galen himself and some of his gymnastic rivals. We see a vivid glimpse of that context toward the end of the treatise, where he describes a hysterical public tirade directed against him by an ignorant *gymnastês* (46, K5.895).

Having established the subordinate role of the *gym-*

[33] See Smith (1979, 106–14); König (2005, 277–79).
[34] See König (2005, 267–74).

nastês, Galen then proceeds to reassert his own control over the art of medicalized regimen, in another important work, the *De sanitate tuenda* (usually translated as *On the Preservation of Health,* or sometimes as *Hygiene*),[35] which several times refers to the conclusions of the *Thrasybulus,* as if imagining a reader who is familiar with that earlier work (see *De sanitate tuenda* 1.4, K6.12; 2.8, K6.136). The work opens in 1.1 with an account of the distinction between the two branches of medicine, the therapeutic and the "hygienic" or preservative (later, in 2.8, K6.135–36 he states his preference for the term *hygieinos* as the practitioner of the latter, criticizing those who instead use the term *gymnastês*). He then outlines the continual tendency of the human constitution to deteriorate from perfect balance between hot, cold, moist, and dry (1.1, K6.2) and defines correction and prevention of that deterioration as the primary goal of the science of *hygieinikê* (i.e., the expertise of the *hygieinos*). Exercise, he makes clear, is one of many different techniques for maintaining correct balance, and the second half of Book 2 comprises a painstaking categorization of different types of exercise and their effects, with extensive subdivision of each category, offering, for example, a range of different varieties of "vigorous" exercise (2.9) and a range of different varieties of "swift" exercise (2.10). He does repeatedly mention the exercises of the gymnasium, and even the experience of athletes, but he also makes it clear that gymnasium exercise is only one type of many. For example, at 2.8 he gives

---

[35] See van der Eijk (2008, 297–300); Wöhrle (1990, 213–48).

PHILOSTRATUS

equal weight to the kinds of exercise linked with work:
"digging, rowing, plowing, pruning, burden bearing, reap-
ing, riding, fighting, walking, hunting, fishing . . . house
building, bronze working, shipbuilding, plow making"
(2.8, K6.134). Here the exclusively athletic style of train-
ing for competition associated with the *gymnastês* and the
paidotribês is kept very much at arm's length (see 3.2.168–
69 for a passage that makes that distinction explicit). The
De sanitate tuenda makes it clear, then, that we should not
overstate Galen's hostility to gymnastic exercise as a part
of regimen. It is in fact by far the most ambitious of all
surviving ancient writings on regimen[36] and is in itself
heavily influenced by earlier writing on diet and massage
and exercise, although even in this text he sometimes
criticizes earlier gymnastic writers for their logical and
physiological misunderstandings.[37] His hostility is di-
rected not against those who use exercise as one of many
techniques for maintaining a healthy balance in the hu-
man body but instead against those who set themselves up
as experts in *gymnastikê* without having proper medical

36 See Green (1951) for English translation. See also Plut.
Precepts of Healthcare, for a similar approach, with Van Hoof
(2010, 211–54) and König (forthcoming): like Galen, Plutarch
denigrates the techniques of the athletic trainer while also con-
structing an alternative model of training for good health, based
on dietetic traditions, rather than rejecting physical exercise out-
right.

37 Especially Theon's writings on massage; see further below,
n. 74; also *Thrasyboulos* 47 (K5. 898) for further brief criticism
of Theon.

knowledge and with the primary goal of enhancing athletic performance rather than health.

3. ATHLETIC TRAINING AS A FORM OF SOPHIA IN *GYMNASTICUS* 1–2 AND 14–16

Philostratus' *Gymnasticus* reacts against this long-standing strand of ambivalence about the value of athletic trainers in Greek thought, especially, but not exclusively, in their guise as quasi-medical experts: his use of the word *gymnastês* for trainer throughout the work aligns him firmly with that medicalized strand of training and regimen. It also seems likely that he is reacting more specifically against Galen,[38] not least in the very opening passage of the work, where Philostratus' characterization of *gymnastikê* as a type of *sophia* goes provocatively against Galen's view. For example, in the closing paragraphs of Galen's *Protrepticus* as it survives, we find the following categorization:

> Given that there is a distinction between two different types of art (*technê*)—some of them are rational and highly respected, whereas others are contemptible, and centered around bodily labor, in other words the ones we refer to as banausic or manual—it is better to take up one of the first category . . . In

[38] For a longer account, see König (2005, 315–25); cf. Jüthner (1909, 118–20) for the argument that Philostratus does not know the work of Galen, and König (2005, 315n45 and 329n70) for doubts about Jüthner's interpretation of the passage (*Gym.* 42) on which he bases that claim.

the first category are medicine, rhetoric, music, geometry, arithmetic, logic, astronomy, grammar and law; and you can also add sculpting and drawing if you wish. (14 [K1.38–9])

Athletic training, by contrast, has already been rejected as a false art in *Protrepticus* 9–14. Other imperial Greek writers too conspicuously decline to categorize athletic training with other types of wisdom. One particularly striking example is Pollux, in *Onomasticon* 3.140–55, where words connected with athletic training are included at the very end of Book 3, and conspicuously excluded from the discussion of different kinds of *technê* which follows on immediately as the central subject of Book 4.[39]

Philostratus' opening paragraph gives a different impression:

> Let us regard as types of wisdom, on the one hand, things like philosophy and skillful speech and engaging in poetry and music (ποιητικῆς τε ἅψασθαι καὶ μουσικῆς) and geometry, and by Zeus astronomy, so long as it is not carried to excess. On the other hand, the organization of an army is a form of wisdom, and in addition things like the following: the whole of medicine and painting and modeling, and the various types of sculpting and gem cutting and metal engraving . . . As for athletic training, we assert that it is a form of wisdom, and one that is inferior to none of the other skills. (*Gym.* 1)

[39] Cf. *Onom.* 7.17 for his inclusion of athletic training among other low-status, banausic areas of expertise.

The similarity in their list of skills suggests that Philostratus may well have had Galen's *Protrepticus* passage in mind. However, it is important to stress that Philostratus' comparison of athletic training with other kinds of wisdom is not simply a response to Galen. For one thing, this passage includes one very precise Platonic reminiscence in the phrase "engaging in poetry and music" (ποιητικῆς τε ἅψασθαι καὶ μουσικῆς). That phrase closely recalls Plato's recommendation of a healthy balance between athletics and music in *Republic* Book 3 (411c), a passage that Galen himself had used, opportunistically, to bolster his own negative characterization of athletic training. It is as if Philostratus is reminding us here, in opposition to Galen, that Plato had in fact allowed the possibility of a positive version of athletic activity, and suggesting that his own vision of *gymnastikê* is in line with Platonic precedent.[40] Philostratus' list of *technai* here has other precedents too, in addition to Plato and Galen. There was also a long philosophical tradition of attacking the *technai*. Many ancient technical treatises, like the *Gymnasticus*, anticipate this kind of criticism by situating the discipline they are treating in relation to a long list of other disciplines that similarly deserve to be categorized as *technai*. And Philostratus' catalog of types of wisdom here includes many that had been standard fixtures in lists of this type.[41]

[40] See König (2005, 321–22) for that point.

[41] See Boudon (2000, 16–35) for discussion of Galen's ranking of the arts in the *Protrepticus*; Blank (1998, xvii–xxxiv) for the long tradition of attacking, defending, and defining *technai*, which stretches as far back as Plato and Hippocrates (and see esp. xviii–xx on evidence in the Hippocratic treatises for defense of the art

That is a good example of the way in which the *Gymnasticus* demands to be read not only within the context of other athletic or even medical works but also within the much broader context of the technical, compilatory prose that forms such a large part of the surviving literature of the Roman empire, and which had its own rich generic conventions.[42]

The technique of offering comparison with other disciplines is also used again by Philostratus in one of his other works, the *Imagines,* where he defends the art of painting in strikingly similar terms in the opening lines of the work (1.1):[43]

---

of medicine against attack); and at most length Nesselrath (1985, 123–239) for the history of writing about *technai* as it informs Lucian's *Parasite,* discussed further below.

[42] For the general argument about the generic conventions of technical prefaces in imperial prose, see König (2009b); and for the *Gymnasticus* specifically, see Jüthner (1909, 97–107) on the context of *eisagogic* (i.e., introductory) and epideictic writing (the latter discussed further below). See also Billault (1993) for a positive view of the work's miscellaneous structure, which he links with the trend toward "encyclopedic" writing in the Roman empire; and Mestre (1991, 323–34) for examination of the *Gymnasticus* in the context of what she refers to as "essay" writing traditions in imperial Greek literature.

[43] Painting was represented in positive terms as a *technê* in a number of Socratic passages (e.g., Pl. *Prt.* 312c–d, *Grg.* 503e; Xen. *Oec.* 6.13), but it was also a standard target in attacks on the *technai* by later writers: e.g., see Sen. *Ep.* 88.19. Cf. Philostr. *VA* 8.7.3 for a similarly high valuation of painting (along with sculpting, navigating, and agriculture), which is represented as being almost deserving of the category of wisdom (ascribed by Philos-

Whoever does not welcome painting is unjust to truth and unjust to the wisdom (ἀδικεῖ τὴν σοφίαν) that has been bestowed on poets—for both poets and painters make an equal contribution to our understanding of the deeds and appearance of heroes —and also fails to give due praise to symmetry (ξυμμετρίαν), by which the skill of painting partakes of reason (δι' ἣν καὶ λόγου ἡ τέχνη ἅπτεται) . . . Wise men discovered it, and called it both painting and plastic art. There are many kinds of plastic art—modeling itself, and imitation in bronze, and those who carve Lygdian or Parian stone and ivory carving and by Zeus the art of gem cutting is also a plastic art.

Here there are close similarities with the *Gymnasticus* passage, especially in the mention of a series of different types of artistic expertise, which may be a sign that Philostratus intends his two works to be read together.[44] If so, that suggests that the *Gymnasticus* may be part of a wider

---

tratus in this passage to the arts of poetry, music, astronomy, and nonforensic rhetoric).

[44] The association between painting and athletic training has parallels both in Philostratus' work and elsewhere. For example, Sen. *Ep.* 88.19–20, denies the status of both painting and athletics as liberal arts in quick succession (he also attacks music, mathematics, and astronomy among others, all of which are also included in *Gym.* 1 and Gal. *Protrepticus* 14). See also *Gym.* 25 for the suggestion that the trainer's assessment of the proportions of the body has much in common with the sculptor's understanding of bodily proportion.

preoccupation in Philostratus' work with seeking manifestations of traditionally Greek wisdom in places one might not initially expect to find them.[45]

In the opening paragraphs of the *Gymnasticus*, then, Philostratus sets out his determination to reclaim a position of intellectual respectability for the athletic trainer as a professional, against the views of Galen and others. From there, in *Gym.* 3 to 13, he changes tack to survey some key moments from athletic history, discussed further in the section following. In *Gym.* 14 to 16 he then returns to the topic of the categorization of *gymnastikē* from a slightly different angle. As we have seen, Galen, in his *Thrasybulus*, had offered a belittling portrait of athletic training, portraying it as a tiny subsection of the wider art of medicine, in such a way as to make the trainers' claims to rival the doctors in expertise seem absurd. Philostratus, by contrast, offers a common-sense remapping of these disciplines, arguing that we need to think of *gymnastikē* as a valid art in its own right, which draws on medical expertise as well as on the expertise of *paidotribikē* (training in the techniques used for competition in the various events), but combines them into an independent and distinctive set of skills: "What, then, should one think about the art of athletic training? What else except to believe that it is a type of wisdom combining both the art of medicine and the art of the *paidotribēs*?" (14). He also associ-

---

[45] See Elsner (2009, 15) for an argument along those lines; also Newby (2005, 324–26) on the way in which this passage raises questions, which are important for the rest of the work too, about the degree to which the painter's skill should be viewed as intellectual as well as technical.

ates *gymnastikê* particularly with preventative medicine, contrasted with therapeutic medicine, which is characterized as the province of the doctor: "Doctors cure the illnesses we refer to as catarrh and dropsy and consumption, and the various types of epilepsy, by prescribing irrigations or potions or dressings, whereas athletic training checks such conditions by the use of diet and massage."

In both 1–2 and 14–16, then, it is clear that Philostratus takes a very different view from Galen of the status of the trainer's art. That said, it is important to stress that Philostratus is not unequivocally hostile to Galen's position. For one thing Philostratus' discussion of particular types of regimen—for example massage and diet—in the second half of the work may well be influenced by Galen's *De sanitate tuenda*, although that is hard to demonstrate definitively. Certainly, they have a great deal in common, not least in their shared insistence on treating each of their subjects as an individual rather than applying blanket prescriptions.[46] Philostratus also criticizes the athletic trainers of the present day and suggests that they have been responsible for a decline:

> The training of our fathers' time produced athletes who were less impressive than these but nevertheless remarkable and worthy of commemoration. But the kind of training which prevails today has so far changed the nature of athletes that the majority of people are irritated even by lovers of the gymna-

[46] Cf. Gal. *De sanitate tuenda* 3.1 (K6.164), 3.8 (K6.214), 5.1 (K6.306), for similar criticism of inflexible training methods that do not take account of differences between individuals.

sium. I have decided to make clear the causes of this degeneration and to contribute for trainers and their subjects alike everything I know. (1–2)

His criticism becomes even more vehement at *Gym.* 44:

When the situation changed, and when athletes became inexperienced in warfare rather than combatants, sluggish rather than energetic, and soft rather than hardened, and when Sicilian gastronomy became popular, then the stadia became enfeebled, and all the more so since the art of flattery was introduced into athletic training.

That attack on the luxury of contemporary athletic trainers is in fact reminiscent of some of Galen's more vehement assaults in the *Protrepticus* and elsewhere.[47] In some respects, then, Philostratus is happy to align himself with Galen's views. The key difference is that he takes a more optimistic view of the potential for athletic training to be a valuable profession in its own right, standing independently of medicine.

4. ATHLETIC HISTORY IN *GYMNASTICUS* 3–13 AND 17–24

Gym. 1–2 and 14–16 suggest that Philostratus' main topic will be the quasi-medical art of the *gymnastês*. At first sight then it seems odd that immediately after the opening paragraphs of the work he launches into an account of the

---

[47] E.g., see criticism of athletic overeating at Gal. *Protrepticus* 11.

origins of all the traditional Greek athletic events. What is the function of that excursus into Olympic history?

One obvious answer is that it helps to provide a history for the discipline Philostratus is presenting to his readers here. That too—like the comparison with other *technai* discussed above—was a standard technique within ancient technical writing.[48] It is also used ingeniously in a number of other surviving works that offer a defense of a particular *technê* using the praise traditions of epideictic rhetoric. Jüthner (1909), for example, has influentially cited Lucian's work *On Dance* as a text that draws on both of those closely connected strands and in that sense closely parallels Philostratus' work in generic terms.[49] That work

---

[48] See Pl. *Prt.* 316d–17a for Protagoras' claim that the art of the sophist is an ancient one (but that the early sophists disguised themselves under the cover of other professions). See also the preface to Columella, *Rust.* for another example that is strikingly close to the *Gymnasticus* not just in setting out a history for agriculture (preface 13–19, for an idealization of the farmer-politicians of the late Republic) and in comparing agriculture to other disciplines (3–6), but also in complaining about recent decline in agricultural skill, linked with the increasing luxury of Roman society (13, 15–16; cf. *Gym.* 2, 44–45), and in setting out to defend nature against the accusation that the ineffectiveness of present-day agriculture is her fault (1–3; cf. *Gym.* 2).

[49] Jüthner (1909, 97–100); he discusses Lucian's text as an example of eisagogic (i.e., introductory) literature, citing Horace's *Ars poetica* as a closely related example, and suggests that these works (like Philostratus' *Gymnasticus*) are characterized by a tendency to treat the art itself (including its history) in the first half and the practitioner in the second (for transition between the two, see *Gym.* 15; cf. Lucian, *On Dance* 35). However, see also

gives a very inventive defense of the art of pantomime, which most commentators would have been reluctant to categorize as an intellectually respectable profession. In the process Lucian, like Philostratus for *gymnastikê*, makes an elaborate and ingenious attempt to give pantomime a history, citing a wide range of precedents from Greek myth and epic.[50] Lucian's *Parasite* offers an even more blatantly parodic version of that same motif:[51] he represents the art of the parasite as superior to philosophy and rhetoric and traces it back to the heroes of the *Iliad* and other famous figures from the classical past,[52] for example, by representing Nestor as a parasite who earns his place at King Agamemnon's table through his entertaining conversation (*Parasite* 44–45).[53]

Those parallels with Lucian are helpful, so long as we do not go too far in assuming that the *Gymnasticus* is simply an ingenious rhetorical exercise for Philostratus.[54]

Billault (1993, 148) for skepticism about the importance of the *ars-artifex* distinction and especially about the relevance of the comparison with Horace.

[50] Lucian, *On Dance* 8–16.

[51] See Nesselrath (1985).

[52] Lucian, *Parasite* 44–48.

[53] The *Heroicus* too engages closely with works like *On Dance* and *Parasite*, although in that case the key point of overlap is the way in which all of these texts represent an interlocutor being converted from skepticism to belief or acceptance (belief in the existence of the heroes, in the *Heroicus,* or in the value of dance and parasitism, in the case of the Lucianic works): see *Her.* Introduction §7, above.

[54] See Anderson (1986, 268–72) for a view of the work along

The evidence of his other work, especially his *Life of Apollonius*, suggests that he cared deeply about defending traditional Greek culture, often in a way that involved quite an archaizing and even quite an exoticized view of the classical past, and often in a way that involved celebration of traditional festival culture.[55] That love of archaizing, exoticizing detail is also on show in these opening sections of the *Gymnasticus*.[56] The version of athletic history Philostratus offers us in *Gym.* 1–13 in many respects seems to draw closely on traditional sources. Much of the information he presents is close to passages in Pausanias, although also often with odd divergences, which have led some people to argue that he was not aware of Pausanias' work, but which may also conceivably be deliberate.[57] He

---

those lines, linking the *Gymnasticus* with the traditions of "adoxography," in other words, rhetorical exercises involving praise of things that are difficult to praise.

[55] E.g., see Swain (1999) on the theme of defending Hellenism in Philostratus' *Life of Apollonius*, and König (2007) on the many scenes in that text where Apollonius travels around the Greek world correcting the observance of festival ritual, trying to bring present-day customs more closely in line with what he views as a more ancient, more virtuous original (e.g., 3.58, 4.5–9, 4.19, 4.27–9, 5.25), and on the way in which that attitude closely parallels the attitude to the athletic past we find in the *Gymnasticus*.

[56] Cf. Billault (1993, 149–50) on Philostratus' fascination with the past in this work.

[57] See Rusten (2004) for similar discussion of the possibility that Philostratus has read Pausanias, in relation to the *Heroicus*; and cf. p. 362 below, on the relationship between Philostratus' anecdotes about trainers and the equivalent stories in Pausanias.

also seems to draw heavily on the Olympic victory-list tradition that dates back to Aristotle and Hippias and others.[58] In line with Pausanias—and to a much greater degree than the victory lists—Philostratus gives us a glimpse of a world that is quite alien to the Roman present, defined, for example, by the omnipresence of military activity in the Peloponnese of the fifth and fourth centuries BC. In *Gym.* 8, for example, we hear the following:

> The best of the hoplite races was thought to be the one in Plataea in Boeotia because of the length of the race and because of the armor, which stretches down to the feet covering the athlete completely, as if he were actually fighting; also because it was founded to celebrate a distinguished deed, their victory against the Persians, and because the Greeks devised it as a slight against the barbarians; and especially because of the rule concerning competitors that Plataea long ago enacted: that any competitor who had already won victory there, if he competed again, had to provide guarantors for his body; for death had been decreed against anyone who was defeated in that circumstance.

That brief account (which is not paralleled elsewhere) conjures up an image of a ruthless and heavily militarized

---

[58] See Jüthner (1909, 60–70); and for a broader account of the tradition, see Christesen (2007, esp. 178–79 on Philostratus; also 210–11, where he suggests that Philostratus has misread one of his sources); and see *Gym.* 2 for mention of "the records of the Eleans" as a key source, which may be a reference to official victory records, with discussion by Jüthner (1909, 109–16).

culture. This defamiliarizing vision of the past is further intensified later in the work, for example in the description of heroic athletes sleeping in the open air and competing against animals in *Gym.* 43.[59] At first sight it seems that these heroic figures inhabit a very alien world, although the whole thrust of Philostratus' *Gymnasticus* is that we can in fact recapture something of that ancient virtue through a reinvigoration of the art of training and that we can in that sense paradoxically find ways of celebrating the links between archaic past and imperial present, despite the apparent distance between them.[60] Philostratus' interest in presenting what seems to be a stylized, archaizing view of the Greek past should of course make us cautious about taking at face value his versions of the origins of the various events he describes, or indeed in accepting his broader vision of a decline from a pure, ancient past to a degenerate present.[61]

[59] Cf. the description of Heracles Agathion in *VS* 552–54, who similarly lives in the countryside and trains in competition with wild animals; also Philostr. *Her.* 10–13 for Protesilaus training in the open air and helping the vinedresser with his work in the fields, and 33.41 for Palamedes sleeping in the open air.

[60] Cf. Swain (2009, 39–40) on the way in which Philostratus' call for a return to nature is central to his desire to revive the virtues of the past in the *Gymnasticus*.

[61] See König (2007) for the argument that Philostratus' model of decline is rather implausible, given the evidence for the continued flourishing and popularity of athletic festivals under the Severan emperors; also Billault (2000, 68–69) on decline as a commonplace sophistic topic, although he then goes on to endorse Philostratus' vision of increasing professionalization and degeneracy in ancient athletic culture. See also Gardiner (1930,

One might argue that these sections of the work are simply ineffective if they are designed to present the reader with a history of the art of athletic training, since *gymnastikê* is barely mentioned in the course of Philostratus' account of the origins of the events he discusses. However there are two passages from toward the end of this section that suggest he is aware of that problem and keen to overcome it as far as possible. The first is from the beginning of 12: "It is said that these events were not brought into the contests all at the same time but one after another, as they were invented and perfected by the art of athletic training." That claim makes *gymnastikê* responsible for the whole evolution of the Olympic program, as if it has a kind of supervisory role. The second instance is at the end of 13: "It seems to me that these events would not have been introduced in this way, one at a time, nor would they have won the enthusiasm of the Eleans and all the Greeks, if the art of athletic training had not undergone improvement, and if it had not trained them (εἰ μὴ γυμναστικὴ ... ἤσκει αὐτά)."[62] There the art of *gymnastikê* is said, with rather odd phrasing, to "train" the various events (ἤσκει can also mean "worked" or "perfected,"

115–16), who similarly cites Philostratus in support of that view, and Kyle (2010) for Gardiner's views on what he saw as a decline from amateur sport to corrupt professionalism in the Hellenistic and Roman periods, set in the context of Gardiner's commitment to early twentieth-century amateurist ideology (although he also points out [p. 305] that Gardiner did not use Philostratus as much as one might expect).

[62] Cf. 12: καὶ ἀνδρῶν πάλην ἤσκησεν ἡ ὀγδόη ἐπὶ δέκα Ὀλυμπιάς.

but the athletic resonances would surely be dominant for most readers in the context of this treatise), again as if it exercises its developmental, supervisory powers over the contests themselves, just as it does over the athletes. Admittedly, Philostratus is vague here about exactly what involvement for athletic training he envisages. Nevertheless, he does seem to be insisting on the centrality of training even to this early history of Olympic development, in a way that might have been surprising to contemporary readers used to the much barer listing of the development of the Olympic festival program in the writing of the Olympic chronographers.

In 17–25, Philostratus' goal of giving a new prominence to the figure of the athletic trainer then becomes much more conspicuous. He talks there about the need for the trainer to be at least competent in his use of words: "neither garrulous nor untrained in speech" (25).[63] What he seems to have in mind is not so much a full-scale rhetorical training but rather the power of a few well-chosen words addressed to the athlete for motivational purposes.[64] He also offers his readers a number of anecdotes to illustrate those qualities. In doing so he portrays the trainers as key members of the Olympic community, reminding us vividly of their presence at the

[63] Cf. the verbal skills of the trainer Melesias in Pind. *Nem.* 4.94–96; also Pl. *Prt.* 316d for sophists disguising themselves as athletic trainers, and as other kinds of professionals, with mention of Iccus and Herodicus.

[64] Cf. *Her.* 14–15 for anecdotes about Protesilaus giving advice—again in just a few well-chosen words—to athletes who come to consult his oracle on how to win victory.

games, which tends to get lost from view in many other ancient portrayals of Olympia. Several of these anecdotes are accordingly set in specific areas of the Olympic site, for example, in the gymnasium or the stadium. It is striking also that earlier versions of these same stories, for instance in Pausanias, often do not involve trainers. For example, the story of Glaucus of Carystus being encouraged to victory by his trainer in *Gym.* 20 also appears in Paus. 6.10.1–2, except that there the athlete is encouraged by his father. And the story of Arrichion in *Gym.* 21, who prefers victory to death, in response to the encouragement of his trainer on the sidelines, also occurs in Paus. 8.40.2, but there again with no mention of a trainer. It seems perfectly possible that Philostratus has invented the contributions of these trainers himself.[65] There is also a negative version of a trainer's expertise (or lack of it) on show within the Olympic sanctuary in the second half of the work, in the story (not attested elsewhere) of the death of an athlete called Gerenus in *Gym.* 54 (discussed further in the section following): Philostratus tells us that he died in the Olympic gymnasium, having been overexercised by his trainer, who misjudged his condition when he turned up to training with a hangover from celebrating an Olympic victory the night before.

[65] By contrast, Nicholson (2005, 119–21) suggests (to my mind less plausibly) that these are the original versions of these stories and that the contributions of the trainers were suppressed by Pindar and Bacchylides and other sources used by Pausanias in order to avoid detracting from the glory of their clients (he also acknowledges at 132 the possibility that they may be late inventions).

One other aspect of festival culture Philostratus is particularly fascinated by in his other works, and which is surely relevant to this portrayal of the trainers displaying their expertise at Olympia, is the tradition of intellectuals speaking to the assembled Greeks in the context of Panhellenic festivals. Apollonius' series of visits to the important religious sites of Greece is one example of that. In the *Life of Apollonius* (8.15), for example, Philostratus describes Apollonius' second visit to Olympia in the work as follows: "An incessant and eager rumor took hold of the Hellenic world (τὸ Ἑλληνικόν) that the man was alive and that he had arrived at Olympia"; the rumor is confirmed, and Philostratus tells us that "Greece (ἡ Ἑλλάς) had never before come together in such a state of excitement as it did for him then." That motif is even more prominent in the *Lives of the Sophists,* where Philostratus repeatedly describes classical orators like Isocrates and Gorgias,[66] and also the sophists of the Roman Empire like Herodes Atticus,[67] speaking at Olympia. In addition, he repeatedly uses this idea of "the Greeks" as the implied audience for sophistic speech making, even when these occasions are not taking place in Olympia and other festive sites. For example, his sophists are repeatedly described as speaking to "the Greeks" even when they are not performing at Olympia or Delphi or other equivalent venues, and their students and admirers are often referred to as "Hellenes" or "Hellenic" or even "Hellas," as if a notion-

---

[66] VS 1.9, 493 (Gorgias); 1.11, 495–96 (Hippias of Elis); 1.17, 505 (Isocrates).

[67] E.g., see VS 1.25, 539 for a good example involving Herodes Atticus, or 2.27, 618 for Hippodromus.

ally festive, Panhellenic quality is one of the defining features of sophistic speech.[68]

There are perhaps traces of that interest in intellectual display at Olympia in Philostratus' portrayal of the trainer as an Olympic expert, whose contributions have lain at the heart of Olympic history for nearly a millennium (on Philostratus' account) by the time Philostratus is writing. The trainer is, of course, a rather unusual version of the Olympic intellectual—apart from anything else, he is not an orator—but as we have seen he does nevertheless make use of the skills of speech, and also powerful skills of physiological analysis, based on a sophisticated, even virtuosic understanding of the way in which outward signs on the surface of the athletic body reveal that body's underlying condition (more on those skills in the section following). The trainer too, in other words, is another (rather idiosyncratic) example of Philostratus' repeated celebration of the figure of the Panhellenic intellectual.

Similarly significant is Philostratus' repeated comparison between the athletic trainers and the *hellanodikai*, the Olympic judges, who were trained for overseeing the games for ten months in the Hellanodikaion building in Elis before the beginning of the festival and who similarly had the task of scrutinizing athletes (although in their case in order to determine which age category they belonged to).[69] In two passages (*Gym.* 18 and 25) Philostratus even

[68] For more detailed discussion, see Follet (1991, 206–8), and cf. Tell (2007) and Tarrant (2003) for similar links between wisdom and athletic activity and festival culture in classical Greek culture.

[69] E.g., see Paus. 6.23.2.

suggests that the trainer should be viewed as superior to the *hellanodikês* in some respects.[70] That comparison too bolsters the sense that *gymnastikê* should be viewed as a distinctively Olympic kind of expertise and also helps to portray the athletic trainer, like the *hellanodikês*, as a kind of guardian figure, in charge of a very old and important body of knowledge.

5. MEDICINE AND PHYSIOGNOMY IN *GYMNASTICUS* 25–58

From *Gym.* 25 onward, it becomes increasingly clear that the trainer also has a level of intellectual, physiological sophistication that the first half of the work has only hinted at. Here Philostratus turns away from the public face of the athletic trainer to concentrate instead on a much more private, intimate kind of expertise, exercised over the bodies of individual athletes within the gymnasium. In doing so he draws on the conventions of ancient scientific writing in order to stress the complexity of the discipline of athletic training, offering us many subdivisions and subcategorizations of different types of body and different types of regimen.[71] He also insists that the trainer has to take account of many different variables in making his judgments: these are not principles that can just be ap-

[70] The *hellanodikai* are mentioned also at *Gym.* 54.
[71] Cf. Barton (1994, esp. 151–67) on similar techniques of subdivision in Galen; and see Jouanna (1999, 167–68) on the beginnings of that technique in the Hippocratic writings, for example, in *Regimen* Book 3.

plied in a mechanical fashion; each individual case, each athlete, is different.[72]

The very final chapter of the *Gymnasticus* as it survives is typical. It gives detailed instructions for sunbathing:

> Some athletes take sunbaths in an ignorant fashion, in every kind of sun and all in the same way; others, by contrast, sunbathe with understanding and rationally, not in all circumstances, but rather waiting for the most beneficial types of sunshine. The kinds of sunshine that accompany the north wind and come on windless days are clean and healthily sunny because they come from a clear sky, but those that accompany the south wind or come on overcast days are moist and burn excessively, and are liable to enfeeble those in training rather than warming them. The days with good types of sunshine I have described. But phlegmatic athletes should be exposed to the sun more often, so as to sweat out excessive secretions, whereas choleric athletes should be kept away from the sun so that fire is not poured over fire. Those who are advanced in age should sunbathe while lying idle, exposed to the sun as if they are being roasted, whereas those who are in their prime should be active while they sunbathe and should be trained in all types of exercise, following the custom of the Eleans.

[72] See Harris-McCoy (2013, esp. 160–61, for a similar approach in Artemidorus' *Oneirocritica*, and 161n20, for parallels from other technical writing in imperial culture).

Here Philostratus differentiates between different types of sunshine caused by different environmental conditions and different types of athletes with different combinations of humors, each of whom needs to be exposed to the sun in a different way. That is typical of the way in which many scientific disciplines in imperial culture use subdivisions in order to insist on their own complexity.

Admittedly, it is important to stress that the complexity of Philostratus' work falls a long way behind what we find in Galen's *De sanitate tuenda*, and indeed in many of Galen's other works. Their very different treatments of massage bring out that difference vividly. Philostratus discusses massage only quite briefly and cryptically in two separate passages, referring to the categorizational complexity of ancient theories of massage in passing, without any attempt at systematic coverage. The first passage is in *Gym.* 46:

> One should train boys in movement, as in the *palaistra*; by movement I mean the kind of passive movement produced in the legs by a softening massage and the kind of movement produced in the arms by a hardening massage. And the boy should keep time by clapping, since that makes these exercises more energetic.

The second is in *Gym.* 50:

> Athletes who have overeaten, whether they happen to be light athletes or competitors in the heavier events, are to be treated by massage of the kind which moves downward, so that the excess in the most important parts of the body can be eliminated

> . . . Both light and heavy athletes should be softened
> by the trainer in the same way, with massages that
> use a moderate amount of oil, especially on the up-
> per body; and when he applies the oil he must wipe
> it off.

Galen, by contrast, offers an enormously long and system-
atic treatment of the subject, mapping out the many dif-
ferent varieties of massage systematically in an account
that takes up more than half of Book 2 of his *De sanitate
tuenda*[73] and criticizing the gymnastic writer Theon for
oversimplifying in his works on the subject.[74]

Philostratus thus falls a long way short of Galen in his
use of these techniques. Some commentators have also
argued convincingly that Philostratus is not closely famil-
iar with many of the techniques he discusses.[75] But even
if it is unlikely that he had spent years of his life working
with athletes himself, that does not mean that we should
take his engagement with earlier gymnastic writing to
be superficial. Introductory treatment of specialist disci-
plines for general readers is common in the scientific and

---

[73] *De sanitate tuenda* 2.1–7 (K6.90–133); the uses of massage
are mentioned repeatedly in later books too (e.g., see 3.13 on
morning and evening massage).

[74] Engagement with Theon at *De sanitate tuenda* 2.3–4
(K6.96–119); and for discussion of the strategy of extensive sub-
divisions in this passage specifically, see Barton (1994, 224–
25n103).

[75] See Poliakoff (1986, 143–47) for a negative view of the
depth of Philostratus' knowledge of athletic vocabulary and com-
bat techniques.

technical writing of the Roman Empire.[76] Even if the *Gymnasticus* is in some respects derivative and imprecise, Philostratus clearly has made a serious attempt to engage with complex medical-gymnastic principles. There seems no reason why it could not have made an innovative and empowering contribution to the way in which the expertise of the athletic trainer was understood by his contemporaries (although there is no sign of it being widely quoted in later classical literature).[77] In that sense it is a powerful reminder of the remarkable range of Philostratus' interests across his oeuvre.

There is also one respect in which Philostratus' contribution is unusual in relation to other surviving writing on training, and that is in his treatment of traditions of physiognomical analysis. Ancient physiognomical writing too, like regimen, had a long prehistory, stretching right back to classical Greece. That earlier physiognomical tradition is concerned primarily with working out how physical appearance can give signs of moral character. There is a considerable amount of physiognomical writing surviving also from the imperial period, most famously the work of

---

[76] Galen's *Protrepticus* is a case in point; cf. Gal. *On the Order of My Own Books* 1 (K19.49), where he explains that some of his works were written at request for friends and others for "young beginners," with suggestions later in the text, e.g., at 2 (K6.54), about the order in which such beginners should read his books; and see also König (2009b) for further discussion of the motif of writing for friends in Galen's work and beyond, which often contributes to the impression that specialist knowledge is being imparted to a nonspecialist reader.

[77] However, see p. 383 below, for quotation of the *Gymnasticus* in three separate scholia on Plato.

Polemo.[78] Philostratus suggests, at the moment of transition between the historical and physiological halves of the work, that the trainer needs to have some understanding of that body of knowledge:

> Let him also take into consideration the whole art of physiognomy . . . The trainer, by contrast, needs to know these things well, being a sort of judge of the athlete's nature. Indeed he should know all the signs of character in the eyes, by which are revealed lazy people, impetuous people, and inactive people and those who are less capable of endurance and lacking in self-control. Some characteristics are associated with people who have black eyes, others with those who have bright, blue or bloodshot eyes, others again with those whose eyes are yellow or flecked, prominent or sunken; for nature has signaled the seasons by the stars, and character by eyes. (*Gym.* 25)

There he stresses the value of knowing about an athlete's character. Later, however, his concerns are rather different and more idiosyncratic: much of the second half of the *Gymnasticus* is taken up with an investigation of how the outward appearance of an athlete reveals not so much his character but rather his physical condition. Many passages in the second half of the work seem to envisage a situation where the trainer needs to be constantly on the alert for the hidden meaning of outward bodily signs, which will affect his decisions about how a particular athlete needs to be trained. The following is a typical example:

[78] See Barton (1994, 95–131); Swain (2007).

Those who have overeaten will be revealed by an overhanging brow and by shortness of breath and by the filling in of the hollows in the collar bones and by the flanks at the side of the body, which will show signs of a certain bulkiness. Athletes who are heavy drinkers can be detected by an oversized stomach, blood that is too lively and moistness in the flank and the knee. (*Gym.* 48)

Philostratus' anecdote about the death of Gerenus, already mentioned above, gives a vivid illustration of what can go wrong:

The trainer became angry and listened furiously and was irritable with him on the grounds that he was relaxing his training and interrupting the tetrads [i.e., a system of training according to a rigid, pre-planned four-day cycle], until he actually killed the athlete through his training, out of ignorance, by not prescribing the exercises he should have chosen even if the athlete had said nothing about his condition. (*Gym.* 54)

Gerenus' trainer, it seems, should have been perceptive enough to work out his condition from his outward bodily appearance.

It is hard to find anything quite like this sustained application of physiognomical method to athletic subjects in earlier Greek or Roman literature. Galen does give great prominence throughout his oeuvre to his own powers of diagnosis, including his own ability to decipher visual clues in order to shed light on underlying condition, and some of his anecdotes have an element of showmanship in their illustration of that quality, drawing attention to his quasi-magical perceptiveness.[79] There are traces of a similar conception even as far back as the Hippocratic writings.[80] Plato, *Leg.* 11, 916a suggests that both *gymnastai* and doctors who purchase a slave with a hidden disease— for example, epilepsy—will have no right of restitution, on the grounds that they should have spotted it before purchase.[81] The idea that the exercising body needs to be closely observed is present in Galen's *De sanitate tuenda*,[82] and there is some material on diagnosis of various types of bodily dysfunction.[83] Philostratus may well be influenced by those medical models of virtuosic diagnosis in his portrayal of the skills required by the athletic trainer. Presumably the many nonsurviving treatises on athletic training also recommended close observation of the athletic body: for example, we have evidence for treatises on different kinds of sweat and on different kinds of tiredness.[84] It also seems possible, however, that the choice to em-

[79] See Nutton (1979).

[80] See Jouanna (1999, 291–322).

[81] Cf. *Gorg.* 464a: both doctors and *gymnastai* should be able to spot health problems.

[82] See Gal. *De sanitate tuenda* 2.12 (K6.160–61) for a good example.

[83] Good examples among others at *De sanitate tuenda* 3.9 (K6.215), 3.10 (K6.219); cf. similar examples in the Hippocratic *On Regimen* Book 3.

[84] E.g., see Theophrastus' treatises on sweat, dizziness, and fatigue: Fortenbaugh, Sharples and Sollenberger (2002), and especially Theophr. *On Sweat* 11, with Jüthner (1909, 16), for passing mention of a work on sweat by a writer called Diotimus. See

phasize visual decipherment of the athletic body so prominently, in a way which borrows from the procedures of physiognomical analysis, may have been partly Philostratus' own innovation.

Even harder to parallel is Philostratus' interest in using outward appearance to determine what kinds of event and what kinds of technique a particular athlete is most suited to. In 35, for example, we hear the following—

> The ideal wrestler should be tall rather than well-proportioned in size, but his body shape should be the same as that of the well-proportioned athlete, having neither a high neck nor a neck which is sunk into the shoulders . . . the neck should be erect like the neck of a beautiful and proud horse and the base of the throat should stretch down to both collar bones. Well-connected upper shoulders and elevated shoulder tips contribute bulk to the future wrestler and nobleness of appearance and strength and help him to wrestle better; for shoulders of this kind, even when the neck is being bent and twisted in the wrestling, are good defenses, by conveying support from the arms to the head

—and so on at great length for wrestling and also for other disciplines. In many cases he uses the standard physiognomical techniques of argument from analogy, especially

---

also Jüthner (1909, 290–92) for a survey of evidence for gymnastic writings on fatigue.

between humans and animals.[85] For example in 40 we hear that "those who are similar to bears are rounded and supple and fleshy and less well structured and stooping rather than upright, and they are hard to wrestle against and good at slipping away and strong in the intertwining that wrestling requires. And their breath splutters like bears when they are running." There is occasional discussion in Galen's *De sanitate tuenda* of the way in which different kinds of body are suited to different kinds of exercise[86] (Galen's main concern is of course the use of exercise for maintenance of health rather than the allocation of athletes to the competitive events to which they are most suited). But there is nothing else in surviving ancient literature that offers anything like such a detailed account of these approaches. The best ancient model is perhaps Xenophon, *On Hunting,* which uses similar techniques to distinguish between the different aptitudes of horses or hunting dogs.[87] Indeed, Philostratus may have had that text in mind as a precedent for his discussion of athletic differentiation, as the following passage (from *Gym.* 26) suggests:

[85] See Barton (1994, 104–6, 124–28), and Boys-Stones (2007, 64–75) on prominent use of animal imagery in the Aristotelian *Physiognomy.*

[86] E.g., see 5.10 (K6.322) for a good example (translated as part of 5.3 by Green [1951, 196–97]) on the asymmetrical body types, in old men, which should not be exercised at all. For brief parallels from classical Greek texts, see Xen. *Symp.* 2.17, and Arist. *Rh.* 1.5.11, 1361b.

[87] See especially Xen. *On Hunting* 4.1–8.

It is not right that there should be so much discussion among hunters and horsemen about dogs and horses—so much so that they do not use the same dogs for every kind of hunting or against every kind of prey, but instead use some for one and others for another, while some horses are made into hunters, some into horses for battle, some into race horses, some into chariot horses, and not simply that but they are assigned to one of the shafts of the chariot or to one of the ropes according to what each is best suited for—but that humans who have to be introduced at Olympia or Pythia in search of victory proclamations to which even Heracles himself aspired, should remain unjudged.[88]

Philostratus may be innovating in this, or he may be drawing on nonsurviving treatises by trainers for these features of his work, and giving them a new prominence.[89] Either way, it is clear that this adaptation of the terminology and logic of the discipline of ancient physiognomy for athletic purposes plays a major role in his project of giving prestige and intellectual respectability to the art of the athletic trainer.

It is striking, too, that Philostratus' interest in that topic is not confined to the *Gymnasticus*. Two of his other works —the *Imagines* and the *Heroicus*—similarly show an in-

[88] The opening paragraph of the Aristotelian *Physiognomy* also draws a brief comparison between physiognomical analysis of humans and the techniques used by hunters for selecting horses and dogs.

[89] As suggested by Jüthner (1909, 127).

terest in quasi-physiognomical descriptions of the athletic body, and several passages from these texts recall the *Gymnasticus* closely.[90] Those similarities have in fact often been used, in combination with a range of other factors, as arguments for common authorship. At one point in the *Heroicus*, to take just one example, Palamedes is described as follows:

> Stripped, they say he was somewhat between a lightweight and heavyweight athlete, and he had a great deal of dirt on his face that was more pleasant than Euphorbus' golden locks; he cultivated the dirt as the result of sleeping wherever he found himself, and of spending many nights, during lulls in the fighting, at the summit of Mt. Ida. (33.41)

That is reminiscent of the tendency to categorize athletes into light or heavy, to varying degrees, throughout the *Gymnasticus*. More specifically, it is reminiscent of the characterization of the ideal pentathlete in *Gym.* 31 as halfway between the two ("The athlete who intends to compete in the pentathlon should be heavy rather than light, and light rather than heavy"). Moreover, the detail about sleeping in the open air links Palamedes with the idealized heroic athletes of *Gym.* 43 ("They washed in rivers and springs, and they trained themselves to lie on the ground, some of them stretched out on skins, others harvesting their beds from the meadows"). In *Imag.* 2.2 we see Achilles as a boy being educated by Cheiron. His

---

[90] See, however, pp. 59–60 above, for the point that the majority of descriptions of heroes in the *Heroicus* focus on the face without description of the body.

athletic potential is as yet unfulfilled but is unmistakable to the practiced eye: "For the boy's leg is straight and his arms come down to his knees; for such arms are excellent assistants in running."[91] In both of those works, subjecting heroes and other figures from Greek mythology to the physiognomical gaze—effectively the gaze of the athletic trainer as Philostratus constructs it in the *Gymnasticus*— is, once again, a way of celebrating the links between past and present, reimagining those figures from the distant past as if they are training in the gymnasia of the Roman Empire, with which Philostratus and his readers were so familiar.

That said, there are also some very striking differences between the *Gymnasticus* and these other two works. Both the *Imagines* and the *Heroicus* draw heavily on traditions of eroticized viewing of the male athletic body. An obvious example is the description of the beauty of Protesilaus in *Her.* 10–11, for instance at 10.4: "He looks most handsome nude, for he is well-proportioned (εὐπα-γής) and graceful (κοῦφος), like the herms one sees at racecourses." The words εὐπαγής (which can mean "well-proportioned" or "solid") and κοῦφος (which can refer to "light" athletes as opposed to heavy, as in the description of Palamedes just quoted, in addition to the more general meaning "graceful") are both used repeatedly in the *Gym-nasticus* and in that sense represent another example of how close the *Heroicus* is to that text in its use of athletic-physiognomical vocabulary. However, the eroticized context of this passage (obvious for example in its mention of

---

[91] For more examples from both works, see König (2005, 338–40).

Protesilaus' passionate love for Laodameia in 11.1) makes it in some respects entirely alien to the physiological descriptions of the *Gymnasticus*.[92] The *Heroicus* also draws on traditions of religious viewing associated with divine epiphanies:[93] the making-present of the past through the appearance of the heroes in the *Heroicus* is a supernatural process that inspires wonder in viewers and narratees alike. That traditional mode of viewing too is absent in the *Gymnasticus*. For example, there is no sign of the supernatural in the description of hero athletes in *Gym.* 43. That absence stands in contrast not just with the *Heroicus* but also with the supernatural details we find in some of the anecdotes about heroized athletes in Pausanias.[94] Philostratus in the *Gymnasticus* thus seems to be experimenting with an entirely different way of analyzing the human body as a marker of the continuing links between past and present, making the viewing of athletic bodies into an act of technical, physiological judgment, separated from any overtones of eroticism or divinity.

Finally, the image of visual and analytical perceptiveness that lies at the heart of Philostratus' celebration of gymnastic expertise also ties the skills of the trainer very

[92] The obvious exception is *Gym.* 45, where we hear that "luxury acts as an acute stimulus also for the sex-drive," but that passage is not linked with the act of viewing; it also describes degenerate contemporary athletic practice, in contrast with the more sober viewing practices Philostratus recommends.

[93] See Platt (2011, 235–52).

[94] For example, see Paus. 6.11.6–8 for the famous story of the statue of Theagenes, and 6.11.9 for his subsequent worship as a hero.

closely to those of Philostratus himself as narrator.[95] That effect is part of a wider equation between narrator and trainer. Philostratus himself shares with the trainers he describes an ingenious, adaptable approach to analysis, where the usefulness and moral value of an utterance often seems to matter as much as its accuracy.[96] The imagery of analysis and visual assessment is also crucial. In *Gym.* 16, for example, we hear the following: "That is the symmetry ($\xi\upsilon\mu\mu\epsilon\tau\rho\iota\alpha$) of the art of training. Its origin ($\gamma\epsilon\nu\epsilon\sigma\iota\varsigma$) lies in the fact that humans are by nature capable of wrestling and boxing and running upright." The word *symmetria* is on the face of it an odd word to use for a *technê*. One of its functions here is surely to equate Philostratus' survey of *gymnastikê* with the trainer's analysis of his charges, given that the words *xymmetros/symmetros* and *xymmetria/symmetria* are used repeatedly in the *Gymnasticus* to describe the bodies of athletes.[97] *Symmetria* is also a word that often has sculptural connota-

---

[95] For more general discussion of the commanding tone of Philostratus as narrator in this work, see Billault (1993, 156–57); cf. Whitmarsh (2004) for similar characteristics in his other work, especially the *Lives of the Sophists*.

[96] See König (2005, 325–37). For other parallels between the vocabulary used to discuss Philostratus' narratorial procedures and the practice of the trainer (all four of them prominently in the first sentence of a new paragraph), see *Gym.* 2, $\xi\upsilon\mu\beta\alpha\lambda\epsilon\sigma\theta\alpha\iota$ $\delta\epsilon$ $\gamma\upsilon\mu\nu\alpha\zeta\sigma\upsilon\sigma\iota$ $\tau\epsilon$ $\kappa\alpha\iota$ $\gamma\upsilon\mu\nu\alpha\zeta\sigma\mu\epsilon\nu\sigma\iota\varsigma$ $\delta\pi\delta\sigma\alpha$ $\sigma\iota\delta\alpha$ (of Philostratus), cf. 20, $\delta\pi\delta\sigma\alpha$ $\delta\epsilon$ $\gamma\upsilon\mu\nu\alpha\sigma\tau\alpha\iota$ $\xi\upsilon\nu\epsilon\beta\alpha\lambda\sigma\nu\tau\sigma$ $\alpha\theta\lambda\eta\tau\alpha\hat{\iota}\varsigma$ (of the trainer); and 35, $^{\prime\prime}I\omega\mu\epsilon\nu$ $\epsilon\pi\iota$ $\tau\sigma\upsilon\varsigma$ $\pi\alpha\lambda\alpha\iota\sigma\nu\tau\alpha\varsigma$ (of Philostratus), cf. 28, $\iota\tau\omega$ δ $\gamma\upsilon\mu\nu\alpha\sigma\tau\eta\varsigma$ $\epsilon\pi\iota$ $\tau\delta\nu$ $\pi\alpha\hat{\iota}\delta\alpha$ $\alpha\theta\lambda\eta\tau\eta\nu$ (of the trainer).

[97] Examples at *Gym.* 10, 33 (twice), 34, 35 (twice), 36, 56.

tions[98] and in that sense perhaps looks ahead to the passage in *Gym.* 25, where we hear that

> the characteristics of the parts of the body are also to be considered, as in the art of sculpture,[99] as follows: the ankle should agree in its measurements with the wrist, the forearm should correspond to the calf and the upper arm with the thigh, the buttock with the shoulder, and the back should be examined by comparison with the stomach, and the chest should curve outward similarly to the parts beneath the hip joint, and finally the head, which is the benchmark for the whole body, should be well proportioned in relation to all of these other parts (πρὸς ταῦτα πάντα ἔχειν ξυμμέτρως).

With that parallel in mind, and given that 14–15 have been focused on the way in which *gymnastikê* includes elements of the art of medicine mixed with elements of the art of the *paidotribês*, it may be that Philostratus means the "symmetry" of the art of training to refer to the relationship between its different constituent parts, just as it refers to the relationship between the different parts of

---

[98] Galen in several passages discusses *symmetria* as the defining feature of the beautiful body as defined by Polyclitus' *Canon*: e.g., see *De placitis Hippocratis et Platonis* 5.3.15–17 (= de Lacy 1978, 308–9).

[99] A reference among others to Polyclitus and his attempt to fix the ideal relations between different parts of the human body in his lost treatise the *Canon* and exemplified in his famous athletic statue, the Doryphoros: see Gal. *De Placitis Hippocratis et Platonis* 5.3, and Plin. *HN* 34.55.

the human body as viewed by the athletic trainer. The trainer and narrator are also paralleled in *Gym.* 16 by their common interest in origins: the use of the word "birth" (γένεσις) in the passage quoted above to describe the origin of athletic training perhaps recalls the following account in *Gym.* 27 to 29 on techniques for understanding the parentage of athletes. Origins are also of course a major focus for the historical half of the work, especially in the section on origins of events in 3 to 13.[100]

There are also two other important later passages where Philostratus' own narratorial activity is given a very visual character. In *Gym.* 26 he announces his transition to a new topic as follows: "Now that I have dealt with these matters, let us not imagine that the topic of training is coming next, but instead we will strip the person who is undergoing training and subject him to an examination of his nature, how it is constituted and for what it is suited." Here the narrator himself, within his text, is performing the actions of stripping and examination that one would normally ascribe to the athletic trainer, and so equating his own written analysis with the perceptive gaze of the ideal *gymnastês*. There is a similar effect at *Gym.* 25: "Let us have a look (σκεψώμεθα) now at the trainer himself, to see what sort of man will supervise the athlete, and what the extent of his knowledge will be." Here, the metaphor of examination, in other contexts a commonplace staple of

---

[100] More generally speaking, that concern with origins aligns the *Gymnasticus* with the concept of *aitia*, which has such a long pedigree as a marker of technical, historiographical, and scientific prose writing as far back as the fifth century BC: see Goldhill (2002, esp. 115) for summary.

technical-philosophical vocabulary, portrays the trainer as an object of visual inspection by Philostratus, just as the athlete is inspected by a trainer.[101] Philostratus in these passages lends his own authority to the trainer and appropriates some of the qualities of the ideal trainer in return, and in doing so reinforces the image of athletic training as a formidably perceptive and intellectually sophisticated body of expertise.

6. MANUSCRIPT TRADITION

There are three manuscripts. The first (Codex Parisinus Suppl. Gr. 1256) (P), dating probably from the fourteenth century, contains all of the surviving text of the *Gymnasticus* together with some of the *Heroicus* and Philostratus' *Dialexis* 1 (possibly by Philostratus' nephew, Philostratus of Lemnos).[102] The manuscript was acquired by Minoides Mynas in the mid-nineteenth century.[103] After editing the text and making copies of it, he left it with a friend in Paris; it was thought lost, until it was sold to the Bibliothèque Nationale in 1898 by the friend's son. The manuscript is in bad condition, with many missing letters and words. A second manuscript (Codex Laurentianus LVIII, 32) (F)

---

[101] At the same time, these passages portray Philostratus as a Socratic figure, by recalling Pl. *Prt* 352a–b, where Socrates compares examining an argument with stripping a patient for medical examination.

[102] See Swain (2009, 41n32), and 500–501 below.

[103] For a brief account of the life and career of Mynas, including his links with the movement for revival of the Olympic festival in mid nineteenth-century Greece, see Kitriniari (1961, 139–44).

contains only a few pages from the final section of the *Gymnasticus*, together with the *Heroicus* and *Imagines*, and several texts by other authors. A third manuscript (Codex Monacensis 242) (M) contains an epitome of the last third of the *Gymnasticus*, followed by a copy of the *Imagines* and various other texts. It is most valuable in the unepitomized sections, where it often improves on P. In addition, two paragraphs of the *Gymnasticus* are cited in scholia: *Gym.* 4, both in Schol. Pl. *Prt.* 335e and in Olympiodorus' scholia on Plato's *Gorgias*, and much of *Gym.* 10, in Schol. Pl. *Resp.* 338e (S^r).[104] For a much more detailed account of the manuscripts, see Jüthner (1909, 75–87).

Some commentators have claimed to identify gaps in the text as it survives. For convincing refutation of those claims, ascribing the odd transitions in the text instead to Philostratus' love of abruptness, see Jüthner (1909, 92–94). Others have suggested that F, whose version of the *Gymnasticus* tails off just before the end of the text as it survives in P and M, but which also has space in the manuscript for additional pages beyond the current, rather abrupt endpoint of *Gym.* 58, may have preserved a longer version. Jüthner (1909, 94) again rejects that possibility, convincingly if not conclusively, on the grounds that P and M share exactly the same endpoint; he suggests instead that F may have contained some other small text after the *Gymnasticus*.

The title of the work as transmitted by P is Περὶ Γυμναστικῆς ("Concerning the art of the athletic trainer"). The *Suda* gives the title of the work as Γυμναστικός (sc.

[104] See Jüthner (1909, 83–84) for details.

logos—i.e., "Treatise concerning athletic training"). The
Latinate form of the latter, *Gymnasticus,* has been taken
as the standard title for the work in most recent scholar-
ship, and I have therefore used it throughout this edition.

7. PREVIOUS EDITIONS AND TRANSLATIONS

The work was edited first by Mynas (1858). Significant
later editors referred to in the apparatus include Darem-
berg (1858), Cobet (1859), and Kayser (1871), all of whom
based their editions on Mynas' copies. But by far the most
important landmark is the edition and translation of Jüth-
ner (1909), whose edition is based unlike those earlier
post-Mynas versions on the rediscovered full manuscript.
Kitriniari's (1961) edition follows Jüthner's text with a few
variations and new conjectures.

Robinson (1955) and Sweet (1987) have both trans-
lated sections into English in their sourcebooks; there are
also shorter sections in Miller (2004) and in a number of
other standard sourcebooks on ancient sport. Nearly all
sections of the text (although with a few exceptions) are
translated in at least one of these three. The only full
translation of the text into English—Woody (1936)—is
unfortunately very inaccessible. In addition, I have fre-
quently consulted translations of the *Gymnasticus* into
other languages, especially Daremberg (1858) (French),
Jüthner (1909) (German), Kitriniari (1961) (modern
Greek), Noccelli (1955) and Caretta (1995) (Italian), Mes-
tre (1996) (Spanish), and Roos (2010) (Swedish). Jüthner's
(1909) commentary is a remarkable piece of scholarship
and indispensable to anyone who wants to study the text

in depth. Kitriniari (1961), Caretta (1995), and Mestre (1996) all include valuable short notes.

8. THIS EDITION AND TRANSLATION

I have followed Jüthner's (1909) text, with occasional adjustments of punctuation, and occasional incorporation of later conjectures by Zingerle (1936) and Kitriniari (1961). In line with the standard Loeb format, it has not been possible to provide a detailed apparatus. Anyone interested in a more detailed account should consult Jüthner (1909). I have included textual notes, and angled brackets to signal attempts by Jüthner and other editors to fill in missing letters and words, only when they are particularly interesting or controversial, or particularly important for translation.

As far as possible, I have kept closely to the sense of the original Greek in my translation. It is important to stress that there are some passages—especially in the physiological sections in the second half—where it is difficult to establish a correct translation beyond doubt. I have occasionally referred to the challenges associated with particular words and phrases in the notes, where they are particularly important for the work as a whole, or where they are often repeated in the course of the *Gymnasticus*, but there is not space to give a full justification of all translation decisions. In cases where the translation is debated, I have most often, though not always, followed Jüthner's (1909) interpretation, and the reader is referred to Jüthner's commentary as the first port of call for explanation of translation decisions that are not explained in full in the notes here.

BIBLIOGRAPHY

Anderson, Graham. 1986. *Philostratus: Biography and Belles Lettres in the Third Century AD*. London.

Barton, Tamsyn S. 1994. *Power and Knowledge: Astrology, Physiognomics, and Medicine under the Roman Empire*. Ann Arbor.

Billault, Alain. 1993. "Le Γυμναστικός [Gymnastikos] de Philostrate: a-t-il une signification littéraire?" *Revue des Etudes Grecques* 106: 142–62.

Blank, D. L. 1998. *Sextus Empiricus, Against the Grammarians*. Oxford.

Boudon, Véronique. 2000. *Galien. Tome 2. Exhortation à l'étude de la médicine. Art médical*. Paris.

Bowie, Ewen. 2009. "Philostratus: The Life of a Sophist." In Bowie and Elsner 2009, 19–32.

Bowie, Ewen, and Jaś Elsner, eds. 2009. *Philostratus*. Cambridge.

Boys-Stones, George. 2007. "Physiognomy and Ancient Psychological Theory." In Swain 2007, 19–124.

Burnett, Anne Pippin. 2005. *Pindar's Songs for the Young Athletes of Aigina*. Oxford.

Caretta, Alessandro. 1995. *Filostrato di Lemno, Il manuale del' allenatore*. Novara.

Christesen, Paul. 2007. *Olympic Victor Lists and Ancient Greek History*. Cambridge.

Cobet, C. G. 1859. *De Philostrati libello recens reperto.* Leiden.

Daremberg, Charles. 1858. *Philostrate, traité sur la gymnastique.* Paris.

de Lacy, Phillip, ed. 1978. *Galen, On the Doctrines of Hippocrates and Plato (Corpus Medicorum Graecorum V, 4, 1.2).* Berlin.

de Lannoy, L. 1997. "Le problème des Philostrate (État de la question)," *Aufstieg und Niedergang der römischen Welt* 2.34.3: 2362–449.

Eijk, Philip van der. 2008. "Therapeutics." In *The Cambridge Companion to Galen*, ed. R. J. Hankinson, 283–303. Cambridge.

Elsner, Jaś. 2009. "A Protean Corpus." In Bowie and Elsner 2009, 2–18.

Flinterman, Jaap-Jan. 1995. *Power, Paideia and Pythagoreanism: Greek Identity, Conceptions of the Relationship between Philosophers and Monarchs and Political Ideas in Philostratus' Life of Apollonius.* Amsterdam.

Follet, Simone. 1991. "Divers aspects de l'hellénisme chez Philostrate." In *Hellenismos: Quelques jalons pour une histoire de l'identité grecque*, ed. S. Saïd, 205–15. Leiden.

Fortenbaugh, William W., Robert W. Sharples, and Michael G. Sollenberger, eds. 2002. *Theophrastus of Eresus: On Sweat, On Dizziness and On Fatigue.* Leiden.

Gardiner, E. Norman. 1930. *Athletics of the Ancient World.* Oxford.

Gauthier, Philippe. 2010. "Notes on the Role of the *Gymnasion* in the Hellenistic City." In König 2010, 87–101. (Translated from Gauthier, Philippe. 1995. "Notes sur le rôle du gymnase dans les cités hellénistiques." In

Stadtbild und Bürgerbild im Hellenismus, ed. Michael Wörrle and Paul Zanker, 1–11. Munich.)

Golden, Mark. 1998. *Sport and Society in Ancient Greece.* Cambridge.

———. 2008. *Greek Sport and Social Status.* Austin, TX.

Goldhill, Simon. 2002. *The Invention of Prose.* Oxford.

Green, Robert Montraville. 1951. *A Translation of Galen's Hygiene (De sanitate tuenda).* Springfield, IL.

Grossardt, Peter. 2002. "Der Ringer Maron und der Pankratiast 'Halter' in epigraphischen und literarischen Quellen: (*SEG* 41, 1407 A und B bzw. Philostr. *Gym.* 36 und *Her.* 14–15)." *Epigraphica Anatolica* 34: 170–72.

Harris-McCoy, Daniel. 2013. "Artemidorus' *Oneirocritica* as Fragmentary Encyclopaedia." In *Encyclopaedism from Antiquity to the Enlightenment,* ed. Jason König and Greg Woolf, 154–77. Cambridge.

Jouanna, Jacques. 1999. *Hippocrates.* Baltimore (translated by M. B. DeBevoise; first published in French 1992).

Jüthner, Julius. 1909. *Philostratos über Gymnastik.* Leipzig.

Kayser, C. L. 1871. *Flavii Philostrati opera,* vol. 2. Leipzig.

Kitriniari, K. S. 1961. ΦΙΛΟΣΤΡΑΤΟΥ ΓΥΜΝΑΣΤΙΚΟΣ. Athens.

König, Jason. 2005. *Athletics and Literature in the Roman Empire.* Cambridge.

———. 2007. "Greek Athletics in the Severan Period: Literary Views." In *Severan Culture,* ed. Jaś Elsner, Stephen Harrison, and Simon Swain, 135–45. Cambridge.

———. 2009a. "Training Athletes and Explaining the Past in Philostratus' *Gymnasticus.*" In Bowie and Elsner 2009, 251–83.

————. 2009b. "Conventions of Prefatory Self-Presentation in Galen's *on the Order of My Own Books.*" In *Galen and the World of Knowledge,* ed. Christopher Gill, Tim Whitmarsh, and John Wilkins, 35–58. Cambridge.

————, ed. 2010. *Greek Athletics.* Edinburgh.

————. forthcoming. "Athletes and Trainers." In *The Oxford Handbook to the Second Sophistic,* ed. William Johnson and Daniel Richter. Oxford.

Kyle, Donald G. 2010. "E. Norman Gardiner and the Decline of Greek Sport." In König 2010, 284–311. (Reprinted from *Essays on Sport History and Sports Mythology,* edited by Donald G. Kyle and Gary D. Stark, 7–44. College Station, TX.)

Lehmann, Clayton Miles. 2009. "Early Greek Athletic Trainers." *Journal of Sport History* 36: 187–204.

Mestre, Francesca. 1991. *L'assaig a la literature grega d'època imperial.* Barcelona.

————. 1996. *Filóstrato—Calístrato: Heroico; Gimnástico; Descripciones de cuadros.* Madrid.

Miller, Stephen G. 2004. *Arete: Greek Sports from Ancient Sources.* Berkeley. (Third revised edition; second edition published in 1991; first edition published in 1979.)

Moretti, Luigi. 1957. "Olympionikai, i vincitori negli antichi agoni olimpici." *Memoria della Classe di Scienze morali e storiche dell' Accademia dei Lincei* 8.2: 55–198.

Mynas, Minoides. 1858. *Philostrate sur la gymnastique.* Paris.

Newby, Zahra. 2005. *Greek Athletics in the Roman World: Victory and Virtue.* Oxford.

Nesselrath, Heinz-Günther. 1985. *Lukians Parasitendialog: Untersuchungen und Kommentar*. Berlin.

Nicholson, Nigel. 2005. *Aristocracy and Athletics in Archaic and Classical Greece*. Cambridge.

Nijf, Onno van. 1997. *The Civic World of Professional Associations in the Roman East*. Amsterdam.

———. 2001. "Local Heroes: Athletics, Festivals, and Elite Self-Fashioning in the Roman East." In *Being Greek under Rome: Cultural Identity, the Second Sophistic and Development of Empire*, ed. Simon Goldhill, 306–34. Cambridge. (Reprinted in König 2010.)

Noccelli, V. 1955. *Filostrato, La ginnastica*. Naples.

Nutton, Vivian. 1979. *Galen, On Prognosis (Corpus Medicorum Graecorum V, 8.1)*. Berlin.

Platt, Verity. 2011. *Facing the Gods: Epiphany and Representation in Graeco-Roman Art, Literature and Religion*. Cambridge.

Poliakoff, Michael. 1986. *Studies in the Terminology of the Greek Combat Sports*. Frankfurt.

Potter, David. 2011. *The Victor's Crown: A History of Ancient Sport from Homer to Byzantium*. London.

Robert, Louis. 1937. *Etudes anatoliennes: Recherches sur les inscriptions grecques de l'Asie mineure*. Paris.

———. 1967. "Sur des inscriptions d'Ephèse. Fêtes, athlètes, empereurs, épigrammes." *Revue de philologie* 41: 7–84 (= *Opera Minora Selecta* 5: 347–424).

———. 1974. "Un citoyen de Téos à Bouthrôtos d'Épire." *Comptes rendus de l'Academie des Inscriptions et Belles-Lettres* 1974: 508–29 (= *Opera Minora Selecta* 5: 675–96).

———. 1984. "Discours d'ouverture." In *Actes du VIIIe congrès international d'épigraphie grecque et latine à*

Athènes, 1982, 35–45. Athens (= *Opera Minora Selecta* 6: 709–19). (Translated in König 2010.)

Robinson, Rachel S. 1955. *Sources for the History of Greek Athletics in English Translation.* Cincinnati.

Roos, Paavo. 2010. *Filostratos, Om tränarkonsten.* Askim.

Rusten, Jeffrey. 2004. "Living in the Past: Allusive Narratives and Elusive Authorities in the World of the *Heroikos.*" In *Philostratus's Heroikos: Religion and Cultural Identity in the Third Century CE*, ed. Ellen Bradshaw Aitken and Jennifer K. Berenson Maclean, 143–58. Atlanta.

Schenkl, K. 1860. Review of Daremberg 1858, Mynas 1858 and Cobet 1859. In *Zeitschrift für österreichische Gymnasien* 11: 791–806.

Schmid, Wilhelm. 1887–97. *Der Atticismus in seinem Hauptvertretern: von Dionysius von Halikarnass bis auf den zweiten Philostratus.* Vol. 4. Stuttgart.

Swain, Simon. 1999. "Defending Hellenism: Philostratus, In Honour of Apollonius." In *Apologetics in the Roman Empire: Pagans, Jews and Christians*, ed. Mark Edwards, Martin Goodman, and Simon Price, 157–96. Oxford.

———, ed. 2007. *Seeing the Face, Seeing the Soul: Polemo's Physiognomy from Classical Antiquity to Medieval Islam.* Oxford.

———. 2009. "Culture and Nature in Philostratus." In Bowie and Elsner 2009, 33–46.

Sweet, Waldo E. 1987. *Sport and Recreation in Ancient Greece: A Sourcebook with Translations.* New York.

Tarrant, H. 2003. "Athletics, Competition and the Intellectual." In *Sport and Festival in the Ancient Greek*

World, ed. David Phillips and David Pritchard, 353–65. Swansea.

Tell, Hakan. 2007. "Sages at the Games: Intellectual Displays and Dissemination of Wisdom in Ancient Greece." *Classical Antiquity* 26: 249–75.

Van Hoof, Lieve. 2010. *Plutarch's Practical Ethics: The Social Dynamics of Philosophy*. Oxford.

Volckmar, C. H. 1862. *Flavii Philostrati de arte gymnastica libellus*. Aurich.

Whitmarsh, Tim. 2004. "Philostratus." In *Narrators, Narratees and Narratives in Ancient Greek Literature*, ed. Irene de Jong, René Nünlist, and Angus M. Bowie, 423–39. Leiden.

Wöhrle, Georg. 1990. *Studien zur Theorie der antiken Gesundheitslehre*. Stuttgart (*Hermes Einzelschriften* 56).

Woody, T. 1936. "Philostratus: *Concerning Gymnastics*." *The Research Quarterly of the American Physical Education Association* 2: 3–26.

Zingerle, J. 1936. "Zum Gymnastikos des Philostratos." *Sonderabdruck aus Wiener Studien* 8: 153–59.

OUTLINE OF THE
GYMNASTICUS

It is hard in any summary to do justice to the richness of
the work, which is full of opinionated authorial asides and
colorful anecdotes. It is hard also to convey its difficulty,
especially the abruptness of some of Philostratus' transi-
tions between different sections, and the oddity (at least
to modern eyes) of many of the explanations and instruc-
tions he chooses to include. Nevertheless a brief précis of
the text may be useful.

Chapters 1–2: Philostratus declares his conviction that
the art of athletic training (*gymnastikê*) is a type of wisdom
(*sophia*) rather than a craft. But he also argues that there
has been a degeneration in the art of training, which has
led to a decline in athletic ability among present-day ath-
letes, and declares his intention to correct that through
this treatise.

3–13: These chapters describe the origins of the main
athletic events—many of which are linked by Philostratus
with famous figures from Greek myth, or with the military
history of the classical Greek world—and the evolution
of the Olympic program. He deals in turn with the pen-
tathlon, the four running events—*dolichos* (long-distance
race), *stadion* (approximately 200 meters), *diaulos* (ap-

proximately 400 meters), and race in armor—then boxing, wrestling, and *pankration*.

14–16: Philostratus turns to the question of how *gymnastikê* is to be defined, stressing that it is a skill (*technê*) in its own right, which has some overlap both with the art of medicine and the practical instruction of the *paidotribês*, but which also stands independently of both.

17–24: The qualities the good trainer needs are discussed, with reference to a series of anecdotes from Olympic history. Philostratus stresses in particular the need for clever speech, which the trainer can use to encourage and inspire his athletes.

25–26: After a final summary of the need for skillful speech, Philostratus suggests that the trainer also needs a full understanding of the art of physiognomy, which will allow him to judge character from physical appearance, and an awareness of the ideal proportions of the athletic body.

27–30: Philostratus affirms the importance of parentage and discusses how to spot an athlete whose constitution is weak through having been born from aged parents; also discussed is the related question of how to spot illness in an athlete.

31–41: This section offers a detailed description of the best body types for the various different types of event, first pentathlon, then running events, then combat sports, followed by an account of some of the other common athletic body types.

42: This section summarizes Philostratus' views on the best mixture of humors and the best ways of training athletes with unbalanced humoral combinations.

43–47: The simple, austere training methods of the

heroic athletes of long ago are compared with the degenerate forms of training that have become common more recently, particularly the introduction of luxury and overeating, which have led in turn to cheating. Others make the mistake of training boy athletes as if they were men, and of using the "tetrad" system, which involves training athletes on a dangerously inflexible four-day cycle, with a different type of exercise on each day.

48–54: Philostratus provides information on how to spot athletes whose condition is damaged in some way—by overeating, excessive drinking, sex, wet dreams—and appropriate ways to train them. This is followed by further critique of the tetrad system through an anecdote about an athlete who turned up for training with a hangover, after celebrating an Olympic victory, and died because his trainer insisted on following the vigorous training methods prescribed for that particular day.

55–58: A range of other equipment and other techniques are discussed: jumping weights, different types of dust and their effects on the body, punching bags, and sunbathing. The text as it survives ends with Philostratus expressing his lack of interest in saunas, which he associates especially with Spartan types of training.

ΠΕΡΙ ΓΥΜΝΑΣΤΙΚΗΣ

1. Σοφίαν ἡγώμεθα καὶ τὰ τοιαῦτα μὲν οἷον φιλοσο-
φῆσαι καὶ εἰπεῖν ξὺν τέχνῃ ποιητικῆς τε ἄψασθαι καὶ
μουσικῆς καὶ γεωμετρίας καὶ νὴ Δί' ἀστρονομίας,
ὁπόση μὴ περιττή, σοφία δὲ καὶ τὸ κοσμῆσαι στρα-
τιὰν καὶ ἔτι τὰ τοιαῦτα· ἰατρικὴ πᾶσα καὶ ζωγραφία
καὶ πλάσται καὶ ἀγαλμάτων εἴδη καὶ κοῖλοι λίθοι καὶ
κοῖλος σίδηρος. βάναυσοι δὲ ὁπόσαι, δεδόσθω μὲν
αὐταῖς τέχνη, καθ' ἣν ὄργανόν τι καὶ σκεῦος ὀρθῶς
ἀποτελεσθήσεται, σοφία δὲ ἐς ἐκείνας ἀποκείσθω μό-
νας, ἃς εἶπον. ἐξαιρῶ κυβερνητικὴν τῶν βαναύσων,
ἐπειδὴ ἄστρων τε συνίησιν[1] καὶ ἀνέμων καὶ τῶν ἀδή-
λων ἅπτεται. ταῦτα μὲν ὦν ἕνεκά μοι εἴρηται, δειχθή-
σεται. περὶ δὲ γυμναστικῆς σοφίαν λέγομεν οὐδεμιᾶς
ἐλάττω τέχνης, ὥστε εἰς ὑπομνήματα ξυνθεῖναι τοῖς
βουλομένοις γυμνάζειν. ἡ μὲν γὰρ πάλαι γυμναστικὴ
Μίλωνας ἐποίει καὶ Ἱπποσθένας, Πουλυδάμαντάς τε

---

[1] συνίησιν Cobet: σύνεσιν P

---

[1] Wrestler from Croton; Olympic victor once in the boys' cat-
egory (540 BC) and five or six times as an adult (536–520 or 516);
renowned for his prodigious strength and his gluttony.

398

PHILOSTRATUS, *GYMNASTICUS*

1. Let us regard as types of wisdom, on the one hand, things like philosophy and skillful speech and engaging in poetry and music and geometry, and by Zeus astronomy, so long as it is not carried to excess. On the other hand, the organization of an army is a form of wisdom, and in addition things like the following: the whole of medicine and painting and modeling, and the various types of sculpting and gem cutting and metal engraving. As for the activities of craftsmen, let us accept that they require skill, by which tools and equipment can be correctly built, but let the label of wisdom be reserved only for those activities I have mentioned. I exempt the piloting of ships from the category of craftsmen's activities, since it requires understanding of the stars and the winds and concerns itself with things that are not evident to the senses. My reasons for saying all of this will become clear. As for athletic training, we assert that it is a form of wisdom, and one that is inferior to none of the other skills, which means that it can be summed up in treatise form for the benefit of those who wish to undertake training. For the old system of athletic training produced men like Milo[1] and Hipposthenes[2]

[2] Wrestler from Sparta; Olympic victor once in the boys' category (632 BC) and five times in the adult category (624–608).

καὶ Προμάχους[2] καὶ Γλαῦκον τὸν Δημύλου καὶ τοὺς
πρὸ τούτων ἔτι ἀθλητάς, τὸν Πηλέα δήπου καὶ τὸν
Θησέα καὶ τὸν Ἡρακλέα αὐτόν· ἡ δ' ἐπὶ τῶν πατέρων
ἥττους μὲν ἢ οἶδε,[3] θαυμασίους δὲ καὶ μεμνῆσθαι ἀξί-
ους· ἡ δὲ νῦν καθεστηκυῖα μεταβέβληκεν οὕτω τὰ τῶν
ἀθλητῶν, ὡς καὶ τοῖς φιλογυμναστοῦσι τοὺς πολλοὺς
ἄχθεσθαι.

2. Δοκεῖ δέ μοι διδάξαι μὲν τὰς αἰτίας δι' ἃς ὑπο-
δέδωκε ταῦτα, ξυμβαλέσθαι δὲ γυμνάζουσί τε καὶ
γυμναζομένοις ὁπόσα οἶδα, ἀπολογήσασθαί τε ὑπὲρ
τῆς φύσεως ἀκουούσης κακῶς, ἐπειδὴ παρὰ πολὺ τῶν
πάλαι οἱ νῦν ἀθληταί· λέοντάς τε γὰρ καὶ νῦν βόσκει
φαυλοτέρους οὐδέν, τῶν τε κυνῶν τε καὶ ἵππων καὶ
ταύρων ταὐτὸν χρῆμα, καὶ τὸ εἰς δένδρα δὲ αὐτῆς
ἧκον ἄμπελοί τε ὅμοιαι ἔτι καὶ συκῆς δῶρα, χρυσοῦ
τε καὶ ἀργύρου καὶ λίθων οὐδὲν παρήλλαξεν, ἀλλ' ὡς

---

[2] Προμάχους Daremberg: πρωτομάχους P
[3] ἢ οἶδε Kitriniari: οἶδε P, Jüthner

---

[3] Pancratiast from Thessaly; Olympic victor in 408; men-
tioned again below, chs. 22 and 43.
[4] Pancratiast from Pellene; Olympic victor in 404, defeating
Poulydamas, as described in ch. 22.
[5] Boxer from Carystus; Olympic victor in the boy's category
(date uncertain), as discussed further below, in chs. 20 and 43.
[6] Father of Achilles; on his athletic skill, see further below,
ch. 3.
[7] Theseus was particularly associated with wrestling, for ex-
ample in his defeat of Cercyon, who challenged travelers on the

and Poulydamas[3] and Promachus[4] and Glaucus[5] the son of
Demylus, and other athletes who were alive even before
these, like Peleus[6] and Theseus[7] and Heracles[8] himself.
The training of our fathers' time produced athletes who
were less impressive than these but nevertheless remark-
able and worthy of commemoration. But the kind of train-
ing that prevails today has so far changed the nature of
athletes that the majority of people are irritated even by
lovers of the gymnasium.[9]

2. I have decided to teach the causes of this degenera-
tion and to contribute for trainers and their subjects alike
everything I know, and to defend nature, which is criti-
cized because the athletes of today are inferior to those
of former times. For nature even today nourishes lions
that are not at all inferior, and dogs and horses and bulls
have the same qualities as they did before. As for her treat-
ment of trees, the vines are still the same and the gifts of
the fig tree, and she has made no change in the quality of
gold and silver and precious stones. Instead, nature pro-

road to Megara to wrestling matches and killed them; see Paus.
1.39.3 for that story and for the claim that Theseus was the inven-
tor of wrestling. He was also the legendary founder of the festivals
of the Panathenaia and the Isthmia and was often commemorated
by statues in gymnasia.

[8] Many of Heracles' labors involved hand-to-hand fighting.
He is said to have refounded the Olympic festival and to have won
the wrestling and *pankration* in that festival on the same day.
Many other athletic festivals were held in his honor, and statues
of Heracles were common in gymnasia.

[9] Philostratus seems to mean here nonspecialist enthusiasts,
rather than full-time competitive athletes.

αὐτὴ ἐνόμισε, τοῖς προτέροις ὅμοια φύει τὰ πάντα.
ἀθλητῶν δέ, ὁπόσαι περὶ αὐτοὺς ἦσάν ποτε ἀρεταί,
οὐχ ἡ φύσις ἀπηνέχθη—φέρει γὰρ δὴ ἔτι θυμοειδεῖς,
εὐειδεῖς, ἀγχίνους· φύσεως γὰρ ταῦτα—τὸ δὲ μὴ
ὑγιῶς γυμνάζεσθαι μηδὲ ἐρρωμένως ἐπιτηδεύειν
ἀφείλετο τὴν φύσιν τὸ ἑαυτῆς κράτος. καὶ ὅπως μὲν
ξυνέβη ταῦτα, δηλώσω ὕστερον· πρῶτον δὲ ἐπισκεψώ-
μεθα δρόμου αἰτίας καὶ πυγμῆς καὶ πάλης καὶ τῶν
τοιούτων καὶ ἐξ ὅτου ἤρξατο ἕκαστα καὶ ἀφ᾽ ὅτου.
παρακείσεται δὲ ἁπανταχοῦ τὰ Ἠλείων· δεῖ γὰρ περὶ
τὰ τοιαῦτα ἐκ τῶν ἀκριβεστάτων φράζειν.

3. Ἔστι τοίνυν ἀγωνίας ξυμπάσης τὰ μὲν κοῦφα
ταῦτα· στάδιον, δόλιχος, ὁπλῖται, δίαυλος· τὰ βαρύ-
τερα δὲ παγκράτιον, πάλη, πύκται. πένταθλος δὲ ἀμ-
φοῖν συνηρμόσθη· παλαῖσαι μὲν γὰρ καὶ δισκεῦσαι
βαρεῖς, τὸ δὲ ἀκοντίσαι καὶ πηδῆσαι καὶ δραμεῖν

10 Chs. 44–47.　11 Official records of the games, kept by
the city of Elis, which was responsible for the festival, are repeat-
edly mentioned by Pausanias (e.g., 3.21.1, 5.21.9, 6.2.3, 6.13.10).
The exact nature of these records is not clear, but they probably
included an Olympic victor list, which may well have provided
much of Philostratus' information in chs. 12–13, below. For de-
tailed discussion of the problem, see Jüthner (1909, 109–16).

12 The distinction between heavy and light events is a com-
mon feature of ancient writing on athletics; e.g., see Paus. 6.24.1.

13 Sprint race of one track length, approx. 200 meters; the
word is also used as English "stadium" and as a unit of mea-
surement (often translated as "stade") of 600 ancient feet.

14 Long-distance race; the exact distance is uncertain and may

duces all things the same as before, as she originally decreed. As far as athletes are concerned, and the virtues that were once associated with them, it is not nature who has abandoned them—for she still produces men who are spirited and well formed and quick witted; these are all natural attributes. Instead, it is the lack of healthy training and vigorous exercise that have deprived nature of her strength. How this happened, I will reveal later.[10] But first let us examine the origins of running and boxing and wrestling and things of that sort, looking at when and how each of them came into being. The records of the Eleans will be kept at hand in each case.[11] For it is important in such matters to make reference to the most accurate sources possible.

3. The light events, taking the whole of athletic competition into account, are these:[12] the *stadion*,[13] the *dolichos*,[14] the hoplite race[15] and the *diaulos*.[16] The heavy events are the *pankration*,[17] wrestling and boxing. The pentathlon was formed by combining the two: for wrestling and discus throwing are heavy events, while javelin throwing and jumping and running are light events. Be-

anyway have varied between festivals; possibly twenty-four track lengths (i.e., approx. 4,500 meters) at Olympia.

[15] Race in armor, usually of *diaulos* length (i.e., two track lengths), originally in full armor but later with just a shield; one possible exception is the hoplite race at the Eleutheria at Plataea, which seems to have been raced in full armor even in the Roman period; cf. ch. 8.

[16] Sprint race of two track lengths; the runners would turn around a turning post at the halfway point, at the end of the track.

[17] The third of the ancient combat events, together with wrestling and boxing, combining elements of both.

κοῦφοί εἰσι. πρὸ μὲν δὴ Ἰάσονος καὶ Πηλέως ἅλμα
ἐστεφανοῦτο ἰδίᾳ καὶ δίσκος ἰδίᾳ, καὶ τὸ ἀκόντιον
ἥρκει ἐς νίκην κατὰ τοὺς χρόνους οὓς ἡ Ἀργὼ ἔπλει·
Τελαμὼν μὲν κράτιστα ἐδίσκευε, Λυγκεὺς δὲ ἠκόντι-
ζεν, ἔτρεχον δὲ καὶ ἐπήδων οἱ ἐκ Βορέου, Πηλεὺς δὲ
ταῦτα μὲν ἦν δεύτερος, ἐκράτει δὲ ἁπάντων πάλῃ.
ὁπότ' οὖν ἠγωνίζοντο ἐν Λήμνῳ, φασὶν Ἰάσονα Πη-
λεῖ χαριζόμενον συνάψαι τὰ πέντε καὶ Πηλέα τὴν
νίκην οὕτω συλλέξασθαι πολεμικώτατόν τε νομισθῆ-
ναι τῶν ἐφ' ἑαυτοῦ διά τε τὴν ἀρετήν, ᾗ ἐχρῆτο εἰς
τὰς μάχας, διά τε τὴν εἰς τὰ πέντε ἐπιτήδευσιν οὕτω
πολεμικὴν οὖσαν ὡς καὶ ἀκοντίζειν ἐν τοῖς ἄθλοις.

4. Δολίχου δὲ αἰτία ἦν ἥδε· δρομοκήρυκες ἐξ Ἀρ-
καδίας ἐφοίτων εἰς τὴν Ἑλλάδα τῶν πολεμικῶν ἄγγε-
λοι καὶ ἀπείρητο αὐτοῖς μὴ ἱππεύειν, ἀλλ' αὐτουργοὺς
εἶναι τοῦ δρόμου. τὸ ἀεὶ οὖν ἐν βραχεῖ τῆς ἡμέρας
διαδραμεῖν στάδια ὁπόσα ὁ δόλιχος δρομοκήρυκας
εἰργάζετο καὶ ἐγύμναζε τῷ πολέμῳ.

5. Στάδιον δὲ ὧδε εὕρηται· θυσάντων Ἠλείων
ὁπόσα νομίζουσι, διέκειντο μὲν ἐπὶ τοῦ βωμοῦ τὰ

[18] Cf. Pind. *Isthm.* 1.26–27 for the claim that the pentathlon did not exist in the mythical age. [19] Calais and Zetes.

[20] For the tradition that the Argonauts competed in athletic contests during their stay with the female-only community on the island of Lemnos, see also Pind. *Ol.* 4.19–28 and *Pyth.* 4.253.

[21] The precise means by which victory was won in the ancient pentathlon is much debated: see Miller (2004, 73–74 for brief discussion, and 259 for extensive bibliography).

fore the time of Jason and Peleus the jump won a crown
on its own, as did the discus, and the javelin too was
enough for victory at the time when the Argo was sailing.[18]
Telamon was the strongest discus thrower, Lynceus the
best javelin thrower, the best jumpers and runners were
the sons of Boreas,[19] while Peleus was second best in these
events, but strongest of all in wrestling. Therefore, when
they held contests in Lemnos,[20] they say that Jason, in
order to please Peleus, joined the five events together and
that Peleus in this way accumulated victory[21] and gained
the reputation for being the most warlike of his contem-
poraries, not only because of his bravery in battle but also
because of his devotion to the pentathlon, which was so
warlike that the contests even included javelin throwing.

4. The origin of the *dolichos* was as follows: couriers
from Arcadia used to go backward and forward into the
rest of Greece as messengers on matters concerning war-
fare;[22] they were forbidden to use horses and instead were
made to depend on their own ability as runners. And so
the process of continually running, in the brief course of
every day, as many stades as are in the *dolichos* made them
into couriers, and trained them for war.[23]

5. The *stadion* was invented as follows: when the El-
eans had sacrificed in the accustomed way, the offerings

---

[22] Possibly a reference to the messengers from Elis (viewed
as part of Arcadia by some ancient authors; cf. Paus. 5.1.1), who
announced the Olympic truce (*ekecheiria*), i.e., the arrangement
that allowed spectators and athletes to travel to the games without
military interference.

[23] The whole of ch. 4 is quoted in Schol. Pl. *Prt.* 335e in order
to explain Socrates' use of the word ἡμεροδρόμος (day runner).

ἱερά, πῦρ δὲ αὐτοῖς οὔπω ἐνέκειτο. στάδιον δὲ οἱ δρο-
μεῖς ἀπεῖχον τοῦ βωμοῦ καὶ εἱστήκει πρὸ αὐτοῦ ἱε-
ρεὺς λαμπαδίῳ βραβεύων· καὶ ὁ νικῶν ἐμπυρίσας τὰ
ἱερὰ ὀλυμπιονίκης ἀπήει.

6. Ἐπεὶ δὲ Ἠλεῖοι θύσειαν, ἔδει μὲν καὶ τοὺς ἀπαν-
τῶντας Ἑλλήνων θύειν θεωρούς. ὡς δὲ μὴ ἀργῶς ἡ
πρόσοδος αὐτῶν γίγνοιτο, ἔτρεχον οἱ δρομεῖς ἀπὸ τοῦ
βωμοῦ στάδιον οἷον καλοῦντες τὸ Ἑλληνικὸν καὶ
πάλιν ἐς ταὐτὸν ὑπέστρεφον οἷον ἀγγέλλοντες, ὅτι
δὴ ἀφίξοιτο ἡ Ἑλλὰς χαίρουσα. ταῦτα μὲν οὖν περὶ
διαύλου ⟨αἰτίας.⟩

7. Δρόμοι[4] δὲ ὁπλῖται παλαιοὶ[5] μὲν καὶ μάλιστα οἱ
κατὰ Νεμέαν, οὓς ἐνόπλους τε καὶ ἱππίους ὀνομάζου-
σιν, ἀνάκεινται δὲ τοῖς ἀμφὶ Τυδέα τοῖς ἑπτά. ὁ δέ γε

---

[4] διαύλου ⟨αἰτίας.⟩ Δρόμοι Jüthner: διαύλου· οἱ ἄδρομοι P
[5] παλαιοὶ Jüthner: πολλοὶ P: ποικίλοι Kayser

---

[24] This etiology is not paralleled in any other ancient source.
[25] Throughout the history of the Olympic festival, the Eleans
would send envoys around the Greek world to announce the fes-
tival, and Greek cities would send envoys to the festival in turn to
offer sacrifice.   [26] Philostratus characteristically uses a num-
ber of different phrases for "Greece" and "the Greeks." In this
case, the phrase is *to hellenikon*, used by Hdt. 8.144 and fre-
quently by Philostratus elsewhere, often with overtones of cul-
tural as well as ethnic Hellenism; it is prominent especially in the
Lives of the Sophists (e.g., 2.3, 567; 2.10, 587; 2.27, 617; cf. VA
8.15), where he regularly describes the sophists speaking to as-
sembled audiences which stand for the whole of the Greek world:
see Introduction for further discussion.

were placed on the altar, but with no fire yet applied to them. The runners stood one stade away from the altar and a priest stood in front of it as umpire, holding a torch; and the winner of the race, having set fire to the offerings, went away as Olympic victor.[24]

6. When the Eleans had sacrificed, any envoys from the Greeks who were present were also required to make a sacrifice.[25] In order that their approach to the altar should not be without ceremony, runners ran away from the altar as if inviting the Greeks[26] to sacrifice, and then ran back again as if announcing that Greece would be glad to come. So much on the origin of the *diaulos*.[27]

7. Hoplite races are ancient events, especially the one in Nemea, which they call the "armor race" as well as the "horse race,"[28] and which is dedicated to Tydeus and the rest of the Seven.[29] By contrast the Olympic hoplite race,

[27] This etiology is not paralleled in any other ancient source.

[28] The distinction here seems to be one of length, the "armor" race being two stades, and the "horse" race four, i.e., the equivalent of two lengths of the hippodrome. See Paus. 6.16.4 for evidence that this latter length was used at both the Isthmian and Nemean games, although he seems to be talking about a race without armor.

[29] The Seven, the heroes who fought against Thebes, are said in many ancient accounts to have been the founders of the Nemean games, one of the four great festivals of the *periodos*, the others being the Olympic, Pythian, and Isthmian festivals. The usual story is that they were funeral games in honor of the boy Opheltes/Archemorus who had been killed by a snake; but other accounts suggest that the games were founded by Heracles to celebrate his defeat of the Nemean lion.

Ὀλυμπικὸς ὁπλίτης ὡς μὲν Ἠλεῖοί φασιν ἐτέθη διὰ
ταῦτα· πόλεμον Ἠλεῖοι Δυμαίοις ξυνῆψαν οὕτω τοι
ἀκήρυκτον, ὡς μηδὲ τὰ Ὀλύμπια ἀνοχὰς εἶναι· νικών-
των δ' αὐτῶν [Ἠλείων] κατὰ τὴν τῶν ἄθλων ἡμέραν
ὁπλίτης λέγεται τῶν ἀπὸ τῆς μάχης ἐσδραμεῖν εἰς τὸ
στάδιον εὐαγγέλια ἀπάγων τῆς νίκης. ταυτὶ δὲ πι-
θανὰ μέν, ἀκούω δ' αὐτὰ καὶ Δελφῶν, ἐπειδὴ πρὸς
ἐνίας τῶν Φωκίδων ἐπολέμησαν, καὶ Ἀργείων, ἐπειδὴ
πολέμῳ ξυνεχεῖ πρὸς Λακεδαιμονίους ἐτρίβοντο, καὶ
Κορινθίων, ἐπειδὴ καὶ ἐν αὐτῇ Πελοποννήσῳ καὶ
ὑπὲρ τὰ ὅρια τοῦ Ἰσθμοῦ ἐπολέμουν. ἐμοὶ δὲ ἕτερα
περὶ ὁπλίτου δοκεῖ· φημὶ γὰρ νενομίσθαι μὲν αὐτὸν
ἐκ πολεμικῆς αἰτίας, παριέναι <δ'> ἐς τοὺς ἀγῶνας
πολέμου ἀρχῆς ἕνεκα δηλούσης τῆς ἀσπίδος ὅτι πέ-
παυται μὲν ἐκεχειρία, δεῖ δὲ ὅπλων. εἰ δὲ μὴ ῥαθύμως
ἀκούεις τοῦ κήρυκος, ὁρᾷς ὡς ἐπὶ πάντων κηρύττει

30 The identity of this conflict is not clear; one candidate is the
war between Elis and the western cities of Greece recorded for
668 BC, but that is well before the date when the hoplite race is
said to have been added to the Olympic program; see ch. 13 on
the first hoplite race, in the 65th Olympiad, in 520 BC.

31 The athletic contests at Olympia were originally confined
to a single day, whereas by Philostratus' time they were distrib-
uted among the five days of the festival.

32 Probably a reference to the first Sacred War, which ended
in 586 BC and was followed by the foundation of the Pythian
festival in 582, which involved the addition of athletic contests to
the already existing musical competitions.

according to the Eleans, was included for the following reason. The Eleans embarked on a war with the people of Dyme,[30] a conflict so truceless that not even the Olympic festival brought any break in hostilities. When the Eleans were winning, on the day of the Olympic contests,[31] a hoplite from the battle is said to have run into the stadium, bringing the good news of victory. This explanation is plausible, but I have head the same story from the Delphians, about the time when they were at war with some of the cities of Phocis[32] and from the Argives, about the time when they were being worn down by constant warfare with the Spartans,[33] and from the Corinthians, about a time when they were fighting both in the Peloponnese itself, and also beyond the boundaries of the Isthmus.[34] But my opinion about the hoplite race is different, for I agree that it was invented originally for military reasons, but I believe that it is included in the contests as a reminder of the resumption of warfare, and that the shield signifies that the truce is over[35] and that weapons are necessary again.[36] If you listen to the herald carefully, you will notice that he announces to the assembled people that the

[33] Probably a reference to the conflict that led to Argos' defeat at the hands of Cleomenes in 494.

[34] The identity of this conflict is not clear.

[35] Cf. n. 22, above, on the Olympic truce; it was not, contrary to what Philostratus appears to suggest here, a suspension of all fighting in the Greek world.

[36] On the final place of the hoplite race in the Olympic program, cf. Plut. *Quaest. conv.* 2.5, 639e, who gives a similar explanation, and Paus. 3.14.3.

λήγειν μὲν τὸν τῶν ἄθλων ταμίαν ἀγῶνα, τὴν σάλ-
πιγγα δὲ τὰ τοῦ Ἐνυαλίου σημαίνειν προκαλουμένην
τοὺς νέους εἰς ὅπλα· κελεύει δὲ τουτὶ τὸ κήρυγμα καὶ
τοὔλαιον ἀραμένους ἐκποδών ποι φέρειν, οὐχ ὡς ἀλει-
φομένους, ἀλλ' ὡς πεπαυμένους τοῦ ἀλείφεσθαι.

8. Ἄριστος δὲ ὁ κατὰ Βοιωτίαν καὶ Πλάταιαν ὁπλί-
της ἐνομίζετο διά τε τὸ μῆκος τοῦ δρόμου διά τε τὴν
ὅπλισιν ποδήρη οὖσαν καὶ σκεπάζουσαν τὸν ἀθλη-
τήν, ὡς ἂν εἰ καὶ μάχοιτο, διά τε τὸ ἐπ' ἔργῳ λαμπρῷ
κεῖσθαι τῷ Μηδικῷ διά τε τὸ νομίσαι ταῦτα Ἕλλη-
νας κατὰ βαρβάρων καὶ μὴν καὶ διὰ τὸν νόμον τὸν
ἐπὶ τοῖς ἀγωνιουμένοις κείμενον, <ὃν ἔθετο πάλαι ἡ>
Πλάταια.⁶ τὸν γὰρ ἤδη παρ' αὐτοῖς ἐστεφανωμένον,
εἰ ἀγωνίζοιτο αὖθις, ἐγγυητὰς ἔδει καταστῆσαι τοῦ
σώματος· θάνατος γὰρ ἡττωμένῳ προσετέτακτο.

9. Πυγμὴ δὲ Λακωνικὸν εὕρημα καὶ εἰς Βέβρυκάς
ποτε βαρβάρους ἦλθεν ἄριστά τε αὐτῇ Πολυδεύκης

---

⁶ Suppl. Jüthner: [..........] Πλάται[.] P

---

37 These sentences seems to paraphrase the traditional her-
ald's announcement at the end of the games; the phrase "the
dispenser of prizes" seems to be a direct quotation.

38 I.e., Ares, the god of war.

39 It was standard practice to rub oneself with olive oil before
athletic activity; the phrase οἱ ἀλειφόμενοι (those who anoint
themselves) came to be used regularly, as in this passage, to de-
scribe those engaged in athletic training.

contest, the dispenser of prizes,[37] is coming to an end, and that the trumpet is giving the signal of Enyalius,[38] calling the young men to take up arms. This announcement also orders them to pick up the oil and take it away, acting not as people who anoint themselves,[39] but as people who have ceased to do so.

8. The best of the hoplite races was thought to be the one in Plataea in Boeotia because of the length of the race[40] and because of the armor, which stretches down to the feet covering the athlete completely, as if he were actually fighting; also because it was founded to celebrate a distinguished deed, their victory against the Persians,[41] and because the Greeks devised it as a slight against the barbarians; and especially because of the rule concerning competitors that Plataea long ago enacted: that any competitor who had already won victory there, if he competed again, had to provide guarantors for his body; for death had been decreed for anyone defeated in that circumstance.[42]

9. Boxing is a Spartan invention. It was adopted at some stage by the barbarian Bebrycians. Polydeuces was best at

[40] The length of the race in Plataea (presumably at least as long as the four stades attested for Nemea; cf. n. 28, above) is given neither by Philostratus nor by any other ancient source.

[41] The festival in question is the Eleutheria at Plataea, founded to commemorate the defeat of the Persians there in 479 BC and held every four years; cf. Paus. 9.2.6 on the prominence of the Eleutheria, and of its armor race, into the Roman Empire.

[42] This rule is not attested by other authors; but see also ch. 24, which implies that the guarantor himself risks execution if the athlete loses, or perhaps if the athlete absconds in order to avoid punishment after losing.

ἐχρῆτο, ὅθεν οἱ ποιηταὶ αὐτὸν ἐκ τούτων ᾖδον. ἐπύκτευον δὲ οἱ ἀρχαῖοι Λακεδαιμόνιοι διὰ τάδε· κράνη Λακεδαιμονίοις οὐκ ἦν οὐδ᾽ ἐγχώριον ἡγοῦντο τὴν ὑπ᾽ αὐτοῖς μάχην, ἀλλ᾽ ἦν ἀσπὶς ἀντὶ κράνους τῷ μετ᾽ ἐπιστήμης φέροντι. ὡς οὖν φυλάττοιντο μὲν τὰς κατὰ τοῦ προσώπου πληγάς, πληττόμενοι δὲ ἀνέχοιντο, πυγμὴν ἐπήσκησαν καὶ τὰ πρόσωπα οὕτως ἐξεγυμνάζοντο. προϊόντες δὲ μεθῆκαν τὸ πυκτεύειν καὶ τὸ παγκρατιάζειν ὁμοίως, αἰσχρὸν ἡγούμενοι διαγωνίζεσθαι ταῦτα, ἐν οἷς ἔστιν ἑνὸς ἀπειπόντος διαβεβλῆσθαι τὴν Σπάρτην ὡς μὴ εὔψυχον.

10. Ὥπλιστο δὲ ἡ ἀρχαία πυγμὴ τὸν τρόπον τοῦτον· εἰς στρόφιον οἱ τέτταρες τῶν δακτύλων ἐνεβιβάζοντο καὶ ὑπερέβαλλον τοῦ στροφίου τοσοῦτον, ὅσον εἰ συνάγοιντο πὺξ εἶναι, ξυνείχοντο δὲ ὑπὸ σειρᾶς, ἣν καθάπερ ἔρεισμα ἐβέβλητο ἐκ τοῦ πήχεος. νυνὶ δὲ αὖ μεθέστηκε· ῥινοὺς γὰρ πιοτάτων βοῶν δέψοντες⁷ ἱμάντα ἐργάζονται πυκτικὸν ὀξὺν καὶ προεμβάλλοντα, ὁ δέ γε ἀντίχειρ οὐ ξυλλαμβάνει τοῖς

⁷ δέψοντες Cobet: ἔψοντες P, Sʳ

43 E.g., see Hom. *Il.* 3.237 and *Od.* 11.300 for the phrase πὺξ ἀγαθὸν Πολυδεύκεα. Polydeukes was famous above all for his defeat of the Bebrycian king Amycus, hence Philostratus' reference to the Bebrycians (from Bithynia); e.g., see Theoc. 22.1–134; Ap. Rhod. *Argon.* 2.1–97.

44 This claim is not paralleled in any other ancient source.

it, which is why the poets celebrate him for that accomplishment.[43] The ancient Spartans used to box for this reason: they did not have helmets nor did they think that fighting beneath helmets was appropriate for their country;[44] instead a shield could serve in place of a helmet for anyone who used it with skill. Therefore in order that they might protect themselves from blows to the face and endure when struck, they practiced boxing and trained their faces in that manner. In time, however, they abandoned boxing and likewise the *pankration*,[45] believing that it was disgraceful to compete in these events, in which it is possible, through just one person admitting defeat, for the whole of Sparta to be reproached for lack of courage.

10. The ancient style of boxing used the following equipment. The four fingers were wrapped in a band, and projected beyond the band far enough to be formed into a fist when clenched together.[46] They were then held together in a fist shape by a strap, which the athletes attached to the forearm as a support. Now, however, the equipment has changed. For these days they knead the hide of the fattest cows in order to make a sharp, projecting boxing glove; and the thumb does not join the fingers

[45] The Spartan ban on boxing and *pankration* (cf. *Gym.* 58, below) seems to have applied to competition only, not to training. It is elsewhere ascribed to Lycurgus, on the grounds that these were the only two events in which it was possible for a defeated competitor to give a signal acknowledging his defeat, e.g., Plut. *Lyc.* 19.

[46] This seems to have been a soft band, often perhaps made of soft leather (cf. Paus. 8.40.3), in contrast with the hardened leather boxing gloves described below.

δακτύλοις τοῦ πλήττειν ὑπὲρ συμμετρίας τῶν τραυ-
μάτων, ὡς μὴ πᾶσα ἡ χεὶρ μάχοιτο. ὅθεν τοὺς ἱμάν-
τας τοὺς ἀπὸ τῶν συῶν ἐκκρίνουσι τῶν σταδίων ὀδυ-
νηρὰς ἡγούμενοι τὰς ἀπ' αὐτῶν πληγὰς καὶ δυσιάτους.

11. Πάλη δὲ καὶ παγκράτιον ὡς ἐς τὸ πρόσφορον
τῷ πολέμῳ εὕρηται, πρῶτον μὲν δηλοῖ τὸ Μαραθῶνι
ἔργον διαπολεμηθὲν οὕτως Ἀθηναίοις, ὡς ἀγχοῦ πά-
λης φαίνεσθαι [προσόντος πολέμου τῷ ἔργῳ],[8] δεύτε-
ρον δὲ τὸ ἐν Θερμοπύλαις, ὅτε Λακεδαιμόνιοι κλα-
σθέντων αὐτοῖς ξιφῶν τε καὶ δοράτων πολλὰ ταῖς
χερσὶ γυμναῖς ἔπραξαν. ὁπόσα τέ ἐστιν ἐν ἀγωνίᾳ
προτετίμηται πάντων τὸ παγκράτιον καίτοι συγκείμε-
νον ἐξ ἀτελοῦς πάλης καὶ ἀτελοῦς πυγμῆς· προτετί-
μηται δὲ παρ' ἑτέροις, ὡς Ἠλεῖοί γε τὴν πάλην καρ-
τερὰν νενομίκασι καὶ ἀλεγεινὴν κατὰ τοὺς ποιητὰς οὐ
μόνον ἐπὶ ταῖς διαπλοκαῖς τῶν παλαισμάτων, αἷς δεῖ
τοῦ σώματος ὑγροῦ καὶ εὐκόλου, ἀλλὰ καὶ τῷ παρ'
αὐτοῖς ἀγωνίζεσθαι τρίς, ἐπεὶ δεῖ τοσούτων διαπτω-
μάτων. παγκράτιον γοῦν καὶ πυγμὴν [καὶ πάλην][9]

8 Del. Jüthner
9 Del. Cobet

47 The precise design of Greek boxing gloves, and their devel-
opment over time, is much debated; see Poliakoff (1986, 68–79)
and Miller (2004, 51–52) for detailed discussion.
48 For close-quarters fighting against the Persians at the battle
of Marathon (490 BC), see Hdt. 6.112–13; but I know of no an-

in striking, in order to avoid excessive wounding, and so that the whole hand should not be involved in fighting.[47] For this reason too they ban from the stadium boxing gloves made from pigs, thinking that blows from these are painful and hard to heal.

11. That wrestling and *pankration* were devised for their usefulness for warfare is clear first of all from the achievement at Marathon,[48] where the battle was fought by the Athenians in such a way that it seemed almost like a wrestling contest, and secondly from the events at Thermopylae, where the Spartans, when their swords and spears were broken, accomplished much with their bare hands.[49] Of all the contests the *pankration* is the most highly respected, even though it is a combination of imperfect wrestling with imperfect boxing. Or at any rate it is honored most highly among all but the Eleans, who consider wrestling to be a test of strength and, as the poets put it, "grievous":[50] not only because of the twisting involved in wrestling holds, which need a supple and agile body, but also because it is necessary for wrestlers at Olympia to compete three times, since that is the number of falls one needs for victory.[51] They think it is a terrible

cient parallel for Philostratus' comparison of the fighting with wrestling.

[49] For the broken spears and the use of hands in battle at Thermopylae (480 BC), see Hdt. 7.224–25.

[50] A reference to Hom. *Il.* 23.701 (the same word is used for boxing at 23.653) and *Od.* 8.126.

[51] Philostratus is characteristically imprecise: three is the minimum number of rounds, five the maximum.

PHILOSTRATUS

ἀκονιτὶ στεφανοῦν δεινὸν ἡγούμενοι τὸν παλαιστὴν
οὐκ ἀπελαύνουσιν, ἐπειδὴ ὁ νόμος τὴν τοιάνδε νίκην
μόνῃ ξυγχωρεῖν φησι τῇ γυρᾷ καὶ ταλαιπώρῳ πάλῃ.
καὶ σαφὴς ἔμοιγ᾽ οὖν ἡ αἰτία, δι᾽ ἣν ὁ νόμος οὕτω
προστάττει· τοῦ γὰρ δὴ ἀγωνίσασθαι ἐν Ὀλυμπίᾳ
δεινοῦ ὄντος χαλεπώτερον ἔτι τὸ γυμνάζεσθαι δοκεῖ.
τὰ μὲν οὖν τῶν κούφων γυμνάσεται ὁ δολιχοδρόμος
ὀκτώ που ἢ δέκα στάδια καὶ ὁ πένταθλος τὸ δεῖν᾽ ἀπὸ
τῶν κούφων,¹⁰ οἱ δρομεῖς δίαυλον ἢ στάδιον ἢ ἄμφω
ἀπὸ τῶν τριῶν. χαλεπὸν ἀπὸ τῶν τοιούτων οὐδέν· ὁ
γὰρ τρόπος τῶν κούφων γυμνασίων ὁ αὐτός, ἤν τε
Ἠλεῖοι γυμνάζωσιν, ἤν τε ἕτεροι· ὁ δὲ βαρύτερος
ἀθλητὴς γυμνάζεται μὲν ὑπὸ Ἠλείων κατὰ τὴν ὥραν
τοῦ ἔτους, ὅτε μάλιστα ὁ ἥλιος τὴν ἰλὺν¹¹ ἐν κοίλῃ
Ἀρκαδίᾳ αἴθει, κόνιν δὲ ἀνέχεται θερμοτέραν τῆς

¹⁰ κούφων Jüthner: αὐτῶν P ¹¹ ἰλὺν Daremberg: ὕλην P

---

52 Victory without contest (literally, "without dust": ἀκονιτί)
occurred when all the other competitors withdrew or when no
other competitors entered the contest; victories of this type are
listed regularly on inscriptions celebrating athletic victory in all
the combat events. There are several recorded exceptions to the
rule Philostratus states here, i.e., cases where victory without
contest seems to have been awarded in other events at Olympia;
e.g., see Paus. 5.21.14 (a boxer) and 6.11.4 (a pankratiast).
53 Like other major festivals, the Olympic festival had its own
laws; e.g., see Paus. 6.24.3 on the building in Elis where the
Olympic judges (hellanodikai) were instructed in their duties by
the guardians of the law (nomophylakes) for ten months before

416

thing for a crown to be awarded without a contest[52] in the case of *pankration* and boxing, but they do not rule it out for the wrestler; for their law[53] explicitly allows that kind of victory only for curved[54] and misery-causing wrestling. It is clear to me why the law prescribes this: for even though competing in Olympia is a fearful matter, the training seems even harder.[55] In the light events, the *dolichos* runner will train by running eight or ten stades, the pentathlete will practice one or other of the light events, those runners who specialize in the other three running events together[56] will train by running the *diaulos* or *stadion* or both. There is nothing difficult in such exercises. For the training techniques for the light events are the same whether the Eleans are in charge of the training or others. But the heavy athlete is trained by the Eleans at the time of year[57] when the sun most of all burns the mud in the lowlands of Arcadia, and he must endure dust hotter than

the festival. For other mentions of the laws in this text, see chs. 12 and 55 (on rules for particular events), 17 (on rules governing the behavior of the athletes' trainers), and 25 (on eligibility to compete).   [54] Probably a reference to the hunched, forward-leaning posture of ancient wrestlers; perhaps also to the curving and intertwining of limbs in combat.   [55] Competitors at Olympia were required to arrive in Elis at least a month before the festival in order to undergo a period of official training (e.g., see ch. 54; Paus. 6.23.1) and to swear an oath that they had been in training for at least ten months (see Paus. 5.24.9).

[56] For athletes who compete in all three of the shorter running events—hoplite race, *stadion*, and *diaulos*—see ch. 33.

[57] The Olympic festival took place at the second full moon after the summer solstice, so this training period was always some time between early July and early September.

Αἰθιόπων ψάμμου, καρτερεῖ δὲ ἐκ μεσημβρίας ἀρξά-
μενος. καὶ τούτων οὕτω ταλαιπώρων ὄντων τὸ ἐπιπο-
νώτατον οἱ παλαισταί εἰσιν· ὁ μὲν γὰρ πύκτης, ἐπει-
δὰν ὁ τοῦ σταδίου καιρὸς ἥκῃ, τρωθήσεται καὶ τρώσει
καὶ προσβήσεται ταῖς κνήμαις, γυμναζόμενος δὲ
σκιὰν τῆς ἀγωνίας ἐπιδείξεται, καὶ ὁ παγκρατιαστὴς
ἀγωνιεῖται μὲν πάντα τρόπον, ὁπόσοι ἐν τῷ παγκρα-
τίῳ εἰσί, γυμνάσεται δὲ ἄλλοτε [καὶ] ἄλλῳ, πάλη δὲ
ταὐτὸν μὲν ἐν προάγωνι, ταὐτὸν δὲ καὶ ἐν ἀγῶνι· παρ-
έχεται γὰρ ἑκατέρα πεῖραν, ὁπόσα οἶδε καὶ ὁπόσα
δύναται, γυρά τε εἰκότως εἴρηται· γυρὸν γὰρ πάλης
καὶ τὸ ὀρθόν. ὅθεν Ἠλεῖοι στεφανοῦσι τὸ γυμναστι-
κώτατον κἀκ μόνου τοῦ γεγυμνάσθαι.¹²

12. Παρελθεῖν δὲ ταῦτα οὐχ ὁμοῦ πάντα ⟨φασὶν⟩
ἐς τοὺς ἀγῶνας, ἐπ' ἄλλῳ δὲ ἄλλο εὑρισκόμενόν τε
ὑπὸ τῆς γυμναστικῆς καὶ ἀποτελούμενον. ἦν μὲν γὰρ
πάλαι Ὀλύμπια εἰς τὴν τρίτην ἐπὶ δέκα Ὀλυμπιάδα

¹² κἀκ μόνου τοῦ Kayser, Kitriniari: καὶ μόνον το Jüthner:
καὶ μόνου τοῦ P

58 According to Paus. 6.24.1, the trainers worked with the light
athletes in the morning and the heavy athletes in the afternoon.
59 It does seem to be the case that kicking was allowed in
ancient boxing, but its infrequent attestation suggests that it was
viewed as a relatively marginal feature; cf. ch. 34 and occasional
references in other sources, e.g., Euseb. *Praep. evang.* 5.34.
60 Either a reference to shadowboxing, which is attested else-
where, or to practice combat against training partners, with softer
coverings for the hands than those used in competition; cf. Paus.
6.23.4.

Ethiopian sand, holding out from midday onward.[58] Of all these misery-causing exercises the most strenuous are those practiced by the wrestlers. For the boxer, whenever the time to compete in the stadium arrives, will be wounded and will wound in turn, and will kick against his opponent's shins,[59] but in training will perform only a shadow of real competition;[60] the pankratiast will compete with all the techniques associated with the *pankration*, but in training he will practice sometimes one and sometimes another. But wrestling is the same both in the precontest training and in competition. For each of them gives a test of how much a man knows and of his ability, and wrestling is rightly described as "curved"; for even the upright variety of wrestling is "curved."[61] For that reason the Eleans award the crown to this most training-intensive discipline even for training alone.

12. It is said that these events were not brought into the contests all at the same time but one after another, as they were invented and perfected by the art of athletic training. For the ancient Olympic festival, up to the thirteenth Olympiad,[62] consisted of the *stadion* only, and

---

[61] A reference to the two different possible phases of a wrestling bout, which would characteristically start with "upright" combat and then move to "rolling" combat, on the ground; see Poliakoff (1986, 20–27) on the latter.   [62] 728 BC. For the most part, Philostratus' list of victors in this chapter and the one following agrees with our other sources (e.g., Julius Africanus and Pausanias) although with some minor discrepancies, including omission of the boys' wrestling and misdating of the introduction of the boys' *stadion*: both of those events were introduced in the 37th Olympiad, in 632 BC, according to our other sources; see Christesen (2007, 209–10 and table 13).

σταδίου μόνου καὶ ἐνίκων ἐν αὐτοῖς Ἠλεῖοι τρεῖς,
ἑπτὰ Μεσσήνιοι, Κορίνθιος, Δυμαῖος, Κλεωναῖος, ἄλ-
λος ἄλλην Ὀλυμπιάδα, δύο δὲ οὐδεὶς ὁ αὐτός. ἐπὶ δὲ
τῆς τετάρτης ἐπὶ δέκα δίαυλος μὲν ἤρξατο, Ὑπήνου
δὲ ἐγένετο Ἠλείου ἡ ἐπ' αὐτῷ νίκη. μετ' ἐκείνην δολί-
χου ἀγὼν καὶ ἐνίκα Σπαρτιάτης Ἄκανθος. ἀνδρῶν δὲ
πένταθλον καὶ ἀνδρῶν πάλην ἤσκησεν ἡ ὀγδόη ἐπὶ
δέκα Ὀλυμπιάς, ἐνίκα δὲ πάλην μὲν Εὐρύβατος Λου-
σιεύς, τὰ δὲ πέντε Λάμπις Λάκων· εἰσὶ δ' οἳ καὶ τὸν
Εὐρύβατον Σπαρτιάτην γράφουσιν. ἡ δὲ τρίτη καὶ
εἰκοστὴ Ὀλυμπιὰς ἄνδρα ἤδη ἐκάλει πύκτην καὶ κρα-
τίστως ὁ Σμυρναῖος Ὀνόμαστος πυκτεύσας ἐνίκησεν
ἐπιγράψας τὴν Σμύρναν ἔργῳ καλῷ· ὁπόσαι γὰρ πό-
λεις Ἰωνικαί τε καὶ Λύδιοι, ὅσαι καθ' Ἑλλήσποντόν
τε καὶ Φρυγίαν, καὶ ὁπόσα ἔθνη ἀνθρώπων ἐν Ἀσίᾳ
εἰσί, ταῦτα ὁμοῦ ξύμπαντα ἡ Σμύρνα ὑπερεβάλετο
καὶ στεφάνου Ὀλυμπικοῦ πρώτη ἔτυχε· καὶ νόμους
ἔγραψεν ὁ ἀθλητὴς οὗτος πυκτικούς, οἷς ἐχρῶντο οἱ
Ἠλεῖοι διὰ σοφίαν τοῦ πύκτου, καὶ οὐκ ἤχθοντο οἱ
Ἀρκάδες, εἰ νόμους ἔγραψέ τις αὐτοῖς ἐναγωνίους ἐξ
Ἰωνίας ἥκων τῆς ἁβρᾶς. κατὰ δὲ τὴν τρίτην καὶ τρι-
ακοστὴν Ὀλυμπιάδα παγκράτιον μὲν ἐτέθη μήπω
τεθέν, Λύγδαμις δὲ ἐνίκα Συρακούσιος. μέγας δὲ οὕτω
τις ὁ Σικελιώτης ἦν, ὡς τὸν πόδα ἰσόπηχυν εἶναι· τὸ

three Eleans won victory in it, seven Messenians, and one each from Corinth and Dyme and Cleonae; each of them in a different Olympiad, none of them twice. In the fourteenth Olympiad,[63] the *diaulos* was introduced, and victory in that event was won by Hypenus from Elis. At the next Olympiad came the *dolichos* event, won by the Spartan Acanthus.[64] The eighteenth Olympiad[65] introduced the men's pentathlon and the men's wrestling; Eurybatus from Lousoi won the wrestling, and Lampis from Sparta the pentathlon, although there are some who record that Eurybatus was a Spartan. The 23rd Olympiad[66] then summoned competitors in the men's boxing, and Onomastus from Smyrna won the victory, having boxed most strongly, so linking the name of Smyrna with a glorious deed. For all the cities of Ionia and Lydia, all the cities along the Hellespont and in Phrygia, all the races of men in Asia, Smyrna surpassed all of these together and was the first to win an Olympic crown.[67] And this athlete wrote down rules for boxing, which the Eleans adopted because of the boxer's wisdom, and the Arcadians were not upset by the fact that someone from the luxurious land of Ionia had written down for them rules of competition. In the 33rd Olympiad[68] the *pankration* was introduced, not having been included before, and Lygdamis from Syracuse was the victor. This Sicilian was so big that his feet were a cubit in length; at any rate he is said to have measured out

---

[63] 724 BC   [64] 720 BC

[65] 708 BC   [66] 688 BC

[67] Philostratus refers here to the fact that Onomastus was the first Olympic victor from outside the Greek mainland.

[68] 648 BC

γοῦν στάδιον ἀναμετρῆσαι λέγεται τοσούτοις ἑαυτοῦ
ποσίν, ὅσοι τοῦ σταδίου πήχεις νομίζονται.

13. Φασὶ καὶ παίδων πένταθλον παρελθεῖν ἐκεῖ
κατὰ τὴν ὀγδόην καὶ τριακοστήν, ὅτε νικῆσαι μὲν
Εὐτελίδαν[13] Λακεδαιμόνιον, τὴν δὲ ἰδέαν ταύτην μη-
κέτι ἀγωνίσασθαι παῖδα ἐν Ὀλυμπίᾳ. ὁ δὲ νικήσας
τὸ τῶν παίδων στάδιον κατὰ τὴν ἕκτην καὶ τεσσαρα-
κοστὴν Ὀλυμπιάδα—τότε γὰρ πρῶτον ἐτέθη—παῖς
ἦν αἰπόλος Πολυμήστωρ ὁ Μιλήσιος, ὃς τῇ ῥύμῃ τῶν
ποδῶν λαγὼν ἔφθανε. πυγμὴν δὲ παίδων οἱ μέν φα-
σιν ἐπὶ τῆς πρώτης καὶ τεσσαρακοστῆς ἄρξασθαι
καὶ Φ<ιλύταν Συ>βαρίτην[14] νενικηκέναι, οἱ δὲ ἐπὶ τῆς
ἑξηκοστῆς λέγουσιν, ἐνίκα δὲ <κατ' αὐτοὺς Λεο->
κρέων[15] ἐκ Κέω τῆς νήσου. Δαμάρετος[16] δὲ κατὰ τὴν
ἑξηκοστὴν πέμπτην πρῶτος ὁπλίτου λέγεται τυχεῖν
Ἡραεύς,[17] οἶμαι, ὧν. ἑκατοστῇ καὶ τεσσαρακοστῇ καὶ
πέμπτῃ Ὀλυμπιάδι παιδὸς παγκρατιαστοῦ ἐπέγρα-
ψαν <ἀγῶνα>[18] οὐκ οἶδα ἐξ ὅτου βραδέως αὐτὸν νομί-
σαντες[19] εὐδοκιμοῦντα ἤδη παρ' ἑτέροις· ὀψὲ γὰρ τῶν
Ὀλυμπιάδων Αἰγύπτου ἤδη στεφανουμένης ἤρξατο,
κἀκείνη τε ἡ νίκη Αἰγυπτία ἐγένετο· Ναύκρατις οὖν

13 Εὐτελίδαν Daremberg: εὐτέαδα P
14 Suppl. Jüthner: φ[.......]βαρίτην P
15 Suppl. Jüthner: κ[.........]κρεων P
16 Δαμάρετος Cobet: δαμάρητος P
17 Ἡραεύς Jüthner: κραεύς P
18 Suppl. Cobet
19 νομίσαντες Volckmar: νοήσαντος P

the stadium, with as many of his own foot lengths as there are thought to be cubits in the stadium.[69]

13. They also say that the boys' pentathlon competition was included there in the 38th Olympiad,[70] when it was won by the Spartan Eutelidas, but that no boy competed in this type of contest again at Olympia after that.[71] The victor of the boys' *stadion* in the 46th Olympiad[72]—for that is when it was first introduced—was the young goat-herd Polymestor from Miletus, who could run faster than hares by the speed of his feet. Some say that the boys' boxing began at the 41st Olympiad,[73] and that Philytas from Sybaris was the victor, others that it began at the 60th,[74] and that it was won by Leocreon from the island of Ceos. Damaretus, who was, I think, from Heraia, is said to have been the first to win the race in armor, in the 65th Olympiad.[75] In the 145th Olympiad they introduced the event of the boys' *pankration*. I do not know why they took so long to adopt it when it was already highly esteemed elsewhere; for it began late in the series of Olympiads, after the time when Egyptians first began to be crowned as victors, and that victory was itself an Egyptian one; and so Naucratis was proclaimed the victorious city, with the

[69] The length of the stadium was 600 feet, or 400 cubits (one cubit = 1.5 feet). The more plausible account of Julius Africanus puts Lygdamis' foot length at one foot (i.e., 32 centimeters) rather than at one cubit (48 centimeters) and suggests that he paced out the Olympic stadium with 600 of his foot lengths rather than with 400. See Gell. *NA* 1.1.2 for the same anecdote told of Heracles.   [70] 628 BC   [71] Cf. Paus. 5.9.1 and 6.15.8.

[72] 596 BC   [73] 616 BC
[74] 540 BC   [75] 520 BC

ἀνερρήθη νικῶντος Αἰγυπτίου Φαιδίμου. ταῦτα οὐκ
ἄν μοι δοκεῖ καθ' ἓν οὑτωσὶ παρελθεῖν εἰς ἀγῶνας,
οὐδ' ἂν σπουδασθῆναί ποτε Ἠλείοις καὶ Ἕλλησι πᾶ-
σιν, εἰ μὴ γυμναστικὴ ἐπεδίδου καὶ ἤσκει αὐτά· καὶ
γὰρ αὗται τῶν ἀθλητῶν αἱ νῖκαι καὶ τοῖς γυμνα-
σταῖς—οὐ μεῖον ἢ τοῖς ἀθληταῖς—πρόσκεινται.

14. Τί οὖν χρὴ περὶ γυμναστικῆς γινώσκειν; τί δ'
ἄλλο ἢ σοφίαν αὐτὴν ἡγεῖσθαι ξυγκειμένην μὲν ἐξ
ἰατρικῆς τε καὶ παιδοτριβικῆς, οὖσαν δὲ τῆς μὲν τε-
λεωτέραν, τῆς δὲ μόριον. ὁπόσον δὲ ἀμφοῖν μετέσχη-
κεν, ἐγὼ δηλώσω. παλαισμάτων εἴδη ὁπόσα ἐστί,
δηλώσει ὁ παιδοτρίβης καιρούς τε ὑποτιθέμενος καὶ
ὁρμὰς καὶ μέτρα καὶ ὅπως ἄν τις ἢ φυλάττοιτο ἢ
φυλαττομένου κρατοίη, διδάξει δὲ καὶ ὁ γυμναστὴς
εἰδότα μήπω τὸν ἀθλητὴν ταῦτα. ἀλλ' ἔστιν ὅπου
μεταχειρίσασθαι δεῖ πάλην ἢ παγκράτιον ἢ καὶ πλε-
ονέκτημα ὑπάρχον ἀντιπάλων διαφυγεῖν ἢ ἐκκροῦ-
σαι, ὧν οὐδὲν ἂν εἰς ἐπίνοιαν ἥει τῷ γυμναστῇ μὴ καὶ
τὰ τῶν παιδοτριβῶν εἰδότι. κατὰ μὲν τοῦτο δὴ ἴσαι
αἱ τέχναι· χυμοὺς δὲ ἀποκαθῆραι καὶ τὰ περιττὰ ἀφε-
λεῖν καὶ λεᾶναι τὰ κατεσκληκότα καὶ πιᾶναί τι ἢ
μεταβαλεῖν ἢ θάλψαι αὐτῶν γυμνασταῖς ἐν σοφίᾳ.

76 Probably a reference to good timing (*kairos*) in the choice
of particular moves in a wrestling bout (cf. ch. 57 on boxing; Paus.
5.14.9 for the altar in honor of *Kairos* near to the entrance to the
stadium at Olympia) rather than to the need for good timing in
the choice of what type of training to do when, although the word
is often used for that latter challenge as well.

victory going to the Egyptian Phaidimus. It seems to me that these events would not have been introduced in this way, one at a time, nor would they have won the enthusiasm of the Eleans and all the Greeks, if the art of athletic training had not undergone improvement, and if it had not trained them. For these victories obtained by the athletes also belong—no less than to the athletes themselves—to the trainers.

14. What, then, should one think about the art of athletic training? What else except to believe that it is a type of wisdom combining both the art of medicine and the art of the *paidotribês*; it is more comprehensive than the latter, and a part of the former. I will show now to what extent it partakes of each. The *paidotribês* will demonstrate all the different types of wrestling move, giving instruction in good timing,[76] in the degree of force to be used, in the limits to be observed in training, and in how one can defend oneself or defeat an opponent who is defending himself, and the trainer (*gymnastês*) too will teach these things to an athlete who does not yet know them. But there are times when it is necessary to turn one's hand to wrestling or the *pankration*, or to the question of how to evade or parry the advantage held by one's opponents, none of which the trainer would be aware of if he did not also know the skills of the *paidotribês*. In those respects the two disciplines are identical. But cleansing the humors and removing excess from the body and smoothing dried-up flesh, and fattening or transforming or warming some part of the body, all of these things belong to the wisdom

ἐκεῖνα ἢ οὐκ ἐπιστήσεται ὁ παιδοτρίβης ἤ, εἰ γινώ-
σκοι τι, πονηρῶς ἐπὶ τοὺς παῖδας χρήσεται βασα-
νίζων ἐλευθερίαν ἀκραιφνοῦς αἵματος. τῆς μὲν δὴ
προειρημένης ἐπιστήμης ἡ γυμναστικὴ τοσούτῳ τελε-
ωτέρα, πρὸς δέ γε ἰατρικὴν ὧδε ἔχει· νοσήματα,
ὁπόσα κατάρρους καὶ ὑδέρους καὶ φθόας ὀνομάζομεν
καὶ ὁπόσαι ἱεραὶ νόσοι, ἰατροὶ μὲν παύουσιν ἐπαν-
τλοῦντές τι ἢ ποτίζοντες ἢ ἐπιπλάττοντες, γυμνα-
στικὴ δὲ τὰ τοιαῦτα διαίταις ἴσχει καὶ τρίψει· ῥή-
ξαντά τι δὲ ἢ τρωθέντα ἢ θολωθέντα τὸ ἐν ὀφθαλμοῖς
φῶς ἢ ὀλισθήσαντά τι τῶν ἄρθρων ἐς ἰατροὺς χρὴ
φέρειν, ὡς οὐδὲν ἡ γυμναστικὴ πρὸς τὰ τοιαῦτα.

15. Ἐκ τούτων μὲν οἶμαι ἀποδεδεῖχθαί μοι ὁπόση
πρὸς ἑκατέραν ἐπιστήμην ἡ γυμναστική, δοκῶ δέ μοι
κἀκεῖνα ἐν αὐτῇ ὁρᾶν· ἰατρικὴν πᾶσαν ὁ αὐτὸς οὐδ<εἰς
γινώσκει, ἀλλ᾽ ὁ μὲν τετρω>μένων²⁰ οἶδεν, ὁ δὲ ξυν-
ιέναι πυρεττόντων, ὁ δὲ ὀφθαλμιώντων, ὁ δὲ φθισικῶν
ὑγιῶς ἅπτεται. καὶ μεγάλου ὄντος τοῦ κἂν σμικρόν τι
αὐτῆς ἐξεργάσασθαι ὀρθῶς φασιν οἱ ἰατρικοὶ πᾶσαν
γινώσκειν. γυμναστικὴν δὲ οὐκ ἂν ἐπαγγείλαιτό τις
ὁμοῦ πᾶσαν· ὁ γὰρ τὰ δρομικὰ εἰδὼς τὰ τῶν παλαι-

---

²⁰ οὐδ<εἰς γινώσκει, ἀλλ᾽ ὁ μὲν τετρω>μένων Jüthner: οὐ-
δ[....................]μένων P

---

⁷⁷ Cf. Gal. *Thrasybulus* 24 for similar discussion of the spe-
cialization of medicine in the Roman Empire and the use of the
term doctor even by individuals with quite a narrow field of
medical expertise.

of the trainer. The *paidotribês* will not understand them, or if he does know something about them, he will use that knowledge in harmful ways on the boys he is training, torturing their free and pure blood. That is the degree to which the art of training is more comprehensive than the aforementioned skill of the *paidotribês*. Its relation to the art of medicine is as follows. Doctors cure the illnesses we refer to as catarrh and dropsy and consumption, and the various types of epilepsy, by prescribing irrigations or potions or dressings, whereas athletic training checks such conditions by the use of diet and massage. But if someone has a break or a flesh wound or clouding of the sight in his eyes or a dislocation of one of his limbs, then he needs to be taken to the doctor, for the art of the athletic trainer does not concern itself with problems of those kinds.

15. With that discussion I believe I have demonstrated how far athletic training is related to each of these two disciplines. But the following points about athletic training also seem to me to be clear. Nobody individually knows the whole discipline of medicine, but some know about treating the wounded, some understand those with fevers, some those with ophthalmia, while others give their attention successfully to those with consumption. And since it is considered a significant achievement to gain knowledge of even a small part of the art of medicine, doctors are right in claiming that they know all of their subject.[77] No one could lay claim to the whole of athletic training together. For the trainer who knows about running will not understand the expertise associated with

PHILOSTRATUS

ὄντων καὶ τῶν παγκρατιαζόντων οὐκ ἐπιστήσεται ἢ ὁ
τὰ βαρύτερα γυμνάζων ἀμαθῶς τῆς ἄλλης ἐπιστήμης
ἅψεται.

16. Ξυμμετρία μὲν τῆς τέχνης ἥδε, γένεσις δὲ
αὐτῆς τὸ φῦναι τὸν ἄνθρωπον παλαῖσαί τε ἱκανὸν καὶ
πυκτεῦσαι καὶ δραμεῖν ὀρθόν· καὶ γὰρ οὐδ᾽ ἂν γένοιτό
τι τῶν τοιούτων μὴ προϋπάρχοντος τούτου, δι᾽ ὃ
γίγνεται. καὶ ὥσπερ χαλκευτικῆς γένεσις ὁ σίδηρος
καὶ ὁ χαλκὸς, καὶ γεωργίας γῆ καὶ τὰ ἐκ τῆς γῆς, καὶ
ναυτιλίας τὸ εἶναι θάλατταν, οὕτως ἡγώμεθα καὶ τὴν
γυμναστικὴν ξυγγενεστάτην τε εἶναι καὶ συμφυᾶ τῷ
ἀνθρώπῳ. καὶ λόγος δὲ ᾄδεταί τις, ὡς γυμναστικὴ
μὲν οὔπω εἴη, Προμηθεὺς δὲ εἴη καὶ γυμνάσαιτο μὲν
ὁ Προμηθεὺς πρῶτος, γυμνάσειε δ᾽ αὖ ἑτέρους Ἑρμῆς
ἀγασθείη τε αὐτὸν τοῦ εὑρήματος, καὶ παλαίστρα γε
Ἑρμοῦ πρώτη καὶ οἱ πλασθέντες ἐκ Προμηθέως ἄν-
θρωποι οἵδε ἄρα [οὗτοι] οἱ ἐν τῷ πηλῷ γυμνασάμενοι
εἶεν [τῷ ἦσαν], οἳ πλάττεσθαι²¹ ὑπὸ τοῦ Προμηθέως
ᾤοντο, ἐπειδὴ τὰ σώματα αὐτοῖς ἡ γυμναστικὴ ἐπι-
τήδειά τε καὶ ξυγκείμενα ἐποίει.

²¹ ἄνθρωποι οἵδε ἄρα [οὗτοι] οἱ ἐν τῷ πηλῷ γυμνασάμενοι
εἶεν [τῷ ἦσαν], οἳ πλάττεσθαι Jüthner: ἄνθρωποι δὲ ἄρα οὗτοι
εἶεν, τῷ πηλῷ γυμνασάμενοι· εἰ ἐν τῷ ἦσαν· ἢ πλάττεσθαι P

78 Cf. Philostratus' positive portrayal of nature in ch. 2.
79 Hermes was regularly linked with gymnastic activity (e.g.,
Pind. Ol. 6.79), and there is extensive epigraphical evidence for
Hermes honored in gymnasia; the regular contests between boys

428

wrestlers or pankratiasts, and the trainer who trains the heavy events will be inexpert in the other parts of the art.

16. That is the symmetry of the art of training. Its origin lies in the fact that humans are by nature capable of wrestling and boxing and running upright.[78] For no activity of this kind would come into being were it not for the preexistence of that through which it comes into being. For just as the origin of metalwork is iron and bronze, the origin of farming is the earth and the things that grow from it, the origin of sailing is the existence of the sea, so let us believe that athletic training too is inborn in and has grown hand in hand with humankind. The story is told that, at a time when athletic training did not yet exist, Prometheus, who was alive at that time, was the first to train himself; they say also that Hermes was the first to train others and that he admired Prometheus for his invention, and that the *palaistra* of Hermes was the first;[79] and finally that the people molded by Prometheus were in fact those men who undertook training in clay, and that they thought they had been molded by Prometheus because of the way in which athletic training made their bodies useful and well formed.[80]

trained in the gymnasium were often known as Hermaea. For another version of Hermes' connection with the origins of the *palaistra* (originally a space used just for wrestling, but later for other athletic training in addition), see Philostr. *Imag.* 2.32, where he is depicted as the father of the girl *Palaistra*.

[80] The link between Prometheus and athletic training, and the ingenious equation between muddy athletes and Prometheus' humans molded in clay, is not paralleled elsewhere in classical literature.

17. Πυθοῖ μὲν οὖν καὶ Ἰσθμοῖ καὶ ὅποι ποτὲ τῆς
γῆς ἦσαν ἀγῶνες, τρίβωνα ὁ γυμναστὴς ἀμπεχόμε-
νος ἀλείφει τὸν ἀθλητὴν καὶ οὐδεὶς ἀποδύσει ἄκοντα,
ἐν Ὀλυμπίᾳ δὲ γυμνὸς ἐφέστηκεν, ὡς μὲν δόξα ἐνίων,
διελέγχοντες Ἠλεῖοι τὸν γυμναστὴν ὥρᾳ ἔτους, εἰ
καρτερεῖν οἶδε καὶ θέρεσθαι, ὡς δὲ Ἠλεῖοί φασι, Φε-
ρενίκη ἡ Ῥοδία ἐγένετο Διαγόρου θυγάτηρ τοῦ πύ-
κτου, καὶ τὸ εἶδος ἡ Φερενίκη οὕτω τοι ἔρρωτο, ὡς
Ἠλείοις τὰ πρῶτα ἀνὴρ δόξαι. εἴ<λ>η<το>²² γοῦν ὑπὸ
τρίβωνι ἐν Ὀλυμπίᾳ καὶ Πεισίδωρον τὸν ἑαυτῆς υἱὸν
ἐγύμνασε. πύκτης δὲ ἄρα κἀκεῖνος ἦν εὔχειρ τὴν τέ-
χνην καὶ μείων οὐδὲν τοῦ πάππου. ἐπεὶ δὲ ξυνῆκαν
τῆς ἀπάτης, ἀποκτεῖναι μὲν τὴν Φερενίκην ὤκνησαν
ἐνθυμηθέντες τὸν Διαγόραν καὶ τοὺς Διαγόρου παῖ-
δας—ὁ γὰρ Φερενίκης οἶκος ὀλυμπιονῖκαι πάντες—
νόμος δὲ ἐγράφη τὸν γυμναστὴν ἀποδύεσθαι καὶ
μηδὲ τοῦτον ἀνέλεγκτον αὐτοῖς εἶναι.

18. Φέρει δὲ καὶ στλεγγίδα ὁ γυμναστὴς ἐκεῖ διὰ
τοῦτο ἴσως· κονίσασθαι²³ παλαίστρᾳ τὸν ἀθλητὴν ἐν
Ὀλυμπίᾳ καὶ πηλοῦσθαι²⁴ ἀνάγκη· ἵν᾽ οὖν μὴ λυμαί-

²² εἴ<λ>η<το> Jüthner: εἴ[.]η[..] P
²³ κονίσασθαι Jüthner: κονίσαι P
²⁴ πηλοῦσθαι Zingerle: ἡλιοῦσθαι P, Jüthner

---

81 Diagoras is the dedicatee of Pind. Ol. 7; he won his first
Olympic victory in 464 BC.
82 Winner of the boys' boxing in 404 BC (named Peisirodus
by Paus. in 5.6.8).

17. At the Pythian and Isthmian festivals, and wherever else in the world there are athletic contests, the trainer oils the athlete wearing a cloak and nobody can make him strip against his will. At Olympia, however, he takes charge naked. Some people think this is because the Eleans want to test the trainer in the summer season and find out whether he can endure and put up with the heat. The Eleans, by contrast, tell the following story: Pherenice, from Rhodes, was the daughter of the boxer Diagoras.[81] Her appearance was so strong that the Eleans at first assumed she was a man. Therefore she wrapped herself in a cloak at Olympia and undertook the training of her son Peisidorus.[82] He too was a boxer, a very dexterous one, and not at all inferior to his grandfather. When they discovered the deception, they hesitated to kill Pherenice out of consideration for Diagoras and his children—for the family of Pherenice were all Olympic victors—but a law was written that the trainer must strip naked, and that not even he should go untested by them.[83]

18. Moreover the trainer at Olympia also carries a strigil,[84] perhaps for the following reason: it is necessary for the athlete in Olympia to dust his body with the sand of the *palaistra* and to be covered in mud.[85] And so, in order that their good condition should not be damaged,

[83] Cf. Paus. 5.6.7–8 for another version of this story and for the claim that any woman found to be watching the games at Olympia risked the death penalty.

[84] The scraping instrument, usually made of metal, used to remove dust, oil, and sweat after exercise or bathing.

[85] For the distinction between mud and dust or sand in wrestling training, cf. ch. 53.

νοιντο τὴν ἕξιν, ἡ στλεγγὶς ἀναμιμνήσκει τὸν ἀθλη-
τὴν ἐλαίου καί φησι δεῖν ἐπάγειν αὐτὸ οὕτως ἀφθό-
νως, ὡς καὶ ἀποστλεγγίζειν ἀλείψαντα. εἰσὶ δ᾽ οἳ
φασιν ὡς γυμναστὴς ἐν Ὀλυμπίᾳ τεθηγμένῃ τῇ
στλεγγίδι τὸν ἀθλητὴν ἀπέκτεινε μὴ καρτερήσαντα
ὑπὲρ τῆς νίκης. καὶ ξυγχωρῶ τῷ λόγῳ· βέλτιον γὰρ
πιστεύεσθαι ἢ ἀπιστεῖσθαι. ξίφος μὲν δὴ ἐπὶ τοὺς
πονηροὺς τῶν ἀθλητῶν στλεγγὶς ἔστω, καὶ ἐχέτω δή
τι ὑπὲρ τὸν ἑλληνοδίκην ὁ γυμναστὴς ἐν Ὀλυμπίᾳ.

19. Λακεδαιμόνιοι δὲ καὶ τακτικὴν ἐβούλοντο πᾶ-
σαν τοὺς γυμναστὰς εἰδέναι μελέτην τῶν πολεμικῶν
τοὺς ἀγῶνας ἡγούμενοι καὶ οὐ χρὴ θαυμάζειν, ὅπου
καὶ τὴν ὄρχησιν, τὸ ῥαθυμότερον τῶν ἐν εἰρήνῃ, Λα-
κεδαιμόνιοι πάντως ἐς τὰ πολεμικὰ ἀνέφερον ὀρχού-
μενοι τρόπον, ὃν φυλάξεταί τις βέλος ἢ ἀφήσει ἢ
ἀρθήσεται ἀπὸ τῆς γῆς καὶ τῇ ἀσπίδι εὐμεταχει-
ρίστως χρήσεται.

20. Ὁπόσα δὲ γυμνασταὶ ξυνεβάλοντο ἀθληταῖς ἢ
παρακελευσάμενοί τι ἢ ἐπιπλήξαντες ἢ ἀπειλήσαντες
ἢ σοφισάμενοι, πολλὰ μὲν ταῦτα καὶ πλείω λόγου,
λεγέσθω δὲ τὰ ἐλλογιμώτερα. Γλαῦκον μὲν τοίνυν τὸν
Καρύστιον ἀφιστάμενον[25] ἐν Ὀλυμπίᾳ τὴν πυγμὴν τῷ

[25] ἀφιστάμενον Volckmar: ἀπιστούμενον P

---

[86] The Olympic judges, ten for each Olympiad for most of the
centuries of Olympic history; cf. n. 53, above.

the strigil reminds the athlete of oil, and tells him that he must apply it so abundantly that it is necessary to scrape himself down after he has oiled himself. But there are some who say that a trainer in Olympia killed his athlete with a sharpened strigil as a punishment for not exercising endurance in pursuit of victory. And I agree with that explanation. For it is better for it to be believed than disbelieved. Let the strigil be a sword against worthless athletes, and let the trainer at Olympia rank in some respects above the *hellanodikai*.[86]

19. The Spartans wanted their trainers in addition to know all about tactics, since they viewed athletic contests as practice for warfare, and one should not be surprised at that, given that the Spartans connected even dancing, the most lighthearted of peacetime activities, in all respects with warfare, and danced in the manner in which one would ward off a missile or launch one or jump up from the ground or use one's shield dexterously.[87]

20. As for cases where trainers have been of use to their athletes, either by encouraging them in something or rebuking them or threatening them or tricking them, there are many of these, too many to recount, but let us mention the more remarkable ones. When Glaucus[88] of Carystus was giving way to his opponent in the boxing at Olympia,

[87] This kind of weapon dance, often given the name *pyrrhichê* in Greek, is attested not just for Sparta (e.g., Ath. *Deipnosophists* 14, 631a) but also for many other ancient cities (e.g., for Athens in the festival of the Panathenaea).

[88] Cf. n. 5, above; and cf. Paus. 6.10.1–2 on this incident (although in Pausanias' version the encouragement comes from his father rather than his trainer).

ἀντιπάλῳ Τισίας ὁ γυμναστὴς εἰς νίκην ἤγαγε παρα-
κελευσάμενος "τὰν ἀπ᾽ ἀρότρου" πλῆξαι. τουτὶ δὲ ἄρα
ἦν ἡ τῆς δεξιᾶς ἐς τὸν ἀντίπαλον φορά· τὴν γὰρ
χεῖρα ἐκείνην ὁ Γλαῦκος οὕτω τοι ἔρρωτο, ὡς ὕνιν ἐν
Εὐβοίᾳ ποτὲ καμφθεῖσαν ὀρθῶσαι σφυρηδὸν τῇ δε-
ξιᾷ πλήξας.

21. Ἀρριχίωνα²⁶ δὲ τὸν παγκρατιαστὴν δύο μὲν ἤδη
Ὀλυμπιάδας νικῶντα, τρίτην δὲ ἐπ᾽ ἐκείναις Ὀλυμ-
πιάδα μαχόμενον περὶ τοῦ στεφάνου καὶ ἤδη ἀπαγο-
ρεύοντα Ἐρυξίας ὁ γυμναστὴς εἰς ἔρωτα θανάτου
κατέστησεν ἀναβοήσας ἔξωθεν, "ὡς καλὸν ἐντάφιον
τὸ ἐν Ὀλυμπίᾳ μὴ ἀπειπεῖν."

22. Προμάχου²⁷ δὲ τοῦ ἐκ Πελλήνης²⁸ ξυνίει μὲν ὁ
γυμναστὴς ἐρῶντος, ἀγχοῦ δὲ Ὀλυμπίων ὄντων, "ὦ
Πρόμαχε,"²⁹ εἶπεν, "δοκεῖς μοι ἐρᾶν." ὡς δὲ εἶδεν ἐρυ-
θριῶντα, "ἀλλ᾽ οὐκ ἐλέγξων," ἔφη, "ταῦτα ἠρόμην,
ξυλληψόμενος δέ σοι τοῦ ἔρωτος· καὶ γὰρ ἂν καὶ δια-
λεχθείην ὑπὲρ σοῦ τῷ γυναίῳ." καὶ διαλεχθεὶς οὐδὲν
ἀφίκετο πρὸς τὸν ἀθλητὴν ἀπάγων λόγον οὐκ ἀληθῆ,
πλείστου δὲ ἄξιον τῷ ἐρῶντι· "οὐκ ἀπαξιοῖ τί σε,"
ἔφη, "τῶν ἑαυτῆς παιδικῶν νικῶντα Ὀλυμπίαζε." καὶ
ὁ Πρόμαχος³⁰ ἀναπνεύσας ἐφ᾽ ὧν ἤκουσεν, οὐκ ἐνίκα

²⁶ Ἀρριχίωνα Cobet: ἀρίωνα P
²⁷ Προμάχου Daremberg: πρωτόμαχου P
²⁸ Πελλήνης Volckmar: πέλλης P
²⁹ Προμάχε Daremberg: πρωτόμαχε P
³⁰ Πρόμαχος Daremberg: πρωτόμαχος P

434

his trainer Tisias led him to victory by encouraging him to strike "the blow from the plow." This meant a right-handed punch against his opponent; for Glaucus was so strong with that hand that he once straightened a bent plowshare in Euboea by hitting it with his right hand like a hammer.

21. Arrichion[89] the pankratiast, having won two Olympic titles already, was competing for the crown in his third Olympiad, following these other two, and when he was just beginning to give up, his trainer Eryxias inspired him with a desire for death by shouting from the sidelines, "What a fine funeral shroud, not to give up at Olympia."

22. The trainer of Promachus[90] from Pellene was aware that Promachus was in love, and when the Olympic festival drew close, he said, "Promachus, you seem to me to be in love." And when he saw him blushing, he said, "I did not ask that in order to disgrace you, but in order to help you in your love; for I could talk to the woman on your behalf." And without actually having spoken to her he then returned to the athlete bringing a message that was not true but that was very valuable for the man in love with her: "She does not think you at all unworthy of her love," he said, "if you win at Olympia." And Promachus, recovering thanks to what he had heard, not only won, but actually

89 Athlete from Phigalia (otherwise known as Arrachion), winner of the Olympic *pankration* in 572 and 568 BC. For longer versions of the story Philostratus alludes to here, where Arrhichion prefers death to victory, cf. Philostr. *Imag.* 2.6, and Paus. 8.40.2, neither of which makes any mention of his trainer.

90 See n. 4, above; and cf. Paus. 7.27.5–7 for a longer account of Promachus' victories, but with no mention of his trainer.

μόνον, ἀλλὰ καὶ Πουλυδάμαντα τὸν Σκοτουσσαῖον
μετὰ τοὺς λέοντας, οὓς ὁ Πουλυδάμας ᾑρήκει παρ᾽
Ὤχῳ τῷ Πέρσῃ.

23. Μανδρογένους δὲ τοῦ Μάγνητος αὐτὸς ἤκουσα
τὴν καρτερίαν, ᾗ ἐκέχρητο ἐφ᾽ ἡλικίας εἰς τὰ παγκρά-
τια τῷ γυμναστῇ ἀνατιθέντος. τεθνάναι μὲν γὰρ τὸν
πατέρα ἔλεγεν, ἐπὶ μητρὶ δὲ εἶναι τὸν οἶκον ἀρρενικῇ
τε καὶ γενναίᾳ, πρὸς ἣν γράψαι τὸν γυμναστὴν ἐπι-
στολὴν τοιαύτην· "τὸν υἱὸν εἰ μὲν τεθνεῶτα ἀκού-
σειας, πίστευσον, εἰ δὲ ἡττώμενον, ἀπίστει." ταύτην
ἔφασκεν αἰδούμενος τὴν ἐπιστολὴν εὐψυχίαν ἐνδείξα-
σθαι πᾶσαν, ὡς μήτε ὁ γυμναστὴς ψεύσαιτο, μήτε ἡ
μήτηρ ψευσθείη.

24. Ὀπτάτος[31] δὲ ὁ Αἰγύπτιος ἐνίκα μὲν ἐν Πλαται-
αῖς δρόμον, κειμένου δ᾽ ὡς ἔφην παρ᾽ αὐτοῖς νόμου
δημοσίᾳ ἀποθνῄσκειν τὸν μετὰ νίκην ἡττώμενον καὶ
μὴ συγγυμνάζεσθαι πρότερον ἢ ἐγγυητὰς καταστῆ-
σαι τοῦ σώματος, οὐδενὸς δὲ ἐγγυωμένου τὸ οὕτω
μέγα, ὑπέθηκεν ἑαυτὸν ὁ γυμναστὴς τῷ νόμῳ καὶ τὸν
ἀθλητὴν ἐπέρρωσεν εἰς νίκην δευτέραν· τοῖς γὰρ
ἅπτεσθαι διανοουμένοις ἔργου μείζονος εὔελπι, οἶμαι,
τὸ μὴ ἀπιστεῖσθαι.

<hr/>

31 Ὀπτάτος Jüthner: ὄπιατος P

<hr/>

91 See n. 3, above; and cf. Paus. 6.5 and Julius Africanus,
Olympionicarum Fasti 93 for his victories and his lion killing and
other exploits.

defeated Poulydamas[91] from Scotoussa following his encounter with the lions, which Poulydamas had overpowered in front of the Persian king Ochus.

23. I have myself heard Mandrogenus[92] of Magnes attributing to his trainer the powers of endurance he displayed in his youth in the *pankration*. For he said that his father had died, and that the whole household came under the authority of his mother, a woman of masculine nobility. To her, he said the trainer wrote a letter of this kind: "If you hear that your son has died, believe it; if you hear that he has been defeated, do not." He said that out of respect for this letter, he displayed all possible courage, in order that neither should his trainer be a liar, nor his mother the victim of deception.

24. Optatus[93] the Egyptian won the running race in Plataea. Since there was a law among the Plataeans, as I said before,[94] that anyone who was defeated, having previously won, should be publicly executed, and that a previous winner should not be allowed to train before providing guarantors for his body, and since no one was willing to provide a guarantee for something so serious, his trainer subjected himself to the law and so gave his athlete the strength for a second victory. For those who intend to undertake a great deed, I believe, not being mistrusted is a source of optimism.

[92] Olympic victor in the *pankration* in AD 213.

[93] The name of this athlete is corrupt in the manuscript; Optatus seems the most likely correction, but no athlete of this name is attested elsewhere in ancient sources.

[94] Cf. ch. 8.

PHILOSTRATUS

25. Ἐπεὶ δὲ ἐπιρρεῖ τῶν τοιούτων ὄχλος ἐγκατα-
μιγνύντων ἡμῶν παλαιοῖς νέα, σκεψώμεθα τὸν γυμνα-
στὴν αὐτόν, ὁποῖός τις ὢν καὶ ὁπόσα εἰδὼς τῷ ἀθλητῇ
ἐφεστήξει. ἔστω δὴ ὁ γυμναστὴς μήτε ἀδολέσχης,
μήτε ἀγύμναστος τὴν γλῶτταν, ὡς μήτε τὸ ἐνεργὸν
τῆς τέχνης ἐκλύοιτο ὑπὸ τῆς ἀδολεσχίας, μήτε ἀγροι-
κότερον φαίνοιτο μὴ ξὺν λόγῳ δρώμενον. φυσιογνω-
μονικήν τε ἐπεσκέφθω πᾶσαν. τουτὶ δὲ κελεύω διὰ
τόδε· παῖδα ἀθλητὴν ἑλληνοδίκης μέν τις ἢ ἀμφι-
κτύων κρίνουσιν ἀπὸ τῶν τοιῶνδε· εἰ φυλὴ τῷδε καὶ
πατρίς, εἰ πατὴρ καὶ γένος, εἰ ἐλευθέρων καὶ μὴ νό-
θος, ἐπὶ πᾶσιν, εἰ νέος καὶ μὴ ὑπὲρ παῖδα· εἰ <δ᾽>
ἐγκρατὴς ἢ ἀκρατής, εἰ μεθυστὴς ἢ λίχνος, εἰ θαρ-
σαλέος ἢ δειλός, οὐδὲ εἰ γιγνώσκοιεν, οὐδὲν οἱ νόμοι
σφίσιν ὑπὲρ τῶν τοιούτων διαλέγονται, τὸν δὲ γυμνα-
στὴν ἐξεπίστασθαι χρὴ ταῦτα φύσεως που κριτὴν
ὄντα. γιγνωσκέτω δὴ τὴν ἐν ὀφθαλμοῖς ἠθικὴν πᾶ-
σαν, ὑφ᾽ ἧς δηλοῦνται μὲν οἱ νωθροὶ τῶν ἀνθρώπων,

95 The *amphiktyones* were officials at the Pythian games, in
other words the Delphic equivalents of the Olympic *hellanodi-
kai*.

96 This process of judging eligibility to compete is widely at-
tested: athletes were required to demonstrate that they were of
free birth, were citizens of a city, and were members of a tribe
(*phyle*) within that city; they were also assigned as appropriate to
the two Olympic age classes (boys and men).

97 "Dissembling" is at first sight the obvious translation for
εἴρωνες, but see Jüthner (1909, 238) for the alternative transla-

438

25. Since a crowd of such examples keeps on pouring out, a mixture of ancient stories with modern ones, let us have a look now at the trainer himself, to see what sort of man will supervise the athlete, and what the extent of his knowledge will be. Let the trainer be neither garrulous nor untrained in speech, so that the effectiveness of his craft may not be reduced because of his talkativeness nor appear too unsophisticated through being performed without proper speech. Let him also take into consideration the whole art of physiognomy. I insist upon that for the following reason. A *hellanodikês* or an *amphiktyon*[95] judges a boy athlete according to the following kinds of criteria: whether he has a tribe and a home city, whether he has a father and a family, whether he is of free birth and not illegitimate, and finally whether he is young and not too old for the boys' age category.[96] But the question of whether he is self-disciplined or immoderate, whether he is a drunkard or a glutton, whether he is courageous or cowardly, even if they knew the answers, their laws do not enter into discussion about such factors at all. The trainer, by contrast, needs to know them well, being a sort of judge of the athlete's nature. Indeed he should know all the signs of character in the eyes, by which are revealed lazy people, impetuous people, and inactive[97] people and those who

tion "sluggish" or "inactive," justified by reference to passages of Photius, *Lexicon* s.v. κατειρωνευσάμενοι, and Hesychius s.v. εἴρων, who give that as an alternative meaning. Kitriniari's (1961) proposed alternative, εἴροντες, by analogy with ch. 40, seems rather forced in this passage; it is a little more plausible in ch. 38, on which see further below.

δηλοῦνται δὲ οἱ ξύντονοι εἴρωνές[32] τε καὶ ἧττον καρ-
τερικοὶ καὶ ἀκρατεῖς· ἄλλα μὲν γὰρ μελανοφθάλμων,
ἄλλα δὲ χαροπῶν τε καὶ γλαυκῶν καὶ ὑφαίμων
ὀφθαλμῶν ἤθη, ἕτερα καὶ ξανθῶν καὶ ὑπεστιγμένων,
προπαλῶν τε καὶ κοίλων· ἡ γὰρ φύσις ὥρας μὲν
ἄστροις ἐσημήνατο, ἤθη δὲ ὀφθαλμοῖς. ἤθη δὲ αὖ
τῶν σώματος ‹μερῶν›[33] ὥσπερ ἐν ἀγαλματοποιίᾳ ὧδε
ἐπισκεπτέον· σφυρὸν μὲν καρπῷ ὁμολογεῖν, κνήμη δὲ
πῆχυν καὶ βραχίονα μηρῷ ἀντικρίνεσθαι καὶ ὤμῳ
γλουτόν, μετάφρενα δὲ θεωρεῖσθαι πρὸς γαστέρα[34]
καὶ στέρνα ἐκκεῖσθαι παραπλησίως τοῖς ὑπὸ τὸ
ἰσχίον, κεφαλήν τε σχῆμα τοῦ παντὸς οὖσαν πρὸς
ταῦτα πάντα ἔχειν ξυμμέτρως.

26. Τούτων ὧδέ μοι εἰρημένων μὴ τὸ γυμνάζειν
ἡγώμεθα ἕπεσθαι τούτοις, ἀλλὰ τὸ ἀποδῦσαι τὸν
γυμναζόμενον καὶ ἐς δοκιμασίαν καταστῆσαι τῆς φύ-
σεως, ὅπη τε σύγκειται καὶ πρὸς ὅ· οὐ γὰρ δὴ[35] κυνῶν
τε καὶ ἵππων τοσοῦτον εἶναι προσήκει λόγον κυνηγε-
τικοῖς τε καὶ ἱππικοῖς, ὡς μὴ ἐς πᾶσαν ἰδέαν, μηδὲ
ἐπὶ πάντα τὰ θηρώμενα τοῖς αὐτοῖς, ἀλλὰ τοῖς μὲν ἐς
τόδε ‹τοῖς δὲ ἐς τόδε›[36] τῶν κυνῶν[37] χρῆσθαι, τῶν τε
ἵππων τοὺς μὲν ξυνθηρατὰς ποιεῖσθαι, τοὺς δὲ μαχί-

---

[32] εἴροντές Kitriniari   [33] Suppl. Jüthner   [34] γαστέρα
Kayser: τὰ ἕτερα P   [35] οὐ γὰρ δὴ Kitriniari: ποῦ γὰρ δὴ
Kayser, Jüthner: ὅπου γὰρ δεῖ P.   [36] Suppl. Mynas   [37] κυ-
νῶν Kayser: κυνηγετικῶν P

---

[98] A reference among others to Polyclitus and his attempt to

are less capable of endurance and lacking in self-control. Some characteristics are associated with people who have black eyes, others with those who have bright, blue or bloodshot eyes, others again with those whose eyes are yellow or flecked, prominent or sunken; for nature has signaled the seasons by the stars, and character by eyes. The characteristics of the parts of the body are also to be considered, as in the art of sculpture,[98] as follows: the ankle should agree in its measurements with the wrist, the forearm should correspond to the calf and the upper arm with the thigh, the buttock with the shoulder, and the back should be examined by comparison with the stomach, and the chest should curve outward similarly to the parts beneath the hip joint, and finally the head, which is the benchmark for the whole body, should be well proportioned in relation to all of these other parts.

26. Now that I have dealt with these matters, let us not imagine that the topic of training is coming next, but instead we will strip the person who is undergoing training and subject him to an examination of his nature, how it is constituted and for what it is suited. For it is not right that there should be so much discussion among hunters and horsemen about dogs and horses—so much so that they do not use the same dogs for every kind of hunting or against every kind of prey but instead use some for one and others for another, while some horses are made into hunters, some into horses for battle, some into race horses, some into chariot horses, and not simply that but they are

fix the ideal relations between different parts of the human body in his lost treatise the *Canon*, and exemplified in his famous athletic statue, the Doryphoros; see Gal. *De Placitis Hippocratis et Platonis* 5.3, and Plin. *HN* 34.55.

μους, τοὺς δὲ ἀμιλλητηρίους, τοὺς δὲ ἀρματηλάτας
καὶ μηδὲ ἁπλῶς τούτους, ἀλλ' ὡς ἕκαστος ἐπιτήδειος
πλευρᾷ τινι ἢ σειρᾷ τοῦ ἅρματος, ἀνθρώπων δὲ ἀκρί-
τους εἶναι, οὓς δεῖ ἐν Ὀλυμπίᾳ ἢ Πυθοῖ ἄγειν ὑπὲρ
κηρυγμάτων, ὧν καὶ Ἡρακλῆς ἦρα. κελεύω δὴ καὶ
ἀναλογίαν μὲν ἐπεσκέφθαι τὸν γυμναστήν,[38] ἣν εἶπον,
πρὸ δὲ τῆς ἀναλογίας καὶ τὰ τῶν χυμῶν ἤθη.

27. Καίτοι καὶ πρεσβύτερον τούτου, ὃ καὶ Λυ-
κούργῳ ἐδόκει τῷ Σπαρτιάτῃ· παριστάμενος γὰρ τῇ
Λακεδαίμονι πολεμικοὺς ἀθλητάς, "γυμναζέσθων,"
φησίν, "αἱ κόραι καὶ ἀνείσθων δημοσίᾳ τρέχειν."
ὑπὲρ εὐπαιδίας δήπου καὶ τοῦ τὰ ἔκγονα βελτίω τί-
κτειν ὑπὸ τοῦ ἐρρῶσθαι τὸ σῶμα· ἀφικομένη γὰρ ἐς
ἀνδρὸς ὑδροφορεῖν οὐκ ὀκνήσει οὐδὲ ἀλεῖν διὰ τὸ
ἠσκῆσθαι ἐκ νέας· εἰ δὲ καὶ νέῳ καὶ συγγυμναζομένῳ
συζυγείη, βελτίω τὰ ἔκγονα ἀποδώσει, καὶ γὰρ εὐ-
μήκη καὶ ἰσχυρὰ καὶ ἄνοσα. καὶ ἐγένετο ἡ Λακεδαί-
μων τοσαύτη κατὰ πόλεμον, ἐπειδὴ τὰ γαμικὰ αὐτοῖς
ὧδε ἐπράττετο.

28. Ἐπειδὴ τοίνυν ἐκ γονῆς ἀνθρώπου προσήκει
ἄρχεσθαι, ἴτω ὁ γυμναστὴς ἐπὶ τὸν παῖδα ἀθλητὴν

---

[38] γυμναστήν Mynas: ποιητὴν P

---

[99] Ancient racing chariots were usually drawn by four horses,
two central ones attached to a yoke and two outer horses attached
by ropes.   [100] Cf. n. 8, above.
[101] Cf. Xen. *Lac.* 1.4; Plut. *Lyc.* 14.

assigned to one of the shafts of the chariot or to one of the ropes according to what each is best suited for[99]—but that humans who have to be introduced at Olympia or Pythia in search of victory proclamations to which even Heracles himself aspired,[100] should remain unjudged. My advice to the trainer is to pay attention to the questions of proportion I mentioned before, but before looking at proportion to pay attention also to the quality of the athlete's humors.

27. That said, there is also an even more ancient consideration than this one, a consideration that seemed important also to the Spartan Lycurgus. For wishing to provide Sparta with warlike athletes, he said, "Let the girls exercise, and let them be allowed to run in public."[101] Doubtless this was for the sake of ensuring good children and to make sure that they would have better offspring by having strong bodies. For a woman with that background, even when she comes to the house of her husband, will not hesitate to carry water and grind grain, because she has exercised from her youth. And if she is married to a young man who is a fellow enthusiast of athletic training she will produce better offspring, for they will be tall[102] and strong and resistant to disease. Sparta became so great in warfare because their marriages were conducted like this.

28. Since, therefore, it is fitting to begin from a person's birth, let the trainer approach the boy athlete and examine

---

[102] The correct translation of the word εὐμήκης in this work is debated. The standard translation, which I have usually followed, is "tall"; others prefer "well-proportioned"; Jüthner (1909) translates "slim." For other examples see chs. 31, 33, 35, and 38.

ἐκ γονέων αὐτὸν ὁρῶν πρῶτον, εἰ νέοι³⁹ ξυνηρμόσθη-
σαν καὶ γενναῖοι καὶ ἄνοσοι νόσων, ὁπόσαι ἐς νεῦρα
ἀπερείδονται καὶ ὀφθαλμῶν ἕδρας καὶ ὦτα ἐκφοιτῶ-
σιν ἢ σπλάγχνα· ταυτὶ γὰρ τὰ νοσήματα καὶ ξυνα-
ποχωρεῖ ποτε τῇ φύσει καὶ παιδία μὲν ὄντα ἀφανῶς
ὑποδέδυκε, προϊόντων δὲ ἐς ἐφήβους καὶ μεθισταμέ-
νων εἰς ἄνδρας καὶ ἀπιούσης ἀκμῆς δῆλα καὶ φανερὰ
γίνεται μεταβολὴν σχόντος τοῦ αἵματος ἐν ταῖς τῆς
ἡλικίας τροπαῖς. νεότης δὲ γονέων, ἢν ἄμφω καὶ γεν-
ναῖοι ξυνέλθωσιν, ἰσχύν τε ξυμβάλλεται καὶ ἀθλητῇ
καὶ αἷμα ἀκήρατον καὶ ὀστῶν κράτος καὶ χυμοὺς
ἀκραιφνεῖς καὶ ἴσον μέγεθος, ἔτι δ' ἂν φαίην, ὅτι καὶ
ὥραν φέρουσιν. ἀγνοείσθων μὴ παρόντες τῷ παιδὶ ἐς
τὴν κρίσιν· πῶς βασανιοῦμεν τὴν σποράν; ἐς εὔηθες
γὰρ ἐκπεσεῖται ὁ λόγος, εἰ τὸν ἀθλητὴν ἐφεστηκότα
ἤδη τῷ σταδίῳ καὶ τοῦ κοτίνου τε καὶ τῆς δάφνης
ἐχόμενον ἐς τὸν πατέρα ἀναβαλλοίμεθα καὶ τὴν μη-
τέρα τάχα που καὶ τεθνεῶτας ἐπὶ νηπίῳ· δεῖ γὰρ θε-
ωρίας, καθ' ἣν ἐς γυμνὸν τὸν ἀθλητὴν βλέψαντες
οὐδὲ τὰ τῶν γονέων ἠγνοηκέναι δόξομεν, ὅπη αὐτῷ
ἔχει. χαλεπὸν μὲν τὸ ἐνθύμημα καὶ οὐ πάνυ τι ῥάδιον,
οὐ μὴν πρόσω γε τῆς τέχνης. παραδίδωμι οὖν αὐτὸ
ἐς γνῶσιν.

³⁹ εἰ νέοι Daremberg: εἶναι· οἱ P

him first of all with reference to his parents, considering whether they were young when they were married and in excellent condition and free from illnesses of the kind which affect the nervous system or arise in the eyes or the ears or the internal organs. For these diseases sometimes disappear from view naturally and conceal themselves unobserved during childhood, but when the children advance to the age of ephebes and make the transition to being men and then go past their prime, then they become obvious and apparent, because of the changes the blood undergoes with the changes of age. The youth of the parents, if they are both in excellent condition when they come together, contributes strength also to the athlete, and pure blood, and strength in the bones and unadulterated humors and even stature, and I would even go so far as to say that it brings beauty. Assuming that the parents are not known about and are not present at the examination of the child, how shall we put the athlete's origins to the test? For the whole procedure will degenerate into absurdity if we make the athlete wait, when he is already standing ready to enter the stadium and within reach of the crown of olive or laurel,[103] while we investigate his father and mother, who may very well have died when he was young. It is necessary to have a method according to which we can look at a naked athlete and feel that we are not ignorant about the condition of his parents and about how it affects him. The reasoning is difficult and not at all straightforward, but it is not beyond the limits of the art. And so I shall reveal it in what follows.

[103] The Olympic victory crown was made of olive, the Pythian of laurel.

29. Ἡ μὲν οὖν γενναία σπορὰ καὶ νεᾶνις ὁποίους
ἀνήσει δεδήλωκα, ἡ δὲ ἐκ τῶν προηκόντων ὧδε ἐλεγ-
κτέα· λεπτὸν μὲν τούτοις τὸ δέρμα, κυαθώδεις δὲ αἱ
κλεῖδες, ὑπανεστηκυῖαι δὲ αἱ φλέβες καθάπερ τοῖς
πεπονηκόσι, καὶ ἰσχίον τούτοις ἄναρμον καὶ τὰ μυ-
ώδη⁴⁰ ἀσθενῆ. γυμναζομένων δὲ πλείους ἔλεγχοι· καὶ
γὰρ νωθροὶ καὶ ὠμοὶ τὸ αἷμα ὑπὸ ψυχρότητος καὶ οἱ
ἱδρῶτες ἐπιπολάζοντες μᾶλλον ἢ τῶν κυρτῶν τε καὶ
κοίλων ἀνίσχοντες καὶ οὐδὲ ἐπανθοῦσιν οὗτοι τοῖς
πόνοις, εἰ μὴ διαπιδύοιμεν⁴¹ τοὺς ἱδρῶτας, οὐδὲ ἐπιτή-
δειοι ἆραι οὐδέν, ἀλλὰ ἀνοχῶν δέονται· ἀναλίσκονται
δὲ καὶ πόνοις ὑπὲρ τὰ πονηθέντα. ἐγὼ δὲ τούτους
πάντων μὲν ἀπαξιῶ τῶν ἐν ἀγωνίᾳ—τὸ γὰρ ἐς ἄνδρα
οὐ βέβαιοι—παγκρατίου δὲ καὶ πυγμῆς μάλιστα· εὐ-
άλωτοι γὰρ πληγαῖς τε καὶ τραύμασιν οἱ μηδὲ τὸ
δέρμα ἐρρωμένοι. γυμναστέοι δ᾽ ὅμως, μᾶλλον δὲ κο-
λακευτέοι τῷ γυμνάζοντι, ἐπειδὴ δέονται τούτου καὶ
πονοῦντες καὶ γυμναζόμενοι. εἰ δὲ κατὰ τὸν ἕτερον
τῶν τοιούτων ἡ σπορὰ παρηβηκυῖα φαίνεται, τὰ μὲν
ἐλαττώματα ἔσται ὅμοια, ἧττον δὲ ἐπίδηλα.

---

⁴⁰ μυώδη Kayser: χυμώδη P
⁴¹ διαπιδύοιμεν Zingerle: ἀπαντλοῖμεν Kayser, Jüthner:
ἀμύητοι μὲν P

---

104 Cf. ch. 48.
105 Bodily warmth was thought to aid digestion, just as heat
aids cooking, with which digestion was often compared; insuffi-
cient warmth in the body was therefore thought to lead to the
absorption of imperfectly digested nutrients into the blood.

29. I have shown what kind of offspring will be produced by excellent and youthful parents. The offspring of parents of advanced age can be detected as follows. Their skin is delicate, their collarbones are hollowed out like cups,[104] their veins stick out like the veins of people who have exerted themselves, their hips are poorly structured and their muscles weak. There are further opportunities to scrutinize them in training. For they are sluggish and raw in their blood[105] because of the coldness of their bodies, and their sweat sits on the surface rather than arising from the curves and hollows of the body; and they do not color when they exercise, unless we are able to draw out their sweat; and they are not capable of picking anything up,[106] but they need periods to rest; and they are exhausted by their efforts out of proportion with their exertion. And I believe that they are not suitable for any kind of athletic contest—for they are not strong in terms of manliness— and especially not for *pankration* and boxing. For they succumb easily to blows and wounds, since even their skin is not strong. Despite that, they should be trained; in the process, however, they ought to be flattered by the trainer,[107] since they need this when they exert themselves and train. And if there are cases of this kind where the athlete's parentage seems to be elderly in relation to just one parent, the defects will be similar, but less obvious.

[106] Lifting of heavy weights is widely attested as a training exercise for ancient athletes, and is especially associated with the early athletes of the archaic period; e.g., see Ael. *VH* 12.22, on Milo of Croton.

[107] Presumably a reference to encouragement and lenient treatment; cf. Plutarch, *How to Tell a Flatterer from a Friend* 58f for a similar use of the word "flatter" in an educational context.

30. Τὰς δὲ νοσώδεις τῶν ἕξεων ἐξελέγξει τὸ αἷμα·
θολερὸν γάρ που ἀνάγκη αὐτὸ φαίνεσθαι καὶ βεβυ-
θισμένον ὑπὸ τῆς χολῆς. τὸ δὲ τοιοῦτον αἷμα κἂν
ἔμπνουν ποτὲ ὑπὸ γυμναστοῦ γένηται, μεθίσταται αὖ
καὶ θολοῦται· χαλεπὰ γὰρ ξυμβαίνει τὰ μὴ εὖ φύντα.
δηλούτω τι καὶ προπαλὴς φάρυγξ καὶ ὤμων πτέρυγες
καὶ αὐχὴν ἀνεστηκὼς καὶ ἄγαν ὑπολισθαίνων καθ᾽ ὃ
ξυμβάλλουσιν αἱ κλεῖδες. καὶ μὴν καὶ οἱ ξυγκεκλει-
μένοι τὰ πλευρὰ καὶ ἀναπεπταμένοι ὑπὲρ τὸ μέτριον
πολλὰ τοῦ νοσώδους ἐπισημαίνουσι· τοῖς μὲν γὰρ
πεπιέσθαι ἀνάγκη τὰ σπλάγχνα καὶ μὴ εὔρουν τὸ
πνεῦμα ἐκφέρειν μηδὲ εὐφορεῖν ἐν τοῖς πόνοις φθορᾷ
τε σιτίων συνεχεῖ ἁλίσκεσθαι, τοῖς δὲ βαρέα τε
[εἰσὶ]⁴² τὰ σπλάγχνα καὶ ἀπηρτημένα ἔσται καὶ ἀμ-
βλὺ τὸ ἀπ᾽ αὐτῶν πνεῦμα καὶ ὁρμῇ ὕπτιοι· καὶ τὰ
σιτία ἧττον ἀναδοθήσεται⁴³ τούτοις ἐς γαστέρα χω-
ροῦντα μᾶλλον ἢ τροφὴν τοῦ σώματος. ταυτὶ μὲν
περὶ σπορᾶς⁴⁴ τῶν ἀγωνιουμένων, τὸν δὲ ἑκάστῳ τῶν
ἀγωνισμάτων πρόσφορον ὧδε χρὴ ἐξετάζειν.

31. Ἔστω ὁ μὲν τὰ πέντε ἀγωνιούμενος βαρὺς
μᾶλλον ἢ κοῦφος, καὶ κοῦφος μᾶλλον ἢ βαρύς, ⟨ἔτι
δ᾽ εὐ⟩μήκης,⁴⁵ εὐπαγής, ἀνεστηκώς, ἀπέριττος τὰ μυ-
ώδη, μὴ κεκολασμένος. ἐχέτω καὶ τοῖν σκελοῖν μα-
κρῶς μᾶλλον ἢ ξυμμέτρως καὶ τῆς ὀσφύος ὑγρῶς τε

---

42 Del. Schenkl   43 ἧττον ἀναδοθήσεται Daremberg:
ἥττονα δοθήσεται P   44 σπορᾶς Jüthner: τροφῆς P
45 Suppl. Jüthner: [.........]μήκης P

30. As for constitutions which are ill, they will be revealed by their blood. For it will necessarily appear muddy and overloaded with bile. This kind of blood, even if it is revived by the trainer, always changes back and becomes muddy again. For whatever is not good by nature causes difficulty. Another sign is a projecting windpipe and shoulder blades, and a neck that is long and sinks down too much at the place where the collar bones come together. Moreover, those who have flanks that are narrow or else unusually wide, these too show many of the signs of illness. For it must be the case that the first group have innards that are cramped, that they do not breathe fluently, that they do not profit from physical exertion and that they are afflicted by continual bad digestion of their food. The other group, by contrast, will have innards that are heavy and loose and their breathing will be dull and they themselves will be sluggish in their movement. And their food will be less well assimilated, contributing more to the expansion of their paunches than the nourishment of their bodies. That is all I have to say on the origins of those who intend to compete. In what follows next it is necessary to examine what qualities are suitable for each of the athletic disciplines.

31. The athlete who intends to compete in the pentathlon should be heavy rather than light, and light rather than heavy.[108] In addition he should be tall, compact and upright, not excessively muscled, but not underdeveloped either. His legs should be long rather than well proportioned and he should have supple and agile loins to help

108 I.e., halfway between the two.

καὶ εὐκόλως διά τε τὰς ὑποστροφὰς τοῦ ἀκοντίου καὶ
τοῦ δίσκου διά τε τὸ ἅλμα· ἀλυπότερον γὰρ πηδήσε-
ται καὶ ῥήξει οὐδὲν τοῦ σώματος, ἢν ὑποκαθεὶς τὸ
ἰσχίον κατερείσῃ τῇ βάσει. καὶ μακρόχειρα χρὴ εἶναι
αὐτὸν καὶ εὐμήκη τοὺς δακτύλους· δισκεύσει τε γὰρ
πολλῷ ἄμεινον, ἢν διὰ μέγεθος τῶν δακτύλων ἐκ κοι-
λοτέρας τῆς χειρὸς ἀναπέμπηται ἡ ἴτυς τοῦ δίσκου,
καὶ εὐκοπώτερον κινήσει τὸ ἀκόντιον, ἂν μὴ τοῦ με-
σαγκύλου ἄνω ψαύωσιν οἱ δάκτυλοι σμικροὶ ὄντες.

32. Ὁ δὲ ἄριστα δολιχοδρομήσων τοὺς μὲν ὤμους
καὶ τὸν αὐχένα κεκρατύσθω παραπλησίως πεντάθλῳ,
σκελῶν τε λεπτῶς ἐχέτω καὶ κούφως ὥσπερ οἱ τοῦ
σταδίου δρομεῖς· ἐκεῖνοι μὲν γὰρ σκέλη χερσὶ κινοῦ-
σιν ἐς τὸν ὀξὺν δρόμον οἷον πτερούμενοι ὑπὸ τῶν
χειρῶν, δολιχοδρόμοι δὲ τουτὶ μὲν περὶ τέρμα πράτ-
τουσι, τὸν ⟨δ'⟩ ἄλλον χρόνον σχεδὸν οἷον διαβαίνου-
σιν ἀνέχοντες ἐν προβολῇ τὰς χεῖρας, ὅθεν ἐρρωμε-
νεστέρων τῶν ὤμων δέονται.

33. Ὁπλίτου δὲ καὶ σταδίου ἀγωνιστὴν καὶ διαύλου
διακρίνει μὲν οὐδεὶς ἔτι ἐκ χρόνων οὓς Λεωνίδας ὁ
Ῥόδιος ἐπ' ὀλυμπιάδας τέτταρας ἐνίκα τὴν τριττὺν

109 In other words, an athlete with long fingers will be able to
curve them over the edge of the discus in order to get a better
grip.

110 An ancient javelin for use in athletic competition would
have a leather strap wound around it in the middle; the javelin
thrower would fix his index and middle finger into the strap to add
more force and precision to his throw. See Miller (2004, 68–73)

with the rocking motion required for the javelin and the discus, and to help with the long jump; for he will jump more painlessly, and he will not break any part of his body, if he can bring his hips down gently so as to gain a solid stance. He should also have large hands and long fingers; for he will throw the discus much better, if the rim of the discus is thrown from a hand which is able to form more of a hollow because of the large size of the fingers,[109] and he will propel the javelin more easily if his fingers do not touch the sling just with their tips,[110] through being small.

32. The athlete who will be best at the *dolichos* should have strong shoulders and a strong neck like the pentathlete, but he should have slender and light legs like *stadion* runners. For they move their legs in a sharp run with their arms, carried along by their arms as if by wings, whereas the *dolichos* runners do this at the end of the race, but for the rest of the race they run almost as though they are walking with their arms held up in a boxing stance, for which reason they need more powerful shoulders.

33. Nobody now draws distinctions between the competitors in the armor race and the *stadion* and the *diaulos,* not since the time when the Rhodian Leonidas won this triple at four Olympiads.[111] Nevertheless one should dis-

for detailed discussion, with reference to a wide range of images from ancient vases. Philostratus suggests that this process will be more effective if the fingers are long enough to get a good grip on the strap, just as long fingers allow a better grip on the discus.

111 Leonidas won all three events at four Olympic festivals in a row (164, 160, 156, and 152 BC); cf. Paus. 6.13.4 for the claim that he was the most famous of ancient runners.

ταύτην, διακριτέοι δ᾽ ὅμως οἵ τε καθ᾽ ἓν ἀγωνιούμενοι
ταῦτα καὶ οἱ ὁμοῦ πάντα. τὸν μὲν δὴ ὁπλιτεύσοντα
πλευρά τε εὐμήκη παραπεμπέτω ὦμος <τ᾽> εὐτραφὴς
καὶ σιμὴ ἐπωμίς,[46] ἵν᾽ εὖ φοροῖτο ἡ ἀσπὶς ἀνεχόντων
αὐτὴν τούτων. σταδιοδρόμοι δέ, τὸ κουφότατον τῶν ἐν
ἀγωνίᾳ, κράτιστοι μὲν καὶ οἱ ξύμμετροι, βελτίους δὲ
τούτων οἱ μὴ ὑπερμήκεις, ἀλλὰ μικρὸν τῶν ξυμμέ-
τρων εὐμηκέστεροι· τὸ γὰρ ὑπερβάλλον μῆκος ἁμαρ-
τάνει τοῦ βεβαίου, καθάπερ τῶν φυτῶν τὰ ὑψοῦ ἀνε-
στηκότα. ξυγκείσθων δὲ εὐπαγεῖς, ἀρχὴ γὰρ τοῦ εὖ
δραμεῖν τὸ εὖ στῆναι. ἁρμονία δὲ αὐτῶν ἥδε· τὰ
σκέλη ἰσόρροπα εἶναι τοῖς ὤμοις, τὸν θώρακα εἶναι
μείω ξυμμέτρου καὶ εὔσπλαγχνον, ἐλαφρὰν ἐπιγου-
νίδα, κνήμην ὀρθήν, χεῖρας ὑπὲρ τὸν λόγον· ἔστω δὲ
αὐτοῖς καὶ τὸ μυῶδες ξύμμετρον, οἱ γὰρ περιττοὶ μύες
δεσμοὶ τοῦ τάχους. διαύλου δὲ ἀγωνισταὶ κατεσκευ-
άσθων ἐρρωμενέστεροι μὲν <ἢ>[47] οἱ τὸ στάδιον, κου-
φότεροι δὲ τῶν ὁπλιτευόντων. οἱ δὲ τῶν τριῶν ἀγωνι-
σταὶ δρόμων ἀριστίνδην συντετάχθων, συγκείμενοι
ἐκ πλεονεκτημάτων, ὧν οὗτοι κατὰ ἕνα. τουτὶ δὲ μὴ
τῶν ἀπόρων ἡγείσθω τις, δρομεῖς γὰρ δὴ καὶ ἐφ᾽
ἡμῶν τοιοῦτοι ἐγένοντο.

34. Ὁ δὲ πυκτεύων μακρόχειρ ἔστω καὶ εὔπηχυς
καὶ τὸν βραχίονα μὴ ὑποσφριγῶν[48] καὶ τοὺς ὤμους

[46] ἐπωμίς Zingerle: ἐπιγουνίς P, Jüthner
[47] Suppl. Daremberg
[48] ὑποσφριγῶν Zingerle: * ...ριγγὴς Jüthner: [..]φριγγὴς P

tinguish between those who compete in just one of those contests and those who compete in all three. The athlete who intends to compete in the armor race should be distinguished by good-sized flanks, a well developed shoulder and a rounded upper shoulder, so that the shield can be carried easily, supported by these parts of the body. Among runners in the *stadion*—which is the lightest of all the events—well proportioned athletes are very strong, but even better than these are athletes who are not oversized but who are nevertheless a little taller than the well proportioned. For excessive height leads to a lack of stability, as in the case of plants which have grown tall. Their build should be solid, for the key to good running is good standing. Their body shape should be as follows: the legs should correspond to the shoulders; the trunk should be less than regular size, and with good internal organs; the knees should be nimble, the shins straight, the hands larger than usual. Their muscles should be moderate in bulk, for excessive muscles are a hindrance to speed. As for the competitors in the *diaulos,* let them be more powerful than the *stadion* runners, but lighter than those who compete in the race in armor. Those who compete in all three races should be assembled by merit, made up of all the good qualities which these single-race competitors hold individually. Let no one think that this is something impossible, for there have been runners of that kind even in our own time.

34. The boxer should have large hands and well-built forearms, and upper arms which are not lacking in vigor

εὔλοφος καὶ ὑψαύχην. καρποὶ δὲ πήχεων οἱ μὲν πα-
χεῖς βαρύτεροι ἐς τὸ πλήττειν, οἱ δ᾽ ἧττον παχεῖς[49]
ὑγροί τέ εἰσι καὶ σὺν ῥᾳστώνῃ παίοντες. ἐρειδέτω δὲ
αὐτὸν καὶ ἰσχίον εὐπαγές· ἡ γὰρ προβολὴ τῶν χει-
ρῶν ἀποκρεμάννυσι τ<ο σ>ὡ<μα εἰ>[50] μὴ ἐπὶ βεβαίου
ὀχοῖτο τοῦ ἰσχίου. παχυκνήμους δὲ οὐδ᾽ ἄλλου
<μὲν>[51] οὐδενὸς τῶν ἐν ἀγωνίᾳ ἀξιῶ, πυγμῆς δὲ ἥκι-
στα· καὶ γὰρ δὴ καὶ προσβῆναι ταῖς τῶν ἀντιπάλων
κνήμαις ἀργοὶ καὶ εὐάλωτοι τῷ προσβάντι. ἐχέτω δὴ
κνήμην μὲν ὀρθὴν καὶ ξύμμετρον[52] μηρῶν ἀπηλλαγ-
μένων τε καὶ διεστηκότων· ὁρμητικώτερον γὰρ τὸ
σχῆμα τοῦ πυκτεύοντος, ἢν μὴ ξυμβαίνωσιν οἱ μη-
ροί. γαστὴρ δὲ ἀρίστη μὲν ὑπεσταλμένη· κοῦφοι γὰρ
δὴ οἱ τοιοίδε[53] καὶ τὸ πνεῦμα ἀγαθοί. ἔστι δ᾽ ὅμως τι
καὶ παρὰ τῆς γαστρὸς ὄφελος τῷ πυκτεύοντι, τὰς
γὰρ τοῦ προσώπου πληγὰς ἡ τοιάδε γαστὴρ ἐρύκει
προεμβάλλουσα τῇ φορᾷ τοῦ πλήττοντος.

35. Ἴωμεν ἐπὶ τοὺς παλαίσοντας. ὁ παλαιστὴς ὁ
κατὰ λόγον εὐμήκης μὲν ἔστω μᾶλλον ἢ ξύμμετρος,
ἡρμόσθω δὲ ὥσπερ οἱ ξύμμετροι, μήθ᾽ ὑψαύχην μήτε
ὤμοις τὸν αὐχένα ἐπεζευγμένος· τουτὶ γὰρ δὴ προσ-

[49] παχεῖς Volckmar: βαρεῖς P
[50] τὸ σῶμα, εἰ Kayser: τ[ֹ]ὡ[. . . . .] P
[51] Suppl. Kayser
[52] ξύμμετρον Jüthner: ξυμμέτρως P
[53] οἱ τοιοίδε Cobet: οὕτω οἴδε P

and strong shoulders and a high neck. Thick wrists give a heavier punch; those that are less thick are flexible and punch with ease. Let him also be supported by well-built hips, for the forward projection of the hands drags the body downward, unless it is supported on firm hips. I think that those who have bulky calves are not well suited to any of the disciplines, but least of all to boxing. For these athletes will be slow to kick against the shins of their adversaries, and easily kicked in turn. The boxer should have calves that are straight and well proportioned, while the thighs should be well distanced and separate from each other. For the shape of the boxer is more suited to attack if his thighs do not come together. The best kind of stomach for a boxer is slim; for these athletes are light and have good breathing. Nevertheless there is some advantage in the stomach for a boxer, for a stomach of this kind can ward off blows against the face by sticking out in a way that impedes the forward motion of the punching opponent.[112]

35. Let us move on to those athletes who intend to compete in the wrestling. The ideal wrestler should be tall rather than well-proportioned in size, but his body shape should be the same as that of the well-proportioned athlete, having neither a high neck nor a neck which is sunk into the shoulders.[113] That latter body shape is suitable, to be sure, but it looks more like someone who is de-

112 Philostratus presumably thinks that a large stomach can prevent one's opponent getting close enough to land a good blow, not that the stomach itself can get in the way of the punch.

113 Cf. Philostr. Her. 49.3 for a free-standing neck as a sign of athletic training; Imag. 2.21.4 for a sunken neck linked with brute strength.

φυὲς μέν, παραπλήσιον δὲ κεκολασμένῳ μᾶλλον ἢ
γεγυμνασμένῳ τῷ γε ξυνιέντι καὶ τῶν Ἡρακλείων
ἀγαλμάτων, ὅσῳ ἡδίω καὶ θεοειδέστερα τὰ ἐλευθέριά
τε καὶ μὴ ξυντράχηλα. ἀλλ᾽ ἔστω αὐχὴν μὲν ἀνεστη-
κὼς ὥσπερ ἐν ἵππῳ καλῷ καὶ ἑαυτοῦ ξυνιέντι, καθ-
ήκουσα δὲ ἐς κλεῖν ἑκατέραν ἡ βάσις τῆς δέρης. συν-
αγωγοὶ δὲ ἐπωμίδες <καὶ>[54] κεφαλαὶ ὤμων ἀνεστηκυῖαι
μέγεθός τε ξυμβάλλονται τῷ παλαίσοντι καὶ γεννναι-
ότητα εἴδους καὶ ἰσχὺν καὶ παλαίειν ἄμεινον· οἱ γὰρ
τοιοίδε ὦμοι καὶ καμπτομένου τοῦ αὐχένος καὶ στρε-
βλουμένου ὑπὸ τῆς πάλης ἀγαθοὶ φύλακες προσερεί-
δοντες τὴν κεφαλὴν ἐκ τῶν βραχιόνων. βραχίων εὔ-
σημος ἀγαθὸν πάλης· βραχίονα δὲ καλῶ εὔσημον
τὸν τοιόνδε· εὐρεῖαι φλέβες ἄρχονται μὲν ἐξ αὐχένος
καὶ δέρης μία ἑκατέρωθεν, ἐπιβᾶσαι δὲ τοῦ ὤμου κα-
τίασιν ἐπὶ τὼ χεῖρε βραχιοσί τε καὶ ὠλέναις ἐμπρέ-
πουσαι. οἷς μὲν δὴ ἐπιπόλαιοί τέ εἰσι καὶ τοῦ μετρίου
ἐπιφανέστεραι, οὔτε ἰσχὺν παρ᾽ αὐτῶν ἄρνυνται καὶ
ἀηδεῖς ἰδεῖν αἵδε φλέβες ὥσπερ οἱ κιρσοί· οἷς δ᾽ ἂν
βαθεῖαι τύχωσι καὶ ὑποκυμαίνουσαι,[55] λεπτόν τε ἐκ-
προφαίνουσι τούτοις καὶ ἴδιον τῶν χειρῶν πνεῦμα,
καὶ τὸν βραχίονα προηκόντων μὲν ὑπονεάζουσι, νεα-

54 Suppl. Jüthner
55 ὑποκυμαίνουσαι Cobet: ἐπικυμαίνουσαι P

114 Presumably Philostratus has in mind here a contrast be-
tween the ideal athletic statue type of the classical period and the
more "realistic," bulky athletic statues that became common from

formed than someone who has been trained, at any rate
for those who perceive, also in the case of statues of Her-
acles, how much more pleasant and godlike are noble bod-
ies which do not have their heads sunk into their shoul-
ders.[114] Rather, the neck should be erect like the neck of
a beautiful and proud horse and the base of the throat
should stretch down to both collar bones. Well-connected
upper shoulders and elevated shoulder tips contribute
bulk to the future wrestler and nobleness of appearance
and strength and help him to wrestle better; for shoulders
of this kind, even when the neck is being bent and twisted
in the wrestling, are good defenses, by conveying support
from the arms to the head. An arm which is well marked
is an advantage for wrestling. And this is the kind of arm
I refer to as well marked. In the human body wide veins
run from the neck and the throat, one on each side, pro-
ceed to the shoulders and from there go down conspicu-
ously to the hands along the arms and the elbows. Those
who have veins that are on the surface and more con-
spicuous than normal do not take strength from them; not
only that but these veins are unpleasant to look at, like
varicose veins. But those who happen to have deep veins
that swell only a little show signs, by these veins, of a
delicate and distinctive *pneuma*[115] in their hands; and
veins of this type bring new life to the arms of those who

the Hellenistic period onward, most famously the "Farnese Her-
cules."

115 *Pneuma* (literally translated, "breath") is in much ancient
medical thought the substance that sustains life in all animal bod-
ies; it was thought to be distributed particularly through the arter-
ies to all parts of the body.

ζόντων δὲ λέγουσιν ὁρμητήν τε φαίνεσθαι καὶ ἐν
ἐπαγγελίᾳ πάλης. στέρνα μὲν ἀμείνω τὰ προέχοντά⁵⁶
τε καὶ ἐκκείμενα· τὰ γὰρ σπλάγχνα αὐτοῖς ὥσπερ ἐν
οἰκίσκῳ <ἁδρ>ῷ⁵⁷ τε καὶ εὐσχήμονι ἵδρυται γενναῖα
ἰσχυρὰ ἄνοσα θυμοειδῆ ξὺν καιρῷ. χαρίεντα δὲ τῶν
στέρνων καὶ τὰ μετρίως μὲν ἐκκείμενα, περιεσκλη-
κότα δὲ σὺν γραμμαῖς· ἰσχυρά τε γὰρ ταῦτα καὶ εὔ-
φορα καὶ παλαῖσαι μὲν ἥττονα, παλαιστικώτερα δὲ
τῶν ἄλλων. κοῖλα δὲ στέρνα καὶ εἰσέχοντα οὔτε ἀπο-
δύειν ἀξιῶ οὔτε γυμνάζειν· καὶ γὰρ στομάχοις ἁλί-
σκονται καὶ οὐκ εὔσπλαγχνοι καὶ τὸ πνεῦμα στενοί.
γαστὴρ δὲ ὑπεστάλθω μὲν παρὰ τὸ ἦτρον—οὐ γὰρ
χρηστὸν ἄχθος ἡ γαστὴρ τῷ παλαίοντι—ἐποχείσθω
δὲ μὴ κενοῖς τοῖς βουβῶσιν, ἀλλ᾽ ἔστω τι κἀκείνων
εὐτραφές· οἱ γὰρ τοιοίδε βουβῶνες συνδῆσαί τε ἱκα-
νοὶ πᾶν, ὅπερ ἡ πάλη παραδιδῷ καὶ ξυνδεθέντες ἀνιά-
σουσι μᾶλλον ἢ ἀνιάσονται. νῶτα δὲ χαρίεντα μὲν
ὀρθά, γυμναστικώτερα δὲ τὰ ὑπόγυρα, ἐπειδὴ καὶ
προσφυέστερα τῷ τῆς πάλης σχήματι⁵⁸ γυρῷ τε ὄντι
καὶ προνεύοντι. κρινέτω δ᾽ αὐτὰ μὴ κοίλη ῥάχις· ἐπι-

---

⁵⁶ προέχοντά Mynas: προσέχοντά P
⁵⁷ Suppl. Jüthner: [. . .]ῷ P
⁵⁸ σχήματι Jüthner: ὀχήματι P

---

¹¹⁶ Presumably especially the lungs in this case.
¹¹⁷ Literally, "with lines," and presumably meaning "well-de-
fined"; cf. ch. 38 for a similar use of the word εὔγραμμοι.

are advanced in age, while in the case of young athletes they announce that the arm seems ready for action and promises much for wrestling. The better kinds of chest are those which project forward and stick out; for the innards[116] are contained in them as if in a solid and shapely chamber and are kept in excellent condition and strong and free from disease and spirited, with a good sense of timing. Also graceful is the type of chest that sticks out to a moderate degree and is lean and lined;[117] for chests of this type are strong and agile and less good for wrestling than the type just mentioned, but nevertheless more suitable for wrestling than all the others. Those who have chests that are hollow and concave should not strip or train, in my opinion; for they can suffer from ill health in their stomachs, and they do not have sound internal organs, and they are constricted in their breathing. And let the stomach be restricted in its lower parts—for the stomach is not a useful weight for a wrestler—and let it be supported by a groin which is not lacking in substance but which should rather be quite well developed. For a groin of that kind is able to crush whatever it encounters in a wrestling bout, and having been squeezed together will cause trouble for the opponent rather than undergoing injury itself.[118] Straight backs are graceful, but the type that are slightly curved are more athletic, since they are better adapted for the shape of wrestling, which is curved and forward leaning. They should be divided in two by a spine that is not hollow, for that will mean it is lacking in

118 For a good example, see Philostr. *Imag.* 2.6.4, where the pankratiast Arrichion traps his opponent by squeezing him in his groin.

λείψει γὰρ μυελοῦ τοῦτο, καὶ οἱ σπόνδυλοι ἐκεῖ κάμ-
πτοιντο καὶ προσαναγκάζοιντο ὑπὸ τῶν παλαισμά-
των καὶ ὀλισθῆσαί τί ποτε εἰς τὸ ἔσω· ἀλλ᾽ ὑπονοείσθω
καὶ δὴ μᾶλλον ἢ ἔστω. τὸ δὲ ἰσχίον οἷον ἄξονα ἐμ-
βεβλημένον τοῖς ἄνω τε καὶ κάτω μέλεσιν ὑγρόν τε
εἶναι χρὴ καὶ εὔστροφον καὶ ἐπιστρεφές· τουτὶ δ᾽ ἐρ-
γάζεται μῆκός τε αὐτοῦ καὶ νὴ Δί᾽ εὐσαρκία περιττο-
τέρα τοῦ λόγου. τὰ δὲ ὑπὸ τῷ ἰσχίῳ μήτε ὑπόλισφα
ἔστω μήτ᾽ αὖ περιττά—τὸ μὲν γὰρ ἀσθενές, τὸ δ᾽
ἀγύμναστον—ἀλλ᾽ ἐκκείσθω σφοδρῶς τε καὶ προσ-
φυῶς τῷ παλαίσοντι. πλευρὰ δὲ εὐκαμπὴς καὶ προσ-
γυροῦσα⁵⁹ τὸ στέρνον ἱκανοὺς ποιεῖ παλαίειν τε καὶ
παλαίεσθαι· καὶ γὰρ ὑποκείμενοι τοῖς ἀντιπάλοις
δυσάλωτοι οἱ τοιοίδε καὶ οὐκ εὔφοροι ὑποκειμένοις.
γλουτοὶ δὲ οἱ μὲν στενοὶ ἀσθενεῖς, οἱ δὲ εὐρύτεροι
ἀργοί, οἱ δ᾽ εὐάγωγοι ἱκανοὶ ἐς πάντα. μηρὸς δὲ εὐ-
παγὴς καὶ ἐς τὸ ἔξω ἐπεστραμμένος ξὺν ὥρᾳ ἔρρωται
καὶ ἀνέχει εὖ πάντα, καὶ μᾶλλον εἰ μηδαμοῦ ἐκκλί-
νουσα κνήμη φέροιτο, ἀλλ᾽ ὀρθῆς ὁ μηρὸς ἐποχοῖτο⁶⁰
τῆς ἐπιγουνα‹τ›ίδ‹ος. τὰ› δὲ μ‹ὴ ὀρθὰ⁶¹ τῶν σφυρῶν,
ἀλλὰ λοξά τε καὶ εἰς τὸ εἴσω διωλισθηκότα σφάλλει
τὸ σῶμα καθάπερ τοὺς ἑδραίους τῶν κιόνων μὴ ὀρθαὶ
βάσεις. τοιόσδε μὲν ὁ παλαιστής καὶ παγκρατιάσει
γε ὁ τοιόσδε τὸ κάτω παγκράτιον, ἀκροχειριεῖται δὲ

---

⁵⁹ προσγυροῦσα Zingerle: προσεγείρουσα P, Jüthner
⁶⁰ ἐποχοῖτο Mynas: ἐνοχοῖτο P   ⁶¹ ἐπιγουνα‹τ›ίδ‹ος.
τὰ› δὲ μ‹ὴ ὀρθ›ὰ Jüthner: ἐπιγουνα[.]ίδ[. . . .]δε μ[. . . .]ὰ P

marrow, and the vertebrae in it are likely to be twisted and wrenched by the wrestling holds and some part might even occasionally slip inward; but that last point is more a matter of conjecture than fact. The hip should be fluid and flexible and supple, like an axle positioned between the limbs above and below; this is achieved by large size and, by Zeus, exceptional fleshiness in the hip. However, the part below the hip should not be flat nor should it be excessively bulky—for the one is weak, while the other is unsuitable for training—but it should project powerfully and in a way that is suitable for the future wrestler. A flank that is curved and makes the chest rounded[119] helps wrestlers to be good both in attack and defense; for when they are underneath their opponents, athletes of this kind are hard to defeat, and they are not an easy load to bear for those who are underneath them. Narrow buttocks are weak, buttocks that are too wide are sluggish, well-formed buttocks are suitable for everything. A thigh that is compact and turned outward is both strong and beautiful and supports the rest of the body well, and all the more so if the shin which props it up is not bent outward but instead the thigh is held up by a knee that is straight. Ankles that are not straight but instead slanting and turned inward make the body fall, just as uneven bases do even in the case of steady columns. That is what the wrestler is like. This kind of athlete will also compete in the parts of the *pankration* that take place on the ground but he will have

[119] Cf. Philostratus Minor, *Imag.* 14.4 for a good parallel, where a rounded chest is associated with good breathing.

ἧττον. τελεώτεροι τῶν παγκρατιαστῶν οἱ ξυγκείμενοι παλαιστικώτερον μὲν ἢ οἱ πύκται, πυκτικώτερον δὲ ἢ οἱ παλαίσοντες.

36. Γενναῖοι τῶν ἀθλητῶν καὶ οἱ ἐν μικρῷ μεγάλοι. τούτους δὲ ἡγώμεθα τοὺς ὑποδεεστέρους μὲν τὸ μέγεθος ἢ τετράγωνοί τε καὶ σύμμετροι, τὸ δὲ σῶμα διηρθρωμένους μεγαλοειδῶς τε καὶ ὑπερφυεστέρως τοῦ μήκους καὶ μᾶλλον, ἢν μὴ κατεσκληκέναι δοκῶσιν, ἀλλὰ καὶ τοῦ εὐσάρκου τι ὑποφαίνωσι. κηρύττει δὲ αὐτοὺς πάλη μᾶλλον· εὔστροφοί τε γὰρ καὶ πολύτροποι καὶ σφοδροὶ καὶ κοῦφοι καὶ ταχεῖς καὶ ὁμότονοι, καὶ πολλὰ τῶν ἀπόρων τε καὶ δυσπαλαίστων διαφεύγουσιν ἐπιστηριζόμενοι τῇ κεφαλῇ, καθάπερ βάσει· παγκρατίου δὲ καὶ πυγμῆς οὐκ ἀγαθοὶ προστάται τῷ τε πλήττοντι ὑποκείμενοι καὶ γελοίως ἀπὸ τῆς γῆς ἑαυτοὺς προσαίροντες, ὁπότε αὐτοὶ πλήττοιεν. παράδειγμα δὲ ποιώμεθα τῶν ἐν μικρῷ μεγάλων τὰς εἰκόνας τοῦ παλαιστοῦ Μάρωνος, ὃν Κιλικία ποτὲ ἤνεγκε. παραιτητέον δὲ τούτων καὶ τοὺς μακροθώρακας· διαφυγεῖν μὲν γὰρ ⟨τὰ τῆς⟩[62] πάλης ἱκανοὶ καὶ οἵδε, καταπαλαῖσαι δὲ ἀχρεῖοι διὰ τὸ ἐπικαθῆσθαι τοῖς σκέλεσι.

[62] Suppl. Jüthner

---

[120] Cf. n. 61, above, on the standard distinction between the two phases of wrestling ("upright" and "rolling"). This passage implies a similar distinction for the *pankration,* and cf. ch. 57.

less success in the hand-to-hand fighting.[120] The more perfect pankratiasts are those who have a more wrestler-like body type than the boxers, and a more boxer-like body type than those who wish to be wrestlers.

36. Another excellent type of athlete is those who are known as "big in small."[121] We should view these as athletes who are smaller in size than those who are squarely built or well proportioned, but who nevertheless have well structured bodies that are large in appearance and more bulky than is normal for people of their size, and all the more so if they do not give an impression of being emaciated but actually reveal a certain amount of fleshiness. Wrestling shows off their skills best; for they are flexible and versatile and vigorous and light and quick and uniform, and they are able to escape from many situations that are impossible and hard to fight out of by supporting themselves on their heads as if on their feet. In *pankration* and boxing, however, they are not good fighters, since they are hit from above by their opponents and have to raise themselves up in the air in a comical fashion whenever they themselves throw punches. We can take as an example of the "big in small" athletes the images of the wrestler Maron,[122] who once lived in Cilicia. Within that category, those with large chests should also be rejected; for these athletes too are able to escape from their opponents' wrestling holds, but they are useless at throwing their opponents because of the weight which presses on their legs.

[121] In other words, as the rest of the paragraph makes clear, stocky athletes, of relatively small stature but strong and heavily built. [122] See Grossardt (2002) and *Her.* 14.4n54, above.

37. Λεοντώδεις δὲ καὶ ἀετώδεις καὶ σχιζίαι καὶ οὓς ἐπονομάζουσιν ἄρκτους,[63] τοιάδε ἀθλητῶν εἴδη. οἱ λεοντώδεις εὔστερνοι μὲν καὶ εὔχειρες, ὑποδεέστεροι δὲ κατόπιν, <οἱ δ' ἀετώδεις>[64] τὸ μὲν σχῆμα τούτοις <ὅμοιοι>,[65] διάκενοι δὲ τοὺς βουβῶνας ὥσπερ τῶν ἀετῶν οἱ ὀρθούμενοι. ἄμφω δὲ οἵδε τολμητάς τε ἀποφαίνουσι καὶ σφοδροὺς καὶ ἀθρόους, ἀθυμοτέρους γε μὴν τὰς διαμαρτίας· καὶ οὐ χρὴ θαυμάζειν ἐνθυμουμένους τὰ λεόντων τε καὶ ἀετῶν ἤθη.

38. Σχιζίαι τε <καὶ>[66] ἱμαντώδεις εὐμήκεις μὲν ἄμφω καὶ μακροὶ τὰ σκέλη καὶ ὑπέρχειρες, διενηνόχασι δὲ ἀλλήλων μικρά τε καὶ μείζονα· οἱ μὲν γὰρ στρυφνοί τε καταφαίνονται καὶ εὔγραμμοι καὶ πολυσχιδεῖς, ὅθεν οἶμαι καὶ ἡ ἐπωνυμία αὐτοῖς ἥκει, οἱ δὲ μανοί τέ εἰσι καὶ ἀνειμένοι μᾶλλον, καὶ ὑγ<ροὶ τὸ σῶμα, ὁμοιούμενοι δι' αὐτὰ> ταῦτα[67] τοῖς μάσθλησιν. εἰσὶ δ' αὐτῶν οἱ μὲν ἰταμώτεροι τὰς συμπλοκάς, οἱ δὲ ἱμαντώδεις συνεκτικώτεροί τε καὶ εἴ<ρων>ες.[68]

---

[63] ἄρκτους Kayser: ἄκουσον P
[64] Suppl. Jüthner
[65] Suppl. Jüthner
[66] Suppl. Mynas
[67] Suppl. Jüthner: ὑγρ[...............................] ταῦτα P
[68] εἴ<ρω>νες Mynas: εἴροντες Daremberg, Kitriniari: εἴ[...] ες P

464

37. "Leonine" and "eagle-like" and "splinter-like" and those known as "bears," these are all types of athlete. Leonine athletes have well built chests and arms, but are lacking in the hind part of the body, while eagle-like athletes are similar to these in their appearance, but are thin in their groin region, like eagles when they stand up straight. Both of these categories display athletes who are daring and forceful and impetuous, but apt to lose heart when things go badly; and one should not be surprised at that, when one thinks about the nature of lions and eagles.[123]

38. The athletes who are "splinter-like" and "strap-like" are both tall, with long legs and larger than average arms, but they differ from each other in both small and larger details. For the former look rigid, well defined and with the different parts of the body well distinguished from each other—hence, I think, the name—whereas the latter are looser and more relaxed, and flexible in their bodies, and are compared because of that to leather straps. The former are more daring in hand-to-hand wrestling, whereas the latter, the strap-like, are harder to disentangle and inclined to inactivity in their wrestling holds.[124]

---

[123] Cf. Introduction on comparison between humans and animals as a common feature of ancient physiognomical reasoning.

[124] Cf. ch. 25 for Jüthner's (1909) translation of εἴρωνες as "sluggish" or "inactive" (contrasted in this case with the word ἰταμώτεροι, i.e., more daring) rather than as the more conventional "dissembling." In this case the alternative reading εἴροντες, proposed by Daremberg (1858) and Kitriniari (1961) by analogy with ch. 40, and meaning in this context "good at intertwining," also seems plausible, although Jüthner points out that it is too long for the gap in the manuscript.

39. ‹Καρ›τ‹ε›ρικῶν τε ἀθλητῶν εἴδη ‹σκληρο›ί, μυ-
ώδεις, κοῖλοι τ‹ὸ ἰσχίον, ἀ›νεσκιρτηκότες τὴν ὄψιν.⁶⁹
‹ἐνιαχ›οῦ μὲν ἐοίκασι καὶ ἀ‹νάλ›ω‹τοι›,⁷⁰ ἀσφαλέ-
στεροι δ' αὐτῶν οἱ φλεγματώδεις· οἱ γὰρ ἐπίχολοι
σφῶν οἷοι [καὶ]⁷¹ διὰ τὸ ἕτοιμον τῆς φύσεως καὶ μα-
νικῶς παραλλάξαι.

40. Οἱ δὲ ταῖς ἄρκτοις ὁμοιούμενοι στρογγύλοι τέ
εἰσι καὶ ὑγροὶ καὶ εὔσαρκοι καὶ ἧττον διηρθρωμένοι
καὶ περιεχεῖς μᾶλλον ἢ ὀρθοί, δυσπάλαιστοί τε καὶ
διολισθαίνοντες, καρτερῶς ‹δ'›⁷² εἴροντες. καὶ σφαρα-
γεῖ⁷³ δὲ τούτοις τὸ πνεῦμα καθάπερ ταῖς ἄρκτοις ἐν
τοῖς δρόμοις.

41. Οἱ δὲ ἰσόχειρες, οὓς περιδεξίους ὀνομάζουσι,
σπάνιον εὕρημα φύσεως ὄντες τήν τε ἰσχὺν ἄρρηκτοί
εἰσι⁷⁴ καὶ δυσφύλακτοι καὶ ἀκμῆτες· τουτὶ γὰρ αὐτοῖς
δίδωσι τὸ ἰσοδέξιον αὐτὸ τοῦ⁷⁵ σώματος πλέον ἰσχύον
τῶν ἀρτίων. τουτὶ δὲ ὁπόθεν, λέγω· Μῦς ὁ Αἰγύπτιος,
ἐγὼ τῶν πρεσβυτέρων ἤκουον, ἀνθρώπιον μὲν ἦν οὐ
μέγα, ἐπάλαιε δὲ πρόσω τέχνης. τούτῳ νοσήσαντι
ἐπέδωκε τὰ ἀριστερά· τοῦ δὲ ἀθλεῖν ἀπεγνωκότι ὄναρ
ἐγένετο θαρρεῖν τὴν νόσον, ἰσχύσειν γὰρ πλέον τοῖς

---

⁶⁹ Suppl. Jüthner: [. . .]τ[.]ρικῶν τε ἀθλητῶν εἴδη [. . . . . .]ί,
μυώδεις, κοῖλοι τ[. . . . . . .]νεσκιρτηκότες τὴν ὄψιν P
⁷⁰ Suppl. Zingerle: [. . . .]οῦ μὲν ἐοίκασι καὶ ἀ[. . . .]ωτ[. .] P,
Jüthner   ⁷¹ Del. Kayser   ⁷² Suppl. Daremberg
⁷³ σφαραγεῖ Volckmar: σπαράζει P
⁷⁴ ἄρρηκτοί εἰσι Mynas: ἄρρητοί[. .]σι P
⁷⁵ αὐτὸ τοῦ Jüthner: αὐτοῦ P

39. The types of athlete who endure well are those who are hard, muscular, with lean hips and animated faces; sometimes they even seem undefeatable. The more dependable of these much-enduring athletes are those who are phlegmatic; for choleric athletes in this category can even fall into madness because of the active quality of their natures.

40. Those who are similar to bears are rounded and supple and fleshy and less well structured and stooping rather than upright, and they are hard to wrestle against and good at slipping away and strong in the intertwining that wrestling requires. And their breath splutters like bears when they are running.

41. Those athletes who are ambidextrous and are known as having "two right hands" are a rarity in nature; they have an unbreakable strength and they are hard to defend against and untiring. And it is their bodily ambidextrousness which in itself gives them these qualities, being more powerful than normal types of bodily condition. Where that information comes from, I shall explain. The Egyptian, Mys,[125] so I have heard from some older informants, was a little chap of no great size, but he wrestled beyond the normal limits of the art. At one point after he had been ill his left side grew bigger; he had decided to give up competing when a dream appeared to him telling him to have no fear of the illness, for he would be stronger in the damaged parts of his body than in those

---

[125] Not attested elsewhere, and to be distinguished from the boxer Mys from Tarentum, Olympic victor in 336 BC.

πεπηρωμένοις ἢ τοῖς ἀκεραίοις τε καὶ ἀτρώτοις. καὶ
ἀληθὴς ἡ ὄψις· τὰ γὰρ δυσφύλακτα τῶν παλαισμά-
των τοῖς βεβλαμμένοις τῶν μερῶν διαπλέκων χαλε-
πὸς ἦν τοῖς ἀντιπάλοις καὶ ὤνητο τῆς νόσου τῷ τοῖς
διεφθορόσιν ἐρρῶσθαι. τοῦτο θαυμάσιον μέν, εἰρή-
σθω δὲ μὴ ὡς γιγνόμενον ἀλλ' ὡς γενόμενον καὶ θεοῦ
δοκείτω μᾶλλον ἐνδεικνυμένου τι ἀνθρώποις μέγα.

42. Περὶ μὲν δὴ σώματος ἀναλογίας, καὶ εἴτε ὁ
τοιόσδε βελτίων εἴτε ὁ τοιόσδε, εἰσί που καὶ λεπταὶ[76]
ἀντιλογίαι[77] παρὰ τοῖς μὴ ξὺν λόγῳ διεσκεμμένοις
ταῦτα, περὶ δὲ κράσεων, ὁπόσαι εἰσίν, οὔτε ἀντείρη-
ταί πω οὔτε ἀντιλεχθείη ἂν τὸ μὴ οὐκ ἀρίστην κρά-
σεων τὴν θερμήν τε καὶ ὑγρὰν εἶναι· ξύγκειται γὰρ
ὥσπερ τὰ πολυτελῆ τῶν ἀγαλμάτων ἀκηράτου τε καὶ
καθαρᾶς ὕλης. ἐλεύθεροι μὲν πηλοῦ τε καὶ ἰλύος καὶ
χυμῶν περιττῶν, οἷς τὸ τοῦ φλέγματος καὶ τὸ τῆς
χολῆς σπανίζει[78] νᾶμα, εὐκάματοι δὲ ἃ χρὴ μοχθεῖν,
καὶ εὔσιτοι καὶ νοσοῦντες μὲν ὀλιγάκις, ταχὺ δ' ἐκ
τῶν νόσων ἀναφέροντες, εὐαγωγοί τε καὶ εὐήνιοι
γυμνάσαι ποικίλως δι' εὐμοιρίαν κράσεως. οἱ δ' ἐπί-
χολοι τῶν ἀθλητῶν θερμοὶ μέν, ξηροὶ δὲ τὴν κρᾶσιν
καὶ ἄκαρποι τοῖς γυμνάζουσι καθάπερ τοῖς σπείρου-
σιν αἱ θερμαὶ ψάμμοι. ἔρρωνται δ' ὅμως τῷ τῆς γνώ-
μης ἑτοίμῳ· περίεστι γὰρ αὐτοῖ‹ς› τούτου. οἱ δὲ φλεγ-

[76] λεπταὶ Jüthner: δεκταὶ P
[77] ἀντιλογίαι Cobet: ἀναλογίαι P
[78] σπανίζει Zingerle: ἐπαντλεῖ P, M

that were unharmed and undamaged. And the dream was right; for he used the damaged parts of his body to make wrestling holds which were very hard to defend against, and that made him very difficult for his opponents to deal with, and he benefited from his disease through being strengthened in the afflicted parts of the body. This is an amazing thing, and let us take it as a one-off incident rather than as something that happens regularly, and let it be viewed more as the work of a god revealing a great sign to humans.

42. As far as the topic of bodily proportions is concerned, and the question whether one kind is best or another kind, there are some minor disagreements among those who have not examined the matter rationally. But as far as the mixture of the humors is concerned it has never been disputed, nor would it ever be disputed, that the best type of mixture of all those that exist is the warm and moist one. For it is composed, like expensive statues, from material that is unmixed and pure. For those who have a sparse supply of phlegm and bile are consequently free of impurities and dregs and excessive humors; they also endure easily whatever hard work is necessary, have good digestion, are rarely ill and recover quickly from illness, and they are submissive and easy to train in a variety of different ways, thanks to their fortunate mixture of humors. Choleric athletes are on the one hand warm in temperament but also dry in their mix of humors and fruitless to trainers, just as hot sand is to those sowing crops. Despite that, they are formidable because of their mental boldness; for they have a very abundant supply of that.

ματώδεις βραδύτεροι τὴ>ν ἕξιν[79] ὑπὸ ψυχρότητος. γυμναστέοι τε οὗτοι συντόνως μ<ὲν κινούμενοι, οἱ δὲ> ἐπίχολοι[80] βάδην καὶ διαπνέοντες—τοῖς μὲν γὰρ δεῖ κέντρου, τοῖς δ᾽ ἡνίας—χρὴ δὲ τοὺς μὲν ξυνάγειν τῇ κόνει, τοὺς δὲ τῷ ἐλαίῳ ἐπαιονᾶν.[81]

43. Ταῦτα εἰρήσθω μοι περὶ κράσεως ἐκ τῆς νῦν γυμναστικῆς, ὡς ἡ ἀρχαία γε οὐδὲ ἐγίνωσκε κρᾶσιν, ἀλλὰ μόνην τὴν ἰσχὺν ἐγύμναζεν. γυμναστικὴν δὲ οἱ παλαιοὶ καὶ αὐτὸ τὸ ὁτιοῦν γυμνάζεσθαι· ἐγυμνά- ζοντο δὲ οἱ μὲν ἄχθη φέροντες οὐκ εὔφορα, οἱ δ᾽ ὑπὲρ τάχους ἁμιλλώμενοι πρὸς ἵππους καὶ πτῶκας, οἱ δ᾽ ὀρθοῦντές τε καὶ κάμπτοντες σίδηρον ἐληλαμένον εἰς παχύ, οἱ δὲ βουσὶ συνεζευγμένοι καρτεροῖς τε καὶ ἁμαξεύουσιν, οἱ δὲ ταύρους ἀπαυχενίζοντες,[82] οἱ δ᾽ αὐτοὺς λέοντας. ταῦτα δὲ δὴ Πολυμήστορες καὶ Γλαῦκοι καὶ Ἀλησίαι καὶ Πουλυδάμας ὁ Σκοτουσ- σαῖος. Τίσανδρον δὲ τὸν ἐκ τῆς Νάξου πύκτην περὶ

---

[79] Suppl. Jüthner: αὐτοῖ[..............................]ν
ἕξιν P   [80] Suppl. Jüthner: μ[...................] ἐπίχολοι P
[81] ἐπαιονᾶν Schmid: ἐπαιονεῖν M: ἐπαινεῖν P
[82] ἀπαυχενίζοντες Kayser: ἐπαυχενίζοντες P, M

---

[126] Training was thought to heat and dry the body; Philostra- tus therefore suggests that it can exaggerate still further the dry and warm temperaments of choleric athletes, i.e., those over- supplied with bile, hence the requirement that they should be trained in leisurely fashion. For phlegmatic athletes, by contrast, he suggests that energetic training can compensate for the natural coldness of the body.

Phlegmatic athletes are slower in their makeup because of their coldness. These must be trained with energetic movements, whereas choleric athletes must be trained in a leisurely fashion and with breaks[126]—in other words the former require a goad, the latter reins—and it is necessary to dry out the former by the application of dust, while moistening the latter with oil.[127]

43. That is all I wish to say about the mixture of humors as modern *gymnastikê* describes them. For the old *gymnastikê* did not even know about the mixtures of humors but trained only strength. By *gymnastikê* the men of the past meant any exercise whatsoever.[128] Some trained themselves by carrying weights that were hard to lift, some by competing for speed with horses and hares, others by straightening or bending thick pieces of wrought iron, while some yoked themselves with powerful, wagon-drawing oxen, and others wrestled bulls and even lions by the throat. That is what training involved for men like Polymestor[129] and Glaucus[130] and Alesias[131] and Poulydamas from Scotussa.[132] Tisandrus the boxer from Naxos[133] used

[127] Dust was generally associated with drying properties and oil with moistening properties.   [128] Cf. Gal. *Thrasybulus* 9 for a similarly positive portrayal of this kind of exertion in day-to-day life outside the gymnasium.   [129] Cf. ch. 13.

[130] Cf. chs. 1, esp. n. 5, and 20, esp. n. 88.

[131] Possibly the same as the athlete Amesinas, victor in the Olympic wrestling in 460 BC, who is said by Julius Africanus to have taken a bull with him to Olympia as a training partner.

[132] Cf. chs. 1, esp. n. 3, and 22, esp. n. 91.

[133] Cf. Paus. 6.13.8, who tells us that Tisandrus was four times victor in the boxing at Olympia and also that he came from the city of Naxos in Sicily rather than the island of Naxos as here.

471

τὰ ἀκρωτήρια τῆς νήσου νέοντα παρέπεμπον αἱ
χεῖρες ἐπὶ πολὺ τῆς θαλάσσης [παραπεμπόμεναι][83]
γυμναζόμεναί τε καὶ γυμνάζουσαι. ποταμοί τε αὐτοὺς
ἔλουον καὶ πηγαὶ καὶ χαμευνίαν ἐπήσκουν, οἱ μὲν ἐπὶ
βυρσῶν ἐκταθέντες, οἱ δ' εὐνὰς ἀμήσαντες ἐκ λειμώ-
νων. σιτία δὲ αὐτοῖς αἵ τε μᾶζαι καὶ τῶν ἄρτων οἱ
ἄπτιστοι[84] καὶ μὴ ζυμῆται καὶ τῶν κρεῶν τὰ βόειά τε
καὶ ταύρεια καὶ τράγεια τούτους ἔβοσκε καὶ δόρκοι
κότινου τε <καὶ>[85] φυλίας ἔχριον αὐτοὺς λίπα· ὅθεν
ἄνοσοί τε ἤσκουν καὶ ὀψὲ ἐγήρασκον. ἠγωνίζοντό τε
οἱ μὲν ὀκτὼ Ὀλυμπιάδας, οἱ δὲ ἐννέα, καὶ ὁπλιτεύειν
ἀγαθοὶ ἦσαν, ἐμάχοντό τε ὑπὲρ τειχῶν οὐδὲ ἐκεῖ
πίπτοντες, ἀλλὰ ἀριστείων τε ἀξιούμενοι καὶ τρο-
παίων, καὶ μελέτην ποιούμενοι πολεμικὰ μὲν γυμνα-
στικῶν, γυμναστικὰ δὲ πολεμικῶν ἔργα.

44. Ἐπεὶ δὲ μετέβαλε ταῦτα καὶ ἀστράτευτοι μὲν
ἐκ μαχομένων, ἀργοὶ δὲ ἐξ ἐνεργῶν, ἀνειμένοι δὲ ἐκ
κατεσκληκότων ἐγένοντο Σικελική τε ὀψοφαγία ἴσχυ-
σεν, ἐξενευρίσθη τὰ στάδια, καὶ πολλῷ μᾶλλον,
ἐπειδὴ κολακευτική γε ἐγκατελέχθη τῇ γυμναστικῇ.

---

[83] Del. Kayser   [84] ἄπτιστοι Jüthner: ἄπιστ[ ].ι P:
ἄπεπτοι M   [85] Suppl. Mynas

---

[134] Cf. Hom. *Od.* 5.482.   [135] Barley was a major staple
of the peasant diet in antiquity, partly because it was much easier
to grow than wheat; refined wheat breads were usually associated
with the wealthy.   [136] These meats are depicted in some
ancient medical writing as hard to digest; pork, by contrast (see

to swim around the headlands of the island and his arms carried him great distances through the sea, training both his body and themselves. They washed in rivers and springs, and they trained themselves to lie on the ground, some of them stretched out on skins, others harvesting their beds from the meadows.[134] Their food was barley cake,[135] or unsifted, unleavened bread, and the meat that nourished them was from cows and bulls and goats and deer,[136] and they oiled themselves abundantly with oil from wild olives and oleasters. Thus they trained without falling ill and were slow to grow old. Some of them competed for eight Olympiads, some for nine,[137] and they were good also at fighting as hoplites, and they fought in defense of their city walls; nor did they fall there but were thought worthy of rewards and trophies, using warfare as training for athletics and athletics as training for warfare.

44. When the situation changed, and when athletes became inexperienced in warfare rather than combatants, sluggish rather than energetic, and soft rather than hardened, and when Sicilian gastronomy became popular, then the stadia became enfeebled, and all the more so since the art of flattery was introduced into athletic training.[138]

ch. 44, below), was viewed as easily digestible and good for the humors, and so particularly suitable for athletes; e.g., see Gal. *On the Properties of Foodstuffs* K6.661–6.   [137] There are no attested examples, but a number of famous athletes from the archaic period come close, e.g., Milo and Hipposthenes, the first athletes mentioned by name in ch. 1.   [138] This passage recalls Pl. *Grg.* 464b–66a, in which Socrates describes luxurious cooking as the art that "flatters" medicine, contributing to its degeneration, and cosmetics as the art that "flatters" athletic training.

ἐκολάκευσε δὲ πρῶτα μὲν ἰατρικὴ παραστησαμένη
ξύμβουλον ἀγαθὴν μὲν τέχνην, μαλακωτέραν δὲ ἢ
ἀθλητῶν ἅπτεσθαι, ἔτι τε ἀργίαν ἐκδιδάσκουσα καὶ
τὸν πρὸ τοῦ γυμνάζεσθαι χρόνον καθῆσθαι σεσαγμέ-
νους οἷον ἄχθη Λιβυκὰ ἢ Αἰγύπτια, ὀψοποιούς τε καὶ
μαγείρους ἥδοντας παραφέρουσα, ὑφ' ὧν λίχνοι τε
ἀποτελοῦνται καὶ κοῖλοι τὴν γαστέρα ἄρτοις τε μη-
κωνίαις καὶ ἀπεπτισμένοις ἑστιῶσα, ἰχθύων παρα-
νομωτάτης βρώσεως ἐμφοροῦσα καὶ φυσιολογοῦσα
τοὺς ἰχθῦς ἀπὸ τῶν τῆς θαλάσσης δήμων—ὡς παχεῖς
μὲν οἱ ἐξ ἰλύων, ἁπαλοὶ δὲ οἱ ἐκ πετρῶν, κρεώδεις δὲ
οἱ πελάγιοι, λεπτούς τε βόσκουσι θαλίαι, τὰ φυκία δὲ
ἐξιτήλους—ἔτι τε τὰ χοίρεια τῶν κρεῶν σὺν τερατο-
λογίᾳ ἄγουσα· μοχθηρὰ μὲν γὰρ ἡγεῖσθαι κελεύει τὰ
ἐπὶ θαλάττῃ συβόσια διὰ τὸ σκόρδον τὸ θαλάττιον,
οὗ μεστοὶ μὲν αἰγιαλοί, μεσταὶ δὲ θῖνες, φυλάττεσθαι
δὲ καὶ τὰ ἀγχοῦ ποταμῶν διὰ τὴν καρκίνων βρῶσιν,
μόνων δὲ ἀναγκοφαγεῖν τῶν ἐκ κρανείας τε καὶ βα-
λάνου.

45. Τὸ δ' οὕτω τρυφᾶν δριμὺ μὲν καὶ ἐς ἀφροδισίων
ὁρμήν, ἦρξε δὲ ἀθληταῖς καὶ τῆς ὑπὲρ χρημάτων
παρανομίας καὶ τοῦ πωλεῖν τε καὶ ὠνεῖσθαι τὰς νί-
κας· οἱ μὲν γὰρ καὶ ἀποδίδονται τὴν ἑαυτῶν εὔκλειαν
δι' οἶμαι τὸ πολλῶν δεῖσθαι, οἱ δ' ὠνοῦνται τὸ μὴ ξὺν
πόνῳ νικᾶν διὰ τὸ ἁβρῶς διαιτᾶσθαι. καὶ ἀργυροῦν

139 For stereotypes of greedy athletes, see, among many oth-
ers, Ath. *Deipnosophists* 10, 412e, and Gal. *Protrepticus* 13.

The first flattery was perpetrated by medicine in offering, in an advisory role, an art that was good to be sure, but too soft to be of use to athletes, and that moreover taught them idleness and encouraged them to spend the time before training sitting stuffed like Libyan or Egyptian grain sacks, and brought in pastry makers and pleasure-bringing cooks, who made them gluttonous and greedy[139] by feeding them with poppy seed bread made from dehusked wheat, stuffing them with an unnatural diet of fish, and pronouncing on the nature of fish from their habitat in the sea:[140] saying that those from swampy places are fat; the soft ones come from near cliffs, fleshy ones from the deep sea; that algae produces thin ones and seaweed tasteless ones. It even treats the meat of pigs in a similarly fantastical way, for it instructs them to believe that herds of pigs pastured by the sea are of poor quality because of the sea garlic, of which the shoreline and the beach are full, and that they should guard against pigs pastured near rivers because of their consumption of crabs, and that they should confine themselves, as part of their forced diet, to pigs fed with cornelian cherries and acorns.

45. This kind of luxury acts as an acute stimulus also for the sex drive. In addition it started the habit of rule breaking among athletes for the sake of money and the buying and selling of victories.[141] For some athletes actually sell their own good reputation, I assume because of their great need, whereas others buy victories gained

[140] Cf. Hippoc. *On Diet* 2.48–49 for a classification of fish along similar lines.

[141] Cf. Paus. 5.21.2–17 for similar examples of bribery and other kinds of wrongdoing at Olympia.

μὲν ἢ χρυσοῦν περισπῶντι ἀνάθημα ἢ διαφθείροντι
ὀργὴν οἱ νόμοι οἱ ἐς ἱεροσύλους ὄντες, στέφανον δ᾽
Ἀπόλλωνος ἢ Ποσειδῶνος, ὑπὲρ οὗ καὶ αὐτοί γε οἱ
θεοὶ μέγα ἤθλησαν, ἄδεια μὲν ἀποδίδοσθαι, ἄδεια δὲ
ὠνεῖσθαι, πλὴν ὅσα Ἠλείοις ὁ κότινος ἄσυλος μένει
κατὰ τὴν ἐκ παλαιοῦ δόξαν· οἱ δὲ ἄλλοι τῶν ἀγώνων,
τόδε[86] μὲν ἐκ πολλῶν εἰρήσθω μοι, ἐν ᾧ πάντα. παῖς
ἐνίκα [κατὰ][87] πάλην Ἴσθμια τρισχιλίας ἑνὶ τῶν ἀντι-
πάλων ὁμολογήσας ὑπὲρ τῆς νίκης· ἥκοντες οὖν τῆς
ὑστεραίας εἰς τὸ γυμνάσιον ὁ μὲν ἀπῄτει τὰ χρή-
ματα, ὁ δ᾽ οὐκ ὀφείλειν ἔφη, κεκρατηκέναι γὰρ δὴ
ἄκοντος. ὡς δ᾽ οὐδὲν ἐπέραινεν, ὅρκῳ ἐπιτρέπουσι[88]
καὶ παρελθόντες ἐς τὸ τοῦ Ἰσθμίου[89] ἱερὸν ὤμνυε δη-
μοσίᾳ ὁ τὴν νίκην ἀποδόμενος πεπρακέναι μὲν τοῦ
θεοῦ τὸν ἀγῶνα, τρισχιλίας δ᾽ ὁμολογεῖσθαί οἱ· καὶ
ὡμολόγει ταῦτα λαμπρᾷ τῇ φωνῇ μηδὲ τῇ εὐφήμῳ
εἴ>πας·[90] ὅσῳ γὰρ ἀληθέστερα, εἰ οὐδ᾽ ἄνευ μαρτύ-
ρων, τοσῷδε ἀνιερώτερα καὶ ἐπιρρητότερα· ὤμνυε δὲ

---

86 τόδε Jüthner: ὧδε P
87 Del. Cobet
88 ἐπιτρέπουσι Cobet: τρέπουσι P
89 Ἰσθμίου Daremberg: ἰσθμοῦ P
90 Suppl. Jüthner: τῇ εὐ[......]πας P

---

142 I.e., at the Pythian or Isthmian festivals, respectively.
143 No other ancient source recounts contests between the
gods at the Pythian or Isthmian festivals, but see Paus. 5.7.10 on
contests between the gods at Olympia.

without exertion because of their own habits of soft living. The laws against temple robbers decree anger against those who steal or destroy a gold or silver offering, but license is given to sell or to buy the crown of Apollo or Poseidon,[142] over which even the gods themselves competed vigorously,[143] with the exception that among the Eleans the olive remains inviolate according to the traditional judgment;[144] but as for the other contests, let me tell this one story, of many possible stories, that sums everything up. A boy won the Isthmian wrestling after agreeing with one of his opponents a price of three thousand drachmas for victory. When they came next day to the gymnasium, the defeated contestant demanded his money but the other said that he did not owe it, given that he had won the victory over an opponent who had been unwilling to lose. And since their argument remained unresolved they entrusted the matter to an oath and came to the temple of the Isthmian god,[145] and the one who had sold the victory swore an oath in public that he had sold the contest of the god and that three thousand drachmas had been promised to him. And he admitted to all this in a clear and unrestrained voice. And the more truthful the story is, through being not without witnesses, the more unholy and infamous it is. For he took that oath at the

[144] Philostratus presumably does not mean that cheating did not happen at Olympia, where the victory crown was made of olive leaves; his point is rather that there was a significant deterrent in the rule that competitors could be fined for misconduct. In these cases the money was used to pay for statues of Zeus, known as Zanes; see Paus. 5.21.2.

[145] I.e., Poseidon.

Ἰσθμοῖ ταῦτα καὶ κατ' ὀφθαλμοὺς τῆς Ἑλλάδος. τί μὲν οὐκ ἂν ἐν Ἰωνίᾳ, τί δ' οὐκ ἂν ⟨ἐν Ἀσίᾳ⟩[91] γένοιτο ἐπ' αἰσχύνῃ ἀγῶνος. οὐκ ἀφίημι τοὺς γυμναστὰς αὐτοὺς ἐπὶ τῇ διαφθορᾷ ταύτῃ· πα⟨ρόντες⟩[92] μὲν γὰρ μετὰ χρημάτων ἐπὶ τὸ γυμνάζειν καὶ δανείζοντες τοῖς ἀθληταῖς ἐπὶ τόκοις μείζοσιν ἢ ὧν ἔμποροι θαλαττεύοντες, τῆς μὲν τῶν ἀθλητῶν δόξης ἐπιστρέφονται οὐδέν, τοῦ δὲ πωλεῖν τε καὶ ὠνεῖσθαι ξύμβουλοι γίγνονταί σφισι προνοοῦντες τοῦ ἑαυτῶν κέρδους ἢ γὰρ δάνεσιν ὠνουμένων ἢ πεπρακότων ἀπολήψει. καὶ ταυτὶ μὲν κατὰ καπηλευόντων εἰρήσθω μοι, καπηλεύουσι γάρ που τὰς τῶν ἀθλητῶν ἀρετὰς τὸ ἑαυτῶν εὖ τιθέμενοι.

46. Ἁμαρτάνουσι δὲ κἀκεῖνο. παῖδα ἀθλητὴν ἀποδύσαντες γυμνάζουσιν ὡς ἤδη ἄνδρα τήν τε γαστέρα προβαρύνειν κελεύοντες καὶ βαδίζειν μεταξὺ τοῦ γυμνάζεσθαι καὶ ἐρεύγεσθαι κοῖλον. δι' ὧν ὥσπερ οἱ κακῶς παιδεύοντες ἀφελόντες τὸν παῖδα τὸ νεοτήσιον σκίρτημα ἀργίαν γυμνάζουσι καὶ ἀναβολὰς καὶ νωθροὺς εἶναι καὶ ἀτολμοτέρους τῆς αὑτῶν ἀκμῆς. κίνησιν ἐχρῆν γυμνάζειν ὡς ἡ παλαίστρα· κίνησιν δὲ λέγω τήν τε ἀπὸ τῶν σκελῶν ὁπόση ἐκ μαλαττόντων

91 ⟨ἐν Ἀσίᾳ⟩ Jüthner: [......]ᾳ P
92 Suppl. Jüthner: πα[....] P

---

146 Philostratus' point must be that if these things can happen in the old festivals of mainland Greece, they are all the more likely in other less prestigious athletic centers, where such misbehavior

Isthmus and before the eyes of the Greeks. Who knows what might not happen in Ionia and in Asia, to the disgrace of the contests.[146] And I do not absolve the trainers themselves from responsibility for this corruption. For they turn up at training sessions with money, and they make loans to the athletes at levels of interest higher than those normal among seagoing merchants, and they pay no attention to the reputation of the athletes but instead act as their advisers in buying and selling, out of a concern for their own profit, which they secure either by giving loans to those who want to make purchases or by taking repayments from those who have made sales. That is what I have to say against these traffickers—for they traffic, as it were, the virtue of the athletes while profiting in their own affairs.

46. They commit the following error in addition. Having stripped the boy athlete they train him as if he were already a man, and they tell him to load his stomach in advance and then during training to go for walks[147] and belch cavernously.[148] By these measures, just like bad teachers, they take away from the boy his youthful vigor and train him in laziness and procrastination and in being sluggish and more timid than he should be at his age. One should train boys in movement, as in the *palaistra*; by movement I mean the kind of passive movement produced in the legs

would be less conspicuous, and especially in Ionia, which traditionally had a reputation for luxury.

[147] Cf. Plut. *Quaest. Rom.* 40.274d for another criticism of walking as a damaging form of training.   [148] Cf. Gal. *Commentary on Hippocrates' Epidemics* K17a.967–68 on belching as exercise for the stomach.

τήν τε ἀπὸ τῶν χειρῶν ὁπόση <ἐκ σκληρυνόντων>.[93]
καὶ παρακροτείτω ὁ παῖς, ἐπειδὴ ἀγερωχότερα τὰ
τούτων γυμνάσια. τὸν Φοίνικα Ἕλικα ἤδε ἰδέα
ἐγύμναζεν οὐκ ἐν παισὶ μόνον, ἀλλὰ καὶ εἰς ἄνδρας
ἥκοντα, καὶ λόγου θαυμασιώτερος ἐγένετο παρὰ πάν-
τας, οὓς οἶδα τὴν ῥᾳστώνην ἐκμελετῶντας ταύτην.

47. Προσεκτέα δὲ οὐδὲ ταῖς τῶν γυμναστῶν τετρά-
σιν, ὑφ᾽ ὧν ἀπόλωλε τὰ ἐν γυμναστικῇ πάντα. ἡγού-
μεθα δὲ τὴν τετράδα κύκλον ἡμερῶν τεττάρων ἄλλο
ἄλλην πράττουσαν· ἡ μὲν γὰρ παρασκευάζει τὸν
ἀθλητήν, ἡ δ᾽ ἐπιτείνει, ἡ δὲ ἀνίησιν, ἡ δὲ μεσεύει.
ἔστι δὲ τὸ παρασκευάζον γυμνάσιον σύντονος πρὸς
βραχὺ καὶ ταχεῖα κίνησις ἐγείρουσα τὸν ἀθλητὴν καὶ
[σὺν] τῷ μέλλοντι μόχθῳ ἐφιστᾶσα, τὸ δὲ ἐπιτεῖνον
ἔλεγχος ἀπαραίτητος τῆς ἐναποκειμένης ἰσχύος τῇ
ἕξει, ἡ <δ᾽> ἄνεσις [ὡς] ὥρα κίνησιν [καὶ] ξὺν λόγῳ
ἀνακτωμένη, ἡ δὲ μεσεύουσα τῶν ἡμερῶν διαφεύγειν
μὲν τὸν ἀντίπαλον, διαφυγόντος δὲ μὴ ἀνιέναι. καὶ
τὴν τοιάνδε ἰδέαν πᾶσαν ἁρμονικῶς γυμνάζοντες καὶ
τὰς τετράδας ταύτας ὧδε ἀνακυκλοῦντες ἀφαιροῦνται
τὴν ἐπιστήμην τὸ ξυνιέναι τοῦ ἀθλητοῦ τοῦ γυμνοῦ.
καὶ γὰρ λυπεῖ μὲν σιτία, λυπεῖ δὲ οἶνος, κλοπαί τε
τῶν σιτίων καὶ ἀγωνίαι καὶ κόποι καὶ πλείω ἕτερα, τὰ

[93] Suppl. Jüthner

---

[149] An athlete of Philostratus' own day; see p. 339 above.

by a softening massage and the kind of movement pro-
duced in the arms by a hardening massage. And the boy
should keep time by clapping, since that makes these ex-
ercises more energetic. This was the type of exercise used
by the Phoenician Helix,[149] not only when he was a boy,
but also when he had come into the men's age category,
and he was an indescribably wonderful athlete, more so
than any of those whom I know to be practicing that kind
of recreation.

47. Nor should one pay attention to the tetrads' of the
trainers, a system by which the whole of athletic training
has been brought to ruin.[150] We take the tetrad system to
be a circle of four days, where the athlete does different
things on different days. One of the days prepares the
athlete, the next makes him exert himself, the next relaxes
him, and the next keeps him on a middle path. The pre-
paratory exercise is short and intense, consisting of a fast
movement which arouses the athlete and makes him ready
for the toil which is to follow; the intensive exercise is an
irrefutable test of the strength of his constitution; the day
of relaxation is a time for starting up his activity again in a
moderate way; and the middling day teaches the athlete
to flee from his opponent, and not to relax when his op-
ponent is fleeing. And in training the athletes systemati-
cally according to this complete form of training, and in
repeating these tetrads over and over again they take away
from the art of training all understanding of the naked
athlete. For food can damage the athlete, and wine and
secret eating of food, and stress and tiredness, and many
other factors, some of which are voluntary and some not.

[150] Cf. Gal. *Thrasybulus* 47 for similar criticism of this system.

μὲν ἑκούσια, τὰ δὲ ἀκούσια. πῶς ἰασόμεθα τοῦτον τετράζοντες καὶ κληροῦντες;

48. Τοὺς μὲν δὴ ὑπερσιτήσαντας ὀφρύς τε δηλώσει βαρεῖα καὶ κοῖλον ἆσθμα καὶ κύαθοι κλειδῶν ἀνεστηκότες καὶ οἱ πλάγιοι κενεῶνες ὄγκου τι ἐνδεικνύμενοι. τοὺς δ᾽ ὑποίνους γαστήρ τε ἑρμηνεύσει περιττὴ καὶ αἷμα ἱλαρώτερον καὶ ἱκμὰς ἡ μὲν κενεῶνος ἡ δὲ ἐπιγουνίδος. τοὺς δ᾽ ἐξ ἀφροδισίων ἥκοντας γυμναζομένους μὲν πλείω ἐλέγξει· τὴν ἰσχύν τε γὰρ ὑποδεδυκότες καὶ στενοὶ τὸ πνεῦμα καὶ τὰς ὁρμὰς ἄτολμοι καὶ ἀπανθοῦντες τῶν πόνων καὶ τὰ τοιαῦτα ἁλίσκεσθαι· ἀποδύντας δὲ κλεῖς τε ἂν ἐνδείξαιτο κοίλη καὶ ἰσχίον ἄναρμον καὶ πλευρὰ ὑποχαράττουσα καὶ ψυχρότης αἵματος. οὕς, εἰ[94] ἐφαπτοίμεθα, οὐδ᾽ ἂν στέφοι ἀγωνία. λεπτὰ μὲν τούτοις ὑπώπια, λεπτὴ δὲ πήδησις καρδίας, λεπτοὶ δ᾽ ἱδρώτων ἀτμοί, λεπτοὶ δ᾽ ὕπνοι ἰθύνοντες τὰ σῖτα βολαί τε ὀφθαλμῶν πεπλανημέναι καὶ τὸ ἐρᾶσθαι δοκεῖν[95] ἀποσημαίνουσαι.

49. Οἱ δὲ ὀνειρώττοντες ἀποκάθαρσις μὲν τῆς ἐπιπολαζούσης εὐεξίας, ὁρῶνται δ᾽ ὅμως ὕπωχροι καὶ δροσίζοντες καὶ ὑποδεέστεροι μὲν τὴν ἰσχύν, εὐτραφεῖς δὲ ὑπὸ τοῦ καθεύδειν καὶ ἀνεύθυνοι[96] τὸ ἰσχίον καὶ διαρκεῖς τὸ πνεῦμα. ἐν χώρᾳ τε τῶν ἀφροδισιαζόντων ὄντες ⟨οὐ⟩[97] ταὐτόν εἰσιν· οἱ μὲν γὰρ καθαί-

94 οὕς εἰ Jüthner: εἰ P: ὧν εἰ M
95 δοκεῖν Jüthner: δοκούντων P, M
96 ἀνεύθυνοι Kitriniari   97 Suppl. Kayser

482

How shall we cure an athlete in this position by following tetrads and assigning training methods by lot?[151]

48. Those who have overeaten will be revealed by an overhanging brow and by shortness of breath and by the filling in of the hollows in the collar bones and by the flanks at the side of the body, which will show signs of a certain bulkiness. Athletes who are heavy drinkers can be detected by an oversized stomach, blood that is too lively and moistness in the flank and knee. Those who come to the gymnasium straight after sex are exposed by a greater number of indicators when they train, for their strength is diminished and they are short of breath and lack daring in their attacks, they fade in color in response to exertion, and they can be detected by signs of that sort; and when they strip their hollow collarbones give them away, their loose hips, the conspicuous outline of their ribs, and the coldness of their blood. These athletes, even if we dedicated ourselves to them, would have no chance of being crowned in any contest. The part beneath the eyes is weak, the beating of their hearts is weak, their perspiration is weak, their sleep, which controls digestion, is weak, and their eyes glance around in a wandering fashion and indicate their awareness of being loved.

49. Those who have wet dreams are actually being cleansed of an excess of good condition. Nevertheless they are pale in appearance and sweaty and lacking in strength, although well nourished by sleep and with irreproachable hips and ample breath. Athletes who have wet dreams are close to those who indulge in sex but not identical, for the

[151] Cf. ch. 54 for an example of the dangers of that kind of approach.

ρονται τὴν ἕξιν, οἱ δὲ τήκονται. κόπων δὲ ἀγαθὴ μάρ-
τυς ἥ τε ἔξωθεν περιβολὴ τοῦ σώματος λεπτοτέρα
ἑαυτῆς δοκοῦσα καὶ ἀνοιδοῦσα φλὲψ καὶ κατηφὴς
βραχίων καὶ τὰ μυώδη κατεσκληκότα.

50. Οἱ μὲν δὴ ὑπερσιτήσαντες, ἥν τε κοῦφοι τύχω-
σιν ἥν τε τῶν βαρυτέρων ἀγωνισταί, μεταχειριστέοι
ταῖς ἐς τὸ κάτω τρίψεσιν, ἵνα τῶν κυριωτέρων τὰ
περιττὰ ἀπάγοιτο. γυμναστέοι δὲ πένταθλοι μέν τι
ἀπὸ τῶν κούφων, δρομεῖς δὲ μὴ ξυντείνοντες, ἀλλὰ
σχολαῖοι καὶ μεῖζόν τι διαβαίνοντες, πύκται δὲ ἀκρο-
χειριζέσθων ἐλαφροὶ καὶ ἀεῤίζοντες. πάλη δὲ καὶ
παγκράτιον ὀρθοὶ μὲν καὶ οἵδε, ἀλλὰ ἀνάγκη κυλίε-
σθαι. κυλιέσθων μέν, ἀλλ' ἐπικείμενοι μᾶλλον ἢ ὑπο-
κείμενοι καὶ μηδαμῇ περικυβιστῶντες, ὡς μὴ ἀνιῷτό
τινι ἕλκει τὸ σῶμα. μαλ‹λατέσ›θων⁹⁸ τε γυμναστῇ
κοῦφοί τε ὁμοίως καὶ βαρεῖς ‹διὰ› τῶν διὰ με‹τρίου
τ›ρίψεων⁹⁹ τῶν ‹ἄνω› μάλιστα,¹⁰⁰ καὶ τοῦτ' ἀπομάτ-
τειν δ‹εήσε›ι¹⁰¹ λιπαίνοντα.

51. Οἶνος δὲ περιττεύσας ἀθλητῶν σώμασιν, ἱδρῶ-
τος ἀνα‹χοὴν› τὰ μεσεύοντα¹⁰² τῶν γυμνασίων ἐκκα-
λεῖται· οὔτε γὰρ ἐπιγυμνάζειν χρὴ τοὺς τοιούτους

⁹⁸ Suppl. Jüthner: μαλ[. . . . .]θων P
⁹⁹ Suppl. Jüthner: με[. . . . . .]ρίψεων P
¹⁰⁰ Suppl. Jüthner: τῶν [. . .] μάλιστα P
¹⁰¹ Suppl. Jüthner: δ[. . . .]ι P
¹⁰² ἀνα‹χοὴν› τὰ μεσεύοντα Jüthner: ἀνα[. . .]τὰ μεστοῦ
ὄντα P

former have their condition cleansed, whereas in the latter it is diminished. A good indication of exhaustion[152] is when the outer surface of the body appears more delicate than usual and when the veins are swollen and the arms flabby and the muscles withered.

50. Athletes who have overeaten, whether they happen to be light athletes or competitors in the heavier events, are to be treated by massage of the kind that moves downward, so that the excess in the most important parts of the body can be eliminated. Pentathletes in this situation must be trained in one of the light events; runners in a way that does not strain them, but in a leisurely fashion and lengthening their stride just a little; whereas boxers should exercise with outstretched arms, lightly punching the air. As for wrestling and *pankration*, these too are upright events, but it is necessary also to roll on the floor; they must train by rolling, but keeping on top of the opponent rather than under him and certainly not somersaulting over, in case the body should be injured. Both light and heavy athletes should be softened by the trainer in the same way, with massages that use a moderate amount of oil, especially on the upper body; and when he applies the oil he must wipe it off.

51. When wine is absorbed in excessive quantities by the bodies of athletes, the medium-strength exercises cause an outpouring of sweat. Athletes suffering from that kind of excess should neither be exercised excessively nor

---

[152] There was an extensive ancient medical literature on the identification and treatment of different kinds of exhaustion (κό-πος); e.g., see Gal. *De sanitate tuenda* Book 4; also 3.5 (K6.190), where he mentions a whole book on the subject by Theophrastus.

περιττεύσαντας οὔτε ἀνιέναι· τὸ γὰρ διεφθορὸς ὑγρὸν
ἀποχετεύειν ἄμεινον, ὡς μὴ τὸ αἷμα ἀπ᾽ αὐτοῦ κα-
κουργοῖτο. ἀποματτέτω δὴ ὁ γυμναστὴς καὶ ἀπο-
στλεγγιζέτω ξυμμέτρῳ χρώμενος, ὡς μὴ ἀποφράττοι-
ντο αἱ ἐκβολαὶ τοῦ ἱδρῶτος.

52. Εἰ δ᾽ ἐξ ἀφροδισίων, ἀμείνους μὲν μὴ γυμνά-
ζειν· οἱ γὰρ στεφάνων καὶ κηρυγμάτων αἰσχρὰν ἡδο-
νὴν ἀλλαξάμενοι ποῦ ἄνδρες; εἰ δ᾽ ἄρα γυμνάζοιντο,
ὑπὲρ νουθεσίας γυμναζέσθων ἐλεγχόμενοι τὴν ἰσχὺν
καὶ τὸ πνεῦμα· ταυτὶ γὰρ μάλιστα αἱ τῶν ἀφροδισίων
ἡδοναὶ ἐπικόπτουσιν. ἡ δὲ τῶν ὀνειρωττόντων ἕξις
ἀφροδίσια μὲν καὶ ταῦτα, ἀκούσια δ᾽ ὡς ἔφην· γυμνα-
στέοι δὴ ξὺν ἐπιμελείᾳ καὶ τὴν ἰσχὺν ὑποθρεπτέοι[103]
μᾶλλον, ἐπειδὴ ἐπιλείπει σφᾶς, κἀξικμαστέοι τοὺς
ἱδρῶτας, ἐπειδὴ περιττοὶ τούτοις. ἔστω δὲ ἐνδοσιμώ-
τερα μὲν τὰ γυμνάσια, προηγμένα δὲ ἐς μῆκος, ἵνα
τὸ πνεῦμα ἐγγυμνάζοιτο. δεῖ δὲ αὐτοῖς ἐλαίου ξυμμέ-
τρου καὶ πεπαχυσμένου τῇ κόνει· τουτὶ γὰρ τὸ φάρ-
μακον καὶ ξυνέχει τὸ σῶμα καὶ ἀνίησιν.

53. Ἀγωνιῶντες δὲ ἀθληταὶ θεραπευέσθων μὲν καὶ
τὰς γνώμας λόγῳ παραθρασύνοντί τε αὐτοὺς καὶ
παριστάντι, γυμναζέσθων δ᾽ ἐν χώρᾳ[104] τῶν ἀϋπνούν-
των τε καὶ μὴ εὐσίτων. εὖ τούτοις ἔχει τὸ ἁρμονικὸν
γυμνάσιον· αἱ γὰρ περιδεεῖς γνῶμαι προθυμότεραί

[103] ὑποθρεπτέοι Jüthner: ἀποθρεπτέοι P, M
[104] γυμναζέσθων δ᾽ ἐν χώρᾳ Volckmar: γυμναζέσθω δὲ ἡ
χώρα P

486

allowed to relax; for it is better to draw off the corrupted moisture, so that the blood is not harmed by it. The trainer should wipe and scrape them down with only a moderate amount of oil, so that the outflowing of sweat is not blocked.

52. If an athlete has just had sex, it is better for him not to exercise. In what sense are they men, those who exchange crowns and victory announcements for disgraceful pleasures? But if they must undergo training, let them be trained as a warning, in a way that tests their strength and their breathing; for these are the areas most damaged by the pleasures of sex. The condition of those who have wet dreams is also sexual in character, but involuntarily so, as I have said. These athletes should be exercised with care, and their strength needs to be built up all the more because it is lacking, and their sweat needs to be driven out of them, since they have an excessive supply of it. Their exercises should be easier but spread out over a long period, so that their breathing is exercised. They should use a moderate amount of oil thickened with dust, for that is a remedy that maintains the body and refreshes it.

53. Athletes who are anxious should also be cared for mentally, through words of encouragement and support; and they should be trained together with those who suffer from insomnia and bad digestion. These athletes benefit from the systematic method of training.[153] For timid minds are more eager to learn what one needs to guard

[153] Philostratus seems to be referring to a more intelligent version of the system of regular training denounced in ch. 47.

εἰσι μανθάνειν ἃ προσήκει φυλάττεσθαι. κόποι δὲ οἱ
μὲν αὐτόματοι νόσων ἀρχαί, καὶ ἀπόχρη τοὺς μὲν
πηλῷ καὶ παλαίστρᾳ πονήσαντας ἀνιέναι [χρή][105] μα-
λακῶς τε καὶ ὡς εἶπον, τοὺς δὲ ἐν κόνει πεπονηκότας
ἐπιγυμνάζειν τῆς ὑστεραίας ἐν πηλῷ ξὺν μικρᾷ ἐπι-
τάσει· ἡ γὰρ ἀθρόα μετὰ τὴν κόνιν ἄνεσις ἰατρὸς
πονηρὸς κόπων,[106] οὐ γὰρ θεραπεύει τὴν ἰσχὺν, ἀλλ᾽
ἀποκρεμάννυσιν. ἡ μὲν δὴ σοφωτέρα γυμναστικὴ καὶ
ξυντείνουσα εἰς τὸν ἀθλητὴν τοιάδε εἴη ἄν.

54. Ἔλεγχος δὲ τῶν τετράδων, ἃς παρῃτησάμην,
καὶ ἡ ἐπὶ Γερήνῳ τῷ παλαιστῇ διαμαρτία, οὗ τὸ
σῆμα Ἀθήνησιν ἐν δεξιᾷ τῆς Ἐλευσινάδε ὁδοῦ. Ναυ-
κρατίτης μὲν γὰρ ἦν οὗτος καὶ τῶν ἄριστα παλαισάν-
των, ⟨ὡς αἱ νῖκαι⟩ δηλοῦ⟨σιν, ἃς ἐνίκησεν⟩[107] ἀγωνι-
σάμενος. ἐτύγχανε μὲν ἐν Ὀλυμπίᾳ νενικηκώς, τρίτῃ
δ᾽ ἀπ᾽ ἐκείνης ἡμέρᾳ ἀποινῶν[108] τὴν ἑαυτοῦ νίκην καί
τινας τῶν γνωρίμων ἑστιῶν ὀψοφαγίᾳ ἀήθει χρησά-
μενος ἀπηνέχθη τοῦ ὕπνου. ἥκων οὖν τῆς ὑστεραίας
ἐς τὸ γυμνάσιον ὡμολόγει πρὸς τὸν γυμναστὴν ὠμός

105 Del. Mynas
106 πονηρὸς κόπων Daremberg: πονηρίας κόπτων P
107 Suppl. Jüthner: [..........]δηλοῦ[.............] P
108 ἀποινῶν Zingerle: πίνων P, Jüthner

154 Cf. Hippoc. *Aphorism* 2.5.
155 Presumably a reference back to ch. 47.
156 The central (usually open-air) space of the *palaistra* in an
ancient gymnasium was usually covered with dust or sand, but

against. Tiredness that arises spontaneously is the beginning of illness,[154] and in these cases it is enough for those who have toiled in mud in the *palaistra* to relax, in a gentle fashion, in the way I have indicated,[155] while those who have toiled in dust should be trained again on the next day in mud, and with a small increase of intensity.[156] For complete rest after exercising in dust is a poor doctor for tiredness, since it slackens one's strength rather than maintaining it. The wisest kind of training, and the kind that gives attention to each individual athlete, would be like that.

54. Evidence against the tetrad system, which I have already rejected, also comes from the great error made in the case of the wrestler Gerenus,[157] whose tomb lies in Athens on the right of the road to Eleusis. For this man was from Naucratis and was one of the best wrestlers, as demonstrated by the victories he won in competition. He happened to win at Olympia, and on the third day after that[158] he celebrated his victory and gave a feast for some of his friends, eating more luxuriously than he was used to, and was deprived of sleep. When he came to the gymnasium the next day he admitted to his trainer that he was

there is also evidence for separate rooms with floors covered with mud or earth for practicing the parts of wrestling that took place on the ground.

157 Not attested elsewhere.

158 In other words, two days after his victory. The combat events took place on the last day of competition, and the day after that was reserved for the official celebrations, including a banquet for victors; the day following was therefore the first one on which a victorious athlete was free to hold his own victory celebrations.

PHILOSTRATUS

τε εἶναι πονηρῶς τε ἔχειν πη. ὁ δ' ἠγρίαινέ τε καὶ ξὺν
ὀργῇ ἤκουε καὶ χαλεπὸς ἦν ὡς ἀνιέντι καὶ τὰς τετρά-
δας διασπῶντι, ἔστε ἀπέκτεινε τὸν ἀθλητὴν ἐν αὐτῷ
τῷ γυμνάζειν ἀγνωσίᾳ, οὐ προειπὼν[109] ἃ γυμνάζειν
ἔδει καὶ σιωπῶντος. τοιῶνδε μὲν δὴ τετράδων οὐ-
σῶν[110] καὶ ὧδε ἀγυμνάστου καὶ ἀπαιδεύτου γυμνα-
στοῦ[111] οὐ μέτρια πάθη[112]· τὸ γὰρ τοιοῦδε ἀθλητοῦ
ἁμαρτεῖν τὰ στάδια πῶς οὐ βαρύ; οἱ δὲ ἀσπαζόμενοι
τὰς τετράδας τί χρήσονται αὐταῖς ἐς Ὀλυμπίαν ἥκον-
τες,[113] παρ' οἷς κόνις μέν ὁποίαν εἴρηκα, γυμνάσια δὲ
προστεταγμένα, γυμνάζει δὲ ὁ ἑλληνοδίκης οὐδ' ἐκ
προρρήσεως, ἀλλ' ἐπεσχεδιασμένα πάντα τῷ καιρῷ,
μάστιγος καὶ τῷ γυμναστῇ ἐπηρτημένης, εἴ τι παρ'
ἃ κελεύουσι πράττοιτο. κελεύουσι δὲ ἀπαραίτητα, ὡς
παραιτουμένοις ταῦτα ἕτοιμον Ὀλυμπίων εἴργεσθαι.
περὶ μὲν δὴ τῶν τετράδων[114] τοσαῦτα, οἷς ἑπόμενοι
σοφίαν τε γυμναστικὴν ἐνδειξόμεθα καὶ τοὺς ἀθλη-
τὰς ἐπιρρώσομεν καὶ ἀνηβήσει τὰ στάδια ὑπὸ τοῦ εὖ
γυμνάζειν.

109 οὐ προειπὼν Jüthner: οὐ προειπόντος M: προειπόντος P
110 οὐσῶν Kayser: τούτων P
111 ἀγυμνάστου καὶ ἀπαιδεύτου γυμναστοῦ Volckmar:
ἀγυμνάσταις καὶ ἀπαιδεύτον γυμνοῦ P
112 οὐ μέτρια πάθη Daremberg: μετρίω πάθει P
113 ἐς Ὀλυμπίαν ἥκοντες Cobet: ἐς Ὀλύμπια νικῶντες P
114 τετράδων Mynas: τετραπόδων P

159 In other words, the trainer should have been perceptive

suffering from indigestion and that he was unwell in some way. The trainer became angry and listened furiously and was irritable with him on the grounds that he was relaxing his training and interrupting the tetrads, until he actually killed the athlete through his training, out of ignorance, by not prescribing the exercises he should have chosen even if the athlete had said nothing about his condition.[159] The damage caused by this kind of tetrad system, and by a trainer who is so untrained and uneducated, is not inconsiderable. How can it not be a bad thing that the stadia should lose an athlete of that caliber? And as for those who welcome the tetrad system, how will they make use of it when they come to Olympia, where the dust is of the kind I have already mentioned,[160] and the training is fixed, and the *hellanodikês* is in charge of training not in a premeditated fashion but improvising everything to fit the occasion, and where the whip is raised against the trainer[161] if he does anything contrary to what the *hellanodikai* order? They give orders that cannot be ignored, so that anyone who rejects them faces the prospect of being excluded from the Olympic festival. That is all I have to say concerning the tetrad system; and if we follow the advice I have given, we will demonstrate that athletic training is a variety of wisdom, and we shall give strength to the athletes, and the stadia will regain their youth thanks to good training practices.

enough to work out Gerenus' condition from his outward bodily appearance.   [160] Cf. chs. 11 and 18.

[161] Several ancient sources mention officials who acted as festival police and carried switches or whips in order to keep order: e.g., see Lucian *Hermot.* 40.

PHILOSTRATUS

55. Ἁλτὴρ δὲ πεντάθλων μὲν εὕρημα, εὕρηται δὲ ἐς τὸ ἅλμα, ἀφ᾽ οὗ δὴ καὶ ὠνόμασται· οἱ γὰρ νόμοι τὸ πήδημα χαλεπώτερον ἡγούμενοι τῶν ἐν ἀγῶνι τῷ τε αὐλῷ προσεγείρουσι τὸν πηδῶντα καὶ τῷ ἁλτῆρι προσελαφρύνουσι· πομπός τε γὰρ τῶν χειρῶν ἀσφαλὴς καὶ τὸ βῆμα ἑδραῖόν τε καὶ εὔσημον εἰς τὴν γῆν ἄγει. τουτὶ δὲ ὁπόσου ἄξιον οἱ νόμοι δηλοῦσιν· οὐ γὰρ ξυγχωροῦσι διαμετρεῖν τὸ πήδημα, ἢν μὴ ἀρτίως ἔχῃ τοῦ ἴχνους. γυμνάζουσι δὲ οἱ μὲν μακροὶ τῶν ἁλτήρων ὤμους τε καὶ χεῖρας, οἱ δὲ σφαιροειδεῖς καὶ δακτύλους. παραληπτέοι δὲ καὶ κούφοις ὁμοίως καὶ βαρέσιν ἐς πάντα γυμνάσια πλὴν τοῦ ἀναπαύοντος.

56. Κόνις δὲ ἡ μὲν πηλώδης ἱκανὴ ἀπορρύψαι καὶ ξυμμετρίαν δοῦναι τοῖς περιττοῖς, ἡ δὲ ὀστρακώδης ἀνοῖξαί τε ἐπιτηδεία καὶ ἐς ἱδρῶτα ἀγαγεῖν τὰ μεμυκότα, ἡ δὲ ἀσφαλτώδης ὑποθάλπειν τὰ ἐπεψυγμένα· μέλαινα δὲ καὶ ξανθὴ κόνις γεώδεις μὲν ἄμφω καὶ ἀγαθαὶ μαλάξαι τε καὶ ὑποθρέψαι, ἡ δὲ ξανθὴ κόνις καὶ στιλπνοὺς ἐργάζεται καὶ ἡδίων ἰδεῖν ὡς περὶ γενναίῳ τε καὶ ἠσκημένῳ σώματι. ἐπισκεδαννύναι δὲ χρὴ τὴν κόνιν ὑγρῷ τῷ καρπῷ καὶ διεστῶσι τοῖς δακτύλοις διαρραίνοντα μᾶλλον ἢ ἐπιπάττοντα, ἵν᾽ ἐς τὸν ἀθλητὴν ἡ ἄχνη πίπτοι.

---

162 *Haltêres* were weights made from stone or lead, usually around 2 kilograms each, one for each hand: see Miller (2004, 63–68) for more detailed discussion of jumping technique, with images.

163 Flute accompaniment was associated especially with the

492

55. The jumping weight (*haltêr*) is an invention of the pentathletes, and it was invented for jumping (*halma*), from which it takes its name.[162] For the rules regard jumping as one of the more difficult of the contests, and therefore stimulate the jumper with flute playing,[163] and lighten him further by the use of the jumping weight; for it is a reliable guide for the hands and it produces a stable and precise landing on the ground. The laws make clear how valuable that is; for they refuse to measure the jump unless the footprint is perfect. Long jumping weights are used to exercise the shoulders and the hands, whereas round ones are used to exercise the fingers in addition.[164] They should be used by light and heavy athletes alike in all their exercises, except for those exercises that are used during a period of relaxation.

56. As far as types of dust are concerned, the type made from clay is suitable for cleansing and for restoring a harmonious balance in cases of excess; the kind made from brick dust is good for opening closed pores and bringing out sweat; and the type that is full of asphalt is useful for warming chilled parts of the body. Black and yellow dust are both like earth and are good for softening and nourishing the body; yellow dust also makes the body gleam and is more pleasant to look at when it is on a noble and well trained body. It is necessary to sprinkle the dust with a supple wrist and with the fingers spread, sprinkling rather than spreading it, so that the light dust falls over the athlete.

long jump (cf. Paus. 5.7.10 and 6.14.10) but is attested for a wide range of other events too.

    [164] Here Philostratus moves on from jumping with *haltêres* to discuss the use of the *haltêr* for weight training.

57. Κώρυκος δὲ ἀνήφθω μὲν καὶ πύκταις, πολὺ δὲ μᾶλλον τοῖς ἐπὶ τὸ παγκράτιον φοιτῶσιν. ἔστω δὲ κοῦφος μὲν ὁ πυκτικός, ἐπειδὴ καιροῦ γυμνάζονται μόνου[115] αἱ τῶν πυκτῶν χεῖρες, ὁ δὲ τῶν παγκρατιαστῶν ἐμβριθέστερος καὶ μείζων, ἵνα γυμνάζοιντο μὲν τὴν βάσιν ἀνθιστάμενοι τῇ τοῦ κωρύκου ἐπιφορᾷ, γυμνάζοιντο δὲ ὤμους τε καὶ δακτύλους ἐς ἀντίπαλόν τι παίοντες. ἡ κεφαλὴ ἐναραττέτω καὶ πάντα ὁ ἀθλητὴς ὑποκείσθω τοῦ παγκρατίου τὰ ὀρθὰ εἴδη.

58. Εἰληθεροῦσι[116] δὲ οἱ μὲν ἀμαθῶς αὐτὸ πράττοντες ἐν ἅπαντι τῷ ἡλίῳ καὶ πάντες, οἱ δὲ ξὺν ἐπιστήμῃ καὶ λόγῳ οὔτε ἀεὶ καὶ ὁπόσοις λῷον· οἱ μὲν γὰρ βόρειοι τῶν ἡλίων καὶ οἱ νήνεμοι καθαροί τέ εἰσι καὶ εὔειλοι ἅτε δὴ λευκοῦ ἐκβάλλοντες τοῦ αἰθέρος, οἱ δὲ νότιοί τε καὶ ἐκνεφίαι ὑγροί τέ εἰσι καὶ ὑπερκάοντες, οἷοι ἐπιθρύψαι[117] μᾶλλον τοὺς γυμναζομένους ἢ θάλψαι. τὰς μὲν δὴ εὐηλίους τῶν ἡμερῶν εἴρηκα, ἡλιωτέοι δὲ οἱ φλεγματώδεις μᾶλλον, ἵνα τοῦ περιττοῦ ἐξικμάζοιντο, ἐπιχόλους δὲ ἀπάγειν χρὴ δὴ τούτου, ὡς μὴ πυρὶ πῦρ ἐπαντλοῖτο. καὶ ἡλιούσθων οἱ μὲν

---

[115] μόνου Jüthner: μόνους P: μόναι F
[116] εἴδη. Εἰληθεροῦσι Cobet: εἴδη· θέρους F
[117] ἐπιθρύψαι P: ἐπιψύξαι F, M

---

[165] Exposure to the sun was thought to have an effect on the humoral balance of the body, most obviously because it had a warming effect; it also had a drying effect, through the process of sweating, which Philostratus mentions later in the chapter. It is

57. A punching bag should be hung up also for boxers, but all the more so for those who compete in the *pankration*. The punching bag for the boxers should be light, since the hands of boxers are to be trained only for opportune punching, but the punching bag for pankratiasts should by heavier and bigger, so that they might be trained to keep their footing by standing up to the impact of the bag, and so that they might train their shoulders and their fingers in striking against an opposing weight. The athlete should also dash his head against the bag and submit to all the upright procedures of the *pankration*.

58. Some athletes take sunbaths in an ignorant fashion, in every kind of sun and all in the same way;[165] others, by contrast, sunbathe with understanding and rationally, not in all circumstances, but rather waiting for the most beneficial types of sunshine. The kinds of sunshine that accompany the north wind and come on windless days are clean and healthily sunny because they come from a clear sky, but those that accompany the south wind or come on overcast days are moist and burn excessively, and are liable to enfeeble those in training rather than warming them. The days with good types of sunshine I have described. But phlegmatic athletes should be exposed to the sun more often, so as to sweat out excessive secretions, whereas choleric athletes should be kept away from the sun so that fire is not poured over fire. Those who are

therefore represented by Philostratus as appropriate for phlegmatic athletes, who have a wet and cold temperament, but not advisable for choleric athletes, whose temperament is dry and warm.

προήκοντες ἀργοὶ κείμενοι καὶ πρόσειλοι κατὰ ταὐτὰ
ὀπτωμένοις, οἱ δὲ σφριγῶντες ἐνεργοὶ καὶ γυμναζόμε-
νοι πάντα καθάπερ Ἠλεῖοι νομίζουσι. τὸ δὲ πυρι-
ᾶσθαι καὶ ξηραλοιφεῖν, ἐπειδὴ τῆς ἀγροικοτέρας
γυμναστικῆς ἔχεται, Λακεδαιμονίοις ἀφῶμεν, ὧν τὰ
γυμνάσια οὔτε παγκρατίῳ οὔτε πυγμῇ εἴκασται.
φασὶ δὲ αὐτοὶ Λακεδαιμόνιοι μηδὲ ἀγωνίας ἕνεκεν
γυμνάζεσθαι τὴν ἰδέαν ταύτην, ἀλλὰ καρτερίας μό-
νης, ὅπερ δὴ μαστιγουμένων ἐστίν, ἐπειδὴ νόμος
αὐτοῖς ἐπὶ τοῦ βωμοῦ ξαίνεσθαι.

---

166 In other words, in the thirty days of preliminary training
before the contests: see ch. 11, esp. n. 55.

167 Effectively, saunas: many baths and gymnasia had small
heated rooms for heating the body and encouraging sweat. The
invention of this practice was ascribed to the Spartans in a num-
ber of ancient texts.

advanced in age should sunbathe while lying idle, exposed to the sun as if they are being roasted, whereas those who are in their prime should be active while they sunbathe and should be trained in all types of exercise, following the custom of the Eleans.[166] The practice of taking vapor baths[167] and dry-anointing,[168] since they belong to the more uncultivated style of training, let us leave them to the Spartans, whose exercises resemble neither the *pankration* nor boxing.[169] But the Spartans themselves say that they exercise in that way not for the sake of contest but solely for the sake of strength, and that is certainly the case for their practice of being whipped, since their law prescribes that they should be lacerated at the altar.[170]

[168] This expression usually refers to precisely the kind of oiling in the gymnasium that Philostratus seems to take for granted as an essential part of athletic training elsewhere in this work, as opposed to oiling of the body in the course of taking a bath. In this passage, however, Philostratus seems to be using it more specifically to refer to the oiling that took place in the sauna room, again by contrast with oiling of the body in the baths.

[169] In other words, their contests are fought as free-for-alls, without reference to the rules of competition used in the rest of the Greek world; cf. Philostr. *Imag.* 2.6.3, on the Spartan acceptance of biting and gouging in the *pankration*.

[170] A reference to the annual contest in which boys were whipped at the altar of Artemis Orthia in Sparta as a test of endurance.

DISCOURSES

INTRODUCTION

The *dialexis*—a brief discourse usually on a philosophical or rhetorical topic and pitched somewhere between a strict investigation and a "ramble" (λαλιά)—was a form of rhetorical display popular in Philostratus' era, sometimes composed as a prologue to a more formal exercise (cf. Men. Rhet. *Treatise II* [388.16–394.31]; it had been in the sophistic repertory during the fifth century and further developed by Plato and other Socratics in the fourth.[1]

Two such discourses are preserved under the name of Philostratus. *Discourse 1* treats epistolary style,[2] with comments on notable practitioners;[3] it may be by Philostratus' homonymous nephew if it is the same work referred to in *VS* 628 as a letter meant to instruct Aspasius, newly appointed as imperial secretary, on the niceties of

---

[1] The term derives from the verb διαλέγεσθαι (*dialegesthai*), "to converse," "to discuss," "to discourse (on)": see M. B. Trapp, *Maximus of Tyre, The Philosophical Orations* (Oxford, 1997), xl.

[2] For this topic, see Abraham J. Malherbe, *Ancient Epistolary Theorists* (Atlanta, GA, 1988). He gives his own translation on p. 43.

[3] The collection of love letters ascribed to Philostratus himself is edited and translated in A. R. Benner and F. H. Fobes, *Alciphron, Aelian and Philostratus: The Letters*, Loeb Classical Library 383 (Cambridge, MA, 1949).

epistolary style. *Discourse 2* suggests reasons for thinking that Nature and Culture are not, as is customarily thought, polar opposites, but rather "closely akin" and interpermeable.[4]

The text is Kayser's, repunctuated and translated by Jeffrey Rusten.

[4] *Discourse 2* is translated and discussed also in S. Swain, "Culture and Nature in Philostratus," in *Philostratus*, ed. Ewen Bowie and Jaś Elsner (Cambridge, 2009), 33–46.

ΔΙΑΛΕΞΕΙΣ

I.

Τὸν ἐπιστολικὸν χαρακτῆρα τοῦ λόγου μετὰ τοὺς πα-
λαιοὺς ἄριστά μοι δοκοῦσι διεσκέφθαι φιλοσόφων
μὲν ὁ Τυανεὺς καὶ Δίων, στρατηγῶν δὲ Βροῦτος ἢ
ὅτῳ Βροῦτος ἐς τὸ ἐπιστέλλειν ἐχρῆτο, βασιλέων δὲ
ὁ θεσπέσιος Μάρκος ἐν οἷς ἐπέστελλεν αὐτός, πρὸς
γὰρ τῷ κεκριμένῳ τοῦ λόγου καὶ τὸ ἑδραῖον τοῦ ἤθους
ἐντετύπωτο τοῖς γράμμασι, ῥητόρων δὲ ἄριστα μὲν
Ἡρώδης ὁ Ἀθηναῖος ἐπέστελλεν, ὑπεραττικίζων δὲ
καὶ ὑπερλαλῶν ἐκπίπτει πολλαχοῦ τοῦ πρέποντος
ἐπιστολῇ χαρακτῆρος. δεῖ γὰρ φαίνεσθαι τῶν ἐπιστο-
λῶν τὴν ἰδέαν ἀττικωτέραν μὲν συνηθείας, συνηθε-
στέραν δὲ ἀττικίσεως καὶ συγκεῖσθαι μὲν πολιτικῶς,
τοῦ δὲ ἁβροῦ μὴ ἀπᾴδειν. ἐχέτω δὲ τὸ εὔσχημον ἐν

---

[1] For the preserved letters of Apollonius of Tyana, see the
introduction, text, and translation of C. P. Jones, *Philostratus, the
Life of Apollonius of Tyana*, Loeb Classical Library 458 (Cam-
bridge, MA, 2006), 2–79.

[2] Five letters ascribed to Dio of Prusa are translated in *Dio
Chrysostom,* vol. 5, tr. H. Lamar Crosby, Loeb Classical Library
385 (Cambridge, MA, 1951), 354–59.

DISCOURSES

I.

It seems to me that, after the ancients, those who have engaged best in the epistolary style of discourse are the man of Tyana[1] and Dio[2] among philosophers, Brutus among generals (or whoever Brutus employed to write letters),[3] among emperors the divine Marcus[4] in the letters he wrote himself, since in addition to his exquisite style he also left an impression in his writing of the stability of his character; among rhetoricians Herodes of Athens wrote letters best, but in his hyperatticism and chattiness he often lapses from the style that suits a letter. For the form of letters must be more attic than the everyday style, but more everyday than the attic style, and be composed seriously, yet not depart from delicacy. Let its elegance

[3] Thirty-five short letters of the tyrannicide are preserved in multiple manuscripts and known to Plutarch (*Brutus* 22–23, 29). Christopher P. Jones, "The Greek Letters Ascribed to Brutus," *Harvard Studies in Classical Philology* (forthcoming), argues for their genuineness and gives a translation and historical commentary on the letters from 43–42 BC.

[4] See G. Cortassa, "Fozio, Filostrato di Lemno e le lettere greche di Marco Aurelio," *Sileno* 20 (1994): 193–200.

τῷ μὴ ἐσχηματίσθαι, εἰ γὰρ σχηματιοῦμεν, φιλοτι-
μεῖσθαι δόξομεν, φιλοτιμία δὲ ἐν ἐπιστολῇ μειρακιῶ-
δες. κύκλον δὲ ἀποτορνεύειν ἐν μὲν ταῖς βραχυτέραις
τῶν ἐπιστολῶν ξυγχωρῶ, ἵνα τούτῳ γοῦν ἡ βραχυλο-
γία ὡραΐζοιτο ἐς ἄλλην ἠχὼ πᾶσα στενὴ οὖσα, τῶν
δὲ ἐς μῆκος προηγμένων ἐπιστολῶν ἐξαιρεῖν χρὴ κύ-
κλους, ἀγωνιστικώτερον γὰρ ἢ κατὰ ἐπιστολὴν τοῦτο,
πλὴν εἰ μή που ἐπὶ τελευτῆς τῶν ἐπεσταλμένων ἢ
ξυλλαβεῖν δέοι τὰ προειρημένα ἢ ξυγκλεῖσαι τὸ ἐπὶ
πᾶσι νόημα. σαφήνεια δὲ ἀγαθὴ μὲν ἡγεμὼν ἅπαντος
λόγου, μάλιστα δὲ ἐπιστολῆς· καὶ γὰρ διδόντες καὶ
δεόμενοι καὶ ξυγχωροῦντες καὶ μὴ καὶ καθαπτόμενοι
καὶ ἀπολογούμενοι καὶ ἐρῶντες ῥᾷον πείσομεν, ἢν
σαφῶς ἑρμηνεύσωμεν· σαφῶς δὲ ἑρμηνεύσομεν καὶ
ἔξω εὐτελείας, ἢν τῶν νοηθέντων τὰ μὲν κοινὰ καινῶς
φράσωμεν, τὰ δὲ καινὰ κοινῶς.

II.

Οἱ τὸν νόμον τῇ φύσει ἀνθομοιοῦντες ἀντικεῖσθαι μὲν
ταῦτά φασιν ἀλλήλοις, καθάπερ τὸ λευκὸν τῷ μέλανι
καὶ τὸ μανὸν τῷ πυκνῷ καὶ τὸ μελιχρὸν τῷ πικρῷ καὶ
τὸ ψυχρὸν τῷ θάλποντι, εἶναι δὲ φύσεως μὲν ἔργα
ζῷα καὶ ἄστρα καὶ ποταμοὺς καὶ ἴδας καὶ πεδία καὶ
ἰσθμοὺς καὶ πορθμοὺς καὶ καθάπαξ τὸ ὑπὲρ τέχνην,
νόμου δὲ ἔργα τείχη καὶ νεώσοικοι καὶ ναῦς καὶ
ἀσπὶς καὶ λήια καὶ πᾶν τὸ ὑπὸ χεῖρα.

καὶ τὰ μὲν τῆς φύσεως ἄφθαρτα εἶναι τὸν ἀεὶ

consist in not being encoded, since if we encode we seem vain, and vanity in a letter is juvenile. As for rounding off a period, I concede it in shorter letters, so that at least in this its concision may seem beautiful, whereas in other sound effects it remains entirely narrow; but from letters that reach some length one must remove periods, since that style is too aggressive for a letter, unless of course at the end of one's missive one has either to summarize the preceding, or set on it all a concluding observation. A good guide to every style is clarity, and especially for a letter; whether we are granting or petitioning, or yielding or not, or finding fault or defending ourselves, or in love, we will persuade more easily if our expression is clear; and our expression will be clear and avoid parsimony if we set forth common thoughts with novelty, and novel ones with a common touch.

II.

Those who contrast Custom with Nature state that these are opposed to each other just as white to black or sparse to dense or sweet to bitter or cold to warm; and that the works of Nature are animals, stars, rivers, trees, plains, isthmuses, straits and whatever cannot be fabricated, while those of Custom are walls, ship sheds, a ship, a spear, crops and everything produced by hand.

And (they say) that the things of Nature are eternally

χρόνον, τήν τε θάλατταν μένειν, ὁπόση ἐγένετο, καὶ
τὴν γῆν, ὁπόση ὡρίσθη, καὶ τὸν αἰθέρα, ὡς ἔφυ,
ἄστρα τε καὶ ὥρας, ὡς ἐκείνων κύκλος, καὶ τὸ ἐπὶ ζῷα
δὲ αὐτῆς ἧκον φθείρεσθαι μὲν αὐτὰ τὰ τικτόμενα, τὸ
δὲ ἀεὶ τίκτον παρέχειν τῇ φύσει τὸν τοῦ ἀκηράτου
λόγον,

    τὰ δὲ τοῦ νόμου φθαρτά τε εἶναι καὶ (χρόνῳ)
ἁλωτά, τείχη τε γὰρ καὶ ἱερὰ τὰ μὲν ἁλίσκεσθαι, τὰ
δὲ φθείρεσθαι σὺν χρόνῳ, οἰκίαν δὲ τὴν εὖ κατεσκευα-
σμένην δῆλον εἶναι, ὅτι οὐκ ἀεὶ ἑστήξει καὶ τὸ ναυ-
πηγηθὲν οὐκ εἶναι βέβαιον ὅτι μηδ᾽ ἡ θάλαττα βε-
βαία ἀνθρώποις, τεκτονικήν τε καὶ χαλκευτικὴν
πᾶσαν φθαρτὰ ἐργάζεσθαι τῷ νόμῳ, καὶ τὸν μὲν νό-
μον οὐκ ἂν δημιουργῆσαι ζῷον ἔμψυχον οὐδέν, οὐδ᾽
ἄστρον, οὐδ᾽ αἰθέρα, οὐδ᾽ ἄλλο τι τῶν ὧδε θεσπεσίων
καὶ μεγάλων, τὴν φύσιν δὲ ὁμοιοῦσθαι πολλαχοῦ
τοῖς τοῦ νόμου εἴδεσι, χωρία τε γὰρ ὀχυροῦν τείχεσιν
ἀσφαλεστέροις τῶν ποιηθέντων ἄντρα τε κισσηρεφῆ
κατανοιγνύναι ἡδίω οἴκων καί που καὶ ἄγαλμα διδό-
ναι πέτρᾳ συμφυὲς σατυρικόν τι ἢ Πανὶ ὅμοιον, ὅρη
τε καὶ σκοπιὰς ὁμοιοῦν ζῴοις, οἷον [τῆς] αὐτῆς ὁ ἐν
Λήμνῳ δράκων καὶ ὁ ἐν Κρήτῃ λέων καὶ ἡ βούκρανος
ἡ πρὸς Χίῳ, ἀγαλματοποιούσης τε κατὰ τὸν νόμον
καὶ τὰς νεφέλας ἐς εἴδη ζῴων ἀγούσης· βλέψαντι
γοῦν ἐς αὐτὰς λύκοις τε ὁμοιοῦνται καὶ παρδάλεσι
καὶ κενταύροις καὶ ἅρμασι, καὶ οὐδὲ ὁ κύκλος τῆς
σελήνης ἄσημος, ἀλλὰ κἀκείνῳ τι ἐντετύπωται πρόσ-
ωπον οἷον γραφῆς ἀρρήτου·

imperishable—the sea endures as it came into being, the land as it was ordained, the heaven as it was born, and the stars and the cycle of the seasons, and as to the part of Nature relating to animals, those that are born themselves die, but what eternally gives birth provides to Nature its unmixed essence.

Whereas (they say) the things of Custom are perishable and subject to time, for walls and temples may be captured, or crumble with age, and it is clear that even a well-constructed house will not stand forever, and that a well-built ship is not secure because for men the sea is not secure either, and that all architecture and bronze-working produce things that are perishable by Custom. And they say that whereas Custom could not manufacture any living animal, or star, or the sky, or any other things so divine and great, nevertheless Nature is everywhere assimilated to the appearance of Custom: for she fortifies territories with walls that are more secure than those made by hand, and opens up ivy-covered caves that are sweeter than houses, and produces a statue growing upon a rock, something like a satyr or resembling Pan, and she likens mountains and rock towers to animals, for example the Dragon on Lemnos, and the lion on Crete, and the Ox skull on Chios, since she is a maker of statues to match Custom and brings on clouds in the shapes of animals—at least, when you look at them they resemble wolves and leopards and centaurs and chariots; the circular moon is not unrecognizable either, a face like an ineffable painting has been carved on it.

ἐμοὶ δὲ νόμος καὶ φύσις οὐ μόνον οὐκ ἐναντίω φαίνεσθον, ἀλλὰ καὶ ξυγγενεστάτω καὶ ὁμοίω καὶ διήκοντε ἀλλήλοιν· νόμος τε γὰρ παριτητέος ἐς φύσιν καὶ φύσις ἐς νόμον καὶ καλοῦμεν αὐτοῖν τὸ μὲν ἀρχήν, τὸ δ' ἐπόμενον, κεκληρώσθω δὲ ἀρχὴν μὲν φύσις, νόμος δὲ τὸ ἔπεσθαι, οὔτε γὰρ ἂν νόμος ἐτειχοποίησεν ἢ ὑπὲρ τείχους ὥπλισεν, εἰ μὴ φύσις ἔδωκεν ἀνθρώπῳ χεῖρας, οὔτ' ἂν ἡ φύσις (τι) τῶν ἐνεργούντων ἔδειξεν, εἰ μὴ τέχναι ἐνομίσθησαν, ἔδωκέ τε φύσις μὲν νόμῳ θάλατταν αἰθέρα ἄστρα, νόμος δὲ αὖ φύσει γεωργίαν ναυτιλίαν ἀστρονομίαν καὶ ὀνόματα κεῖσθαι ταῖς ὥραις, ἄργυρόν τε καὶ χρυσὸν καὶ ἀδάμαντα καὶ μάργαρον καὶ τὰ ὧδε σπανιστὰ φύσις μὲν εὗρε, νόμος δ' ἐτίμησε. περιωπήσαις δ' ἂν καὶ τὰ ἀνθρώπου ὁμοίως ἔχοντα· φύσις μὲν ἔννουν δημιουργεῖ τὸν ἄνθρωπον καὶ λογικὸν καὶ εὐφυᾶ πάντα, νόμος δὲ παιδεύει καὶ ὁπλίζει καὶ ὑποδεῖ καὶ ἀμφιέννυσιν, ἐπειδὴ γυμνὸς αὐτῷ παρὰ τῆς φύσεως πέμπεται, προτίθησι δὲ ὁ νόμος καὶ ἀρετῆς ἆθλα ἀνθρώποις, οἷον τιμῶν τὴν φύσιν.

καὶ μὴ τὸν νόμον ἀφαιρώμεθα τὸν τοῦ ἀθανάτου λόγον, καὶ γὰρ εἰ καὶ φθαρτὰ ἐργάζεται, ἀλλ' ἀθάνατά γε αὐτὰ ποιεῖ, ὄνομα δὲ αὐτῷ τέχνη. ἠπείρου δὲ ἀπορραγεῖσα νῆσος καὶ νήσῳ ξυμβαλοῦσα ἤπειρος καὶ Πηνειὸς Ὀλύμπου διεκπεσὼν οὐ φύσεως ταῦτα οὐδὲ νόμου ἔργα· ἔστι τι ἀμφοῖν μέσον, ὃ καλεῖται συμβεβηκός, ὑφ' οὗ ὁ νόμος ὁμοιοῦται φύσει καὶ φύσις μεταβάλλει ἐς νόμον.

But to me Custom and Nature not only do not seem opposed, but actually most closely akin and similar and permeating each other. For the road to Nature leads through Custom and vice versa, and we call one of them the starting point and the other the consequence—let the start be allotted to Nature, the follow up to Custom. For neither would Custom have built a wall or armed men to breach it unless Nature had given men hands, nor would Nature have revealed anything that was effective, if their crafts had not existed by Custom. Nature gave to Custom the sea, the sky and the stars, whereas Custom in turn gave to Nature farming, seafaring and astronomy and the naming of the seasons; it was Nature that discovered gold and silver and adamant and pearls and substances so rare, but it took Custom to prize them. You could behold human behavior in the same way: Nature makes a man conscious and rational and talented in everything; Custom educates him and arms him and give him shoes and clothing (since he is naked when sent to him by Nature). Custom institutes prizes for human superiority, as if to pay Nature a compliment.

And let us not deprive Custom of its immortal essence, for even if its products are perishable, nevertheless this makes them immortal; its name is Art. When an island breaks away from the coast or the coast crashes into an island or Peneius falls from Olympus, these are the deeds of neither Nature nor Custom; there is something between the two which is called coincidence by which Custom is made similar to Nature, and Nature changes into Custom.

INDEX TO *HEROICUS*

References to the Introduction (*Introd.*) are by page number; references to the translation and notes of the *Heroicus* (*Her.*) are by chapter and section number.

27.1n96, 5; 33.28n135;
38.1–2

Aeolia/Aeolians, *Her.* 8.6; 28.10;
33.48

Aepytos, *Her.* 8.12n40

Aeschylus, *Introd.* 52, 56; *Her.*
6.5n23; 27.2n98; 28.1n102;
51.7n183

Aetolians, *Introd.* 68

Agamemnon, *Introd.* 17, 49, 52,
54n137; *Her.* 23.30, 30n80;
26.9; 27.6, 10, 10n101;
29.1, 2n110, 3; 31.2, 2–3, 7;
33.12n129; and Achilles,
Her. 48.6–9; and Palame-
des, *Her.* 33.13, 24–33

Agathion, *Introd.* 32, 59

agora (Athens), *Introd.* 22

Aiaia, *Her.* 34.5

Aianteion, *Her.* 20.2

Aidoneus, *Her.* 25.9

Aithiopis, Introd. 64; *Her.*
26.16n91, 18n95;
56.11n212

Ajax (son of Telamon [the
greater]), *Introd.* 23n75,
34, 58, 58n148, 61; *Her.*
8.1, 1n30; 12.1; 18.3–5;
19.8–20.2; 23.18–19,
21–22; 27.8; 30.3; 31.6;
33.3n125, 30n136, 33–34,
39; 35.1–15, 15n154; 37.2;
48.20n179, 20–22; 49.2;
55.3; and Achilles, *Her.*
35.5; 48.22; madness of,
Her. 18.3, 3n65; 35.12; and
Palamedes, *Her.* 33.33;
statue, *Introd.* 34n108;
Her. 35.7; tomb, *Introd.* 34;

Her. 8.1, 1n30; 18.4; 19.9.
See also Aianteion

Ajax Locrian (lesser), *Her.* 12.1;
23.20; 31.1n115, 1–6;
33.30; 35.1; 43.7; 49.2;
funerary ship burning,
Introd. 61–62; *Her.* 31.8–9

Akesa, *Her.* 28.6

Alcaeus, *Introd.* 64

Alcestis, *Her.* 11.8

Alcidamas, *Introd.* 53n136; *Her.*
43.7n165

Alcmaeon, *Introd.* 44; *Her.* 54.5

Alcmene, *Introd.* 20; *Her.* 7.5

Aldus Manutius, *Introd.* 68

Alexander, *Her.* 40.1, 1n160. *See
also* Paris

Alexander Severus, *Introd.* 10,
41n117; *Her.* 53.22n201

Alexander the Great, *Introd.* 9,
24n76, 29, 34, 49, 55; *Her.*
10.5n49; 53.16

Alkyoneus, *Her.* 8.15

Aloadae, *Her.* 8.14

Amaltheia, *Her.* 7.7

Amazons, *Introd.* 23n75, 55, 67;
Her. 23.26; 29n79;
54.2n204; 56.11–57.17;
57.3n216

Amphiaraus, *Introd.* 44; *Her.*
16.5n61; 17.1, 1n62

Amphilochus, *Introd.* 24, 28,
44; *Her.* 17.1, 1n62

Amphion, *Introd.* 18

Amphipolis, *Introd.* 23n73; *Her.*
17.5n64

Anagyros, *Introd.* 47n126

Anaxilas, *Her.* 37.3n156

Anchises, *Her.* 45.3

INDEX TO *GYMNASTICUS*

References to the Introduction (*Introd.*) are by page number; references to the translation and notes of the *Gymnasticus* (*Gym.*) are by paragraph number.